# WATER RESOURCES
# AND THE
# NATIONAL WELFARE

## by

# WALTER U. GARSTKA

Water Resources Publications
Fort Collins, Colorado 80552, USA

For information and correspondence:

WATER RESOURCES PUBLICATIONS
P. O. Box 303
Fort Collins, Colorado 80522 U

WATER RESOURCES AND THE NATIONAL WELFARE

By

Walter U. Garstka - Consultant in Hydrology and
Visiting Professor in Natural Resources

ISBN No. 0-918334-19-5
U.S. Library of Congress Catalogue Card No. 77-074260

Published by Water Resources Publications, P. O. Box 303,
Fort Collins, Colorado 80522 U.S.A.

This book is printed and bound by LithoCrafters, Chelsea,
Michigan, U.S.A.

To my wife, Ruth

In appreciation of
her devotion and endurance

TABLE OF CONTENTS

# ACKNOWLEDGMENTS

Acknowledgment is made of the cooperation extended the author by many professional societies and Federal, State, and private organizations, in providing published material and references. Personal communications are specifically credited in the lists of references of each Topic. Librarians in charge and members of their staffs in the following libraries provided invaluable information: Park County Library, Bailey, Colorado; Central Region Library of the U.S. Geological Survey, Denver, Colorado; the Library of the Engineering and Research Center, U.S. Bureau of Reclamation, Denver, Colorado; the Reference Room of the U.S. Dept. of Energy's Regional Office, Denver, Colorado; and the Denver Public Library and its Conservation Library, Denver. The assistance of Douglas E. Becker of Ridgway's, a reproduction specialty firm, Denver, Colorado, in the preparation of photographs and charts for printing, is appreciated. The review of the sub-sections on Nuclear Fission and Nuclear Fusion in Topic 90, made by Wade Ballard, Assistant Director for Fuel Cycle Development, Nuclear Power Development Division, U.S. Dept. of Energy, Washington, D.C., is appreciated. Acknowledgment is made to Dr. Vujica Yevjevich, Professor of Civil Engineering, Colorado State University, Fort Collins, for suggestions relating to the preparation of this book for printing and especially for his review of Topics 1 through 80. Ruth K. Garstka edited the book and typed the camera-ready manuscript.

Credit is given to the American Society of Civil Engineers for permission to use copyrighted material from publications of the Society. Each illustration appears with complete reference citation. Other copyrighted material, which is included with permission of the copyright holders, is identified as follows: John Wiley and Sons, Inc., and Dr. Ernest F. Brater, Table 30-1 and Figure 15-1; Science Magazine and Dr. F. H. Bormann, Figure 34-2; University of Hawaii and Dr. Doak Cox, Figure 44-4; Denver Museum of Natural History, Denver, Colo., Figure 47-1; Miami Conservancy District, Dayton, Ohio, Figure 72-1; and Public Works Magazine, Ridgewood, New Jersey, Figures 73-3, 73-4, 73-5, and 73-6. Figure 60-1 is from the archives of the Yale University School of Forestry and Environmental Studies, New Haven, Connecticut.

Walter U. Garstka

July, 1978

# PREFACE

This volume is an outgrowth of an assembly of lecture summaries which were prepared under the title, "Water Resources and the National Welfare", for use in teaching courses in Engineering Hydrology, General Hydrology, Hydrology and the National Welfare, Watershed Management, Wildland Hydrology, and Forest Hydrology, at both undergraduate and graduate levels. The first printing of the lecture summaries in 1973, which totaled 60 Topics, was done by Ball State University through the interest of Dr. Clyde Hibbs, Chairman of the Department of Natural Resources, Ball State University, Muncie, Indiana. The second version of this book was published as an assembly of 63 Topics in 1974 primarily for use as a text in the teaching of Forest Hydrology and General Hydrology. Although prepared initially for use as a college text, a large part of the second edition was purchased by consulting engineers and government agencies.

A great many of the problems facing the Nation, such as land use, population migration trends, energy, food and fiber production, and the quality of the environment, are intimately enmeshed with decisions relating to water resources. Legislators, administrators, financiers, and citizens may be required at one time or another to make sometimes irreversible decisions on water resources without having been given an opportunity to learn about the subject. The importance of this problem was recognized and the National Academy of Science published the final report of the National Resource Council's Work Group on Education and Training of the U.S. National Committee for the International Hydrological Decade. This 70-page report, which presents 16 recommendations, was published in 1976 under the title, "Education in Hydrology and Water Resources in the United States - 1965-1974 - An Overview with Recommendations".

This volume is not simply a revision of previous editions but is a completely new book expanded into 95 Topics. It has been written not only as a textbook but to provide a working knowledge of the water resource for those who will be responsible for the management of our environment in which the water resource forms a critical and often dominant role.

Walter U. Garstka

July, 1978

xii

ABOUT THE AUTHOR:

Walter Urban Garstka is a professional interdisciplinarian. All of his professional endeavors were and continue to be related to the water resource. His academic degrees are: Bachelor of Science in Forestry with a minor in Soils, Pennsylvania State University; Master of Forestry, Yale University School of Forestry and Environmental Studies; Master of Science in Irrigation Engineering, Colorado State University. In addition he has pursued graduate studies at Michigan State University, the Graduate School of the U.S. Department of Agriculture, and the University of California at Berkeley. He has been employed as a forester, soil technologist, civil, hydraulic, hydrologic, and general engineer in a long career with the Federal Government, which included research, teaching, and administration. He has worked with the State of Michigan, U.S. Forest Service, U.S. Soil Conservation Service, Tennessee Valley Authority, and the U.S. Bureau of Reclamation. Prior to his retirement at an early option while serving as Chief of the Office of Atmospheric Water Resources of the Bureau of Reclamation, he was granted the U.S. Department of Interior's Distinguished Service Award.

His college teaching experience includes positions at Pennsylvania State University, Fort Lewis College, and Ball State University in addition to short assignments at four other universities. At Colorado State University he has served as Professor of Civil Engineering, Professor of Watershed Management, and Director of the International School for Water Resources Environmental Management. At the Yale University School of Forestry and Environmental Studies he served as Visiting Professor of Forest Hydrology; as Visiting Professor in Hydrology and Water Resources and of Watershed Management in the Department of Hydrology and Water Resources, College of Earth Sciences, and in the School of Renewable Natural Resources, College of Agriculture, University of Arizona, Tucson.

He has contributed over 30 publications, 3 patents, and this textbook and its 2 predecessors. He served as a Lecturer for the Sigma Xi - RESA National Lectureship Bureau in 1973 and 1974. He is a Registered Professional Engineer in the State of Colorado. In addition to memberships in numerous professional and scientific societies he is a Fellow of the American Association for the Advancement of Science.

INTRODUCTION

One does not need to be an engineer or a watershed
management specialist to use this book. The science and
art underlying water resource management is Hydrology. The
improvement and perpetuation of a favorable environment, the
well-being of mankind, and the future of our civilization,
all depend on intelligent management of the water resource.

Courses in hydrology and water resources at most
universities require such extensive prerequisites in physics,
hydraulics, and mathematics that it is very difficult for
those not majoring in engineering or watershed management to
have the opportunity to learn about water resources. This
book has been used in the teaching of no-prerequisite
courses ranging from 2 to 5 semester-hour credits. The
treatment of the subject by Topics permits the reader or
the instructor to organize their approach as desired.

My experience has shown that each offering of a course
at various universities at which I taught was attended by
students of such a diversity of backgrounds as to require a
judicious selection of Topics and the detail in which they
were presented. The problems, none of which require a
knowledge of mathematics beyond arithmetic, have been included to illustrate fundamental concepts. For those
interested in a more profound pursuit of any of the Topics,
numerous references, many of a highly technical nature, have
been included with each Topic.

Although laboratory exercises and field trips are not
described in detail in this volume, effectiveness of the
teaching of the subject can be expanded by laboratory experiments, field trips, and the use of slides and motion
pictures. Superb 16 mm color and sound motion pictures are
available from many Federal agencies. The American Meteorological Society and the American Water Works Association
have prepared excellent films as have many universities and
private companies. The audio-visual departments of most
colleges and the larger libraries have lists of motion
pictures available.

Dr. Donald E. Van Meter of Ball State University has
prepared a "Manual of Laboratory and Field Experiences" (1977)
dealing with natural resources. These include outlines for
visits to gravel pits, municipal water and wastewater treatment plants, and forest industry, soil science, wildlife
resources, and outdoor recreation exercises among others.
Field trips to power plants and dams have been found to be
instructive. Visits to agricultural and forest experiment

stations and watersheds are also recommended.

Naylon and Vogt of the Minnesota Environmental Sciences Foundation, Inc., Golden Valley, Minnesota, have prepared a comprehensive assembly of suggested teaching units with laboratory and field exercises entitled, "Natural Resources Management", (undated). This 115-page series contains sections on moving water, lakes, ponds, and marshes, among other sections relating to water.

Stapp and Liston (1975) in their book "Environmental Education - A Guide to Information Sources" present a 225-page assembly giving the addresses of professional societies, government agencies, magazines, journals, newsletters, and privately-funded foundations dealing with the environment. Many of the listings are directly related to the water resource.

For the advanced student and for the reader having a professional interest in water resources the assembly of problems prepared by Schulz (1976) is highly recommended.

## References

Naylon, Michael J., and Carl E. Vogt, "Natural Resources Management", Suggested Teaching Units for Agricultural Education prepared for the Minnesota Dept. of Education, Div. of Vocational-Technical Education, St. Paul, Minn., 115 pp, undated.

Schulz, E. F., "Problems in Applied Hydrology", Water Resources Publications, Fort Collins, Colo., 501 pp, 1973, rev. 1976.

Stapp, William B., and Mary Dawn Liston, "Environmental Education - A Guide to Information Sources", Gale Research Co., Book Tower, Detroit, Mich., 225 pp, 1975.

Van Meter, Donald E., "Manual of Lab and Field Experiences - Introduction to Natural Resources", 3d edition, 104 pp, Aug. 1977. (This book available at Ball State Univ. Bookstore, Muncie, Ind.)

SECTION I

HISTORICAL BACKGROUND

Topic 1    Anthropological and Archeological Backgrounds

The history of water resource management and the history
of the human race are inseparable.  In Durant's (1935) estimation civilization was and continues to be conditioned by
certain factors which are geologic, geographic, and economic.
Under geographic conditions Durant says, "Rain is necessary;
for water is the medium of life, more important even than the
light of the sun; the unintelligible whim of the elements may
condemn to desiccation regions that once flourished with
empire and industry, like Nineveh or Babylon, or may help to
swift strength and wealth cities apparently off the main line
of transport and communication, like those of Great Britain or
Puget Sound."

Social organizations, law, economics, and commerce are all
related to the water resource.  Biswas (1967) traces reported
interest in meteorological phenomena as far back as 3000 B.C.
The interrelationships between meteorological and hydrologic
phenomena and politics and agricultural economics are reported
in connection with the work of Kautilya (also known as
Vishnugupta Chanakya) in his book "Arthasastra" which was probably written at the end of the 4th century B.C. in India,
according to Biswas.  The necessity for measuring rainfall
arose for two reasons:  lands were taxed according to the
amount of rainfall they received; and, the superintendent of
agriculture required data on rainfall for use in making decisions on agronomic practices.

Bennett (1974) has written a very informative overview of
anthropological relationships referring in detail to many
cultures and many lands.

Biswas (1970) in the table on page 3 of this reference
lists hydrologic engineering for the period 3200 B.C. to
600 B.C.  The management of the water resources of the Nile
from which the development of mathematics, surveying, and
astronomy have been traced has been extensively studied as
have been many other river basins of the ancient world.

Hammurabi of Mesopotamia dealt with water rights in his
Code as described by Biswas (1970, pp 19-22).  Hammurabi
decreed that each man must keep his own part of the dike and
ditch system in repair and if not he had to recompense the
neighboring farmers whose lands might suffer through flooding.
One of the earliest records (equivalent to a modern tax

1

assessor's map) is the tablet depicted by Kazmann (1972) of a
baked clay property record from Nippur in Mesopotamia dated
about 1300 B.C.

An intelligent system of groundwater development is also
one of the oldest methods of water utilization. The Quanats
(also referred to as Qanat, Kanat, or Khanat) were tunnels and
galleries developed by the people in the Iranian Plateau and
were reported as early as 714 B.C. In the Tehuacan Valley of
Mexico the new world counterparts of the Quanats, referred to
in Mexico as Galerias, were developed as reported by Kirkby
(1969).

Mention is made in numerous chapters of the book edited
by Chorley (1969) of anthropological and archeological relationships to water resource management. George Perkins Marsh
(1965) in his book originally published in 1864, presents an
extensive discussion on pages 281-381 of the interactions between man and water resources for the lands in the Mediterranean Sea area.

One of the outstanding examples of the management of a
desert water resource is that of the Hohokam an Indian Tribe
which lived in the Southwest in what is now Arizona, in the
period approximately 300 B.C. to about 1300 A.D. An article
by Haury and Teiwes (1967) on the Hohokam is illustrated with
many photographs and artist Peter V. Bianchi's conceptions of
how they may have worked and lived. The Casa Grande Ruins National Monument has been able to preserve one of the structures
built by the Hohokam as described by Valkenburgh (1962).

The astonishing attainment of the Hohokam however was the
development of an extensive 125-mile irrigation canal system
in the Salt River Valley of Arizona. They built 22 villages,
irrigated about 140 thousand acres of land and prospered for
about 1400 years. The modern canal systems of the Salt River
Valley follow very closely those built about 2,000 years ago
by the Hohokam and the current irrigated acreage depending on
the Salt River is not much greater than that of the Hohokam.
Hubert and Kemper (date unknown) prepared a series of four
paintings as an illustration of the Hohokam era which ended
approximately 600 years ago for reasons not as yet understood.

In ancient times people either traveled as nomads to
springs and oases or lived along river courses. This is true
even now in many parts of the world. Diversions of streamflow
as developed in many parts of the world including the Hohokam
made it possible to use water other than on lands immediately
adjacent to the river channel. The Hohokam canal system, extensive as it was, had no carry-over storage and they could
only convey water when it was available in the river channel.
This is also true of all the ancient usage of river flow for

irrigation. Stewart (1940) conducted a study of both old, about 1300 A.D., and modern water conservation practices in Pueblo agriculture of the Southwest. In his article, illustrated with numerous maps and photographs, he describes the extensive flood water diversion, water retention, and irrigation systems developed in the Southwest, a region characterized by high summer temperatures, extremely variable rainfall, and with long periods of moisture deficiencies with recurring extensive droughts.

Rohn (1963) presents in considerable detail with surveys and sketches the extensive check dam and water spreading systems and terraces developed on the Chapin Mesa in the Mesa Verde National Park area. As of 1963 over 900 recognizable dams were recorded on the surveyed portion of Chapin Mesa. These developments included relatively large stone dams at the heads of several canyons which served to impound water for storage and to permit it to soak into the bedrock sandstone to feed springs some of which have been found in the cliff dwellers' caves. Mummy Lake, described by Rohn (1963) as a circular depression about 90 feet in diameter originally about 14 feet deep, provided domestic water allowing about 1200 A.D. a population concentration unusual for an arid area. Mummy Lake was engineered with an unusual inflow system which decreased sediment intake and allowed bypass of flows (Rohn, 1963, pages 449-451).

Although the ancient Pueblo did not attain massive carryover storage they certainly were headed in that direction.

References

Bennett, John W., "Anthropological Contributions to the Cultural Ecology and Management of Water Resources", chap. 2, pp 34-81, in MAN AND WATER, L. Douglas James, Editor, the University of Kentucky Press, Lexington, 1974.

Biswas, Asit K., "Development of Rain Gages", Jour. Irrigation & Drainage Div., Proceedings ASCE, pp 99-124, Sept. 1967.

Biswas, Asit K., "History of Hydrology", American Elsevier Publishing Co., Inc., New York, N.Y., 1970.

Chorley, Richard J., Editor, "Water, Earth and Man", Methuen & Co. Ltd., London (Distributed in the USA by Barnes & Noble Inc.) 1969.

Durant, Will, "Our Oriental Heritage", The Story of Civilization: Part 1, Simon and Schuster, New York, 1954.

Haury, Emil W., and Helga Teiwes, "First Masters of the American Desert - The Hohokam", National Geographic, vol. 131, no. 5, pp 670-695, May, 1967.

Hubert, Virgil and Charles O. Kemper, A series of four 17-inch by 22-inch paintings on the Hohokam Indians of the Salt River Valley, Arizona. Originals in the Heard Museum of Anthropology and Primitive Art, Phoenix, Ariz. Reduced-size reproductions were published by the Salt River Project, Phoenix. (Date unknown)

Kazmann, R. G., "Modern Hydrology", 2nd ed., Harper & Row, New York, 1972.

Kirkby, Anne V., "Primitive Irrigation", chap. III(ii) pp 209-212 in WATER, EARTH, AND MAN", Richard J. Chorley, Editor Methuen & Co., Ltd, London (Distributed in the USA by Barnes & Noble Inc.) 1959.

Marsh, George Perkins, "Man and Nature", Originally pub. in 1864. The Belknap Press of Harvard University Press, edited by David Lowenthal, Cambridge, Mass., 1965.

Rohn, Arthur H., "Prehistoric Soil and Water Conservation on Chapin Mesa, Southwestern Colorado", American Antiquity, vol. 28, no. 4, pp 441-455, Apr. 1963.

Stewart, Guy R., "Conservation in Pueblo Agriculture", The Scientific Monthly, vol. LI, pp 201-220 and 329-340, Oct. 1940.

Valkenburg, Sallie Van, "The Casa Grande of Arizona as a Landmark on the Desert, A Government Reservation, and a National Monument", The Kiva, vol. 27, no. 3, pp 1-31, Feb. 1962.

History of Hydrology

The term hydrology is relatively new. At the turn of the Century the term was used in connection with groundwater. Much of the early work, now considered to be hydrologic in nature, dealt in essence with fluid dynamics, physics, instrumentation, and natural philosophy. Since about 1930 the currently accepted divisions of hydrology came into general usage.

Until recently hydrology has been considered to be exclusively in the domain of civil engineering. However much of the knowledge of hydrology is based upon research and experience in many related fields such as geology, meteorology, oceanography, biology, zoology, soil science, agronomy, agriculture, and watershed management.

The U.S. Federal Council for Science and Technology in 1962 published the following definition of hydrology: "Hydrology is the science that treats of the waters of the Earth, their occurrence, circulation, and distribution, their chemical and physical properties, and their reaction with their environment, including their relation to living things. The domain of hydrology embraces the full life history of water on the Earth."

Chow (1964) classifies the historical development of hydrology into the following periods:

        A. Speculation     (Ancient - 1400 A.D.)
        B. Observation     (1400 - 1600)
        C. Measurement     (1600 - 1700)
        D. Experimentation (1700 - 1800)
        E. Modernization   (1800 - 1900)
        F. Empiricism      (1900 - 1930)
        G. Rationalization (1930 - 1950)
        H. Theorization    (1950 - date)

Ancient structures and water-management practices, many of which would be impressive attainments even today, are described by Vallentine (1967) in his Chapter 2.

The modern science of hydrology which underlies all water resource management began during the periods of observation and measurement. Leonardo Da Vinci was among the first to achieve a correct understanding of the hydrologic cycle. Biswas (1968) describes the early work in hydrology of the French naturalist, Perault, the French physicist, Mariotte, and the English astronomer, Halley.

A scholarly and fascinating 336-page History of Hydrology is that prepared by Biswas (1970) embracing a time span from

3200 B.C. to the current era.

Section 1 of Sopper and Lull (1967) touches upon the history of forest hydrologic research in Austria, Australia, Belgium, Canada, Czechoslovakia, Denmark, East and Central Africa, Finland, West Germany, Greece, Israel, Japan, The Netherlands, New Zealand, South African Republic, Sweden, Switzerland, Taiwan, United Kingdom, and the United States of America.

Baker, Rae, Minor, and Connor (1973) assembled a 205-page historical survey and a guide to historic sites pertaining to the development of water for the Southwest. Lavender's (1975) book on the Rocky Mountain region includes much history of water resource as related to the development of the West.

In the more humid portions of the United States municipal water supply, waste disposal, harbor management, inland navigation, hydropower, and land drainage were and in many instances continue to be matters of more pressing concern than year-around availability of water.

In the United States the first hydrologic land-use experiment was begun in 1909 by foresters and meteorologists (not by engineers) in the headwaters of the Rio Grande in Colorado. This is known as the "Forest and Streamflow Experiment at Wagon Wheel Gap". Reports on the investigation were published by Bates and Henry in 1922 and 1928.

## References

Baker, T. Lindsay, Steven R. Rae, Joseph E. Minor, Seymour V. Connor, "Water for the Southwest - Historical Survey and Guide to Historic Sites", Amer. Soc. of Civil Engineers, ASCE Historical Pub. No. 3, 1973.

Bates, C. G., and A. J. Henry, "Streamflow Experiment at Wagon Wheel Gap, Colo: Preliminary Report on Termination of First Stage of Experiment", Monthly Weather Review, Supp. No. 17, 1922.

Bates, C. G., and A. J. Henry, "Forest and Streamflow Experiment at Wagon Wheel Gap, Colo; Final Report on Completion of Second Phase of the Experiment", Monthly Weather Review, Supp. No. 30, 1928.

Biswas, Asit K., "Beginning of Quantitative Hydrology", Jour. Hydraulics Div., Proceedings ASCE, pp 1299-1316, Sept. 1968.

Biswas, Asit K., "History of Hydrology", American Elsevier Publishing Co., Inc., New York, 1970.

Chow, Ven Te, "Hydrology and its Development", Section 1 in
     HANDBOOK OF APPLIED HYDROLOGY, Ven Te Chow ed-in-chief,
     McGraw-Hill Book Co., New York, 1964.

Lavender, David, "The Rockies", rev. edition, Harper & Row,
     New York, 1975.

"Scientific Hydrology", Ad Hoc Panel on Hydrology, U.S. Feder-
     al Council for Science and Technology, Washington, D.C.,
     June, 1962.

Sopper, Wm. E., and Howard W. Lull, editors, "Resumes of Forest
     Hydrology Research", Session 1, pp 3-103 in INTERNATIONAL
     SYMPOSIUM ON FOREST HYDROLOGY, Pergamon Press, New York,
     1967.

Vallentine, H.R., "Water in the Service of Man", Penguin Books,
     Baltimore, Md., 1967.

     For the conterminous United States as a whole, according
to the Select Committee on National Water Resources (1959), the
average precipitation is 30 inches of which 21 inches returns
to the atmosphere through evaporation.  Included in the 21
inches is the water needed to support the forests, the grasslands, and cultivated crops.  Of the remaining 9 inches 6
inches flows directly into the ocean and 3 inches supplies urban population and endeavors.  Of this 3 inches, 2 inches returns to the streamflow network and one inch is consumed.

     The National Water Commission (1973) defines consumptive
use in the Section entitled, "Glossary", as follows:

     "Consumptive use - water withdrawn from a supply which,
     because of absorption, transpiration, evaporation, or in-
     corporation in a manufactured product, is not returned
     directly to a surface or groundwater supply; hence, water
     which is lost for immediate further use.  Also called
     'consumption'."

     In his 568-page volume on "Water Resources of the World"
van der Leeden (1975) includes on pages 343-374 information on
the water supply of the United States.

     Although the average annual precipitation for the United
States appears to be more than sufficient to satisfy all of the
anticipated national demands for some time to come this sim-
plistic interpretation is completely unrealistic.  The problem
with the water resource is that there is not sufficient water
to supply not only anticipated demands but in many instances
current demands for water of the quality we have become accustomed to in the places where we wish to live, at the times we
believe we need water, and, in the quantities desired.

     The following table of water use is based upon page 8 of
The Select Committee (1959):

Table 3-1    Percentage Distribution of Utilization of Water

| Irrigation - 46% | Industrial - 46% | Public - 8% |
|---|---|---|
| of which: | of which: | of which: |
| 60% is consumptive, | 2% is consumptive | 10% is consumptive, |
| 40% non-consumptive | 98% non-consumptive | 90% non-consumptive |

     Water resources regions as used in "The Nation's Water
Resources" (1968) are shown in Figure 3-1.  Geraghty, Miller,
van der Leeden, and Troise have prepared a very informative
Water Atlas of the United States (1973).

Figure 3-1
Water Resource
Regions

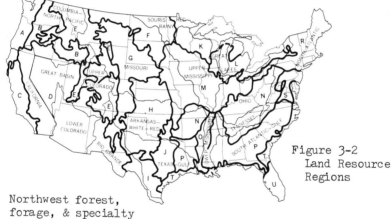

Figure 3-2
Land Resource
Regions

A  Northwest forest, forage, & specialty crop
B  Northwest wheat & range
C  Calif subtropical fruit, truck & specialty crop
D  Western range & irrigated
E  Rocky Mt. range & forest
F  Northern Great Plains spring wheat
G  Western Great Plains Range & irrigated
H  Central Great Plains winter wheat and range
I  Southwestern plateau & plains range & cotton
J  Southwestern prairies cotton & forage
K  Northern Lake states forest & forage

L  Lake States fruit, truck & dairy
M  Central feed grains & livestock
N  East & central general farming & forest
O  Mississippi Delta cotton & feed grains
P  So. Atlantic & Gulf slope cash crop forest & livestock
R  Northeastern forage & forest
S  North Atlantic slope truck, fruit and poultry
T  Atlantic & Gulf Coast lowland forest & truck crop
U  Florida subtropical fruit, truck crop & range

9

It is to be observed that there is a marked similarity between the boundaries of water resource regions and the land use regions. Although the physiography, climate, and soil characteristics are important the dominant factor in determining land use is usually the water resource. Trends in major land use for the period 1900-1965 are summarized in Table 3-2 taken from "The Nation's Water Resources" (1968).

Table 3-2   Trends in Major Land Uses, Conterminous United States, 1900-1965

(Million acre units)

| Land Use | 1900 | 1920 | 1940 | 1960 | 1965 |
|---|---|---|---|---|---|
| Cropland[1] | 389 | 480 | 467 | 458 | 444 |
| Pasture and range[2] | 761 | 652 | 650 | 630 | 636 |
| Forest[3] | 610 | 614 | 630 | 637 | 638 |
| Total agricultural land | 1,760 | 1,746 | 1,747 | 1,725 | 1,718 |
| Nonagricultural land[4] | 142 | 156 | 155 | 177 | 184 |

[1] Cropland harvested, crop failure, cropland idle or fallow, and cropland used for pasture.
[2] Grassland pasture and other nonforested grazing land.
[3] Includes grazed forest land and reserved forest lands.
[4] Includes special land uses, such as urban areas, highways and roads, and parks and so on.

Most of the land area of the United States is available for some type of agricultural or wildland purpose. The type of management and the degree of utilization varies widely. There has been very little fluctuation in the total acreage in agricultural land in the past 70 years. Crop lands have declined from a peak of 480 million acres in the period 1920-1930 to an estimated 440 million acres in 1965. There has been a moderate decline in pasture and range land. A steady increase has been observed in special use such as urban areas, highways, roads, and parks. Twenty-six states had at least 50 percent of their people living in metropolitan areas. California has the highest share of metropolitan area development with 86 percent of its people living in metropolitan areas.

R. M. Davis, Administrator of the Soil Conservation Service, (1976) reports that as of mid-1976 farm land is being swallowed up by urban development at the rate of 2 million acres per year. The reasons for the concentration on agricultural land are many. They are usually fertile, well-drained, and served by roads, power lines, and communication especially near expanding metropolitan centers.

Earl Butz (1975) gives additional reasons for the withdrawal of 2 million acres annually of agricultural land.

10

Whereas in the past urban expansion consisted of single houses or subdivisions now new satellite towns may range up to 20 thousand acres in size. While 40 acres was more than enough for ordinary power plants, nuclear power plants may require 5 thousand acres for cooling lakes and a nuclear center may take up to 64 thousand acres of land.

Transfer of land from agriculture to energy and industrial usage results in an extremely complicated adjustment in the management of the water resources. In the past the naturally available surface water and springs were the dominant factors in determining land use, urbanization, and industrial development.

With the construction of Hoover Dam a new era unprecedented in history developed. Hoover Dam and its related system of reservoirs and aqueducts made possible the development of centers of civilization, industries, agriculture, and urbanization in an environment not naturally suited for such use. The systems of reservoirs and their related engineering structures have made it possible to store water not only from a wet season to a dry season but also from a succession of wet years for release during a period of dry years. This massive carry-over storage project is presented by Garstka (1972).

The quality of the environment in which we live and work, the adequacy and dependability of our food supply, and the production and distribution of energy are all interrelated not only with one another but especially with water resources.

Whereas in the past when population centers were in areas of naturally adequate and dependable water supply the water resource was taken for granted and the decisions on development were left to the specialists. Now everyone is concerned and involved in how, where, and for what purpose the water resource is developed and managed.

There are certain laws of nature which are just becoming recognized and the future impact of decisions on the water resource is becoming more and more difficult to understand and to foresee. This book has been prepared to provide not only an explanation but also a working knowledge of the natural phenomena, the physical and mathematical bases, and engineering technology all of which interact with political and social factors in our management of the water resource.

References

Butz, Earl L., "Perspectives on Prime Lands", Background papers for Seminar on the Retention of Prime Lands July 16-17, 1975, sponsored by the USDA Committee on Land Use. 257 pages paperback, pub. by U.S. Dept. of Agriculture.

Davis, R. M., "What's Left of Our Cropland 'Frontier'?", Soil
Conservation, vol. 42, no. 1, Aug. 1976.

Garstka, Walter U., "Water Resources in the West", pp 8-14,
from Watersheds in Transition, Proceedings of a Symposium
held at Fort Collins, Colo., June 19-22, 1972. Edited by
S. C. Csallany, T. G. McLaughlin and W. Striffler, Proceedings Series No. 14, American Water Resources Assn.,
Urbana, Ill., 405 pp, Sept. 1972.

Geraghty, J. J., D. W. Miller, F. van der Leeden, and
F. L. Troise, "Water Atlas of the United States", A Water
Information Center Publication, Port Washington, N.Y.,
122 plates, 1973.

van der Leeden, Frits, "Water Resources of the World", Water
Information Center, Inc., New York, 568 pp, 1975.

"The Nation's Water Resources", Parts 1-7, The First National
Assessment of the Water Resources Council, Washington,
D.C., 1968.

"Water Policies for the Future", Final Report to the President
and to the Congress of the United States by the National
Water Commission. 579 pp, Washington, D.C., June, 1973.

"Water Resources Activities in the United States", Committee
Print No. 1, Select Committee on National Water Resources,
U.S. Senate, puruant to Senate Resolution 48, 86th Cong-
ress, 1st Session, Aug. 1959.

SECTION II

THE HYDROLOGIC CYCLE, METEOROLOGY AND CLIMATOLOGY

Topic 4  Units of Measurement and Methods of Expression

From prehistoric times attempts have been made to describe dimensions, weights, and time. Each rising civilization designed its own units and it was not until international commerce developed coupled with taxation that there was any attempt made to standardize the definitions. A fascinating history of the masterpieces, mysteries, and muddles of measurements has been written by Klein (1974).

The United States, which inherited the English system of measurement, is currently in the throes of conversion to the "International System of Units" which was developed by the General Conference on Weights and Measures at its 11th meeting in 1960. The International System of Units has an international abbreviation of SI.

The SI is not entirely the same as the metric system the original of which dates back more than 175 years. The American Society of Testing Materials in its very comprehensive 37-page publication, "Standard for Metric Practice", ASTM E 380-76, describes the SI system as being divided into three classes: base units, supplementary units, and derived units. In the SI system there are only 7 well-defined base units which by convention are regarded as independent. These units are listed in the following table taken from page 2 of ASTM E 380-76.

| "Quantity | Unit | Symbol |
|---|---|---|
| length | metre | m |
| mass | kilogram | kg |
| time | second | s |
| electric current | ampere | A |
| thermodynamic temperature | kelvin | K |
| amount of substance | mole | mol |
| luminous intensity | candela | cd    ". |

The definition and inclusion of supplementary and derived units are beyond the scope of this book. These can be found together with conversion factors in the above publication. An interim metric guide in which are assembled both U.S. customary units and SI units pertinent to Water Resources is the booklet available at no charge entitled, "Standard for Commonly Used International System (SI) Units in Bureau of Reclamation Practice", (1976). Appendix A lists conversion factors.

In our daily lives and in water resource management the use of an expression of temperature is common. The entrancing history of temperature measurements is given by Klein (1974) in his Chapters 26 through 29. The SI unit of temperature is the kelvin (K). The U.S. measure of temperature has been the degree Fahrenheit.

In normal activities temperature is expressed in degrees Celsius. On the Celsius scale the freezing point of water is $0^{o}C$ and the boiling point of water is $100^{o}C$. These correspond respectively to the Fahrenheit temperatures of $32^{o}F$ and $212^{o}F$.

A temperature of one degree Celsius equals one degree kelvin exactly. Therefore $0^{o}C$ is 273.15 K and $100^{o}C$ is 373.15 K.

Conversion equations are

$$^{o}C = \frac{5}{9} \; (^{o}F - 32) \tag{1}$$

$$^{o}F = \frac{9}{5} \; (^{o}C + 32) \tag{2}$$

A "grade" is one-hundredth of a right angle as used in Europe in the late 1700's and early 1800's (see Klein, 1974, pages 114-115) and the "centigrade" is one hundredth of a "grade". The use of the word centigrade with reference to temperature is not only incorrect but also obsolete.

Inherent in all measurements is the expression of accuracy. A cloth tape is acceptable in dressmaking but no one would think of using it for precise measurement as in the layout for machining of a crank-case which must be accurate to a thousandth of an inch. In water resource management very few measurements justify expression to 4 significant places. Certain rules have been adopted for rounding off numerical expressions.

The general rule for rounding is: if the digit in the decimal place to be eliminated is 5 or greater, increase the digit in the next decimal place to the left by 1; if the digit to be eliminated is less than 5, retain the numerical value of the next digit to the left unchanged.

It is a requirement of the rounding procedure that consideration be given only to the first digit to the right of the position of the digit expressing the degree of accuracy desired. A chain reaction procedure starting at the extreme right digit and rounding off progressively to the left is not correct. For example

```
0.1414 rounded to thousandths is   0.141
3.147 rounded to tenths is          3.1    (not 3.2)
0.345 rounded to tenths is          0.3
2346    rounded to hundreds is     2300
```

There are specific rules for rounding when data are to be added, subtracted, divided, or multiplied. Time is saved and the chances for making mistakes are reduced if not more than one significant digit beyond the least accurate factor is used in the computation and the answer is rounded off as indicated by the significance of the least accurate factor. A detailed discussion is given in Section 4 of ASTM E 380-76.

When dealing with very large numbers it is common in scientific endeavors to use a form of notation which will incorporate an expression of the number of significant figures without using ponderous numbers. Scientific notation using powers of 10 is summarized in the following table:

| American system expression | Multiples and submultiples | Prefix | Symbol |
|---|---|---|---|
| Quintillion | $10^{18}$ | exa | E |
| Quadrillion | $10^{15}$ | peta | P |
| Trillion | $10^{12}$ | tera | T |
| Billion | $10^{9}$ | giga | G |
| Million | $10^{6}$ | mega | M |
| Thousand | $10^{3}$ | kilo | k |
| Hundred | $10^{2}$ | hecto | h |
| Ten | $10^{1}$ | deka | da |
| Tenth | $10^{-1}$ | deci | d |
| Hundredth | $10^{-2}$ | centi | c |
| Thousandth | $10^{-3}$ | milli | m |
| Millionth | $10^{-6}$ | micro | $\mu$ |
| Billionth | $10^{-9}$ | nano | n |
| Trillionth | $10^{-12}$ | pico | p |
| | $10^{-15}$ | femto | f |
| | $10^{-18}$ | atto | a |

Large numbers up to and including a million have the same definitions in the American system of expression as they do in the French, British, and German systems. According to Webster (1971, p 1549) the term "billion" in the American system is equal to 1,000 million or $10^9$. In the European system, usually referred to as British, a billion is one million million, $10^{12}$, which is equivalent to the American "trillion", $10^{12}$. The British trillion is $10^{18}$. This confusion can be avoided by using powers of 10 when dealing with figures above one million.

An example of methods of expression is Albert Einstein's fundamental mass-energy equation of 1905

$$E = mc^2. \tag{3}$$

The symbols in one expression of Einstein's equation are defined on page 209 of the Encyclopedia of Science and Technology (1971) as follows:

> $E$ is energy in ergs
> $m$ is mass in grams
> $c$ is the speed of light; $3 \times 10^{10}$ cm/sec.

Selby (1967) defines the speed of light in a vacuum as being:

$(2.997925 \pm 0.000002) \times 10^{10}$ centimeters per second.

Then $c^2$ is $8.987554 \times 10^{20}$ which rounded is $9 \times 10^{20}$.

Moller (1972, p 30) defines $c = 3 \times 10^8$ meters per second. It is extremely important when changing the definition of units or converting terms in an equation that all other terms be adjusted to retain homogeneity and that there be acknowledgment of the number of significant places.

## References

"Encyclopedia of Science and Technology", Vol. 8, McGraw-Hill Book Co., New York, 1971.

Klein, H. Arthur, "The World of Measurements", Simon and Schuster, New York, 1974.

Moller, C., "The Theory of Relativity", 2nd edition, Clarendon Press, Oxford, 1972.

"Standard for Commonly Used International System (SI) Units in Bureau of Reclamation Practice", Engineering and Research Center, Bur. of Recl., Bldg. 67, Denver Federal Center, Denver, Colo. 80225, Sept. 1976, available at no charge.

"Standard for Metric Practice", ASTM E 380-76[e], American Soc. for Testing Materials, 1916 Race St., Phila. Pa. 19103 with editorial corrections as of July, 1976.

"Standard Mathematical Tables", Samuel M. Selby, editor, 15th ed., The Chemical Rubber Co., Cleveland, Ohio, 1967.

"Webster's Third New International Dictionary of the English Language - Unabridged", Philip Babcock Gove, ed-in-chief, G. C. Merriam Co., 1971.

Bellamy (Topic 4, p 39) proposes the "Geospheric System of Units" for Meteorology to supplement deficiencies in the SI System.

Water Substance

Water substance, commonly considered to consist of two
atoms of hydrogen and one of oxygen ($H_2O$), is a most unique
substance.  Its molecular structure with flexible bonds endows
it with a unique array of physical and chemical properties.
It is one of the very few substances found in the human environment in the three states, vapor, liquid, and solid.  The
nature of life and much of the non-living aspects of our environment are the direct result of the unique properties of water.

A basic reference on water is the compendium by Dorsey
(1940).  The Geological Survey prepared in 1972 a condensed but
very informative pamphlet entitled, "What is Water".  An informative condensed review of the electrons, protons, neutrons,
chemical and nuclear changes involving isotopes and emissions
is Chap. 3 in the book by Moran, Morgan, and Wiersma (1973).

A detailed discussion illustrated with drawings of molecular models was prepared by Buswell and Rodebush (1956).  Their
paper includes a diagram depicting the 33 different substances
which exist as a result of different combinations of three isotopes of hydrogen:  ordinary hydrogen ($H^1$), deuterium ($H^2$), and
tritium ($H^3$), and of the three oxygen isotopes, ordinary oxygen
($O^{16}$), oxygen 17, and oxygen 18.  These common isotopes yield
18 different combinations.  The remaining of the 33 water substances are various ions.

Eisenberg and Kauzmann (1969) present in their 296-page
volume a discussion of water substances under five general
headings:  (1) the water molecule; (2) the real vapor; (3) ice;
(4) properties of liquid water; and, (5) models of liquid
water.

Water is one of the few substances which expands as it
changes from the liquid to the solid state.  Liquid water has a
density of 1 whereas the ordinary Ice Ih has a density of 0.916
at $0^\circ$ C and one atmosphere pressure.  There are nine forms of
ice as discussed by Hobbs (1974).  Water has a very high specific heat which is the amount of heat necessary to change the
temperature of a substance without a change in state.  The specific heat of water is 8 times as great as that of iron and
over 32 times that of lead.  The latent heat of fusion of water
is also very great.  It takes 13 times as much heat to melt a
gram of ice as it does a gram of lead.

A tabulation comparing the thermal characteristics of
water with that of other substances has been prepared by
Garstka (1964).  The latent heat of fusion is 79.7 calories per
gram at $0^\circ$ C.  The latent heat of vaporization of water at the
boiling point is 539.6 calories per gram.  The latent heat of

vaporization of water at 0° C is 596 calories per gram. The latent heat of sublimation of ordinary Ice Ih to form ordinary water vapor at 0° C is 676 calories per gram.

When water vapor condenses to form liquid water the latent heat of vaporization is released as sensible heat. When water freezes the latent heat of fusion is similarly released tending to slow down the rate of formation of ice. Conversely adding ice cubes to water cools the liquid as the liquid supplies the latent heat of fusion. The abstraction and release of the vast quantities of heat involved in the changes of state of the Earth's water substance are fundamental to meteorology and limnology.

Water has a very high surface tension a quality which has been used to explain the fact that sap has been lifted as high as 300 feet in trees as discussed by Veihmeyer (1964). Water is considered to be a universal solvent especially on polar compounds where its ability to ionize and form complex ions is especially important to all life, as discussed by Moran, Morgan and Wiersma (1973). Water makes up about 65 percent of the weight of a human body. Man can live for weeks without food but a loss of only 12 percent of the body's water content, which can occur in just a few days, is fatal.

There is an impressive and ever-expanding knowledge about water. The series edited by Felix Franks "Water - A Comprehensive Treatise" amounts to a total of 2,957 pages in 5 volumes issued between 1972 and 1975.

References

Buswell, Arthur M. and Worth H. Rodebush, "Water", Scientific American, vol. 194, no. 4, Apr. 1956.

Dorsey, N. Ernest, "Properties of Ordinary Water-Substance", American Chemical Society Monograph Series, Reinhold Publishing Corp., New York, 1940.

Eisenberg, D., and W. Kauzmann, "The Structure and Properties of Water", Oxford University Press, New York & Oxford, 1969.

Franks, Felix, Editor, "Water - A Comprehensive Treatise", Plenum Press, New York, London. This is a series of volumes:

Volume 1, "The Physics and Chemistry of Water, 596 pages, 1972.

Volume 2, "Water in Crystalline Hydrates - Aqueous Solutions of Simple Nonelectrolytes, 684 pp, 1973.

Volume 3, "Aqueous Solutions of Simple Electrolytes, 472 pages, 1973.

Volume 4, "Aqueous Solutions of Amphiphiles and Macromolecules, 839 pages, 1975.

Volume 5, "Water in Disperse Systems", 366 pages, 1975.

Garstka, Walter U., "Snow and Snow Survey", Section 10 in HANDBOOK OF APPLIED HYDROLOGY, Ven Te Chow, ed-in-chief, McGraw-Hill Book Co., New York, 1964.

Hobbs, Peter V., "Ice Physics", Oxford University Press, London, 1974.

Moran, Joseph M., Michael D. Morgan, James H. Wiersma, "An Introduction to Environmental Sciences", Little, Brown and Co., Boston, 1973.

Veihmeyer, Frank J., "Evapotranspiration", Section 11 in HANDBOOK OF APPLIED HYDROLOGY, Ven Te Chow, ed-in-chief, McGraw-Hill Book Co., New York, 1964.

"What is Water?", Folder by U.S. Geological Survey, Government Printing Office, Washington, D.C. (Stock No. 2401-2193) 1972.

The water resource is the product of the operation of the
hydrologic cycle.  A broad definition of hydrology is quoted
from the Transactions of the American Geophysical Union (1962):
"Hydrology is the science that treats of the waters of the
Earth, their occurrence, circulation and distribution, their
chemical and physical properties, and their reaction with their
environment including their relation to living things.  The
domain of hydrology embraces the full life history of water on
the Earth."

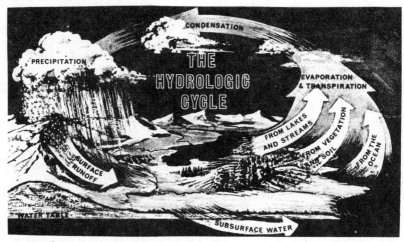

Figure 6-1  The Hydrologic Cycle

This figure is an artist's conception taken from the U.S.
Geological Survey's folder, "The Hydrologic Cycle" (1973).
This is one of many hydrologic charts in the engineering and
hydrologic literature.  Figure 6-2 on page 21 includes currently applied water resource management concepts.

Essentially the hydrologic cycle is a boiler and distillation plant with the energy supplied by the sun.  It is a
closed system with practically no water being lost or gained
for the Earth as a whole.  Philosophers from times immemorial
have been conjecturing about the hydrologic cycle.  Biswas
(1965) traces some of the recorded history of the hydrologic
cycle to Thales who is estimated to have lived during the
period 624 to 598 B.C.

The estimated water supply of the Earth is so vast that
it is usually reported in cubic miles.  Table 6-1 from USGS
Circular 601-1 (1973) is an accounting for the World's estimated water supply.  The oceans of the World account for 97.2
percent of the total.  Fresh water lakes account for 0.009

Figure 6-2   This figure is available free in two sizes: 22 x
15 inches and 66 x 42 inches from the Bureau of
Reclamation, Engineering and Research Center, Code 922,
P.O. Box 25007, Denver Federal Center, Denver, Colo.
80225.

21

percent.  The average flowing in stream channels accounts for
0.0001 percent; total estimated groundwater accounts for 0.62
percent, and the ice caps and glaciers account for a surprisingly large 2.15 percent of the total water.  The atmosphere
at sea level accounts for only 0.001 percent.  The water in
the unsaturated zone of subsurface water which includes soil
moisture accounts world-wide for 0.005 percent and this is the
soil moisture upon which all plant life, and indirectly, all
animal life depends.  It is to be seen that our National welfare is founded on extremely small percentages of the Earth's
total water supply.

| Location | Surface area (square miles) | Water volume (cubic miles) | Percentage of total water |
|---|---|---|---|
| **Surface water:** | | | |
| Fresh-water lakes ------------- | 330,000 | 30,000 | 0.009 |
| Saline lakes and inland seas ----------------- | 270,000 | 25,000 | .008 |
| Average in stream channels ---- | ---------- | 300 | .0001 |
| **Subsurface water:** | | | |
| Water in unsaturated zone (includes soil moisture) ----- | | 16,000 | .005 |
| Ground water within a depth of half a mile --------- | 50,000,000 | 1,000,000 | .31 |
| Ground water—deep lying ----- | | 1,000,000 | .31 |
| **Other water locations:** | | | |
| Icecaps and glaciers ----------- | 6,900,000 | 7,000,000 | 2.15 |
| Atmosphere (at sea level) ------ | 197,000,000 | 3,100 | .001 |
| World ocean ----------------- | 139,500,000 | 317,000,000 | 97.2 |
| Totals (rounded) ------------ | ---------- | 326,000,000 | 100 |

Figure 6-1   World's Estimated Water Supply (Feth, 1973)

Of direct concern in everyday endeavors are three facets
of the hydrologic cycle: the average annual precipitation is
shown in Figure 6-3; the average annual runoff in Figure 6-4;
and the annual average lake evaporation is shown in Figure 6-5.
These figures are taken from "The Nation's Water Resources"
(1968).  Average flows in cubic feet per second of the large
rivers of the United States are shown in Figure 6-6 taken from
Iseri and Langbein (1974).

The character of the environment, the type of agriculture,
and the location of industry, all are predicated on the interaction at a particular site of precipitation, runoff, and
evaporation.

Appendix B is a glossary taken from "Water Policies for
the Future" (1973) defining terms in common usage as they apply
to the hydrologic cycle and water resource management.  A list
of many of the books dealing with hydrology is included.

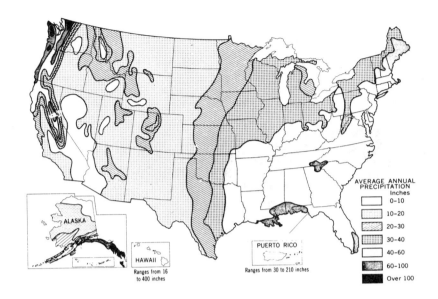

Figure 6-3          Average Annual Precipitation

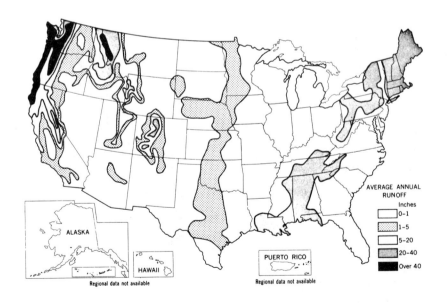

Figure 6-4          Average Annual Runoff

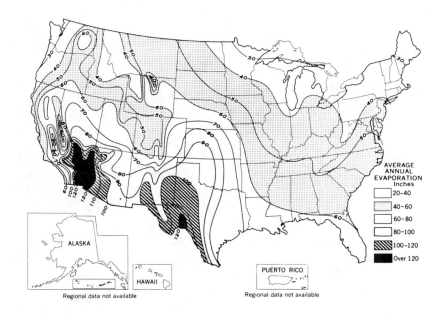

Figure 6-5     Average Annual Lake Evaporation

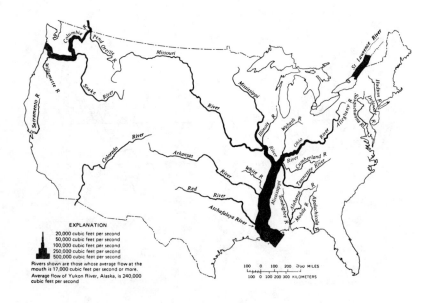

Figure 6-6  Average Flow of Large Rivers of the United States

## References

Biswas, Asit K., "The Hydrologic Cycle", Civil Engineering, pp 70-74, Apr. 1965.

"Definition of Hydrology" as prepared by the Federal Council of Science and Technology in June, 1972 and published in the Transactions of the American Geophysical Union, vol. 43, no. 4, p 493, Dec. 1962.

Feth, J. H.,"Water Facts and Figures for Planners and Managers" U.S. Geological Survey Circular 601-I, 1973.

Iseri, K. T., and W. B. Langbein, "Large Rivers of the United States", U.S. Geological Survey Circular 686, 1974.

"The Nation's Water Resources", Water Resources Council, Parts 1-7, 1968.

"The Hydrologic Cycle", U.S. Geological Survey Folder, INF - 73-2 (R-1), 1973.

"The Hydrologic Cycle", an 8-page folder, U.S. Dept. of Commerce, Environmental Science Services Admin., ESSA/PI 670003, June, 1967.

## List of Books Dealing With Hydrology

Ackerman, Edward A., and George O. G. Lof, "Technology in American Water Development", pub. for Resources for the Future Inc., by the John Hopkins Press, Baltimore, 710 pp, 1959.

Butler, S. S., "Engineering Hydrology", Prentice-Hall, Inc., Englewood Cliffs, New Jersey, 1957.

Chorley, Richard J., ed., "Water, Earth, and Man - A Synthesis of Hydrology, Geomorphology, and Socio-Economic Geography", Methuen & Co., Ltd., London, 558 pp, 1969.

Chorley, Richard J., ed.,"Introduction to Geographical Hydrology", Methuen & Co., Ltd., London, 1969. (This 206-page paperback consists of selected chapters extracted from the preceding reference.) Paperback published in 1971.

Chow, Ven Te, ed. in chief, "Handbook of Applied Hydrology", McGraw-Hill Book Co., New York, 1964. (Pages 1-16 to 1-22 list titles of many publications on hydrology in languages other than English.)

Eagleson, Peter S., "Dynamic Hydrology", McGraw-Hill Book Co., New York, 462 pp, 1970.

Gray, Donald M., ed. in chief, "Handbook on the Principles of Hydrology", pub. by the Secretariat, Canadian Natl. Committee for the International Hydrological Decade, Natl. Research Council of Canada, 1970. (Reprinted under agreement by the Water Information Center, Inc., Port Washington, N.Y., 1973.)

Heindl, L. A., "The Water We Live By - How to Manage it Wisely" Coward-McCann, New York, 1970.

Hewlett, John D., and Wade L. Nutter, "An Outline of Forest Hydrology", Univ. of Georgia Press, Athens, 1969.

"Hydrological Maps", A Contribution to the International Hydrological Decade, pub. jointly by the United Nations Educational, Scientific and Cultural Organization, Paris, France, and the World Meteorological Organization, Geneva. Printed in Switzerland. ISBN 92-3-101260-6, 1977.

"Hydrology Handbook", Manuals of Engineering Practice - No. 28, American Society of Civil Engineers, Adopted Jan. 17, 1949, reprinted 1952 and 1957.

Kazmann, R. G., "Modern Hydrology", Harper and Row, New York, 2nd ed., 1972.

Leopold, L. B., and W. B. Langbein, "A Primer on Water", U.S. Govt. Printing Office, Washington, D.C., 1960.

Leopold, Luna B., and Kenneth S. Davis, "Water", Life Science Library, Time-Life Books, 1960 and 1970. Reprinted 1972.

Linsley, R. K., M. A. Kohler, and J. L. H. Paulhus, "Applied Hydrology", McGraw-Hill Book Co., New York, 1949.

Linsley, R. K., M. A. Kohler and J. L. H. Paulhus, "Hydrology for Engineers", McGraw-Hill Book Co., New York. (A condensed version of the preceding reference. 2nd ed. 1975)

Meinser, O. E., "Hydrology  vol. IX of Physics of the Earth, McGraw-Hill Book Co., Inc., New York, 1942. (Reprinted by Dover Publications Inc., New York, 1949.)

Meyer, Adolph F., "The Elements of Hydrology", John Wiley and Sons, Inc., 1st ed., 1917.

Pereira, H. C., "Land Use and Water Resources - In Temperate and Tropical Climates", Cambridge Univ. Press, paperback 246 pp, 1973.

Rodda, John C., editor, "Facets of Hydrology", John Wiley and Sons, Ltd., ISBN 0 471 01359 5. Printed in Great Britain, 1976.

Satterlund, Donald R., "Wildland Watershed Management", The Ronald Press Co., New York, 370 pp, 1972.

Sopper, Wm. E., and Howard W. Lull, editors, "Forest Hydrology" Proceedings of a Natl. Science Foundation Advanced Science Seminar, Aug. 29-Sept. 10, 1965, Pergamon Press, 1st ed. 813 pp., 1967.

Todd, David Keith, editor, "The Water Encyclopedia", Water Information Center, Port Washington, N.Y., 559 pp, 1970.

Vallentine, H. R., "Water in the Service of Man", Penguin Books, Baltimore, Md., paperback No. A852, 1967.

van der Leeden, Frits, compiler and editor, "Water Resources of the World - Selected Statistics", Water Information Center Inc., Port Washington, N.Y., 568 pp, 1975.

Viessman, Warren Jr., Terence E. Harbaugh, John W. Knapp, "Introduction to Hydrology", Intext Educational Publishers, New York, 415 pp, 1972.

"Water, Yearbook of Agriculture, 1955", U.S. Dept. of Agriculture, 751 pp, 1955.

Ward, R. D., "Principles of Hydrology", McGraw-Hill Pub. Co., London, 403 pp, 1967.

Wisler, C. O., and E. F. Brater, "Hydrology", John Wiley & Sons Inc., New York, 2nd edition, 408 pp, 1949, 3d printing 1965.

The atmosphere is a layer of a mixture of gases completely enveloping the earth. This mixture which is invisible and odorless sustains life. It is the transporting mechanism for the operation of the hydrologic cycle. The composition of air varies. Table 7-1 from Petterssen (1964) gives the composition of dry air below 15 miles (25 kilometers).

Table 7-1    Composition of Dry Air Below 15 miles (25 Km)

| Gas | Volume Percent |
| --- | --- |
| Nitrogen, $N_2$ . . . . . . . . . . . . | 78.09 |
| Oxygen, $O_2$ . . . . . . . . . . . | 20.95 |
| Argon, Ar . . . . . . . . . . | 0.93 |
| Carbon dioxide, $CO_2$ . . . . . . . | 0.03 |
| Total . . . . . . . . . . | 100.00 (approx.) |

All other gases amounting to 0.003 percent consist of traces of neon, helium, krypton, hydrogen, xenon, ozone, and radon among others. Although ozone ($O_3$) makes up only less than one part in 400,000 by weight it is extremely important to all life since ozone prevents harmful ultraviolet radiation from reaching the surface of the Earth where life exists. The composition of the air above 5 thousand miles is made up about equally of hydrogen and helium.

Carbon dioxide, although small in percentage content, is very important to all life since it is a raw material in the photosynthesis. With very few exceptions practically all of the life forms on Earth depend for their energy on combustion of substances the end product of which is carbon dioxide. Carbon dioxide produces a "green house" effect in that it interferes with the departure of long-wave radiation from the surface of the Earth. This could result in a temperature rise of the atmosphere and increase melting of polar ice caps.

The layers of the atmosphere are shown in Figure 7-1 from the "Pilots' Weather Handbook" (1955), on the following page. Almost all clouds, storms, and horizontal winds are in the lowest-lying layer, the troposphere, in which temperature decreases with elevation. The thickness of the troposphere is about 54,000 feet over the equator and about 28,000 feet over the poles.

Practically all of the water vapor exists in the atmosphere below about 25,000 feet. About one-half of the weight of the air is below 18,000 feet (500 millibars); about three-fourths is below 36,000 feet (250 millibars); and the remaining one-fourth is spread out through the above-lying 500 miles.

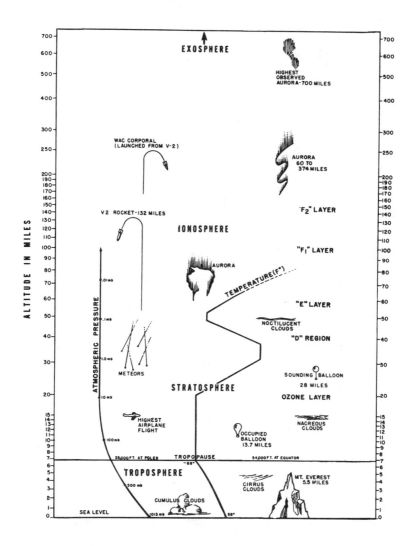

Figure 7-1    Layers of the Atmosphere and Altitude-
             Pressure Relationships

Dry air is a rarity on the surface of the earth.  The
presence of free water surfaces in the oceans and lakes and
the vegetal cover of the earth result in evaporation which is
a change of state from solid or liquid water to a water vapor.
Vast quantities of energy are either abstracted or released
when the water substance goes through changes in its three
states, solid, liquid, and vapor and this procedure coupled
with the radiation imbalance on the surface of the Earth as it
rotates, going progressively through night and day cycles, with

29

complications introduced by the Coriolis effect results in a flow of air masses of dissimilar composition and density. Water has one of the largest latent heats of fusion and specific heats as discussed by Garstka (1964).

Except for the water vapor content the composition of the atmosphere up to 15 miles is remarkably uniform throughout the globe. The water vapor content however is continually varying. An understanding of what is happening in the air-water-vapor relationship can be shown through a review of the basic gas laws of physics as they pertain to partial pressures in a mixture of gases. See Petterssen (1964).

In meteorology the unit of pressure commonly used is the millibar. The millibar is equal to 1,000 dynes per square centimeter. The barometric height of 75.01 centimeters at $0^\circ$ Celsius is equivalent to 1,000 millibars usually written "mb". One millibar equals 0.0143 psi or 0.0295 inch of mercury. For average conditions one atmosphere is equal to 1013.25 mb. In may applications 1000 mb is used to simplify computations.

The vapor pressure of water in the air expressed in millibars is usually symbolized by the small, italicized, letter "e". List (1963) has assembled psychrometric tables together with a wealth of other information. Various slide rules and alignment charts have been developed for specific uses of psychrometric data.

The weight of the atmosphere exerts a pressure upon the surface of the Earth. This amounts to 2,116 pounds per square foot or 14.7 pounds per square inch and the weight of the atmosphere at sea level resting upon a 2,000-square-foot house is 4,232,000 pounds if the interior were a vacuum.

Pressure exerted at sea level under standard conditions is called one atmosphere. This pressure balances in vacuum a column of mercury 76 centimeters or 29.92 inches in height. By common accord this pressure is expressed as the barometric height of the column of mercury in terms of sea-level equivalent the actual elevation of the point of observation notwithstanding. The common altimeter is a mechanical aneroid barometer whose dial is expressed in elevations instead of barometric pressures.

The amount of water vapor in the air exacts a profound effect upon the processes of life. The same amount of water vapor may result in widely varying micro-climatic impacts depending upon temperature and pressure.

Relative Humidity (RH) is the ratio, expressed as a percentage, of the amount of moisture in the air as compared to the amount of moisture that air would hold if it were saturated at the same dry bulb temperature.  RH is a dimensionless expression.  For example, with no change in the amount of water vapor RH of 24 percent at 80° F would become 48 percent at 60° F and, if the temperature were to drop to 40° F the RH would be 100 percent or the "dew point" for that parcel of air.

The relative humidity expression is especially important since it expresses the livability of a microclimate such as is found in our working places and homes.  Techniques for the measurement of the water vapor in the air are discussed in another Topic.  Figure 7-2, which appears on page 32, is a copy of Table 4 from Schroeder and Buck (1970).  This table permits conversion of observations of wet bulb and dry bulb temperatures to dew point temperatures and relative humidity percentages and is applicable at elevations between 101 and 1900 feet above sea level.  Psychrometric tables for use at other elevations have been assembled by Rechard (1967).

Depending upon the location on the surface of the Earth a mass of air characterized by temperature and especially water vapor content acquires an individuality which it tends to maintain unless modified by changes of temperature due to radiation and to changes of water vapor content through precipitation or evaporation.

Certain portions of the surface of the Earth produce recognizably distinct air masses which then flow around the globe in a never-ending but never precisely attained thermal balance of the Earth as a whole.  Since water vapor is only 5/8ths as heavy as dry air any mixture of dry air and water vapor will weigh less than dry air.  Cold dry air is dense and heavy; warm dry air is comparatively lighter.  Therefore an air mass made up of warm air with a large water vapor content will weigh considerably less than a cold air with a very low water vapor content.  Dry air at a temperature below the freezing point of water can contain a relatively very small amount of water vapor so that the colder the air becomes the heavier it is.

Because of the distinct density difference the air masses tend to flow across the surface of the Earth producing the "highs" and "lows" which are shown on weather maps.  The point of contact between two air masses is called a "front" usually described as a "cold" or "warm" front.  The cold air masses originate in the arctic or subarctic regions and the warm fronts start in the equatorial regions.  An artist's conception of the air masses is shown in Figure 7-3 from Weather for Air Crews (1962) on page 33.  The winds about a moving cold front are shown in Figure 7-4 from Weather for Aircrew Trainees (1944) on page 33; a warm front is shown in Figure 7-5 from the same reference also on page 33.

31

WET BULB TEMPERATURES °F

Relative humidity and dew-point table for
use at elevations between 501 and 1900 feet
above sea level.

Upper entry is Dew Point in °F

Lower entry is Relative Humidity,
Percent

Example: for 75° F Dry
Bulb and 60° F Wet Bulb

RH is 41 percent and
Dew Point is 50° F.

DRY BULB
TEMPERATURES
°F

Figure 7-2 Relative
Humidity and Dew-
Point Relationship

32

Figure 7-3

Cross Sections of
Typical Air Masses
of the Northern
Hemisphere. The
Jet Stream Meanders
with the Movement
of the Tropical and
Polar Air Masses.

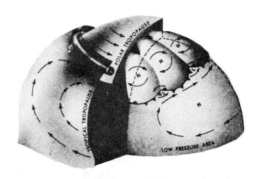

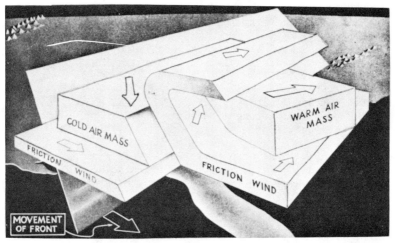

Figure 7-4   Winds in Relation to a Movement of a Cold Front

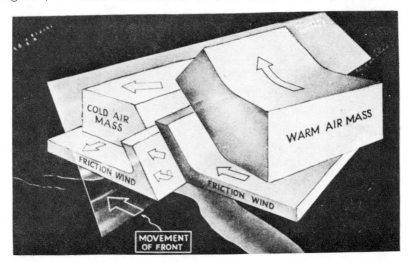

Figure 7-5   Winds in Relation to a Movement of a Warm Front

References

Garstka, Walter U., "Snow and Snow Survey", Section 10 in
    HANDBOOK OF APPLIED HYDROLOGY, Ven Te Chow, ed-in-chief,
    McGraw-Hill Book Co., New York, 1964.

List, Robert J., "Smithsonian Meteorological Tables", 6th ed.,
    2nd reprint, Pub. No. 4014 of the Smithsonian Institution,
    Washington, D.C., 1963.

Petterssen, Sverre, "Meteorology", Section 3 in HANDBOOK OF
    APPLIED HYDROLOGY, Ven Te Chow, ed-in-chief, McGraw-Hill
    Book Co., New York, 1964.

"Pilots' Handbook of Aeronautical Knowledge", Dept. of Trans-
    portation, Federal Aviation Administration, 207 pp,
    paperback, 1971.

"Pilots' Weather Handbook", C.A.A. Technical Manual No. 104,
    143 pp, Civil Aeronautics Admin., U.S. Dept. of Commerce,
    revised Dec. 1955.

Rechard, Paul A., "Psychrometric Tables for Wyoming (High
    Elevations)", Water Resources Series No. 6, Water
    Resources Research Institute, Univ. of Wyoming, Laramie,
    31 pp, Aug. 1967.

Schroeder, Mark J., and Charles C. Buck, "Fire Weather", U.S.
    Dept. of Agriculture, Forest Service, Agriculture Hand-
    book 360, 229 pp, May, 1970.

"Weather for Aircrews", Dept. of the Air Force, AF Manual
    105-5, 1 September 1962.

"Weather for Aircrew Trainees", Air Forces Manual No. 6,
    154 pp, 14 February 1944.

Topic 8                    Meteorology

Meteorology is concerned with the changes of state and the
dynamic processes of the gaseous envelope of the earth. Insofar as hydrology is concerned the processes involved are based
upon thermodynamics although physical and chemical changes
assume increasing importance in the endeavor to manage the
quality of the atmosphere.

This subject considers those portions of the hydrologic
cycle which comprise the evaporation of water, primarily from
the oceans, its transport in the form of water vapor by the
global circulation pattern of the atmosphere, and its conversion to precipitation available for deposition on the sea and
land surfaces of the earth. Riehl (1972) has prepared an excellent presentation of meteorology in a text which does not
require higher mathematics or thermodynamics. Thompson and
O'Brien (1965) have prepared a superbly illustrated semi-
technical treatment of weather.

The polar and the tropical air masses originate primarily
over the oceans. When they impinge upon the continent a number
of extremely complex thermodynamic reactions occur. The movement of a polar air mass originating in the northwest and
traveling toward the southeast is shown in Figure 8-1 from
"Weather for Aircrew Trainees" (1944). As the maritime polar
air mass moves over the Pacific Ocean it picks up moisture.
When the air mass impinges upon the Cascade Mountains it is
forced upward. The reduction of pressure cools the air mass so
that its relative humidity attains 100 percent and at the dew
point level temperature the flat bases of the clouds can be
seen.

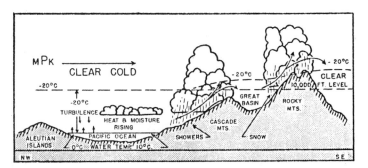

Figure 8-1   Movement of Maritime Polar Air Southeastward

Continued elevation results in rainfall and snowfall and as
the air mass continues in the southeasterly direction it de-
scends and is compressed and heated. This results in a
decrease in the relative humidity and a water vapor deficit.

35

Therefore as the air mass moves on it can no longer yield precipitation. In fact it becomes a drying wind as depicted in Figure 8-2 taken from "Weather for Aircrews" (1962). The descending air can become extremely dry and such winds have been given the local names of foehn in the European Alps; Chinook in the Northwest and the western slope of the Rocky Mountains; and Santa Ana in Southern California. Dust storms are often associated with such descending air flows and the danger of forest fires is greatly increased.

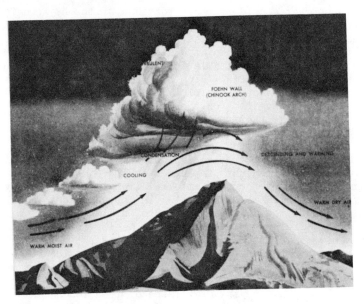

Figure 8-2    An Air-Flow Pattern With Associated Clouds
Which Produces a Dry Down-Slope Foehn Wind

The position of the jet stream (see Figure 7-3, page 33) which occurs between the polar and the tropical tropopauses is very important in meteorology. These narrow, meandering, high-velocity air currents may be identified by observing the clouds as described by Schaefer (1953).

If the precipitation of the central United States depended only on the water transported from the northwest the area would be very dry. However much of the precipitation east of the Rocky Mountains and throughout the Great Plains comes from the Gulf of Mexico. Holzman (1937) presented a condensed discussion of sources of moisture for precipitation in the United States.

The changes in temperature of an air mass as it flows over an orographic barrier or is elevated by convective vertical movement is described by meteorologists in terms of "lapse rate". Barometric pressure drops with increase in elevation in the troposphere. By common accord barometric readings are all expressed in terms of mean sea level equivalent instead of actual pressure. Therefore the actual barometric pressure at Denver, Colorado, is around 25 inches even when the dials of aneroid barometers show 30 inches. As the air expands with altitude its temperature drops. The rate of change of temperature with height in the free atmosphere is the lapse rate. Should an increase in temperature occur with altitude a "temperature inversion" condition prevails. The presence of a temperature inversion interferes with the rise of air currents creating stagnation leading to smog conditions.

Three terms are commonly used in referring to the type of lapse rate:

(a)  Adiabatic or dry-adiabatic lapse rate prevails when no heat is added or subtracted to the column of air rising in the free atmosphere; this is 5.4 degrees Fahrenheit per 1,000 feet.

(b)  Saturated-adiabatic lapse rate prevails when saturated air is lifted while the dew-point temperature of the water vapor is being reached. At the dew point water vapor releases about 596 calories per gram of water condensed, thereby heating the parcel of air and compensating for the dry-adiabatic rate of cooling. The saturated lapse rate is about $3^0$ F per thousand feet at low altitudes.

(c)  Pseudo-adiabatic lapse rate prevails when saturated vapor condenses and releases heat and water which falls to the ground while carrying some heat away from the parcel of air. The pseudo-adiabatic lapse rate has no fixed value since the lapse rate would depend upon temperature, precipitation rate, and rate of rise of air column among other factors. The average lapse rate is about $3.6^0$ F per thousand feet. In hydrology, the pseudo-adiabatic rather than the saturated-adiabatic lapse rate is usually used.

A rising or descending air column in nature seldom persists for any length of time since the extremely complex interactions of condensation and radiation interacting with frontal passages and as modified by the Coriolis effect come into play.

Another characteristic of air masses especially over smaller areas is that of stability. Stability and dynamic instability are related to lapse rate. The lapse rate expresses the vertical distribution of temperature in the atmosphere. If the vertical distribution is such that a parcel of air resists displacement the air is in a stable condition. This condition can be observed on relatively windless days around sunrise and sunset when the incoming radiation from outer space, including

the sun, and the back radiation from the earth, are in exact
balance.  Under such stable conditions smoke from a trash bur-
ner or steam from a condenser cooler at a thermal electric power
plant will rise, cooling adiabatically, until the expansion
with elevation cancels the density difference created by the
input of heat.  Upon attaining that height the smoke or steam
will flatten out or make an abrupt turn in the direction of the
general local air movement.

If a small parcel of air, upon being induced to rise, continues to rise from that point at an increasing vertical velocity, the condition is said to be unstable.  A temperature inversion may suppress its penetration by rising air columns.
Instability leads to the creation of convective cells which are
one of the principle mechanisms of the precipitation process.
Stability of the air affects the flow as air is lifted over a
mountain as shown in Figure 8-3 from Schroeder and Buck (1970).

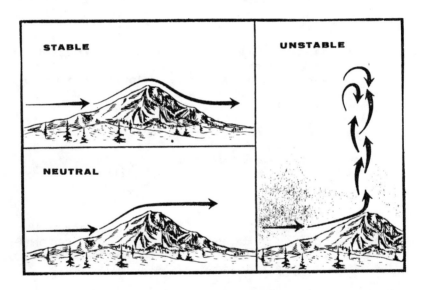

Figure 8-3  As air is lifted over mountains the resulting air
flow may yield a foehn wind as shown in the upper
left.  Unstable air could set up a convective cell,
as shown in the upper right, which could yield precipitation if there is sufficient moisture in the
incoming air.

The September, 1970 issue of Scientific American is in
effect a symposium on the Biosphere.  Penman's article is a
discussion of the water cycle in relation to energy and plant
growth.  In addition to Penman's discussion papers are included by other authors on the oxygen, carbon, nitrogen, and mineral cycles and on the energy cycles of the Earth and of the

Biosphere.

Battan (1974) has prepared a highly informative non-mathematical treatment of meteorology in his booklet, "Weather". Another booklet by Lehr, Burnett, and Zim (1965) showing meteorological instruments on pages 118 through 130, is also called "Weather". A standard professional reference is the compendium edited by Malone (1951). Maunder (1970) discusses economic, social, physiological, political, and legal aspects of weather. The folder entitled "Clouds" (1974) shows photographs printed in color of cloud forms and is highly recommended.

How a person reacts to exposure to wind depends upon a complex interaction of variables among which are air temperature, wind speed, relative humidity, solar radiation, type of clothing, health condition, and personal metabolism. The integrated effect is "wind chill". Arkin (1974) presents a nomogram and a table in his review of the subject. Wind chill describes the relative rate of cooling. For example, a combination of $20^\circ$ F and a 10-mile-per-hour wind has the same cooling effect as a temperature of $3^\circ$ F and a 4-mph wind.

Some of the shortcomings in meteorology and aeronautics of the SI system of units (see Topic 4) are discussed by Bellamy (1972) in the proposal of his "Geospheric System of Units".

Weather folk-lore goes back to prehistoric times. Nomads, herdsmen, farmers, woodsmen, and sailors have long observed the actions of animals, birds, and insects, as they react to coming weather changes. Garriott (1903) has assembled weather folklore and local weather signs for selected cities in the United States.

## References

Arkin, M. A., "Wind Chill (Equivalent Temperatures)", Environmental Information Summaries, C-3, NOAA, National Climatic Center, Asheville, North Carolina, Sept., 1974.

Battan, Louis J., "Weather", Prentice Hall, Inc., Inglewood Cliffs, New Jersey, paperback, 136 pp, 1974.

Bellamy, John C., "Meteorological Aspects of the Units Problem" Bulletin of the American Meteorological Society, vol. 53, no. 2, pp 102-120, Feb. 1972.

"Clouds", A 7-inch by $10\frac{1}{2}$-inch folder, printed in color, U.S. Dept. of Commerce, Natl. Oceanic and Atmospheric Admin., NOAA/PA 71012, U.S. Govt. Printing Office, 35¢, 1974.

Garriott, E. B., "Weather Folk-Lore and Local Weather Signs", U.S. Dept. of Agri. Weather Bureau, Bull. No. 294, 1903.

Holzman, Benjamin, "Sources of Moisture for Precipitation in
    the United States", U.S. Dept. of Agriculture, Tech. Bull.
    No. 589, 42 pp, Oct. 1937.

Lehr, Paul E., R. Will Burnett, and Herbert S. Zim, "Weather",
    Golden Press, New York, 160 pp, 1965.

Malone, Thomas F., editor, "Compendium of Meteorology", pre-
    pared by H. R. Byers, H. E. Landsberg, H. Wexler,
    E. Haurwitz, A. E. Spilhaus, H. C. Willett, and
    H. G. Houghton, Amer. Meteorological Society, Boston,
    Mass., 1334 pp, 1951.

Maunder, W. J., "The Value of the Weather", Methuen and Co.,
    Ltd. London, 388 pp, paperback, 1970.

Penman, H. L., "The Water Cycle", Scientific American, Sept.,
    1970, vol. 223, no. 3, pp 99-108, Sept. 1970.

Riehl, Herbert, "Introduction to the Atmosphere", McGraw-Hill
    Book Co., New York, 2nd edition, 516 pp, 1972.

Schaefer, Vincent J., "The Use of Clouds for Locating the Jet
    Stream", The Aeroplane, Oct. 30, 1953.

Schroeder, Mark J., and Charles C. Buck, "Fire Weather", U.S.
    Dept. of Agriculture, Forest Service, Agriculture Hand-
    book 360, 229 pp, May, 1970.

Thompson, Philip D., and Robert O'Brien, "Weather", Life
    Science Library, Time Inc., New York, 200 pp, 1965.

"Weather for Aircrews", Dept. of the Air Force, AF Manual
    105-5, 1 September 1962.

"Weather for Aircrew Trainees", Air Forces Manual No. 6,
    154 pp, 14 February 1944.

The following is a quotation from page 4 of "Climate and
Man" (1941): "The distinction between climate and weather is
more or less artificial, since the climate of a place is
merely a build-up of all the weather from day to day and the
weather is merely a day-by-day break down of the climate. It
seems to be a useful distinction, however, and there will probably continue to be meteorologists concentrating on the daily
weather and climatologists concentrating on the longer time
range." This reference, consisting of 1,238 pages, continues
to be one of the outstanding treatments of the subject.

Its title notwithstanding, the book by Conway, May and
Armstrong, (1963) is in effect an assembly of climatological
data. It contains numerous tabulations of temperatures, precipitation, and other data not only for the United States but
also for stations in many other parts of the world. There are
several maps of the world and 58 maps of the conterminous
United States presenting in graphic form various climatological
characteristics.

"The Water Atlas" by Geraghty, Miller, van der Leeden, and
Troise (1973) is made up of 122 plates dealing with climatology
and the water resource. Todd (1970) presents in the first 57
pages climatological data for the United States. Pages 431-451
of van der Leeden's computation (1975) tabulate temperatures
and precipitation data for representative world-wide stations.
"Climatic Atlas of the United States" was prepared by the
Environmental Science Services Administration in June, 1968.

Entrancing discussions of the early history of the development of climatological instruments are presented in a number
of chapters by Biswas (1970). At one time it was considered
adequate to observe the total amounts of rainfall, including
snow depths, the daily maximum-minimum temperatures, to report
the earliest and latest dates of killing frosts, to estimate
the percentage of cloud cover, and to mention the direction
from which the wind was blowing. Increased appreciation for
the need for more detailed climatological data has led to the
continuing development of complex meteorological and climatological instruments.

Charles Denison (1893), Professor of Diseases of the Chest
and of Climatology, University of Denver, prepared a book on
climates of the United States.

The very comprehensive compilation containing data assemblies printed out by a computer from storage in tapes of the
climate of Arizona is given by Sellers and Hill (1974). Benci
and McKee (1977) have summarized monthly temperature and

precipitation data for Colorado for the period 1951-1970. "Climates of the States" (1974) is a two-volume compilation prepared by NOAA.

Observations at weather stations staffed by professional personnel are made in accordance with "Federal Meteorological Handbook No. 1 - Surface Observations", which was first issued in January, 1970. There have been four changes and a Part B has been issued. The total assembly of these releases is almost one-inch deep. Detailed descriptions are given in the References.

The climatological records of the United States are based upon the observations made currently in accordance with the December, 1972 revision of the "National Weather Service Observing Handbook No. 2 - Substation Observations - Supersedes Circular B". (The first edition of Circular B-C was released as a revision in 1892.) Observing Handbook No. 2 is a 77-page publication containing numerous photographs and drawings of instruments and installations.

The National Weather Service Observing Handbook No. 2, revised December, 1972, states in the Preface that 12,000 volunteer observers regularly contribute their time gathering climatological data with instruments provided by the NWS and that approximately 1400 other persons and agencies provide the NWS gratuitously with climatological data from their own instruments. The most recent count of cooperative observers and agencies supplying climatological data to the NWS was made in July, 1977 at which time there were 11,000 volunteer observers and 823 other personnel and agencies (Clark, 1977).

While the importance of climatological data in the Nation's water and air resource management is steadily increasing the observing networks are shrinking at an alarming rate. This disturbing trend will no doubt continue to the detriment of the management of the quality of the environment. When the climatological observations were of interest chiefly to agriculture the Weather Bureau was able to secure the cooperation of unpaid observers throughout the country.

At one time the Weather Bureau's concept of an adequate network was one observing station per county. This might have been satisfactory in the populous East where many of the counties are about 50 miles wide but it was found to be inadequate in other parts of the United States. With the development of commercial aviation many observing stations were financed by the Federal Aviation Administration for a time. Various Federal action agencies such as the Forest Service, Soil Conservation Service, U.S. Army Corps of Engineers, Tennessee Valley Authority, National Park Service, Bureau of Land Management, and the Bureau of Reclamation cooperated with the Weather

42

Bureau as did private power companies and flood control and engineering districts and numerous Universities and State agencies. The volunteer climatological observing network has been shrinking as the old observers move away or retire. Also many cooperating governmental and private interests have found it undesirable to continue the operation of stations on a free basis as their personnel are assigned to duties more closely related to the objectives of their organization.

One of the problems which all users of climatological data have encountered is that of fragmentary, sporadic records. Often data came from stations not maintained at the same location. Very seldom has concurrent operation been done at old and new sites to provide a basis for correlation. Although extrapolation and interpolation can be attempted by statistical techniques such synthesized figures are a poor substitute for observations.

Data yielded by the observing networks are currently assembled by the Environmental Data Service, NOAA, Dept. of Commerce, at the National Climatic Center, Asheville, North Carolina 28801. The Center publishes for each state 13 issues of a series entitled, "Climatological Data", consisting of a separate issue for each month and an annual summary prepared after the end of a calendar year. The National Climatic Center is the repository of all official records going back to the very beginning of observations. Very few libraries in the country have a complete and unbroken series of Climatological Data.

The Federal Government subsidizes commercial aviation, railroads, highway systems, inland waterways, and many other activities related to environmental management. The time has come for an acknowledgement of the fact that the important and necessary climatological networks are in serious trouble. Only a reorganization including detailed assignment of responsibility and financial support can guarantee perpetuation of climatological networks.

A constructive plan for the continuation of this activity could be the assignment of responsibility for field operation of climatological networks to the County Commissioners or their equivalent and that the Counties be provided with Federal funding.

References

Benci, John F., and Thomas B. McKee, "Colorado Monthly Temperature and Precipitation Summary for Period 1951-1970", Dept. of Atmospheric Science, Colo. State University, Fort Collins, Colo., Climatology Report No. 77-1, March, 1977.

Biswas, Asit K., "History of Hydrology", American Elsevier Publishing Co., New York, 1970.

Clark, Robert A., Associate Director, National Weather Service (Hydrology), communication of Aug. 12, 1977 in reply to request for information.

"Climate and Man", Yearbook of Agriculture, 1941, Dept. of Agriculture, Government Printing Office, Washington, D.C. 1941.

"Climates of the States", Water Information Center, Inc., Port Washington, N.Y., 1974 in two volumes:
    Vol. 1.  Eastern States including Puerto Rico and the U.S. Virgin Islands, pp 1-480 and appendix
    Vol. 2.  Western States including Alaska and Hawaii, pp 481-975 plus appendix.
There are individual authors for each State with data and references included.

"Climatic Atlas of the United States", 80 pages, 18" x 24", Environmental Data Service, Environmental Science Services Admin., U.S. Dept. of Commerce, June, 1968.

Conway, H. McKinley, Jr., Stancel L. May, Jr., Evan Armstrong, Jr., "The Weather Handbook - A Summary of Weather Statistics for Principal Cities Throughout the United States and Around the World", Conway Publications, Atlanta, Ga. 1963.

Denison, Charles, "Climates of the United States - In Colors", The W. T. Keener Company, Chicago, Ill., 1893.

"Federal Meteorological Handbook No. 1 - Surface Observations", Change No. 3 Includes Changes 1 and 2, effective July 1, 1975.
    Change No. 4, effective Jan. 1, 1976
    Part B (Additional Natl. Weather Service Instructions) effective July 1, 1975.
Changes Nos. 3 and 4 prepared jointly by U.S. Dept. of Commerce, U.S. Dept. of Defense, and U.S. Dept. of Transportation.
    Part B prepared by Natl. Weather Service, NOAA, U.S. Dept. of Commerce.

Geraghty, James J., D. W. Miller, F. van der Leeden, and F. L. Troise, "Water Atlas of the United States", Water Information Center, Port Washington, New York, 1973.

"Observing Handbook No. 2, Substation Observations", Supersedes Circular B, National Weather Service, NOAA, U.S. Dept. of Commerce, 77 pages, Revised Dec. 1972.

Sellers, William D., and Richard H. Hill, "Arizona Climate
    1931-1972", The University of Arizona Press, Tucson, Ariz.
    revised 2nd edition, 616 pages, 1974.

Todd, David Keith, Ed., "The Water Encyclopedia", Water Inform-
    ation Center, Port Washington, New York, 1970.

van der Leeden, Frits, "Water Resources of the World", Water
    Information Center, Port Washington, New York, 568 pp,
    1975.

Topic 10    Extremes of Precipitation and Related Phenomena

A knowledge of extremes of precipitation and other climatological phenomena is of importance in agriculture, industry,
commerce, transportation and the National defense.

There is no doubt that extremes other than those reported
might have occurred at some time and in some place where there
were no instruments or personnel to record the occurrence. Not
all extremes are of equal scientific veracity. New instruments
are being developed, the best instruments might not be in cali-
bration, and human errors in observation and transcription undoubtedly occur. Whenever an extreme phenomena takes place it
is suggested that the observer report immediately to the National Weather Service or other scientific authority and that
the equipment or instrument which produced the record not be
touched until they can be inspected and their performance
verified.

van der Leeden (1975) presents in his Table 7.2, pages
431-451, temperature and precipitation data for representative
world stations listing extremes of minimum and maximum temperatures. In his precipitation tabulations he has endeavored to
use a standard period of 30 years 1931 to 1960 for locations in
the United States and for some other countries. The length of
record of extreme maximum and minimum temperatures includes all
available years of data for a given location and is usually for
a longer period.

Ludlum (1971) lists the outstanding weather events for the
United States and Canada for the period 1871 to 1970. His book
includes numerous photographs.

The listing in the paragraphs that follow is condensed
from "Weather Extremes Around the World" (1974). This reference lists citations to documents in support of the data
entered.

Rainfall

World, 1-minute, 1.23 inches, Unionville, Maryland, 4 July 1956

World, 20-minute, 8.10 inches, Curtea-de-Arges, Romania,
    7 July 1889

World, 42-minute, 12 inches, Holt, Missouri, 22 June 1947

World, 24-hour, 74 inches, Cilaos, La Reunion I.,
    15-16 March 1952

Yankeetown, Florida, had a 24-hour rainfall of 39 inches,
    5-6 September 1950

Canada, 24-hour, 19 inches, Ucluelet, British Columbia,
6 October 1967

World, 12-month, 1042 inches, Cherrapunji, India, August 1860
to July 1861

U.S., 12-month, 624 inches, Mt. Waialeale, Kauai, Hawaii,
24 July 1947 to 27 July 1948

World, Greatest Average Yearly Precipitation, 460 inches during a 32-year period, Mt. Waialeale, Kauai, Hawaii

North America, Greatest Average Precipitation, 262 inches
during a 14-year period, Henderson Lake, British Columbia

Europe, Greatest Average Precipitation, 183 inches during a
22-year period, Crkvice, Yugoslavia

Arica, Chile, had no rain for more than 14 consecutive years,
October 1903 through December 1917

U.S. Longest Dry Period, 767 days, Bagdad, California,
3 October 1912 to 8 November 1914

World's Lowest Average Yearly Precipitation, Arica, Chile,
0.03-inch during a 59-year period

North America Lowest Average Yearly Precipitation, 1.2 inches
during a 14-year period, Bataques, Mexico

U.S. Lowest Average Yearly Precipitation, 1.63 inches, Death
Valley, California

Europe, Lowest Average Precipitation, 6.4 inches during a 25-
year period, Astrakhan, U.S.S.R.

Snowfall - greatest depths

North America, 24-hour, 76 inches, Silver Lake, Colorado,
14-15 April 1921

Alaska, 24-hour, 62 inches, Thompson Pass, 29 December 1955

Canada, observation day, 44 inches, Livingston Ranger Station,
Alberta, 29 June 1963

North America, one storm, 189 inches, Mt. Shasta Ski Bowl,
California, 13-19 February 1959

North America, one season, 1122 inches, Rainer Paradise Ranger
Station, Washington, 1971-72.

Canada, one season, 880 inches, Kemano, Kildala Pass, British
Columbia, 1956-57

U.S. greatest depth of snow on the ground, 451 inches, Tamarack
California, 11 March 1911

Temperature - Highest

World, 136° F, El Azizia, Libya, 13 September 1922

Western Hemisphere and United States, 134° F, Death Valley,
California, 10 July 1913

Australia, 128° F, Cloncurry, Queensland, 16 January 1889

Europe, 122° F, Seville, Spain, 4 August 1881

Canada, 113° F, Midale and Yellow Grass, Saskatchewan, 5 July
1937

U.S. warmest winters, 70° F, average, Key West, Florida

Western Hemisphere hottest summers, 98° F, average, Death
Valley, California

Temperature - Lowest

World, -127° F, Vostok, Antarctica, 24 August 1960

Northern Hemisphere, -90° F, Verkhoyansk, U.S.S.R., 5 and 7
February 1892; and Oimekon, U.S.S.R., 6 February 1933

U.S., -80° F, Prospect Creek, Alaska, 23 January 1971

U.S., excluding Alaska, -70° F, Rogers Pass, Montana,
20 January 1954

U.S. lowest annual mean, 10° F, Barrow, Alaska

U.S. coolest summers, 37° F, average, Barrow, Alaska

U.S. coldest winters, -16° F, average, Barter Island, Alaska

Temperature Variations

U.S. largest 2-minute temperature rise, 49F° (-4 to 45),
Spearfish, South Dakota, 22 January 1943

U.S. largest 24-hour temperature fall, 100F° (44 to -56),
Browning, Montana, 23-24 January 1916

Rapid City, South Dakota, had three temperature rises and two
falls of 40F° or over during a period of 3 hours, 10
minutes, 22 January 1943

Verkhoyansk, U.S.S.R., has a difference of 183F° (93.5 to
-89.7) between highest and lowest recorded temperatures

## Miscellaneous

U.S. largest hailstone, <u>17.5 inches</u> circumference, Coffeyville, Kansas, 3 September 1970

World, highest sea-level air pressure, 32.01 inches, Agata, U.S.S.R., 31 December 1968

North America, highest sea-level air pressure, <u>31.52</u> inches, Medicine Hat, Alberta, 24 January 1897

World, lowest sea-level air pressure, <u>25.90 inches</u>, estimated by aerial reconnaissance in the eye of Typhoon Ida at 19° N, 135° E, 24 September 1958

World, highest wind speed peak gust, <u>231 miles per hour</u>, Mt. Washington, New Hampshire, 12 April 1934

Port Martin, Antarctica, had a 24-hour mean of <u>108 miles per hour</u>, 21-22 March 1951 and a mean monthly of <u>65 miles per hour</u>, March 1951

U.S. highest annual mean, <u>35 miles per hour</u>, Mt. Washington, New Hampshire

Malange, Angola, had <u>113 langleys</u> of solar radiation in 1 hour, 7 November 1961

## References

Ludlum, David M., "Weather Record Book - The Outstanding Events 1871-1970", Weatherwise, Inc., Box 230, Princeton, N.J., 1971.

van der Leeden, Frits, "Water Resources of the World", Water Information Center, Inc., New York, 568 pp, 1975.

"Weather Extremes Around the World", (Revision of NLABS Report TR-70-45-ES), Report No. ETL-TR-74-5, U.S. Army Topographic Labs., Fort Belvoir, Virginia, 52 pp, Apr. 1974.

Atmospheric moisture is converted to precipitation by two mechanisms differing with the temperatures of the water droplets forming the cloud. A cloud air temperature of below 32° F does not signify that the water is in the form of ice since microscopic-size droplets will remain in the super-cooled liquid state to temperatures as low as -39° F (or 39° C).

The vapor pressure of super-cooled water is greater than that of an ice crystal at the same temperature. A cloud of super-cooled water droplets devoid of crystallization nuclei will not yield precipitation unless it is cooled to -39° F at which temperature crystallization will take place. The formation of ice crystals from super-cooled water droplets is shown in Figure 11-1 taken from page 19 of the "Avalanche Handbook" by Perla and Martinelli (1976). The same crystallographic process takes place in the metamorphism of snow on the ground.

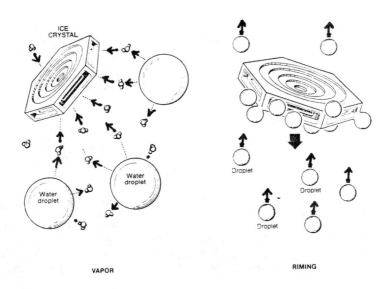

Figure 11-1    Ice-Crystal Formation from Super-Cooled Droplets

There is a fascinating history of a scientific assignment concerned with the practical problem of gas mask filters for the removal of smoke particles and for the creation of screening fogs for obscuring military activities and protection of cities as part of the Nation's efforts during World War II. Schaefer (1960) recounts how this assignment led to the serendipitous attainment of weather modification.

Schaefer (1946) reported the production of ice crystals in a cloud of super-cooled water droplets in the laboratory using a small commercial freezing unit. The last paragraph of his article is quoted in full: "It is planned to attempt in the near future a large-scale conversion of super-cooled clouds in the atmosphere to ice crystal clouds, by scattering small fragments of dry ice into the cloud from a plane. It is believed that such an operation is practical and economically feasible and that extensive cloud systems can be modified in this way."

In accordance with this announced plan Schaefer carried out the first experiment in modifying a cloud in the free atmosphere on November 13, 1946. A four-mile super-cooled alto stratus cloud having a temperature of minus 18.5 C with no trace of ice crystals was seeded with six pounds of solid carbon dioxide (dry ice). The seeding was performed in a small monoplane flying at an altitude of 14,000 feet above Mt. Greylock, Massachusetts.

Figure 11-2 shows 3 photographs of this unprecedented attainment. Figure 11-3 was taken over the Rome, New York, airport during Flight 53 of General Electric Company's "Project Cirrus". This attainment ushered in extensive attempts at weather modification, chiefly rain-making. A review of this era was prepared by Garstka (1963).

When an ice crystal or an aggregation of crystals in the shape of a snowflake falls through a warm layer of air nearer the ground it melts forming rain. If the air column is cold snow falls. In a thundercloud there may be alternate melting and freezing as the ice crystals fall and then may be lifted by the violent updrafts into levels of available super-cooled water droplets where they grow in size and weight. The up-and-down shuttle may be repeated numerous times creating hail sometimes of great size as reported in Topic 10.

In 1930, according to Thompson and O'Brien (1965) page 89, five German glider pilots soared into a thunderhead in the Rhon Mountains. Because of extremely violent updrafts all 5 bailed out and immediately were turned into hailstones as they were trapped in the up-and-down shuttle. Four fell to Earth frozen stiff with only one surviving.

One of the objectives of the South Dakota weather modification program, as described by Schleusener and Boyd (1972), is that of reducing hail. Many organizations have been engaged in hail suppression research but the results to date have been inconclusive as summarized by Atlas (1977).

"Cloud Seeding Principles and Techniques" (1971) is a condensed discussion of findings established concerning the behavior of natural and seeded clouds. The following figures,

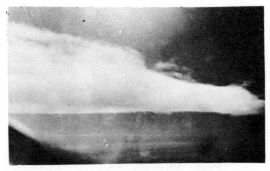

CLOUD BEFORE SEEDING.  BASE AT 13,600 FT. TEMP. -1.5° F.
SOUTHERN END OF CLOUD 4 MILES LONG ABOVE GRAYLOCK MT., MASS.
10:34 A.M., NOV. 13, 1946.

SAME SECTION OF CLOUD ABOVE FIVE MINUTES AFTER SEEDING.  NOTE
LONG DRAPERIES OF SUN.

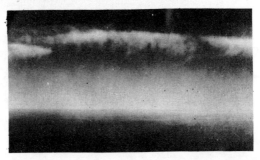

MID SECTION OF 4-MILE CLOUD ABOUT 15 MINUTES AFTER SEEDING.

Figure 11-2  The three photographs show the very first
     modification of a cloud as performed and photographed by
     Dr. Vincent J. Schaefer above Mt. Graylock, Mass. on the
     morning of Nov. 13, 1946. The alto-stratus cloud was
     modified by the release of six pounds of $CO_2$ pellets from
     aircraft.  Photographs supplied by Dr. Schaefer.

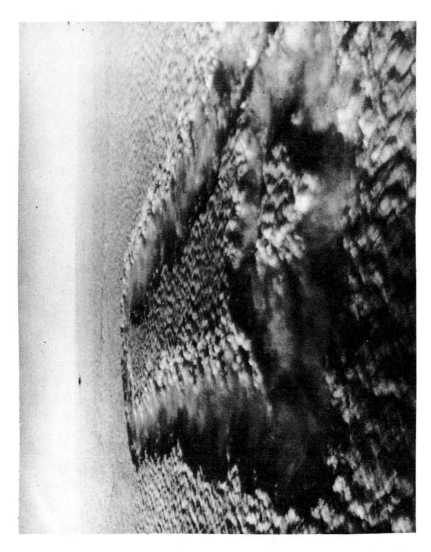

Figure 11-3 Eastern New York over Rome Airport, Nov. 24, 1948.
Racetrack pattern produced in a super-cooled stratus
cloud. The pattern in a solid overcast resulted from
seeding with crushed dry ice at a rate of 1.7 pounds per
mile. Long legs are ten miles long. The view of the
seeded area was photographed 24 minutes after seeding.
U.S. Signal Corps Engineering Laboratory photo, Flight 53
of Project CIRRUS. The photograph is taken from page 125
of "Final Report - Project CIRRUS, Part 1, Laboratory,
Field, and Flight Experiments", by Vincent J. Schaefer.
General Electric Laboratory Report No. RL-785,
Schenectady, N.Y., 170 pp, Mar. 1953.

11-4 through 11-8, are taken from this reference with updating
of temperatures as of September, 1977.

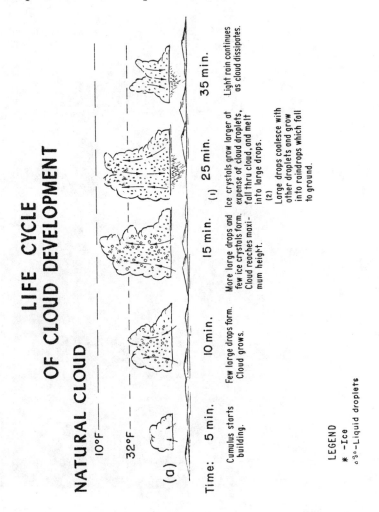

Figure 11-4    Natural Cumulus Super-Cooled Cloud Life Cycle

Figure 11-4 illustrates a 35-minute life cycle of a natural cumulus, super-cooled cloud and Figure 11-5 shows the life-
cycle development of modified clouds.  Orographic clouds are
shown in Figure 11-6 in which a cloud seeding performed for
increasing snowfall is illustrated.

A monograph on winter seeding of orographic clouds has
been prepared by Vardiman and Moore (1977).  The studies they
report were conducted in the Rocky Mountains and Pacific Coast

areas. Depending on stability, moisture content, temperature, and atmospheric mixing, increases in precipitation ranging from 20 percent to about 50 percent were demonstrated with decreases of about 50 percent under certain unfavorable conditions. Statistical analyses of the results are given by the authors indicating that the chances were 98 or 99 out of 100 that the results were real.

Ever since Schaefer (see Figure 11-2) modified a cloud, scientists and engineers have been facing the problem of evaluation of weather modification activities. One of the early

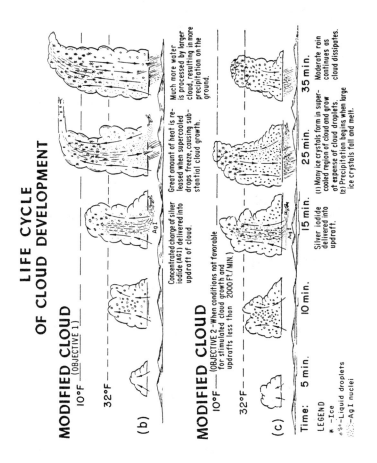

Figure 11-5    Life Cycles of Modified Super-Cooled Cumulus Clouds. The modification (b) is considerably more effective in augmenting precipitation than is modification (c).

55

analyses performed in 1952 is described in the "Report by the Committee for Evaluation of Bonneville Power Administration Cloud-Seeding Operations in the United States Portion of the Pend Oreille River Basin".

When the cloud-top temperatures are colder the -22° F seeding with a sublimation nucleating agent, such as silver iodide, may decrease the snowfall from that cloud as shown in Figure 11-7. Hobbs and Radke (1973) have shown that this technique can be used for deliberate cloud modification to carry moisture over an orographic barrier. Their case study describes work they performed in the Cascade Mountains of the State of Washington.

## NATURAL MOUNTAIN CLOUD

(Top Temperature:   -9° F to -22° F)

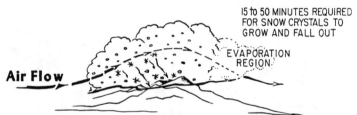

Relatively few snow crystals form & fallout. Most cloud water remains aloft in the form of tiny supercooled droplets

## SEEDED MOUNTAIN CLOUD

(Top Temperature:   -9° F to -22° F)

Many snow crystals form in seeded clouds, thus depositing most of the cloud water on the ground.

Figure 11-6   Natural and Seeded Mountain Clouds Modified to Increase Snowfall

Since much of the rainfall in the central and western portions of the United States and in other parts of the world may be released by the mechanisms triggered by hygroscopic agents rather than through the ice-crystal phenomena, extensive research is being conducted by many public and private organizations.

The release of rain from a warm cloud is shown in Figure 11-8. The modification of warm clouds, potentially of great world-wide importance, is a challenge to cloud physicists since the processes which cause large drops to form in a warm cloud are not as yet understood. Since probably most of the World's precipitation falls from warm clouds intensive research is being conducted by many organizations on the hygroscopic seeding processes.

## NATURAL MOUNTAIN CLOUD

(Top Temperature Colder Than -22° F)

Cloud is cold enough for many snow crystals to form naturally, thus depositing most of the cloud water on the ground.

## SEEDED MOUNTAIN CLOUD

(Top Temperature Colder Than -22° F)

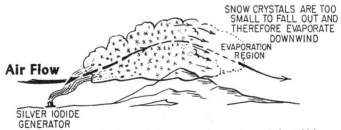

Seeding very cold clouds produces excessive snow crystals, which compete for available moisture. This limits their size which prevents them from falling to the ground.

Figure 11-7    Natural and Seeded Mountain Clouds Modified to Transport Moisture Over an Orographic Barrier (See Hobbs and Radke, 1973)

A program directed at increasing precipitation from summer cumulus in the Great Plains is described by Kahan, Todd, Howell, and Silverman (1976). This project has as its objective the verification of techniques with as rapid as possible an application of proven procedures to operational programs of weather modification under local control.

Over a period of about 45 years the people of Santa Clara County, California, have been storing surface runoff in extensive aquifers which underly much of the County. In a region of seasonal precipitation weather modification must be performed when clouds are available. Dennis and Kriege (1966) found a

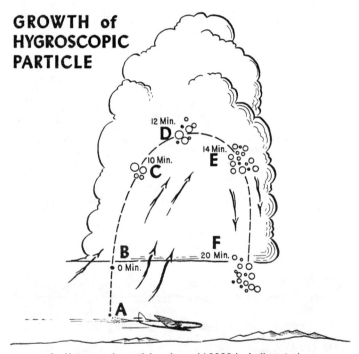

**GROWTH of HYGROSCOPIC PARTICLE**

A - Hygroscopic particle released (.0008 inch diameter)

B - Particle grows by condensation to .003 inch diameter

C - Particle grows by coalescence to .2 inch diameter and breaks up into smaller drops

D & E - Drops formed at C grow and break up again when diameter = .2 inch

F - Drops fall out the base of cloud

Figure 11-8    Modification of a Warm Cloud with Hygroscopic Agents

net increase in precipitation and that seeding effects were most evident down wind of the crest of the Santa Cruz Mountains.

The design of the Colorado River Basin Pilot Project is described by Hurley (1972). Howell (1972) discussed the impact of weather modification on planning activities in the Rio Colorado and the Rio Grande to the year 2020.

It was concluded by Aubert, Malhotra and Spiegler (1972) that management of the atmospheric water resource of the Connecticut River Basin in New England would offer definite advantages to domestic and industrial usages and to electric utilities in the region.

Not all weather modification is deliberate. There is increasing evidence that inadvertent modification of the atmosphere resulting from air pollution caused by industrial activity and emissions from internal combustion engines and thermal power plants may be exerting a much more profound effect on the human environment than has been attained by deliberate cloud-seeding operations. An example of an increasing literature on this subject is the article by Schaefer (1969).

Landsberg (1970) in his discussion of man-made climatic changes, deals with the impacts of ozone, carbon dioxide, air pollution particulates, and, especially, condensation and freezing nuclei produced by motor vehicles and other combustion processes. He believes that man-made aerosols may constitute a more acute problem than carbon dioxide. He cautions against complacency since man-made climatic changes may affect the global climate of the future.

Implications of the fascinating, long-range objective, that of managing the atmospheric circulation for World peace are explored by Garstka (1967).

Changnon(1976) in his review, with a total of 52 references one of which is as early as 1956, of inadvertent weather modification concludes that during the past 30 years the development of megalopolises in the United States has resulted in serious urban effects on meso-scale weather and climate. His analyses include the southern part of Lake Michigan and the St. Louis, Missouri, area in addition to other urban centers.

Huff (1977) analyzed the network of 225 recording rain gages over a 5,200 $km^2$ in the St. Louis, Missouri, area. He found a definite enhancement of high-intensity rainfall producing cells. He concludes that urban-induced, short-duration rainfall-intensity increase is so great as to merit inclusion of the inadvertent weather modification in the design and operation of hydrologic systems especially with regard to the control of flood flows.

Weather modification activities, although originally aimed at increasing rainfall and snowfall, are also being conducted for many other purposes. Among these are hail control, fog control especially at airports, the suppression of forest fires, reduction of the incidence of wildland fires set by lightning unaccompanied by precipitation, and hurricane and tornado control.

Farnes (1976) summarizes possible impacts of precipitation modification on watershed management with reference to soil moisture, snowmelt rates, volumes and intensity of runoff, snow loads, forest management practices, travel in mountain areas, and lightning control.

Weather modification activities are being conducted World-wide and the volume of literature published each year is extremely large and increasing rapidly. The following Federal organizations are active in weather modification in the United States: The National Science Foundation, Washington, D.C.; The Division of Atmospheric Water Resource Management of the Bureau of Reclamation, Denver, Colorado; and various divisions of the National Oceanic and Atmospheric Administration, Washington, D.C. Many irrigation districts, municipal water supply organizations and private agricultural and power interests participate.

The first man-made rain to reach the ground in Australia occurred in February, 1947 according to Watson (1976). His article is an excellent and very condensed summary of cloud physics research, weather modification experiments, and cloud-seeding operations in Australia.

The ownership of moisture in the clouds has been the subject of extensive discussion and many states now require licensing of cloud-seeding operators and special permission for this activity. The submission of detailed reports is also required. The University of Arizona's College of Law has prepared a 248-page monograph on legal implications (Oct. 1968).

At the American Association for the Advancement of Science annual meeting held in Denver, Colorado, February 20-25, 1977 a Symposium entitled "Technical and Legal Aspects of Weather Modification" was sponsored jointly by the AAAS and the American Bar Association. Kahan (1977) offers some thought-provoking and choice comments on the interaction of scientists and lawyers concerning weather modification.

In order to foster the development of a legislative uniformity and to provide for an effective information exchange the North American Interstate Weather Modification Council, NAIWMC, was formed. Twenty-three states from the United States three provinces in Canada, and Mexico participated in the formation of NAIWMC. The workings of this organization are described by Keyes (1977).

Hess (1974) edited an 842-page volume entitled, "Weather and Climate Modification". This book consists of 22 monographs written by recognized authorities on various aspects of weather modification. Chapter I, "History of Weather Modification", by Horace R. Byers refers back to Plutarch in the first century A. D. Another book, "Collected Reprints 1975-76, Weather Modification Program Office". (1977) is an assembly of 78 reprints of papers contributed by scientists of the National Oceanographic and Atmospheric Administration dealing primarily with cloud physics, hurricane and tornado meteorology, and precipitation augmentation in Florida.

An appraisal of the current state of knowledge and attainments and of possible future trends of weather modification was prepared by Sax, Changnon, Grant, Hitschfeld, Hobbs, Kahan, and Simpson (1975). This paper, the reading of which is highly recommended, deals with inadvertent weather and climate modification, hail suppression, augmentation of orographic precipitation, convective cloud modification, hurricane modification, weather modification and water management, and fog modification.

The Bureau of Reclamation (1977) has prepared a very comprehensive statement, "Project Skywater - Final Environmental Statement - A Program of Research in Precipitation Management". This statement, consisting of 3 volumes which stack up to a 2-inch depth, reviews proposed actions and past field programs. It discusses general experimental procedures and deals with weather modification in relation to climates in various regions and the possible effects both favorable and possibly adverse on vegetation, fish and wildlife, recreation, ecology, hydrology, erosion, transportation, and human activities. Both for short and long-terms the impact of weather modification is considerable.

Weather modification for augmenting rain and snow can only be successful if the atmospheric circulation brings into the desired area clouds possessing the proper characteristics. It is not to be expected that a seedable cloud may somehow appear just when a particular crop needs more soil moisture. In many parts of the World the water-bearing atmospheric moisture transport is out of phase with agricultural and economic periods of demand. The future of productive precipitation augmentation lies in weather modification activities managed in conjunction with runoff storage either in reservoir systems or in groundwater aquifers since the storage of water as soil moisture is inadequate for other than short periods of time.

References

Atlas, David, "The Paradox of Hail Suppression", Science, vol. 195, no. 4274, pp 139-145, Jan. 14, 1977.

Aubert, Eugene J., Gurbachan P. Malhotra, and David B. Spiegler "Potential of Precipitation Modification", Jour. of the Irrigation and Drainage Div., ASCE, pp 49-64, Mar. 1972.

Changnon, Stanley A., Jr., "Inadvertent Weather Modification", Water Resources Bulletin, vol. 12, no. 4, pp 695-718, Aug. 1976.

"Cloud Seeding Principles and Techniques - Skywater", Bureau of Reclamation, USDI, Div. of Atmospheric Water Resources Mgmt., Denver, Colo., Nov., 1971.

"Collected Reprints - 1975-76, Weather Modification Program Office", Environmental Research Laboratories, NOAA, Boulder, Colo., and Miami, Fla., 667 pp, May, 1977.

Dennis, A. S., and D. F. Kriege, "Results of Ten Years of Cloud Seeding in Santa Clara County, California", Jour. of Applied Meteorology, vol. 5, pp 684-691, Oct. 1966.

Farnes, Phillip E., "Watershed Management: State of the Practice Precipitation Modifications", Proceedings of the 5th Workshop of the United States/Australia Rangelands Panel, entitled Watershed Management on Range and Forest Lands, ed. by H. F. Heady, D. H. Falkenborg, and J. P. Riley, pp 175-180, pub. by College of Engineering, Utah State Univ., Logan, March, 1976.

Garstka, Walter U., "Recent Research Developments in Weather Modification", a paper presented at the 32d Annual Convention Oct. 24, 1963 at Sun Valley, Idaho, published in the Proceedings by the Natl. Reclamation Assn., pp 55-68, 1963.

Garstka, Walter U., "Weather Modification - Avenue to World Peace", GeoScience News, vol. 1, no. 2, pp 4-6 and 22-25, Nov. - Dec., 1967.

Hobbs, Peter V., and L. F. Radke, "Redistribution of Snowfall Across a Mountain Range by Artificial Seeding: A Case Study", Science, vol. 181, pp 1043-1045, Sept. 14, 1973.

Hess, W. N., "Weather and Climate Modification", John Wiley and Sons, New York, 842 pp, 1974.

Howell, Wallace E., "The Impact of Weather Modification on U.S. Planning for the Rio Colorado and Rio Grande", a paper presented at the International Symposium on the Planning

of Water Resources, Mexico City, Dec. 4-7, 1972 and published in the Proceedings, vol. 2, <u>Final Papers</u>, by the
Secretariat of Hydraulic Resources, Mexico, D.F. (Undated)

Huff, F. A., "Effects of the Urban Environment on Heavy Rainfall Distribution", Water Resources Bulletin, vol. 13,
no. 4, pp 807-816, Aug. 1977.

Hurley, Patrick A., "Colorado Pilot Project: Design Hydrometeorology", Jour. of the Hydraulics Div., Proceedings ASCE,
pp 811-826, May, 1972.

Kahan, A. M., C. J. Todd, W. E. Howell, and B. A. Silverman,
"Project Hiplex - Plans, Progress and Approach", Proceed-
ings of the 2nd World Meteorological Organization
Scientific Conference on Weather Modification of Aug. 2-6,
1976 held at Boulder, Colorado. Pub. by IAMAT - AMS,
WMO Headquarters, Geneva, Switzerland, pp 28-34, (Undated)

Kahan, Archie M., "Interaction of Scientists and Lawyers About
Weather Modification", a paper presented at the Symposium,
Technical and Legal Aspects of Weather Modification,
Feb. 22, 1977, sponsored jointly by the AAAS and the Amer.
Bar Foundation, to be published by AAAS as Proceedings,
Weather Modification, Technology and Law, R. J. Davis,
and L. O. Grant, editors. In press as of Oct. 1977.

Keyes, C. G., Jr.., "NAIWMC - Impact on Hydrometeorologic
Measurements", Proceedings Western Snow Conference, April
1977, 45th Annual Meeting, pub. by Colo. State University,
Fort Collins, 1977.

Landsberg, Helmut E., "Man-Made Climatic Changes", Science,
vol. 170, no. 3964, pp 1265 - 1274, Dec. 18, 1970.

Perla, Ronald I., and M. Martinelli, Jr., "Avalanche Handbook",
Forest Service, USDA, Agri. Handbook 489, 238 pp,
July, 1976.

Project Skywater - Final Environmental Statement - A Program of
Research in Precipitation Management", in three volumes,
vol. 1, Statement, vol. 2, Appendices A-J, vol. 3,
Appendix K, Div. of Atmospheric Water Resources Mgmt.,
Bur. of Reclamation, USDI, Denver, Colo., 1977.

"Report by the Committee for Evaluation of Bonneville Power
Administration Cloud-Seeding Operations in the United
States Portion of the Pend Oreille River Basin", prepared
by a Committee of individuals, Milton S. Sachs, Chairman,
BPA, C. C. McDonald, USGS, Walter U. Garstka, USBR, and
H. C. S. Thom, USWB. Pub. by US Dept. of Interior,
Washington, D.C., July, 1952.

Sax, R. I., S. A. Changnon, L. O. Grant, W. F. Hitschfeld, P. V. Hobbs, A. M. Kahan, and J. Simpson, "Weather Modification: Where Are We Now and Where Should We be Going? An Editorial Overview", Jour. of Applied Meteorology, vol. 14, no. 5, pp 652-672, Aug. 1975.

Schaefer, Vincent J., "The Production of Ice Crystals in a Cloud of Super-cooled Water Droplets", Science, vol. 104 no. 2707, pp 457-459, Nov. 15, 1946.

Schaefer, Vincent J., "Serendipity and the Development of Experimental Meteorology", Jour. of the Irrigation and Drainage Div., Proceedings ASCE, pp 1-16, March, 1960.

Schaefer, Vincent J., "The Inadvertent Modification of the Atmosphere by Air Pollution", Bulletin Amer. Meteorological Soc., vol. 50, no. 4, pp 199-206, Apr. 1969.

Schleusener, Richard A., and Edwin I. Boyd, "Weather Modification Program for South Dakota", Jour. Hydraulics Div., Proceedings ASCE, pp 1515-1526, Sept. 1972.

"The Legal Implications of Atmospheric Water Resources Development and Management", prepared for the Bureau of Reclamation by the Weather Modification Law Project Staff, Univ. of Arizona, College of Law, 248 pp, Oct. 1968.

Thompson, Philip D., and Robert O'Brien, and the Editors of Life, "Weather", Time Inc., New York, 200 pp, 1965.

Vardiman, Larry, and James A. Moore, "Generalized Criteria for Seeding Winter Orographic Clouds", Skywater Monograph Report No. 1, Div. of Atmospheric Water Resources Mgmt., Bur. of Reclamation, USDI, Denver, Colo., 91 pp, and appendices, July, 1977. Summary Report under same title, 12 pp, March, 1977 is available.

Watson, B., "A Review of Cloud Seeding in Australia and its Potential Impact on Water Resources Management", Proceedings 5th Workshop of the United States/Australia Rangelands Panel, entitled Watershed Management on Range and Forest Lands, ed. by H. F. Heady, D. H. Falkenborg, and J. P. Riley, pp 181-192, pub. by College of Engineering, Utah State Univ., Logan, March, 1976.

Topic 12          Precipitation Measurement

The priests of the ancient Babylon culture 3000 to 1000 B.C. were interested in hydrology as part of their religious practices according to Biswas (1967). This reference deals with the development of rain gages from ancient times. Also in this reference mention is made of the construction of a recording rain gage, actually a meteorograph, invented by the famous architect Sir Christopher Wren. Among his architectural achievements was the design for the rebuilding of St. Paul's Cathedral in London. He is also credited with inventing the tipping-bucket rain gage a concept in use to this day.

Figure 12-1 shows an 8-inch non-recording precipitation gage and also one type of intensity-recording gage. This figure is taken from the "Observing Handbook" No. 2 (1972). The 8-inch non-recording precipitation gage is the United States standard. There is no concurrence internationally concerning the exact design of a rain gage.

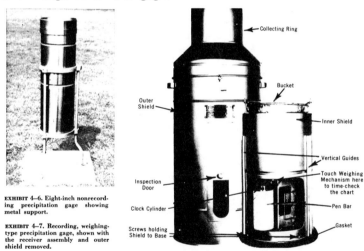

EXHIBIT 4–6. Eight-inch nonrecording precipitation gage showing metal support.

EXHIBIT 4–7. Recording, weighing-type precipitation gage, shown with the receiver assembly and outer shield removed.

Figure 12-1   U.S. Standard Non-recording Precipitation Gage on the Left and One Type of Intensity-Recording Gage on the Right

When stream floods occur it is seldom that the rainfall which produced the floods centered over an officially-approved rain gage. While the flood flow is receding it is common practice for hydrologists to comb the area performing "bucket" surveys by measuring the catchment in sumps, watering troughs, tin cans, or any structure which could permit them to compute the depth of rainfall which caused the flood.

Musgrove (1963) concluded that if the receiver ring of the

65

gage is thin or has a sharp edge the rainfall gage is adequate regardless of the size of the gage. Four sizes were compared: standard 8-inch Weather Bureau sharp-edge gage; 2.8-inch aluminum can with 0.02-inch wall thickness and square-edge receiver; 0.85-inch glass tube with 0.06-inch wall thickness and round-edge receiver; and 0.65-inch plastic tube with sharp-edge receiver.

Rainfall records are usually assumed to refer to precipitation which fell in the liquid state as rain. In many parts of the world a considerable portion of the precipitation may fall as snow or in some form intermediate between rain or snow. Where practically all of the winter precipitation falls as snow, storage gages are sometimes used. However, where the snow does not melt during the winter it is common practice to measure the water equivalent of snow on the ground through the performance of snow surveys, according to Garstka (1964).

In areas where the snow does not persist unmelted throughout the winter, such as in the northeastern United States, it has been found necessary to convert precipitation which fell as snow to a water equivalent. A common "rule of thumb" is that 10 inches depth of snow as measured at time of fall has an average water equivalent of one-inch depth of water. Weather Bureau Technical Paper No. 50 (1964) presents data on frequency of maximum water equivalent of March snow cover in the northeastern United States.

The measurement and estimation of precipitation on experimental watersheds, many of which are forested watersheds, is reviewed in a very comprehensive manner by Corbett (1967). His review includes the discussions of the accuracy of point measurements, the effect of shielding, the reliability of rain-gage measurements, and the importance of site selection. He refers to the variability in the design of rain gage networks introduced by precipitation formation processes. He deals with tilted gages, which are especially useful in mountain watersheds, provided enough gages are installed.

Johnson (1970) reports on the analyses of rain gage networks at the Sleepers River Experimental Watersheds of the Agricultural Research Service, USDA, near Danville, Vermont. The results indicate that a placement of gages with due regard to the main direction of storm travel over the area produces a more accurate measurement than does a simple equal-area grid.

Mueller and Kidder (1972) performed a study of rain gage catch variation based upon wind tunnel observations coupled with computer simulation of the movement of rain drops. They concluded that the error in the amount of precipitation measured can be large if the free stream velocities are above 25 feet per second. At 40 feet per second the deviation of the

66

catch could be as much as minus 80 percent for the one-milli-
meter drop size; 25 percent for two-millimeter drops; and practically no deviation for three- to five-millimeter drop sizes.

Extensive research is currently underway on unattended
automatic transmitting meteorological and hydrologic installations. Some of the systems have provisions for either time-
cycle control or on-call transmittal of data either on telephone lines or by radio. Large multiple-purpose complex river
basin projects such as the Columbia and Colorado Rivers and the
Missouri River Basin have been provided with microwave communication facilities which operate under extremes of weather and
at times of floods when the usual communication facilities may
break down.

Communication satellites are being used for the transmittal of hydrologic data. A development which makes possible
the practically instantaneous transmission of data on ocean
currents, precipitation levels, river and lake water levels, smog
content and radiation levels together with surface data is
being transmitted for distances up to 1,200 miles through the
use of the meteor-burst communication system. According to
Leader (1974) billions of ionized meteor trails are produced
daily in the earth's atmosphere in heights up to 80 to 120 kilometers (about 50 to 75 miles). The trails disappear within a
few seconds but during their brief existence they reflect radio
waves in the VHF frequency ranges. The physics of the system
are described by Leader. Further discussion of the meteor-
burst system is included in Topic 16, Snow Measurement.

Scientific instrument developers and commercial suppliers
of meteorological and hydrologic equipment are very active in
developing and improving precipitation measuring devices. The
aerodynamics at the gage orifice vary with each configuration
and size of the rain gage. In order to provide for the compar-
ability of data by common accord hydrologists have accepted the
standard 8-inch rain gage catchment as the "true" value. In
hydrologic analyses and research the catchment of other gages
such as the tipping-bucket and various recording gages is adjusted by a factor so that their total catchment corresponds to
the standard gage before intensity computations are made.

Although precise measurement of rainfall remains to be
demonstrated, hydrologists accept and use the values as observed in standard instruments operated by qualified observers.

In most litigations the observations of a standard 8-inch
non-recording gage located at a site approved by a hydrometeorological inspector of the National Weather Service and operated
by an approved observer are accepted as a statement of fact.
Observations from other instruments and sources may not be
legally acceptable.

References

Biswas, Asit K., "Development of Rain Gages", Jour. of Irrigation and Drainage Div., Proceedings of the ASCE, pp 99-124
Sept. 1967.

Corbett, Edward S., "Measurement and Estimation of Precipitation on Experimental Watersheds", pp 107-129 in International Symposium on Forest Hydrology, ed. by Wm.E. Sopper
and Howard W. Lull, Pergamon Press, New York, 1967.

"Frequency of Maximum Water Equivalent of March Snow Cover in
North Central United States", Tech. Paper No. 50, Weather
Bureau, U.S. Dept. of Commerce, Washington, D.C., 1964.

Garstka, Walter U., "Snow and Snow Survey", Section 10 in
HANDBOOK OF APPLIED HYDROLOGY, Ven Te Chow, ed-in-chief,
McGraw-Hill Book Co., New York, 1064.

Johnson, Martin L., "Research on Sleepers River at Danville,
Vermont", Jour. of Irrigation and Drainage Div., Proceedings of the ASCE, pp 67-88, March, 1970.

Leader, Ray E., "Meteor Burst Communications", Proceedings 42nd
Annual Meeting, Western Snow Conference of Apr. 16-20,
1974, Anchorage, Alaska, pp 29-36, printed by Colo. State
University, Fort Collins, Colorado, 1974.

Mueller, Charles C., and Ernest H. Kidder, "Rain Gage Catch
Variation Due to Airflow Disturbances Around a Standard
Rain Gage", Water Resources Research, vol. 8, no. 4,
pp 1077-1082, Aug. 1972.

Musgrove, R. H., "Accuracy of Three Non-Standard Rain Gages",
U.S. Geological Survey Water Supply Paper No. 1669-Z,
Selected Techniques in Water Resources Investigations,
pp 45-47, 1963.

"Observing Handbook No. 2 - Substation Observations", National
Weather Service, NOAA, U.S. Dept. of Commerce, 77 pages,
Revised, Dec. 1972.

Topic 13   Determination of Precipitation Over an Area

For engineering, agricultural, environmental management, and land use applications, the rainfall observed by a network of individual raingages must be converted to depths over a drainage basin.  The mechanisms of precipitation formation and of its release over an area operate in such a complex manner that the distribution of precipitation on the surface of the Earth during any one storm varies greatly over the area.  Figure 13-1 from "Thunderstorm Rainfall" (1947) shows how differently the distribution of rainfall over a drainage basin may appear depending on the number of raingages used to compute the average precipitation. Figure 13-1 follows:

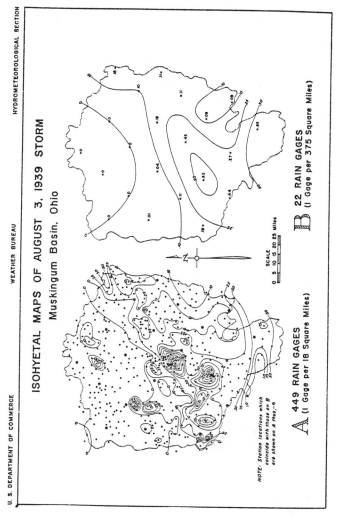

Figure 13-1  Appearance of Isohyetal Maps as Computed for Different Densities of Rain Gages for the Same Storm

69

The area of the orifice of the 8-inch diameter, U.S. standard raingage is about 1/80,000,000th of a square mile. The catchment by a single raingage in a network density of one gage per 375 square miles as shown in map B of Figure 13-1 is an extremely small sampling but map B has many more raingages than are to be found in many important drainage basins.

Todd (1970), page 53, presents a tabulation of density of raingage networks for 28 selected countries of the world as of 1960. Israel ranked first with a density of 10.4 raingages per 100 square miles; the United States ranked 21st with a density of 0.3 raingages per 100 square miles. The United States ranked above Thailand, the Philippines, Pakistan, Greece, Turkey, Burma and Viet Nam. Insofar as hydrologic networks are concerned the United States is one of the developing countries. Please refer to Topic 9, Climatology.

There are three commonly used methods of computing the average precipitation: the Arithmetic Mean, the Thiessen (or Polygon) method, and the Isohyetal method. The advantage of the Arithmetic Mean method is its simplicity. It assigns equal weight to each gage. The Thiessen method provides a weighting for gages in a non-uniformly distributed system in proportion to an assumed area of influence for each gage. The Isohyetal method also weights the value of each individual gage but it does so by assigning the raingage observations to portions of the total area assumed to have equal precipitation amounts.

Arithmetic averages are seldom indicative because of non-uniform distribution of gages, physiographic effects, and characteristics of each gage location. A comparison of the three methods is shown on page 83 of Linsley, Kohler, and Paulhus (1975). According to this example the average precipitation was determined to be 3.09 inches by the Arithmetic Mean; 2.34 inches by the Theissen method; and 2.61 inches by the Isohyetal method.

Bethlahmy (1976) proposes a 2-axis method in which each station is assigned a weight based upon measurement of angles between stations and the average precipitation is calculated from the products of corresponding station weights and measured precipitation. Bethlahmy states that the method is impersonal, efficient, and is readily computerized.

Singh (1976) proposed a rapid method of estimating mean areal rainfall by linear functional calculation in which coordinates are assigned to individual raingages. He compares his method with the three traditional methods (the Arithmetic Mean, the Thiessen Polygon, and the Isohyetal) for an area in New Mexico and two rivers in Great Britain. He concludes that his method is not as well suited as is the Isohyetal for physiographically complex regions.

Chang (1977) evaluated precipitation gage intensity in a topographically complex area of West Virginia. He used a 25-year period for computing average standard errors of the estimate for stations within 50 miles distant and 1000-foot elevation differences. The Arithmetic Mean and the Theissen methods lend themselves readily to use of electronic computers whereas the Isohyetal method requires more work. Nicks (1967) deals with an application of computer usage to rainfall analyses.

The Isohyetal method is considered to be the most accurate. It is especially suited for mountainous terrain but it has the disadvantage of being costly and time-consuming since each storm requires the preparation of a separate Isohyetal map. This requires judgment and experience. The Isohyetal method requires a determination of areas between the contour-like lines of identical rainfall depth.

Planimeters are commonly used in determining such areas. The Amsler polar planimeter and similar instruments are expensive and may not be readily available. Sparks (1932) describes the use of the Hatchet Planimeter for which he submits rigorous mathematical proof. Properly used the Hatchet Planimeter is just as accurate as the expensive mechanical integrators. Figure 13-2 is a photograph showing one form of the Hatchet Planimeter. The description of this figure provides detailed instructions.

Figure 13-2 The Hatchet Planimeter (See Sparks 1932).

A knife can serve as a hatchet planimeter. The tracer point is placed at a roughly-estimated center of the area and the sharp blade is pressed into the paper to make an indentation. The tracer point is moved along a pencil line which has been drawn from the estimated center to the perimeter of the area. The tracer point then moves along the perimeter and then back along the radius to the starting point. It will be observed that the sharp blade has changed its location. The end is pushed again to make another indentation.

The area of the figure is computed by multiplying the distance between the 2 indentations by the distance between
either one of the indentations and the tracer point.  The
answer will be given in whatever units of measurement were
used to measure the distances.  The longest dimension of
the figure should preferably be not more than a quarter of
the length of the tracer point to the blade point.  If the
greatest length of the figure is equal to the length of
the knife, the error would be about 6 percent.  Large
areas can be divided into sections.

Determinations of areas with an accuracy equal to or
superior to the planimeter can be attained with the dot-grid
method as described by Barrett and Philbrook (1970).  The dot-
grid transparency must be dropped repeatedly so that it is positioned at random before the dots are counted.

Frederick, Myers, and Auciello (1977) report upon digit-
izing of radar data of precipitation in Oklahoma to produce
what amounts to an Isohyetal plotting of depths of precipitation yielding depth-area curves in a progress report on their
research.

## Problem Assignment - Weight and Volume of Rainfall

An informative problem assignment is that of computing the
amount of precipitation over an area delineated in a campus or
urban location and calculating the amounts of water deposited
in various English and SI units.  The answers are to be submitted with due regard to Topic 4.  Conversion units are given in
Appendix A.

Problem A   What would a depth of water of 1.00 inch (2.54 cent-
            imeters) over a horizontal area as assigned (or one
            square mile) amount to in the units listed?

            a.  Imperial gallons    e.  Liters
            b.  U.S. gallons        f.  Cubic meters
            c.  Acre feet           g.  Kilograms
            d.  Pounds

## Problem Assignment - Average Depth of Rainfall

A preliminary Isohyetal map for the Big Thompson flash
flood of July 31-August 1, 1976 is shown as Figure 13-3 taken
from Natural Disaster Survey Report 76-1 (1976).  A detailed
report, 10-7/8 inches by 17 inches, consisting of 78 pages
prepared by Grozier, McCain, Lang, and Merriam (1976) contains
numerous photographs of the Big Thompson Canyon before and
after this rare hydrologic event.  Some of the pictures were
taken on the ground but most of them were taken from aircraft.
Page 5 in this report describes the flood flow which amounted

72

to 31,200 cubic feet (880 cubic meters) per second at the "mouth of the Canyon".

The heavy runoff-contributing area as determined during field observations by personnel of the U.S. Geological Survey is delineated in Figure 13-3 by the line of dashes. The boundary of the drainage area is shown by the dotted line. Very little runoff-producing rain fell west of Estes Park.

Problem B    (1)  Calculate the average depth of precipitation for the heavy runoff area in the Big Thompson River drainage basin.

(2)  Compute the volume in acre-feet of the average precipitation.

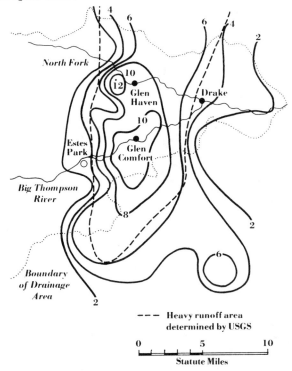

Figure 13-3  Total precipitation (inches) July 31-
Aug. 2, 1976 based on climatologic network
and supplemented by unofficial observations.

References

Barrett, J. P. and J. S. Philbrook, "Dot Grid Area Estimates: Precision by Repeated Trials", Jour. of Forestry, vol. 68, no. 2, pp 149-151, March 1970.

Bethlahmy, Nedavia, "The Two-Axis Method: A New Method to Calculate Average Precipitation Over a Basin", Hydrological Sciences-Bulletin-des Sciences Hydrologiques, XXI, pp 379-385, March, 1976.

Natural Disaster Survey Report 76-1, "Big Thompson Canyon Flash Flood of July 31 - August 1, 1976", NOAA, U.S. Dept. of Commerce, Rockville, Md., 41 pp, Oct.-Nov. 1976.

Chang, Mingteh, "An Evaluation of Precipitation Gage Density in a Mountainous Terrain", Water Resources Bulletin, vol. 13, no. 1, pp 39-46, Feb. 1977.

Frederick, Ralph H., Vance A. Myers, and Eugene P. Auciello, "Storm Depth-Area Relations From Digitized Radar Returns", Water Resources Research, vol. 13, no. 3, pp 675-679, June, 1977.

Grozier, Richard U., Jerald F. McCain, Larry F. Lang, and Danny C. Merriman, "The Big Thompson River Flood of July 31 - August 1, 1976, Larimer County, Colorado", pub. by the Colorado Water Conservation Board, Denver, Colo., Oct. 1976.

Linsley, R. K., M. A. Kohler, and J. L. H. Paulhus, "Hydrology for Engineers", McGraw-Hill Book Co. New York, 2nd ed., 1975.

Nicks, Arlin D., "A Computer Mapping Method for Analysis and Summary of Rainfall Data", USDA Agricultural Research Service, Pub. ARS 41-135, Aug. 1967.

Singh, Vijay P., "A Rapid Method of Estimating Mean Areal Rainfall", Water Resources Bulletin, vol. 12, no. 2, pp 307-315, April, 1976.

Sparks, Robert, "The Hatchet Planimeter", Jour. of The Franklin Institute, vol. 213 - nos. 1273-1278 (107th year) pp 611-667, Jan. - June, 1932.

"Thunderstorm Rainfall", Hydrometeorological Report No. 5, Part 2 - Figures, pub. by Waterways Exp. Station, Corps of Engineers, U.S. War Dept. Vicksburg, Miss., 1947.

Todd, David Keith, editor, "The Water Encyclopedia", Water Information Center, Port Washington, N.Y., 559 pp., 1970.

Precipitable Water

The changes in temperature as a parcel of air is lifted in
the atmosphere interacting with changes of state of water substance which may or may not be contained in the parcel of air
were discussed under lapse rate in Topic 8. The three lapse
rates are: dry adiabatic, saturated adiabatic and the pseudo-
adiabatic. The latter prevails when saturated vapor condenses
and releases heat and water which falls to the ground while
carrying some heat away from the parcel of air.

Eagleson (1970) presents a mathematical analysis of atmospheric moisture. His Section 4-4, pages 59-65, deals with vapor pressure and density, virtual temperature, phase changes,
latent heats, humidity, and pseudoadiabatic processes.

Professional meteorologists have prepared a complex chart
which deals in part with lapse rate computations. The title of
the chart is, "USAF SKEW T, log p DIAGRAM", (1957). Certain
portions of this chart have been extracted by hydrologists to
simplify computations.

As has been discussed in Topics 7 and 8 a column of air
over any part of the surface of the Earth at any time contains
a certain amount of water substance. This total amount of
water vapor in the air is expressed in terms of the depth of
the water which would be yielded if all of the water vapor were
to be condensed. Admittedly there is no natural physical process or combination of processes which would precipitate the
entire moisture content of the air.

The concept of precipitable water is very useful in water
resource management. It is the starting point for deciding
whether or not cloud formations might be amenable to weather
modification. Huff (1963) studied relationships between atmospheric water and surface precipitation especially with reference to heavy rainstorms in Illinois. He also studied relationships between atmospheric moisture and both short-period
and extended droughts. He concluded that for Illinois allevi-
ation of severe extended drought conditions by cloud seeding
was not feasible because of deficiency of precipitable water.

The precipitable water concept is especially valuable in
computation of rainfall which could possibly result in
extreme floods. The hydrologic data gathering networks are so
scattered and the periods of record are of such short duration
that statistical extrapolations of observed storms have been
found to be not nearly as realistic as the hydrometeorological
approach. This technique, which requires the services of professional meteorologists, transposes observed storms such as
those discussed in Topic 13 to drainage basins under

consideration by applying adjustments for air mass movements, distances from moisture sources, elevations, and with due regard to shapes of isohyetal patterns. A compilation of recorded storms is given in "Greatest Known Areal Storm Rainfall Depths for the Contiguous United States" (1976).

An understanding of this subject can be approached through the working of the following problem dealing with an actual event. The information in Table 14-1 was supplied by Dr. James Rasmussen of the Colorado State University Dept. of Atmospheric Science. The data are based on readings at the Colorado Agricultural Experiment Station's Weather Station, located at 5,004 feet above mean sea level.

Table 14-1    Convective Storm of July 11, 1967

| Time | Temperature $^{\circ}F$ | | | Precipitation | |
|------|----------|----------|-----------|------|--------|
| MST | Dry Bulb | Wet Bulb | Dew Point | Type | Amount in Inches |
| 3:00 p.m. | 73.3 | 66.6 | 64 | (Before storm) Intense rain | 0 1.07 |
| 5:05 p.m. | 60.0 | 60.0 | 60 | Drizzle begins | |
| 6:59 p.m. | 61.0 | 61.0 | 61 | Drizzle continues | |
| 8:55 p.m. | 61.0 | 61.0 | 61 | Drizzle continues | |
| 11:05 p.m. | 60.0 | 59.7 | 60.0 | Drizzle ends | .03 |
| | | | | Total for storm | 1.10 |

The convective storm ended before 5:05 p.m.

Pseudoadiabatic charts such as the "USAF SKEW T, log p DIAGRAM" and Figures 14-2 and 14-3 are for sea level-based computations. Since Fort Collins is at 5,004 feet elevation there is no atmospheric water at that point below that elevation. Therefore the observed dew point temperatures at Fort Collins must be adjusted for sea-level equivalents before Figures 14-2 and 14-3 are used.

This conversion is accomplished through the use of Figure 14-1. For example, the temperature of 65° F and 6000 feet intersect the slanting line which is labeled 78° F on the horizontal axis toward the right-hand edge. This means that a 65° F dew point temperature at 6000-foot elevation would be equivalent to a 78° F temperature at sea level. Figures 14-1, 14-2, and 14-3 are taken from "Design Storms", Chapt. 6.5 (1948).

Problem:  Calculate precipitable water to the 32,000-foot elevation before and after the convective storm of July 11, 1967. Compare with observed rainfall and discuss your results. Show all computations.

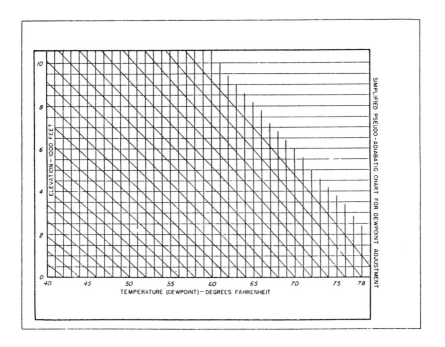

Figure 14-1    Chart for Converting Observed Dew-Point
               Temperature to Sea-Level Equivalent

References

"Design Storms", chap. 6.5, part 6, Flood Hydrology, vol. IV
     Water Studies, Bureau of Reclamation Manual, USDI,
     originally prepared in 1948 with continuing revisions.

Eagleson, Peter S., "Dynamic Hydrology", McGraw-Hill Book Co.,
     New York, 462 pp, 1970.

Huff, Floyd A., "Atmospheric Moisture-Precipitation Relations",
     Jour. of the Hydraulics Division, Proceedings of the ASCE,
     pp 93-110, Nov., 1963.

"USAF SKEW T, log p DIAGRAM", published by the Aeronautical
     Chart and Information Center, United States Air Force,
     St. Louis, Mo., July, 1957.  (ACIC)

# DEPTHS OF PRECIPITABLE WATER IN A COLUMN OF
# AIR OF GIVEN HEIGHT ABOVE 1000 MILLIBARS

**Assuming Saturation with a Pseudo-Adiabatic Lapse**

**Rate for the Indicated Surface Temperatures**
Adapted from U.S. Weather Bureau Hydrometeorological Report No. 23

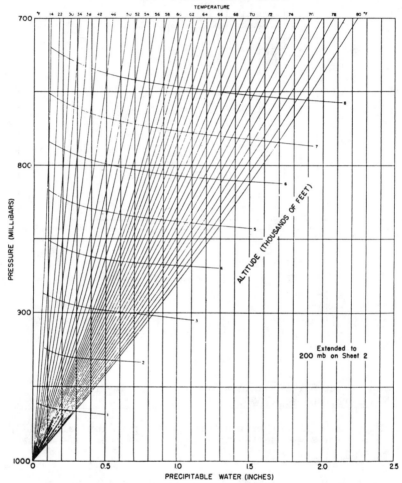

Figure 14-2   Depth of Precipitable Water in the Range of
1000 millibars to 700 millibars Pressure and
Sea Level to 8000-foot Elevation

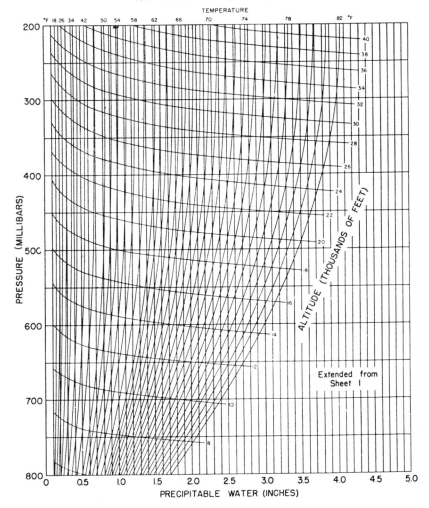

## DEPTHS OF PRECIPITABLE WATER IN A COLUMN OF
## AIR OF GIVEN HEIGHT ABOVE 1000 MILLIBARS

### Assuming Saturation with a Pseudo-Adiabatic Lapse
### Rate for the Indicated Surface Temperature
Adapted from U S Weather Bureau Hydrometeorological Report No. 23

Figure 14-3     Depth of Precipitable Water in the Range of
800 millibars to 200 millibars Pressure and
8000-foot to 40,000-foot Elevation

Example     For the 76° F sea level dewpoint, precipitable water is 3.04" to 200 mb and precipitable water is
1.91" to the 10,000-foot elevation.

Topic 15   Precipitation Depth-Intensity-Duration Analyses

Three Isohyetal maps were included in Topic 13.  For hydrologic analyses dealing with land use it is necessary to have some estimate of the recurrence interval of depths, intensities and durations of intense rainfalls for drainage basins of various sizes.  Such information is fundamental to the assignments of land usage in relation to the management of flood flows.

Comprehensive treatment of space-time characteristics of rainfall and the use of such information in hydrology is given by Gilman (1964).  A very useful work pertaining to the United States is that prepared by Hershfield (1961).  Bruce (1968) has prepared an atlas of rainfall intensity-duration frequency data for Canada.

Bell (1969) has demonstrated that the physics and thermodynamics of convective storms produce rainfall-duration-frequency relationships which are practically identical, as based upon his analyses of such storms in the United States, South Africa, Australia, Hawaii, Alaska, and Puerto Rico.

In order to provide a density of raingages capable of yielding data in the detail necessary a system of 300 recording raingages, some telemetering, are being installed on a grid system in an area of 4000 square miles in and around Chicago, Illinois.  This area has also two sophisticated weather radar systems using both 10-cm and 3-cm wavelengths.  The 10-cm system is used to measure rainfall; the 3-cm system to observe snowfall with the 10-cm wavelengths as a backup.

Huff and Changnon (1977) state that this system is to be used for providing data on depth-intensity-duration characteristics of both summer and winter precipitation necessary to operate one of the most complex land use and urban water management systems in major metropolitan areas.

Although it would be reasonable to expect that a superbly planned research program of such immediate practical value would be financed by NOAA.  This is not so.  This project is being funded by the State of Illinois and the RANN Program of the National Science Foundation.

Shipe and Riedel (1976) have prepared an extensive compilation of greatest known areal storm rainfall depths for the contiguous United States for winter, spring, summer, and fall seasons.  Depths are included for areas ranging from 100 to 10,000 square miles (259 to 25,900 square kilometers) and for duration ranging from 6 to 48 hours.

Problem Assignment - Depth-Intensity-Duration Analyses

Cumulative precipitation data for the storm of August 17, 1926 at Detroit, Michigan, is entered in Table 15-1. Detailed analyses of this storm are given by Wisler and Brater (1959) on pages 92-96.

Table 15-1          Cumulative Precipitation

| Time (Minutes) | Depth (Inches) | Time (Minutes) | Depth (Inches) |
|---|---|---|---|
| 0 | 0.00 | 40 | 2.44 |
| 5 | 0.08 | 45 | 2.59 |
| 10 | 0.13 | 50 | 2.60 |
| 15 | 0.23 | 60 | 2.61 |
| 20 | 0.67 | 80 | 3.41 |
| 25 | 1.45 | 100 | 3.78 |
| 30 | 2.04 | 120 | 3.86 |
| 35 | 2.29 | | |

Problem A   Plot cumulative precipitation on the y-axis vs time on the x-axis on Cartesian coordinate paper. This is called a mass curve.

Problem B   Convert the precipitation data to intensities in inches per hour and plot appropriate time intervals on the same sheet on which the maximum curve was plotted. This graph shows the pattern of intensity distribution on a real time scale. This plotting called a "hyetograph" is shown in Figure 15-1.

Problem C   Using the information available to you based upon previous analyses plot on Cartesian coordinate paper maximum average intensities of precipitation in inches per hour on the y-axis vs duration in minutes on the x-axis. This graph is an intensity-duration curve and the time factor is no longer real for the storm event.

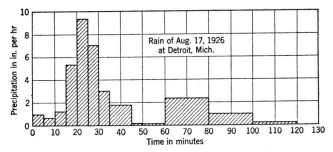

Figure 15-1  Hyetograph (From Wisler and Brater, 1959, p. 94)

## References

Bell, Frederick C., "Generalized Rainfall-Duration-Frequency Relationships", Jour. Hydraulics Div., Proc. American Society of Civil Engineers, pp 311-327, Jan. 1969.

Bruce, J. P., "Atlas of Rainfall Intensity-Duration Frequency Data for Canada", Climatological Studies No. 8, Dept. of Transport, Meteorological Branch, Ottawa, Canada, 1968.

Gilman, Charles S., "Rainfall", Sec. 9, Handbook of Applied Hydrology, Ven Te Chow, ed-in-chief, McGraw-Hill Book Co., New York, 1964.

Hershfield, D. M., "Rainfall Frequency Atlas of the United States for Durations from 30-Minutes to 24-Hours and Return Periods from 1 to 100 Years", Tech. Paper No. 40, U.S. Weather Bureau, Washington, D.C., 1961.

Huff, F. A., and S. A. Changnon, Jr., "A Hydrometeorological Research Program", Water Resources Bulletin, vol. 13, no. 3, pp 573-581, June, 1977.

Shipe, Albert P. and John T. Riedel, "Greatest Known Areal Storm Rainfall Depths for the Contiguous United States", Natl. Weather Service, Office of Hydrology, Silver Spring, Md., NOAA Tech. Memorandum NWS HYDRO-33, Dec. 1976.

Wisler, C. O., and E. F. Brater, "Hydrology", John Wiley and Sons, Inc., New York, 2nd edition, 408 pp, 1959. (Third printing, Mar. 1965.)

Topic 16                      <u>Snow</u>

<u>Measurement of Snow</u>

Snow is defined by Dr. Vincent J. Schaefer (1956) as
follows:

"Snow is the solid form of water which grows while floating
rising, or falling in the free air of the atmosphere."

Since it is a principle of crystallography that the vapor pressure of a sharp edge or point tends to be greater than that of
a flat surface, in the presence of even microscopically-thin
films of water the stellar form of snow commonly thought of as
being the true snow crystal retains its geometric shape for a
very short period of time.

Seligman's (1936) book on snow structure and ski fields
deals with snow metamorphism. The "International Classification for Snow" (1954) was prepared by the Commission on Snow
and Ice of the International Association of Hydrological
Sciences. Summerfield (1976) has prepared an illustrated pamphlet for the classification of snow on the ground. Perla and
Martinelli (1976) include on their pages 20 and 21 sketches and
various classification of snow crystals of which 90 forms are
described. The book "Snow Crystals" by Bentley and Humphreys
(1931) and (1962) contains over 2000 microphotographs of snow
crystals taken by Bentley in Vermont. A classic work is
"Historja Naturalna Lodu" by Dobrowolski (1923). A general
treatment of snow hydrology, snow surveying, and water-yield
forecasting is given by Garstka (1964) in Section 10 of the
Handbook of Applied Hydrology.

A technique for making transparent replicas, in plastic,
of individual snowflakes in three dimensions is described by
Schaefer (1956).

Figure 16-1
Photomicrograph of
a snow crystal taken
by W. A. Bentley of
Jericho, Vermont.
From page 195 of
Bentley and Humphreys
(1931 and 1962)

In hydrology the depth of snow as measured at the time of fall has limited value. The water equivalent and the distribution of densities are hydrologically important. Snow density is a ratio between the volume of the water equivalent of a snow sample and the initial volume of that sample. A snowpack under natural conditions seldom possesses uniform density. Snow at the time of fall may have a density as low as 0.01 or as high as 0.15. In hydrology where snow surveys are not available or where rain-gage catchments or snow-board measurements are not physically converted to water equivalents by melting, it is common to assume that the snow fell at a density of 0.10. Therefore a snowfall of 10 inches in depth, as measured at the time of fall, is assumed to have a water equivalent of one inch. Snow when ripe and when yielding water usually has a density of about 0.45.

Judy, Meiman, and Friedman (1970) concluded that the deuterium variations in an annual snowpack in the Central Rocky Mountains of Colorado were largely reduced in their initial variability as a result of metamorphism.

Snow is measured in a number of ways:

a.  By rain gages both standard and recording.
    The density of snow at the time of fall, the prevailing temperature and especially wind, have very complex interactions in the vicinity of a rain gage resulting in catchment which may be far different than that as measured on the ground. Seasonal storage gages have been developed which contain a charge of antifreeze and an evaporation retardant. One type of a shielded gage is shown on page 26 in the Bulletin by Washichek, Stockwell and Evans (1963).

b.  By snow boards.
    Snow boards are used to measure, for each storm, the depth of snow at time of fall. Total snowfall for a winter, as reported at a weather station, is a sum of the measurements made at the time of fall. It is not to be expected that the depth reported would be in evidence at any one time at the reporting station.

c.  Snow stakes.
    Some years ago in many western states extensive observations were made of snow depths. This data has been shown to possess but little hydrologic significance unless there happened to be a snow course or an observation station in the vicinity at which water equivalents were determined. Snow depths are of importance to transportation, recreation, ecology, and wildlife management. A specialized form of snow stake is the aerial marker which is discussed on pages 23-25 in the Bulletin by Washichek, Stockwell and Evans (1963). This trellis-like structure yields depth-of-snow information when viewed or photographed from flying aircraft. Systems of aerial markers installed as part of a

snow-course system yield data on the distribution of snow depths over a drainage basin at many more sampling points than might be available from snow courses.

Larson, Ffolliott and Moessner (1974) found that a scale of 1 to 15,840 was best when using aerial photography to measure forest overstory and topography to estimate peak snowpack.

d.  Snow course.
In hydrology the basic measurement of snow is that performed at a snow course. Colorado Snow Course 5K3, Berthoud Pass, is platted on Page 15 of the Washichek, Stockwell, and Evans 1963 reference. In this same reference the form used for recording the data is shown on page 18 and the improved Mount Rose snow sampling outfit is shown in detail on pages 12 and 13. The measurement and management of watershed snowpacks was reviewed by Work (1955). Environment Canada has prepared a bilingual manual of standards for procedures entitled "Snow Surveying" (1973).

Dr. James E. Church, a pioneer in snow surveying, in his articles published in 1912 described the Mount Rose Observatory and the design of a snow sampler. According to Poulton (1964) Dr. Church was a Latin and Greek scholar and a critic of art at the University of Nevada.

Figure 16-2  Snow Surveyors Using the Mount Rose Snow Sampler
The surveyor on the left is reading the depth of snow. Between the surveyors the spring balance for determining water equivalent is shown hanging from two ski poles. From page 20, Washichek, Stockwell and Evans, 1963.

e.  Radioisotope snow gages.
    Snow courses require on-the-ground measurements.  Inaccess-
    ibility under adverse weather conditions and the cost of
    frequent surveys (if they could be performed) have led to
    the development of remotely-located, unattended radio-
    reporting equipment.  The development of radioisotope snow
    gages is described by Gerdel and Mansfield (1950), Doremus
    (1951), Itagaki (1959), and Robinson (1960).  Most snow-
    depth radioisotope gages use Cobalt 60.

    James L. Smith (undated) developed a snow-density water-
    content gage making use of radioisotope Cesium 137.  This
    is a profiling gage which can determine snow characteris-
    tics in half-inch sections of snow without disturbing the
    snowpack.  Bissell and Burson (1974) suggest using cosmic
    radiation for measuring the snow-water equivalents of deep
    snows.

f.  Snow pillows.
    This instrument was developed by scientists and engineers
    of the Soil Conservation Service as described by Beaumont
    (1965).  It consists of a pillow-shaped, liquid-filled con-
    tainer made of an impervious but flexible material connect-
    ed to a manometer.  Remote control radio-reporting facili-
    ties have been developed to convert the level of the liquid
    in the manometer to a radio signal.  Kerr (1976) found that
    snow pillows could be used effectively in monitoring the
    changes of water equivalents in shallow depths of snow such
    as found in Alberta, Canada.

Telemetering

    Reynolds (1972) analyzed the results of 46 telemetering
precipitation stations having capacities of from 36 to 70 inches in the Wasatch Mountains of Utah.  Some of the stations,
operated primarily in winter, are more than 100 miles from the
base station and a few are at altitudes of above 10,000 feet.
The experimental design of the project provides for both case
studies of storm events and for statistical testing.  Chadwick
(1972) describes a variable inductance transducer which is
frictionless.  This device is used in the radio-reporting telemetry system described by Reynolds.

    Barton (1975) described the proposed program of establish-
ing an on-call radio-reporting telemetering system called
SNOTEL ultimately to include over 500 snow courses in the
Western United States.  Further information concerning this
project is provided in the paper by Barton and Burke (1977).
The area to be covered by SNOTEL is estimated to be greater
than 2,000,000 square kilometers.

    The radio components of the system are described in the

65-page booklet, "Western Union's Meteor Burst Communications" (1977). A lower VHF frequency, for example 40.530 MHz, is used at the master station. This frequency is reflected or re-radiated by the ionized meteor trails billions of which occur daily at elevations of 80-120 km above the Earth. The communications paths are visible at distances up to about 2000 km.

A remote data aquisition station in this example would respond at 41.530 MHz following a reciprocal path. The two master stations are located at Boise, Idaho, and Ogden, Utah, chosen by extensive field propagation and performance tests. Eleven SNOTEL sites are to be active in Colorado alone for the winter of 1977-78 and about 160 sites are scheduled for the initial part of the system.

## Travel Over Snow

Access to snow courses, maintenance of hydrologic and weather instruments, and water resources project operations and maintenance under winter conditions, were among the interests which led to the development of over-snow vehicles. Fish and wildlife, forest, and recreational interests, and those engaged in mineral industries, had an interest in common with hydrologists in developing over-snow vehicles.

The American Indian is credited with the invention of the snowshoe first applying the principle expressed by Bekker (1950). Travel over snow is like travel over soil except that snow is much less cohesive and much less dense but the basic principles are parallel. Bekker pointed out that the resistance to collapse of a surface under a vehicle loading increased directly with increased length of the loaded surface and also increased as the square of the width of the loaded surface.

Over-snow vehicles attempt to attain a loading of about one-half pound per square inch either through increasing length or width or both, of the area of contact with the snow. The Tucker Sno-Cat shown on Page 28 of the reference by Washichek, Stockwell and Evans, slides on ski-like pontoons the propulsive effort being provided by a ladder-like track moving around the periphery of the pontoons. The track-laying vehicles are similar to the Caterpillar tractors consisting of one or more belts.

There has been a tremendous growth during recent years of the two-passenger snowmobiles. Several hundred thousand of these vehicles are now in service. The original research and development on this small, single-track, vehicle was done by snow surveyors. Kirk (1978) in her enthusiastic, non-technical illustrated book on snow includes a chapter on travel over snow with sled dogs and reindeer.

Avalanches

A natural phenomena of special interest to forest hydrologists is the avalanche. This awesome spectacle unleashes some tremendous forces. Speeds of descent of avalanches have been observed to exceed two hundred miles per hour. Avalanche control makes use of structural engineering and of forest practices. A classic publication dealing with snow structure and avalanches is Seligman's (1936) book.

Frutiger (1964) discusses avalanche problems in mountain highways in Colorado. Massive concrete snow chutes and tunnels have been constructed in high-avalanche risk areas. The Eisenhower Tunnel under Loveland Pass on Interstate 70 west of Denver, Colorado, was built because of avalanche hazards.

Perla and Martinelli (1976) have prepared an outstanding avalanche handbook which includes sections on meteorology, snow physics, snow mechanics, avalanche movement, control measures, and life-saving procedures among other subjects. This handbook is recommended for study by anyone interested in snow, especially in cross-country skiing.

Williams (March, 1975) analyzes in detail 76 avalanche accidents in the United States during the period 1967-71. In a supplemental report Williams (Sept. 1975) presents information for the period 1950-75. In the last 25 years deaths due to avalanches averaged 6 per year but this figure increased to 12 per year in the last 5 years. About three-fourths of all victims are recreationists.

Martinelli (1974) has assembled photographs and sketches dealing with the identification and evaluation of avalanche sites.

"Avalanche Protection in Switzerland" (1975) is a translation of 16 articles by Swiss avalanche experts. It contains numerous photographs, sketches, tables, and engineering drawings.

Snow Loads

An avalanche is the result of snow loading exceeding the mechanical properties of the snowpack at that site. The maximum weight which a snowpack may attain is of direct concern to structural engineering. On March 28, 1952 the snow load at Donner Summit, California, was 426 pounds per square foot according to Brown (1970). Tobiasson and Redfield (1977) report that during the extreme winter of 1976-77 at Buffalo, New York, snow-drift loads on roofs exceeding 200 pounds per square-foot ($976.6$ Kg/m$^2$) were measured.

Frequency analyses have been made of snow-water equivalents for Colorado and New Mexico snow courses by Washichek and Moreland (1974).

Snow-load design requirements are specified in many national, state, and local building codes. Evidence of lack of uniformity has led the U.S. Army Corps of Engineers to organize an extensive program to update both research and practice on snow loads as described by Tobiasson and Redfield (1977). Data from more than 9000 observation stations is to be used. Their paper includes 20 references to snow-load criteria for both the United States and Canada.

Sources of hydrologic data, including snow, are listed in Appendix C.

## References

"Avalanche Protection in Switzerland", Translation by the U.S. Army, CRREL, of Lawinenschutz in der Schweiz. This is a collection of 16 articles by Swiss Avalanche experts. Published by Rocky Mt. Forest and Range Exp. Station, Fort Collins, Colo. General Tech. Report RM-9, 168 pp, Mar., 1975.

Barton, Manes, "SNOTEL: Automated Snow Surveys", Proc. 43d Western Snow Conf., Apr. 23-25, 1975, Coronado, Calif., pp 6-9, pub. by Colo. State Univ., Fort Collins, 1975.

Barton, Manes, and Michael Burke, "SNOTEL: An Operational Data Acquisition System Using Meteor Burst Technonology", Proceedings, Western Snow Conf., Apr. 18-21, 1977, Albuquerque, N.M., pp 82-87, pub. by Colo. State Univ., Fort Collins, 1977.

Beaumont, R. T., "Mt. Hood Pressure Pillow Snow Gage", Jour. of Applied Meteorology, vol. 4, pp 626-631, 1965.

Bekker, M. G., "Soil-Vehicle Concepts Found Impeding Design", Jour. Society of Automotive Engineers, vol. 58, no. 5, pp 20-24, May, 1950.

Bentley, W. A., and W. J. Humphreys, "Snow Crystals", originally pub. by McGraw-Hill Book Co., 1931; reprinted by Dover Pub. Inc., New York, 227 pp, 1962.

Bissell, Vernon C., and Zolin G. Burson, "Deep Snow Measurements Suggested Using Cosmic Radiation", Water Resources Research, vol. 10, no. 6, pp 1243-1244, Dec. 1974.

Brown, John W., "An Approach to Snow Load Evaluation", Western
    Snow Conf., 38th Annual Meeting, Victoria, B.C., Apr. 21-
    23, 1970, pp 52-60, pub. by Colo. State Univ., Fort
    Collins, 1970.

Chadwick, Duane G., "Precipitation Telemetry in the Mountainous
    Areas", Water Resources Research, vol. 8, no. 1, pp 255-
    258, Feb. 1972.

Church, James E., "The Progress of Mount Rose Observatory,
    1906-1912", Science, N.S., vol. XXXVI, no. 936, pp 796-
    800, Dec. 6, 1912.

Dobrowolski, Antoni Boleslaw, "Historja Naturalna Lodu",
    (Natural History of Ice), pub. in Warsaw, Poland, 1940 pp,
    1923.

Doremus, J. A., "Telemetering System for Radioactive Snow Gage"
    Electronics, vol. 25, pp 88-91, 1951.

Frutiger, Hans, "Snow Avalanches Along Colorado Mountain High-
    ways", U.S. Forest Service Research Paper RM-7, Rocky Mt.
    Forest and Range Exp. Station, Fort Collins, July, 1964.

Garstka, Walter U., "Snow and Snow Survey", Chap. 10, Handbook
    of Applied Hydrology, Ven Te Chow, ed-in-chief, McGraw-
    Hill Book Co., New York, 1964.

Gerdel, R. W., and C. W. Mansfield, "The Use of Radioisotopes
    in Research on Snowmelt and Runoff", Proc. Western Snow
    Conf., Boulder City, Nev., pp 5-17, Apr. 1950.

"International Classification for Snow (With Special Reference
    to Snow on the Ground)", issued by the Commission on Snow
    and Ice of the International Assn. of Hydrology, Tech.
    Memo. No. 31, Associate Comm. on Soil and Snow Mechanics,
    Natl. Research Council, Ottawa, Canada, Aug. 1954.

Itagaki, K., "An Improved Radio Snow Gage for Practical Use",
    Jour. of Geophysical Research, vol. 64, no. 3, pp 375-
    383, March, 1959.

Judy, Clark, James R. Meiman, and Irving Friedman, "Deuterium
    Variations in an Annual Snowpack", Water Resources
    Research, vol. 6, no. 1, pp 125-129, Feb. 1970.

Kerr, W. E., "Snow Pillow Experiences in a Prairie (Alberta)
    Environment", Proc. 44th Western Snow Conf., Apr. 20-22,
    1976, Calgary, Alberta, Canada, pp 39-47, pub. by Colo.
    State Univ., Fort Collins, 1976.

Kirk, Ruth, "Snow", Wm. Morrow & Co., New York, 320 pp, 1978.

Larson, Frederic R., Peter F. Ffolliott, and Karl E. Moessner, "Using Aerial Measurements of Forest Overstory and Topography to Estimate Peak Snowpack", Rocky Mt. Forest and Range Exp. Station Research Note RM-267, 4 pp, Fort Collins, Colo., July, 1974.

Martinelli, M., Jr., "Snow Avalanche Sites, Their Identification and Evaluation", Forest Service, USDA, Agricultural Information Bulletin No. 360, 28 pp, Feb. 1974.

Perla, Ronald I., and M. Martinelli, Jr., "Avalanche Handbook", Forest Service, USDA, Agri. Handbook 489, 238 pp, July, 1976.

Poulton, Helen, J., "James Edward Church: Bibliography of a Snow Scientist", Bibliographical Series No. 4, 35 pp, Univ. of Nevada Press, 1964.

"Proceedings of the Workshop on Snow and Ice Hydrology", James R. Meiman, editor, Colo. State Univ., Aug. 18-22, 1969. Pub. by Colo. State Univ., Fort Collins, as a U.S. contribution to the International Hydrological Decade, 1970.

Reynolds, George W., "Weight Capacity Requirements for Precipitation Measurements in the Wasatch Mountains", Water Resources Research, vol. 8, no. 1, pp 249-254, Feb. 1972.

Robinson, D., "Gamma Radiation Gauges Snow Pack Water Content", Elec. World, vol. 154, no. 17, Cover photo and pp 82-83, Oct. 24, 1960.

Schaefer, Vincent J., "The Preparation of Snow Crystal Replicas VI", Weatherwise, vol. 9, no. 4, pp 132-135, Aug., 1956.

Schaefer, Vincent J., "Snow", Encylopaedia Britannica, vol. 20, page 854, 1956.

Seligman, G., "Snow Structure and Ski Fields: With an Appendix on Alpine Weather by C. K. M. Douglas", MacMillan and Co., Ltd., London, 1936.

Smith, James L., "Snow Research in the Sierra Nevada, California", an 8-page pamphlet published by the U.S. Forest Service, Pacific Southwest Forest and Range Exp. Station, Berkeley, Calif. (Undated).

"Snow Surveying", (Releves Nivometriques) Manual of Standards, Snow Surveying Procedures, 2nd edition, Atmospheric Environment, Environment Canada, Toronto, Ontario, Canada, April, 1973.

Summerfield, R. A., "Classification Outline for Snow on the Ground", Forest Service, USDA, Research Paper RM-48 (1969) Rocky Mountain Forest and Range Exp. Station, Fort Collins, 24 pp, reissued June, 1976.

Tobiasson, Wayne, and Robert Redfield, "Update on Snow Load Research at CRREL", presented at the 34th Eastern Snow Conf., 3-4 Feb. 1977, Belleville, Ontario. Reprint pub. by Cold Regions Research and Engineering Lab., Corps of Engineers, U.S. Army, Hanover, N.H., Apr. 1977.

Washichek, Jack N., Homer J. Stockwell, and Norman A. Evans, "Snow Surveys in Colorado", Colo. State Univ., General Series No. 795, 1963.

Washichek, Jack N., and Ronald E. Moreland, "Snow Frequency Analysis for Colorado and New Mexico Snow Courses", Soil Conservation Service, USDA, Denver, Colo. 59 pp, Apr. 1974.

"Western Union's Meteor Burst Communications", Govt. Systems Div., Western Union, McLean, Va., 65 pp, Jan. 1977.

Williams, Knox, "The Snow Torrents: Avalanche Accidents in the United States, 1967-71", Forest Service, USDA, Gen. Tech. Report RM-8, Rocky Mountain Forest and Range Exp. Station, Fort Collins, Colo., 190 pp, March, 1975.

Williams, Knox, "Avalanche Fatalities in the United States, 1950-75", Forest Service, USDA, Research Note RM-300, Rocky Mountain Forest and Range Exp. Station, Fort Collins Colo., 4 pp, Sept. 1975.

Work, R. A., "Measurement and Management of Watershed Snow Packs", Proceedings, Society of American Foresters Meeting, 1955, pp 195-198, 1955.

# SECTION III

## MATHEMATICAL AND STATISTICAL TREATMENTS

An appreciation of mathematical statistics is necessary in water resource management. The accuracy of measurements, the significance of results, the validity of sampling systems, the probability of recurrence of hydrologic events such as floods and droughts, and the calculation of risks, all require mathematical statistical analyses. The topics in Section III will serve to establish an acquaintanceship with the philosophy underlying water resource applications. Knowledge of this field of water resources is extensive and extremely specialized and should a problem arise it would be desirable to secure the advice and services of those who are professionally competent in mathematical statistics as they apply to water resources.

Topic 17      The Normal Distribution Concept

The arithmetic mean yields no information concerning the extent to which each of the values averaged departs from the mean. The median is the central value of an array of values and it may or may not be numerically equal to the mean. The basic information about the extent of values around the mean can be expressed by the standard deviation, which is computed from the squares of the individual deviations from the mean, by the following equation taken from Butler, Section 4-11 (1957):

$$s = \sqrt{\frac{\Sigma (y - \bar{y})^2}{n - 1}}$$

in which

s  is the standard deviation  $\bar{y}$  is the mean
y  is the item                n  is the total number
                                 of items

The coefficient of variation (c.v.) also expresses the extent to which items vary about the mean. The coefficient of variation is the ratio of the standard deviation to the mean, or:

$$c.v. = \frac{s}{\bar{y}}$$

In a great many applications of statistical analyses it has been found that the data plotted will depict the normal distribution yielding a symmetrical bell-shaped curve as is shown in Figure 17-1 on the following page.

A distribution graph in which the peak of the curve does not coincide with the mean and which is not necessarily bell-shaped is called a "skewed" distribution. Complex mathematical treatments are required for skewed distribution.

93

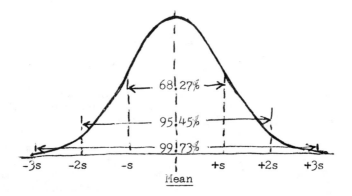

Figure 17-1   Probability Density Function of the Normal
Distribution

The area under the normal distribution curve shows the
dispersion of the data.   Therefore by determining the area
under the curve as measured between the mean and an ordinate
erected at any plus or minus value and measured in  s  units
along the  x  axis, probabilities can be computed for any selected range.   Plus or minus one standard deviation can be interpreted to mean that 68.27 times out of 100 the value will be
between plus or minus one standard deviation.   95.45 percent of
the items are included between ± 2s and 99.73 items are included between ± 3s.

By choosing the proper multiplier other probabilities can
be selected.   For example, plus or minus 1.645 times the standard deviation yields the 90 percent limits.   In hydrologic
forecasting the "quartile" dispersion often is used.   This is
another expression of the 50 percent probability limits.   The
normal distribution curve goes to infinity on both the plus and
the minus sides of the mean.   A table of multipliers for areas
under the curve is given by Ford (1959).

Many natural phenomena do not yield the normal distribution symmetrical bell-shaped curve.   Eight examples of frequency curves are shown on page 31 in a reference by Spiegel (1961).
The concepts of computation of probabilities as developed for
the symmetrical curve do not apply directly to non-symmetrical
or skewed distributions, treatment of which requires complex
mathematical statistics.

A concise treatment of fundamentals of statistics is presented by Crow, Davis, and Maxfield, (1955).   Spiegel (1961) in
his Chapter 4 discusses the standard deviation and other measures of dispersion.   Included in his Chapter 4 are 82 problems
with answers.

Riggs (1968) presents a brief discussion of symmetrical and non-symmetrical distributions together with a review of methods of regression analyses with special reference to hydrology.

## References

Butler, Stanley S., "Engineering Hydrology", Prentice-Hall, Inc., Englewood Cliffs, New Jersey, 1957.

Crow, Edwin L., Frances A. Davis, and Margaret W. Maxfield, "Statistics Manual", U.S. Naval Ordnance Test Station, China Lake, Calif., 1955. (Navord Report 3368 Nots 948).

Croxton, Frederick E., and Dudley J. Cowden, "Applied General Statistics", Prentice-Hall, Inc., New York, 1939, (17th printing 1949).

Ford, Perry M., "Multiple Correlation in Forecasting Seasonal Runoff", Engineering Monograph No. 2, Bureau of Reclamation, USDI, 2nd revision, June, 1959.

Riggs, H. C., "Some Statistical Tools in Hydrology", Surface Water Techniques, Hydrologic Analysis, Book 4, Chapt. A1, Geological Survey, USDI, 1968.

Spiegel, Murray R., "Statistics", Schaum Pub. Co., New York, 359 pp, 1961.

Topic 18         <u>Simple Correlation Analysis</u>

The basic concept underlying mathematical expression of a relationship is the derivation of the equation of a line. A fundamental case is that of one independent variable, X, which is correlated with the dependent variable, Y.

The general statement of the equation is: $Y = mX + b$, in which m is the slope of the line and b is a constant, also called the intercept. Figure 18-1 is a graph with solution to illustrate the derivation of the equation of a line.

The equation derived in the example is from a line drawn through points A and B. It therefore expresses in a mathematical statement only the personal judgment of the analyst and says nothing about the statistical relationships of the data plotted as points A, B, C, and D.

Figure 18-1

Example of procedure for derivation of equation of a line connecting 2 points

$Y = mX + b$          (1)

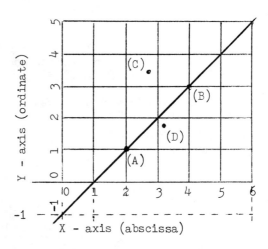

X - axis (abscissa)

Point (A) is $X_2 Y_1$                    Point (B) is $X_4 Y_3$

Slope $m = \dfrac{Y_3 - Y_1}{X_4 - X_2} = \dfrac{3 - 1}{4 - 2} = \dfrac{2}{2} = 1$, or Slope $m = 1$     (2)

Solving the equation for b yields:     $b = -mX + Y$

$b = (-1 \times 4) + 3 = -1$
or $b = (-1 \times 2) + 1 = -1$     Therefore:  $b = -1$

$Y = mX + b$; or: $Y = (1 \times X) -1$; or: <u>$Y = X - 1$</u>          (3)

Verification: Let $X = 3$, then $Y = 2$, which is on the graph.

A very much more indicative analysis of a simple correlation is the derivation of the equation of the line by the Method of Least Squares. The Least Squares computation results not only in the equation for the line but also yields the coefficient of correlation either with or without adjustment for the number of degrees of freedom, and the standard error of the estimate can be derived.

This will make it possible, assuming that the data will plot into a normal probability curve, to compute confidence limits which can be interpreted as probability percentages.

An example of a simple correlation analysis with derivation of the equation by the Method of Least Squares is presented in Figure 18-2. The graph, Figure 18-3, depicts the precipitation-runoff correlation and shows the position of the line as plotted from the equation: $Y = 5.068X - 18.773$. These two figures are from "Seasonal Runoff Forecasting" (1948).

When the dependent variable is the result of the interaction of two or more independent variables it is possible to express the relationship through the use of statistical multiple correlation analyses which are outlined by Ford (1959).

Madkour (1968) has appended to his paper on the precision of adjusted variables by least squares a selected bibliography of 21 general references. Numerous computer programs are available for least squares analyses.

There are numerous general and specialized texts on statistics. Spiegel (1961) may be very useful to those who wish to review their background in statistics. In addition to condensed reviews of statistical concepts the reference includes 875 problems completely solved in detail.

References

Ford, Perry M., "Multiple Correlation in Forecasting Seasonal Runoff", Engineering Monograph No. 2, Bureau of Reclamation, USDI, 2nd revision, June, 1959.

Madkour, Mohamed F., "Precision of Adjusted Variables by Least Squares", Jour. Surveying and Mapping Div., Proceedings ASCE, pp 119-136, Sept. 1968.

"Seasonal Runoff Forecasting", chap. 8.1, of part 8, Operating Problems vol. IV, Water Studies, Bureau of Reclamation Manual, USDI, originally prepared in 1948 with continuing revisions.

Spiegel, Murray R., "Statistics", Schaum Pub. Co., New York, 859 pp, 1961.

## I

I = April-July, incl. Runoff 10,000 A.F. units
X = Total precipitation, Oct.-Mar. average of five stations, inches.

| Year | X | Y | X² | XY | Y² |
|---|---|---|---|---|---|
| 1936 | 15.84 | 58.4 | 250.91 | 925.06 | 3,410.56 |
| 37 | 8.81 | 29.1 | 77.62 | 256.37 | 846.81 |
| 38 | 16.24 | 78.8 | 263.74 | 1,279.71 | 6,209.44 |
| 39 | 11.88 | 31.4 | 141.13 | 373.03 | 985.96 |
| 1940 | 14.43 | 38.6 | 208.22 | 557.00 | 1,489.96 |
| 41 | 9.85 | 35.2 | 97.02 | 346.72 | 1,239.04 |
| 42 | 12.08 | 42.8 | 145.93 | 517.02 | 1,831.84 |
| 43 | 22.01 | 103.6 | 484.44 | 2,280.24 | 10,738.96 |
| 44 | 7.67 | 31.8 | 58.83 | 243.91 | 1,011.24 |
| 45 | 12.09 | 40.5 | 166.15 | 522.04 | 1,640.25 |
| 46 | 17.53 | 71.3 | 307.30 | 1,249.89 | 5,083.69 |
| 47 | 16.04 | 49.0 | 257.28 | 785.96 | 2,401.00 |
| 48 | 12.88 | 46.8 | 165.89 | 602.78 | 2,190.24 |
| 49 | 15.60 | 51.7 | 243.36 | 806.52 | 2,672.89 |
| 1950 | 14.93 | 67.0 | 222.90 | 1,000.31 | 4,489.00 |
| Total | 208.68 | 776.0 | 3,090.72 | 11,746.56 | 46,234.88 |
| Mean | 13.912 | 51.733 | Number of Years of Record n = 15 | | |

## II

### Derivation of Equation of line

$(M_x)^2 = (13.912)^2 = 193.54$

$(M_y)^2 = (51.733)^2 = 2,676.30$

$M_x M_y = 739.71$

$$b = \frac{\Sigma(XY) - n(M_x M_y)}{\Sigma(X^2) - n(M_x)^2} = \frac{11,746.56 - 15(739.71)}{3,090.72 - 15(193.54)}$$

$$b = \frac{11,746.56 - 10,795.65}{3,090.72 - 2,903.10} = \frac{950.91}{187.62} = 5.068$$

$a = M_y - bM_x = [51.733 - 5.068(13.912)] = -18.773$

Equation:

$Y = a + bX$

$Y = -18.773 + 5.068(X)$

## III

### Calculation of Coefficient of Correlation

$$r = \frac{\Sigma(XY) - n(M_x M_y)}{\sqrt{[\Sigma(X^2) - n(M_x)^2][\Sigma(Y^2) - n(M_y)^2]}}$$

$$= \frac{11,746.56 - 15(739.71)}{\sqrt{(3,090.72 - 2,903.10)(46,234.88 - 40,144.50)}}$$

$$= \frac{950.91}{\sqrt{1,142,677.10}} = \frac{950.91}{1,068.9}$$

$r = 0.890 \qquad r^2 = 0.792$

$\bar{r}^2 = 1 - \left[(1 - r^2)\left(\dfrac{n-1}{n-2}\right)\right]$

$\bar{r}^2 = 1 - \left[(1 - 0.792)\left(\dfrac{15-1}{15-2}\right)\right] = 1 - (0.208)(1.077)$

$\bar{r}^2 = 1 - 0.224 = 0.776$

$\bar{r} = 0.881$

## IV

### Calculation of Standard Error of Estimate

$$S = \sqrt{\frac{\Sigma(Y^2) - n(M_y)^2}{n - 1}(1 - r^2)}$$

$$= \sqrt{\frac{46,234.88 - 40,144.50}{15 - 1}(1 - 0.776)}$$

$$= \sqrt{(435.03)(0.224)}$$

$$= \sqrt{97.447}$$

$S = 9.87$ or $98,700$ acre-feet

$1.645 \, S = 162,400$ acre-feet

## V

### Summary of Forecast Computation. April 1st.

South Fork of the Boise River at Anderson Ranch, Idaho.

Equation: $Y = 5.068(X) - 18.773$

where

Y = April-July, inclusive, run-off, in 10,000 acre-foot units

X = total precipitation, Oct.-Mar., inclusive, average of five stations: Arrowrock, Atlanta, Hill City, Idaho City, Obsidian.

Parameters:

$\bar{r} = 0.881$

$S = 98,700$ acre-feet

$1.645 \, S = 162,400$ acre-feet

The chances are one to twenty that the observed flow may fall above the +1.645 S line; and one in twenty that the observed flow may fall below the -1.645 S line.

Figure 18-2    An Example of a Procedure for Computation of a Simple Correlation by the Method of Least Squares

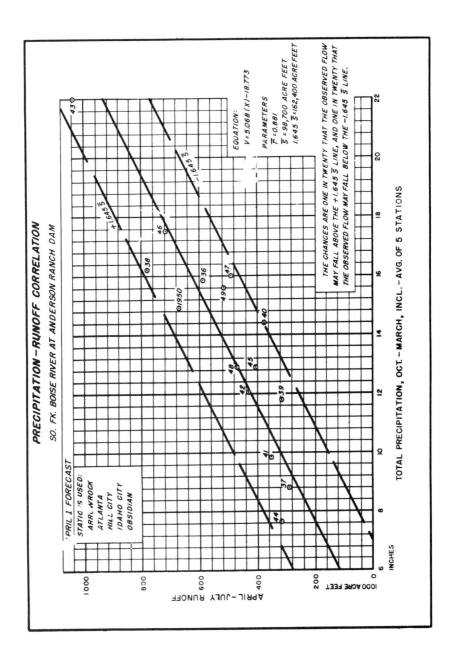

Figure 18-3  Graph Depicting the Precipitation-Runoff Correlation of the Least Squares Computation Outlined in
Figure 18-2

99

A number of terms dealing with frequency analyses are in common use:

Frequency Distribution. The mathematical relationship between the size of an event and its return period or probability.

Annual Series. A general term for a set of any kind of data in which each item is the maximum in a year. Also used if the data are minimums or sums or averages of years.

Partial Series. An array of all events larger than some arbitrary size or lower limit regardless of the years in which they occur. It may consist of several events from some years and no events from other years.

Full Series. The full series includes all records. It is not suitable for frequency analyses. The full series is used in the computation of duration curves.

"Method of Flow Frequency Analysis" (1966) defines the "recurrence interval" (sometimes referred to as the "return period") as follows:

"recurrence interval - (1) The average time interval between actual occurrences of a hydrological event of a given or greater magnitude. (2) In an annual flood series the average interval in which a flood of a given size recurs as an annual maximum. (3) In a partial duration series, the average interval between floods of a given size, regardless of their relationship to the year or any other period of time. This distinction holds even though for large floods recurrence intervals are nearly the same on both scales (ASCE)".

There is no uniformity on the symbol used for the return period, $T_r$, T and others being used in various publications and textbooks. However the relationships stated deal with the same concepts.

One of the simplest of the formulas for estimating the recurrence interval by plotting, which can be done either on cartesian or preferably on semi-log paper with the arithmetic scale on the y-axis, is the so-called "California" method:

$$T_r = \frac{n}{m}$$　　　in which:　$T_r$ = return period in years　　(1)
　　　　　　　　　　　　　　　$n$ = number of years of record
　　　　　　　　　　　　　　　$m$ = rank or number of event
　　　　　　　　　　　　　　　　　　($m = 1$ for largest, $m = 2$
　　　　　　　　　　　　　　　　　　for second largest, etc.)

One of the valuable approaches to frequency analyses consists of the double exponential extreme value distribution now generally known as the "Gumbel" method. A condensed discussion of the Gumbel method is given by Linsley, Kohler, and Paulhus (1975). There is an extensive literature on the Gumbel method for which a basic reference was written by Gumbel (1968).

Chow (1964) and Benson (1962) have prepared informative papers on frequency analyses. The Proceedings of the International Hydrology Symposium (1967) include numerous papers and discussions dealing with this subject.

When making frequency analyses of annual series of hydrologic events for projecting extensions to long recurrence intervals, the Weibull formula is used for computing plotting points on the Gumbel Frequency Distribution paper which was developed by Powell on the basis of the theory of largest values. It is not a log paper and is not to be used for plotting points for partial series computed with other formulas. The Weibull formula is

$$T_r = \frac{n + 1}{m} \tag{2}$$

The extreme value distribution as computed according to the Gumbel method is not symetrical about the mean but has a fixed skew. The arithmetic mean of the distribution occurs at the 2.33-year recurrence interval. Therefore when using the Gumbel paper it is customary that the arithmetical mean of the annual values be plotted at the 2.33-return period. The hydrologist then chooses (as a personal decision) a point in the upper or higher value portions of the paper to fix the position of his line.

A "frequency distribution" is the mathematical expression, usually as plotted, between the size of an event and its recurrence interval, which is sometimes expressed in terms of probability.

Probability of occurrence, j, of an event with a recurrence interval of $T_r$ or larger in an interval of n years, is computed by

$$j = 1 - (1 - \frac{1}{T_r})^n \tag{3}$$

Percent chance is the probability multiplied by 100.

The probability of non-occurrence is

$$1 - j = (1 - \frac{1}{T_r})^n \tag{4}$$

Massive investment of Federal funds either from direct appropriations or from repayment accounts or trust funds has called attention to flood damage risk. If adequate provision is not made it is possible that Federal funds may not be made available for financing developments in high-risk areas. A further step in this direction is a recommendation for "A Uniform Technique for Determining Flood Flow Frequencies" (1967) which in this reference is the Pearson Type III method.

Bobee and Robitaille (1977) compared the results of the use of Pearson Type 3 and the Log Pearson Type 3 distributions as applied to a total of 28 river stations. Eleven stations in Canada with periods of record varying from 48 years to 65 years and drainage basin areas varying from 3,680 to 203,000 square kilometers were used. Seventeen river stations outside of Canada with periods of record varying from 45 to 162 years and drainage basins varying in areas from 17,090 to 578,300 square kilometers also were used. They concluded that the Pearson Type 3 distribution conforms better generally to annual flood data than does the Log Pearson Type 3.

The problems in frequency analyses indicate the importance of long and unbroken records of hydrologic events. The mathematical statistical methods discussed were developed as part of the endeavor to divine the future. Riggs (1968) has prepared a very useful review of frequency curves.

Eagleson (1972) presents a highly mathematical treatment of flood frequency computations. He derives, on a theoretical basis, a flood frequency equation which he proposes be used in the absence of streamflow records for extrapolating empirical estimates based upon short records. His comparison of a theoretical regional flood frequency function compares favorably with observations of mean annual floods from 44 Connecticut catchments.

Estimates of the recurrence interval and of probabilities of hydrologic events are matters of decision since there exist as yet no mathematical methods for proving the validity of a particular decision.

## Problem Assignment - Flood

On June 17, 1965 a flood which peaked at 47,000 cfs occurred on Fountain Creek at Pueblo, Colorado. The table lists peak rates of discharge for a year and the date of occurrence as observed on Fountain Creek which has a drainage area of 926 square miles above the Pueblo, Colorado, gaging station.

The 34,000 cfs peak rate which is listed as having taken place on June 4, 1921 was a backwater from a flood in the Arkansas River.

Table 19-1    Peak Rate of Discharge for a Year and Date
              of Occurrence

Fountain Creek at Pueblo, Colorado - Drainage Area: 926 sq. mi.

| Peak rate of discharge cfs | Date | Peak rate of discharge cfs | Date |
|---|---|---|---|
| 47,000 * | June 17, 1965 | 6,110 | Aug. 6, 1964 |
| 35,000 | May 30, 1935 | 5,880 | July 8, 1947 |
| 34,000 | June 4, 1921 | 5,800 | Aug. 6, 1954 |
| 17,800 | July 10, 1945 | 5,250 | Aug 10, 1956 |
| 16,500 | Aug. 26, 1946 | 5,170 | Aug 28, 1952 |
| 12,900 | Aug. 4, 1944 | 5,140 | Aug. 7, 1922 |
| 12,000 | Oct. 3, 1923 | 3,750 | Aug. 5, 1958 |
| 11,600 | July 30, 1951 | 3,730 | Aug 16, 1953 |
| 11,500 | Aug. 6, 1955 | 2,530 | July 13, 1960 |
| 11,000 | Aug. 14, 1942 | 2,520 | July 11, 1962 |
| 9,600 | July 28, 1950 | 2,500 | July 19, 1925 |
| 9,290 | June 12, 1948 | 1,590 | June 5, 1949 |
| 8,800 | Aug. 12, 1963 | 1,150 | Apr 29, 1941 |
| 6,200 | Aug. 11, 1961 | 324 | May 22, 1943 |
| 6,180 | May 15, 1957 | 204 | Apr 11, 1959 |

*Peak rates of discharge are from Patterson (1964) except for
the 47,000 cfs for June 17, 1965 which is from Snites (1974).

Problem A   Using the Gumbel frequency distribution compute the
            probability of occurrence and the percent chance of
            the 47,000 cfs flood occurring within the next five
            years.

Problem B   Estimate the 25-year, the 100-year, and the 500-year
            values for the peak rate of discharge for Fountain
            Creek, at Pueblo, Colorado.

Problem Assignment - Rainfall

     Twelve storms of one-hour duration which occurred inde-
pendently as convective rainstorms during a 42-year period at a
hypothetical station are listed in Table 19-2.

Table 19-2    Rainfall Depths for Storms of One-Hour Duration

| Date | | Rainfall (inches) | Date | | Rainfall (inches |
|---|---|---|---|---|---|
| 1925 | June 4 | 1.21 | 1941 | June 28 | 1.01 |
| 1926 | July 7 | 1.06 | | Aug. 21 | 0.98 |
| | Aug. 15 | 0.81 | 1942 | July 6 | 0.86 |
| 1934 | Aug. 10 | 0.80 | 1953 | Sept. 10 | 0.97 |
| 1935 | July 13 | 0.83 | 1961 | July 28 | 0.89 |
| 1937 | June 4 | 1.25 | 1966 | Aug. 1 | 0.92 |

Problem C

Plot the frequency distribution for one-hour rainfall by the California method and draw the line.

Problem D

Estimate 10-year, 25-year, and 100-year values from the line.

References

"A Uniform Technique for Determining Flood Flow Frequencies", Hydrol. Comm. Water Resources Council, Bulletin 15, Dec., 1967, pub. by Water Resources Council, Washington, D.C.

Benson, M. A., "Evolution of Methods for Evaluating the Occurrence of Floods", USGS Water Supply Paper 1580-A, 1962.

Bobee, Bernard B. and Roland Robitaille, "The Use of the Pearson Type 3 and Log Pearson Type 3 Distributions Revisited", Water Resources Research vol. 13, no. 2 pp 427-443, Apr. 1977.

Chow, Ven Te, "Frequency Analysis", Sec. 8-I Handbook of Applied Hydrology, Ven Te Chow, ed-in-chief, McGraw-Hill Book Co., New York, 1964.

Eagleson, P. S., "Dynamics of Flood Frequencies", Water Resources Research, vol. 8 no. 4, pp 878-898, Aug. 1972.

Gumbel, E. J., "Statistical Theory of Floods and Droughts", Jour. Institute of Water Engineers, vol. 12, no. 3, pp 157-184, May, 1958.

Linsley, R. K., M. A. Kohler, and J. L. H. Paulhus, "Hydrology for Engineers", McGraw-Hill Book Co., New York, 2nd edition, 1975.

"Methods of Flow Frequency Analysis", prepared under the auspices of the Sub-committee on Hydrology, Inter-Agency Committee on Water Resources, Notes on Hydrologic Activities, Bull. no. 13, Apr. 1966.

Patterson, James L., "Magnitude and Frequency of Floods in the United States - Part 7. Lower Mississippi River Basin", USGS Water Supply Paper 1681, 1964. (Data for recent years secured from publications of the Colo. State Engr.)

Proceedings, International Hydrology Symposium, Sept. 6-8, 1967, Fort Collins, Colo. Vol. 1, preprints of papers issued in June, 1967, 671 pp. Vol. 2, presentations of the general reporters and discussions, 433 pp. Published by Colorado State University, Sept. 1967.

Riggs, H. C., "Frequency Curves", Chapter A2 of Book 4, Hydrologic Analyses and Interpretation of Techniques of Water Resources Investigations of the USGS, 1968. (2nd printing 1969.)

Snites, R. J., and others, "Floods of June, 1965 in Arkansas River Basin, Colorado, Kansas, and New Mexico", USGS Water Supply Paper 1850-D, 97 pp, 1974.

Extreme values of rainfall, of floods, and of droughts, are of great importance in water resources development. Sufficient lengths of record of hydrologic observations of the necessary quality are practically non-existent. Therefore, the hydrologists use a number of methods which could possibly improve the reliability of the estimation of extreme values. Among these are:

a. Extending the actual record with estimates based upon other events such as extending runoff records of a short duration by correlations with precipitation records of greater length.

b. Pooling information by regional analyses, an example of which is the station-year method.

c. Extending the effective length of a record by interpreting evidence of extreme values from historical documents, glacier advances and recessions, varves in lake deposits, isotopes, and dendrochronology.

d. Ice cores from Greenland analyzed for the ratios of Oxygen 16 and 18 isotopes are being used to interpret temperature variations for the past 120,000 years; a sea core from the bottom of the North Atlantic shows evidence of ice ages and tropical climates extending back more than 3 million years, according to Matthews (1976) page 584.

e. Comparison of estimates of extremes computed statistically with floods synthesized through hydrometeorological storm transpositions.

f. Synthesized estimates of long hypothetical records using stochastic generating processes. In this it should be kept in mind that a 20-year record expanded into a 200-year "record" is still a 20-year record of natural events.

Gilman (1964) presents on page 5-59 a diagram of "calculated risk". He discusses the relationship between the calculated risk and the design return period prepared from theoretical computations. Therefore if a design engineer wants to be approximately 90 percent certain that a 10-year or greater rainfall does not occur in the next 10 years he should design for the 100-year rainfall.

A comprehensive treatment of flood frequency analyses is Dalrymple's Water Supply Paper (1960). Five sections in the Handbook of Applied Hydrology edited by Chow (1964) deal with various facets of the problem of extreme values. An example of literature on extreme values is the article by Huxham and McGilchrist (1969). Millan and Yevjevich (1971) report upon their investigations of probabilities of occurrence of observed droughts.

Shen (1976) serves as editor for lecture notes on 28 presentations given at an Institute at Colorado State University. Several of the presentations dealt with risk, uncertainty, generation of data on rainfall, floods, droughts, and on extreme values.

Extreme values are chosen. They are not computed since at this time there is no impersonal, precise mathematical technique for the computation, with proof, of extreme values.

## References

Dalrymple, Tate, "Flood Frequency Analyses", USGS Water Supply Paper 1543-A, 80 pp, 1960.

Gilman, Chas. S., "Rainfall", Sec. 9, Handbook of Applied Hydrology, Ven Te Chow, ed-in-chief, McGraw-Hill Book Co., New York, 1964.

"Handbook of Applied Hydrology", Sections 8, 9, 14, 18, and 25, Ven Te Chow, ed-in-chief, McGraw-Hill Book Co., New York, 1964.

Huxham, S. H., and C. A. McGilchrist, "On the Extreme Value Distribution for Describing Annual Flood Series", Water Resources Research, vol. 5, no. 6, pp 1404-14-5, Dec. 1969.

Matthews, Samuel W., "What's Happening to Our Climate", National Geographic, vol. 150, no. 5, pp 576-615, Nov. 1976.

Millan, J., and V. Yevjevich, "Probabilities of Observed Droughts", Hydrology Paper No. 50, Colorado State Univ., June, 1971.

Shen, H. W., editor, "Stochastic Approaches to Water Resources", in 2 volumes based essentially on lecture notes of the Institute on Application of Stochastic Methods to Water Resources Problems, Colo. State Univ., Fort Collins, June 30-July 11, 1975. Water Resources Publications, Fort Collins, Colo., 1976.

Topic 21          Stochastic Hydrology

The solar system is proof of the existence of an order in the makeup of the universe. However many thinkers on the subject claim that the laws of chance are the basic laws of the universe.

Pollard (1958) a physicist who helped develop the first atomic bomb and who later became an ordained minister wrote a philosphical treatise on the subject, "Chance and Providence".

The term "stochastic hydrology" applies to a consideration of the laws of chance as they pertain to hydrology. The opposite of stochastic is "deterministic" sometimes called "parametric" hydrology. Some publications refer to "statistical" as meaning "stochastic" and "scientific" as referring to non-stochastic. Those immersed in thinking about stochastic processes consider every physical system under precise control as a special case of a stochastic system. It is man's mastery of these special cases which has developed his control of the environment now reaching out beyond the confines of the Planet Earth.

The random or stochastic input of precipitation, temperature, etc., may be such in many parts of the world as to set a definite limit beyond which the hydrologist must admit that he has no knowledge of the future trend of events. At this point stochastic hydrology becomes extremely valuable since the techniques, now in an evolving state, provide for the generation of projections into the future. A brief but comprehensive review of the subject is given by Chow (1964).

The shortness of the duration of records in most river basins has led to the extensive consideration of stochastic hydrology in relation to long-range water resources project planning. The publication by Maass and associates (1962) is a very important contribution to the subject. Works dealing with the design of storage reservoir systems are to be found in papers by Jeng and Yevjevich (1966) and Yevjevich (1966).

Rapid advances in our knowledge of astrophysical-meteorological interrelationships raise the question as to the length of a cycle to be investigated in the analyses of sequences of hydrologic events as discussed by Garstka (1967). Yevjevich (1969) summarizes concisely the thinking in stochastic hydrology.

Todorovic and Zelenhasic (1970) obtained reasonably good agreement between theoretical and observed results of their investigation of a stochastic model for flow analysis of the 72-year record of the Susquehanna River at Wilkes-Barre,

Pennsylvania.

Burges and Linsley (1971) used the second generation of digital computers in their search for methods that could account for the expected variation of inflow sequences in reservoirs. They conclude that: "Great care should be exercised in the application of, and in the interpretation of, results from stochastic analysis particularly when demand levels are high, inflow variability is large, and apparent large correlations exist."

Duckstein, Fogel, and Kisiel (1972) discuss the problem of the use of a stochastic model to introduce a rainfall input before the runoff output can be predicted as part of the approach to the evaluation of the effects of the modification of watersheds which may take place either through natural processes such as erosion or forest fires or through human influences such as urbanization.

Thompson (1973) reviews the history of analyses of correlating sunspots and solar cycles with the occurrence of droughts in the mid-west. All indications point to a recurrence of a drought period in the late 1970's or early 1980's. Thompson advocates that the late Henry Wallace's concept of an "Ever Normal Granary" be reconsidered since our National policy has committed us to export quantities of grain which we could not produce in an extended dry cycle.

Yevjevich (1972) discusses and illustrates with problem assignments in his textbook methods of analyzing hydrologic sequences governed by the laws of chance.

Gottschalk, Lindh, and deMare (1977) have edited 25 papers from International sources dealing with stochastic approaches to water resource management, risk analyses, and simulations.

References

Burges, S. J., and R. K. Linsley, "Some Factors Influencing Required Reservoir Storage", Jour. Hydraulics Div., ASCE, pp 977-991, July, 1971.

Chow, Ven Te, "Statistical and Probability Analysis of Hydrologic Data", Sec. 8-I, Handbook of Applied Hydrology, Ven Te Chow, ed-in-chief, McGraw-Hill Book Co., New York, 1964.

Duckstein, Lucien, Martin M. Fogel, and Chester C. Kisiel, "A Stochastic Model of Runoff-Producing Rainfall for Summer-Type Storms", Water Resources Research, vol. 8, no. 2, pp 410-421, April, 1972.

Garstka, Walter U., "Discussion of Paper No. 51, 'Cyclic Fluctuations of Variability in Hydrologic Phenomena', by
Oldrich Vitha and Vladimir Soucek, and Paper No. 52, 'Sunspots and Hydrologic Time Series', by I. Rodriguez and
V. Yevjevich", in Proceedings, The International Hydrology
Symposium, Sept. 6-8, 1967, Fort Collins, Colo., vol. 2,
pp 298-301, Sept. 1967.

Gottschalk, Lars, Gunnar Lindh, and Lennart de Mare, editors,
"Stochastic Processes in Water Resources Engineering",
Proceedings, 2nd International IAHR Symposium on Stochas-
tic Hydraulics, Lund Institute of Technology, Univ. of
Lund, Lund, Sweden, Aug. 2-4, 1977, 558 pp, Water
Resources Publications, Fort Collins, Colo., 1977.

Jeng, R. I., and V. M. Yevjevich, "Stochastic Properties of
Lake Outflows", Hydrology Paper No. 14, Colorado State
University, April, 1966.

Maas, Arthur, M. M. Hufschmidt, Robert Dorfman, H. A. Thomas,
Jr., S. A. Marglin, and G. M. Fair, "Design of Water-Resource Systems", Harvard Univ. Press, Cambridge, Mass. 1962.

Pollard, William G., "Chance and Providence", Charles Scribners
Sons, New York, 190 pp, 1958.

Thompson, Louis M., "Cyclical Weather Patterns in the Middle
Latitudes", Jour. of Soil and Water Conservation, vol. 28,
no. 2, March-April, 1973.

Todorovic, P., and E. Zelenhasic, "A Stochastic Model for Flood
Analysis", vol. 6, no. 6, Water Resources Research,
pp 1641-1648, December, 1970.

Yevjevich, V. M., "Design of Storage Reservoirs", Water
Research, ed. by A. V. Kneese and S. C. Smith, The Johns
Hopkins Press, pp 375-411, 1966.

Yevjevich, V., "Some Aspects of Education and Research in Stochastic Hydrology", The Progress of Hydrology, Proceedings
1st International Symposium for Hydrology Professors,
vol. 1, pp 316-333, Dept. of Civil Engineering, Univ. of
Illinois, Urbana, July, 1969.

Yevjevich, Vujica, "Stochastic Processes in Hydrology", Water
Resources Publications, Fort Collins, Colo. 1972.

According to Webster's Third International Dictionary a
drought is a period of dryness especially protracted and causing extensive damage to crops or preventing their successful
growth.  Most agricultural practices are related to the growing
of domesticated plants and animal husbandry in most instances
is being practiced in areas and in concentrations not a part of
the natural ecology and environment.  It can be reasoned that
droughts as they affect our civilization are a product of this
civilization since under natural conditions all forms of terrestrial life tend to be in balance with the available water
supply.

As it affects plant production a drought is a period when
there is a deficiency of soil moisture for profitable crop
production.  Most of the cultivated plants are mesophytes (see
Topic 46).  A mesophyte is a plant which requires that some
soil moisture be available at all times to at least part of its
root system.  A deficiency of soil moisture at definite times
during the growing season might not necessarily kill the plants
but the yield might be so greatly reduced as to be economically
a failure.

There are other interpretations of a drought.  Deficiency
of precipitation and runoff may reduce streamflow to such low
flows as to seriously affect fish and wildlife, recreation,
usage of reservoirs, lakes, and streams, and to seriously
affect the economy of a region depending on hydro-electric
power.  This type of drought may have a minor effect on the
natural vegetal cover in a drainage basin.

From the time before written history when the human race
began to cultivate food crops, droughts have been of critical
concern since they affected survival.  It has been observed
that a period of deficiency in precipitation in one part of the
country may occur at the same time of excessive precipitation
elsewhere.  A drought at·a local level tends to persist for a
few years whereas large area variations may be much slower and
more difficult to define.  In mathematical analyses of droughts
in various localities the stochastic processes, especially the
Markov chain, has been found to be indicative.  (See Topic 21)

Complex statistical analyses of drought occurrence intervals and persistence have invoked the use of advanced mathematical concepts which are described by Hudson and Hazen (1964)
and by Chow and Yevjevich (1964).  There is no doubt but that
many natural phenomena occur in cycles such as day and night
and the progression of the seasons of a year.

Although some cycles are harmonic like teeth on a handsaw,

a great many cycles appear to be non-harmonic. If it were possible to show a harmonic property of cycles which appear to be non-harmonic then it would be mathematically straight-forward to make predictions. Langbein (1960) describes procedures for fitting curves to cyclic data including five different methods: moving arithmetic average, moving parabolic and quartic arcs, fitting polynomial by least squares, double integration, and fitting Fourier (sine and cosine) series. One of the problems associated with a mathematical search for harmonic cycles is that a spurious finding may be made which results from the analytical technique rather than the data itself.

Until the development of dendrochronology the search for harmonic cycles which produced both droughts and periods of excessive rainfall was based upon observations or reconstructions of historical anecdotes. With the advent of dendrochronology the timing of climatic variations became a science.

The native vegetation, especially trees, are very sensitive to the response to the availability of water not only for a year but at various times during the annual growth cycle. An excellent introduction to dendrochronology is the pamphlet "Tree Rings" (1976). The Laboratory of Tree Ring Research at the University of Arizona at Tucson has assembled a list of "Selected References on Dendrochronology" (1977) for the period 1950-1976. Stockton and Jacoby, Jr., (1976) using tree-ring data and complex statistical analyses has calculated the virgin flow of the Colorado River at Lee Ferry as far back as 1564.

Lee's Ferry, Arizona, is a place. Lee Ferry is the computed Colorado River Compact division point between the Upper and the Lower Basin States. The flow at Lee Ferry is the sum of the flows of the Colorado River and the Paria River as measured on the Colorado River one mile below the mouth of the Paria River. Stockton and Jacoby's reconstructed hydrograph is shown in Figure 22-1. The historic measured flow of the Colorado River at Lee Ferry for the period 1922-1974 is shown in Figure 22-2. It is interesting to note that when the moving 10-year average of Figure 22-2 is examined in Figure 22-1 the period of very high yield preceding 1922 when the Colorado River Compact was drafted appears to the highest of any time since 1564, according to the authors. The national and international implications of this analysis are extremely far-reaching since the Colorado River Compact legally divided water which may not be physically present in the Colorado River Basin.

Bannister and Robinson (1975) in their review of tree-ring dating in archeology refer to work underway in the United Kingdom, Ireland, Western Germany, Eastern Europe, the Near East, South America, Mexico, and our Southwest. These investigations are yielding data for paleoclimatic applications. They report on the resolution of discrepancies between $C^{14}$ dating and tree-

ring results.  It is now known that the concentration of radio-
carbon in the atmosphere has not remained constant as
previously thought.

ESTIMATED VIRGIN FLOW

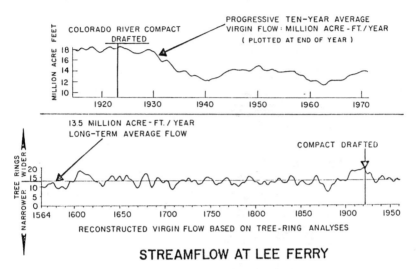

STREAMFLOW AT LEE FERRY

Figure 22-1   Virgin Flows of the Colorado River

Amino acids, which are components of all living systems,
occur in pairs of chemically-identical molecules which are
mirror images of each other.  The vast majority of amino acids
in living organisms are in the levo- or left-rotating form.
This form is recognized by its property of rotating a beam of
polarized light to the left.  With the passage of time some of
the isomers change to the dextro- or right-rotating isomers
until ultimately both levo- and dextro-isomers are in balance.

A determination of the ratio of the two isomers can dis-
close, as yet within somewhat wide limits, not only the age of
the sample but also indicate paleoclimatic conditions when the
sample was alive.  An early reference to this process, which
is called racemization, is the article by Abelson (1954).
Recent investigations have been conducted by Bada, Schroeder
and Carter (1974) and Hare (1974).  The Laboratory of Tree Ring
Research at Tucson, Arizona, is working on the amino acid
racemization starting with tree-ring data of known ages.

An outstanding discussion of climatic cycles and variations is the article by Matthews (1976).  Pages 584, 585, and
586 depict climatic clues such as sea shell spiraling in sea
bottom cores which suggest climatic changes of 3 million years
ago, ice cores from Greenland which span a period of

113

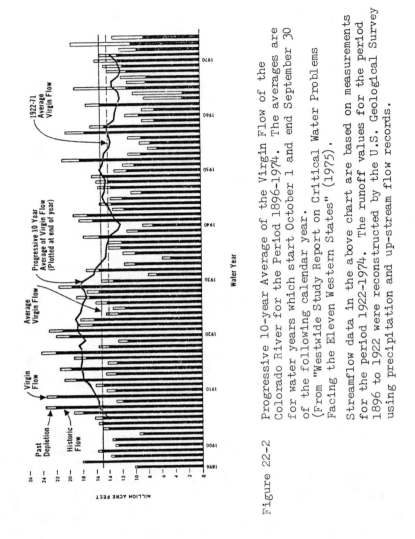

Figure 22-2  Progressive 10-year Average of the Virgin Flow of the
Colorado River for the Period 1896-1974. The averages are
for water years which start October 1 and end September 30
of the following calendar year.
(From "Westwide Study Report on Critical Water Problems
Facing the Eleven Western States" (1975).

Streamflow data in the above chart are based on measurements
for the period 1922-1974. The runoff values for the period
1896 to 1922 were reconstructed by the U.S. Geological Survey
using precipitation and up-stream flow records.

120,000 years and dendrochronology records extended back to
about 2000 B.C.  A study of Matthews' article is highly
recommended.

The American Association for the Advancement of Science
held a Symposium on American Droughts at the Annual Meeting of
February 20-25, 1977 in Denver. One of the papers presented
was the History of American Droughts by Bark (1977) in which he
refers to tree-ring analyses, diaries of early explorers and

quotes from Great Plains newspapers of the 1870's.

Weakly (1965) reconstructed the occurrence and duration of droughts in Western Nebraska for a 748-year period, 1210-1958. This work is based on dendrochronology using native red cedars and a few western yellow pines. The average time between 21 droughts was 20.9 years and the average duration of the drought was 12.8 years. The cycles were definite non-harmonic with intervals between droughts ranging from 3 to 38 years and the duration of droughts ranging from 5 to 38 years. Weakly concluded that it was not possible to mathematically predict the time of occurrence of serious droughts.

Schneider (1977) in a presentation at the February, 1977 AAAS Symposium stated that a major drought for many parts of the United States, especially the high plains east of the Rocky Mountains, is highly probable but not exactly predictable and that "the best that can be done is to assess the intuition of the experts".

Stockton and Meko (1975) have prepared a history of drought occurrence from 1700 A.D. to 1970 in the area roughly west of the Mississippi River. They compared tree-ring data with values of the calculated PDSI. Palmer's (1965) Drought Severity Index is computed from temperature and precipitation data incorporating not only data for a given month but also for several preceding months. They conclude that the period 1907-1916 was the wettest decade since 1700 and that the driest single year since 1700 was 1934.

Since all of the Earth's energy comes from the sun recent astro-physical research has been concentrated on the solar-terrestrial interactions. Observations of sun spots go back to Galileo but it is only during the past few decades that there has been any detailed information as to the structure of solar radiation.

Matthews (1976) on his pages 587, 588, and 589 includes an artist's conception of solar-terrestrial relationships as they might influence atmospheric circulation.

It has become evident that droughts are the result of changes in the circulation pattern of the Earth's atmosphere (see Topic 9) since the incoming solar radiation impinging on the Earth is practically a constant and since only a few mechanisms such as volcanic dust have been shown to date to influence the incidence of radiation at the surface of the continents and oceans.

Dr. Hurd C. Willett (1974), Professor of Meteorology at the Massachusetts Institute of Technology, has been studying sun spot-weather correlations for many decades. His forecasts of the severity of droughts and the coldness of winters have been borne out by experience.

For reasons not yet understood the sunspots move across a solar hemisphere in one direction during a cycle which averages about 11 years, and in the opposite direction during a subsequent 11 years; thus the complete sunspot cycle averages 22 years although it ranges from 16 to 30 years indicating that this is not a true harmonic cycle. The Bruckner cycle which averages about 35 years was the subject of much study especially in Europe.

Just why changes in the circulation pattern should occur has not been ascertained. These changes result not only in wet and dry periods but also in warm and cold periods. It is becoming evident that some of the circulation patterns are the result of temperatures of the surface waters of the oceans which in turn interact with the air modifying the atmospheric moisture and, through changes in density, affect the circulation pattern. An example of the result of a major but not unprecedented shift in the circulation pattern was the extreme winter of 1976-77 in the Northeastern United States. This was coupled with deficiency in precipitation and abnormally high temperatures in the Rocky Mountain regions and in the Northwest. Another example of the impact in the change in the circulation pattern was the extreme drought in the Sahel region of Africa.

Time magazine for January 31 and February 7, 1977 published informative reports on the severe weather in the Central States and in the Northeast. Page 27 of the January 1st article includes a map of North America above Mexico showing the unusual atmospheric circulation pattern which caused extremely high temperatures in Alaska as the warm weather blew north and then made an almost hairpin turn coming straight south into Central Canada and the United States before swinging with another turn toward the Northeast.

This type of circulation pattern is not unprecedented. A possible explanation for the severe weather of 1948-49 in the Central and Western Unites States is presented by Garstka (1949). Snow is one of the few substances capable of reflecting instant short-wave solar radiation. The reflectance (albedo of snow) may be 85 percent whereas bare ground or vegetation reflects only about 5 percent. As the cold air masses travel southward if they carry sufficient moisture the path they travel will become snow covered and therefore there will be no warming. When these air masses enter the United States they are extremely cold.

Nace and Pluhowski (1965) describe the drought of the 1950's. They include maps depicting the severity and extent of

116

droughts in the mid-continent. The drought of the 1950's did not have as great an impact on the economy of the area as did the drought of the 1930's.

Rosenberg (1977) at the AAAS meeting of February, 1977 in Denver listed technologies to minimize the effects of drought. Among these are irrigation, plant breeding, soil conservation, wind breaks, anti-transpirants and minimum tillage. A research assessment of drought hazards in the United States including a description of social consequences and responses and recommending agricultural and urban drought-effect mitigation research has been prepared by Warrick (1975).

An extremely severe drought persisted from 1968 to 1974 in the Sub-Sahara area of Africa which affected millions of people and either directly or indirectly resulted in tens of thousands of deaths, according to Hidore (1977). Englebert (1974) describes the impacts of this drought on the inhabitants of the area in an article illustrated with striking photographs.

Physical models of the Earth's atmospheric circulation pattern have been studied for about 25 years as described by Fultz, Loy, Owens, Bohan, Taylor and Weil (1958). Lacher, McArthur, and Buzyna (1977) describe their physical model study of abrupt changes in large-scale atmospheric circulation patterns. They used a doughnut-shaped dish in which changes in the circulation pattern were delineated by suspensions of aluminum flakes in a silicone fluid as the dish was heated.

Reid A. Bryson of the University of Wisconsin at Madison, as interviewed by Young (1977), is the proponent of a hypothesis that the wobble of the Earth's axis of rotation, which occurs every 13 to 15 months, may have a major impact on the atmospheric circulation. This wobble known according to Bryson as the Chandler motion, although it amounts to only a few feet, is sufficient to affect the oceans. Bryson's hypothesis is that it may also affect the atmospheric circulation pattern.

Inigo Jones (1943), an Australian astronomer and meteorologist, who has conducted extensive research world-wide on sun spot-weather relationships proposed a provocative hypothesis about the possible effect of the positioning in their orbits of the planets, Uranus, Neptune, Saturn, Jupiter, and the Earth. Jones stated that the cycle of the electromagnetic field of Jupiter is 11.862 years long. The double sun-spot cycle is roughly 22 years and the Bruckner cycle is about 35 years both of which are almost multiples of the Jupiter cycle. Jones said that the double cycle of Saturn is 58.916 years which is about 5 times the Jupiter cycle. According to Jones the magnetic cycle of Uranus is 84.015 years which is almost half of the magnetic cycle of Neptune which is stated to be 164.788 years.

Jones found that a repeated wide combined passage of Jupiter and Saturn during the periods 1865-70 and 1924-29 showed positive results with reference to sun-spot activity. Writing in 1943 Jones forecasted 1959-60 as times of another close passage. Was his forecast verified?

With the fantastic advances in equipment for astrophysical research perhaps another exploration should be organized on Inigo Jones' imaginative reasonings. Chapman (1977) has included in his Executive Summary of a 5-year plan for Solar-Terrestrial Programs of the National Aeronautics and Space Administration a section on Atmospheric Physics.

The physical reasons underlying changes in the atmospheric circulation patterns are the subject of intensive world-wide research. A review of some recent work on solar structure and terrestrial weather is given in the article by Wilcox (1976). He reviews the work of Roberts and Olson (1973) who studied, at the National Center for Atmospheric Research (NCAR) at Boulder, Colorado, days of sizable increase in geomagnetic activity, assumed to result from solar activity. They found that low-pressure troughs moving from the Gulf of Alaska across the continental United States were significantly larger than troughs associated with intervals of quiet geomagnetic conditions.

Alexander (Sept. 1977 and Oct. 1977) has written an excellent non-technical treatment illustrated with charts and photographs of the atmospheric circulation patterns and of the effects of droughts and extremely cold winters. His discussion of ice-age progressions is informative.

Since persistence is a recognized characteristic of weather trends it is quite likely that an extremely wet, dry, cold, or warm year will be followed by a somewhat similar weather pattern for the subsequent few years in the same continental region.

As more knowledge becomes available on the physical bases and changes in the circulation pattern it is reasonable to expect that great improvements will follow in the understanding and forecasting of occurrence and persistence of climatic extremes especially of droughts.

Problem Assignment

Select a drainage basin for which preferably at least 50 years of records of precipitation and streamflow are available. Compute 5-year, 11-year, and 15-year progressive averages. Prepare charts similar to Figure 22-2 for each progressive average period plotting both precipitation and streamflow together with observed annual data. Ascertain whether or not any cycles are shown either by precipitation or by runoff data. If so, observe whether or not there is a time lag between the precipitation and the runoff cycles. Explain.

## References

Abelson, Philip H., "Amino Acids in Fossils", Science, vol. 119 p 576, 1954.

Alexander, George, "Drought - Our Changing Weather: Part 1", Popular Science, vol. 211, no. 3, pp 90-94, Sept. 1977.

Alexander, George, "Colder Winters Ahead - Our Changing Weather, Part 2", Popular Science, vol. 211, no. 4, pp 100-103 and 180, Oct. 1977.

Bada, Jeffery L., Roy A. Schroeder, and George F. Carter, "New Evidence for the Antiquity of Man in North America Deduced from Aspartic Acid Racemization", Science, vol. 184, no. 4138, May 17, 1974.

Bannister, Bryant, and William J. Robinson, "Tree-ring Dating in Archaeology", World Archaeology, vol. 7, no. 2, pp 210-225, Routledge & Kegan Paul, London, Oct., 1975.

Bark, L. Dean, "History of American Droughts", a paper presented at the Symposium on American Droughts, AAAS annual meeting in Denver, Feb. 21, 1977.

Chapman, Robert D., "Solar Terrestrial Programs - A Five-Year Plan - Executive Summary", Office of Space Science, Natl. Aeronautics and Space Admin., 17 pp, Jan. 1977.

Chow, Ven Te, "Frequency Analysis", Section 8-I, pp 8-1 to 8-42 in The Handbook of Applied Hydrology, ed. by Ven Te Chow, McGraw-Hill Book Co., New York, 1964.

Englebert, Victor, "Drought Threatens the Tuareg World", National Geographic, vol. 145, no. 4, pp 544-571, Apr. 1974.

Fultz, D., R. Loy, G. Owens, W. Bohan, R. Taylor, and J. Weil, "Studies of Thermal Convection in a Rotating Cylinder With Some Implications for Large-scale Atmospheric Motions", Meteorological Monograph 4:77-101, 1958.

Garstka, Walter U., "Why the Snow?", The Reclamation Era, vol. 35, no. 6, pp 126-127 and 137, June, 1949.

Hare, P. E., "Amino Acid Dating - A History and an Evaluation", MASCA Newsletter, vol. 10, no. 1, July, 1974.

Hidore, John J., "Acceleration of Dessication and Population Trauma in Sub-Saharan Africa", Water Resources Bulletin, vol. 13, no. 4, pp 783-794, Aug. 1977.

Hudson, H. E., Jr, and Richard Hazen, "Droughts and Low Streamflow", Section 18, Handbook of Applied Hydrology, Ven Te Chow, ed-in-chief, pp 18-1 to 18-26, McGraw-Hill Book Co., New York, 1964.

Jones, Inigo, "Long Range Weather Forecasting", Queensland Geographical Journal (New Series), vol. XLVIII, 27 pp, 1943.

Lacher, R. C., Robert McArthur, and George Buzyna, "Catastrophic Changes in Circulation Flow Patterns", American Scientist, vol. 65, no. 5, pp 614-621, Sept. Oct. 1977.

Langbein, W. B., "Fitting Curves to Cyclic Data", pp 59-66, in USGS Water Supply Paper 1541-B, Double Mass Curves, by James K. Searcy and Clayton H. Hardison, U.S. Govt. Printing Office, 1960.

Matthews, Samuel W., "What's Happening to Our Climate?", National Geographic, vol. 150, no. 5, pp 576-615, Nov. 1976.

Nace, R. L., and E. J. Pluhowski, "Drought of the 1950's with Special Reference to the Midcontinent", USGS Water Supply Paper 1804, 88 pp, USDI, U.S. Govt. Printing Office, 1965.

Palmer, W. C., "Meteorological Drought", U.S. Weather Bureau Research Paper 45, U.S. Dept. of Commerce, Washington, D.C., 58 pp, 1965.

Roberts, Walter Orr, and Roger H. Olson, "Geomagnetic Storms and Wintertime 300 mb Trough Development in the North Pacific-North America Area", Jour. of Atmospheric Science, vol. 30, no. 1, pp 135-140, Jan. 1973.

Rosenberg, Norman J., "Recent Technological Advances to Minimize the Effects of Drought", a paper presented at the Symposium on American Droughts, AAAS Annual Meeting in Denver, Feb. 21, 1977.

Schneider, Stephen H., "Forecasting Future Droughts: Is It Possible?", a paper presented at the Symposium on American Droughts, AAAS Meeting in Denver, Feb., 1977.

"Selected References in Dendrochronology", for the period 1950-1976, Laboratory of Tree-Ring Research, Univ. of Arizona, Tucson, 18 pp, Mar. 1977.

Stockton, Charles W., and Gordon C. Jacoby, Jr., "Long-Term Surface-Water Supply and Streamflow Trends in the Upper Colorado River Basin Based on Tree-Ring Analyses", Lake Powell Research Bulletin No. 18, Natl. Science Foundation Research Applied to National Needs, 70 pp, March, 1976. (Copies obtainable from: Institute of Geophysics and Planetary Physics, Univ. of California, Los Angeles, Calif. 90024.)

Stockton, Charles W., and David M. Meko, "A Long-Term History of Drought Occurrence in Western United States as Inferred from Tree Rings", Weatherwise, pp 245-249, Dec. 1975.

"The Big Freeze", Time magazine, pp 22-28, Jan. 31, 1977.

"The Great Winter Hits Again", Time magazine, pp 29-32, Feb. 7, 1977.

"Tree Rings - Timekeepers of the Past", a pamphlet, 16 pp, U.S. Geological Survey, INF-73-15, USDI, Govt. Printing Office, 1976.

Warrick, Richard A., with Patricia B. Trainer, Earl J. Baker, Waltraud Brinkmann, "Drought Hazard in the United States: A Research Assessment", Program on Technology, Environment and Man, Monograph No. NSF-RA-E-75-004, Institute of Behavioral Science, Univ. of Colorado, 199 pp, 1975.

Weakly, Harry E., "Occurrence of Drought in the Great Plains During the Last 700 Years", Agricultural Engineering, p 85, Feb. 1965.

"Westwide Study Report on Critical Problems Facing the Eleven Western States", USDI, Washington, D.C., 457 pp, Apr. 1975. (This reference is supplemented by an "Executive Summary", 85 pp, Apr. 1975).

Wilcox, John M., "Solar Structure and Terrestrial Weather", Science, vol. 192, no. 4241, pp 745-748, May 21, 1976.

Willett, Hurd C., "A Frigid, Snowy Winter Ahead for Most of the Nation", an interview in U.S. News and World Report, pp 35-36, Nov. 4, 1974.

Yevjevich, Vujica M., "Regression and Correlation Analysis", Section 8-II, pp 8-43 to 8-67, in the Handbook of Applied Hydrology, ed. by Ven Te Chow, McGraw-Hill Book Co., New York, 1964.

Young, Patrick, "The Long-Range Forecast - Western Drought Worsens, Bodes Ill for Food, Power, Business", National Observer, p 4, May 30, 1977. (Dr. Bryson is interviewed).

HYDRAULICS AND FLUID MECHANICS

Topic 23          Hydraulics and Fluid Mechanics

## Hydrostatics and Flotation

A fluid is a substance which is capable of flowing and
which conforms to the shape of the vessel containing the fluid.
Fluids offer little resistance to change in form and they cannot sustain shear forces.  Liquids and gases are fluids and the
general subject dealing with them is called Fluid Mechanics.
Hydraulics deal only with liquids.  The forces exerted by a
liquid on a plane area is equal to the specific weight of the
liquid and the depth to the center of gravity of the area.
Water weighs 62.4 pounds per cubic foot.  Therefore the pressure exerted on a square foot under a 10-foot head of water is
624 pounds and under a 100-foot head of water it would be 6240
pounds per square foot.  The mercurial barometer, the manometer
and the snow pillow are applications of hydrostatic forces in
balance exerted by fluids, sometimes of dissimlar densities.

According to Archimedes' principle, known for over 2000
years, a body fully immersed in a liquid is acted upon by an
upward force equal to the weight of the liquid which it displaced.  A partially immersed body will float when the weight
of water which it displaces equals the total weight of the
body.  Thus steel ships float.  In order to float in a stable
position, the center of gravity of the whole body must lie below the center of buoyancy of the displaced liquid.

## Flow Through Orifices and Over Weirs

Toricelli over 300 years ago propounded the theorem that
water discharging from an orifice under a constant head, h, has
a theoretical velocity equal to the velocity of a body, in a
vacuum, falling freely through a vertical distance, h.

$$h = \frac{v_t^2}{2g} \qquad \text{or:} \qquad v_t = \sqrt{2gh} \qquad (1)$$

in which

   h is the head on the center of the orifice in feet,

   $v_t$ is the theoretical velocity in feet per second,

   g is the acceleration due to gravity, 32.16 feet
      per second per second.

The relationships of equation (1) are shown in Figure 23-1.

Because of viscosity, inertia forces, friction, and shear within the liquid, the actual velocity attained is less than the theoretical velocity.

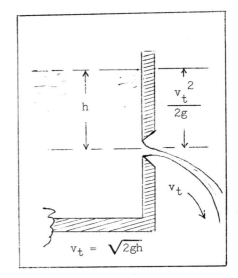

Figure 23-1  Flow Through an Orifice Under a Constant Head

The computation of discharge through an orifice makes use of the area of the water jet at its least diameter rather than using the area of the orifice.

$$Q = a' v_o \tag{2}$$

in which

Q   is discharge of the orifice in cubic feet per second,

a'   is the area of the cross-section of the jet at the vena contracta, and

$v_o$   is the mean velocity of the jet at the vena contracta.

Then
$$Q = a' v_o = C_c C_v a v_t \tag{3}$$

in which

$C_c$   is the coefficient of contraction,
$C_v$   is the coefficient of velocity, and
a   is the area of the orifice.

Subsituting
$$Q = C a \sqrt{2 gh} \tag{4}$$

The new coefficient C combines $C_c$ and $C_v$.

The coefficient C is usually determined by measuring, either gravimetrically or volumetrically, the actual discharge from an orifice of known dimensions and of area "a". Therefore C is the ratio of the actual discharge to the theoretical discharge. For sharp-edged orifices $C_v$ is 0.98 and $C_c$ is 0.62. Then C becomes 0.61 and the equation becomes:

$$Q = 0.61 \, a \, \sqrt{2gh} \qquad (5)$$

In a weir $a = L \, t_h$ in which L is the length and $t_h$ is the flow-producing head. Through the use of the calculus, the general equation $Q = a \, \sqrt{2gh}$ serves as the basis for the general theoretical formula without coefficients for free discharge without correction for velocity of approach under constant head over a rectangular weir.

$$Q = \frac{2}{3} L \, \sqrt{2g} \, h_2^{3/2} \qquad (6)$$

in which

    L   is the width, in feet, of the rectangular orifice, and

    $h_2$  is the head in feet of the water above the lower edge of the rectangular weir.

For a standard suppressed rectangular weir, neglecting velocity of approach, the Francis formula is

$$Q = 3.33 \, L \, H^{3/2} \qquad (7)$$

The Cone formula for small standard 90° contracted V-notch weirs is

$$Q = 2.49 \, H^{2.48} \qquad (8)$$

## Open Channel Flow

When a free surface of a liquid flowing in a conveyance conduit, either natural or man-made, is open to atmospheric pressure the flow is called "open-channel flow". A flow in a smooth conduit or in an open channel is subjected to a loss of velocity due to friction which depends upon the surface characteristics of the material, the geometry of the channel cross-section, and upon the nature of obstructions, such as trees, bridges, etc.

Many situations arise where it is not possible to measure the velocity. Nevertheless the hydrologist must calculate a discharge. Chezy in 1775 proposed the following formula for velocity

$$v = C \, \sqrt{RS} \qquad (9)$$

in which

    v   is the mean velocity in feet per second

    C   Chezy's resistance factor

    R   is the mean hydraulic radius in feet, which is computed by dividing the cross-sectional area of the stream in square feet, by the wetted perimeter in feet

    S   is the average head loss, due to friction, per foot. It is computed by dividing the total head loss in feet in a channel length, expressed in feet. S is dimensionless. It expresses the slope of the energy gradient. If the flow is uniform S is the slope of the water surface and, if the bed of the channel is smooth, S expresses the slope of the channel bottom. In the Chezy formula S is commonly referred to as the slope.

Chezy thought that C was a constant but it soon became evident that the numerical value of C depended to a considerable extent upon the degree of roughness of the channel in addition to being influenced by R and S.

Ganguillet and Kutter published in 1869 a relationship, commonly called the Kutter formula, which defined Chezy's C as follows:

$$C = \frac{41.65 + \frac{0.00281}{S} + \frac{1.811}{n}}{1 + \frac{n}{\sqrt{R}} (41.65 + \frac{0.00281}{S})} \tag{10}$$

in which

n is the roughness coefficient.

In 1890 Manning published his formula for Chezy's C, as follows:

$$C = (\frac{1.486}{n}) R^{1/6} \tag{11}$$

The $\frac{1.486}{n}$ in Manning's formula was designed to make the value of n correspond numerically to the values of Kutter's n.

Substituting Equation (11) in Equation (9) the completed Chezy expression becomes:

$$v = (\frac{1.486}{n}) R^{2/3} S^{1/2} \tag{12}$$

then

$$Q = A (\frac{1.486}{n}) R^{2/3} S^{1/2} \tag{13}$$

Williams (1970), as a result of a review of the history of the derivation of the formula in equation (13) concludes that the credit for the first derivation in 1867 of that relationship rightfully belongs to P. G. Glauckler, an engineer for the Ponts et Chaussees at Colmar. Rouse and Ince (1957) have written an informative history of hydraulics.

Values of "n" appear in many publications. A convenient source is the table on page 446 as assembled by Linsley, Kohler, and Paulhus (1975). Barnes (1967) presents cross-sections, photographs in color, and descriptions of 50 stream channels for which values of "n" were determined. Chow (1959) has written a standard textbook on open channel hydraulics.

Dalrymple and Benson (1968) prepared a manual illustrating the computation of peak discharge by the slope area method. The Water Measurement Manual (1974) contains a wealth of detail on the design, including dimensions, of various weirs and control meters. It also contains numerous tabulations which can be very helpful in reducing the labor required in making flow computations. Appendix A, pp 305-319, of this reference is entitled "Hydraulics for the Novice". The U.S. Bureau of Reclamation issued in 1971 a Metric Supplement to the "Water Measurement Manual".

## Equation of Continuity

Under steady flow conditions in a channel the discharge is constant. If the cross-sectional area changes, the velocity adjusts so that the product of the two always equal the same $Q$.

Then
$$Q = A_1 V_1 = A_2 V_2 = A_3 V_3 = \ldots \qquad (14)$$

This equation (14) is called the Equation of Continuity. In this form it applies only when there is no addition to or depletion from the amount of discharge.

## The Energy Equation

In open channel flow the energy contained in the flow is a total of the velocity energy plus the energy resulting from the pressure at a particular depth. In simplified form the energy equation becomes:
$$\text{Total energy} = \frac{v^2}{2g} + d \qquad (15)$$

in which           $d$ is the depth of the water measured in feet from the bottom of the channel.

The phenomena ascribed to the energy equation for a flow in a pipe are different from the phenomena of flow in an open channel. In pipe flow pressure changes occur as the flow velocity changes. When a constriction occurs in a pipe so that the velocity increases the pressure will decrease so that the total energy from one point to another point in the pipe system, neglecting head losses, remains constant. Albertson, Barton, and Simons (1960) present in Chapt. 3 a comprehensive discussion of fluid dynamics including the energy equation.

Under open channel conditions, when the flow accelerates so that more of the supply of energy goes into the velocity head, the depth of the flow must decrease. Conversely when the velocity is reduced, the depth must increase so that the total energy, neglecting various losses, remains constant. The energy equation serves as the basis for many flow-measuring devices.

126

## Hydraulic Machinery

Propellors, pumps, turbines, fluid couplings, torque converters, pressure regulators, sprayers, water distribution systems for supply, heating, and cooling, transportation systems, and innumerable industrial usages are all based upon the application of the fundamental laws of Hydraulics and Fluid Mechanics. Anatomists and engineers have found the circulatory systems of living organisms to be fascinating.

Hjorth, Jonsson and Larsen (1977) have edited a report on 28 papers presented in, "Hydraulic Problems Solved by Stochastic Methods", at an international symposium in Sweden. Kibosbocskoi and Szabo (1975) are the editors of a 1260-page proceedings in two volumes containing 114 papers presented at a conference in Hungary on Fluid Machinery, held in 1975.

Water and wastewater systems within domiciles are designed and built in compliance with local building codes. The design of complex and extensive water conveyance systems is in the realms of hydraulic, civil, mechanical, and chemical engineering rather than in hydrology.

Vallentine (1967) has written an excellent non-technical treatment, "Water in the Service of Man", in which he discusses and illustrates with informative diagrams and drawings the development of theory, water at rest, viscosity, flow in channels and in pipes, waves, and hydraulic machinery such as pumps and turbines.

Giles (1962) has prepared an excellent review of Hydraulics in which he includes 475 problems with solutions given in detail. Brater (1976) has brought up-to-date one of the classic Handbooks of Hydraulics the first edition of which was published by King in 1918.

## References

Albertson, Maurice L., James R. Barton, and Daryl B. Simons, "Fluid Mechanics for Engineers", Prentice-Hall, Inc., Englewood Cliffs, New Jersey, 1960.

Barnes, Harry H., Jr., "Roughness Characteristics of Natural Channels", USGS Water Supply Paper 1849, 1967.

Brater, Ernest Frederick and Horace Williams King, "Handbook of Hydraulics for the Solution of Hydraulic Engineering Problems", McGraw-Hill Book Co., New York, 6th ed., 591 pp, 1976.

Chow, Ven Te, "Open-Channel Hydraulics", McGraw-Hill Book Co., New York, 680 pp, 1959.

Dalrymple, Tate, and M. A. Benson, "Measurement of Peak Discharge by the Slope-Area Method", book 3, chap. A2, Techniques of Water-Resources Investigations of the USGS, 1967. 2nd printing, 1968.

Giles, Ranald V., "Fluid Mechanics and Hydraulics", Schaum's Outline Series, Theory and Problems, Schaum Pub. Co., New York, 2nd ed., 1962.

Hjorth, Peder, Lennart Jonsson, and Peter Larsen, eds. "Hydraulic Problems Solved by Stochastic Methods", Proceedings, 2nd International IAHR Symposium on Stochastic Hydraulics, Lund Institute of Technology/Univ. of Lund, Lund, Sweden, Aug. 2-4, 1977, 608 pp, Water Resources Pub., Fort Collins, Colo., 1977.

Kibosbocskoi, L., and A. Szabo, eds., "Proceedings of the Fifth Conference on Fluid Machinery", pub. by Hungarian Academy of Sciences (Akademiai Kiado), Budapest, Hungary, in two volumes, 1260 pp, distributed by Water Resources Pub., Fort Collins, Colo., 1975.

Linsley, R. K., M. A. Kohler, and J. L. H. Paulhus, "Hydrology for Engineers", McGraw-Hill Book Co., New York, 2nd ed. 1975.

"Metric Supplement to Water Measurement Manual", Bureau of Reclamation, USDI, Denver Federal Center, Denver, Colo., 224 pp, 1971.

Rouse, Hunter, and Simon Ince, "History of Hydraulics", Iowa Institute of Hydraulic Research, State Univ. of Iowa, 269 pp, 1957. Reprinted by Dover Pub., Inc., New York, 1963.

Vallentine, H. R., "Water in the Service of Man", Penguin Books, Baltimore, Md., Paper-back No. A852, 224 pp, 1967.

"Water Measurement Manual", Bureau of Reclamation, USDI, Bldg. 67, Denver Federal Center, Denver, Colo., 327 pp, 2nd ed., 1967. Revised reprint issued 1974.

Williams, Garnett P., "Manning Formula - A Misnomer?", Jour. Hydraulics Div., Proceedings of the American Soc. of Civil Engineers, pp 193-200, Jan. 1970.

The first systematic stream-gaging station in the United
States was established near Embudo, New Mexico, on the Rio
Grande in 1889 and is still active. The history of this in-
stallation is given by Frazier and Heckler (1972).

Among various methods of measuring streamflow are the
following:  weir stations, control meter stations, power plants,
and velocity-area stations. General treatments of the subject
have been prepared by Corbett (1943), Grover and Harrington
(1966), and Boyer (1964).

Control meters usually consist of mathematically-shaped
constrictions placed in the flow of water. The constrictions
are so designed as to cause a hydraulic jump or critical depth
change in the flow. Depending on the design, at an appropriate
place, a measurement or a record is made of the depth of water.
In some cases two or even four depths may be observed. An example of the control meter station is the widely-used measuring
device developed by Parshall (1950).

A comprehensive treatment of water measurement, including
many tables, is the "Water Measurement Manual" (1974) for which
there is available a Metric Supplement (1971).

Velocity-area stations require field surveys. Velocity
may be determined with meters such as the revolving-cup type or
the direct-acting propellor type. Other techniques of attaining values for the velocity are:  salt-velocity method, salt-
dilution method, and the total-count method using radioisotopes
or materials susceptible to neutron activation. The methods
which use a tracer substance whether it is salt, dye or radioisotopes require a means for identifying concentrations at various times as the substances are carried downstream by the flow.

Barron (1963) discusses new instrumentations for surface
water investigations:  the electro-magnetic velocity meter,
acoustic velocity meter, the "bubble" gage surface follower,
the sonic flood-measuring assembly, the velocity-azimuth-depth
assembly (Vada), and the two-speed timer. There are various
commercially-available meters used in water works and in sewage
works and specialized meters and recorders used in the chemical
engineering industry.

An ingenious device based upon sound fluid dynamics for
measurement of velocity of streamflow in the range between one-
foot and 8-feet per second is the Velocity-Head Rod, in effect
a specially shaped stick, developed by Wilm and Storey (1944).
Heede (1974) recommends usage of this device in urban runoff investigations where channel cross sections may resemble plain

geometric figures and where flows may be smooth.  Heede does
not recommend the Velocity-Head rod for steep, boulder-strewn
turbulent mountain streams.

Where water stage records have been discontinued but maximum heights, otherwise known as crest-stages or peak-stages,
are still desired, crest-stage indicators have been installed.
In valleys known to be subjected to sudden and violent flooding
many organizations establish systems of crest-stage indicators
usually two or three feet in length.  Systems of these indicators are installed so that they overlap, thereby giving a continuous depth coverage.  Crest-stage indicators consist of
glass or transparent-plastic tubes stoppered at both ends with
plugs with small holes drilled in them.  The tubes contain
small amounts of cork dust.  The dust tends to adhere to the
highest elevation attained by the water leaving a ring in the
tube at the meniscus.  Crest-stage gages are discussed by Frye
(1963) and Mills (1963).

Dickinson (1967) performed an exhaustive review of the
literature regarding both qualitative and quantitative aspects
of the accuracy of discharge measurements.  This bibliography
contains 110 items.  A mathematical representation was given to
the stage-discharge relationship and found to account for vir-
tually all the variability in sample data for nine mountain
stream-gaging stations in Colorado.

Using surveying instruments it is possible, with the slope-
area method (discussed in Topic 23) to determine streamflow
without direct measurement of velocity.  However, except for
surveys subsequent to a flood, a direct determination of velocity by one of the established techniques is recommended.  The
U.S. Geological Survey is preparing a series of publications
primarily intended for use by members of its Surface Water
Branch.  An example of this series is the paper by Somers and
Selner (1965).

The Geological Survey has conducted extensive investigations of automating the whole process of streamflow measurement,
computation, and reporting.  Recent Water Supply Papers are reproduced from tables typed by automatic data processing machinery components.  Isherwood (1963) describes some of the equipment capable of performing this work.

Although first published in 1935 and reprinted in January,
1959, the Circular entitled "Measuring Irrigation Water" by
Scott and Houston continues to be an excellent reference on the
subject.  James R. Barker of the Utah State Agricultural College Extension Service prepared a 4-page pamphlet identified as
No. 31, also entitled, "Measuring Irrigation Water", (undated).
This concise pamphlet contains all the information needed to
construct and operate a rectangular weir having a range of

130

measurement of discharge in cubic feet per second from 0.11 to 9.48. The 4½-inch by 7-inch pamphlet "Irrigation Water Measurement" (Oct. 1966) was prepared as a handbook for ditch riders and irrigators and has been approved for use in Colorado, Nevada, Oklahoma, Oregon, Utah, and Wyoming. It contains drawings presenting in detail critical dimensions for a number of easily-built devices for water measurement together with tables and graphs for determining flows from as low as 0.008 cfs (or 3.6 gallons per minute) to as high as 175 cfs.

Thomas and Cervione (1970) in their re-evaluation and proposal for expansion of streamflow data for Connecticut recommended that environmental data on channel geometry, flood profiles, land use, time of travel, and aquifers hydraulically connected to streams, be obtained. Much additional environmental information is needed to provide a base for intelligent development of Connecticut's water resources.

Maytin and Henderson (1970) are quoted (page 179): "Any scheme for water resources development must eventually focus on hydrology and meteorology. Past and present streamflow data and weather records furnish the basic raw material so necessary to the prognostic methods which reduce them to probability levels. To that effect, we must accept the inescapable fact that as the amount of data increases, so does the effectiveness of statistical inference. In plain words then, we need more data collection stations and programs throughout the country."

## References

Barker, James R., "Measuring Irrigation Water", Utah State Agricultural College Extension Service Fact Sheet, No. 31, (Undated).

Barron, E. G., "New Instruments for Surface Water Investigations", in Selected Techniques in Water Resource Investigations, USGS Water Supply Paper 1669-Z, pp 1-12, 1963.

Boyer, Marion C., "Streamflow Measurement", Sec. 15, Handbook of Applied Hydrology, Ven Te Chow, ed-in-chief, McGraw-Hill Book Co., New York, 1964.

Corbett, Don M., & others, USGS Water Supply Paper No. 888, 1943.

Dickinson, W. T., "Accuracy of Discharge Determinations", Hydrology Paper No. 20, Colo. State University, Fort Collins, Colo., June, 1967.

Frazier, Arthur H. and Wilbur Heckler, "Embudo, New Mexico, Birthplace of Systematic Stream Gaging", USGS Prof. Paper 778, 23 pp, 1972.

Frye, Prentis M., "Establishment of Crest-Stage Gages at Discontinued Gaging Stations", pp 25-26, USGS Water Supply Paper 1669-Z, 1963.

Grover, N. C. and A. W. Harrington, "Stream Flow", originally pub. by John Wiley and Sons, 1943. Reprinted with a new introduction by Ven Te Chow by Dover Publications, Inc., New York, 1966.

Heede, Burchard H., "Velocity-Head Rod and Current Meter Use in Boulder-Strewn Mountain Streams", USDA Forest Service Research Note RM-271, Rocky Mountain Forest and Range Exp. Station, Fort Collins, Colo., Aug. 1974.

"Irrigation Water Measurement", (A Handbook for Ditch Riders and Irrigators), Mountain States Regional Pub. 1R. Available from Extension Services of the Agri. Exp. Stations of the cooperating states. Ref. copy obtained from Colo. State Univ., Fort Collins, Colo. 50 pp, Oct. 1966.

Isherwood, W. L., "Digital Water Stage Recorder in Selected Techniques in Water Resources Investigations", USGS Water Supply Paper 1669-Z, pp 13-16, 1963.

Maytin, Iury I. and Peter B. Henderson, "Hydrologic Data Acquisition and the Instrumentation Gap", Water Resources Bulletin, Jour. Amer. Water Resources Assn. vol. 6 no. 2, pp 178-188, Apr. 1970.

Mills, Willard B., "Use of Plastic Tubes for Peak-Stage Gages on Reservoirs", pp 27-28, USGS Water Supply Paper 1669-A 1963.

Parshall, R. L., "Measuring Water in Irrigation Channels With Parshall Flumes and Small Weirs", USDA Cir. 843, May, 1950.

Scott, Verne H., and Clyde E. Houston, "Measuring Irrigation Water", Calif. Agri. Exp. Station Ext. Service Cir. 473, 52 pp, 1935, reprinted Jan. 1959.

Somers, W. P., and G. I. Selner, "Computer Technique for Slope-Area Measurements", Surface Water Techniques, Book I, Chap. 15, Hydraulic Measurement and Computation, USGS, 1965.

Thomas, Mendall P. and Michael B. Cervione, Jr., "A Proposed Streamflow Data Program for Connecticut", prepared by USGS in coop. with Connecticut Water Resources Commission as Report No. 23, 1970.

"Water Measurement Manual", Bur. of Reclamation, USDI, Denver, Colo., 327 pp, 2nd ed., 1967. Revised reprint 1974.

Wilm, H. G., and H. C. Storey, "Velocity-Head Rod Calibrated for Measuring Streamflow. Civil Engineering, vol. 14 pp 475-476, 1944.

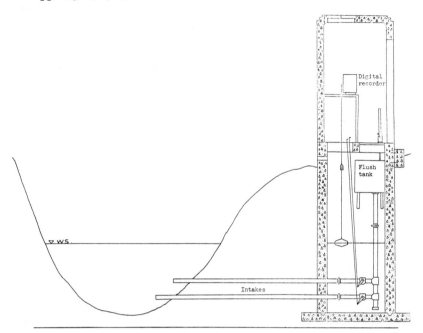

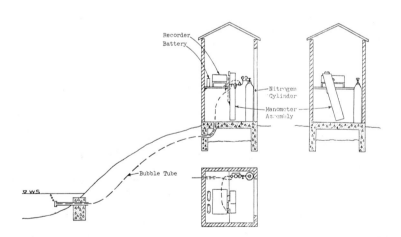

Figure 24-1  Typical Stream-Gaging Installations: Stilling-well type above; bubble-gage type below. From Geological Survey, USDI, "Stream-Gaging Manual" 1963 with continuing revisions.

Precipitation is ultimately disposed of in four major catagories:  evaporation loss (including evapotranspiration), soil
moisture, runoff, and groundwater.  A basic water loss is that
exerted by the soil.  It is that fraction of the precipitation
retained by the soil which sustains vegetal growth.  The results of exhaustive research in many fields of endeavor have
shown that all of the water retained as soil moisture in the
layers of soil penetrated by roots is lost by the end of the
growing season.  Differences have been observed in the rates of
loss from depths of the soil from which these losses take
place.

It has been established that water loss from bare soil
will take place by vapor phase transfer of water molecules from
depths down to 12 inches.  This fact is fundamental to the success of the so-called "dry-land" agriculture practiced in many
parts of the world.  Dry-land agriculture produces a crop for
which one-year's precipitation is insufficient by storing precipitation from alternate years as soil moisture under a bare,
clean-cultivated surface.

To an engineer concerned with the design of water conveyance structures, water losses are of minor concern since he is
primarily interested in the water yielded from a drainage basin
from "rainfall excess" after all of the water losses have been
satisfied.  The ecologist, agronomist, and forest hydrologist,
on the other hand may be primarily interested in the propor-
tionate distribution of the rainfall (including snow) among the
various water loss processes.  An example of an extensive literature in both Agronomy and Forestry, dealing with water loss
distribution is in an article by Voigt (1960).  A general
treatment of water losses is given by Wisler and Brater (1959).

The disposition of storm rainfall is presented in a schematic diagram on page 264 of the book by Linsley, Kohler, and
Paulhus (1975).  A detailed discussion of the interaction of
forests with precipitation is given on pages 107-244 in the
Proceedings edited by Sopper and Lull (1967).  This chapter
consists of eleven papers and a summary.  Included are discussions of interception, stemflow, and throughfall of both rain
and snow.

Satterlund (1972) discusses water losses in relation to
wildland watershed management.  Interception loss is that part
of the precipitation, either rain, snow, fog drip, or dewdrop,
which is retained by vegetation.  Some intercepted precipitation may reach the ground as stemflow or drip but much of the
interception is lost to the atmosphere.  For low-intensity,
short duration storms interception may absorb all of the

precipitation. Rime is a form of cloud drip which occurs when super-cooled droplets attach themselves to a surface which could be vegetation or man-made structures.

When precipitation falls on a drainage basin water losses may interact in a very complex and dynamic manner. Low intensity rains of the type referred to as "potato soakers" may replenish soil moisture without producing any runoff. The same amount of precipitation if it should fall at very high intensity for a very short duration may result in "gully-washer" type of runoff often accompanied by erosion.

References

Linsley, R. K., M. A. Kohler, and J. L. H. Paulhus, "Hydrology for Engineers", McGraw-Hill Book Co., New York, 2nd ed. 1975.

Satterlund, Donald R., "Wildland Watershed Management", The Ronald Press Co., New York, 370 pp, 1972.

Sopper, Wm. E., and Howard W. Lull, editors, "Forest Hydrology" Proceedings of a Natl. Science Foundation Advanced Science Seminar, Aug. 29-Sept. 10, 1965, Pergamon Press, 1st ed. 813 pp, 1967.

Voigt, G. K., "Distribution of Rainfall Under Forest Stands", Forest Science, vol. 6, pp 2-10, 1960.

Wisler, C. O., and E. F. Brater, "Hydrology", 2nd ed., John Wiley and Sons, Inc., New York, 1959. (Third printing 1965).

A hydrograph is a chart of rates of discharge on the y-axis plotted with their time of occurrence plotted on the x-axis. Although hydrographs are usually plotted to an arithmetic scale on the time axis, the discharge could be in either arithmetic or logarithmic scales depending on the purpose for which the graph has been prepared.

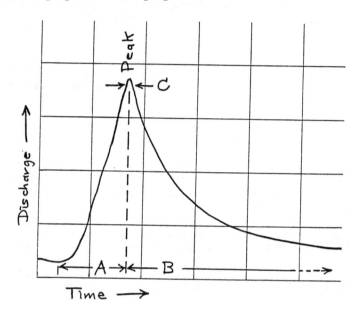

Figure 26-1        Segments of the Hydrograph

The dimension "A" shown on the schematic sketch in Figure 26-1 encompasses the Rising Limb of the hydrograph. This is the length of time elapsed from the instant at which the rate of discharge increases either to the instantaneous peak or to a portion called the Crest Segment shown by dimension "C". The length of persistence of "C" depends upon many characteristics of the drainage basin and of the storm.

The portion of the hydrograph designated by dimension "B" is called the Falling Limb often referred to as the Recession Limb or simply, the Recession.

A detailed discussion of the hydrograph is given in Section VII of the book edited by Gray (1970). Holtan, Minshall and Harrold (1968) describe in detail, with illustrations, various techniques and procedures used in measuring precipitation, runoff, temperatures, and many other hydrologic parameters. This reference also contains examples of chart transcription procedures and of data reduction and computation procedures.

## References

Gray, Donald M., ed., "Handbook on the Principles of Hydrology, A General Text with Special Emphasis on Candian Conditions", originally published in 1970 by the Natl. Research Council of Canada. Reprinted in 1973 by Water Information Center, Port Washington, New York.

Holtan, H. N., N. E. Minshall, L. L. Harrold, "Field Manual for Research in Agricultural Hydrology", Agriculture Handbook No. 224, Agri. Research Service, USDA, June, 1962. Reviewed and reprinted Oct. 1968.

## Problem Assignment - Plotting the Hydrograph

A portion of a rating table is given in Table 26-1 and a print of part of a runoff recorder chart is given in Fig. 26-2.

a.* Plot stage-discharge curve, using cartesian coordinates, the gage height on the y-axis and discharge on the x-axis.

b. Prepare tabulation of gage height and discharge. Use enough points from the chart record to reproduce the hydrograph shape.

c. Plot the hydrograph.

d. State time of occurrence of peak and discharge at the peak.

e. Compute acre-feet and cubic meters of water yielded between 4:00 p.m. July 25, 1955 and the time of peak. Compute acre-feet and cubic meters of water yielded between the time of the peak and midnight, July 26, 1955.

f. Compute inches and centimeters depths over the drainage basin for the periods specified in Paragraph e.

---

*There are times when it is desired to extend a rating curve usually above but sometimes below stages for which discharge measurements were made. Two references are suggested:

Linsley, R. K., M. A. Kohler, and J. L. H. Paulhus, "Hydrology for Engineers", pages 127-128, McGraw-Hill Book Co., 482 pp, 2nd edition, 1975.

Wisler, C. O. and E. F. Brater, "Hydrology, 2nd edition, pages 391-394, John Wiley and Sons, Inc., New York, 1959. (Third printing 1965).

Table 26-1    Transcription of a portion of the USGS Form 9-210
(Sept. 1952) "Rating Table" for Douglas Creek
above Keystone, Wyoming, drainage area 22.10 sq.
mi. for the period May 1, 1955 to Apr. 30, 1957.

9–210
(Rev. 2–67)

UNITED STATES DEPARTMEN
GEOLOGICAL SURVEY (WATER

Rating table for Douglas Creek above Keystone, Wyoming, drainage area 22.10 square miles

from May 1, 1955 to Apr. 30, 1957 , from to

| Gage height | Discharge | Difference | Gage height | Discharge | Difference | Gage height | Discharge | Difference | Gage height | Discharge |
|---|---|---|---|---|---|---|---|---|---|---|
| Feet | Cfs | Cfs | Feet | Cfs | Cfs | Feet | Cfs | Cfs | Feet | Cfs |
| .00 | | | 2.00 | 52 | 11 | 4.00 | 510 | 40 | .00 | |
| .10 | | | .10 | 63 | 11 | .10 | 550 | 40 | .10 | |
| .20 | | | .20 | 74 | 13 | .20 | 590 | 50 | .20 | |
| .30 | | | .30 | 87 | 14 | .30 | 640 | | .30 | |
| .40 | | | .40 | 101 | 14 | .40 | | | .40 | |
| .50 | | | .50 | 115 | 15 | .50 | | | .50 | |
| .60 | | | .60 | 130 | 15 | .60 | | | .60 | |
| .70 | | | .70 | 145 | 20 | .70 | | | .70 | |
| .80 | | | .80 | 165 | 20 | .80 | | | .80 | |
| .90 | 1.5 | 1.5 | .90 | 185 | 20 | .90 | | | .90 | |
| 1.00 | 3.0 | 2.0 | 3.00 | 205 | 25 | .00 | | | .00 | |
| .10 | 5.0 | 2.0 | .10 | 230 | 25 | .10 | | | .10 | |
| .20 | 7.0 | 2.5 | .20 | 255 | 25 | .20 | | | .20 | |
| .30 | 9.5 | 3.5 | .30 | 280 | 30 | .30 | | | .30 | |
| .40 | 13 | 4 | .40 | 310 | 30 | .40 | | | .40 | |
| .50 | 17 | 5 | .50 | 340 | 30 | .50 | | | .50 | |
| .60 | 22 | 6 | .60 | 370 | 30 | .60 | | | .60 | |
| .70 | 28 | 7 | .70 | 400 | 35 | .70 | | | .70 | |
| .80 | 35 | 8 | .80 | 435 | 35 | .80 | | | .80 | |
| .90 | 43 | 9 | .90 | 470 | 40 | .90 | | | .90 | |

This table is applicable for open-channel conditions.   It is based on _____ discharge measuren
Above stage of 3.3 feet. This table ____ and is _____ well defin
the same as that dated 6/11/56 (extended) _____

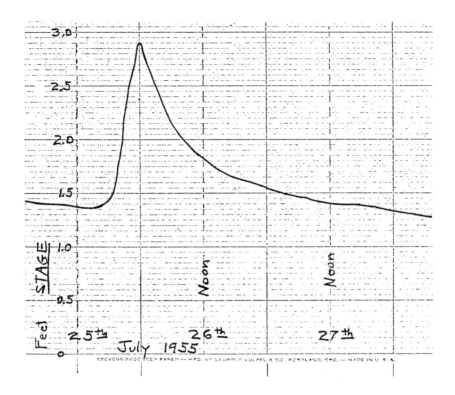

Figure 26-2    Print of a Portion of the Runoff Recorder Chart.
               Douglas Creek above Keystone, Wyoming, drainage
               area 22.10 square miles.  This gaging station is
               among those for which records are available at
               the Small Watershed Hydrology Program repository
               of data, Dept. of Civil Engineering, Colo. State
               Univ., Fort Collins, Colo.  This station is des-
               ignated in that program as
               Watershed No. 1-50-07-01-00.  The gaging station
               is located at Latitude 41-11-10
                              Longitude 106-16-20.

The recorder chart trace included in Figure 26-2
has been redrawn from the original record for the
event of July 25-27, 1955.  Redrawing was necessary because of a weak pen trace on a rising limb
of the hydrograph and of evidence of possible
wind action causing float oscillations near the
peak.

139

The components of a hydrograph consist mainly of surface runoff, interflow (sometimes referred to as sub-surface runoff) and groundwater.  A separation of the hydrograph into the three components is based upon the established facts that these components depart from the drainage area and enter the stream channel under different fluid dynamics processes.  Hewlett and Nutter (1969) give on pages 92-93 a more detailed classification of flow components.

Surface runoff follows the laws of open-channel flow.  It is the flow which causes water-borne erosion.  Surface flows, if of sufficient magnitude and rate of runoff, produce the destructive floods in channels and valley bottoms.  Surface runoff departs from a drainage area in a matter of minutes or hours.  True surface or overland flow forms but a very small portion of the annual yield of a drainage basin.

Interflow is that portion of the hydrograph which flows just beneath the surface.  It departs from the drainage area in a matter of hours or days.  Interflow does not follow the hydraulic loss of open channel flow.  It is the flow of a fluid through a porous medium and this flow departs from a drainage basin in accordance with Darcy's law.

Groundwater flow also follows Darcy's law.  However groundwater departs from the basin in a matter of months, years or decades.  The transition from one component of flow to another is not sudden; it could be compared to changes of color in a rainbow.

Although hydrologists have studied base-flow recessions for a period of more than 100 years, the delineation of the separate components of the hydrograph eludes as yet precise mathematical evaluation.  Hall (1968) presents an excellent status statement which is quoted from page 980: "An obvious need is to determine more clearly the components that make up a stream hydrograph.  Base flow should either be defined in a meaningful way or the term should be abandoned, and the same should be done for what is commonly called interflow.  A more useful way of defining the hydrograph might be in terms of the delay or lag times of the components, without implication of the origin.  Another facet to be examined is the matter of linear versus non-linear response.  Two distinct aspects are involved:  one arises from linear or non-linear differential equations and solutions thereof, and the other from the shape of a recession curve.  The solutions are valid only if all assumptions and boundary conditions are satisfied.  On the other hand, it still remains to be demonstrated that the real basin fits the mathematical system, even if the recession curve fits a solution. In other words, uniqueness of fit must be proved. Furthermore, it seems likely that most, if not all, natural hydrologic systems are non-linear, and the basic questions are to what extent and why."

Hewlett and Nutter (1972) present a philosophical discussion of various conceptual models dealing with components of the hydrograph.

The separation of the components is based upon the analytical recognition of the types of flow. The mathematics of the separation is performed through the derivation of the slope of a line (see Topic 18). Since very few are able to derive without extensive review the slope of a line as plotted on semilogarithmetic paper, the technique suggested in the Problem Assignment has been prepared to perform the separation with arithmetic.

Barnes (1942) stated an equation for a single-valued recession above a horizontal base line:

$$Q = Q_0 K_r^t \tag{1}$$

in which

$Q$ is the flow in cfs at time t
$Q_0$ is the flow in cfs at the beginning of the computation period, or when time t equals 0 days
$t$ is time in days
$K_r$ is the daily runoff recession coefficient

This equation makes it possible to compute Q for any length of time $t$ in one step but it requires that $K_r$ be known.

If the daily average discharge $Q_0$ of the preceding day is plotted on the x-axis using Cartesian (arithmetic) coordinate paper, and the daily average discharge of the day is plotted on the y-axis, the slope of the line will be m in the basic equation: $y = mx + b$ (See Topic 18). Also m is a ratio as is explained in the following paragraph. $K_r$, the recession coefficient, is arithmetically the same as the slope m. This simplified derivation of $K_r$ is illustrated in Figure 27-1 taken from Garstka, Love, Goodell, and Bertle (1958).

If it is known that a stream is in groundwater recession flow, it is possible to compute the value of $K_r$ by performing a series of computations of daily ratios since when t = 1 day, then $K_r = Q/Q_0$. The average of the ratios having approximately the same value will yield groundwater $K_r$.

When computing the ratio Q divided by $Q_0$ it is necessary to exercise judgment so that the transition between two components of flow is not included in the average $K_r$.

141

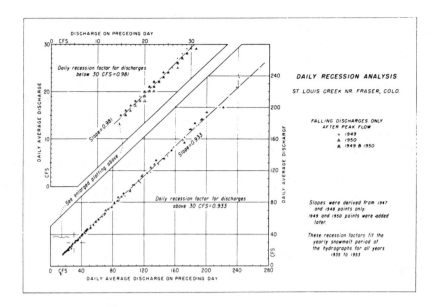

Figure 27-1    Daily Recession Analysis, St. Louis Creek Near
               Fraser, Colo.  Check of Recession Slopes Derived
               from 1947-48 Data with Observed 1949-50 Flows.

## Problem Assignment - Separation of Components

Table 27-1 lists mean daily flows from U.S. Geological
Survey Water Supply Paper 1565 (1960) at the Arroyo Valle gaging station at Pleasanton, California, which has an area of 171
square miles for the drainage basin.

Table 27-1    Daily Average Discharges, Arroyo Valle, at Pleas-
              anton, Calif., drainage area 171 square miles.

| Date 1958 | Flow cfs | Date 1958 | Flow cfs | Date 1958 | Flow cfs |
|-----------|----------|-----------|----------|-----------|----------|
| Apr  5 | 1030 | Apr 14 | 173 | Apr 23 | 66 |
| 6 | 1370 | 15 | 148 | 24 | 62 |
| 7 | 964 | 16 | 132 | 25 | 58 |
| 8 | 584 | 17 | 118 | 26 | 55 |
| 9 | 415 | 18 | 102 | 27 | 53 |
| 10 | 335 | 19 | 92 | 28 | 51 |
| 11 | 273 | 20 | 84 | 29 | 49 |
| 12 | 230 | 21 | 78 | 30 | 47 |
| 13 | 198 | 22 | 72 | May  1 | 45 |
|  |  |  |  | 2 | 43 |

This is an exercise in the separation of a hydrograph into its components: surface runoff, interflow, and groundwater. Components are shown on page 228 in the book by Linsley, Kohler, and Paulhus (1975).

a.  Construct a table having the following column headings: Date, Total Flow, Groundwater Flow, Surface Runoff Plus Interflow, Interflow, Groundwater Plus Interflow, and Surface Runoff.

b.  Plot the total flow (surface runoff plus interflow plus groundwater flow) recession data (Q = 964 cfs to 43 cfs) on Cartesian coordinate graph paper (Scales: 1 inch = 100 cfs, 1 inch = 4 days). Plot the total flow on 3-cycle semi-log graph paper (log Q = 1-10-100-1000 cfs, 1 inch = 4 days). The points may be connected by straight lines.

c.  The total flow near the lower end of the recession curve may reasonably be assumed to be groundwater flow only. On the semi-log graph, extend the straight-line groundwater recession back under the total flow curve. Tabulate the mean daily groundwater flow data and plot these data on the Cartesian graph.

d.  Calculate the mean daily combined surface runoff and interflow data. Plot these data on the semi-log graph and determine if a reasonably straight-line relationship exists in or near the center portion of the plot. Extend this straight-line interflow recession back under the plotted "curve" and tabulate the interflow data.

e.  Calculate the combined groundwater and interflow data and plot these data on the semi-log graph. The difference between this combination and the hydrograph is surface runoff. The total flow recession is now separated into its components. It is apparent that considerable interflow exists in this watershed and that, for this event, there was little surface runoff. Barnes (1942) developed an exponential equation for a single-valued recession, as discussed previously. Recession coefficients for surface runoff may vary considerably depending upon the shape of the watershed and the distribution of rainfall as the storm moves across the watershed. The chief value of recession coefficients is in connection with interflow and groundwater components.

f.  Complete the plotting on Cartesian coordinates of the four hydrographs for the runoff event showing on one sheet separate curves for the actual hydrograph and for its components: surface runoff, interflow, and groundwater. Plot the same separations on the semi-log paper used in your analyses.

143

g.  Derive separate $K_r$ recession coefficients for groundwater, interflow, and surface runoff.

## References

Barnes, B. S., "Discussion of Analysis of Runoff Characteristics", Trans. ASCE, vol. 105, p. 106, 1940 and vol. 107, pp 836-841, 1942.

Garstka, W. U., L. D. Love, B. C. Goodell, F. A. Bertle, "Factors Affecting Snowmelt and Streamflow", prepared jointly by Bureau of Reclamation and U.S. Forest Service, Govt. Printing Office, 189 pp, 1958.

Hall, Francis R., "Base-Flow Recessions - A Review", Water Resources Research, vol. 4, no. 5, pp 973-983, Oct. 1968.

Hewlett, John D., and Wade L. Nutter, "An Outline of Forest Hydrology", Univ. of Georgia Press, Athens, 1969.

Hewlett, John D., and Wade L. Nutter, "The Varying Source Area of Streamflow From Upland Basins", pp 65-83 in Proceedings of a Symposium, Interdisciplinary Aspects of Watershed Management, Bozeman, Mont., ASCE, Aug. 3-6, 1970, published, 1972.

Linsley, R. K., M. A. Kohler, and J. L. H. Paulhus, "Hydrology for Engineers", McGraw-Hill Book Co., 482 pp, 2nd ed. 1975.

"Water Supply Paper 1565 - Surface Water Supply of the United States 1958 - Part 11, Pacific Slope Basins in California", USGS 1960.

According to Newman (1976) the Earth is at least four and
a half billion years old.  The surface of the Earth is forever
changing as a result of the action of vast forces which have
resulted in various non-harmonic cycles of upthrusts and sink-
ings.  The land masses exposed on the surface of the Earth have
been acted on by tides,  ocean currents, the winds of the atmospheric circulation, and, chiefly, by the movement of water
through the hydrologic cycle.  Therefore the configuration of
the Earth's surface is a result of a complex interaction of
geophysical activities, surface relief, slope, and the amount
of water available under the prevailing climate, including ice
ages, of any particular geologic era.  Figures 28-1 and 28-2
are taken from Newman (1976).

The changes in the North American continent through the
geologic eras, periods, and epochs are described very informa-
tively in "Our Changing Continent" (1969).  "Land Forms of the
United States" (1969) includes a map of the physiographic regions and provinces of the conterminous United States.  A volume superbly illustrated with photographs, cross sections, and
landscape features of land forms has been prepared by Shimer
(1972).  The geology in and to the west of Denver, Colorado, is
described in "Mountains and Plains - Denver's Geologic Setting"
(1969).  This folder includes photographs and artist's conceptions of cross-sections of mountains and plains together with a
road log of an 8.4-mile trip which takes in the features near
Red Rocks Park.

The science of geomorphology includes the study of the
processes forming the land.  Fluvial geomorphology deals primarily with the interactions of the land surface with streamflow.  Chorley (1969) has prepared a very well illustrated review of the extensive findings dealing with the drainage basin
in relation to hydrology.  A thorough review of the subject
with special reference to channel networks was prepared by
Strahler (1964).  Hewlett and Nutter (1969) have prepared a
brief but informative discussion of the subject of drainage
basin geomorphology.

Stream orders are shown in Figure 28-3.  Comparative hydrographs yielded by a feather-shaped and an oval-shaped drainage basin are shown in Figure 28-4.  Common drainage patterns
are shown in Figure 28-5.

Schumm (1967) in his paper on Paleohydrology has prepared
a number of entrancing charts, especially Figures 3 and 4 on
page 193 of vol. 1, which present hypothetical curves depicting
assumed relationships between precipitation and runoff and precipitation and relative sediment yield for four geologic times:

before the appearance of land vegetation; following the appearance of primitive vegetation; following the appearance of flowering plants and conifers; and following the appearance of grasses.

Geomorphologic descriptions of drainage basins may be very valuable in the selection of areas for land use and hydrologic experiments. Stream orders, bifurcation ratios, drainage patterns, drainage densities, and channel patterns are usually described in addition to pertinent watershed characteristics. Snyder (1938) has developed a technique for deriving the shape of a hydrograph for an ungaged stream. His method is based on geomorphologic drainage basin characteristics.

The drainage basin pattern is of direct value in land-use planning with special reference to hydrology. The nature of the stream order and the drainage basin pattern, of which a few examples are shown, bear a direct influence on the times of occurrence of peak flows and of the shape of the hydrographs which result from rainfall excess produced by the storm paths. There may be very great differences in the peak rate of discharge and in the shape of the hydrograph yielded by storms which may traverse a basin in different directions as shown in Topic 29.

As detailed hydrologic records including rainfall depth-intensity-duration data (see Topic 15) and streamflow records (see Topic 24) are rarely to be found, hydrologists are conducting exhaustive research on techniques of synthesizing flow (see Topic 31).

Shreve (1974) correlated basin area with mainstream length for 461 rivers in the world. He found that the slope of the trend was 0.6 for the smaller basins and about 0.5 for the largest basins. Onesti and Miller (1974) investigated 16 hydromorphic variables with observations grouped by third, fourth, fifth, and sixth order stream tributaries all of which are in the Pecatonica River Basin, area 710 kilometers, in the driftless area above Darlington in southern Wisconsin. Their principal components analysis showed that the interrelationship between drainage basin and stream channel characteristics improved with increasing stream order.

Murphey, Wallace and Lane (1977), as a result of an exhaustive study relating hydrograph rise time, duration, mean peak discharge, volume, peak-volume ratio, and maximum flood to physical basin parameters such as area, shape, slope, drainage density, basin relief, stream length, and combinations thereof found that a parameter expressing basin shape and size served to be as good a predictor as other more complex approaches. The study area was the Walnut Gulch Experimental Watershed surrounding Tombstone, Arizona. Their suggested approach is recommended for intermountain drainage basins up to 60 square miles in area in the Mexican Highland section of the Basin and Range province of Arizona, New Mexico, Texas, Sonora, Chihuahua and Coahuila.

References

Chorley, R. J., "II, The Drainage Basin as the Fundamental Geomorphic Unit", in Water, Earth and Man, R. J. Chorley, ed. Methuen and Co. Ltd., 1969.

Hewlett, John D., and Wade L. Nutter, "An Outline of Forest Hydrology", Univ. of Georgia Press, Athens, 1969.

"Land Forms of the United States", Geological Survey, USDI, 16-page pamphlet, 1969.

"Mountains and Plains - Denver's Geologic Setting", a folder, Geological Survey, USDI, 1969.

Murphey, J. B., D. E. Wallace, and L. J. Lane, "Geomorphic Parameters Predict Hydrograph Characteristics in the Southwest", Water Resources Bulletin, vol. 13, no. 1, Feb.1977.

Newman, William L., "Geologic Time", Geological Survey, USDI, 20 pp, 1970, revised 1976.

Onesti, Lawrence J., and Theodore K. Miller, "Patterns of Variation in a Fluvial System", Water Resources Research, vol. 10, no. 6, pp 1178-1186, Dec. 1974.

"Our Changing Continent", a folder, Geological Survey, USDI, 16 pages, 1969.

Schumm, S. A., "Paleohydrology: Application of modern hydrologic problems of the ancient past", Proc. International Hydrology Symposium, Sept. 6-8, 1967, Fort Collins, Colo., pub. by Colo. State Univ. vol. 1, pp 185-193, Sept. 1967.

Shimer, John A., "Field Guide to Landforms in the United States", The Macmillan Co., New York, 272 pp, 1972.

Shreve, Ronald L., "Variations of Mainstream Length With Basin Area in River Networks", Water Resources Research, vol. 10 no. 6, pp 1167-1177, Dec. 1974.

Snyder, F. F., "Synthetic Unit-Graphs", Trans. American Geophysical Union, vol. 19, pp 447-454, 1938.

Strahler, Arthur N., "Part 4-II - Quantitative Geomorphology of Drainage Basins and Channel Networks", Sec. 4, Handbook of Applied Hydrology, Ven Te Chow ed., McGraw-Hill, 1964.

Figure 28-1 An artist's conception showing geologic periods
with related life forms and climatic conditions during
various periods for the Earth. The age of the Earth is
estimated to be between 5.5 and 6 billion years. This
chart is taken from pages 18-19 of Newman (1976). The
major divisions of geologic time are described and the
related index fossils are shown in Figure 28-2.

# MAJOR DIVISIONS of GEOLOGIC TIME

## INDEX FOSSILS

|  |  |  |  |
|-----|--------|-------------|---------|
| CENOZOIC ERA (Age of Recent Life) | Quaternary Period | The several geologic eras were originally named Primary, Secondary, Tertiary, and Quaternary. The first two names are no longer used; Tertiary and Quaternary have been retained but used as period designations. | NEPTUNEA tabulata; VENERICARDIA planicosta; PECTEN gibbus; CALYPTRAPHORUS velatus |
| | Tertiary Period | | |
| MESOZOIC ERA (Age of Medieval Life) | Cretaceous Period | Derived from Latin word for chalk (creta) and first applied to extensive deposits that form white cliffs along the English Channel. | INOCERAMUS labiatus; SCAPHITES hippocrepis |
| | Jurassic Period | Named for the Jura Mountains, located between France and Switzerland, where rocks of this age were first studied. | NERINEA trinodosa; PERISPHINCTES tiziani |
| | Triassic Period | Taken from word "trias" in recognition of the threefold character of these rocks in Europe. | MONOTIS subcircularis; TROPITES subbullatus |
| PALEOZOIC ERA (Age of Ancient Life) | Permian Period | Named after the province of Perm, U.S.S.R., where these rocks were first studied. | PARAFUSULINA bosei; LEPTODUS americanus |
| | Pennsylvanian Period | Named for the State of Pennsylvania where these rocks have produced much coal. | LOPHOPHYLLIDIUM proliferum; DICTYOCLOSTUS americanus |
| | Mississippian Period | Named for the Mississippi River valley where these rocks are well exposed. | PROLECANITES gurleyi; CACTOCRINUS multibrachiatus |
| | Devonian Period | Named after Devonshire County, England, where these rocks were first studied. | PALMATOLEPIS unicornis; MUCROSPIRIFER mucronatus |
| | Silurian Period | Named after Celtic tribes, the Silures and the Ordovices, that lived in Wales during the Roman Conquest. | HEXAMOCERAS hertzeri; CYSTIPHYLLUM niagarense |
| | Ordovician Period | | TETRAGRAPTUS fructicosus; BATHYURUS extans |
| | Cambrian Period | Taken from Roman name for Wales (Cambria) where rocks containing the earliest evidence of complex forms of life were first studied. | BILLINGSELLA corrugata; PARADOXIDES pinus |
| PRECAMBRIAN ERA | - - - - - - - | The time between the birth of the planet and the appearance of complex forms of life. More than 80 percent of the Earth's estimated 4½ billion years falls within this era. | |

Figure 28-2 Geologic Time and Related Fossils.

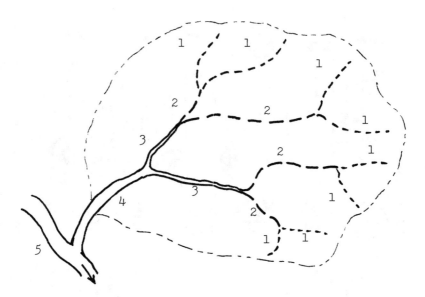

Figure 28-3   Stream Orders, after Strahler (1964).

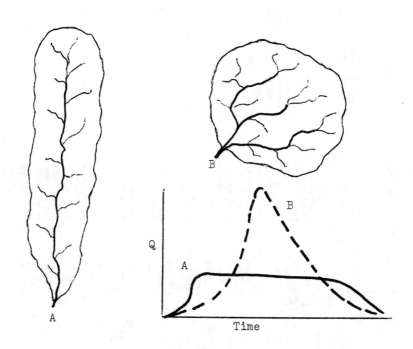

Figure 28-4   Comparative Hydrographs, assuming uniform rainfall on equal areas.   See Topic 29, Elemental Hydrographs.

150

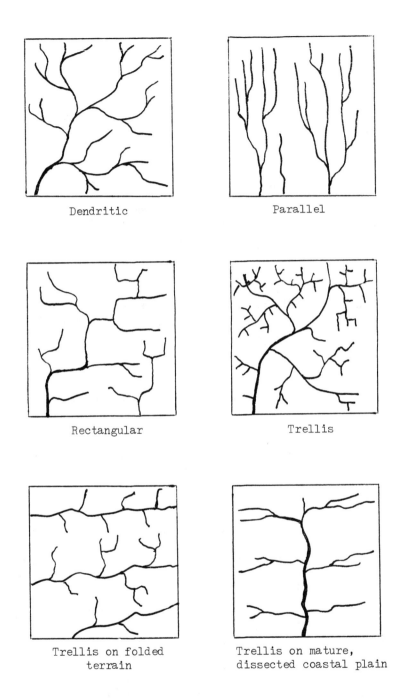

Figure 28-5  Common Drainage Patterns.

151

The elemental hydrograph illustrates how rainfall is converted to runoff under idealized conditions of uniform rainfall intensity, uniform surface velocity of runoff, and under the assumption that there is no surface detention, infiltration, or interflow or groundwater interactions with the surface runoff.

Water leaving the watershed (outflow) at any instant is that which had time to reach the outlet subsequent to its having fallen. Therefore at any instant the outflow consists of water which fell at the outlet at that instant plus all unit quantities of water which previously fell on the watershed at a time equivalent to the runoff time for each individual unit of water.

At any time following the beginning and prior to the end of the rainfall water is being contributed to the outlet by an area bounded by a distance from the outlet equivalent to the product of the runoff velocity and the time since the rain began. The rate of outflow (cfs) at any time is then the product of the area contributing (sq. mi.), the uniform rainfall intensity (inches/hour), and a conversion factor.

At any time following the end of the rain, water having fallen on an area bounded by a distance from the outlet equivalent to the runoff velocity and the time since the rain ended, will already have run off. The outflow at that time is therefore the water which had fallen on the remainder of the watershed. The rate of outflow (cfs) is then the product of the area contributing (total area minus the "bounded area" in sq. mi.), the uniform rainfall intensity (in./hr), and a conversion factor.

In those cases where the storm is moving the same general procedure applies but must be modified to account for this movement. The area contributing at any time is that portion of the watershed area on which rain had fallen at a time equivalent to the product of the runoff velocity and the time since rain started to fall on the area.

It is not understood precisely how rainfall becomes runoff. A laboratory facility at the University of Illinois at Urbana is described by Chow (1967) who uses a 40-foot square drainage basin on which storm movement intensity and duration can be controlled by a computer.

Dickinson, Holland, and Smith (1968) describe a unique outdoor experimental rainfall-runoff facility in which natural storm events can be compared with the behavior of the drainage basin under artificially-created storms.

The elemental hydrographs problem assignment was prepared
by Dr. Walter F. Rowland, Professor of Civil Engineering,
California State University at Fresno, Calif.

References

Chow, Ven Te, "Laboratory Study of Watershed Hydrology", Proc-
    eedings, International Hydrology Symposium held at Colo.
    State Univ., Fort Collins, Sept. 6-8, 1967, pp 194-202,
    vol. 1, 671 pp, June, 1967.

Dickinson, W. T., M. E. Holland, G. L. Smith, "An Experimental
    Rainfall-Runoff Facility", Hydrology Paper No. 25, Colo.
    State Univ., Fort Collins, Sept. 1967. (This publication
    includes a bibliography of parametric hydrology consisting
    of abstracts of 226 references.)

Problem Assignment - Elemental Hydrographs

Assume: a uniform rainfall intensity of 1 inch per hour;
starting instantaneously over the entire watershed, continuing
at a uniform intensity for 2 hours, then stopping instantaneously; a uniform surface runoff velocity of 5 miles per hour
with no surface retention, detention, infiltration, interflow,
or groundwater recharge. The storms moving at a uniform 5
miles per hour over a plane-surfaced hypothetical "Table Watershed" 5 miles wide and 10 miles long with the runoff falling
over a 5-mile-wide straight-edged cliff on the East or right-
hand side.

Problem A  Construct hydrographs of flow (Q in cfs). One-inch
           depth per hour multiplied by 645 = cfs per sq. mi.

1.  Rainfall moving laterally across the watershed towards
    the South.
2.  Rainfall moving up the watershed towards the West.
3.  Rainfall moving down the watershed towards the East.

Problem B  For each storm compute the total volume of runoff
           in: cfs-hours, acre-feet, and cubic meters.

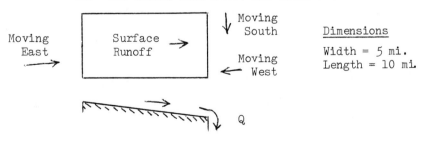

Figure 29-1        Table Watershed

153

L. K. Sherman (1932) and (1942) described the unit hydrograph concept which has been found to be extremely valuable in hydrology. The term "unit" is no longer considered as applying to any particular volume of runoff such as one inch, although in practice for larger storms there are advantages in dealing in units of one inch of runoff for a given basin.

Dooge (1959) gives a highly mathematical general theory of the unit hydrograph. Chow (1964) presents additional and increasingly intricate discussions of extensions of the unit hydrograph concept. Dickinson and Ayers (1965) give a detailed analysis of storm characteristics as they influence the unit hydrograph. A thorough discussion of the unit hydrograph concept as used in hydrologic practices is given by Barnes (1965).

The basic assumptions of the unit hydrograph concept are:
a.  The hydrograph of runoff produced by rainfall excess (which is assumed to be uniformly distributed for its duration over its drainage basin) of a unit time will show a characteristic shape integrating all of the physical characteristics of the drainage basin.

b.  Differences in amounts of rainfall excess will result in differences in peak rates of runoff with the time remaining a constant. This will be true providing that the rainfall excess is equal to or less than the hydrograph rise time.

In practice long complex storms on large drainage basins are treated by the unit hydrograph concept by dividing large basins into smaller basins and by considering long storms to be a series of unit rainfall durations suitable for converting to the total storm hydrograph through the application of the distribution graph technique.

An example of complex mathematical analyses and treatments of the unit hydrograph concept is Diskin's (1969) proposal of a method which can be carried out numerically so that the analysis of the convolution derivatives for the derivation of an instantaneous unit hydrograph may be programmed and the analysis performed by a digital computer.

Newton and Vinyard (1967) have developed a computer technique using matrix operations which make it possible to develop a unit hydrograph from three or four complex storms. They conclude that this is not a push-button technique and that the hydrologist must exercise judgment in the selection of flood data and in the interpretation of the computer-produced results. Laurenson and O'Donnell (1969) perform an analysis of five factors which could introduce deviations in the accuracy of derivation of unit hydrographs from complex storms.

Singh (1976) derived for comparison unit hydrographs by two methods, linear programming and least squares, for four storms over the North Branch of the Potomac River near Cumberland, Maryland. The linear programming method minimizes the sum of absolute deviations while the least squares method minimizes the sum of the squares of deviations.

Problem Assignment - Unit Hydrograph

The data in Table 30-1 is taken from Wisler and Brater (1959), page 252. It pertains to the storm of June 28, 1940 over a small drainage basin having an area of 76.5 acres at the North Appalachian Experimental Watershed near Coshocton, Ohio, operated by the Agricultural Research Service, USDA.

Table 30-1    Storm of June 28, 1940

| 10-min Interval | Discharge Inches per hr. | Distribution Graph Percentages |
|---|---|---|
| 1 | 0.06 | 2.7 |
| 2 | 0.43 | 19.3 |
| (Peak) | (0.67) | (30.0) |
| 3 | 0.59 | 26.5 |
| 4 | 0.43 | 19.3 |
| 5 | 0.31 | 13.9 |
| 6 | 0.17 | 7.6 |
| 7 | 0.08 | 3.6 |
| 8 | 0.05 | 2.2 |
| 9 | 0.04 | 1.8 |
| 10 | 0.03 | 1.3 |
| 11 | 0.02 | 0.9 |
| 12 | 0.01 | 0.5 |
| | 0.01 | 0.4 |
| Sum | 2.23 | 100.0 |

Problem A  For the storm of June 28, 1940 plot distribution graph on Cartesian coordinates with cumulative time on the x-axis and individual percent on y-axis.

Problem B  Plot the hydrograph for the storm totalling 2.23 in/hr.

Problem C  Plot the hydrograph which would result if another storm began at end of Interval 3 of the first storm. This second storm, based upon previously established rainfall-runoff relationships, was estimated to produce a sum of 3.00 in/hr discharges.

155

Problem D   State peak rate of discharge and time of its occurrence for the combined storms.

References

Barnes, B. S., "Unitgraph Procedures", Hydrology Branch, Div. of Project Planning, Bureau of Reclamation, Denver, Colo. Nov. 1952; Revised Aug. 1965.

Chow, Ven Te, "Runoff", Sec. 14, Handbook of Applied Hydrology, Ven Te Chow, ed-in-chief, McGraw Hill Book Co., New York, 1964.

Dickinson, W. T., and H. D. Ayers, "The Effect of Storm Characteristics on the Unit Hydrograph", Trans. Engineering Institute of Canada, Paper No. EIC-65-CIV 5, vol. 8 no. A-15, Dec. 1965.

Diskin, M. H., "Evaluation of Segmented IUH Derivatives", Jour. Hydraulics Div., Proc. ASCE, pp 329-346, Jan. 1969.

Dooge, James C. I., "A General Theory of the Unit Hydrograph", Jour. Geophysical Research, vol. 64, no. 2, pp 241-256, Feb. 1959.

Laurenson, E. M., and T. O'Donnell, "Data Error Effects in Unit Hydrograph Derivation", Jour. Hydraulics Div., Proc. ASCE, pp 1899-1917, Nov. 1969.

Newton, D. W., and J. W. Vinyard, "Computer-Determined Unit Hydrograph from Floods", Jour. Hydraulics Div., Proc. ASCE pp 219-235, Sept. 1967.

Sherman, L. K., "Streamflow from Rainfall by the Unit-graph Method", Engineering News Record, vol. 108, pp 501-505, 1932.

Sherman, L. K., "The Unit Hydrograph Method", Chap. XI of Hydrology - Physics of the Earth, ed by O. E. Meinzer, McGraw-Hill Book Co., New York, 1942. (Reprinted by Dover Publications, Inc., New York, 1949.)

Singh, Krishan P., "Unit Hydrographs - A Comparative Study", Water Resources Bulletin, vol. 12, no. 2, pp 381-392, Apr. 1976.

Wisler, C. O., and E. F. Brater, "Hydrology", 2nd ed., John Wiley and Sons, Inc., New York, 1959, 3d printing 1965.

Topic 31         Synthesis of a Hydrograph

    Climatological and hydrologic installations yielding
sufficient data to be of use in detailed rainfall-runoff hydrograph analyses are relatively scarce, especially for the smaller drainage basins. Since it is necessary for many purposes
to derive the shape of a hydrograph for an ungaged stream, a
great deal of effort has been expended by practicing hydrologists and by research organizations in developing methods for
synthesizing a hydrograph.

    Extensions of the unit hydrograph principle have been pro-
ductive although there are many other methods available to the
hydrologist. One of the most useful techniques is that derived
by Snider (1938). He expressed the results of his study of
basins in the Appalachian Mountain regions in the following
equation:

$$t_p = C_t \ (L \ L_c)^{0.3} \tag{1}$$

in which

$t_p$   is the lag time from the centroid of effective
      rainfall of duration $t_r$ to the peak of a unit
      hydrograph in hours

$C_t$   is a coefficient related to the basin character-
      istics. Its numerical value varies from 1.8 to
      2.2 in the Appalachian Mountain region. For
      other values see Page 14-23 of Chow (1964).

L    is the length of the main stream from the out-
      let to the upstream limits of the divide in
      miles,

$L_c$   is the distance from the outlet to a point on
      the stream nearest to the centroid of the drain-
      age basin in miles.

In order to apply the equation it is necessary that the peak
flow be computed. For this an initial step is to assume a
standard duration of the rain. For rains in the Appalachian
Mountain region Snider used the following relationship:

$$t_r = \frac{t_p}{5.5} \tag{2}$$

With appropriate modifications, and accepting Snider's formula
for $t_r$, the peak discharge of the synthetic unit hydrograph
would be

$$q = \frac{640 \ C_p \ A \ P}{t_r} \tag{3}$$

in which

    q  is the peak discharge in cubic feet per second

for a given amount of rainfall falling over time $t_r$,

640   is the conversion factor to give q in cfs for the drainage area in square miles,

$C_p$   is a coefficient related to basin characteristics having a value in the Appalachian Mountain region between 0.56 and 0.69,

A   is area in square miles,

P   is inches of precipitation on a saturated watershed over time $t_r$.

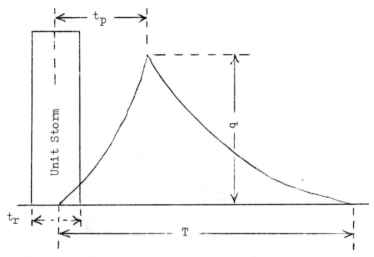

Figure 31-1     Synthesis of a Hydrograph

In order to establish the time base in days of the synthetic hydrograph Snider used the following relationship:

$$T = 3 + 3\ \frac{t_p}{24} \quad \text{in which:} \quad T = \text{time in days} \quad (4)$$

The values of the constants 3 and 24 in Snider's procedure were based upon a separation of the base flow from the direct runoff. The realism of the synthesis depends to a considerable extent upon the values of $C_t$ and $C_p$. A logical approach to the selection of values is to compute them for nearby comparable basins for which hydrologic data are available.

The equations given can be used to establish the lag time, the peak rate of discharge, and the total time, thereby making it possible to synthesize a hydrograph from physical characteristics of the drainage basin.

Kent (1972) gives a detailed discussion of travel time,

158

time of concentration, and lag. Snider (1972) classifies hydrographs used in watershed work into four categories: natural, synthetic, unit, and dimensionless. He states that difficulties with hydrograph synthesis stem chiefly from estimation of runoff from rainfall and determination of the paths of flow.

Extensive research has been conducted introducing additional parameters describing the physical characteristics of a drainage basin. "Research Data Assembly for Small Watersheds" (1967) defines over 30 expressions of physiographic characteristics of a drainage basin; Holland (1967) has prepared a condensation of this reference.

Sangal (1967) describes a method of computing peak discharge from rainfall excess in his discussion of a triangular unit hydrograph for which he has assumed an isosceles shape so that the rise time and the recession time are equal.

Overton's article (1968) is an example of work on extracting unit hydrographs from complex storms through the application of least squares techniques by using a procedure which is the reverse of the usual synthesis of a complex hydrograph by a summation of successive unit hydrographs. (See Topic 30.) A review of the science of geomorphology with a discussion of an analogy between landscape evolution and thermodynamics is discussed by Scheidegger (1969).

A computer program for mathematical modeling of the relationship of watershed characteristics and flood hydrographs for basins in Connecticut has been prepared by Green (1971). Based on studies of 22 Connecticut streams this model takes into account the percentage of stratified drift in the basin, antecedent moisture, and groundwater recession coefficient. The results combined by a unit hydrograph technique produce a storm hydrograph.

Hedman, Moore and Livingston (1972) developed a method for computing mean annual runoff and peak rates of discharge based on the relationships of the width and average depth of cross sections selected between depositional bars in the stream channel. This statistical computation, based on 53 gaged locations on perennial streams in the mountain regions of Colorado, is performed so that peak rates of discharge can be calculated for ungaged streams.

Topic 28, Drainage Basin Geomorphology, includes several references to the synthesis of a hydrograph. Murphey, Wallace, and Lane (1977) is especially pertinent. Most approaches of this type require maps of the drainage basins to provide information on parameters.

Land forms, soils, and vegetal cover are primarily the

result of the climate. This basic ecological principle can be applied by the hydrologist when dealing with drainage basins for which practically no geomorphic or hydrologic data are available. If ecological complexes look alike they will behave hydrologically in a parallel manner. Therefore, as a broad assumption, the hydrologic performance of a watershed for which detailed records are available may be transposed to the undeveloped areas under consideration.

References

Chow, Ven Te, "Runoff", Sec. 14 in Handbook of Applied Hydrology, Ven Te Chow, ed-in-chief, McGraw Hill Book Co., New York, 1964.

Green, Ralph F., "Mathematical Modeling of Relationships Between Watershed Characteristics and Flood Hydrographs for Basins in Connecticut", The Center for the Environment and Man, Inc., Hartford, Conn. 1971.

Hedman, E. R., D. O. Moore, and R. K. Livingston, "Selected Streamflow Characteristics as Related to Channel Geometry of Perennial Streams in Colorado", USGS Water Resources Div., Colo. District, Open-File Report, Lakewood, Colo. May, 1972.

Holland, Melvin E., "Discussion of Paper No. 70, 'Purpose and Performance of Peak Predictions', by Brian M. Reich and Lourens A. V. Hiemstra", Proceedings International Hydrology Symposium, Sept. 6-8, 1967, Fort Collins, Colo. vol. 2 pp 382-388, Sept. 1967.

Kent, Kenneth M., "Chapter 15. Travel Time, Time of Concentration and Lag", Soil Conservation Service, USDA, National Engineering Handbook, Sec. 4, Hydrology. Aug. 1972.

Murphey, J. B., D. E. Wallace, and L. J. Lane, "Geomorphic Parameters Predict Hydrograph Characteristics in the Southwest", Water Resources Bulletin, vol. 13, no. 1, Feb. 1977.

Overton, D. E., "A Least-Squares Hydrograph Analysis of Complex Storms on Small Agricultural Watersheds", Water Resources Research, vol. 4, no. 5, pp 955-963, Oct. 1968.

"Research Data Assembly for Small Watersheds, Part II", Colo. State Univ., Small Watershed Hydrology Program, CER 67-68-13, Colo. State Univ. Exp. Sta., General Series 856, Fort Collins, Colo., Sept. 1967.

Sangal, B. P., "Discussion of Paper No. 70, 'Purpose and Performance of Peak Predictions', by Brian M. Reich and Lourens A. V. Hiemstra", Proc. Inter. Hydrology Symposium, Sept. 6-8, 1967, Fort Collins, Colo. vol. 2, pp 378-381, 1967.

Scheidegger, Adrian E., "Geomorphology", The Progress of Hydrology, Proc. First International Seminar for Hydrology Professors, July 13-25, 1969, pub. by Dept. of Civil Engineering, Univ. of Illinois at Urbana, pp 777-786, 1969.

Snider, Dean, "Chap. 16, Hydrographs", Soil Conservation Service, USDA, National Engineering Handbook, Sec. 4, Hydrology, Aug. 1972.

Topic 32          Erosion and Sedimentation

The processes of erosion have shaped and continue to shape
the surface of the Earth.  Water, wind, temperature, and human
activity are the agents of erosion which can be defined as a
wearing away of the land.  Normal erosion is erosion of the
land surface under natural conditions undisturbed by man.  Geologic norm of erosion occurs usually whether or not man-made
endeavors such as the construction of dams, the channelization
of rivers, the construction of harbors and highways, mining operations, gravel pits, municipal and industrial land-leveling,
clean-cultivated bare soil, and irrigated agriculture are involved.  Most of man's activities in the past tended to result
in greatly accelerated erosion.  General references to erosion
are to be found in publications by Leopold and Maddock (1953)
and Leopold and Langbein (1966).  Bennett (1955) gives a general discussion of soil erosion and its importance.  Young and
Wiersma (1973) found that decreasing rainfall impact energy by
89 percent without reducing rainfall intensity decreased soil
losses by 90 percent or more.

Water acts in many ways.  The energy of falling water has
been estimated by Dr. R. H. Brooks of the Agricultural Research
Service stationed at Colorado State University to approximate
roughly 100 horse-power on an acre during a 0.1-inch per hour
rainfall.  This energy operates to break up soil aggregates at
the soil surface and to initiate the erosion process.  In land
management two kinds of soil erosion by water are recognized:
sheet erosion which is a suspension of soil material and its
removal by overland flow; and channel erosion which is transport of material by a confined hydraulic flow.  Gulley formation is a result of channel flow.  Heede (1971) describes the
processes of soil piping in gullies.  It is a tendency of nature to protect soil surface against sheet erosion.  Man's
activities such as the plowing of soil exposing a bare surface,
over-grazing, logging, and wildfires both grassland and forest,
are among the examples of disturbances which cause accelerated
sheet erosion.

Sheet erosion and gulley formation contribute to the sediment load of channel flows.  Stream-bank, flood plain, and
stream-bed scour, are all aspects of channel erosion.  Sediment
transport is of direct interest to water resources development
activities as treated in Topic 33, "Sediment Transport in
Alluvial Channels".

Wind erosion has been of tremendous significance in the formation of loessial soil in past geologic times. Wind erosion continues to be a major problem in many parts of the world.

Free (1911) wrote a 173-page review of the movement of soil by the wind drawing upon observations from many parts of the world. Stuntz and Free (1911) prepared an extensive bibliography of eolian geology. An 8-page report "Facts About Wind Erosion and Dust Storms on the Great Plains", (1966) describes with numerous photographs the wind erosion of the dust bowl era during the period 1931-1938.

The formation of glacial cirques, the scouring of glacial valleys, sediment transport of water released by the melting of glaciers, the cracking of rocks, the ice-shove against dams and shore-line construction, are important examples of ice erosion. Meier (1964) has prepared a concise review of glaciers.

Gravity, of course, is a component of all the other processes of erosion. It is directly evident in sloughing, land slides, mud flow, and cave-ins. Williams and Guy (1971) describe land slumps which they refer to as debris avalanches, a geomorphic hazard, which has been occurring for a very long time in the Appalachian Mountains.

Any general changes in the volume of flow, and in the distribution of velocities in the cross section, result in changes in the sediment transporting capabilities of the flow. A rule of thumb which applies generally to the flow of water bearing only a suspended load consisting of particles of fine soil, with no bed load, is that the carrying power of the flow varies as the 4th to the 6th power of its velocity. This can be seen in any ditch in soil where practically imperceptible changes in velocity result in clearly evident changes in deposition or erosion of soil material.

Flowing water transports sediment either in suspension throughout the flow or by pushing a portion of the material down the channel as a bed load. There have been developed tractive-force type formulae for a bed load movement only. General references pertinent to the subject are in Gottschalk (1964), Einstein (1964), Dawdy (1961), Kennedy (1963), Lane (1955), Richardson, Simons, and Haushild (1962), Simons and Richardson (1965), Simons and Richardson (1966), and Chang, Simons and Richardson (1965).

Geologically speaking a lake is an evanescent feature and a reservoir is a man-made lake. In the case of any body of water, whether it is the result of natural processes or of man-made activity, sooner or later the lake will become filled with sediment and become a plain. In order to ascertain how rapidly the deposition of sediment is reducing the capacity of a reservoir, "Sedimentation Surveys" are performed periodically. At one time it was estimated that the life of Lake Mead would be about 375 years. (Since the closure of Glen Canyon Dam the sediment life of Lake Mead has been extended to an estimated 1,000 years.) The life of the reservoir formed by Norris Dam of the Tennessee Valley Authority has been estimated to be about 2,700 years. Garstka (1972) analyzes the long-range implications of reservoir sedimentation.

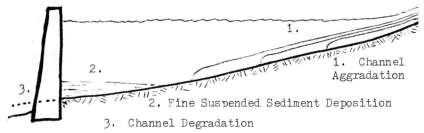

1. Channel Aggradation

2. Fine Suspended Sediment Deposition

3. Channel Degradation

Figure 32-1   Longitudinal Cross Section of a Reservoir

In a river system development there is a tendency for the bed load and much of the suspended load to be deposited in the upper reaches of a reservoir. This causes a delta formation which may result in lifting or aggradation of the bottom of the channel. An example of this is the Rio Grande. Sediment deposits in Elephant Butte Reservoir have caused deposition which lifted the bottom of the channel so much that it has been necessary to build dykes to confine the flows.

An example of an exhaustive report on a very well organized and thoroughly analyzed sedimentation survey on Lake Mead was done by Smith, Vetter, Cummings, and others (1960). Lara's (1971) report on the 1967 Altus Reservoir sediment survey includes numerous photographs, charts, and sedimentation profiles. Guy and Norman (1970) have prepared a 59-page detailed manual of field methods for the measurement of fluvial sediment.

The Water Resources Council (expected release in 1978) has appointed an inter-agency work group engaged in the preparation of a revised and enlarged "National Handbook of Recommended Methods for Water Data Acquisition". This handbook is expected to include a Chapter on Reservoir Surveys in which are to be a Section on Reservoir Sediment Surveys and another Section on Reservoir Sampling. Many professional Societies have committees actively working on subjects related to erosion and sedimentation.

A sedimentation bibliography (1968) contains a thousand entries in the third volume of the series. Source languages for this volume are: Bulgarian, Chinese, Czech, Danish, Dutch, English, French, German, Hebrew, Hungarian, Italian, Japanese,

Norwegian, Polish, Romanian, Russian, Serbo-Croat, Slovak, Spanish, Swedish, and Ukranian. It does not include articles published in the United States. This reference is one of a series of translations and compilations of information from foreign sources prepared under the general sponsorship of the National Science Foundation and available from the U.S. Dept. of Commerce, Clearinghouse for Federal Scientific and Technical Information, Springfield, Virginia.

Egypt's Aswan Dam project is bound to be a classic in the field of erosion and sedimentation. A very informative review of this project has been prepared by Turner (1971). Before the dam was built the Nile River carried about 134 million tons of suspended matter each year. As a result of the annual flooding the sediment deposited enriched the soil and made the Nile Valley agriculturally productive for thousands of years. With the closure of the dam sediment is no longer deposited on the fields and artificial fertilizers have become necessary. The absence of sediment transport to the Eastern Mediterranean Sea has reduced the food supply for the sardine catch which has fallen from about 18,000 tons before the dam closure to about 500 tons per year. An extremely serious result which will have far-reaching political and economical effects is the channel degradation, not only in the Valley of the Nile, but also in the shoreline of the Eastern Mediterranean. Turner refers to the publication by Abdel Aziz Ahmed in 1960 of a paper predicting many of the effects now being observed. By that time Egypt's commitments on various economic and political programs were assumed to be so inflexible that Ahmed's warnings were not given consideration.

When an original soil, made up of particles of different sizes, is subjected to either wind or water erosion, the smallest particles are removed first. Larger particles, too heavy to be carried away, remain to form a protective layer known as "desert pavement" or "erosion pavement" asdescribed by Shaw (1929). Hammad (1972) has calculated that the small percentage of coarse sand and gravel in the alluvium of the Nile River basin may be sufficient to build up a natural protective erosion pavement armoring the channel against progressively increasing degradation.

Guy (1970) reviews various fluvial sediment concepts involving physical characteristics, sediment transport and deposition, geomorphic considerations, economic aspects, and data needs and program objectives. A thorough study of this reference is recommended. Holeman (1968) summarizes sediment yield of major rivers of the world.

A major problem facing water resources developers is that of estimating sediment yield under ultimate operating conditions especially with regard to the total amount of sediment to be provided for and the rate of loss of reservoir capacity. Smith, Davis, and Fogel (1977) propose a method using the Bayesian Decision Theory and the determination of sediment yield by transferring rainfall data.

Simons and Senturk (1976-1977) have written an exhaustive 807-page treatise on sediment transport technology.

There has been an extensive public education campaign relating to environmental degradations caused by erosion and sedimentation. Some of the less desirable environmental effects of control measures to reduce erosion much below the natural norm must be recognized. Stall (1972) and Guy (1973) point out an underloaded stream could be highly erosive and could result in drastic environmental, biological, and ecological changes.

## References

Bennett, H. H., "Elements of Soil Conservation", McGraw-Hill Book Co., New York, 1955.

Chang, F. J., D. B. Simons, and E. V. Richardson, "Total Bed-Material Discharge in Alluvial Channels", USGS Water Supply Paper 1498-I, 1965.

Dawdy, D. R., "Depth-Discharge Relations of Alluvial Streams - Discontinuous Rating Curves", USGS Water Supply Paper 1498-C, 1961.

Einstein, Hans Albert, "River Sedimentation", Sec. 17-11, Handbook of Applied Hydrology, Ven Te Chow, ed-in-chief, McGraw-Hill Book Co., New York, 1964.

"Facts About Wind Erosion and Dust Storms on the Great Plains", USDA Leaflet No. 394, 8 pp, reprinted July, 1966.

Free, E. E., "The Movement of Soil Material by the Wind", pp 1-173 in USDA Bureau of Soils Bulletin No. 68, June 15, 1911.

Garstka, Walter U., "Water Resources in the West", pp 8-14, from Watersheds in Transition, Proc. of a Symposium held at Fort Collins, Colo., June 19-22, 1972. Ed. by S. C. Csallany, T. G. McLaughlin and W. Striffler, Proc. Series No. 14, American Water Resources Assn., Urbana, Ill., 405 pp, Sept. 1972.

Gottschalk, Louis C., Section 17-1, "Reservoir Sedimentation", Handbook of Applied Hydrology, Ven Te Chow, ed-in-chief, McGraw-Hill Book Co., New York, 1964.

Guy, Harold P. and Vernon W. Norman, "Field Methods for Measurement of Fluvial Sediment", Techniques of Water-Resources Investigations of the USGS, Chap. C2, Book 3, Government Printing Office, 1970.

Guy, Harold P., "Fluvial Sediment Concepts", Chap. C1, Book 3, Techniques of Water-Resources Investigations of the USGS, Government Printing Office, 1970.

Guy, Harold P., "Sediment and Soil Conservation", Jour. of Environmental Quality, vol. 2, no. 2, p 316, 1973.

Hammad, Hammad Y., "River Bed Degradation After Closure of Dams", Jour. Hydraulics Div., Proceedings ASCE, pp 591-607 Apr. 1972.

Heede, Burchard H., "Characteristics and Processes of Soil Piping in Gullies", USFS Rocky Mt. Forest & Range Exp. Station, Fort Collins, Colo., Research Paper RM-68, 15 pp, March, 1971.

Holeman, J. H., "The Sediment Yield of Major Rivers of the World", Water Resources Research, vol. 4, no. 4, pp 737-747, Aug. 1968.

Kennedy, J. F., "The Mechanics of Dunes and Antidunes in Erodible-bed Channels", Fluid Mechanics Jour. vol. 16, pt. 4, pp 521-544, 1963.

Lane, E. W., "The Importance of Fluvial Morphology in Hydraulic Engineering", Amer. Soc. of Civil Engineers, Proc. vol. 81 no. 745, pp 1-17, 1955.

Lara, Joe M., "The 1967 Altus Reservoir Sediment Survey", Bur. of Reclamation Engineering and Research Center Report REC-ERC-71-21, 41 pp, March, 1971.

Leopold, Luna B., and Thomas Maddock, Jr., "The Hydraulic Geometry of Stream Channels and Some Physiographic Implications", USGS Prof. Paper 252, USDI, 1953.

Leopold, Luna B., and Walter B. Langbein, "River Meanders", Scientific American, vol. 214, no. 5, pp 60-70, June, 1966.

Meier, Mark F., "Ice and Glaciers", Sec. 16, Handbook of Applied Hydrology, Ven Te Chow, ed-in-chief, McGraw-Hill Book Co., New York, 1964.

Richardson, E. V., D. B. Simons, and W. L. Haushild, "Boundary Form and Resistance to Flow in Alluvial Channels", Inter. Assn. Scien. Hydrology Bulletin 1, vol. 7, 1962.

"Sedimentation - Annotated Bibliography of Foreign Literature, 1965-1967, Survey No. 3", prepared for the U.S. Dept. of Agriculture and the National Science Foundation by the Israel Program for Scientific Translations, 1968. Report No. TT-67-51412 available from U.S. Dept. of Commerce, Clearinghouse for Federal Scientific Information, Springfield, Va., 1968.

Shaw, Charles F., "Erosion Pavement", The Geophysical Review, vol. XIX, no. 4, pp 638-641, Oct. 1929.

Simons, D. B., and E. V. Richardson, "A Study of Variables Affecting Flow Characteristics and Sediment Transport in Alluvial Channels", reprint from Proc. of the Federal Inter-Agency Sedimentation Congress, 1963, Misc. Publ. No. 970, Agri. Research Service, June, 1965.

Simons, D. B. and E. V. Richardson, "Resistance to Flow in Alluvial Channels", USGS Prof. Paper 422-J, 1966.

Simons, Daryl B. and Fuat Senturk, "Sediment Transport Technology", Water Resources Publications, Fort Collins, Colo., 807 pp, 1976-1977.

Smith, Jeffrey, Donald R. Davis, and Martin Fogel, "Determination of Sediment Yield by Transferring Rainfall Data", Water Resources Bulletin, vol. 13, no. 3, pp 529-541, June, 1977.

Smith, W. O., C. P. Vetter, G. B. Cummings, and others, "Comprehensive Survey of Sedimentation in Lake Mead, 1948-49, USGS Prof. Paper 295, 1960.

Stall, John B., "Effects of Sediment on Water Quality", Jour. Environ. Quality, 1:353-360, 1972.

Stuntz, S. C. and E. E. Free, "Bibliography of Eolian Geology", pp 174-272 in The Movement of Soil Material by the Wind, USDA Bureau of Soils Bulletin No. 68, June 15, 1911.

Turner, Darrell J., "Dams and Ecology - Can they be made compatible?", Civil Engineering, vol. 41, no. 9, pp 76-80, Sept. 1971.

Water Resources Council, Chap. on Reservoir Surveys with a Sec. on Reservoir Sediment Surveys and another Sec. on Reservoir Sampling in "National Handbook of Recommended Methods for Water Data Acquisition". Expected date of release 1978.

Williams, Garnett P. and Harold P. Guy, "Debris Avalanches - A Geomorphic Hazard", Chapt. 2, pp 25-46, in Environmental Geomorphology, D. Coates, editor, 262 pp, State Univ. of New York at Binghamton, 1971.

Young, R. A. and J. L. Wiersma, "The Role of Rainfall Impact in Soil Detachment and Transport", Water Resources Research, vol. 9, no. 6, pp 1629-1636, Dec. 1973.

Topic 33    Sediment Transport in Alluvial Channels

Research in sedimentation has as its objectives the increase of understanding of factors influencing sediment transport in streams and the development of methods for computing
sediment discharge.  Such information is fundamental to the
design and maintenance of channels; for forecasting rates of
scour or fill in natural or artificial channels; for providing
a basis for evaluating the environmental impact of land use
changes; for computation of annual sediment transport at a contemplated dam site to provide a basis for the allocation of
reservoir storage for sediment deposition.

At any cross section of a stream the sediment discharge is
affected by a complex interaction of the following:  depth,
width, velocity, energy gradient, temperature, the wetted perimeter, roughness, turbulence, rate of flow; on the size, density, shape, and cohesiveness of the particles in the banks and
in the streambed at the cross section and in upstream channels;
on the geomorphology, geology, meteorology, topography, soil
and subsoil structures; and to a very considerable extent on
the vegetal cover of the drainage area and the character of the
streambank vegetation.  The interactions, many of them dealing
with transients not expressible directly as rigorous digital
mathematical equations, are so complex that no precise technique has as yet been evolved to encompass all conditions found
in nature.

Sediment transport in channels is of continuing importance
to water resources management since it affects the design and
operation and maintenance of conveyance structures, influences
the allocation of space in reservoirs and the economics of project planning, and controls the useful life of reservoirs.

About 80 to 90 percent of canals are in effect sand bed
channels.  A great many irrigation supply canals are built of
natural material usually in a trapezoidal section and without
lining.  At the practically flat slopes irrigation canals may
carry up to 500 parts per million in sediment.  If a greater
sediment concentration is found in the water diverted into the
canal deposition will occur and the canal will tend to fill with
sediment.  Conversely, if slopes are too steep and velocity too
great, the flows will erode the banks of the canal.

Many problems have been encountered in lined canals.  In
the past it was usual to design a canal to carry sediment when
the flow was at the full designed capacity of the canal.  A
lined canal designed with a value of "n" of 0.0135 may adequa-
tly transport both water and sediment as anticipated but at reduced flow the relative roughness increases, velocity is

170

reduced, sediment is deposited on the bed and develops into
dunes increasing the  n  value to 0.035. This reduces the discharge capacity and additional sediment deposition may occur.

The basic relationship in sediment transport is that
stated by the late Professor E. W. Lane of Colorado State University:

$$Q \times S \quad \propto \quad Q_S \times d \qquad (1)$$

in which

| | | |
|---|---|---|
| Q  is flow | (is proportional to) | $Q_S$  is sediment discharge |
| S  is slope | | d  is size of sediment |

Whenever any one of the four values is changed a readjustment
must be made in the others. The equation is a proportionality
and not a mathematically rigorous expression. However, it can
be used to approximate the effect of river engineering works
and water resources development on the river basin.

The ever-growing delta of the Mississippi River is lifting
the bed to such an extent as to offer serious threats to navigation. River-bank lands previously almost worthless are now
selling for many thousands of dollars per foot of frontage at
New Orleans. Increased freight traffic is estimated to result
in the foreseeable future in a demand for a 20-foot minimum
depth of navigation channel up the river to St. Louis, Missouri.
At present the Corps of Engineers maintains a 12-foot channel
to St. Louis. This is being performed under increasing difficulties in river regulation and sediment management. It is to
be expected that design, construction, and maintenance of a 20-
foot deep channel would place tremendous demands on the
engineers.

A widely-used technique which applies to steady-flow conditions and not to variable rates of flow is that described by
Colby (1964). This reference contains a number of alignment
charts the use of which makes it possible to compute sand discharge in tons per day per foot of width for alluvial stream
channels. On pages A31, A36, A37, and A39, Colby describes the
procedure. An interesting problem assignment is possible to
illustrate his procedure. His method has been found to work,
within limits of plus or minus 50 percent, in flumes, canals,
and river flows varying in depth from a few tenths of a foot to
about 100 feet.

Wigham (1970) includes in his section on sediment transportation 36 equations dealing with soil erosion, sediment
transport, bed load, and total load calculation. He warns that
none of the equations predict accurately short-term estimates
of sediment transport volumes and rates.

Water flowing in a channel carries a suspended load and

pushes a bed load. The combination of the two is described as
total sediment transport. The subject cuts across many engineering activities. One activity is concerned with the measurement, control, and disposition of transported sediment. One
other, and a new and expanding field, is related to the ecological and pollution aspects of the subject.

Most engineering problems require knowledge of sediment
transport and control. Flowing water tends to pick up any
loose material in the channel up to the limit of its transport
capacity. Channels not only convey the water but in many instances must also be designed to convey sediment. Experience
has shown that the placement of a diversion from a major channel is very important with respect to sediment.

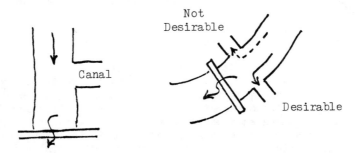

Figure 33-1    Canal Diversions in Relation to Sediment
               Transport

Most successful diversions from rivers are on the outside
of a bend. Diversions on the inside result in large sediment
loads in the canal and complex sediment problems. This introduction of excess sediment to the canal is due to unequal distribution of velocity, secondary circulation, and sediment
transport ability of a stream cross section as it flows around
the bend.

Canal intake structures and canal systems may be designed
either for the exclusion of excess sediment, that is, to keep
it from entering the canal, or with ejection systems to get rid
of the excess sediment in the canal flow. Examples of the
latter are tunnel-ejectors in the bottom of canals to get rid
of bed load, and desilting basins for settling of suspended
sediment.

Brown and Ritter (1971) describe a 10-year study of the
Eel River Basin in Northern California. This is the region of
the California Redwoods; some of the tallest trees in the world
are in the Eel River Basin. This river at Scotia carries about
4,330 tons of sediment each year from each square mile. The
average rate of erosion per square mile per year is at least

13 times the national average. During a 10-year period of study beginning in October, 1957, more than 310,000,000 tons of rock and soil were eroded away from the Basin.

In most years over half of the sediment load is carried away in less than 6 days mostly during winter storms. The average annual precipitation is 59 inches and the average annual runoff is 35 inches. A combination of soil types, geology, steep slopes, and heavy precipitation produce slumps and land slides. Sediment discharge figures are based upon measured, computed, and estimated rates of transport. Computer programs were used as prepared for the Eel River.

Kordas (1963) describes a computation procedure, based on the Chezy-Manning formula, for designing of river bed cross sections taking into account bed-load transportation.

Channel degradation and aggradation are especially important in urban areas as they affect the stability of the metropolitan area's structures, drainage patterns, and land use. Kresan (1974) in his thought-provoking analysis of flood hazards in the Tucson, Arizona, area described a technique attributed to Bull and Scott (1974) for direct observation of changes in the stream channel bottom using a tier of metal link chains, the lower most having been buried deeply below current bottom elevation.

The interaction between a flowing stream and its channel is dynamic; there is no way whatsoever of preserving in perpetuity the current appearance of a stream. Both natural phenomena, such as slumps (see "Landslides" 1974), dunes, earthquakes and geophysical trends, and changes resulting from manmade land-use assignments and river channel control engineering practices result in a response by the stream.

Flowing water refuses to store energy which it acquires with increasing velocity. If the water is flowing in a hard rock channel or in a lined canal the water will expend the energy in a hydraulic jump (in accordance with the Law of Continuity: $Q = A^1 V^1 = A^2 V^2$ etc.) or in standing waves or as white water in a boulder-strewn stream bottom. If the stream bottom or banks are erodible the water will pick up and transport a sediment load thereby expending excess energy. Conversely, as velocity is reduced the sediment load will decrease resulting in aggradation.

Schumm (1969) anticipates that great changes, some of which may take place over a time span of decades or even centuries, are inescapable as river metamorphosis develops in response to man's activities in the management of the water resource.

# References

Brown, W. M. III, J. R. Ritter, "Sediment Transport and Turbidity in the Eel River Basin, California", USGS Water Supply Paper No. 1986, Govt. Printing Office, 1971

Bull, W. B. and Kevin M. Scott, "Impact of Mining Gravel from Urban Stream Beds in the Southwestern U.S., " Geology,

Colby, Bruce R., "Discharge of Sands and Mean-Velocity Relationships in Sand-Bed Streams", USGS Prof. Paper 462-A, Government Printing Office, 1964.

Kordas, Boleslaw, "Designing of River Bed Cross Sections Taking into Account Bed Load Transportation", Gospodarka Wodna, vol. 23, no. 10, pp 383-385, 1963. (Trans. from Polish Report TT 67-56044, pub. for the U.S. Dept. of Interior and the Natl. Science Foundation by the Scientific Pub. Foreign Cooperation Center of the Central Institute for Scientific, Technical and Economic Information, Warsaw, Poland, 1968.)

Kresan, Peter L., "Flood Hazards in the Tucson Area - A Discussion and Self-Guided Tour of Flood Hazards in the Tucson Basin, Arizona, Dept. of Geosciences, College of Earth Sciences, Univ. of Ariz., Tucson, 11 pp, Oct. 1974.

"Landslides", an 8-page pamphlet, U.S. Geological Survey, Washington, D.C. 1974.

Schumm, Stanley A., "River Metamorphosis", Jour. Hydraulics Div., Proceedings ASCE, pp 255-273, Jan. 1969.

Wigham, John M., "Sediment Transportation", Sec. XI, of Handbook on the Principles of Hydrology, Donald M. Gray, editor, pub. 1970 by Canadian Natl. Committee for the IHD, reprinted 1973 under agreement with National Research Council of Canada by Water Information Center, Port Washington, N.Y.

Topic 34        Soil Science and Soil Mechanics

To a geologist the soil is decomposed rock; an engineer considers soil to be a material; to a soil scientist soil is a fascinating entity which is the end product of the interaction of a parent material, vegetal cover, the biological complexes and climate. The parent geologic material may be a rock exposed in place or material transported by various processes: through glacial action; by gravity; by water erosion and transportation laid down as sediment deposits in alluvial flood plains or beneath the surfaces of lakes and oceans; by wind to form loess; or by volcanic action.

## Soil Science

The vegetal cover which occupies the surface of the land (where the water supply permits the growth of such a cover) deposits on the surface litter consisting of cast-off leaves, branches and stems. This litter provides food for an ecological system made of fungi, mycorrhiza, viruses, phages, bacteria, protozoa, actinomycetes, diatoms, earth worms, insects, shrews, rodents, to enumerate but a few. As the biota digest the litter (and each other) they secrete substances which help break down the geologic parent material. Waksman (1966) has given a very informative review of the importance of microbes to the survival of man on Earth.

Infiltrating and percolating waters seep through the geologic material and become organized into horizontal layers generally parelling the soil surface, called horizons. Five general horizons are recognized as shown in Figure 34-1 on the following page.

An excellent discussion of the fundamentals of soil science is given in the Year Book of Agriculture for 1938, "Soils and Men", Part IV. The terms used to describe values of soils in this publication have since been replaced by a much more detailed classification requiring a great number of created words having precise scientific meanings. The current soil taxonomy system is described in Agriculture Handbook No. 436 (1975) a 754-page publication. Appendix I of this handbook defines on pages 459-463 three O horizons, seven A horizons, five B horizons, and a C and an R horizon, with a list of 14 subordinate symbols. Such detailed differentiations are of interest to those specializing in soil classification.

| Depth (approximate) | Horizon | Characteristics |
|---|---|---|
| 0 to about 100 cm | O | **Litter**, leaves and organic debris partly decomposed at surface of Horizon A |
| 15 cm to 25 cm thick | A | **Topsoil** Layer of Eluviation Gray in Spodosols, brown in Alfisols, red in Oxisols and black in Mollisols. |
| 50 cm to 100 cm thick | B | **Subsoil** Layer of Accumulation Dark brown Spodosols, brown in Alfisols, usually dark in Mollisols, various colors in other major groups. |
| Up to 100 meters thick | C | **Parent Material**, partly weathered and disintegrating rock. May have layers of calcium accumulation in Mollisols. |
| Possibly thousands of meters thick | R | **Rock or any stratum** not showing evidence of weathering or disintegration |

Figure 34-1  Generalized Principal Horizons of a Soil Profile
(not to scale)

As the vegetal cover is the result of the climate, the land surfaces of the hemispheres are characterized by bands of ecosystems. Each of these climatological-ecological entities results in the formation of a broad zonal group of soils. In the following paragraphs a few broad classifications of soils will be given using both the older and the current general terms.

The podzol soils, (spodosols), have developed in the colder regions and are found primarily under coniferous or mixed forests or under heath vegetation in temperate to cold moist climates. The spodosol soils may be covered by a layer up to many centimeters in thickness of newly fallen litter which decomposes very slowly because of the resinous character of the litter and the low temperatures with short growing seasons. The decomposition processes include many fungi which do not produce a complete breakdown of the organic matter. Low temperatures and somewhat uniform distribution of precipitation result in a percolation from the organic layers of a water which dissolves the iron oxide and aluminum from the A horizon producing a light gray ash-like layer.

Ugolini, Dawson, and Zachara (1977) present direct evidence in photographs taken with a scanning electron microscope at magnifications of x 450 and x 5400 of particle migration in a soil solution containing fulvic acid from the A to the B horizons in a podzol soil located in the Findley Basin in the Central Cascades in Washington.

When these dissolved materials together with some organic matter come in contact with soil particles in the B horizon they are participated often forming a distinct chocolate-brown layer which slowly merges into the C horizons. Podzol soils are not very productive of food and fiber partly because of the shortness of the growing season where they are formed.

The second broad zonal group of soils are the brown earth forest soils (alfisols) which may be undergoing some podzolization but in which the eluviation of the iron oxides and aluminum is not dominant. These soils develop under deciduous forests in temperate humid zones and may be slightly acid with a moderately high content of calcium and soil colloids. There is seldom a very distinct visible delineation between the A and B horizons. Decomposition of organic litter is accomplished by bacteria, earth worms, and micro flora with the fungi having a very minor part. This type of decomposition produces a complex substance called "humus" which is one of the final degradation products of vegetal and animal material. Humus has the ability to cement into clusters collodial-size soil particles. These soil aggregates improve greatly the water-holding capacity of the soil and also are very efficient in retaining nutrient ions and preventing their removal by leaching.

The fertility of a soil depends to a considerable extent on the humus. Waksman (1936 and 1938) prepared an exhaustive treatment of the origin, chemical composition, and importance in nature of humus.

While studying the decomposition of organic matter, including forest litter, on and in the soil Dr. Waksman observed antagonistic effects upon the growth of certain micro organisms in the presence of other organisms. His further pursuit of this effect ultimately resulted in his development of actinomycin, streptomycin and neomycin for which he was awarded the Nobel Prize in Physiology or Medicine in 1952.

In the brown earth soils of the temperate zones, as the plant nutrients accumulate in the humus-soil complex, they produce a soil of increasing fertility so that vegetal associations higher in the ecological scale tend to develop. Garstka (1932) found the calcium content of Connecticut forest litter showed an increase in the content as the forest type progressed toward the climax.

The relationships between forests and soils are so fundamental to soil taxonomy, agronomy and land management that
there is a highly specialized field of endeavor dealing with
wildland and forest soils.  Lutz and Chandler (1946) prepared a
textbook of forest soils.  Bernier and Winget have edited the
Proceedings of a Symposium on "Forest Soils and Forest Land
Management (1975).  "Forest-Soil Relationships in North
America" were the subject of a conference held at Corvallis,
Oregon, in 1963 which have been edited by Youngberg (1965).

Eyre (1963) has written a very informative book presenting
a world picture of vegetation and soils in both the northern
and southern hemispheres.  Eyre's book is illustrated with 32
photographs of various forests and ecological complexes and
with 30 figures and maps.

Bormann, Likens, and Meilello (1977) present in quantitative detail the nitrogen budget for the northern hardwood
ecosystem.  Their chart of the annual nitrogen budget as worked
out for the Hubbard Brook Experimental Forest in the White
Mountains of New Hampshire is given as Figure 34-2.

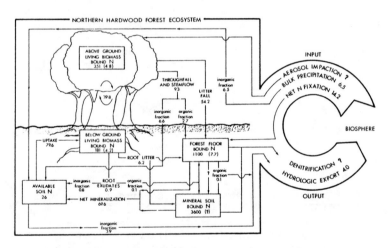

Figure 34-2  Annual nitrogen budget for an undisturbed northern
        hardwood forest ecosystem at Hubbard Brook.  The values in
        boxes are in kilograms of nitrogen per hectare.  The rate
        of accretion of each pool (in parentheses) and all trans-
        fer rates are expressed in kilograms of nitrogen per
        hectare per year.

Likens, Bormann, Pierce, Eaton, and Johnson (1977) have
prepared a thorough treatise on the biogeochemistry of the
Hubbard Brook Experimental Forest which has been maintained by
the U.S. Forest Service in the Northern Hardwoods ecosystem in
New Hampshire since 1956.  Their treatise takes into account

the chemistry of precipitation and stream water. They analyze
seasonal and monthly variations and discuss hydrogen ion,
chloride, calcium sulfur, and nitrogen cycles. A reading of
their treatise is recommended.

A third major zonal group of soils in the world is the
laterite soils (oxisol). Laterite soils are found in the
tropics and in only a few areas in the United States. They
form under a tropical forest in a hot moist climate with moderate to high rainfall. The organic matter falling to the surface of the soils is broken down with extreme rapidity so that
there is very little to be found as litter on the surface.
Under this ecological climatic complex the soil-forming process
is the opposite of the podsol. Silicon dioxide is dissolved
from the A horizon leaving a layer rich in hydrous alumina and
iron oxide or both. This produces red soils which are commonly
seen in the tropics.

Laterite soils are very low in organic matter and humus.
They have very little capacity to resist removal of plant nut-
rients by leaching and are poor producers of food and fiber.
Many of the agricultural plans being proposed or applied in the
tropical areas have been based on an application to the later-
ite soils of agronomic practices developed in the brown earths.
The success of this approach remains to be demonstrated (see
Topic 38).

A fourth major zonal group of the world is the prairie
soils (mollisols) which are found in the prairies, steppes, and
pampas. This zonal group of soils develops under tall grasses
in temperate to relatively humid climates. The soils may be
dark brown to almost black in color and may be many feet in
depth.

The desert soils (aridisols) comprise another broad zonal
group. These soils may show immature profile development sometimes millions of years old and are to be found in the desert
regions of the Earth. The flow of soil moisture may be by
capillary rise toward the surface. Because of the very great
difference between the potential evapotranspiration and the
actual precipitation, in some instances, desert soils have
accumulated large amounts of salt at the surface. The excess
salts must be leached out by using techniques paralleling those
developed by Holland for the reclamation of polders which are
fields from which ocean waters have been excluded by the construction of dykes. In some cases the desert soil when subjected to the application of water by irrigation may change the
crystallographic nature of the clays possibly becoming unsuitable for irrigation. Thorne and Peterson (1949) discuss the
fertility and management of irrigated soils.

An exhaustive 1180-page treatise consisting of an assembly

of chapters by specialists is the "Irrigation of Agricultural Lands" (1967) in which Maletic and Hutchings (1967) have prepared Chapter 10, pages 125-173, on the selection and classification of irrigable land.

Another broad zonal group is the <u>organic</u> soils (<u>histosols</u>). These are the peat and the muck soils developed in extinct lakes, behind beaver dams, and on side-hill seepage areas and wherever detentions to surface runoff may occur. Organic soils were much more prominant ages ago than they are now. The coal seams are the result of great forests during the Carboniferous ages (see Figure 28-1) of tree ferns, giant horse tails, great club mosses, and also the ancestors of present-day conifers. Three informative textbooks on soils have been prepared by Foth and Turk (1972), Brady (1974), and Donahue, Miller, and Shickluna (1977).

Holtan, England, and Whelan (1967) list hydrologic characteristics of 96 samples of 40 soil types. This subject is discussed in further detail in Topic 55, Design Floods.

As of 1971 about 9500 soil series were recognized in the United States. Beginning in 1897 an extensive accumulation of reports and soil maps, many of them obsolete, have been published by various bureaus of.the U.S. Dept. of Agriculture. These maps have been very useful not only in agriculture, range management and forestry, but also in land use and municipal planning, recreation, waste disposal, and in construction and operation of industrial operations, canals, conduit, pipelines, power lines, and highways. Currently soil surveys are performed and reports and maps published by the Soil Conservation Service of the U.S. Dept. of Agriculture in accordance with the "Soil Survey Manual" (1951).

## Soil Mechanics

The earth material engineer uses soils without regard to the horizon characteristics. He is interested in the behavior of the earth material usually under conditions having no resemblance to soils in their natural state. Foundation engineering is aimed at finding out the safe limit to which a soil may be loaded without failure.

In water resources development, dykes, levees, canals, and dams are built of earth material. The usual objective is to design a structure which will retain either flowing or still water at certain velocities and heads. Holtz (1969) has written a very informative and well-illustrated report on soil as an engineering material and the reading of this report is recommended.

An outstanding, highly-technical reference on soil

mechanic fundamentals and applications is the 810-page Bureau
of Reclamation's "Earth Manual" (1974). This manual has been
translated into several languages. Figure 34-3 (on the following page) is the chart which faces page 12 of this Manual.
This chart contains an engineering classification of soil as
adopted by the U.S. Army Corps of Engineers and the U.S. Bureau
of Reclamation in January, 1952.

Many dams in different parts of the world have been built
of earth materials. In many locations the cost of a concrete
dam would be prohibitive especially when suitable earth materials can be secured locally. A dam site may not be suitable
for any structure other than an earth dam. Hydraulics of the
design of earth-filled dams can be stated in disarmingly simple
terms; the friction exerted on water tending to flow through
the interstices below and around the dam must be greater, as
expressed in hydraulic head, than is the static head of the impounded water. Both heads are to be expressed as a dimension
of depth. (See Topic 23).

Some of the desert soils in the Central Valley of California have existed in the absence of water for an extremely
long time. When irrigation water is applied to such soils the
collapse of the soil structure has resulted in a subsidence in
some instances amounting to 13 feet as shown by Holtz (1969) in
his figure 34, page 25, taken at the Mendota test site. Gibbs
and Bara (1962) describe a procedure for predicting surface
subsidence from basic soil tests. To induce consolidation an
accepted engineering practice is to pond the building sites in
advance of the building of large or heavy structures.

A classic reference on theoretical soil mechanics is the
book written by Terzaghi (1943). A revision of this book was
prepared by Terzaghi and Peck (1968). Tschebotarioff (1973)
has written a textbook on foundations, retaining, and earth
structures. Craig (1974) of the University of Dundee deals
with soil mechanics.

The fundamental physical concepts and mathematical treatments developed by earth materials engineers have been found to
apply to avalanche control as discussed in Topic 16.

## References

Bormann, F. H., G. E. Likens, and J. M. Melillo, "Nitrogen
    Budget for an Aggrading Northern Hardwood Forest Ecosytem"
    Science, vol. 196, no. 4293, pp 981-983, May 27, 1977.

Brady, Nyle C., "Nature and Properties of Soils", 639 pp,
    8th edition, McMillan Pub. Co., New York, 1974.

# UNIFIED SOIL CLASSIFICATION
## INCLUDING IDENTIFICATION AND DESCRIPTION

| | FIELD IDENTIFICATION PROCEDURES (Excluding particles larger than 3 inches and basing fractions on estimated weights) | GROUP SYMBOLS | TYPICAL NAMES | INFORMATION REQUIRED FOR DESCRIBING SOILS | LABORATORY CLASSIFICATION CRITERIA |
|---|---|---|---|---|---|
| **COARSE GRAINED SOILS** — More than half of material is larger than No 200 sieve size / **GRAVELS** More than half of coarse fraction is larger than No 4 sieve size (For visual classifications, the ¼ size may be used as equivalent to the No 4 sieve size) / CLEAN GRAVELS (Little or no fines) | Wide range in grain size and substantial amounts of all intermediate particle sizes | GW | Well graded gravels, gravel-sand mixtures, little or no fines | Give typical name, indicate approximate percentages of sand and gravel; max. size, angularity, surface condition, and hardness of the coarse grains, local or geologic name and other pertinent descriptive information, and symbol in parentheses. | $C_u = \dfrac{D_{60}}{D_{10}}$ Greater than 4    $C_c = \dfrac{(D_{30})^2}{D_{10} \times D_{60}}$ Between one and 3 |
| | Predominantly one size or a range of sizes with some intermediate sizes missing | GP | Poorly graded gravels, gravel-sand mixtures, little or no fines | | Not meeting all gradation requirements for GW |
| GRAVELS WITH FINES (Appreciable amount of fines) | Non-plastic fines (for identification procedures see ML below) | GM | Silty gravels, poorly graded gravel-sand-silt mixtures | For undisturbed soils add information on stratification, degree of compactness, cementation, moisture conditions and drainage characteristics. | Atterberg limits below "A" line, or PI less than 4 | Above "A" line with PI between 4 and 7 are borderline cases requiring use of dual symbols |
| | Plastic fines (for identification procedures see CL below) | GC | Clayey gravels, poorly graded gravel-sand-clay mixtures | EXAMPLE:— Silty gravel, gravelly, about 20% hard, angular gravel particles ½-in maximum size, rounded and subangular sand grains coarse to fine, about 15% non-plastic fines with low dry strength, well compacted and moist in place, alluvial sand, (SM) | Atterberg limits above "A" line with PI greater than 7 |
| **SANDS** More than half of coarse fraction is smaller than No 4 sieve size (The No 200 sieve size is about the smallest particle visible to the naked eye) / CLEAN SANDS (Little or no fines) | Wide range in grain sizes and substantial amounts of all intermediate particle sizes | SW | Well graded sands, gravelly sands, little or no fines | Give typical name, indicate degree and character of plasticity, amount and maximum size of coarse grains, color in wet condition, odor if any, local or geologic name, and other pertinent descriptive information, and symbol in parentheses. | $C_u = \dfrac{D_{60}}{D_{10}}$ Greater than 6    $C_c = \dfrac{(D_{30})^2}{D_{10} \times D_{60}}$ Between one and 3 |
| | Predominantly one size or a range of sizes with some intermediate sizes missing | SP | Poorly graded sands, gravelly sands, little or no fines | | Not meeting all gradation requirements for SW |
| SANDS WITH FINES (Appreciable amount of fines) | Non-plastic fines (for identification procedures see ML below) | SM | Silty sands, poorly graded sand-silt mixtures | For undisturbed soils add information on structure, stratification, consistency in undisturbed and remolded states, moisture and drainage conditions. | Atterberg limits below "A" line or PI less than 4 | Above "A" line with PI between 4 and 7 are borderline cases requiring use of dual symbols |
| | Plastic fines (for identification procedures see CL below) | SC | Clayey sands, poorly graded sand-clay mixtures | EXAMPLE:— Clayey silt, brown, slightly plastic, small percentage of fine sand, numerous vertical root holes, firm and dry in place, loess, (ML) | Atterberg limits above "A" line with PI greater than 7 |

**IDENTIFICATION PROCEDURES ON FRACTION SMALLER THAN No. 40 SIEVE SIZE**

| | DRY STRENGTH (CRUSHING CHARACTERISTICS) | DILATANCY (REACTION TO SHAKING) | TOUGHNESS (CONSISTENCY NEAR PLASTIC LIMIT) | GROUP SYMBOLS | TYPICAL NAMES |
|---|---|---|---|---|---|
| **FINE GRAINED SOILS** — More than half of material is smaller than No 200 sieve size / SILTS AND CLAYS Liquid limit less than 50 | None to slight | Quick to slow | None | ML | Inorganic silts and very fine sands, rock flour, silty or clayey fine sands with slight plasticity |
| | Medium to high | None to very slow | Medium | CL | Inorganic clays of low to medium plasticity, gravelly clays, sandy clays, silty clays, lean clays |
| | Slight to medium | Slow | Slight | OL | Organic silts and organic silt clays of low plasticity |
| SILTS AND CLAYS Liquid limit greater than 50 | Slight to medium | Slow to none | Slight to medium | MH | Inorganic silts, micaceous or diatomaceous fine sandy or silty soils, elastic silts |
| | High to very high | None | High | CH | Inorganic clays of high plasticity, fat clays |
| | Medium to high | None to very slow | Slight to medium | OH | Organic clays of medium to high plasticity |
| **HIGHLY ORGANIC SOILS** | Readily identified by color, odor, spongy feel and frequently by fibrous texture | | | Pt | Peat and other highly organic soils |

Determine percentages of gravel and sand from grain size curve. Depending on percentage of fines (fraction smaller than No 200 sieve size) coarse grained soils are classified as follows:—

Less than 5 % — GW, GP, SW, SP
More than 12 % — GM, GC, SM, SC
5 % to 12 % — Borderline cases requiring use of dual symbols

PLASTICITY CHART
FOR LABORATORY CLASSIFICATION OF FINE GRAINED SOILS

COMPARING SOILS AT EQUAL LIQUID LIMIT
Toughness and dry strength increase with increasing plasticity index

PLASTICITY INDEX

LIQUID LIMIT

ADOPTED BY — CORPS OF ENGINEERS AND BUREAU OF RECLAMATION — JANUARY 1952

Boundary classifications. Soils possessing characteristics of two groups are designated by combinations of group symbols. For example GW-GC, well graded gravel-sand mixture with clay binder

All sieve sizes on this chart are US standard

Figure 34-3 Unified Soil Classification Used in Earth Materials Engineering. See Earth Manual (1974)

Craig, R. F., "Soil Mechanics", Van Nostrand Reinhold Co., N.Y. 275-pp, 1974.

Donahue, Roy L., Raymond W. Miller, and J. C. Shickluna, "Soils-Introduction to Soils and Plant Growth", 4th ed. Prentiss-Hall Inc., Englewood Cliffs, N.J., 587 pp, 1977.

"Earth Manual", (A guide to the use of soils as foundations and as construction materials for hydraulic structures). Bur. of Reclamation, USDI, 810 pp, 2nd edition, 1974.

Eyre, S. R., "Vegetation and Soils - A World Picture", Aldine Publ.Co., Chicago, 324 pp, 1963.

"Forest-Soil Relationships in North America"; Papers presented at the Second North American Forest Soils Conference, 1963 ed. by Chester T. Youngberg, Oregon State Univ. Press, Corvallis, 532 pp, 1965.

"Forest Soils and Forest Land Management", Proceedings of the Fourth North American Forest Soils Conference held at Laval Univ., Quebec, ed. by B. Bernier and C. H. Winget, Les Presser de L'Universite Laval, Quebec, 675 pp, 1975.

Foth, H. D., and L. M. Turk, "Fundamentals of Soil Science", 5th ed., John Wiley & Sons, New York, 454 pp, 1972.

Garstka, Walter U., "Calcium Content of Connecticut Forest Litter", Jour. of Forestry, vol. XXX, no. 4, pp 396-405, April, 1932.

Gibbs, H. J., and J. P. Bara, "Predicting Surface Subsidence from Basic Soil Tests", Field Testing of Soils, ASTM STP 322, pp 231-246, 1962.

Holtan, Heggie N., Charles B. England, and Donald E. Whelan, "Hydrologic Characteristics of Soil Types", Jour. Irrigation and Drainage Div., Proceedings ASCE, pp 33-41, Sept. 1967.

Holtz, Wesley G., "Soil as an Engineering Material", A Water Resources Tech. Pub., No. 17, Bur. of Reclamation, USDI, 45 pp, 1969.

"Irrigation of Agricultural Lands", ed. by R. M. Hagan, H. R. Haise, T. W. Edminster, and R. C. Dinauer, No. 11 in the Agronomy Series, 13 sections containing 62 chapters written by 122 contributors. Amer. Society of Agronomy, Madison, Wis., 1180 pp., 1967.

183

Likens, Gene E., F. Herbert Bormann, Robert S. Pierce, John S. Eaton, and Noye M. Johnson, "Biogeochemistry of a Forested Ecosystem", Springer-Verlag, New York, 1977.

Lutz, Harold J., and Robert F. Chandler, Jr., "Forest Soils", John Wiley and Sons, Inc., New York, 514 pp, 1946.

Maletic, John and T. B. Hutchings, "Selection and Classification of Irrigable Land", Chapt. 10 in Irrigation of Agricultural Lands, ed. by R. M. Hagan, H. R. Haise, T. W. Edminster, and R. C. Dinauer, Amer. Soc. of Agronomy Madison, Wis., pp 125-173, 1967.

"Soil Survey Manual", Soil Survey Staff, Bureau of Plant Industry, Soils and Agricultural Engineering, USDA Handbook No. 18, 503 pp, Govt. Printing Office, Aug. 1951.

"Soil Taxonomy", A basic system of soil classification for making and interpreting soil surveys, Soil Survey Staff, Soil Conservation Service, USDA, Agri. Handbook No. 436, $9\frac{1}{2}$ x $11\frac{1}{4}$ inches, 754 pp, Govt. Printing Office, Dec. 1975.

"Soils and Men", Yearbook of Agriculture, 1938, Govt. Printing Office, 1232 pp, 1938.

Terzaghi, Karl, "Theoretical Soil Mechanics", John Wiley and Sons, New York, 510 pp, 1943.

Terzaghi, Karl, and Ralph B. Peck, "Soil Mechanics in Engineering Practice", 2nd ed., corrected printing, John Wiley and Sons Inc., New York, 729 pp, March, 1968.

Thorne, D. W., and H. B. Peterson, "Irrigated Soils", Their Fertility and Management, The Blakiston Co., Philadelphia and Toronto, 288 pp, 1949.

Tschebotarioff, Gregory P., "Foundations, Retaining and Earth Structures", (Art of design and construction and its scientific basis in soil mechanics), McGraw-Hill Book Co., New York, 2nd ed., 642 pp, 1973.

Ugolini, F. C., H. Dawson, and J. Zachara, "Direct Evidence of Particle Migration in the Soil Solution of a Podzol", Science, vol. 198, no. 4317, pp 603-605, Nov. 11, 1977.

Waksman, Selman A., "Microbes and the Survival of Man on Earth" Agri. Science Review, vol. 4, no. 2, pp 1-14, 2nd quarter, 1966.

Waksman, Selman A., "Humus; Origin, Chemical Composition & Importance in Nature", Williams Wilkins & Co., Baltimore, 1st ed., 494 pp, Jan. 1936. (2nd edition 1938).

Initially infiltration occurs at that instant when rainfall or snowmelt percolates directly into the soil or when
water ceases to be a flow in a continuous phase over a surface
and percolates into the soil.

Although the concept of infiltration as being a process
describing the entrance of water into the surface of the soil
and its movement downward to the groundwater is simple, in nature it is hydrodynamically extremely complex.  Percolating
water is not open-channel flow.  Among the factors affecting
infiltration are:  (a) soil texture, (b) soil structure, (c)
the initial moisture content of the soil at the beginning of a
rainstorm, (d) the distribution of dissimilar moisture contents
in a soil profile due to penetration by roots, (e) turbidity of
the water, (f) the alkalinity of the soil, (g) the presence or
absence of frost, (h) the soil temperature and the water temperature, (i) the distribution of intensities  for a particular
rainstorm, (j) duration of the rainstorm, (k) hydrophobic coatings on soil particles, and (l) entrapped air.

Many of these factors are interrelated.  For example, the
presence or absence of forest litter can exert a major influence on the infiltration characteristics of a soil of a certain
texture.  Soil structure is related to a very great extent to
the type of organic matter incorporated in the soil and to the
maturity of the soil profile.  The initial soil moisture content at the beginning of a storm may have an important influence on the infiltration.  Land-use treatments can influence to
a great extent the behavior of a drainage basin under average
conditions but they have practically no effect under extreme
rainfall excess conditions.

A condensed review of infiltration is given by Bruce and
Clark (1966) on pages 38-44 in which previous work is quoted
giving the results of infiltration measurements of an eroded
Marshall silt loam.  This soil had an infiltration rate after
90 minutes of 1.34 inches per hour with an alfalfa cover; 0.82
inch per hour with a crop of oats; and 0.30 inch per hour for a
bare, cultivated soil.

Kittredge (1948) on his page 207 presents a tabulation of
data from Rowe (1941) of a decrease in infiltration, as shown
in Table 35-1, in an annually burned sandy clay loam in the
foothills of the Sierra Nevadas as the relative wetness increased from below the wilting point to above field capacity.

Table 35-1   Infiltration in Relation to Relative Wetness

| Relative wetness, percent of field capacity | 20 | 40 | 60 | 80 | 100 | 120 |
|---|---|---|---|---|---|---|
| Infiltration, in/hr | 0.91 | 0.43 | 0.26 | 0.17 | 0.11 | 0.08 |

An investigation by Auten (1934) of infiltration on a cherty silt loam in Arkansas is summarized by Kittredge (1948) on his page 207. This summary is given in Table 35-2.

Table 35-2   Infiltration in Relation to Land Use

| Cover | Relative Infiltration |
|---|---|
| Oak  . . . . . . . . . . . . . . . | 100 |
| Old field pine . . . . . . . . . . . | 95 |
| Oak, burned  . . . . . . . . . . . | 25 |
| Open pasture . . . . . . . . . . . | 22 |

Infiltration can be determined in several ways. One is by direct measurement by using infiltrometers some of which include rainfall simulators. Another is by analysis of the hydrograph. Dortignac and Love (1961) describe the result of infiltration experiments conducted at the Manitou Experimental Forest, Colorado, with the so-called "Rocky Mountain Infiltrometer", a photograph of which appears on page 11 of this reference. Musgrave and Holton (1964) give a very comprehensive discussion of infiltration. They discuss three types of infiltrometers and three methods of hydrograph analyses to estimate infiltration.

Experience has shown that infiltrometers do not yield quantitative information on either rates or amounts of infiltration. In a number of instances an amount of water exceeding the annual rainfall has been supplied by infiltrometers without producing any runoff whereas the drainage basin has behaved otherwise. The infiltrometers have performed a very useful purpose in yielding data for qualitative comparisons of various soil surfaces and land use treatments.

In working with actual drainage basins, infiltration must be computed from hydrograph analyses. In addition to the discussion of infiltration by Musgrave and Holtan various aspects of infiltration are discussed in Sections 6, 10, 13, 20, and 22 in the Handbook of Applied Hydrology (1964), the volume in which the Musgrave and Holtan reference is to be found.

In hydrology a basic relationship was that stated by Horton (1940). He was interested in ascertaining the time at which a drainage basin would become so saturated that all subsequent rainfall would become runoff. The hyetograph would be converted into a hydrograph.

186

Horton described three rates of infiltration: ($f_o$) the initial infiltration rate in inches per hour at the beginning of the rainfall; ($f$) the infiltration rate in inches per hour at any time; and ($f_c$) the ultimate slowest constant value of infiltration in inches per hour as controlled by the least permeable layer.

A complex mathematical expression including the three infiltration rates is given in Horton's article (1940). Although each investigator selects his own symbols and definitions, Horton's concepts apply in all studies of infiltration.

There is an extensive literature on infiltration. Much of the laboratory work on percolation columns, most of the infiltrometer work, and a great deal of the very recent highly mathematical treatment of the infiltration concept add to our philosphical knowledge of the infiltration process but they are not a substitute for hydrograph analysis of a particular drainage basin. Analyses of the hydrograph yield a workable value of Horton's $f_c$ which is an integrated expression of the hydrologic interaction of a great complexity of characteristics of a particular drainage basin.

Holtan, England, and Allen (1967) propose a mathematical model " . . . . . . for computing infiltration during intermittent rainfall based upon readily available information on soils and vegetation. The model is adapted to long-term soil-moisture accounting and to the computation of areal and temporal distributions of rainfall excess during a storm in sequences compatible with the hydraulics of overland flow."

Scholl (1971) found that fresh or decomposing organic matter in stands of Utah Juniper greatly increased resistance to wetting of a soil derived from basaltic parent material.

A mathematical analysis of vertical infiltration in dry soil is presented by Brutsaert (1977). He includes expressions for soil water diffusivity and capillary conductivity. Brutsaert concludes that his new infiltration equations are valid not only for short but also for longer times of infiltration.

Fok (1970) presents an algebraic formula based upon Darcy's Law describing a one-dimensional infiltration into layered soils. Soil variability criteria for input parameters in studying models of hydraulic conductivity over a watershed are treated mathematically by Rogowski (1972).

Philip (1957) compared the results of several infiltration equations with data for the Yolo light clay and concluded that his algebraic equation gave the most realistic results.

Morel-Seytoux and Khanji (1974) discuss the importance of the effective capillary head and the viscous correction factor as a function of initial water constant. Based upon mathematical analyses they conclude that these two factors yield both simple and accurate equations for use by the hydrologist.

Bouwer (1976) discussed the situation where a lower horizon is more permeable than horizons near the surface. Such a soil may not become wetted completely throughout if gravity removes water from the lower horizon more rapidly than the infiltration intake, as shown in his mathematical analyses. This is a practical problem in the application of water in irrigation.

In his investigation of the mathematical analyses of data observed in a laboratory model of infiltration into a horizontal sand column, Poulovassilis (1977) found that there were considerable discrepancies possibly introduced by non-Darcian flows. He discusses previous investigations on this subject which bears a practical relationship to canal seepage losses, drainage and irrigation of land, and surface water - ground water interrelationships.

Thorp and Gamble (1972) used deuterium oxide ($D_2O$) as a tracer in studying the movement of water on several soils in Wayne County, Indiana. They found very close relationships between water levels, relative moisture content of the soil as determined by Bouyoucos electrical resistance blocks, and periods of transpiration in a forest. They traced downslope movement of water underground which took 3 weeks to move a maximum distance of 20 feet.

## Problem Assignment  - Infiltration and Percolation

Perform the experiments outlined by Harrold (1963) on water intake. Repeat these experiments with the introduction of a more permeable lower-lying layer as described by Bouwer (1976). Tabulate all data and analyze and interpret your results.

## References

Auten, J. T., "The Effect of Forest Burning and Pasturing in the Ozarks on the Water Absorption of Forest Soils", Central States Forest Experiment Sta. Note 16, U.S. Forest Service, 1934.

Bouwer, Herman, "Infiltration into Increasingly Permeable Soils", Jour. Irrigation and Drainage Div., Proceedings ASCE, pp 127-136, vol. 102, no. IR1, March, 1976.

Bruce, J. P., and R. H. Clark, "Introduction to Hydrometeor-
    olgy", Pergamon Press, London, New York, Toronto, paper-
    back, printed in Great Britain, 319 pp, 1966.

Brutsaert, Wilfried, "Vertical Infiltration in Dry Soil",
    Water Resources Research, vol. 13, no. 2, pp 363-368,
    Apr. 1977.

Dortignac, E. J., and L. D. Love, "Infiltration Studies on
    Ponderosa Pine Ranges of Colorado", Rocky Mt. Forest and
    Range Exp. Station Paper No. 59, U.S. Forest Service,
    Fort Collins, Colo., June, 1961.

Fok, Yu-Si, "One Dimensional Infiltration into Layered Soils",
    Jour. Irrigation and Drainage Div., Proceedings, ASCE,
    No. 7343 - IR2, pp 121-129, June, 1970.

Harrold, Lloyd L., "Water Intake by Soil - Experiments for High
    School Students", Misc. Publication No. 925, ARS, U.S.
    Dept. of Agriculture, 10 pp, Aug. 1963.

Holtan, H. N., C. B. England, and W. H. Allen, Jr., "Hydrologic
    Capacities of Soils in Watershed Engineering", Proceedings
    International Symposium, Sept. 6-8, 1967, Fort Collins,
    Colo., vol. 1, pp 218-226, June, 1967.

Horton, R. E., "An Approach Toward a Physical Interpretation of
    Infiltration-Capacity", Proceedings Soil Science Society
    of America, 5:399-418, 1940.

Kittredge, Joseph, "Forest Influences", McGraw-Hill Book Co.,
    New York, 394 pp, 1948.

Morel-Seytoux, H. J., and J. Khanji, "Derivation of an Equation
    of Infiltration", Water Resources Research, vol. 10, no. 4
    pp 795-800, Aug. 1974.

Musgrave, G. W., and H. N. Holtan, "Infiltration", Sec. 12,
    Handbook of Applied Hydrology, Ven Te Chow, ed-in-chief,
    McGraw-Hill Book Co., New York, 1964.

Philip, J. R., "The Theory of Infiltration: 4. Sorptivity and
    Algebraic Infiltration Equations", Soil Science,
    84:257-264, 1957.

Poulovassilis, A., "Flow Characteristics During Infiltration
    Into a Horizontal Sand Column", Water Resources Research,
    vol. 13, no. 2, pp 369-374, Apr. 1977.

Rogowski, A. S., "Watershed Physics: Soil Variability
    Criteria", Water Resources Research, vol. 8, no. 4,
    pp 1015-1023, Aug. 1972.

Rowe, P. B., "Some Factors of the Hydrology of the Sierra Nevada Foothills",Trans. American Geophysical Union, pp 90-100, Part 1, 1941.

Scholl, David G., "Soil Wettability in Utah Juniper Stands", Proceedings, Soil Science Society of America, vol. 35, no. 2, pp 344-345, Mar.-Apr., 1971.

Thorp, James, and Erling E. Gamble, "Annual Fluctuations of Water Levels in Soils of the Miami Catena, Wayne County, Indiana", Science Bulletin No. 5, Earlham College, Richmond, Ind., pub. by the Stanley W. Hayes Research Foundation, Inc., Richmond, Ind., Feb. 1972.

Topic 36                    Soil Moisture

Soil physicists, soil technologists, forest-soil specialists, and engineers who use soil as a material have developed a large number of definitions of use to their professional endeavors. The hydrologist is concerned with soils under field conditions. A brief review of definitions of various soil characteristics as used with reference to plant-soil relationships is given by Hewlett and Nutter (1969) in their Chapter 5. A detailed discussion of soil-water relationships is given by Kirkham (1964) in his pages 5-9 to 5-19.

"Soil Survey Laboratory Data and Descriptions of Some Soils of the New England States" (1968) is an example of a series of publications which contain detailed information for specific soil types on particle size distribution, textural class, organic matter, electrical conductivity, moisture tensions, cation exchange capacity, detailed descriptions of characteristic profiles, together with moisture percentage at saturation. Although this information may be of great value to soil scientists, agronomists, ecologists, and silviculturists, the hydrologist is usually concerned with the integrated response of the soil mantle on a drainage basin to the precipitation which has fallen upon it.

A very important characteristic of a soil is its field capacity which can be defined as the amount of water based on the total volume of the moist soil retained in a previously saturated soil after it has been allowed to drain two or three days. It is to be noted that the field capacity is based on the total volume of the soil when equilibrium has been reached between the water-retentive forces of the soil and the force of gravity. In hydrologic usage, field capacity is not based upon oven-dry weight or bulk density.

In hydrology, field capacity is expressed in inches depth of water equivalent. Infiltration rates are expressed in inches per hour. The use of this unit makes it possible to consider rainfall, soil moisture, infiltration, and runoff as expressions of the behavior of drainage basins.

Most cultivated crops and food plants are mesophytes (see Topic 46), an ecological class of plants which require that at all times soil moisture be available to their root systems. When soil moisture is no longer available the plant first wilts and if the deficiency persists the plant dies. Figure 36-1 from the "Handbook on Soils" (1961), shows the water available for plant growth in inches per foot of soil for different textured soils.

191

The amount of water available for plant growth having a root depth of 4 feet may be only about 7 to 8 inches under the most favorable humid conditions.

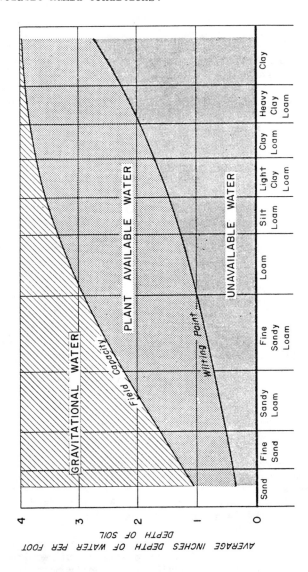

Figure 36-1   Typical Water Characteristics of Different-Textured Soils.  (Forest Service, USDA, 1961)

Another presentation of the interrelationships of soil texture, weight, and moisture properties of five broad physical classes of soils, is given in Figure 36-2 taken from the

"Handbook of Soils" (1961).

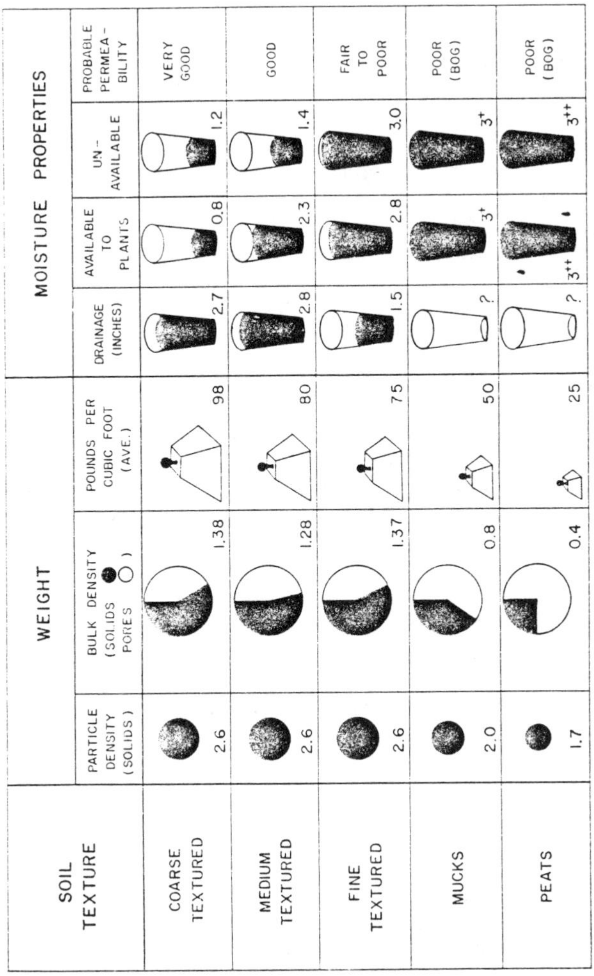


Figure 36-2 Diagrammatic Presentation of Some of the Average Weights and Moisture Properties of Soils of Different Textures. (Forest Service, USDA, 1961)

The food supply for the World's population, not only for humans but also for land-based animals, depends on the surprisingly small amount of water retained by the soil between field moisture capacity and the wilting point. Irrigation practices in arid regions (see Topics 1 and 2) from ancient times served, as they do now, to maintain soil moisture favorable for food production in ecologically unsuitable areas so that crops could be grown without dependence upon natural precipitation.

Only in the temperate zones is there a combination of soil characteristics, seasonal progression of air temperatures, and favorable distribution of precipitation to produce food in sufficient abundance to sustain life throughout the year with an excess to transport for consumption in less productive regions.

Schematic diagrams of the relationships between a plant's root and the soil-water complex are shown in Figure 36-3 from the "Handbook on Soils" (1961). Under conditions A and B the soil is full of water at or above field capacity and evapo-transpirational losses can be fully supplied as demanded by the energy-atmosphere conditions (See Topic 40).

Under condition C the root is extracting water together with dissolved mineral nutrients while growth continues. As the water films become thinner the forces holding the water films to the soil particles increase and the roots extract water with increasing difficulty. Although plants under such moisture stress may survive and remain turgid, crop yield is sharply reduced.

Under condition D, the root can no longer extract water. Since evapotranspirational demands must be met the water comes from the plant tissues. As the cells lose turgidity, like a deflating baloon, the plant structures, first the leaves and then the stems, wilt having lost mechanical stiffness. Unless soil water is increased immediately the cell sap becomes so concentrated as to precipitate the proteins and the plant dies. Additional water supply will not resuscitate that plant.

Carson (1969) has included a number of informative sketches in his Chapter on soil moisture in which he refers to the effects of denudation on soil moisture. He also presents mathematical equations of pore-water pressure in a soil mass in relation to the stability of soil on slopes.

Under the sponsorship of the International Hydrological Decade (IHD) 1965-1974, five international organizations, such as FAO, IAEA, UNESCO, WMO, and AIHS-IASH, attended a Symposium "Water in the Unsaturated Zone", the Proceedings of which were published in 1969.

Schmugge, Meneely, Rango, and Neff (1977) describe the results of the use of a study of near-surface soil moisture variations as determined by satellite observations of micro-wave brightness at the 1.55 cm wavelength. Their Figure 1, page 267, shows the inverse relationship between microwave brightness temperature ($T_B$) and soil moisture in the top centimeter of soil. The soil moisture is expressed as a percentage of field capacity. Since plant growth absorbs this microwave these observations are best suited to bare soil conditions just before the planting season.

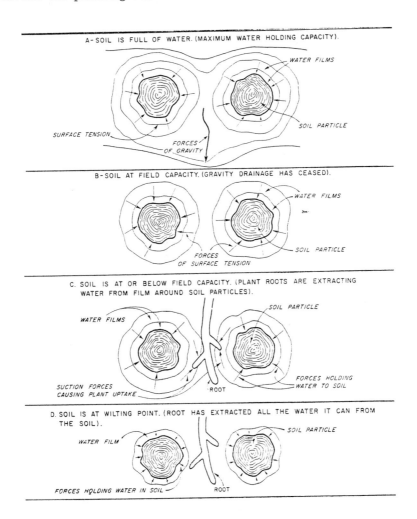

Figure 36-3   Schematic Diagrams of Soil-Moisture Relationships where the root is in contact with water films in the interstices of a soil.   (Forest Service, USDA, 1961)

# References

Carson, M. A., "Soil Moisture", in Water, Earth and Man, ed. by
    R. J. Chorley, pp 185-195, Methuen & Co. Ltd., Great
    Britain, 1969.

"Handbook on Soils", Part 2512.5, Category 2 Handbook, Forest
    Service, USDA, June, 1961 (with subsequent amendments).

Hewlett, John D., and Wade L. Nutter, "An Outline of Forest
    Hydrology", Univ. of Georgia Press, Athens, 1969.

Kirkham, Don, "Soil Physics", Section 5, Handbook of Applied
    Hydrology, Ven Te Chow, ed-in-chief, McGraw-Hill Book Co.,
    New York, 1964.

Schmugge, T. J., J. M. Meneely, A. Rango, and R. Neff,
    "Satellite Microwave Observations of Soil Moisture
    Variations", Water Resources Bulletin, vol. 13, no. 2,
    pp 265-281, April, 1977.

"Soil Survey Laboratory Data and Descriptions for Some Soils
    of . . . . New England States", Soil Survey Investigations
    Report No. 20, Soil Conservation Service, USDA, in cooper-
    ation with Connecticut (Storrs), Maine, Massachusetts,
    New Hampshire, Rhode Island, and Vermont Agricultural Exp.
    Stations, Govt. Printing Office, 1968.

"Water in the Unsaturated Zone", Proceedings of the Wageningen
    Symposium, ed. by P. E. Rijtema and H. Wassink, 2 vol.
    totalling 995 pages, pub. by the International Assn. of
    Scientific Hydrology, Braamstraat 61, Gentbrugge, and by
    UNESCO, Place de Fontenoy, 75 Paris-7[e], 1969.

Topic 37          Plots and Lysimeters

Field plots have been in extensive use in research in
Agronomy and in Forestry for a long time. The fertilizer
treatment plots at Pennsylvania State University are over a
hundred years old. There is an extensive literature dealing
with the use of plots in forest hydrology research which will
be discussed in subsequent topics. In hydrology a plot is an
area within a drainage basin separated by artificial watersheds
to delineate a small fraction of the drainage area primarily to
permit the measurement of runoff. A comprehensive discussion
of hydrologic plot studies is given by Holtan and Minshall
(1968). Instrumentation and techniques dealing with agronomic
and land-use plots are described in detail by Holtan, Minshall,
and Harrold (1962). Harrold, Brakensiek, McGuinness, Amerman,
and Dreibelbis (1962) report upon experiments dealing with the
influence of land use and treatment on the hydrology of small
watersheds, including woodland watersheds, in Ohio.

The dissimilarities in the distribution of runoff between
surface, interflow, and groundwater components of the hydrograph of runoff from the sample plot as compared to the hydrograph from a natural drainage basin, are so great as to cast
serious doubt on the usefulness of sample plots in our understanding of the hydrology of natural drainage basins.

The lysimeter can be looked upon as a special type of
three-dimensional segregated segment of a drainage basin.
Lysimeters are classified according to the construction and
soil content as follows: (a) the monolith or undisturbed soil
block; (b) the Ebermayer, or unconfined; and (c) the filled-in
lysimeter. Beginning with the early 1930's there was a great
resurgence of interest in hydrologic lysimeters.

According to Kohnke, Dreibelbis, and Davidson (1940) the
first report on a lysimeter investigation was that of
Philippe De la Hire, who initiated in 1688 at Runges near
Paris, France, a lysimeter investigation in which he endeavored
to determine the origin of springs. John Dalton, the father of
the atomic theory and the scientist who first expressed the
vapor pressure difference found in evaporation equations, installed a lysimeter near Manchester, England, in 1796. Dalton's
lysimeter was the first with a runoff provision. Ebermayer,
who could be considered one of the first known forest hydrologists, carried out lysimeter studies in relation to Bavarian
forests in 1879.

The first lysimeter in the United States was built by
Sturtevant in 1875 on a farm near Framingham, Massachusetts.
Dr. H. A. Lunt (1937) built in 1932 a small lysimeter

installation at New Haven, Connecticut.

The record is clear that hydrologists invented the
lysimeter. With the advent of chemical fertilizers the agronomists and soil scientists saw the advantages of the lysimeter
technique. Such extensive use has been made of lysimeters in
soil fertility studies that one definition of a lysimeter is:
". . . . . a device for measuring the percolation of water
through soils and determining the soluble constituents removed
in the drainage." (Webster's 1971, page 1351).

Coleman and Hamilton (1947) describe the series of lysimeters built by the U.S. Forest Service at the San Dimas Experimental Forest near Glendora, California. The author designed
the large lysimeter installation and some of the galvanized
iron, filled-in lysimeters at Tanbark Flats of the San Dimas
Experimental Forest. The large lysimeters consist of an alignment of 26 contiguous concrete tanks, each 10.5 feet wide by
20.8 feet long and 6 feet deep. They were back-filled with a
soil rendered extremely uniform with a complex digging-out and
replacement procedure. Each of the large lysimeters holds 64
tons dry weight of the uniform soil.

The author's objective for which the lysimeters were
designed, was to organize a long-term research project in
Forest Soils for the purpose of evaluating the physical, chemical, structural, and hydrologic changes resulting from the
incorporation of both surface and subsurface forest litter of
different species of chaparral shrubs into an originally uniform soil. With the passing of time and changes of personnel
and administrations, the original objective was lost so that
the San Dimas lysimeters became a strictly hydrologic
installation.

Patric (1961) reported that the response of perennial
plants growing in a confined soil mass resulted in a development of the plant different from that attained under unrestric-
ted conditions, so that the evapotranspirational losses observed, especially over long periods for trees, did not appear
to be reasonable in the light of other experiments.

Some of the San Dimas lysimeters were planted to Coulter
Pine and native grasses. Operation of these lysimeters ceased
in 1960 following a wildfire. Patric (1974) has prepared an
informative monograph on these lysimeters. His text is
supplemented by 15 pages of photographs and charts.

It was recognized by the author that back-filled lysimeters of whatever type they might be could hardly be considered
a sample of watershed. This led to the construction of the
monolith lysimeters at the North Appalachian Experimental
Watershed of the U.S. Dept. of Agriculture near Coshocton,

Ohio. These monolith lysimeters have horizontal projected dimensions of 6.22 feet by 14 feet with a depth of 8 feet to the top of the percolation sieves. The whole soil profile is included with about 2 feet of bedrock. The weight of each lysimeter is about 130,000 pounds. The scales have an accuracy of 5 pounds which approximates the weight of 0.01 inch of precipitation over the area. Figure 37-1 taken from Kohnke, Dreibelbis, and Davidson (1940) is a sketch of a Coshocton weighing lysimeter.

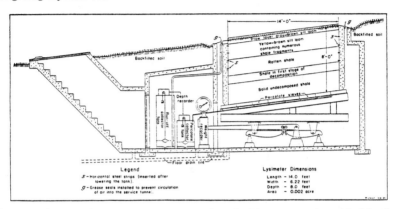

Figure 37-1  Schematic cross-sectional diagram.  A soil-block
    lysimeter with self-recording weighing mechanism.
    (Garstka, 1937 and Kohnke, Dreibelbis, 1940).

The design and the construction technique are described by Garstka (1937). Reports on the research accomplished by the monolith lysimeters were prepared by Harrold and Dreibelbis (1951) and (1967). References to the Coshocton monolith lysimeters appear in numerous other reports emanating from the North Appalachian Experimental Watershed now being operated by the Agricultural Research Service of the U.S. Dept. of Agriculture.

An outgrowth of the Coshocton lysimeters is the installation built by the University of California at Davis, California, as described by Pruitt (1962). The Coshocton and Davis lysimeter installations have yielded data otherwise unobtainable on evapotranspiration losses.

Interest continues world-wide in the use of lysimeters. Romanov (1962) discusses on page 27 the soil-water concept underlying the design of a lysimeter in which an attempt is made to maintain a water level, in a weighing lysimeter, to be hydrologically equivalent to but not the same as the water level in the surrounding soil so that realistic evapotranspiration observations may be made.

Sartz (1963) found that evapotranspiration accounted for

about three-fourths of the precipitation in the lysimeter installations of the Lake States Forest Experiment Station at
La Crosse, Wisconsin. This figure agrees well with other
studies made at La Crosse and with estimates made for Madison,
Wisconsin. The total water yield from the Forest Service lysimeters compared favorably with streamflow records from nearby watersheds. The lysimeters described by Sartz were operated from 1934 to 1942. Each of the 10 lysimeters had the
dimensions 10 feet by 20 feet by 4 feet deep. The undisturbed
soil monoliths were cut from nearby borrow pits and moved into
the lysimeters. Ninety monoliths, each weighing 500 pounds,
were required for each lysimeter.

Barry (1969) includes on page 179 a sketch of the Hancock,
Wisconsin, lysimeters in which the soil block floats in a
tank of water.

An ingenious concept is that of the Base Rock in-place
lysimeters at the Sierra Ancha Experimental Watershed of the
U.S. Forest Service near Globe, Arizona, as described by Rich
(1959). The walls of these lysimeters extend to an impervious
bedrock which serves as the bottom of the 3 lysimeters.

Pruitt, von Oettingen, and Morgan (1972) describe the
results from their weighing-lysimeter installation which on
most days is so sensitive that it is able to measure daily
evapotranspiration with an accuracy of plus or minus one
percent. They were able to determine evapotranspiration frequencies for Central California.

Nixon, Lawless, and Richardson (1972), also using weighing
lysimeters, determined frequency distribution of daily evapotranspiration for the Coastal regions of California.

Scholl and Hibbert (1973) determined evapotranspiration at
a sloping back-filled lysimeter 200.5 feet long, 7.0 feet deep,
and 4.6 feet wide at a slope of 38 percent. Two experiments
were performed. In the first phase a vertical unsaturated
Darcy equation analysis was made when the lysimeter was sealed
with a plastic sheet to eliminate evapotranspiration. In the
second phase evapotranspiration was determined following the
establishment of grass.

The root ball of a Douglas fir tree 28 m (91.8 ft.) high
was encased in-place in a steel container to serve, with a
hydraulic mechanism, as a weighing lysimeter. The construction
in 1971, instrumentation, and initial results of this facility
are described by Fritschen, Cox, and Kinerson (1973). The
total weight of this lysimeter is 28,900 kg (63,000 pounds) at
field-moisture capacity. The sensitivity of this system is
630 grams, which is equivalent to a depth of 0.06 mm (0.002
inch) of water for the lysimeter under still-air conditions.

This lysimeter is in the Cedar River watershed near Seattle, Washington.

The unprecedented sensitivity of this lysimeter made it possible to measure the dew on 2 clear days in May, 1972. According to Fritschen and Doraiswamy (1973) dew amounted to 15 percent and 20 percent of the evaporation. This indicates the importance of dew in the hydrologic balance of Douglas fir forests in the Northwest.

Fritschen, Hsia, and Doraiswamy (1977) found, when analyzing the results of the 1972, 1973, and 1974 summer and fall seasons, that interception was very important at this 28-meter Douglas fir weighing lysimeter. The crown projection at the soil surface of this tree is 30.98 $m^2$ (333.5 sq. ft.) whereas the lysimeter area is 10.5 $m^2$ (113 sq. ft). The authors report in their Table 1 evapotranspiration losses by months in millimeters per unit area of crown projection.

Young, Evans, and Sammis (1975) describe the construction of a 4-meter (13 ft. 4 in.) diameter by 1.0 meter ( 3 ft. 3 in) deep monolith weighing lysimeter constructed around the root ball of a 6-foot high creosote bush (Larrea divaricatta). This bush was growing in the semi-desert near Tucson, Arizona. The total weight of the completed lysimeter is 22,000 kilograms (48,500 lbs). Problems were encountered with the differential pressure hydraulic weighing system.

Progress in developing an electronic transducer system which is not sensitive to temperature or wind pressure disturbances and which in case of failure of an individual strain gage can be easily repaired without collapse of the lysimeter as a whole, is reported by Young, Evans, Sammis, and Constant (1976). The electronic transduces system has a sensitivity of detecting a change of 0.04 mm of water.

References

Parry, R. G., "Evaporation and Transpiration", pp 169-184 in Water, Earth, and Man, ed. by Richard J. Chorley, Methuen and Co. Ltd., Great Britain, 1969.

Coleman, E. A., and E. L. Hamilton, "The San Dimas Lysimeters: Instruments for Evaluating the Water Economy of Chaparral Vegetation, Part 1, The Lysimeter Installation and Research Program", pp 1-14, Calif. Forest and Range Exp. Station, Berkeley, Calif., Forest Research Note No. 47, 33 pp, Dec. 1947.

Fritschen, Leo J., Lloyd Cox, and Russell Kinerson, "A 28-Meter Douglas-fir in a Weighing Lysimeter", Forest Science, vol 19, no. 4, pp 256-261, Dec. 1973.

Fritschen, Leo J., and Paul Doraiswamy, "Dew: An Addition to the Hydrologic Balance of Douglas Fir", Water Resources Research, vol. 9, no. 4, pp 891-894, Aug. 1973.

Fritschen, Leo J., Joe Hsia, and Paul Doraiswamy, "Evapotranspiration of a Douglas Fir Determined With a Weighing Lysimeter", Water Resources Research, vol. 13, no. 1, pp 145-148, Feb. 1977.

Garstka, Walter U., "Design of Automatic-Recording In-Place Lysimeters Near Coshocton, Ohio", Soil Science of America, Proceedings of 1937, pp 555-559, 1937.

Harrold, L. L., and F. R. Dreibelbis, "Agricultural Hydrology as Evaluated by Monolith Lysimeters", Tech.Bulletin No. 1050, Soil Conservation Service, USDA, in coop. with Ohio Agri. Exp. Station, 149 pp, Washington, D.C., Dec. 1951.

Harrold, L. L., D. L. Brakensiek, J. L. McGuinness, C. R. Amerman, and F. R. Dreibelbis, "Influence of Land Use and Treatment on the Hydrology of Small Watersheds at Coshocton, Ohio, 1938-1957", USDA Tech. Bulletin No. 1256, Jan. 1962.

Harrold, L. L., and F. R. Dreibelbis, "Evaluation of Agricultural Hydrology by Monolith Lysimeters 1956-62", USDA in coop. with Ohio Agri. Research and Development Center, Tech. Bulletin No. 1367, 123 pp, Jan. 1967.

Holtan, H. N., N. E. Minshall, and L. L. Harrold, "Field Manual for Research in Agricultural Hydrology", USDA Handbook 224, 1962.

Holtan, H. N., and N. E. Minshall, "Plot Samples of Watershed Hydrology", Agri. Research Service, USDA, Pub. ARS 41-133, Beltsville, Md., Jan. 1968.

Kohnke, Helmut, F. R. Dreibelbis, and J. M. Davidson, "A Survey and Discussion of Lysimeters and a Bibliography on Their Construction and Performance", USDA Misc. Publication No. 372, 68 pp, May, 1940.

Lunt, Herbert A., "Forest Lysimeter Studies Under Red Pine", Connecticut Agri. Exp. Station, New Haven, Bulletin 394, June, 1937.

Nixon, Paul R., G. Paul Lawless, and Gary V. Richardson, "Coastal California Evapotranspiration Frequencies", pp 185-191, Jour. Irrigation & Drainage Div., Proceedings ASCE, June, 1972.

Patric, James H., "A Forester Looks at Lysimeters", Jour. of Forestry, vol. 59, no. 12, pp 889-893, Dec. 1961.

Patric, James H., "Water Relations of Some Lysimeter-Grown Wildland Plants in Southern California", Northeastern Forest Experiment Station, Forest Service, USDA, Upper Darby, Pa., 117 pp plus 15 pp of charts and photographs, 1974.

Pruitt, W. O., "Correlation of Climatological Data with Water Requirements of Crops", Dept. of Irrigation, Univ. of Calif., Berkeley, Calif., Aug. 1962.

Pruitt, W. O., S. von Oettingen, and D. L. Morgan, "Central California Evapotranspiration Frequencies", Jour. of Irrigation and Drainage Div., Proceedings, ASCE, pp 177-184, June, 1972.

Rich, L. R., "Hydrologic Research Using Lysimeters of Undisturbed Soil Blocks", International Assoc. Sci. Hydrology, Symposium of Hannoversch-Munden, pub. 49, 2:139-145, Sept. 1959.

Romanov, V. V., ""Evaporation from Bogs in the European Territory of the USSR", State Hydrological Institute, Leningrad 1962, trans. by N. Kaner, Israel Program for Scientific Translations, Jerusalem, 1968, Trans. No. TT-67-51293, available from Clearinghouse for Federal Scientific and Tech. Information, U.S. Dept. of Commerce, Springfield, Va., 22151.

Sartz, Richard S., "Water Yield and Soil Loss from Soil-Block Lysimeters Planted to Small Trees and Other Crops", Research Paper LS-6, Lake States Forest Exp. Station, Forest Service, USDA, Dec. 1963.

Scholl, David G., and Alden R. Hibbert, "Unsaturated Flow Properties Used to Predict Outflow and Evapotranspiration from a Sloping Lysimeter", Water Resources Research, vol.9 no. 6, pp 1645-1655, Dec. 1973.

"Webster's Third New International Dictionary of the English Language - Unabridged", Philip Babcock Gove, ed-in-chief, G. C. Merriam Co., 1971.

Young, D. W., D. D. Evans, and T. W. Sammis, "Measurement of Evapotranspiration with a Monolith Lysimeter", US/IBP Desert Biome Res. Memo 75-42. Utah State Univ., Logan,1975.

Young, D. W., D. D. Evans, T. W. Sammis, C. Constant, "Measurement of Evapotranspiration With a Monolity Lysimeter", US/IBP, Desert Biome Rpt. 76-34, Utah State Univ., 1976.

The earliest record of the tillage of the soil to produce
crops is lost in antiquity.  As discussed in Topics 1 and 2
management of soil and water pre-dates written history.
McDonald (1941) summarized the writings of early American soil
conservationists.  His publication refers to:  Jared Eliot,
1685-1763; J. Bartram, 1699-1777; Samuel Deane, 1733-1814;
Solomon Drown, 1753-1834; John Taylor, 1753-1824; John Lorain,
about 1764-1819; Isaac Hill, 1789-1851; Nicholas Sorsby, active
1844-1857; and, Edmund Ruffin, 1794-1865.

In the temperate regions most of the cultivated crop land
is in the brown earth soil zone (see Topic 34).  The structure
and the fertility and the soil-water relationships of the brown
earth were the result of the development of the soil profile
with its A and B horizons as a result of the forest growth.
When the first English colonists settled in the Chesapeake Bay
area in 1607 they began felling, and usually burning, the
forest.  Drawing upon the accumulation of nutrients and humus
the soil yielded good crops.  The early agriculturists and conservationists noted that before many years had passed the soils
grew lighter in color and that there was extensive erosion.
References to worn-out land appear in the literature in the
18th Century.  Long before the American Revolution many farmers
abandoned much land and cleared more forests.  According to
McDonald (1941, page 2) the early records in Massachusetts
indicate that most of the land near the coast was abandoned at
least once before 1800.

As discussed in Topic 47, Ecology, even-aged pure stands
of a single specie are extremely rare in nature.  The removal
of the forest growth brought to a standstill the ecological
cycle of the building up of the humus and enriching fertility
through the accumulation and storage of plant nutrients.  The
infiltration characteristics of the soil were changed radically
by the removal of the litter.  The tillage of crops and their
harvesting resulted in the removal of the organic matter from
the area and greatly reducing the formation of humus.  Clean-
cultivated, single-crop agriculture continues to have these de-
grading effects as is summarized in the comprehensive evaluation with 118 references prepared by Pimentel et al (1976).

"Washington, Jefferson, Lincoln, and Agriculture" (1937)
is a 102-page assembly of records, letters, and extracts from
speeches by the three Presidents all of whom were far ahead of
their times in their thinking about the problems of agriculture.
This publication includes the epoch-establishing agricultural
laws of 1862:  the Act signed on May 18, 1862 establishing the
Department of Agriculture; the Act signed on May 20, 1862 known
as the Homestead Act; and the Land-Grant College Act signed on

July 2, 1862. These three Acts were signed by President Lincoln.

The Traveling Exhibition Service of the Smithsonian Institution of Washington, D.C., prepared a bicentennial exhibition entitled, "American Agriculture: A Continuing Revolution", researched by Keith Melder (undated). This exhibition consisted of 45 panels each 30-inches by 40-inches. The following is extracted from the descriptions: 1776, about 90 percent of the American people lived off the land growing food and raw materials for clothing and other necessities; 1790, over 90 percent of the population worked in agriculture; 1820, 72 percent worked in agriculture; 1860, 58 percent; 1890, 43 percent; 1920, 27 percent; 1950, 12.2 percent; and in 1970, 4.6 percent worked in agriculture.

There are many reasons underlying the great reduction in the percentage of people working in agriculture. Among these can be listed the development of the plow and other tillage implements; the replacement of oxen with horses and, in turn, the replacement of horses with steam and then with internal-combustion-engine-powered tractors; expansion of farmland into the prairie followed by the development of irrigation; introduction of electricity, mechanization of poultry and livestock production; the revolution in plant breeding by hybrid crop plants; the development of synthetic chemical fertilizers; tremendous advances in biocides (see Topic 48); and the recent creation of new strains of high-nutrition and high-yield crops as part of the "Great Revolution".

According to Melder (undated) in 1960 the number of people fed by one farm worker was 26 and this increased to 47 people in 1970. A chief reason for this unparalleled efficiency in food production is the availability of energy. Tillage in the early colonial days was probably done with hand tools by women. Human muscle power is very low as analyzed by Krendel (1967) who presented equations for comparing power generated by man and animals. For a short burst of less than one second's duration a man may generate about 6 horsepower. Depending on age and other factors average human power production may amount to only 60 watts.

Subsequently oxen and then horses supplied muscle power. Manure was returned to the fields thereby replacing in part the organic matter needed to serve as the raw material for the formation of humus.

The following quotation is taken from Bartlett (1976) ". . . . A far more fundamental problem becomes apparent when one recognizes that modern agriculture is based on petroleum-powered machinery and on petroleum-based fertilizers. This is reflected in a definition of modern agriculture.

                    Modern agriculture
                    is the use of land
                    to convert petroleum
                    into food."
The above quotation follows Bartlett's discussion of the
history of the world production of crude oil which has increased at an exponential growth of 7.04 percent per year.

    Modern efficiency of food and fiber production would be
practically impossible to attain without extensive use of
biocides (see Topic 48) a great many of which are derived from
petroleum.

    Splinter (1977) said that the great productivity of our
Nation's food rests on the utilization of fossil fuels.  Of the
total energy expenditure in the United States 22 percent goes
for food and fiber production.  According to Splinter there can
be no return to muscle power, either man or animal, since the
work a man can do in a 10-hour day can be obtained from the
drawbar of a tractor for 2.8 cents worth of Diesel fuel priced
at 40 cents per gallon.  To reduce energy consumption Splinter
recommended spot planting instead of plow and disk planting,
reduction of energy requirements for pumping irrigation water
(see Topic 49) and development of alternative fuel sources from
agricultural and forestry products to replace fossil fuels.

    The increasing cost of petroleum has had a very adverse
effect on the standard of living of the developing nations.
Hammond (1977) describes a program which the Brazilian Government is organizing to produce ethyl alcohol.  Less than 2 percent of the land area of Brazil could produce enough fuel to
replace all imported oil.  Strabala (1977) reported that the
State of Colorado is contemplating the construction of an experimental "gasohol" plant in Northeastern Colorado to cost
about $25,000,000.  This would be one of four such plants under
consideration by the U.S. Department of Agriculture.  They
would produce alcohol from low quality or surplus farm products
for blending with gasoline.

    Concern about the balance between population and food
supply is not new.  Thomas R. Malthus, an English economist, in
his first essay on the subject, published in 1798, propounded the thought that population always increases to the
limits of the means of subsistence.  Malthusianism is described
by Webster (1971), "The doctrines of Malthus holding esp. that
population tends to increase at a faster rate than its means of
subsistence and that widespread poverty and degradation of the
lower classes inevitably result unless the population is pre-
ventively checked by moral restraint or positively checked esp.
by disease, famine, or war".

    Mechanization of agriculture, petrochemicals, and energy

from petroleum have changed food production from simple farming to industrial engineering but the basic concepts of Malthusianism remain unchallenged.

Brink, Densmore, and Hill (1977) review the problem of soil deterioration and growing world demand for food. They state that the average American uses about one ton of grain a year, 93 percent of which is utilized indirectly to raise cattle, hogs, and chickens which in turn supply the main nutritional protein sources, meat, milk, and eggs. They state on page 627 that the much-publicized grain sales to the Soviet Union in 1972 resulted from the decision of the Soviet Government to maintain a high level of meat production in spite of a poor cereal crop yield in the USSR. The United States and Canada are now the source of about 80 percent of the food and feed grains imported by the industrialized nations.

All of food production is based on the availability of water. Most cultivated crops are mesophytes (see Topic 46), plants which require that water be available to their root systems at all times. The hybrid plants and the new crops developed in the "Green Revolution" result in high yields only if the soil is adequately supplied with chemical fertilizers and if there is always adequate soil moisture.

The developing nations, most of which are located outside of the temperate zone, simply have not demonstrated the capability of producing food of the type and quantity needed to provide for even the minimal nutrition of their ever-expanding populations. In many of the tropical areas there was practiced in the past the prehistoric system of "shifting" or as it is known in the Philippines, "kaingan" agriculture. This is the same system used by the early colonists. An area of forest or native vegetation would be cleared, usually burned, and for a few years crops were grown on the ash elements released by burning with some fertility provided from the rapidly depleting humus. That area would then be abandoned and another area cleared. This procedure would be repeated in a never-ending cycle.

In many parts of the World under the pressure of increasing population attempts have been made to introduce temperate-zone agriculture with very limited success. In the meantime the population has been steadily growing.

Wittwer (1977) states that about half of the people of the World depend on subsistence agriculture and that 40 percent of the cultivated land of the World is in the hands of subsistence farmers. They live off the land and there is often limited initiative to produce food beyond their needs. Wittwer has prepared an assessment of technology in food production. Cereal grains listed in order of descending importance are:

rice, wheat, maize, sorghum, millett, barley, oats and rye. These are the most valuable food crops since they provide 60 percent of the calories and 50 percent of the protein consumed by man. Another 20 percent comes from the seed legumes: field beans, peanuts, chick peas, pigeon peas, soybeans, cowpeas, mung beans, and broad beans. Root and tuber crops are: potatoes, sweet potatoes, cassava and yams. The sugar crops are: sugar cane and sugar beets. Main tropical crops are bananas and coconuts. Among numerous other crops, fruits, vegetables and berries are grapes, tomatoes and the citrus fruits many of which are seldom reported in economic surveys. Rice, wheat, maize, and potatoes account for as much world total food tonnage as do all other crops combined.

The number of livestock is probably double the human population. Wittwer divides food resources from animals into two catagories: those derived from the ruminants, dairy cattle, beef cattle, water buffalo, sheep, goats, camels, llamas and alpacas; and the monogastrics, swine, poultry, rabbits, and guinea pigs. The ruminants are especially important since with their multiple stomachs they are able to digest cellulose found in grasses and forage plants. Swine and poultry consume many food products not directly edible by man although the diets are essentially similar. Livestock serve as a living food reservoir. For the world as a whole livestock and poultry provide about 25 percent of the protein and 10 percent of man's calorie requirements.

Although the proteins found in meat are considered essential to good nutrition the production of protein in the form of meat is very inefficient when it is realized that it takes about 11 pounds of grain consumed by an animal to produce one pound of meat. Therefore one obvious, but probably not universally acceptible solution at this time to the supply of food for humans would be to restrict the feeding of grain to animals.

Aquatic animals and fish provide about 5 percent of human protein needs according to Wittwer. Where the climate and hydrology are suitable fish production in ponds properly built and managed may yield from 100 to 300 pounds of fish per year for each acre of water surface. This yield is about equal to beef production from average improved grasslands according to the Soil Conservation Service publication, "Ponds for Water Supply and Recreation" (1971).

Othmer and Roels (1973) state that just one major ocean current upwelling (see Topic 42) of the Humboldt Current off the coast of Peru supplies one-fifth of the world's total fish harvest. They propose bringing up very large amounts of deep cold sea water with its high level of nutrients to make possible the practice of mariculture to produce oysters, clams, scallops, lobsters, and seaweed.

Development of biodegradable biocides is becoming a more urgent necessity not only in the technologically-advanced countries but especially in the developing countries. The tonnage of biocides used annually in the technologically-advanced countries is approaching the tonnage of synthetic chemical fertilizers used both of which are derived principally from petroleum.

The use of biocides is intimately related to food and fiber production (see Topic 38). Furtick (1977) summarized the loss of crop production from weeds in the technological advancement and in the developing countries. The adverse effect of weeds and pests on food and fiber production is enormous. Furtick lists the following factors which cause these losses: (a) direct competition for water, light, and nutrients; (b) loss of crop and livestock quality; (c) weeds serving as intermediate hosts for insects and diseases; (d) weeds reducing the value of land or preventing the best land use; (e) weeds increasing production costs especially where high fertility and water supply levels need to be maintained for the new high-yield crops.

Milner, Parpia, and Scrimshaw (1977) list as a priority of the UN University the control of post-harvest losses. Very little international effort has been expended on this problem the reduction of which could have a very great impact on the standard of living in many parts of the Earth. They give as an example that in the years 1953-54 rats in the Philippines were estimated to have consumed 90 percent of the rice, 50 percent of the maize, and 50 percent of the grain. They estimate that quantitative and qualitative food losses are estimated to be between 20 and 40 percent in developing countries the losses occurring during handling, storage, processing, distribution, and ultimate use. Additional instances of tremendous crop losses in Africa are reported on page 38 of "The Bugs are Coming" (1976).

Hendricks (1969) calls attention to the value of productive land and to the importance of water. The following is a quotation from page 74: "Sources of the water are near at hand for many humid regions. Distribution of water for occasional use is the real question - a solvable problem, but at a cost, much like rural electrification and telephone service. The flower bed in the city seldom wants for water though the crops on nearby farms are wilting.

"Water for irrigation in dry and desert regions is quite another matter. Here the source becomes important. Even with complete gathering, all the water of many regions would not be enough to supply the potentially arable land - for example, in

Spain, Israel, Central China, and the Colorado Basin of North America. The Salt River Valley of Arizona has a water deficit of more than 2 million acre-feet per year."

Schneider, with Mesirow (1977) have written a fascinating analysis of the interrelationships of climate, weather modification, ecology, and politics as their interactions affect food production and global survival. Their Chapter 9 presents a number of suggestions including what they call the "Genesis Strategy" (see page 295) based on Joseph's interpretation of the Pharaoh's dreams. This is described on pages 63 and 64 of "The Jerusalem Bible" (1966). Joseph advised the Pharaoh to store crops from years of plenty to be released to the people of Egypt during years of famine.

Schneider and Mesirow propose several World Security Institutes: an Institute of Imminent Dangers, an Institute of Resource Availability, an Institute of Alternative Technologies and an Institute of Policy Options. Their book, the reading of which is recommended, includes Appendix C which consists of 38 figures carefully selected to supplement the text.

In the very far distant future when all of the Earth's fossil sources of energy have been exhausted, man need not revert to the life styles of our distant ancestors who browsed on vegetation and killed the beasts of the wilderness. Solar energy and renewable resources, which come directly or indirectly from photosynthesis through the technology of controlled environment production (see Topic 50) might produce sufficient food and fiber provided that the renewable water resource is managed intelligently on a world-wide basis, to maintain civilization.

Problem Assignment - Pertinent to Section VI, SOILS

A short-duration thunder storm produces precipitation which falls on a grass- and brush-covered area. The vegetal cover was found on a uniform soil having a depth of 10 inches, underlain by a loose gravel. The field moisture capacity of the soil by volume was 10 percent. The rain fell at a uniform intensity of 1-inch per hour. It started and stopped suddenly. The total duration of the storm was 2 hours. The total interception losses for the area were 0.3 inch. It had been determined previously that the infiltration capacity was .2 inch per hour. The soil was dry at the start of the storm.

Compute the following:

a. What is the total amount of rainfall?

b. What is the amount of rainfall reaching the soil during the first hour?

c. At what time did rain reach the surface of the soil?

d.  At what time would surface runoff begin?

e.  How much rainfall would have infiltrated into the soil at the end of the first hour?

f.  What would be the distribution of soil moisture in that soil at the end of the first hour?

g.  What would be the distribution of soil moisture in that soil at the end of the storm?

h.  What would be the groundwater recharge?

Tabulate answers on one page and hand in all work sheets.

## References

Bartlett, Albert A., "The Forgotten Fundamentals of the Energy Crisis", a paper presented at the Third Annual Conf. on Energy, Univ. of Missouri at Rolla, Oct. 12-14, 1976. (Dr. Bartlett is at the Dept. of Physics and Astrophysics Univ. of Colorado, Boulder, Colo.)

Brink, R. A., J. W. Densmore, G. A. Hill, "Soil Deterioration and the Growing World Demand for Food", Science, vol. 197, no. 4304, pp 625-630, 12 August 1977.

Furtick, William R., "Weeds and World Food Production", a paper presented at the Symposium on World Food, Pest Losses, and the Environment, AAAS Meeting, Denver, Colo. Feb. 22, 1977. (Dr. Furtick is Dean, College of Tropical Agriculture, Univ. of Hawaii.)

Hammond, Allen L., "Alcohol: A Brazilian Answer to the Energy Crisis", Science, vol. 195, pp 564-566, Feb. 11, 1977

Hendricks, Sterling B., "Food From the Land", Chap. 4, pp 65-85, in Resources and Man, W. H. Freeman and Co., San Francisco, 259 pp, 1969.

"Jerusalem Bible", Alexander Jones, Gen. Editor, Doubleday and Co., Garden City, N.Y., 1966.

Krendel, E. S., "Man- and Animal-Generated Power", pp 9-209 and 9-210 in Standard Handbook for Mechanical Engineers, 7th ed., T. Baumeister, ed-in-chief, McGraw Hill Book Co., New York, 1967.

McDonald, Angus, "Early American Soil Conservationists", U.S. Dept. of Agriculture, Misc. Pub. 449, 63 pp, Oct. 1941.

Melder, Keith, "American Agriculture: A Continuing Revolution", Smithsonian Institution Traveling Exhibition Service, 8-page folder, undated. (Probably 1976).

Milner, Max, H. A. B. Parpia, and Nevin S. Scrimshaw, "Post
    Harvest Losses - A Priority of the U.N. University", a
    paper presented at the Symposium on World Food, Pest
    Losses, and the Environment, AAAS Meeting, Denver, Colo.
    Feb. 22, 1977. (Dr. Milner is at the Massachusetts Insti-
    tute of Technology, Cambridge, Massachusetts.)

Othmer, Donald F., and Oswald A. Roels, "Power, Fresh Water,
    and Food from Cold, Deep Sea Water", Science, vol. 182,
    no. 4108, pp 121-125, Oct. 12, 1973.

Pimentel, David, Elinor C. Terhune, Rada Dyson-Hudson,
    Stephen Rochereau, Robert Samis, Eric A. Smith, Daniel
    Denman, David Reifschneider, Michael Shepard, "Land
    Degradation; Effects on Food and Energy Resources",
    Science, vol. 194, pp 149-155, Oct. 8, 1976.

"Ponds for Water Supply and Recreation", Soil Conservation Ser-
    vice, USDA, Agri. Handbook No. 387, 55 pp, Jan. 1971.

Schneider, Stephen H., with Lynne E. Mesirow, "The Genesis
    Strategy: Climate and Global Survival", Dell Pub. Co.,
    N.Y., paperback, 419 pp, 1977.

Splinter, William E., A presentation stressing the importance
    of developing fuel sources other than from petroleum so
    that current high-level agricultural activity in the
    United States may continue. Presented at a Symposium on
    Renewable Resource Management for Agriculture and Forestry
    AAAS Meeting, Denver, Colo., Feb. 24, 1977. Waiting
    publication.

Strabala, Bill, "Gasohol Plant Bid Planned", The Denver Post,
    Sun., Dec. 11, 1977.

"The Bugs are Coming", Time, pp 38-46, July 12, 1976.

"Washington, Jefferson, Lincoln, and Agriculture", Bureau of
    Agri. Economics, USDA, 102 pp, Nov. 1937.

"Websters 3d New International Dictionary of the English Lang-
    uage - Unabridged", Philip Babcock Gove, ed-in-chief,
    G. C. Merriam Co., 1971.

Wittwer, Sylvan H., "Assessment of Technology in Food Produc-
    tion", a paper presented at the Symposium on Renewable
    Resource Management for Agriculture and Forestry, AAAS
    meeting, Denver, Colo., Feb. 24, 1977. (Jour. Article
    No. 7967 of the Mich. Agri. Exp. Station, East Lansing.)

Of special interest to this subject is The Scientific American,
vol. 235, no. 3, "Food and Agriculture", Sept. 1976.

# SECTION VII

## EVAPORATION AND EVAPOTRANSPIRATION

Topic 39                    Evaporation

The hydrologist is concerned with evaporation, first in accounting for losses from existing natural bodies of water and in the water resource development; and, second, with estimating what the evaporation losses would be when the naturally occurring water surfaces are modified either by increasing or decreasing the free water surface through water resource developments. As evaporation involves changes of state of water substance the physical and mathematical treatment of evaporation measurement and forecasting involves thermodynamic considerations.

Since in effect all of the energy involved in evaporation comes from the sun, a knowledge of solar radiation is necessary in evaporation and also in evapotranspiration. A publication by Reifsnyder and Lull (1965) on radiant energy in relation to forests is an excellent review of both the physical and practical aspects of solar radiation and radiation exchange. Fritz and MacDonald (1949) have summarized average solar radiation in the United States for the heating and ventilating industries. Harmon, Weiss, and Wilson (1954) have prepared correlations for computing solar radiation from daily sunshine duration. Frank and Lee (1966) in their tabulation of solar irradiation on slopes give information pertinent not only to evaporation and evapotranspiration but also to solar energy applications such as heating.

A historic measurement of evaporation based on observing water loss from a pan is that performed by Edmond Halley in the late 1680's as described by Biswas (1970), pages 223-230.

Various types of evaporation pans, which are indices of evaporation, have been developed throughout the World. One of the designs with long records and with extensive analyses is the U.S. Weather Bureau's Class A evaporation pan. Detailed instructions for the construction and operation of the Class A pan are given in Chapter 5 of the "National Weather Service Observing Handbook, No. 2" (1972) from which Figure 39-1 is taken.

Average annual lake evaporation for the conterminous United States is shown in Figure 6-5 on page 24 of Topic 6. The information presented on this map is based on evaporation pan data.

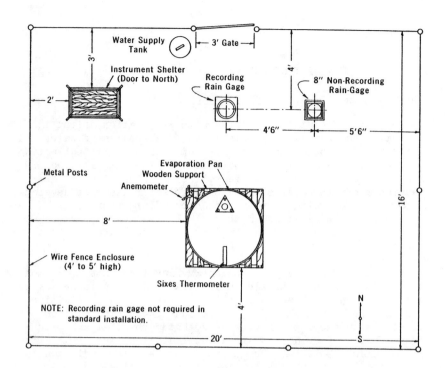

Figure 39-1  Layout of a Class A Evaporation Station Showing
Recommended Dimensions for Enclosure and Spacing of
Instruments.  Distances are in feet and inches.

Comprehensive discussions of evaporation have been prepared by Kohler, Nordenson, and Fox (1955), Veihmeyer (1964),
and Bruce and Clark (1966).  A translation from the Russian of
Konstantinov's book, "Evaporation in Nature", (1963) is a very
thorough treatment of the subject containing numerous tables
and graphs.  It is interesting to note that some of the 843
references listed were originally published in English.

One accurate way to determine evaporation loss would be
through the water budget of an existing reservoir.  Precision
of measurements of various inflow and outflow components for
either the size of the reservoir or the hydrologic complexity
existing at the reservoir location usually requires extensive
and costly installations.  Except for research projects the
installations are not considered justifiable.

The energy budget approach to evaporation loss determination is based upon an accounting procedure.  If all of the heat
entering into and departing from a body of water were to be
measured this approach assumes that any heat not accounted for

was lost from the system by having been removed as latent heat
of vaporization.

Another method of measuring evaporation is through the
measurement of the water vapor content of air as it approaches
and, after it has interacted with the water surface, departs
from the body of water. This method is known as the "mass-
transfer".

An excellent analysis of several of these methods is the
highly mathematical review of evaporation theory by Anderson,
Anderson, and Marciano (1950) as part of the cooperative
research aimed at determing evaporation loss from Lake Mead.

Since the heat exchange between the pan and its surroundings can have a major influence on the stored energy and therefore upon the potential evaporating conditions, it is necessary
to follow precisely the recommendations for installation of any
pan. For example, the Weather Bureau's Class A pan is to be
placed on a 2-inch by 4-inch lumber base and assembled according to a specific pattern. The base permits relatively unre-
stricted flow of air under the pan. If the pan were to be
placed on a concrete base or on soil or on a wood platform not
permitting the flow of air, it would no longer be a Class A
installation.

It was found by experience that pans tended to evaporate
more water than did reservoirs. Accordingly so-called "pan
coefficients" are applied to reduce pan evaporation-measured
losses to an assumed lake-evaporation equivalent. Usage of
pan coefficients should be restricted to full water-year
periods unless specific research has been conducted to establish values for shorter periods.

This has been done for Lake Hefner. This detailed evaporation determination research is described in two reports,
"Water-Loss Investigation - Lake Hefner Studies" (1954) and
its related "Base Data Report" (1954).

Lake Hefner is an off-channel reservoir located about 8
miles northwest of the center of Oklahoma City, Oklahoma. It
is at an elevation of about 1200 feet above sea level when full
and has an area of about 4 square miles. It is located in a
sub-humid area at a longitude of about $97^\circ - 40'$, and latitude
of about $35^\circ - 30'$.

As observed at Lake Hefner the Weather Bureau's Class A
pan coefficient for February, 1951 was 0.13; for November, 1950
1.32; for a full year, 0.69. Linsley, Kohler, and Paulhus
(1975) give on page 169 a summary of pan coefficients for 2
surface and 4 sunken pans at 20 world-wide locations.

Crow and Hottman (1973) compared the accuracy of the determination of Lake Hefner evaporation by the energy budget method. They compared the results based on 1, 5, 11, or 19 temperature-profile stations. They concluded that the optimum number of stations was 5, or 1 station for each 520 acres. If only one temperature profile was taken at the deepest part of the Lake the evaporation error was 8.2 percent, whereas increasing the number of stations from 5 to 19 resulted in an increase of accuracy of the evaporation measurement of only 1 percent.

The Lake Hefner investigations were performed as a preliminary to the determination of the evaporation loss from Lake Mead. Lake Hefner was chosen because it offered promise (which was later demonstrated) of a water budget of sufficient accuracy to make possible evaluation of the hydrologic practicality of the other methods of measuring reservoir evaporation.

A thorough evaporation study which established an average loss of over 7 feet in depth per year at Lake Mead, Arizona-Nevada, is described by Harbeck, Kohler, Koberg, and others (1958). A combination of methods was used to measure the Lake Mead evaporation loss. Depending on the reservoir elevation and corresponding surface area during some years, the evaporation loss from Lake Mead is practically as great as the withdrawal of water from the Lake for municipal use by the City of Los Angeles.

For about 75 years it has been reasoned on theoretical grounds that evaporation and evapotranspiration should vary with changes in elevation above sea level. To date an acceptable mathematical analysis to demonstrate the magnitude of the difference has not been performed. Blaney (1958) reported upon average evaporation losses at a number of high-altitude pan installations. Decreases in evaporation were more closely related to temperature than to altitude.

Peck and Pfankuch (1963) describe in a progress report the organization of a specially-designed network of 13 Class A evaporation stations placed at elevations ranging from 4,400 to 9000 feet in the Wasatch Mountains near Farmington, Utah. Detailed meteorological observations aimed at calculating daily and even hourly evaporation should provide scientific information on this important aspect of water resource management.

Radiative lagoons in connection with thermal power plants offer an approach to the disposal of waste heat without thermal modification of streamflow. Dake (1972) proposed equations for computing evaporation and its consequent energy losses, taking into account hourly changes in meteorological conditions, in his study of evaporative cooling of a body of water.

Ryan, Harleman and Stolzenbach (1974) developed a technique for computing the surface temperature of cooling ponds using energy balance equations.

It has been demonstrated that a compressed monomolecular film of certain straight-chain heavy alcohols such as hexadecanol when applied to a water surface can reduce significantly evaporation loss from a body of water. An informative treatment of the general subject is "Water-Loss Investigations: Lake Hefner 1958 Evaporation Reduction Investigations" (1959).

The importance of reservoir evaporation loss is indicated by the fact that during some years the evaporation loss from Lake Mead alone could be about one-third of the minimum annual inflow of the Colorado River to the Lake. In closed basins such as the Great Salt Lake in Utah and Pyramid Lake in Nevada, all of the inflow is ultimately evaporated. Evaporation loss places a limit on the number of reservoirs that can be built in an arid region river basin.

Timblin, Florey, and Garstka (1962) describe laboratory and field reservoir evaporation reduction investigations. This paper is one of 19 published in "Retardation of Evaporation by Monolayers: Transport Processes" (1962) edited by Victor K. La Mer. Fitzgerald and Vines (1963) refer to earlier work in Australia by W. W. Mansfield in their review of the practical aspects of treatment of large water storages.

World-wide interest in evaporation-loss reduction was evidenced by an international symposium held in Poona, India, in December, 1962, the Proceedings of which were published in a volume, "Symposium on Water Evaporation Control" (1966). This 330-page volume contains 27 papers.

Although interest in reservoir evaporation-loss reduction orginally centered upon monomolecular films it was found that, although reductions of up to about 90 percent were demonstrated in the laboratory, their active life on a reservoir surface was greatly shortened due to wind action and biological degradation. The monomolecular film remains the only technique which does not prevent usage of a reservoir for purposes other than storage. If the physicists and chemists could develop a monomolecular film which would re-form a monolayer after being crumpled by winds or shorelines, a tremendous amount of fresh water could be saved.

Cluff (1977) lists eight methods which have been tested for evaporation control and which are listed in Table 39-1. His paper includes a brief discussion of each of the methods, and, as available, information on the effectiveness in reducing evaporation loss in each of the methods is entered in Table 39-1.

Table 39-1   Methods of Evaporation-Loss Reduction

| | |
|---|---|
| 1. Minimizing the surface-to-volume ratio | 5. Sand or rock-filled reservoirs |
| 2. Destratification | 6. Shading the water surface |
| 3. Surface films, Monomolecular layers | 7. Floating reflective covers |
| 4. Wind barriers | 8. Floating vapor barriers |

Percent effectiveness ranged from an increase in evaporation of about 9 percent in one instance of destratification to a decrease in evaporation loss ranging from about 9 percent to about 57 percent. As discussed by Cluff some of these percentages are based on pan observations; others on reservoir observations.

The following is a quotation from the introduction to the paper by Cluff:

"Reducing surface evaporation may be the most economical way of increasing water supplies in arid lands. The water thus saved is essentially distilled and is normally at the head of existing distribution systems and can be easily utilized. Evaporation loss is perhaps the major deterrent to fully utilize erratic flood flows in arid lands. The other water loss, seepage, can more easily be controlled using several available methods. In some cases, seepage loss can be recovered through wells located in the vicinity of the reservoir."

As a conclusion to this Topic on Evaporation it is urged that the reader study the information given in the following: Figure 6-3, "Average Annual Precipitation"; Figure 6-4, "Average Annual Runoff"; and Figure 6-5, "Average Annual Lake Evaporation", all in Topic 6, "The Hydrologic Cycle".

References

Anderson, E. R., L. J. Anderson, and J. J. Marciano, "A Review of Evaporation Theory and Development of Instrumentation", Report No. 159, U.S. Navy Electronics Laboratory, San Diego, Calif., 71 pp, 1 February 1950.

"Base Data Report", Water-Loss Investigations: Lake Hefner Studies, Geological Survey Prof. Paper 270, USDI, 300 pp, U.S. Govt. Printing Office, 1954.

Biswas, Asit K., "History of Hydrology", American Elsevier Pub. Co., Inc., New York, 336 pp, 1970.

Blaney, Harry F., "Evaporation from Free Water Surfaces at
High Altitudes", Trans. Amer. Soc. of Civil Engr.,
vol. 123, p 385, 1958.

Bruce, J. P., and R. H. Clark, Chap 5, "Evaporation and Evapotranspiration", in Introduction to Hydrometeorology,
Pergamon Press, New York, 319 pp, 1966.

Cluff, C. Brent, "Evaporation Control for Increasing Water
Supplies", a paper presented at Conf. on Alternative
Strategies for Desert Development and Management, held at
Sacramento, Calif. May 31 - June 10, 1977. (Dr. Cluff is
with the Water Resources Research Center, Univ. of Ariz.
Tucson)

Crow, Franklin R., and Steven D. Hottman, "Network Density of
Temperature Profile Stations and Its Influence on the
Accuracy of Lake Evaporation Calculations", Water
Resources Research, vol. 9, no. 4, pp 895-899, Aug. 1973.

Dake, Jonas M. K., "Evaporation Cooling of a Body of Water",
Water Resources Research, vol. 8, no. 4, pp 1087-1091,
Aug. 1972.

Fitzgerald, L. M., and R. G. Vines, "Retardation of Evaporation
by Monolayers: Practical Aspects of the Treatment of
Large Water Storages", Australian Jour. of Applied Science
vol. 14, no. 4, pp 340-346, Dec. 1963.

Frank, E. C., and Richard Lee, "Potential Solar Beam Irradia-
tion on Slopes. Tables for 30° to 50° Latitude", U.S.
Forest Service Research Paper RM-18, Rocky Mt. Forest and
Range Exp. Station, Fort Collins, Colo. Mar. 1966.

Fritz, Sigmund, and T. H. MacDonald, "Average Solar Radiation
in the United States", Heating and Ventilating, vol. 46,
pp 61-64, 1949.

Harbeck, G. Earl, Jr., Max A. Kohler, Gordon E. Koberg, and
others, "Water-Loss Investigations: Lake Mead Studies",
USGS Prof. Paper 298, 100 pp, 1958.

Harmon, R. W., L. L. Weiss, and W. T. Wilson, "Insolation as an
Empirical Function of Daily Sunshine Duration", Monthly
Weather Review, vol. 82, pp 141-146, June, 1954.

Kohler, M. A., T. J. Nordenson, and W. E. Fox, "Evaporation
from Pans and Lakes", Research Paper No. 38, Weather
Bureau, U.S. Dept. of Commerce, 21 pp, 1955.

Konstantinov, A. R., "Evaporation in Nature", originally pub.
in 1963 in Russian. Trans. by I. Shechtman of the Israel

Program for Scientific Translations, Jerusalem, 1966.
Trans. TT 66-51015. Available from the U.S. Dept. of
Commerce, Clearinghouse for Federal Scientific & Technical
Information, Springfield, Va. 22151.

Linsley, Ray K., Jr., Max A. Kohler, and Joseph L. H. Paulhus,
"Hydrology for Engineers", McGraw-Hill Book Co.,
New York, 2nd edition, 481 pp, 1975.

"National Weather Service Observing Handbook No. 2", Substation
Observations, Supersedes Circular B, Natl. Weather Service
NOAA, U.S. Dept. of Commerce, Silver Spring, Md., 1st
ed. 1970, revised, 77 pp, Dec. 1972.

Peck, Eugene L., and Dale J. Pfankuch, "Evaporation Rates in
Mountainous Terrain", Proceedings of the General Assembly
of Berkeley of the International Assn. for Scientific
Hydrology, Committee for Evaporation, Pub. No. 62,
Gentbrugge, Belgium, pp 267-278, 1963.

Reifsnyder, William E., and Howard W. Lull, "Radiant Energy in
Relation to Forests", Forest Service, USDA, Tech. Bulletin
No. 1344, 111 pp, Dec 1965.

"Retardation of Evaporation by Monolayers: Transport Processes"
ed. by Victor K. La Mer, an assembly of 19 papers
presented at a Symposium sponsored by the Division of
Colloid and Surface Chemistry of the Amer. Chemical Soc.
in Sept. 1960. Academic Press, New York and London,
277 pp, 1962.

Ryan, Patrick J., Donald R. F. Harleman, and Keith D. Stolzenbach, "Surface Heat Loss From Cooling Ponds", Water
Resources Research, vol. 10, no. 5, pp 930-938, Oct. 1974.

"Symposium on Water Evaporation Control - Proceedings", an
assembly of 27 papers presented in Dec. 1962 at Poona,
India. Pub. jointly by UNESCO South Asia Science Cooperation Office and Council of Scientific & Industrial
Research, New Delhi, 330 pp, 1966.

Timblin, L. O., Jr., Q. L. Florey, and W. U. Garstka, "Laboratory and Field Reservoir Evaporation Reduction Investigations Being Performed by the Bureau of Reclamation",
pp 177-192, in Retardation of Evaporation by Monolayers:
Transport Processes", ed. by Victor K. La Mer,
Academic Press, New York and London, 277 pp, 1962.

Veihmeyer, Frank J., "Evapotranspiration", Section 11, Handbook
of Applied Hydrology, Ven T. Chow, ed-in-chief, McGraw-
Hill Book Co., New York, 1964.

"Water-Loss Investigations: Lake Hefner Studies, Technical
    Report", Geological Survey Prof. Paper 269, Prepared in
    Collaboration with the U.S. Dept. of the Navy, Bureau of
    Ships, Navy Electronics Lab., U.S. Dept. of the Interior,
    Bureau of Reclamation, U.S. Dept. of Commerce, Weather
    Bureau, U.S. Govt. Printing Office, 158 pp, 1954.

"Water-Loss Investigations: Lake Hefner 1958 Evaporation
    Reduction Investigations", Report by the Collaborators:
    City of Oklahoma City, Okla.; Okla. State Dept. of Health;
    U.S. Dept. of Health, Education & Welfare, Public Health
    Service; U.S. Dept. of Commerce, Weather Bureau; U.S. Dept
    of the Interior, Bureau of Reclamation, pub. by Bureau of
    Reclamation, USDI, Denver, Colo., 131 pp, June, 1959.

Evapotranspiration is the process by which water moves from the surface of the land to the atmosphere. It takes into account all movements from soil surfaces, from rocks, vegetation, and animal life. Conversion of water to water vapor requires heat and all of the physical concepts underlying evaporation apply to evapotranspiration.

The terms transpiration, consumptive use, and irrigation water requirements are not synonymous. Transpiration is that water evaporated by plants and used directly in formation of plant tissues. Consumptive use may include interception, absorption as soil moisture, evaporation, transpiration, or incorporation in a manufactured product; it is water which is not returned to the surface or groundwater. Withdrawal of water for a trans-basin diversion is a consumptive use to the source basin. Irrigation water requirements in addition to evapotranspiration include all conveyance losses such as seepage and evaporation enroute to the point where the water is actually applied to the land.

Ripple, Rubin, and van Hylckama (1972) developed a method which combines meteorological equations with soil water transfer equations for the purpose of computing evaporation losses from the soils under conditions of high water tables. Their treatment, combining as it does the concepts underlying Darcy's law and the mass transfer meteorological equations with a consideration of the thermodynamic relationships, is highly mathematical.

Campbell (1971) reported on evaporation from bare soil as affected by texture and temperature. Six semi-arid regions soils from the Rio Puerco drainage basin in New Mexico were included in pot experiments. Evaporation from initially saturated soils was 0.33-inch per day at 90° F and 0.22-inch per day at 60° F.

Plants and animals and many industrial mechanisms such as cooling towers make use of this latent heat absorption to attempt to maintain their temperatures. Warm-blooded animals, including humans, evaporate water either through their skin or through the lungs to dispel excessive heat.

Gates (1965) reviews mechanisms of heat transfer in plants which attempt to maintain temperature through radiation, transpiration, and convection. Of these processes transpiration and convection are very effective. Gates gives energy budgets for daytime and nighttime. He describes the functioning of stomata as they influence evapotranspiration. Page 84

of his article includes a sketch of a cross-section of a leaf
showing stomata which may be as numerous as 20,000 per square
centimeter of leaf surface. Evapotranspiration by plants
serves a useful purpose in that it brings to the actively-
growing parts of the plant not only the necessary water but
also the dissolved mineral nutrients. The efficiency of the
hydraulics of this system is illustrated by the fact that some
trees lift water 300 feet as described by Bonner (1958).

A comprehensive discussion of the fundamentals underlying
evapotranspiration and of many of the pertinent methods is
given by Veihmeyer (1964). Lull (1964), pages 6-17 through
6-30, has written an excellent review of the ecological
and silvicultural aspects of evapotranspiration. A summary of
10 papers on forests and evapotranspiration is given by Wicht
(1967).

Some years ago extensive work was conducted to establish a
ratio between pounds of dry matter produced by plant growth and
the amount of water required. This approach is seldom used at
present since it has been established that a plant evaporates
water, not because it needs to do so to satisfy its biochemical
processes but because it must evaporate the water to satisfy
the moisture deficit in the atmosphere under the environmental
conditions which prevail.

Thornthwaite (1931) developed a classification of the climates of North America based on his precipitation-evaporation
concept. His basic idea was that a ratio of precipitation divided by evaporation would serve as a single-index expression of
the integration of a great complexity of climatological factors.
He called the total annual precipitation divided by the total
evaporation the P/E quotient. The sum of the P/E ratios for
each of the 12 months of the year he called the P-E index.

For practical purposes food and fiber production depend
on a management of soil moisture so that the soil for most
crops is seldom above field moisture capacity and never below
the wilting point. The computation of these losses for a potential project is among the most important of the professional
services of a hydrologist. The realization of the importance
of this soil moisture management responsibility goes back to
prehistoric times as has been discussed in Topics 1 and 2.

Bulletin No. 1 of the State Agricultural College of
Colorado at Fort Collins (now Colorado State University) is
entitled, "Report of Experiments in Irrigation and Meteorology".
This report was written in 1887 by Elwood Mead who later served
as Commissioner in 1924-36 of what is now the U.S. Bureau of
Reclamation. The reservoir created by Hoover Dam is named Lake
Mead in his honor. Mead's report No. 1 deals with consumptive
use, called in his day, the "duty" of water.

Rosenberg, Hart, and Brown (1968) in their review of research discuss methods of evapotranspiration computation among which are: mass transport; aerodynamic methods (treated under 3 subdivisions); eddy correlation; energy budget and Bowen's ratio (treated under 4 subdivisions); empirical and bookkeeping methods (treated under 4 subdivisions); advection (including discussion of underlying physical theory); and lysimetry (with 5 subdivisions).

Throughout research and practice in evaporation and evapotranspiration this vapor pressure relationship is to be found:

$$E = C \cdot (e_o - e_a) \tag{1}$$

in which

E   is the evaporative flux

C   is an empirical constant, encompassing many factors, chiefly wind speed

$e_o$   is the saturation vapor pressure at the temperature of the evaporating surface

$e_a$   is the actual vapor pressure in the air immediately above that evaporating surface.

This relationship was first stated by Dalton (1798) the father of the atomic theory according to Rohwer (1931), page 21. The relationship differentiates between conditions of equilibrium, evaporation, or condensation.

Most of the methods of evapotranspiration determination are aimed at daily, short-period, monthly, or seasonal totals. Mawdsley and Brutsaert (1973) propose a method for computing regional or basin-wide evapotranspiration by applying the atmospheric science's geostrophic drag concept. The authors report that generally good agreement was found between mean evapotranspiration and evaporation from Class A pans at Greensboro, North Carolina, Little Rock, Arkansas, and Bismarck, North Dakota.

The influence of evapotranspiration on crop growth and food production was so direct that most of the investigations performed by agronomists and engineers in the past related to crop growth. However, an increasing realization of the role of evapotranspiration in influencing drainage basin water yield has resulted in a great increase in the study of evapotranspiration under grassland and forest conditions. A condensed review of the results of comparisons of forest and agricultural lands with respect to evapotranspiration is Baumgartner's paper (1967). His Figure 2 on page 383 discloses a remarkable agreement in shortwave radiation balance of a spruce forest, an alfalfa stand, and a potato field on a summer day near Munich. Although Horton (1973) compiled an extensive bibliography with abstracts aimed primarily at phreatophyte management, his bibliography contains much information on evapotranspiration.

Reifsnyder and Lull (1965) in their very comprehensive discussion of radiant energy in relation to forests, review on pages 82-84 a number of approaches to the estimation of evapotranspiration on the basis of solar radiation data.

The recent approaches to evapotranspiration turn out to be studies of complex astrophysical-meteorological-thermodynamic-ecological interrelationships. An example of this is the work of Jensen and Haise (1963). The Jensen and Haise equation for periods greater than 5 days is

$$E_{tp} = (0.014 \ T - 0.37) \ R_s \ D \tag{2}$$

in which

$E_{tp}$ is potential evapotranspiration in inches per day

$T$ is the mean air temperature in $^{o}F$

$R_s$ is total short-wave solar and sky radiation in inches

$D$ is the number of days.

As direct observations of total short-wave solar and sky radiation are rare, Jensen and Haise in their Tables 5 and 6 give average totals of cloudless short-wave solar and sky radiation by months for selected locations and for Latitude $^{o}N$ from $0^{o}$ to $60^{o}$.

Follett, Reichman, Doering, and Benz (1973) pages 90-92, have prepared a series of nomographs for estimating evapotranspiration based upon modifications of the Jensen-Haise method. They suggest that the procedure could be modified for other geographic areas by replacing a temperature scale with one calculated for a particular area. Their nomographs are prepared for North Dakota. They recommend that the computation be checked against field-water conditions and soil-crop needs prior to the scheduling of irrigation based on the results of their method.

Ostromecki (1965) reviews methods of computation of water requirements of fields and grasslands as developed in Poland. It is interesting to note that everyone of the 21 publications cited in his paper refer to Polish or European literature. A working group on evaporation measurement of the Commission for Instruments and Methods of Observation of the World Meteorological Organization (1968) has prepared an exhaustive comparison and analysis of methods of "Measurement and Estimation of Evaporation and Evapotranspiration", from soil and water surfaces.  Their report presents on pages 113-114 graphs for the computation of evapotranspiration from a soil in millimeters per day from average values of air temperature and humidity (Figure 24) and a graph for computation of evaporation of a land surface for a year from average values of air temperature and humidity (Figure 25).

The American Society of Civil Engineers has published a report, "Consumptive Use of Water and Irrigation Water Requirements", (1973) prepared by a special Technical Committee on Water Requirements of the Irrigation and Drainage Division. This report, edited by Marvin E. Jensen, contains papers on the soil-plant-atmosphere system, energy and water balance, evapotranspiration and potential evapotranspiration, source of evapotranspiration data, among other topics.  Table 6.7 of that report, pages 105 through 110, is titled "Selective Examples of Observed Seasonal Evapotranspiration for Well-Watered, Common Crops in the U.S.A. and Canada".  This table contains 95 entries with citations to 31 authorities responsible for the data given for each entry.

Pages 125 through 138 of Chapter VII contain 50 graphs comparing various methods for:  Aspendale, Australia; Brawley, California; Copenhagen, Denmark; Coshocton, Ohio; Davis, California; Kimberly, Idaho; Lompoc, California; Ruzizi Valley, Zaire; Seabrook, New Jersey; and South Park, Colorado. Figure 40-1 is taken from page 128 of Chapter VII and Figure 40-2 is taken from page 130 of that Chapter. These Figures appear on the following page.

In water resources project planning, which includes irrigation projects and municipal water supply projects, the major unknowns have been infiltration, evapotranspiration, and conveyance losses.  Of these 3 the evapotranspiration loss has been of greatest concern.  Reservoir locations and active capacities, conveyance systems, and distribution systems must be designed to supply a sufficient quantity of water to make the project economically feasible.  Seldom is a project designed to supply water for extremely dry conditions.  Therefore the frequency distribution (see Topic 19) of evapotranspirational demand must be considered in water resources planning and operation.

Extensive frequency analyses have been made.  Rosenberg (1972) reports on such studies for the Central Great Plains; McGuinness and Parmele (1972) have dealt with the East Central United States; Pruitt, von Oettingen, and Morgan (1972) report on frequencies in the Central Valley of California; and Nixon, Lawless, and Richardson (1972) have analyzed the frequencies of evapotranspirational demands for Coastal California.

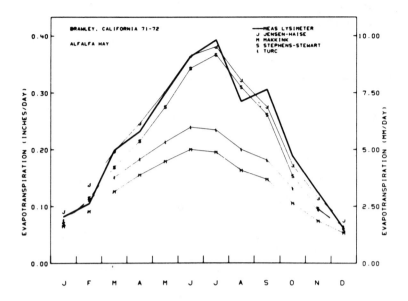

Figure 40-1   Evapotranspiration in Inches Per Day, as Computed
by Radiation Methods at Brawley, California

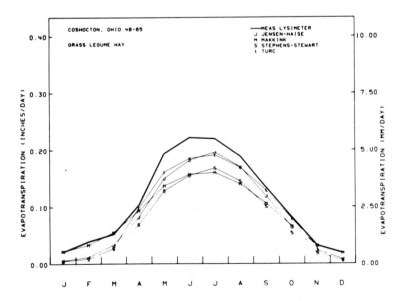

Figure 40-2   Evapotranspiration in Inches Per Day, as Computed
by Radiation Methods at Coshocton, Ohio

Kruse, Kincaid, and Duke (1977) propose a method for making evaporation estimates with modified Penman equations. Their analyses, based chiefly on data from the Grand Valley of Colorado, were aimed to forecast irrigation scheduling for alfalfa and corn. The technique gave good agreement with water use by these crops in lysimeters.

A widely-used method for determining consumptive use of irrigated agricultural land is the one developed by Blaney and Criddle. Their equation as given by Rosenberg, Hart, and Brown (1968), page 40, is

$$U = K_S F = K_M f \tag{3}$$

in which

$U$ = consumptive use in inches during the period of interest

$K_S$ = seasonal or growing period consumptive use coefficient.

$K_M$ = monthly consumptive use coefficient.

$f = \dfrac{t \cdot p}{100}$ = monthly consumptive use factor.

$t$ = monthly mean temperature ($^\circ$F).

$p$ = monthly percent of total annual daylight hours

$F$ = f for the total period.

$u = K_M f$ = monthly consumptive use (inches).

This is a bookkeeping method based on data readily available from Weather Bureau climatological records. A detailed presentation of the method with numerous supporting tables and charts has been prepared by the Soil Conservation Service, "Irrigation Water Requirements, Technical Release No. 21" (1970). It has been found that the Blaney-Criddle method, when supported with locally-derived tables and graphs, yields practically applicable results over a wide range of conditions. This method assumes that there is no deficiency of soil moisture.

There is an increasing volume of literature in the use of substances such as phenylmercuric acetate and decenylsuccinic acid which by closing the stomata reduce transpiration loss. Hart (1969) points out that mercuric compounds can have a toxic effect on animals. This reference is a progress report on his work dealing with quaking aspen stands in Utah. Waggoner and Turner (1971) describe the work they have performed on the reduction of transpiration through the control of stomata in pine forests in Connecticut. Their report contains numerous references to substances used, vegetation treated, and effectiveness attained.

Belt, King, and Haupt (1977) found a 12 percent increase

in streamflow in a 63-day period, in the summer of 1974, following a spraying by helicopter of a 65-acre (26.3 ha) cedar-hemlock drainage basin in Idaho. A 5 percent aqueous emulsion of a silicone oil anti-transpirant, 40 gallons per acre (375 litres/ha), was used. This material is not classified as a pesticide, herbicide, or toxic substance. The 12 percent increase was found to be significant at the 97.5 percent confidence level. This carefully-planned and executed research indicates that there is promise of augmentation of summer streamflow through the application of anti-transpirants.

## Problem Assignment - Evapotranspiration Computation

a. Select an area and crop.

b. Compute evapotranspiration by the Jensen-Haise (1963) method using the nomographs prepared by Follett, Reichman, Doering, and Benz (1973).

c. Compute evapotranspiration using the Blaney-Criddle (1962) method as outlined in "Irrigation Water Requirements - Technical Release No. 21" (1970).

(As an alternate use the procedure outlined by Schulz (1976) in his pages 219-222 and illustrated for Colorado).

d. Prepare a graph comparing the results of the computations and discuss your results.

## References

Baumgartner, Albert, "Energetic Bases for Differential Vaporization from Forest and Agricultural Lands", pp 381-389 in International Symposium on Forest Hydrology, ed. by Wm. E. Sopper and Howard W. Lull, Pergamon Press, New York, 1967.

Belt, G. H., J. G. King, and H. F. Haupt, "Augmenting Summer Streamflow by Use of a Silicone Antitranspirant", Water Resources Research, vol. 13, no. 2, pp 267-272, Apr. 1977.

Blaney, H. F., and W. D. Criddle, "Determining Consumptive Use and Irrigation Water Requirements", USDA Tech. Bulletin No. 1275, 59 pp, 1962.

Bonner, J., "Water Transport: This classical problem in plant physiology is becoming amenable to mathematical analysis", Science, vol. 129, pp 447-450, 1958.

Campbell, Ralph E., "Evaporation from Bare Soil as Affected by Texture and Temperature", USDA Forest Service Research Note RM-190, Rocky Mt. Forest and Range Exp. Station, Fort Collins, 7 pp, 1971.

"Consumptive Use of Water and Irrigation Water Requirements",
ed. by Marvin E. Jensen, A report prepared by the Technical Committee on Irrigation Water Requirements of the
Irrigation and Drainage Div. of the American Society of
Civil Engineers, 215 pp, 1973.

Dalton, J., "Experimental Essays on the Constitution of Mixed
Gases; on the Force of Steam of Vapor from Waters and
Other Liquids in Different Temperatures, Both in a
Torricellian Vacuum and in Air; on Evaporation; and on
the Expansion of Gases by Heat". Mem. Manchester Lit. and
Phil. Soc. 5: 535-602, illus., 1798.

Follett, R. F., G. A. Reichman, E. J. Doering, and L. C. Benz,
"A Nomograph for Estimating Evapotranspiration", Jour.
Soil and Water Conservation, vol. 28, no. 5, pp 90-92,
March-April, 1973.

Gates, David M., "Heat Transfer in Plants", Scientific
American, vol. 213, no. 6, pp 76-84, Dec. 1965.

Hart, Geo. E., "Chemical Sprays? - - - Reducing Water Use by
Trees", Utah Science, pp 55-57, Sept. 1969.

Horton, Jerome S., compiler, "Evapotranspiration and Watershed
Research as Related to Riparian and Phreatophyte Management", Forest Service, USDA, Misc. Publication No. 1234,
192 pp, Jan. 1973.

"Irrigation Water Requirements - Technical Release No. 21",
USDA, Soil Conservation Service, Engineering Division,
Apr. 1967, 88 pp, rev. Sept. 1970.

Jensen, Marvin E., and Howard R. Haise, "Estimating Evapotranspiration from Solar Radiation", Jour. Irrigation and
Drainage Div., Proceedings ASCE, pp 15-41, Dec. 1963.

Kruse, E. Gordon, Dennis C. Kincaid, and Harold R. Duke,
"Et Estimates with the Modified Penman Equation", vol. 1
of the Proceedings ASCE, Irrigation & Drainage Div.,
Specialty Conference, Water Mgmt. for Irrigation and
Drainage, July 20-22, 1977, Reno, Nev., publ. by ASCE,
438 pp, 1977.

Lull, Howard W., "Ecological and Silvicultural Aspects",
Sec. 6, Handbook of Applied Hydrology, ed by Ven T. Chow,
McGraw Hill Book Co., New York, 1964.

Mawdsley, John A., and Wilfried Brutsaert, "Computing Evapotranspiration by Geostrophic Drag Concept", Jour. Hydraulics Div., Proceedings ASCE, pp 99-110, Jan. 1973.

Mead, Elwood, "Report of Experiments in Irrigation and Meteor-
ology", Bull. No. 1, Report of Experimental Work in the
Dept. of Physics and Engineering, The State Agricultural
College of Colo., Fort Collins, pp 3-12, 1887.

"Measurement and Estimation of Evaporation and Evapotranspir-
ation", Tech. Note No. 83 (Report of a Working Group on
Evaporation Measurement of the Commission for Instruments
and Methods of Observation, prepared by M. Gangopadhyaya,
Chairman, G. Earl Harbeck, Jr., Tor J. Nordenson,
M. H. Omar, V. A. Uryvaev) World Meteorological Organiza-
tion Report No. WMO-No. 201.TP.105, 1966. Reprinted in
Geneva, Switzerland, 1968.

McGuinness, J. L., and Leslie H. Parmele, "Maximum Potential
Evapotranspiration Frequency - East Central U.S.", Jour.
Irrigation and Drainage Div., Proceedings ASCE, pp 207-
214, June, 1972.

Nixon, Paul R., G. Paul Lawless, and Gary V. Richardson,
"Coastal California Evapotranspiration Frequencies", Jour.
Irrigation and Drainage Div., Proceedings ASCE, pp 185-
191, June, 1972.

Ostromecki, Jerzy, "Remarks on Methods of Computation of Water
Requirements of Fields and Grasslands", originally pub.
in Prace I Studia Komitetu Inzynierii I Gospodarki Wodnej,
vol. 7, no. 1, 1965, pp 163-184. Trans. by J. Dobrowolski
Trans. No. TT 67-56052. Available from U.S. Dept. of
Commerce, Clearinghouse for Federal Scientific and Tech.
Information, Springfield, Va. 22151.

Pruitt, W. O., Sergius von Oettingen, and D. L. Morgan,
"Central California Evapotranspiration Frequencies",
Jour. Irrigation and Drainage Div., Proceedings ASCE,
pp 177-184, June, 1972.

Reifsnyder, William E., and Howard W. Lull, "Radiant Energy in
Relation to Forests", Forest Service, USDA, Tech. Bulletin
No. 1344, 111 pp, Dec. 1965.

Ripple, C. D., Jacob Rubin, and T. E. A. van Hylckama,
"Estimating Steady-State Evaporation Rates from Bare Soils
Under Conditions of High Water Table", USGS Water-Supply
Paper 2019-A, Govt. Printing Office, 1972.

Rohwer, Carl, "Evaporation from Free Water Surfaces", USDA,
Tech. Bulletin No. 271, 96 pp, Dec. 1931.

Rosenberg, Norman J., Hoyt E. Hart, and Kirk W. Brown,
"Evapotranspiration - Review of Research", MP20, College
of Agri. & Home Ec., Univ. of Nebraska, 80 pp, Nov. 1968.

231

Rosenberg, Norman J., "Frequency of Potential Evapotranspiration Rates in Central Great Plains", Jour. Irrigation and Drainage Div., Proceedings, ASCE, pp 203-206, June, 1972.

Schulz, E. F., "Problems in Applied Hydrology", Water Resources Publications, Fort Collins, Colo., 1973, 501 pp, rev. 1976.

Thornthwaite, C. Warren, "The Climates of North America - According to a New Classification", The Geographical Review, vol. XXI, no. 4, pp 633-655, Oct. 1931.

Veihmeyer, Frank J., "Evapotranspiration", Sec. 11, Handbook of Applied Hydrology, ed. by Ven Te Chow, McGraw-Hill Book Co., New York, 1964.

Waggoner, Paul E., and Neil C. Turner, "Transpiration and its Control by Stomata in a Pine Forest", Bull. of the Conn. Agricultural Exp. Station, New Haven, No. 726, 87 pp, May, 1971.

Wicht, C. L., "Summary of Forests and Evapotranspiration Session", pp 491-494 in International Symposium on Forest Hydrology, ed. by Wm E. Sopper and Howard W. Lull, Pergamon Press, New York, 1967.

SECTION VIII

LIMNOLOGY AND OCEANOGRAPHY

Topic 41                    Limnology

Zumberge and Ayers (1964) in their 33-page discussion of
the hydrology of lakes and swamps include a number of definitions one of which is quoted below:

"A lake is an inland basin filled or partially filled by
a water body whose surface dimensions are sufficiently
large to sustain waves capable of producing a barren
wave-swept shore".

A pond is a small and very shallow body of standing water in
which quiet water and extensive occupancy by higher aquatic
plants are common characteristics. A bog is the end stage in
the life history of a lake although not all lakes may end as
bogs. The distinctive characteristic of a bog is a floating
vegetal mat attached to the shore. A swamp is a vegetated land
area saturated with water. Swamps have also been considered to
be wet prairies.

A salt water tidal marsh, a very complex ecosystem, is a
swamp subjected to periodic fluctuations of brakish or salt
water.

Geologically all lakes are evanescent features ultimately
becoming plains. Since man-made reservoirs are artificial
lakes they also fill with sediment ultimately as has been discussed in the Topic entitled, "Erosion and Sedimentation".

An outstanding work is the 3-volume "Treatise on Limnology"
by Hutchinson. Volume I (1957) deals with Geology, Physics,
and Chemistry; Volume II (1967) is an introduction to Lake Biology and the Limnoplanktons; Volume III (1975) is on Limnological Botany. A study of Hutchinson's Treatise is highly
recommended for the serious worker in limnology.

An oligotrophic lake is one in which nutrient cycling is
low and in which productivity is low. It may be deeper than a
eutrophic lake. The process of accumulation in lakes of sediment and nutrients which sustain living organisms is called
"eutrophication". Natural eutrophication as a lake ages has
been going on for geologic eras of time. Recently observed extremely rapid aging of a lake may be the result of the influx
of effluents from man's activities resulting in a "cultural"
eutrophication as discussed on pages 209-214 by Moran, Morgan,
and Wiersma (1973).

Eutrophication is of continuing interest in water resource management. The University of Wisconsin at Madison as part of its Water Resources Information Program issues a bi-monthly summary of current literature dealing with eutrophication. An example of this series is the 38-page issue No. 42 for May-June, 1974.

Under accelerated eutrophication a lake may become completely depleted in dissolved oxygen. Under these conditions a breakdown of organic materials may be incomplete resulting very often in water of poor quality due to color, taste, and odor. Extensive attention has been directed toward the reaeration of streams and reservoirs. King (1970) has reviewed the physical principles underlying the aeration of reservoirs.

A comprehensive mathematical treatment of the exceedingly complex process of reaeration in open-channel flow is given by Bennett and Rathbun (1972). Symons (1969) compiled 17 papers with discussions on the subject of water quality behavior in reservoirs.

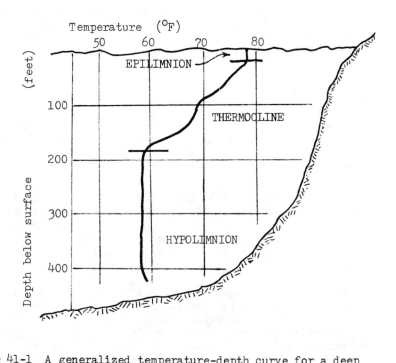

Figure 41-1  A generalized temperature-depth curve for a deep reservoir showing the positions of 3 commonly used terms for describing strata of a reservoir. The diagram is based on page 70 in the reference by Garstka, Phillips, Allen, and Hebert (1958).

The surface layer which has a high dissolved oxygen content and which allows sufficient penetration of light to sustain plant growth and which has high temperatures during the growing season is called "epilimnion". Underlying this layer is a transition zone in which there is a rapid temperature drop. This layer is called the "thermocline". Beneath the thermocline is a relatively stagnant layer with low temperatures, very low dissolved oxygen, and practically no plant growth. This bottom layer is called the "hypolimnion".

Since water attains its highest density at $4^\circ$ C a water approaching the freezing point is at the surface of the lake. The resulting ice cover forms without affecting the heat storage of the remainder of the lake at the time of freezing. If this were not the case lakes would freeze solid.

Hirshburg, Goodling, and Maples (1976) present a mathematical prediction model for diurnal mixing on thermal stratification of deep static impoundments. A nocturnal turnover in the epilimnion is the result of vertical energy transport due to solar radiation, molecular diffusion, and convective mixing.

In the cooler parts of the temperate zones deep lakes and reservoirs are thermally stratified in the summer. In the autumn as the surface waters cool and reach temperatures below those of the hypolimnion the surface layers become more dense and sink to lower depths displacing and bringing up the waters of the hypolimnion. This produces an inverse stratification for the winter. These lakes, called "climictic" by Hutchinson (1957, Vol. I, page 535), are freely circulating twice a year. This phenomenon, commonly referred to as the "fall-turnover", is of great ecological significance since it prevents stagnation and its related oxygen deficiency in the deeper portions of the lake or reservoir.

Because of differences in temperatures of inflowing water at various times of the day and of the year and of dissolved solids and suspended material, density currents may occur in a lake. Changes in energy storage due to incident sunlight, back radiation, and evaporation also produce differences in the density of the surface water. Therefore most lakes are thermally stratified.

Garstka, Phillips, Allen, and Hebert (1958) studied the possibility of reducing evaporation loss from Lake Mead by discharging the surface water which in the summer may attain temperatures of over $80^\circ$ F. They concluded that the hydrodynamics of the withdrawal of water did not permit such an operation of the reservoir.

The temperature of the water being released from a reservoir may be very important for fish and wildlife management, recreation, and for industrial and municipal usages. Extensive research has been conducted on the hydrodynamics of selective withdrawal from a stratified reservoir. A brief discussion of the physical concepts is given by Garstka, Phillips, Allen, and Hebert (1958) on their pages 63-67.

King (1971) described the results of mathematical and physical model studies of proposed selective withdrawal positionings for fish hatchery outlets at Pueblo Dam, Colorado. Johnson (1974) summarized the theory underlying the hydraulics of stratified and developed design curves and formulae for practical application. Pages 13-41 of Johnson's report contain a computer program, "USER'S MANUAL-PRO 1530-STRAH", developed by D. L. King, dated 10/11/73 for determining the theoretical withdrawal layer thickness for stratified reservoirs. This program, written in Fortran IV language for a Honeywell 800 computer, was found to be applicable to investigations of prototype structures.

A problem closely related to forecasting withdrawal from a stratified reservoir is that of predicting the water temperatures in a reservoir as yet not in existence. King and Sartoris (1973) report on verification tests conducted at Horsetooth Reservoir, Colorado, and Flaming Gorge Reservoir, Utah-Wyoming. Using the U.S. Army Corps of Engineers' version of the Water Resources Engineers' procedures which this private concern developed for the California Department of Fish and Game, King and Sartoris found excellent simulation of the 1965 Horsetooth Reservoir temperature profiles and acceptable simulation of 1965 temperature for Flaming Gorge Reservoir.

They conclude that a reliable prediction model for weakly stratified reservoirs remains to be developed. The input data for these temperature predictions is made up of five meteorological variables, two variables each for inflow and outflow, and eight reservoir characteristic variables making a total of 17 variables.

Burt (1974) made comparisons of forecasts of temperatures of outflows before the construction of Brownlee Dam on the Snake River, Idaho-Oregon, with observed temperatures after the dam was built. Brownlee Dam is 240 feet high. The reservoir is stratified. Forecasted and observed temperatures agreed very well for outflows released 141 feet below normal high-water elevation. Agreement was not as good for surface releases.

The interaction of natural stratification and cultural eutrophication may be so complex that under natural conditions a lake or reservoir would rapidly become unfit as a water supply for domestic use. Toetz, Wilhm, and Summerfelt (1972) review various mechanical and hydrodynamic means of inducing destratification and improving the aeration of lakes and reservoirs.

Fast (1973) found that artificial destratification of
El Capitan Reservoir in California resulted in a distribution
of zoobenthos throughout the lake. Ordinarily zoobenthos are
found only to shallow depths during well-stratified times.

The effects of artificial aeration on the chemistry and
algae of two lakes in the Michigan Lower Penninsula are described by Fast, Moss, and Wetzel (1973). A cross-sectional
drawing and a photograph of the hypolimnion aerator is given by
the authors. The depth of one design reached from near the
surface to 15.5 meters (50.84 feet). Compressed air was released to lift the water in this hypolimnion aerator.

Winter (1977) made a classification of the hydrologic
settings of 150 lakes in the North Central United States. He
found that the most important variables in his classification
were: dissolved solids concentration of groundwater, precipitation-evaporation balance, streamflow inlet and outlet, ratio
of the drainage basin area to lake area, and lake depth.

A very informative report entitled, "Man-Made Lakes as
Modified Ecosystems", has been prepared by a working group of
the Scientific Committee on Problems of the Environment (SCOPE)
(1972).

The Proceedings of a Symposium organized by the Scientific
Committee on Water Research on behalf of the International
Council of Scientific Unions and held at Knoxville, Tennessee,
May 3-7, 1971, were published in a monograph entitled, "Man-
Made Lakes: Their Problems and Environmental Effects" (1973).

By 1969 private land users in the United States had built
more than 2.2 million ponds and many more will be needed in the
future. The Soil Conservation Service has prepared an excellent handbook, "Ponds for Water Supply and Recreation" (1971),
which gives detailed information for the development of a pond.
This handbook is based on field experience and observations of
successful land users, experienced engineers, conservationists,
and other professionals. This handbook considers dams less
than 25 feet high located where failure of the dam would not
result in loss of life, damage to homes or commercial structures, or to main highways, railroads, and public utilities.

Problem Assignment - Pond

1. Select a location for a pond to be of not less than 2 acres
   in area, in a region of your choice.
2. State the purposes for which the pond is to be built such

as domestic and livestock water supply, irrigation, recreation, reserve water for fire fighting, etc. The purposes for which the pond is to be built must be in keeping with the climatology and hydrology of the area.

3. Outline steps you would take in your investigation of the suitability of the site with reference to construction material for the dam, possible seepage, and access to the pond.

4. Outline the steps you would take to determine the precipitation-evaporation ratios with reference to seasonal or year around usage.

5. Outline steps you would take to determine the peak rate of discharge which might occur and state the recurrence interval.

6. Outline your approach to the engineering design of the dam, water withdrawal facilities, and the flood spillway provisions.

7. Evaluate the potential damage which could occur downstream should the dam fail.

8. State what might be the environmental impacts of this pond.

9. Summarize all of your considerations and state whether or not you recommend that the pond be built.

## References

Bennett, J. P. and R. E. Rathbun, "Reaeration in Open-Channel Flow", Geol. Survey, USDI, Prof. Paper 737, Govt. Printing Office, Washington, D.C., 75 pp, 1972.

Burt, Wayne V., "Verification of Water Temperature Forecasts for Deep, Stratified Reservoirs", Water Resources Research vol. 10, no. 1, pp 93-97, Feb. 1974.

"Eutrophication: A Bimonthly Summary of Current Literature". For copies of this series and other series dealing with water resources address requests to: Coordinator, Water Resources Information Program, University of Wisconsin, Madison, 1975 Willow Dr., Madison, Wis. 53706.

Fast, Arlo W., "Effects of Artificial Destratification on Primary Production and Zoobenthos of El Capitan Reservoir, California", Water Resources Research, vol. 9 no. 3, pp 607-623, June, 1973.

Fast, Arlo W., Brian Moss, Robert G. Wetzel, "Effects of Artificial Aeration on the Chemistry and Algae of Two Michigan Lakes", Water Resources Research, vol. 9, no. 3, pp 624-647, June, 1973.

Garstka, Walter U., H. Boyd Phillips, Ira E. Allen, and
Donald J. Hebert, "Withdrawal of Water from Lake Mead",
pp 63-75 in Water-Loss Investigations: Lake Mead Studies,
USGS Prof. Paper 298, Govt. Printing Office, Washington,
D.C., 1958.

Hirshburg, R. I., J. S. Goodling, and G. Maples, "The Effects
of Diurnal Mixing on Thermal Stratification of Static
Impoundments", Water Resources Research, vol. 12, no. 6,
pp 1151-1159, Dec. 1976.

Hutchinson, G. Evelyn, "A Treatise on Limnology", Vol. I,
Geography, Physics, and Chemistry, 17 chapters, 1015 pp,
John Wiley & Sons, Inc., New York, 1957.

Hutchinson, G. Evelyn, "A Treatise on Limnology", Vol. II,
Introduction to Lake Biology and the Limnoplankton,
Chapters 18 through 26, 1115 pp, John Wiley & Sons, 1967.

Hutchinson, G. Evelyn, "A Treatise on Limnology", Vol. III,
Limnological Botany, Chapters 27 through 32, 660 pp,
John Wiley and Sons, New York, 1975.

Johnson, P. L., "Hydraulics of Stratified Flow - Final Report -
Selective Withdrawal from Reservoirs", Bureau of Reclama-
tion, USDI, Div. of General Research, Denver, Colo.,
Report No. REC-ERC-74-1, 24 pp, Jan. 1974.

King, D. L., "Reaeration of Streams and Reservoirs - Analysis
and Bibliography", Report No. REC-OCE-70-55, Engineering
and Research Center, Bur. of Reclamation, Denver, Colo.
Dec. 1970.

King, D. L., "Selective Withdrawal Studies for the Fish Hatch-
ery Outlets at Pueblo Dam - Mathematical and Physical
Models", Div. of General Research, Bur. of Reclamation,
USDI, Denver, Colo. Report No. REC-ERC-71-32, 18 pp,
Aug. 1971.

King, D. L. and J. J. Sartoris, "Mathematical Simulation of
Temperatures in Deep Impoundments - Verification Tests of
the Water Resources Engineers, Inc. Model - Horsetooth and
Flaming Gorge Reservoirs", Div. of General Research, Bur.
of Reclamation, USDI, Denver, Colo., Report REC-ERC-73-20,
27 pp, Nov. 1973.

"Man-Made Lakes as Modified Ecosystems", SCOPE Report 2, Paris,
1972, printed by F. Giannini & Figli, Naples, for International Council of Scientific Unions, 1972.

"Man-Made Lakes - Their Problems and Environmental Effects",
    ed. by William C. Ackermann, Gilbert F. White, and
    E. B. Worthington, Proceedings of an International Sympos-
    ium held in Knoxville, Tenn., May 3-7, 1971, Geophysical
    Monograph 17, pub. by Amer. Geophysical Union, Washington
    D.C., 847 pp, 1973.

Moran, Joseph M., Michael D. Morgan, and James H. Wiersma, "An
    Introduction to Environmental Sciences", 389 pp, Little,
    Brown and Co., Boston, 1973.

"Ponds for Water Supply and Recreation", prepared by Soil Cons-
    ervation Service, Agri. Handbook No. 387, USDA, 55 pp,
    Jan., 1971.

Symons, James M., Compiler, "Water Quality Behavior in
    Reservoirs - A Compilation of Published Research Papers",
    U.S. Public Health Service, Pub. No. 1930, Govt. Printing
    Office, Washington, D.C. 1969.

Toetz, Dale, Jerry Wilhm, Robert Summerfelt, "Biological
    Effects of Artificial Destratification and Aeration in
    Lakes and Reservoirs - Analysis and Bibliography", Report
    No. REC-ERC-72-33 prepared for the Bur. of Reclamation by
    Oklahoma State Univ., Stillwater Okla., 117 pp, Oct. 1972.

Winter, Thomas C., "Classification of the Hydrologic Settings
    of Lakes in the North Central United States", Water
    Resources Research, vol. 13, no. 4, pp 753-767, Aug. 1977.

Zumberge, James H., John C. Ayers, "Hydrology of Lakes and
    Swamps", Sec. 23 of Handbook of Applied Hydrology,
    Ven Te Chow, ed-in-chief, McGraw-Hill Book Co., New York,
    1964.

Oceanography was thought of as being the science of the seas but it is much more than that. There are three major divisions each of which is interdisciplinary in character. Dynamic oceanography deals with waves, currents, and tides which in turn involve astrophysics, fluid dynamics, and thermodynamics. Biological oceanography deals with the animal and plant life inhabiting the oceans ranging from microscopic organisms to whales. This involves not only the organisms presently inhabiting the oceans but also takes in paleontology. Physical oceanography encompasses direct observations of the ocean and theoretical studies of the processes involved. This division includes geology, chemistry, physics, mechanics, and engineering. Dynamic and physical oceanography interact with solar radiation and the atmosphere to produce the circulation pattern and the resulting hydrologic cycle upon which all land-based life depends as discussed in Topics 6 and 7.

Oceanography touches upon the geologic concept of continental drift. Hallam (1975) describes the development by Alfred Wegener (a meteorologist with no credentials as a geologist) of the hypothesis of the Continental Drift. This idea, which was not accepted for about 60 years, was first met with resistance and ridicule since it rendered obsolete practically all of the previous and, until then, hallowed concepts of the structure of the earth.

The origin of the ocean is the subject of a paper by Sir Edward Bullard written in 1969 and included as one of 15 papers in a very interesting assembly of reprints from the Scientific American entitled, "Continents Adrift", with an introduction by Wilson (1972). A tantalizing question raised by Bullard is that of the almost complete loss of neon from the Earth whereas the water molecule which has an atomic weight less than that of neon did not escape. The Earth, to the best of our current knowledge, is the only planet with sufficient water to form oceans.

Moore (1971) has written the Preface and Introductions to the five sections of an informative assembly of 41 papers relating to Oceanography the reading of which is recommended.

Davis (1972) has prepared a textbook, "Principles of Oceanography", which he designed for use in a one-semester course in general oceanography. Davis considers Matthew Fontaine Maury (1806-1873) of the U.S. Navy as probably the first full-time oceanographer.

von Arx with Ann F. Martin (1962) list in their Appendix

A, pages 351-395, events that have influenced thoughts in marine science. Their entries span the period from the time of Thales of Miletus, who lived during the period 640 to 546 B.C., up to 1955. Kazimierz Lomniewski's (1973) book on physical oceanography on his page 294 lists 30 international organizations and research programs dealing with oceanography and 27 principal oceanographic institutes in the World. There are over 30 oceanographic textbooks and over 25 periodicals dealing with this subject.

The concept of thermal structure and circulation discussed in Topic 41, Limnology, apply on a vastly increased and complicated scale to the oceans. The patterns of the ocean currents have long been recognized. Benjamin Franklin compiled and published in 1769 a chart of the Gulf Stream which is generally considered to be the first oceanographic publication according to Davis (1972). von Arx (1964) devotes Chapter 11, pages 313-350 to the Gulf Stream problem. Were it not for the Gulf Stream the climate of the British Isles might be similar to that of northern Newfoundland. The circulation patterns of the Atlantic Ocean southeast of the Gulf Stream upon close examination are found to be extremely complicated as described by Kerr (1977).

Munk (1955) gives a chart of the Earth's average surface circulation of the ocean basins as entered on an unusual cartographic projection. In another illustration of an idealized ocean, rectangular in shape, he assumes that this ocean was subjected only to horizontal winds. He uses descriptions for the winds as "westerly", "trade winds", and the "doldrums", terms which originated with mariners in the days of the sailing vessels. This idealized flow is complicated by the presence of continents, density changes due to temperature, and the Coreolis effect. Distribution of winds over oceans is analyzed mathematically by Thom (1973).

Ricker (1969) analyzes the potentiality and significance of food production from sea water in which he includes sea weeds, mollusks, fish, turtles, game birds, and mammals. He considers various ecological levels. He concludes that under the best expected conditions production of food from the sea would supply only about 3 percent of the energy requirements for a population of 3-1/2 billion people. However, food production from the seas can be very important to many people.

Cloud (1969) in his discussion of mineral resources from the sea concludes that by far the most important products from the oceans could be the oil and gas which really come not from the ocean but from geologic structures inundated by ocean waters. Magnesium, sodium, chlorine, bromine, potassium, iodine, strontium, and borax probably can be extracted most effectively from sea water. There are obstacles to the prospecting, development, and commercial utilization of minerals from the ocean environment and Cloud states: "A 'mineral cornucopia' beneath the sea thus exists only in hyperbole. What is actually won from it will be the result of persistent, imaginative research, inspired invention, bold and skillful experiment, and intelligent application and management - and resources found will come mostly from the submerged continental shelves, slopes, and rises. Whether they will be large or small is not known."

Some profound implications with reference to the availability of power, fresh water and food from cold deep sea water is discussed by Othmer and Roels (1973). They analyze the thermodynamics of possible utilization of the temperature differences between ocean waters at dissimilar temperatures and solar energy for the generation of power, referring to the work of G. Claude in 1930. Their concept is worthy of immediate pursuit in this era of increasing energy supply problems.

In the last few decades there have been tremendous advancements in the instrumentation data gathering techniques and analytical procedures in oceanography. Lomniewski's (1973) book contains many illustrations of instruments dealing with the recent approaches to data gathering and research methods. The availability of computers and electronic data processing and plotting facilities has become of inestimable value to oceanography as it has to meteorology and hydrology.

The use of sound waves of various frequencies to determine the position and thickness of the sediment on the ocean floor and the underlying rocks is described in a pamphlet "Marine Geology - Research Beneath the Sea" (1973). Ocean surface currents are being mapped by radar with a precision better than 30 centimeters per second as described by Barrick, Evans, and Weber (1977).

The interaction between the atmosphere and the ocean is illustrated by the effects of the severe winter of 1976-77 in the Northeastern United States on temperatures in the north-western Sargasso Sea of the Atlantic Ocean. Leetmaa (1977) found that the severe winter significantly changed the temperature of the main thermocline in this area. Newly-formed, well-mixed layers of water at $18^\circ$ C ($64.4^\circ$ F) as deep as 550 meters (1800 feet) were observed, and the main thermocline south of the Gulf Stream was 100 to 150 meters (330 to 490 feet) deeper than average.

To the ancients the oceans were a mystery, to the mariners they were a base upon which they navigated, but the shorelines and the estuaries are the areas of interest touching upon man's endeavors. The estuary and the wetlands are of special interest since these are the areas which are extremely productive in harboring water fowl and in producing oysters, clams, crabs, and many fish.

Soucie (1975) reviewed the increasing appreciation of the wetlands. In South Carolina alone the salt marshes have yielded gross profits of about 5 million dollars a year from the oyster beds and the shrimpers have boosted the State's economy by about 10 million dollars a year. According to Soucie the South Carolina Water Resources Commission conservatively estimates that saltwater sports anglers' expenditures amount to at least 15 million dollars in the State.

A rising public awareness of the value of estuarine areas is indicated by the publication by the League of Women Voters of the pamphlet, "Where Rivers Meet the Sea", (1970) which contains a description of estuarine areas, the damage arising from industrial and municipal waste, and damages from physical change especially dredging and filling.

In 1824 Congress made the U.S. Army Corps of Engineers responsible for deepening and maintaining harbor channels in the interest of National defense in the days of sailing vessels. In 1899 Congress made it a requirement that a permit be issued by the Corps for private dredging and dumping in navigable waters. This concept will be discussed further in Topic 66.

Zitta, Shindala, and Corey (1977) describe mathematical models for water quality planning using data from the Pascagoula River basin estuary. The river basin has a drainage area of 9700 square miles in Mississippi.

Not all off-shore development is necessarily destructive to the environment. Lord (1974) describes off-shore developments that minimize environmental impact. He compares the cost of various techniques of reclaiming land from the ocean. The Netherlands began reclamation of land from the ocean to be used for agricultural production as early as the 13th Century and the total area they have reclaimed as of 1962 was approximately 1,800,000 acres (7300 km$^2$). A major portion of the JFK International Airport was reclaimed from the tidal marshes and a large portion of San Francisco Bay has been filled for an airport, recreation, residential purposes, and other developments.

The increasing dependence of the United States on imported oil for energy and for the chemical industries has produced National concern about the ecological dangers of massive oil spills. An interesting exchange of different points of view on the actual damage which may result from massive oil spills such as that of the Argo Merchant which released almost 28,000 metric tons of Diesel fuel oil off Nantucket Island, is presented by Abelson (1977) and Farrington, Sanders, Teal, and Grassle (1977).

Engineers and scientists were aware of the potential dangers of oil spills as is evidenced by the analyses of the dynamics of contained oil slicks treated by Wilkinson (1972), which is illustrated with photographs of physical models of oil slicks using peanut oil with a viscosity of 60 times that of water, and kerosene having a viscosity of twice that of water.

Cross and Cunningham (1973) analyze the design, construction, storage, and performance of booms for the containment of oil under emergency use in harbors. They found that a boom must be deployed around oil spills within minutes of the start of a spill if it is to have a good chance of containing most of the oil in a deep compact pool. The design criteria they present are based upon actual experience in spill control while working with the Marine Division of the Fire Department in the New York Harbor area.

Moran, Morgan, and Wiersma (1973) list effects of either accidental or thoughtless discharges of oil. Water fowl have little chance of survival, fish that depend on their sense of smell become confused, and fish and shellfish acquire a tainted odor, beaches are covered and oil is tracked into buildings and homes. As shipping of oil increases so may the incidence of oil spills.

Sewage discharge from ships transiting coastal salt waters is the subject of a paper by van Hees (1977). He defines sewage as all non-oily waste water generated on shipboard. He describes experiments in which dye concentrations and coliform bacteria were measured. Experiments were conducted near the Norfolk, Virginia, Naval Base and near the coast of San Clemente Island, California. A single ship entering pristine waters should be little cause for concern. However long-range effects from a concentration of traffic are not known. Recent water quality legislation outlaws the discharge of sewage from commercial or recreational vessels in inland waterways or lakes.

The incessant action between the shoreline with tides, waves, and the inflowing rivers results in the creation of deltas, estuaries, beaches, and sedimentary deposits. Certain aspects of fluvial geomorphology are described in the book by Simons and Senturk (1977). Bascom (1959) described with photographs and drawings the hydrodynamics of waves which bear a mathematical relationship to the depth of water. Bascom describes the awesome phenomenon of the "tsunami" or seismic sea wave which may have a wave length of several hundred miles and a velocity of about 450 miles per hour. Tsunamis have been extremely destructive to coastal environments.

Bernstein (1954) in his article on tsunamis reported that in 1896 a Japanese tsunami killed 27,000 people and swept away

245

about 10,000 homes. Tsunamis are rare in the Atlantic. In the Pacific Japan has had 15 destructive tsunamis since 1596. The recurrence interval for severe tsunamis at the Hawaiian Islands averages about 25 years.

The interaction of sediment, wind, waves, and tides is so complex as to defy mathematical expression. The complexity of this problem can be appreciated by a study of the illustrations included in the paper by Bascom (1960) as reprinted in the compilation by Moore (1971).

Shoreline features such as Cape Cod and Martha's Vineyard are evanescent and with time could cease to exist. Harbors for ocean-going vessels are continuously being filled in by sediment deposits. The Beach Erosion Board was created to study the problem. Subsequent to November, 1963 it is known as the Army Coastal Engineering Research Center, Kingman Building, Fort Belvoir, Virginia 22060.

The Corps of Engineers has established the U.S. Army Engineer Waterways Experiment Station, P.O. Box 631, Vicksburg, Mississippi 39180. Both of these centers have at their disposal extensive physical model facilities and they often collaborate on the solution of practical problems of mutual interest.

Since the problems dealing with maintenance of waterways and harbors are world-wide in their scope an extensive literature is available. One example of this is the Proceedings (1977) of the Fifteenth Coastal Engineering Conference, international in scope, held in Honolulu, Hawaii, July, 1976. These Proceedings consist of 4 volumes containing 206 papers.

The Waterway, Port, Coastal, and Ocean Division of the American Society of Civil Engineers sponsored in November, 1977 a Symposium on Coastal Sediments. The 1,113-page Proceedings of this Symposium deal with an appraisal of the state-of-the-art concerning functional design of structural and non-structural solutions to shoreline protection and inlet stabilization.

## Saline Water Demineralization

By far the greatest percentage (97.2 percent) of the Earth's total water is in the oceans. Related to the formation of continents is the question: Why are the oceans salty? An answer, long in vogue, was that the leaching of salts by runoff and groundwater, their transport to the ocean, and concentration by the hydrologic cycle produced the salinity. However this concept failed to account for the geologic time span involved. Macintyre (1970), in the compilation edited by Moore (1971), explains on the basis of geology and physical chemistry how the weathering of igneous rocks ends up as sodium chloride as shown in his chart on page 115. Especially interesting is his chart of carbon dioxide as related to hydrogen-ion concentration (pH). Sea water is extremely corrosive.

The salinity of the ocean averages 35,000 parts per million with a variation of only about 2,000 parts per million. Another way of expressing this is that there are 35 pounds of salt in each thousand pounds of sea water. Over 70 elements have been found in sea water and there is no doubt that every element known on Earth is to be found there. The major components of sea water and of river water are given in Table 42-1 as taken from "Why is the Ocean Salty" (1976). It will be noted that sodium chloride constitutes over 85 percent of the total salt content of ocean water and a little less than 16 percent of the total salt content of river water.

Table 42-1   Composition of Ocean and River Water Generalized

| Chemical Constituent | Percentage of Total Salt Content | |
|---|---|---|
| | Ocean Water | River Water |
| Silica $(SiO_2)$ . . . . . | | 14.51 |
| Iron $(Fe)$ . . . . . . . | | 0.74 |
| Calcium $(Ca)$ . . . . . | 1.19 . . . . | 16.62 |
| Magnesium $(Mg)$ . . . . . | 3.72 . . . . | 4.54 |
| Sodium $(Na)$ . . . . . | 30.53 . . . . | 6.98 |
| Potassium $(K)$ . . . . . | 1.11 . . . . | 2.55 |
| Bicarbonate $(HCO_3)$ . . | 0.42 . . . . | 31.90 |
| Sulfate $(SO_4)$ . . . . . | 7.67 . . . . | 12.41 |
| Chloride $(Cl)$ . . . . . | 55. . . . . | 8.64 |
| Nitrate $(NO_3)$ . . . . . | | . . . . 1.11 |
| Bromide $(Br)$ . . . . . | 0.20 . . . . | |
| Total   . . . . | 100.00 . . . . | 100.00 |

Throughout the Nation there are numerous deposits of rock salt or of brine. Many springs and streams carry such great concentrations of salt as to be unfit for domestic and agricultural usage.

Demineralization, sometimes called desalination, is aimed at reducing the total dissolved solids to yield fresh water. Although there are over 30 different approaches physically or chemically possible for producing fresh water from salt water most do not lend themselves to practical large-scale applications.

In general there are two approaches: one is the removal
of water from the salt as is done by distillation, and the
other is the removal of salt from the water as is accomplished
by electrodialysis. An informative description of the more
promising processes with numerous multi-colored diagrams is
given in the pamphlet, "The A-B-Seas of Desalting" (1968) from
which Figures 42-1 through 42-4 are taken. These Figures
appear on the following pages.

Many techniques for producing fresh water such as distillation have been known and practiced for a very long time and
extensive research had been conducted by both governmental and
private agencies on saline water demineralization. The importance of this activity was finally recognized and in 1952
Congress passed the "Saline Water Conversion Act of 1952",
Public Law 448, 82nd Congress, Second Session as Amended. This
Act has been followed by many others pertaining to saline water.

A continuing problem with land-based saline water demineralization plants is the disposal of the concentrated
solutions. The initial approach of pumping the salt water back
into the groundwater was not acceptable since it would ultimately result in polluting the natural system. Piping the concentrated solutions to the sea is practical for distances up
to about 70 miles. The construction of evaporative lagoons
and the disposal of the salt by transportation to the ocean are
other approaches. Therefore, except for small installations
and for special purposes large-scale inland saline water
demineralization plants are not being considered currently for
extensive use.

Jenkins (1957) as included in Moore's compilation (1971)
described a number of techniques available for demineralization
of water among which are solar stills. An ingenous application
of the solar still is given by Jackson and van Bavel (1967)
who describe the construction of the still using polyvinyl
fluoride film which would provide sufficient water to survive
in the desert securing the water from the soil or from plant
tissues. See Figure 42-5 on page 251.

The Office of Saline Water was combined with the Office of
Water Resources Research both of which were in the U.S. Dept.
of Interior, forming the new organization, the Office of Water
Research and Technology. Reports dealing with saline water de-
mineralization are now available by purchase only from the
National Technical Information Service, Operations Division,
Springfield, Virginia 22151. NTIS listed over one thousand re-
ports on saline water as being available.

As of late 1972 more than 8000 desalting plants having a
capacity of 25 thousand gallons per day or larger were either
in operation or under construction in the United States and in

248

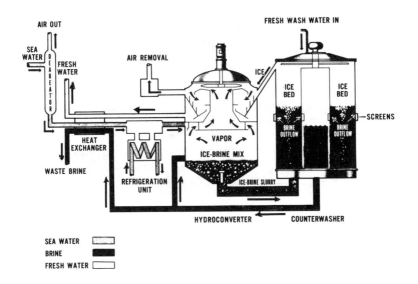

Figure 42-1  Vacuum freezing-vapor compression process from "The A-B-Seas of Desalting" (1968).

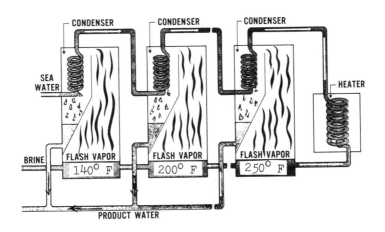

Figure 42-2  Multistage flash distillation process from "The A-B-Seas of Desalting" (1968).

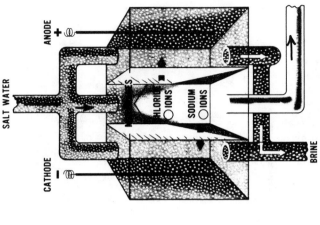

Figure 42-4 An electrodialysis cell for separating salts from water.

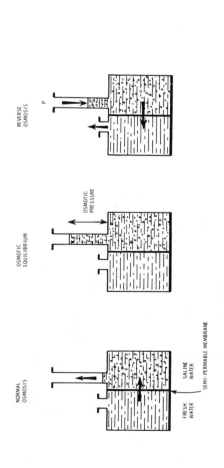

Figure 42-3 Principle of the Reverse Osmosis process.

Both figures are from "The A-B-Seas of Desalting" (1968).

the World as reported in the "1972-73 Saline Water Conversion
Summary Report". The major effort currently is on the construction of large-scale plants.

Todd (1977) reported that the rate of growth of the desalination industry in recent years has been about 20 percent per
annum and this is expected to increase in the near future. The
Multi-Stage Flash (MSF) evaporation process is the "work horse"
of the desalination industry. MSF units of 7,900,000 gallons
per day (30,000 cubic meters) are now in service.

Figure 42-5  A Solar Still to
              Provide Water for
Survival in the Desert.
See Jackson and van Babel
(1967). "Edge of plastic film
is securely weighted down with
soil all around rim of pit.
Rock is placed in center and
pushed down to form the film
into an inverted cone. Rock
must be directly over container. The solar still is now
complete. Wait for a few
hours and then you can take a
drink." The photograph shows
the man securing a drink by
sucking water through a
plastic tube from the receiver.
This technique does not dis-
turb the solar still.

In order to reduce the salinity of Colorado River water to
be delivered to Mexico under the Treaty of February 3, 1944,
the Bureau of Reclamation has built a test facility near Yuma,
Arizona. van Hoek and Mavis report some of the test results
of this facility (1977) which was constructed preliminary to
the ultimate construction of a much larger plant. Engstrom,
Taylor, and Haugseth (1977) describe the design and construction approach for the Yuma desalting plant which will have a
capacity of 100,000,000 gallons per day (378,500 cubic meters)
and will be the largest plant of its type in the World. This
activity is being done under the "Colorado River Basin Salinity
Control Project Act, PL 93-320, Title I ". Not less than 2 or

more than 3 commercially available demineralization processes are to be used. Saline water of 3,200 ppm will be processed to yield demineralized water which could be as low as 254 ppm if needed to supply water to Mexico in accordance with the Treaty.

Although the original objective of the demineralization program was to provide fresh water, the research and development findings have had wide application in industrial engineering, food and medical supply processes, and industrial wastewater treatment, Research is underway to apply the knowledge and experience to sewage effluent treatment as part of water quality management.

Another impact on oceans, notably on estuaries, is thermal modification especially in the vicinity of power plants. Heating of the water may modify the ecology of the immediate environment. The generation of hydroelectric power by harnessing the tides is discussed in Topic 91.

Not very many years ago the ocean was considered to be the ideal repository forever of the debris of civilization including garbage, toxic substances, and the waste products of the nuclear industry, both military and commercial. Increasing knowledge of oceanography has revised our practices with regard to debris. If it were not for the oceans we would not be here.

## References

"A-B-Seas of Desalting", Office of Saline Water, USDI, 40 pp, U.S. Govt. Printing Office, 1968.

Abelson, Philip H., "Oil Spills", Science, vol. 195, no. 4274, p 137, 14 January 1977.

Barrick, D. E., M. W. Evans, and B. L. Weber, "Ocean Surface Currents Mapped by Radar", Science, vol 198, no. 4313, pp 138-144, 14 Oct. 1977.

Bascom, Willard, "Ocean Waves", Aug. 1959, pub. in Oceanography Readings from Scientific American, introduction by J. Robert Moore, W. H. Freeman & Co., pp 45-55, 1971.

Bascom, Willard, "Beaches", Aug. 1960, pub. in Oceanography, Readings from Scientific American, introduction by J. Robert Moore, W. H. Freeman & Co., pp 131-141, 1971.

Bernstein, Joseph, "Tsunamis", Aug. 1954, pub. in Oceanography, Readings from Scientific American, introduction by J. Robert Moore, W. H. Freeman & Co., pp 56-59, 1971.

Bullard, Sir Edward, "The Origin of the Oceans", Sept. 1969, pub. in Continents Adrift, Readings from Scientific American, introductions by J. Tuzo Wilson, W. H. Freeman and Co., San Francisco, pp 88-97, 1972.

Cloud, Preston, "Mineral Resources from the Sea", pub. in Resources and Man, by the Committee on Resources and Man, Natl. Academy of Sciences, Natl. Research Council, W. H. Freeman & Co., San Francisco, pp 135-155, 1969.

"Coastal Sediments '77", Proceedings of a Conference held at Charleston, So. Carolina, Nov. 2-4, 1977, sponsored by the Waterway, Port, Coastal, and Ocean Div. 1113 pp, Amer. Soc. of Civil Engineers, 1977.

Cross, Ralph H., and John J. Cunningham, "Oil Booms for Emergency Harbor Use", Jour. Waterways, Harbors, and Coastal Engineering Div., Proceedings ASCE, pp 27-37, Feb. 1973.

Davis, Richard A., Jr., "Principles of Oceanography", Addison-Wesley Pub. Co., Reading, Mass., 434 pp, 1972.

Engstrom, Fred, I. Taylor, and L. Haugseth, "Yuma Desalting Plant Design", a paper presented at 5th Annual Conference, Natl. Water Supply Improvement Assn., San Diego, Calif., July 20, 1977. To be published by the Association, P.O. Box 8300, Fountain Valley, Calif. 92708.

Farrington, John W., Howard L. Sanders, John M. Teal, and J. Frederick Grassle, "The Argo Merchant Oil Spill", a letter to the editor, Science, vol. 195, p 932, Mar. 11, 1977.

Hallam, A., "Alfred Wegener and the Hypothesis of Continental Drift", Scientific American, vol. 232, no. 2, pp 88-97, Feb. 1975.

Jackson, Ray D., and C. H. M. van Bavel, "A Drink from the Desert", pub. in Outdoors USA, Yearbook of Agriculture, 1967, pp 175-177, U.S. Govt. Printing Office, 1967.

Jenkins, David S., "Fresh Water From Salt", March, 1957, pub. in Oceanography, Readings from Scientific American, introduction by J. Robert Moore, W. H. Freeman & Co., San Francisco, pp 337-345, 1971.

Kerr, Richard A, "Oceanography: A Closer Look at Gulf Stream Rings", Science, vol. 198, no 4315, pp 387-389 and 430, 28 October 1977.

Leetma, Ants, "Effects of the Winter of 1976-1977 on the North-
western Sargasso Sea", Science, vol. 198, no. 4313,
pp 188-189, 14 October 1977.

Lomniewski, Kazimierz, "Physical Oceanography", (Oceanografia
fizyczna), 1971; Translated from Polish by
Halina Dzierzanowska, Translation TT 70-55095. National
Tech. Information Service, Springfield, Va. 22151, 1973.

Lord, Charles J., "Offshore Developments That Minimize Environmental Impact", Jour. Construction Division, ASCE,
pp 159-170, June, 1974.

Macintyre, Ferren, "Why the Sea is Salt", Nov. 1970, pub. in
Oceanography, Readings from Scientific American, intro-
duction by J. Robert Moore, W. H. Freeman & Co.,
San Francisco, pp 110-121, 1971.

"Marine Geology - Research Beneath the Sea", pamphlet, 16 pp,
Geological Survey, USDI, 1973.

Moore, J. Robert, Introductions for "Oceanography - Readings
from Scientific American", W. H. Freeman & Co.,
San Francisco; this is a compilation of 41 reprints
totalling 417 pp, 1971.

Moran, Joseph M., Michael D. Morgan, and James H. Wiersma,
"An Introduction to Environmental Sciences", Little,
Brown and Co., Boston, 389 pp, 1973.

Munk, Walter, "The Circulation of the Oceans", Sept. 1955, pub.
in Oceanography, Readings from Scientific American,
introduction by J. Robert Moore, W. H. Freeman & Co.,
San Francisco, pp 64-69, 1971.

Othmer, Donald F., and Oswald A. Roels, "Power, Fresh Water,
and Food from Cold, Deep Sea Water", Science, vol. 182,
no. 4108, pp 121-125, 12 October 1973.

"Proceedings Fifteenth Coastal Engineering Conference",
held at Honolulu, Hawaii, July, 1976. 206 papers in 4
volumes totalling more than 2600 pp. Amer. Soc. of Civil
Engineers, 1977.

Ricker, William E., "Food From the Sea", pub. in Resources and
Man, by the Committee on Resources and Man, Natl. Academy
of Sciences, Natl. Research Council, W. H. Freeman & Co.,
San Francisco, pp 87-108, 1969.

"Saline Water Conversion Summary Report 1972-1973", Office of
Saline Water, USDI, 70 pp, U.S. Govt. Printing Office,
1973.

Simons, Daryl B., and Fuat Senturk, "Sediment Transport Technology", Water Resources Publications, Fort Collins, Colo., 807 pp, 1977.

Soucie, Gary A., "We Can Still Save Salt Marshes of Georgia, Carolina", Smithsonian, vol. 5, no. 12, pp 82-89, March, 1975.

Thom, Herbert C. S., "Distributions of Extreme Winds Over Oceans", Jour. Waterways, Harbors and Coastal Engineering Div., Proceedings ASCE, pp 1-17, Feb. 1973.

Todd, Brian, "Desalination Industry", Nickel Topics, International Nickel Co., vol. 30, no. 2, p 15, 1977.

van Hees, Willem, "Sewage Discharges from Ships Transiting Coastal Salt Waters", Water Resources Bulletin, vol. 13, no. 2, pp 215-229, Apr. 1977.

van Hoek, C., and J. D. Mavis, Jr., "Test Results at the Yuma Desalting Test Facility", a paper presented at 5th Annual Conf., Natl. Water Supply Improvement Assn., San Diego, Calif , July 20, 1977. To be published by the Assn. P.O. Box 8300, Fountain Valley, Calif. 92708.

von Arx, William S., "An Introduction to Physical Oceanography" Addison-Wesley Pub. Co., Inc., Reading, Mass. 422 pp, 1962.

"Where Rivers Meet the Sea", pub. by The League of Women Voters of the United States in Facts and Issues, Pub. No. 367, 8 pp, Feb. 1970.

"Why is the Ocean Salty?", pamphlet 16 pp, Geological Survey, USDI, U.S. Govt. Printing Office, 1976.

Wilkinson, David L., "Dynamics of Contained Oil Slicks", Jour. Hydraulics Div., Proceedings ASCE, pp 1013-1030, June, 1972.

Wilson, J. Tuzo, Introductions for "Continents Adrift - Readings from Scientific American", W. H. Freeman & Co., San Francisco; this is a compilation of 15 reprints totalling 172 pp, 1972.

Zitta, V. L., A. Shindala, and M. W. Corey, "A Two-Dimensional Mathematical Model for Water Quality Planning in Estuaries", Water Resources Research, vol. 13, no. 1, pp 55-61, Feb. 1977.

SECTION IX

GROUNDWATER

Topic 43          Groundwater Hydraulics

In dealing with groundwater hydraulics a distinction
should be kept in mind between the flow of a fluid through a
porous medium and the flow of the same fluid through pipes or
through fissures in which the cross section of the flow is very
large as compared to the size of pores in a soil or in a porous
sandstone.

Fluid dynamics distinguishes between laminar flow and turbulent flow. Laminar flow occurs in a molecular dimension.
Laminar flow is also referred to as viscous flow or streamline
flow. It can be likened to movement in a bundle of necklaces
in which each bead represents a molecule of water. A pull on
one necklace will result in movement of the beads strung only
to that necklace and none of the other beads on adjacent
strings will be displaced.

In turbulent flow the motion of the fluid is not stream-
lined and any movement results in a very complex readjustment
of the individual molecules of the fluid in such a way that the
exact direction of movement of any one molecule is unpredic-
table. Practically all of our knowledge of the behavior of
fluids to date has been with reference to the turbulent regime
and only recently in dealing with supersonic velocities are we
attaining some understanding of the laminar conditions.

The Reynolds number makes it possible to distinguish between laminar and turbulent flows. The equation in condensed
form for the Reynolds number is

$$Re = \frac{inertial\ forces}{viscous\ vources} = \frac{\rho vL}{\mu} \qquad (1)$$

in which

$\rho$   is the fluid density

$v$   is the velocity

$L$   is a characteristic length, and

$\mu$   is the fluid viscosity.

If the Reynolds number is less than 2,000 the flow is laminar. As Re increases the laminar sublayer is penetrated by
roughness elements and the flow becomes turbulent. Between the
values of 2,000 and 3,500 for Re there is an indefinite transition when the flow changes from laminar to turbulent. Above

256

Re = 3,500 it is commonly assumed when dealing with flow in pipes that the flow is completely turbulent. The numerical value of Re can run into millions.

However under laminar-flow conditions and especially under turbulent-flow conditions there is a boundary layer at the interface between the fluid and the confining structure, whether it be pipe, capillary tube, or soil interstices. Within the boundary layer there is a steep reduction in velocities of flow until a condition of shear of molecular dimensions is attained.

In groundwater hydraulics the value of Reynold's number of less than 10 is accepted as laminar flow; greater than 10 as turbulent flow. In laminar flow the head required varies directly with the velocity. In turbulent flow the head varies approximately as the square of the velocity. The change from laminar to turbulent flow in groundwater results from a combination of increases in velocity, increases in the size of the opening, and decreases in viscosity affected chiefly by temperature.

Henri Darcy in 1856 described the results of his experiments on the flows of water through sands in a report on water supply. He concluded that the flow of water was directly proportional to head loss and inversely proportional to the thickness of the sand. A general statement of Darcy's equation is

$$v = K \frac{dh}{dL} \tag{2}$$

in which

    $v$   is the velocity

  $\dfrac{dh}{dL}$  is the gradient

    $K$   is the coefficient of permeability or the hydraulic conductivity.

Shear resistance is computed by the Darcy-Weisbach equation which was originally derived for flow in pipes. The equation follows

$$h_f = f \frac{L}{D} \frac{v^2}{2g} \tag{3}$$

in which

    $f$  is a resistance coefficient,
    $L$  is a length of pipe in feet,
    $D$  is the diameter in feet,
    $V$  is the mean velocity of flow in ft per second
    $g$  is acceleration due to gravity, 32.2 ft per second per second, and
    $h_f$ is the shear resistance.

The resistance coefficient f depends on the Reynolds number of the flow and the relative roughness as expressed by the ratio e/D, where e is the average size of the roughness element.

When this equation is transformed for the laminar flow condition it becomes

$$V = \frac{k}{\mu} \quad \frac{H}{L} \tag{4}$$

in which

H  is the frictional head loss,
L  is the length,
k  is an expression of permeability, and
μ  is dynamic viscosity.

As applied to groundwater hydraulics it is necessary to depart from a diameter and length concept since the pores in a soil or an aquifer are rarely circular in cross section and cylindrical in shape.

This statement is the general Darcy equation for laminar flow through a porous medium. By making appropriate substitutions in the basic hydraulic equation of Q = AV the initial statement of Darcy's equation as used in groundwater hydrology becomes

$$Q = P I A \tag{5}$$

in which

Q  is discharge in cubic feet per day,
P  is coefficient of permeability in cubic feet per day per square foot,
I  is the hydraulic gradient in feet per foot,
A  is area of cross section of the flow, in square feet.

Various transformations of Darcy's equation are of fundamental importance in hydrology. It is basic to our understanding of infiltration; of the flow of water in soils; of the removal of excess water in soil by drainage systems; of the release of groundwater to a stream, to a spring, or to a well; of the contributions to a stream channel by subsurface flow; and of snowmelt.

In its Q = PIA form, Darcy's equation applies only to the laminar flow condition. Therefore, whenever fissures or faults occur in rocks or cracks or rough channels in the soil, the movement of water through them does not behave according to Darcy's equation.

Each of the terms in Darcy's equation can be expressed as needed for a particular application. If any three terms are

258

known the fourth can be computed. It is extremely important that the definitions of the terms for a particular statement of Darcy's equation be correct for that statement. For example, the U.S. Geological Survey used two definitions of the coefficient of permeability:

| Symbol | Name | Definition |
|---|---|---|
| $K_s$ | The Meinzer Unit (also known as the laboratory or standard coefficient of permeability) | Flow of water at 60° F in gal/day through a medium having a cross-sectional area of 1 sq. ft. under a hydraulic gradient of 1 ft. per ft. |
| $K_f$ | Field coefficient of permeability | Flow of water in gal/day through a cross section of aquifer 1 ft. thick and 1 mile wide under a hydraulic gradient of 1 ft. per mile at field temperature. |
|  | U.S. Bureau of Reclamation Unit of Permeability. | Cubic feet per year through 1 sq. ft. under unit gradient. (This is a volumetric unit, as are others when time is stated.) |

$K_s$ has a value in the range of 10 to 5,000 for most natural aquifers.

The symbol T appears in many groundwater hydraulic formulae. One definition of T is
$$T = K_f\ b \tag{6}$$
in which

T is the coefficient of transmissiblity,
$K_f$ is the field coefficient of permeability, and
b is the aquifer thickness in feet.

Until Theis described his non-equilibrium formula which recognized time as a factor and introduced the coefficient of storage concept, groundwater hydrology was limited to relatively simple applications of Q = PIA. Todd discusses the Theis formula and the "well function" [W(u)] and presents an example of its use. See Todd (1964) pages 13-18, 13-19, and 13-20.

The four books referenced in the following four paragraphs require a considerable background in fluid dynamics, mathematics, and geology. They were written primarily for use as upper-level or graduate study texts and for use by professionals.

Bear, Zaslavsky, and Irmay (1968) have prepared a 465-page

volume on the physical principles of water percolation and seepage. They deal with soil physics, dynamics of soil moisture, unsaturated flow, two-fluid flow, and hydrodynamic dispersion. They present a synthesis of theoretical physical-mathematical models with direct observation in the laboratory or in the field.

Glover's (1974) book on transient groundwater hydraulics is based on material coming from his professional experience including the teaching of graduate-level courses.

Corey (1977) has prepared a textbook with 113 problems dealing with the mechanics of heterogeneous fluids such as water, gas, petroleum including two-phase fluids in porous media.

McWhorter and Sunada (1977) have written a text designed for use in upper-level and graduate courses in groundwater hydrology and hydraulics for students majoring in Agricultural Engineering, Civil Engineering, Geology, and Watershed Science.

## References

Albertson, Maurice L. and Daryl B. Simons, "Fluid Dynamics", Sec. 7, Handbook of Applied Hydrology, ed. by Ven Te Chow, McGraw-Hill Book Co., New York, 1964.

Bear, J., D. Zaslavsky, S. Irmay, editors, "Physical Principles of Water Percolation and Seepage", a UNESCO Publication in the English language, printed in France, 1968.

Butler, Stanley S., "Subsurface Water", Chap. 5; "Hydraulics of Wells", Chap. 7; and "Adaptation of Well Hydraulics to Field Conditions", Chap. 8 in Engineering Hydrology, Prentice-Hall Inc., Englewood Cliffs, N.J., 1957.

Corey, Arthur T., "Mechanics of Heterogeneous Fluids in Porous Media", 259 pp, Water Resources Publications, Fort Collins Colo., 1977.

Ferris, John G., "Ground Water", Chapt. 6 in Hydrology, 2nd edition, C. O. Wisler and E. F. Brater, John Wiley and Sons, New York, 1959.

Glover, Robert E., "Transient Ground Water Hydraulics", 413 pp Water Resources Publications, Fort Collins, Colo. 1974.

Kasmann, Raphael G., "Ground Water", in Modern Hydrology, Harper and Row, New York, 2nd edition, 1972.

Linsley, R. K., M. A. Kohler, and J. L. H. Paulhus, "Subsurface Water", Chap. 6 in Hydrology for Engineers, McGraw-Hill Book Co., New York, 2nd ed. 1975.

McWhorter, David B. and Daniel K. Sunada, "Ground-Water Hydrology and Hydraulics", 304 pp, Water Resources Publications Fort Collins, Colo. 1977.

Theis, C. V., "The Relation Between the Lowering of the Piezometric Surface and the Rate and Duration of Discharge of a Well Using Groundwater Storage", Trans. AGU, vol. 16, pp 519-524, 1935.

Todd, David Keith, "Groundwater", Sec. 13, Handbook of Applied Hydrology, edited by Ven Te Chow, McGraw-Hill Book Co., New York, 1964.

Water Resources Research, vol. 8, no. 1, Feb. 1972, includes papers from a Symposium on Planning and Design of Groundwater Data Programs. The Symposium was held Dec. 8, 1970, in San Francisco, Calif., under the sponsorship of the AGU. Pp 177-211 contain eight papers on groundwater. 1972

Utilization of groundwater pre-dates the development of pumps. About 3,000 years ago, according to Wulff (1968), the ancient Persians learned how to dig tunnels into mountain aquifers. As of 1968 there were about 170,000 miles of underground channels providing about 75 percent of the water used in Iran.

Artificial recharge of groundwater is a prehistoric practice. The American Indians in the Southwest are known to have made use of this practice over a thousand years ago. (See Topic 1.) There is increasing interest in the disposal of waste treatment plant effluent through artificial groundwater recharge techniques. Longenbaugh (1966) reviews requirements of artificial recharge and describes a program conducted on the Arikaree River near Cope, Colorado.

Movement of water between open-channel flow in streams and groundwater is a subject of great importance in water resources development, land-use planning, and water law. An excellent sketch showing a number of the more common groundwater-surface-water interchanges is Eagleson's (1970) figure on his page 266.

An "influent" stream is one which contributes to a groundwater system; it is now being referred to as a "losing" stream. An "effluent" stream is one supplied by water flowing out of a groundwater system; it is now referred to as a "gaining" stream. Concepts of surface-water groundwater interactions are shown in Figure 44-1 from Feth (1973).

"Water in the Unsaturated Zone" (1969) includes in Chapters VI, VII, XII, XIII, and XIV numerous papers which present in condensed form many concepts about groundwater.

A pumped well depresses the groundwater level. If two wells are located too close to each other they will cause a further depression as shown in Figure 44-2 from Bittinger (1967). Aquifer characteristics permitting, the deepest well equipped with the most powerful pumps can dry up shallower wells.

Wells drilled on a stream bank may in effect be supplied by water percolating from a "losing" stream or they may be depleting the groundwater on its way to a "gaining" stream. A very interesting legal and hydrologic problem of continuing interest in Colorado, is that of delineating the interrelationships of groundwater and surface water as they relate to water supply and to water rights. This is described by Farmer (1960). As of late 1977 the issues on pumped water rights have not been resolved. See Topic 66.

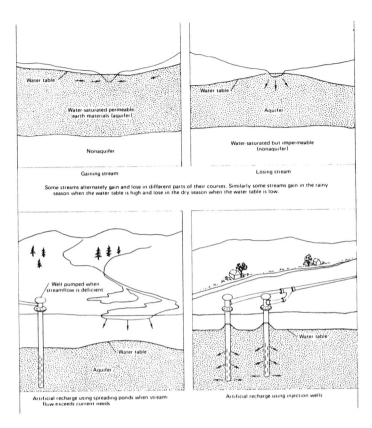

Figure 44-1   Concepts of Surface Water-Groundwater Interactions
Including Artificial Recharge Using Injection Wells.
Feth (1973).

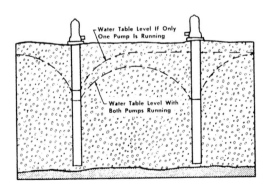

Figure 44-2   Interaction of Water Table Level with Pumping From
Adjacent Wells.  Wells too close together reduce each
others supply.  Bittinger (1967).

Artesian aquifers are shown in Figure 44-3 as prepared by Baldwin and McGuinness (1963). Many areas once endowed with artesian springs or wells have been developed to such an extent that the artesian flows are no longer in evidence.

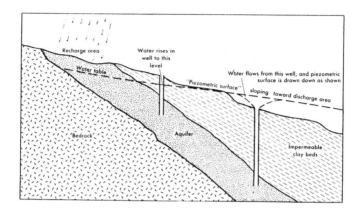

Figure 44-3    Artesian Aquifer and Recharge Area

The recurring questions in groundwater management are: Where does the groundwater come from? and, What is the rate of replenishment in a particular aquifer? Mathematical computations of field data, mathematical modeling by computers, electric analogues, and tracer techniques, all are being used to provide answers. Cabrera and Marino (1976) describe a mathematical analysis of the dynamic response of aquifer systems to localized recharge. Fetter (1977) found through statistical analyses that as much as 85 percent of the streamflow prior to 1959 of the Yahara River near Madison, Wisconsin, was due to effluent discharge.

Simpson, Thorud, and Friedman (1970) used deuterium to distinguish seasonal groundwater recharge in Southern Arizona. They found that winter runoff was most effective in providing water for recharge.

Judy (1972) in reviewing the use of heavy water as a tracer in snow studies, evaporation, and groundwater tracing, calls attention to the advantages of the technique since water is actually being used to trace water so that there are few problems with selective absorption.

Davidson (1973) describes the geohydrology and water resources of the Tucson Basin, Arizona. The 81-page text is supplemented by a folio containing 6 maps. The Tucson groundwater basin does not coincide with the shape and size of the surface drainage pattern. This geohydrologic fact has produced some

extremely complex sociological, economic, and legal situations
for which no resolution is in sight.  The Tucson groundwater
basin will bear watching since much of the water pumped is
fossil water at least 6,000 years old.

A condensed but comprehensive discussion of groundwater is
given by Todd (1964).  Kazmann (1972) presents a well-illustrated discussion of groundwater hydrology.  McGuinness (1963) has
assembled an 1121-page National appraisal of groundwater with
state summaries based on reports by District Offices of the
Groundwater Branch of the U.S. Geological Survey.

The "Proceedings of Hydrology Symposium No. 3 - Groundwater" (1963) includes papers on pertinent subjects with
special reference to Canadian conditions.  Cox (1954) described
the complex groundwater systems of Hawaiian volcanic domes.

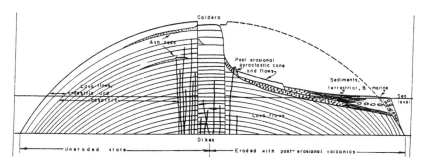

Diagrammatic cross-section of a typical Hawaiian volcanic
dome showing geologic structure.

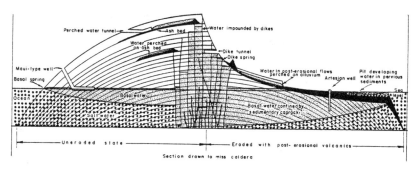

Diagrammatic cross-section of a typical Hawaiian volcanic
dome showing occurrence and recovery of groundwater.

Figure 44-4  Relationship of Hawaiian volcanic dome geology to
occurrence and recovery of groundwater.  Cox (1954)
Reprinted from Pacific Science by permission of the Univ.
Press of Hawaii (formerly Univ. of Hawaii Press).

There has been a great development of groundwater not only in arid regions but also in humid areas, either as the sole source of supply or as a supplement for deficiencies in water from other sources. With very few exceptions serious over-drafts result because of withdrawals at rates in excess of natural recharge. Davis (1960) on page 6 gives the following definitions:

"A 'safe yield' of a groundwater reservoir is the largest amount of water than can be pumped without depleting the supply or making it unprofitable to use. Farmers may think that they are pumping at a safe yield but a drouth period or price decline may prove them wrong.

"On the other hand, they may be causing an overdraft for a time and still be at a safe yield due to the nature of the groundwater reservoir or perhaps cost and price relation-ships. However, if the groundwater reservoir is depleted or permanently damaged in the process, after some point in time the overdraft obviously was no longer a safe yield."

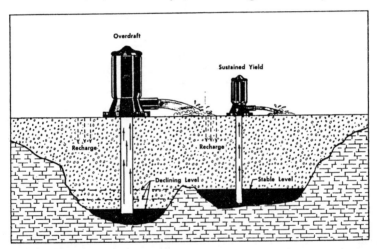

You cannot continue to pump more than the recharge if you want a sustained yield over the years.

Figure 44-5  "Safe Yield" according to Davis (1960, page 7)

Subsurface disposal of industrial wastes in the past was looked upon as an economic and attractive alternative to costly surface treatment. However, knowledge of the diverse geologic and hydrologic conditions to be found at a specific site at which injection is contemplated is necessary if environmental acceptability of such practices is to be attained. Rima, Chase, and Myers (1971) have prepared a 305-page selective annotated bibliography on sub-surface waste disposal. See "Ground Water Manual" (1971) p 291 for sanitary seal casings.

266

A true water table can be found surrounding most lakes. Since a reservoir is a synthetic lake the storage capacity of a reservoir is made up of the visible free water and the ground-water in the soil or strata surrounding the reservoir. This is called "bank storage" and its volume in some instances may form a considerable fraction of the operational capacity of the reservoir. Haimes and Dreizin (1977) deal with a method for solving the problems of conjunctive use of large-scale complex groundwater systems, surface stream networks, and reservoirs, all interacting with each other. Bank storage is also to be found along stream channels.

A problem pertinent to the phenomena under discussion is the interaction between a stream and nearby well. As discussed by Rahn (1968) it has been found that the amount of water which may be removed from a stream by induced streambed infiltration depends primarily upon the geology of the area. Horizontal permeability may be many times greater than vertical permeability. The presence of a well near a stream may or may not deplete significantly the streamflow depending upon interactions between the cone of depression of the draw-down of the well and the rate of streambed infiltration in proportion to the rate of pumping. Rahn's paper describes research performed in the Fenton River Valley which is in part a water supply for the University of Connecticut at Storrs.

Experience has shown that permeability of aquifers determined from core samples, although informative, could result in highly misleading computations of performance of wells. Therefore, the more recent groundwater exploration and groundwater hydraulics studies are based to the fullest extent possible on field data of well performance in nature. Groundwater resources development is among the most important and most rapidly expanding hydrologic activities throughout the world.

The presence of a water "table", in effect an underground reservoir, the phreatic zone, with a horizontal plain surface, a concept which persists in the minds of many people, is practically non-existent. Water tables may be found in a few valleys in an alluvial fill. Because of gaining and losing streams the alluvial valley water tables are seldom horizontal.

The character of a water table depends entirely on the interaction of precipitation, the vegetation, and the geology of the area. In an area of sedimentary stratified rocks, some of which may be impermeable such as in parts of the Appalachian Mountain system, there may be perched water tables completely separate from each other and from the alluvial valley water table. In a system such as is illustrated in Figure 44-3 there may be a water-bearing, porous strata such as the Ogallala formation in the Great Plains in which there is a tremendous water reserve coming from a far-removed recharged area.

In many areas such as parts of the Mississippi Valley there may be a water table near the surface in which the infiltrated precipitation is moving at a slow rate. Such groundwater systems respond to wet and dry cycles in the precipitation and therefore may be undependable. In the igneous crystalline rock areas such as the White Mountains in New England, the Rocky Mountains, and the Sierras, there is no water table. The water in crystalline rocks is in the faults and fissures. In an alluvial valley fill a successful well drilling can be expected. Usually this applies to shallow wells also. In the crystalline rock areas each well drilled is a calculated risk. Dry holes have been drilled hundreds of feet deep. Other drillings only a few yards away may be successful.

Very few well drillers will sign a contract, before drilling, guaranteeing to locate a site which will bring in water of a definite yield at a specified depth and at a fixed cost.

From time immemorial man has attempted to reduce the risk in the search for water. Although some historians are of the opinion that water witching goes back 7000 years the best evidence is that the forked twig divining rod was first reported about 400 to 500 years ago. A background in brief is given in "Water Witching" (1965). Water witching has been the subject of intense interest, religious censure, ridicule, and violent controversy.

An entrancing book on the subject was written by Vogt and Hyman (1959). Their book includes an appendix entitled, "Water Well Location by Scientific Divination", by H. E. Thomas. In spite of learned discourses aimed at discrediting the concept of water witching there has remained an increasingly persistent belief in its efficacy. There is no doubt in the minds of many people that the divining rod has worked. The question has been "why" and "how".

As mankind has advanced in the mastery of the environment through the application of the physical laws of the Universe certain inherent senses have been suppressed. It is known that all forms of life from bacteria to humans respond to certain as yet inexplicable impulses. Brown (1972) presents a condensed review in his article "The 'Clocks' Timing Biological Rhythms". On page 763 he refers to the Earth's electromagnetic fields as contributing not only to organism's external environment but to its internal functioning as well.

It has been surmised that one of the suppressed senses lying dormant in humans is a responsiveness to minute fluctuations in the Earth's electromagnetic field. It has been conjectured for some time that a "water witch" holding a divining rod was a person who, without intellectual acknowledgement or

268

perception, reacted to changes in the electromagnetic field caused by the proximity of groundwater.

Chadwick and Jensen (1971) found some evidence of correlation between magnetic gradient changes and dousing reactions. Chi-square tests showed considerable statistical significance. Their research project was conducted over a period of one year and involved participation of approximately 150 people many of whom had had no previous experience or knowledge of water devining. Magnetic field perturbations measured by geophysical exploration equipment such as the cesium vapor magnetometer were plotted to compare with dousing reactions. The results of one of the studies showed that one dowser possessed an uncanny ability to demonstrate quasi-repeatable results in trials over a long period of time.

The authors point out that no wells were dug in this experiment which was aimed at finding a statistical correlation between the response by dowsers and the magnetic field perturbations. Their over-all conclusion was that the dowser's response was much higher than that which would be expected purely by chance.

In the Proceedings of the Institute of Electrical and Electronic Engineers, Puthoff and Targ (1976) explore and describe in considerable detail paranormal perceptions and parapsychological research. Water witching until recently was considered to be a paranormal "act" but Chadwick and Jensen's work (1971) requires a re-orientation of many old attitudes.

References

Baldwin, Helen L. and C. L. McGuinness, "A Primer on Ground Water", Geological Survey, USDI, 26 pp, U.S. Govt. Printing Office, 1966.

Bittinger, Morton W., "Ground Water in Colorado", Bull. 504-S of the Colorado's Ground-Water Problems series, Colo. State Univ. Exp. Sta. Fort Collins, 28 pp, 1967.

Brown, Frank A., Jr., "The 'Clocks' Timing Biological Rhythms", American Scientist, vol. 60, pp 756-766, Nov.-Dec. 1972.

Cabrera, Guillermo, and Miguel A. Marino, "Dynamic Response of Aquifer Systems to Localized Recharge", Water Resources Bull., vol. 12, no. 1, pp 49-63, Feb., 1976.

Chadwick, Duane G., and Larry Jensen, "The Detection of Magnetic Fields Caused by Groundwater - and the correlation of such fields with water dowsing", Utah Water Research Lab., College of Engineering, Utah State Univ. Logan, Report No. PRWG 78-1, 57 pp, Jan., 1971.

Cox, Doak C., "Research in Ground-Water Hydrology in Hawaii", Pacific Science, pp 230-233, Apr. 1954.

Davidson, E. S., "Water Resources of the Tucson Basin - Geohydrology and Water Resources of the Tucson Basin, Arizona", USGS Water Supply Paper 1939-E, U.S. Government Printing Office, 1973.

Davis, Irving F., Jr., "The Economic Picture", Bull. 506-S of the Colorado's Ground-Water Problems series, Colo. State Univ. Exp. Station, Fort Collins, Colo., 32 pp, 1960.

Eagleson, Peter S., "Dynamic Hydrology", McGraw-Hill Book Co., New York, 462 pp, 1970.

Farmer, Edward J., "Water and the Law", Bulletin 505-S, of the Colorado Ground-Water Problems series, Colorado State Univ. Exp. Station, Fort Collins, Colo., Jan. 1960.

Fetter, C. W., Jr., "Statistical Analysis of the Impact of Ground Water Pumpage on Low-Flow Hydrology", Water Resources Bull., vol. 13, no. 2, pp 309-323, Apr. 1977.

Feth, J. H., "Water Facts and Figures for Planners and Managers", Geological Survey Circular 601-I, USDI, 30 pp, 1973.

"Ground Water Manual - A Guide for the Investigation, Development, and Management of Ground-Water Resources", a Water Resources Tech. Publication, Bur. of Reclamation, USDI, Washington, D.C., 1st ed., 480 pp, 1977.

Haimes, Y. Y., and Y. C. Dreizin, "Management of Groundwater and Surface Water Via Decomposition", Water Resources Research, vol. 13, no. 1, pp 69-77, Feb. 1977.

Judy, Clark H., "Heavy Water - A Natural Tracer", Proceedings of the Indiana Academy of Science for 1971, vol. 81, pp 242-245, 1972.

Kazmann, Raphael G., "Modern Hydrology", Harper and Row, New York, 2nd edition, 1972.

Longenbaugh, Robert A., "Artificial Ground-Water Recharge on the Arikaree River Near Cope, Colorado", Bulletin No. CER66RAL35, Civil Eng. Dept. Engineering Research Center, Colo. State Univ., Fort Collins, 12 pp, June, 1966.

McGuinness, C. L., "The Role of Ground Water in the National Water Situation", USGS Water Supply Paper 1800, 1,121 pp, and 2 plates, 1963.

Proceedings of Hydrology Symposium No. 3 "Groundwater", held
at Univ. of Alberta,Calgary, 8 & 9 Nov., 1962, Subcommit-
tee on Hydrology, Assoc. Comm. on Geodesy and Geophysics,
Natl. Research Council of Canada, Ottawa, 1963.

Puthoff, Harold E., and Russell Targ, "A Perceptual Channel for
Information Transfer Over Kilometer Distances: Historical
Perspective and Recent Research", Proceedings of the
Institute of Electrical and Electronic Engineers, vol. 64,
no. 3, pp 329-354, March, 1976.

Rahn, Perry H., "The Hydrogeology of an Induced Streambed Infiltration Area", Ground Water, vol. 6, no. 3, May-June,
1968.

Rima, Donald R., Edith B. Chase, and Beverly M. Myers, "Sub-
surface Waste Disposal by Means of Wells - A Selective
Annotated Bibliography", USGS Water Supply Paper 2020,
U.S. Govt. Printing Office, 1971.

Simpson, E. S., D. B. Thorud, and Irving Friedman, "Disting-
uishing Seasonal Recharge to Groundwater by Deuterium
Analysis in Southern Arizona", International Assn. of
Hydrology, Proc. of the Reading Symposium, July, 1970,
pp 112-121, 1970.

Todd, David Keith, "Ground Water", Sec. 13, Handbook of Applied
Hydrology, Ven Te Chow, ed-in-chief, McGraw-Hill Book
Co., New York, 1964.

Vogt, Evon Z., and Ray Hyman, "Water Witching, U.S.A.", The
Univ. of Chicago Press, 248 pp, 1959.

"Water in the Unsaturated Zone", Proceedings of the Wageningen
Symposium, ed. by P. E. Rijtema and H. Wassink, 2 volumes,
995 pp, pub. by International Assn. of Scientific Hydrology, Braamstraat 61, Gentbrugge, and by UNESCO, Place de
Fonteroy, Paris, 1969.

"Water Witching", a 14-page pamphlet, Geological Survey, USDI,
1965.

Wulff, H. E., "The Qanats of Iran", Scientific American,
vol. 218, no. 4, pp 94-105, Apr., 1968.

Topic 45    Fresh Water - Salt Water Interactions

The interactions of waters of dissimilar densities are extremely important. Such interactions may take place not only along sea coasts but also wherever waters of different densities may meet. The techniques developed in Holland for the reclamation of lands taken from the ocean to make them suitable for the raising of cultivated crops apply also to the removal of salt from desert land to be brought under irrigation. These principles apply also to the displacement of contaminated water in heavily industrialized areas.

Baldwin and McGuiness (1963) have an excellent condensed review of the general subject of groundwater. Linsley, Kohler, and Paulhus (1975) give in their Chap. 6, pages 192-222, a condensed review of groundwater including definitions of terms used in this branch of hydrology.

Forty-four elements present in sea water, exclusive of dissolved gases, are listed with their concentrations in milligrams per kilogram (commonly called parts per million or ppm) and also in milligrams per liter, on page 413 of "1967 Saline Water Conversion Report". A discussion of inland disposal of blended industrial waste effluent by artificial recharge technique is found on pages 98 through 100 of this reference.

The basic relationship expressing the interaction of waters of different densities is the Ghyben-Herzberg equation. The form included here is taken from Carlson (1968).

$$h_s = \frac{p_f}{p_s - p_f} h_f \qquad (1)$$

in which

$h_s$ is the depth to salt water below the sea level (depth to fresh water-saline water interface),

$h_f$ is the height of the water table above sea level,

$p_f$ is the specific gravity of the fresh water, and

$p_s$ is the specific gravity of sea water.

For example, if $p_s$ is 1.025 grams per cubic centimeter, and $p_f$ is 1.00 gram per cubic centimeter, then $h_s = 40 \, h_f$. This equation is another expression of the hydrostatic principle. In practice it must be modified to take into account the hydraulics of flow of a fluid through a porous medium when movement of the interface takes place.

The Ghyben-Herzberg relationship is shown in Figure 45-1 taken from Carlson (1968) as shown at the top of the following page.

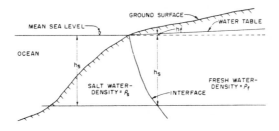

Figure 45-1    The Ghyben-Herzberg Relationship

Figure 45-2 illustrates the manner in which salt water intrusion may take place at the bottom of the well and how a fresh water recharge will reposition the interface. Lee and Cheng (1974) found that their mathematical model of sea water encroachment in the coastal Biscayne aquifer in the Cutler area in Florida gave good qualitative agreement with field data. Figure 45-2 appears on the following page.

Figure 45-3 is a print of the inside of the cover of Carlson's report (1968). It shows how the infiltration and horizontal flow of fresh water displaces saline water into a tile drain as observed in a glass-walled hydraulic laboratory model. It was found that reducing the distance between drains results in a greatly reduced effectiveness in flushing out saline water. Figure 45-3 is shown on page 275.

Groundwater recharge will inevitably become a widely-used practice in heavily populated areas. Many municipalities are now using sewage treatment plant effluent as groundwater recharge. The filtering effect of the soil and of the geologic strata usually yields a very high quality water from effluent reclaimed by this process.

Peters and Rose (1968) describe the water supply situation facing Nassau County, Long Island, New York. Projections of the requirements for potable water indicate that by 1977 the rate of withdrawal will exceed the rate of recharge. Importation of water from the mainland or from adjacent counties is not considered feasible. The alternatives are desalting of sea water or reclamation and reuse of the water following injection into the groundwater.

Fang, Wang, and Harrison (1972) present a highly mathematical treatment describing a model that closely approximates, through two-dimensional finite element techniques, the fluctuations in the water table of an ocean beach. Only small differences appeared between field data and theoretical results.

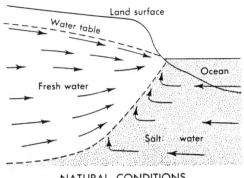

NATURAL CONDITIONS

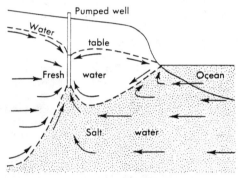

SALT INTRUSION

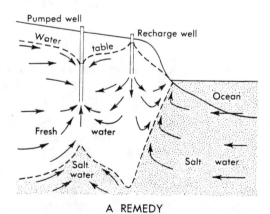

A REMEDY

Figure 45-2  Relation of fresh water to salt water in a coastal
area showing that it is possible to pump salt water some
distance inland although shallower wells nearer the ocean
may yield fresh water.  Baldwin and McGuinness (1963).

274

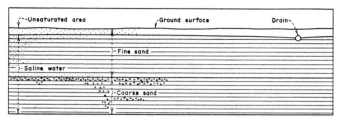

BEFORE IRRIGATION

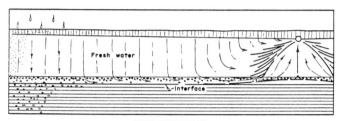

WITH IRRIGATION

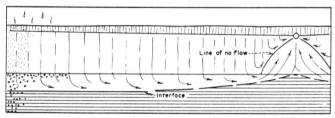

WITH STABILIZED INTERFACE

Figure 45-3    Drainage Patterns of Saline Water in Two-Part
              Aquifer Under Irrigation

Exotic uses of aquifers are reviewed by Kazmann (1971).
He discusses the disposal or storage of liquids, gases, fresh-
water in the vicinity of saline water, and the use of aquifers
as heat sinks and for energy storage.

Ballentine, Reznek, and Hall (1972) state on page 3:
"Sources of subsurface water contamination can generally be
assigned to one of three basic categories:  1) The direct
introduction of pollutants deep within the earth by injection
through wells; 2) percolation of pollutants from surface and
near surface sources such  as septic tanks, leaching ponds,
sanitary landfills, and pesticides and fertilizers used in agricultural practices; and 3) intrusion of salt water into fresh
water aquifers as a result of reductions in fresh water flow in
coastal areas or the breaching of impervious strata in inland
areas."

275

Their report is supplemented by two subsurface water bibliographies, Part I, "Subsurface Waste Injection", and, Part II, "Saline Water Intrusion" (1972).

Kazmann (1971) warned the managers of groundwater basins that they must monitor, make predictions, and protect their groundwater against deliberate or inadvertent pollution or destruction by increasing pressures on land use and natural resource utilization.

References

Anon. "1967 Saline Water Conversion Report", Office of Saline Water, USDI, Government Printing Office, Washington, D.C., 421 pp, 1967.

Baldwin, Helene L. and C. L. McGuinness, "A Primer on Ground Water", U.S. Geological Survey, USDI, Government Printing Office, Washington, D. C., 26 pp, 1963.

Ballentine, R. K., S. R. Reznek, and C. W. Hall, "Subsurface Pollution Problems in the United States", Office of Water Programs, U.S. Environmental Protection Agency, Technical Report TS-00-72-02, 27 pp, May, 1972.

"Subsurface Waste Injection, Part I", Subsurface Water Pollution, A Selective Annotated Bibliography, Office of Water Programs, EPA, 156 pp, March, 1972.

"Saline Water Intrusion, Part II", Subsurface Water Pollution, A Selective Annotated Bibliography, Office of Water Programs, EPA, 161 pp, March, 1972.

Carlson, Enos J., "Removal of Saline Water from Aquifers", A Water Resources Tech. Pub., Research Report No. 13. Bur. of Reclamation, USDI, Denver Federal Center, Denver, Colo. 80225, 1968.

Fang, C. S., S. N. Wang, and W. Harrison, "Groundwater Flow in a Sandy Tidal Beach. 2. Two-Dimensional Finite Element Analysis", vol. 8, no. 1, Feb. 1972.

Kazmann, Raphael G., "Exotic Uses of Aquifers", Jour. Irrigation and Drainage Div., Proceedings ASCE, pp 515-522, Sept. 1971.

Lee, Chun-Hian, and Ralph Ta-Shun Cheng, "On Seawater Encroachment in Coastal Aquifers", Water Resources Research, vol. 10, no. 5, pp 1039-1043, Oct. 1974.

Linsley, R. K., M. A. Kohler, and J. L. H. Paulhus, "Hydrology for Engineers", McGraw-Hill Book Co., 2nd ed., 1975.

Peters, John H. and John L. Rose, "Water Conservation by
    Reclamation and Recharge", Jour. Sanitary Engineering Div.
    Proceedings ASCE, pp 625-639, Aug. 1968.

Ecologists have classified plants in relation to their demands on the environment for water supply as follows:

Hydrophytes - Plants which require continuous immersion in water either floating or rooted, such as water ·lilies, water hyacinths, or algae.

Mesophytes  - Plants which require at all times that some soil moisture be available to at least part of their root system. If soil moisture is inadequate the plants wilt and ultimately die. Most crop and forage plants are mesophytes.

Xerophytes  - Plants which, by morphological adaptations, are able to survive extended periods when no soil moisture whatever may be available to the root systems such as the cactus.

Phreatophytes - Plants which may normally be mesophytes but due to inherent characteristics tend to extend their roots deep into the soil as the soil moisture or groundwater table is depressed. Therefore, under arid conditions, the phreatophytes are able to survive when no soil moisture remains as long as their deep roots descend into the groundwater. Many plants and trees can be either mesophytes or phreatophytes but few true mesophytes will survive when their roots are immersed in the water. The cottonwood, sycamore, tamarisk (salt cedar), and alfalfa are phreatophytes.

Phreatophytes can thrive in arid and semi-arid climates as long as their roots reach the groundwater table. The resulting evapotranspirational losses, estimated to be from 4 feet to about 10 acre feet per year, can result in a major depletion of the water supply. Since phreatophytes tend to grow in valleys and channel bottoms where underground flow may provide a continuous water table condition, their presence impedes runoff, increases sediment deposition, and tends to aggravate flood damage. Therefore, extensive operations of phreatophyte eradication have been conducted using mechanical and chemical means of eradication as described in Robinson (1958) and Lowry (1966) A guide for surveying phreatophyte vegetation prepared by the Phreatophyte Sub-committee of the Pacific Southwest Inter-Agency Committee is the report by Horton, Robinson and McDonald (1964).

Tovey (1969) found that alfalfa can adapt to static high water tables but that fluctuating water table levels reduce yield or kill alfalfa. He compares various methods determining consumptive use by alfalfa.

The following quotation is taken from "Did You Know That..
...." (1969):

"Phreatophytes in the Rio Grande basin consume 85,000 acre-
feet of water a year? In an effort to find solutions to
the chronic water shortage in the Rio Grande Valley the
Bureau of Reclamation is studying the possibility of
clearing the water-greedy plants from about 32,000 acres
of infested land along a 240-mile stretch of the Rio
Grande from Velarde in Northern New Mexico to Elephant
Butte Reservoir in the south. About 58 percent of the
cottonwoods, willows, Russian olives, and salt cedar in
the area would be removed leaving a protective layer along
levees and natural river banks needed for flood control.
This would conserve about 48,000 acre-feet of water a
year. Conservationsists oppose the plan on the ground
that the water involved is worth more supporting wildlife
and scenery than it is for irrigating crops elsewhere."

Bristow (1968) calculated that the hunting of the white-
wing doves on an acre of phreatophytes could add as much as
$880 per year to the economy of Arizona.

A procedure is given by Bouwer (1975) for calculating
seepage from a stream resulting from evapotranspirational
losses in a flood plain. This procedure is aimed at computing
the reduction in seepage losses which might result if phreatophytes were to be removed.

Van Hylckama (1970) found that thinned-out stands of salt
cedar used nearly as much water as unthinned stands. He concluded that thinning and cutting are ineffective methods of
saving water. In thinned-out stands sprouts can increase in
length by as much as 5 cm a day. Only a few plants such as
bamboo and cucumber are reported to grow faster. Van Hylckama
thinks that some of the claims for potential savings of water
by removal of phreatophytes may be overestimated because of
differences in site characteristics especially with reference
to the position of the phreatic surface (groundwater level).
The USGS Professional Papers in the Series 655 with various
letter designations deal with phreatophytes.

Turner (1970) prepared a very informative report on phreatophyte activities as of 1968. Preliminary estimates indicate
that phreatophytes cover about 16 million acres (6.5 million
hectares) in the Western United States and consume about 20 to
25 million acre feet of water annually. Turner's report makes
reference to the use of 24 different biocides in research and
operations.

Maddox (1972) compares the economic value of the agriculture produced by the water saved through phreatophyte removal with the dollar value of the wildlife habitat destroyed by the removal. The comparison is close. He concludes that if phreatophytes were to be removed so that patches of vegetation and of stream meanders would remain, fish and wildlife could continue to use the watershed while at the same time evapotranspiration would be reduced by removal of the phreatophytes.

Hughes (1972) has prepared curves comparing Salt Cedar evapotranspiration loss separately for the months of May, June, and July as measured and as computed by a simulation technique based upon modification of the Penman equation.

Horton (1973) has compiled a 192-page abstract bibliography, international in its scope, on phreatophyte management containing references to 713 papers.

Management of phreatophyte and riparian vegetation for maximum multiple-use values is analyzed by Horton and Campbell (1974). Their informative report includes discussions of methods and techniques of measurement and evaluation of water losses among which are: tanks and evapotranspirometers, the evapotranspiration tent, the heat-pulse method, the pressure-bomb technique, phreatophyte flood plain reaches, riparian reaches, groundwater wells, and energy measurements. Their management recommendations encompass various depths to the water table and continental elevations of drainage basins.

## References

Bouwer, Herman, "Predicting Reduction in Water Losses From Open Channels by Phreatophyte Control", Water Resources Research, vol. 11, no. 1, pp 96-101, Feb. 1975.

Bristow, B., "Statement by Arizona Game and Fish Dept. on Phreatophyte Clearing Projects", Proc. 12th Annual Ariz. Watershed Symposium, pp 41-43, Ariz. State Land Dept., Phoenix, 1968.

"Did You Know That . . .?" Civil Engineering, vol. 39, no. 2, p 33, Feb. 1969.

Horton, J. S., US Forest Service, T. W. Robinson, US Geological Survey, H. R. McDonald, US Bur. of Reclamation, "Guide for Surveying Phreatophyte Vegetation", Agri. Handbook No.266, USFS, Washington, D.C., May, 1964.

Horton, Jerome S., Compiler, "Evapotranspiration and Watershed Research as Related to Riparian and Phreatophyte Management", Forest Service, USDA, Misc. Publication No. 1234, Jan. 1973.

Horton, Jerome S., and C. J. Campbell, "Management of Phreato-
    phyte and Riparian Vegetation for Maximum Multiple Use
    Values", USDA Forest Service Research Paper RM-117, Rocky
    Mt. Forest and Range Exp. Station, Forest Service, USDA,
    Fort Collins, Colo., 23 pp, Apr. 1974.

Hughes, William C., "Simulation of Salt Cedar Evapo-Transpira-
    tion", Jour. Irrigation and Drainage Div., ASCE,
    pp 533-542, Dec., 1972.

Lowry, O. J., "Mechanical and Chemical Control of Phreato-
    phytes", ASCE Water Resources Engineering Conference,
    Denver, Colo., May 16-20, 1966.

Maddox, George E., "Ecologic-Economic Values in Phreatophyte
    Control", Proc. Symposium, Watersheds in Transition,
    pp 257-259, Fort Collins, Colo. June, 1972.  Proceedings
    Series No. 14, Amer. Water Resources Assn. Urbana, Ill.
    Oct. 1972.

Robinson, T. W., "Phreatophytes", USGS Water Supply Paper 1423,
    Washington, D.C., 1958.

Tovey, Rhys, "Alfalfa Water Table Investigations", Jour. Irri-
    gation and Drainage Div., Proc. ASCE, pp 525-535,
    Dec. 1969.

Turner, Philip M., "Annual Report of Phreatophyte Activities -
    1968", Report No. REC-OCE-70-27, Div. of Research, Bur.
    of Reclamation, Denver, Colo., July, 1970.

Van Hylckama, T. E. A., "Water Use by Salt Cedar", Water Res-
    ources Research, vol. 6, no. 3, pp 728-735, June, 1970.

Topic 47                          Ecology

Ecology is the science which deals with the interrelationships of organisms with each other and their environment.
Human ecology is that branch of sociology which deals with the
relationship between humans and their environment. An ecosystem is a community of plants and animals interacting with
their physical environment as an organizational unit to create,
in effect, the life support systems. A biome is the living
portion of a locale such as grasslands, forests, deserts, or
tundras. The biosphere is that part of the Earth containing
life. An excellent and very comprehensive reference is the
"Biosphere", the September, 1970 issue of Scientific American.

Grossman (1970) has written a non-technical discussion of
ecology illustrated with superb black and white and color
photographs. Kuchler (1964) prepared a map of the conterminous
United States classifying the vegetation into plant ecosystems.
Garrison and his co-workers (1975) have written a report on
vegetation and environmental features of forest and range ecosystems. This report, which includes a 19-inch by 28-inch map
in color of the conterminous United States, classifies the land
into 34 ecosystems. The description of each of the ecosystems
deals with the physiography, the climate, the vegetation, the
fauna, the soils, and the land use. The publication is illustrated with 34 photographs. Acquisition of this reference is
recommended to those interested in ecology.

Since climate is one of the most important features
affecting an ecosystem it has been observed that increases in
altitude in a mountain region bring about ecosystems found at
numerically higher latitudes in the hemisphere. A thousand-
foot increase in elevation is roughly equivalent ecologically
to locales between 300 and 400 miles further north in the
northern hemisphere.

Figure 47-1, which shows ecological life zones, is taken
from page 11 of the publication by Moenke (1971). The terms
describing each of the zones are given for the southwestern
mountain regions. Ecologists, not only in the United States
but in other parts of the World, have assigned different names
to altitudinal zones as discussed by Moenke on pages 11-18.
Moenke's report is a handbook describing ecological life zones
displayed in the Walter C. Mead's Ecological Hall of the Denver
Museum of Natural History. The dioramas are so large and constructed with such realism as to create the impression that the

viewer is actually present in the ecosystem presented.

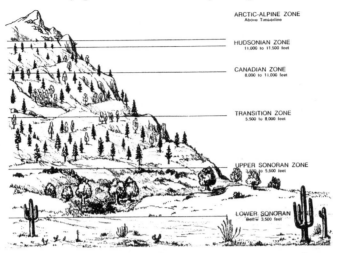

Figure 47-1  Life Zones in the Southwestern United States

Ecosystems may be robust or fragile.  The temperate and
tropical zone lower-elevation ecosystems have demonstrated the
ability to adjust to changes and to recover effectively in
years or decades as is illustrated by a forested area which has
been logged.  Tundra and desert ecosystems are fragile.  Once
disturbed their rate of recovery may be so slow as to require
perhaps centuries before the original ecosystem returns.

Only in the forests and in certain rangelands can there be
seen some evidence of the natural ecosystems.  Silviculture is
basically applied ecology and range management has as its aim
the management of a natural ecosystem for sustained domesticated animal production.  "Silvics of Forest Trees of the United
States" (1965) is a 762-page book describing the ecological
requirements and tolerances of 127 native forest trees.  A Soil
Conservation Service publication, "National Range Handbook"
(1976) describes in detail the treatment of rangeland grazable
woodland and native pasture.

Riparian ecosystems are very important to fish, animals,
and birds and often possess scenic and recreational value.
Kennedy (1977) discusses water as a factor affecting wildlife
conflicts in riparian management.  His article is illustrated
with 8 sketches depicting changes in a grazed area streambottom
over a period longer than 20 years.  Anderson, Engel-Wilson,
Wells and Ohmart (1977) describe techniques and data applica-
bility for ecological studies of southwestern riparian
habitats.

Hynes (1970) in Chapter XXIII of his book on the ecology of running waters, discusses the effects of man on water courses. Odum (1977) in his article on the emergence of ecology as a new integrated system links ecology with the social sciences, technological assessments, economics, and politics.

Helm and Peters (1975) in their Chapter 5 on ecology state: "Public projects, after all, relate to man, and according to ecologic principles man is part of the ecosystem and is regulated and influenced by the same set of principles which regulate all other living organisms. Man's failure to recognize this in the past has often resulted in an endless series of problems, frequently compounded one upon the other, until the resulting megaloproblem seems to defy solution.

"The first step in solving a problem is to recognize that one exists. The successful administration of public projects and programs can depend a great deal on how responsive the decisionmaker is toward ecological principles before deciding upon, designing, and constructing a public works project."

This chapter is an excellent review of ecology as it bears upon public works in the planning, design, construction, and operation and maintenance stages. Irrigation, water supply, power, highway, and river channelization activities are also considered (see Topic 84).

"Ecological Modeling in a Resource Management Framework" was the subject of a Symposium held in July, 1975. The 394-page Proceedings consist of 7 papers, with transcripts of discussions, on lake, estuary, forest, phytoplankton, eutrophication, fish population, and fisheries modeling.

Rapport and Turner (1977) in their thought-provoking article analyze one of the central problems of human ecology, the ways in which scarce resources are allocated among alternative uses and users. This problem is fundamental to economic thinking and the authors delve deeply into the theories of economics. They propose ecological models of economic analyses in place of the usual mechanical models. Their paper, the reading of which is recommended, contains 75 valuable references.

"Biological Effects in the Hydrological Cycle" (1971), an advanced science Seminar, was held under the sponsorship of the National Science Foundation at Purdue University. The 391-page Proceedings contain 31 papers.

Dillard's book, "Pilgrim at Tinker Creek" (1974) is a literary work dealing in a philosophical manner with an ecosystem in the Blue Ridge Mountains of Virginia.

Commoner (1971) in his book, "The Closing Circle", gives

numerous examples of the increasing complexity of human ecology
in an environment into which are being injected increasing
arrays of synthetic substances considered necessary to sustain
nutrition, health, and life as densities of population increase
and as communities numbering into millions of people grow in
areas ecologically unsuited for such concentrations.  In his
Chapter 2 Commoner states his four informal laws of ecology.

"Ecological Impacts of Snowpack Augmentation in the San
Juan Mountains, Colorado" (1976) is a 489-page assembly of 25
separate reports on an exhaustive ecological study of weather
modification activities as they could affect alpine vegetation,
geomorphic processes, pocket gophers, boreal toads, elk movements and calving, small mammals, forest tree species seed ger-
mination, and various ecosystems.

The great increase in the human population inhabiting the
Earth and the food production technology (see Topic 38) have
overwhelmed if not completely eradicated the natural ecosystems
in many parts of the World.  Clean-cultivated, single-specie
hybridized plants, chemically-fertilized, biocide-protected,
irrigated crop production is a total departure from the natural
ecosystems which once prevailed on the cropland.  There is a
limit as to the number and extensiveness of natural ecosystems
which can be "preserved" without interfering with the well-
being, if not the survival, of man.

References

Anderson, Bertin W., Ronald W. Engel-Wilson, Douglas Wells, and
    Robert D. Ohmart, "Ecological Study of Southwestern
    Riparian Habitats: Techniques and Data Applicability",
    pp 146-155 in Importance, Preservation and Management of
    Riparian Habitat: A Symposium, Tucson, Ariz., July 9, 1977
    Rocky Mt. Forest & Range Exp. Station, Forest Service,
    USDA, Fort Collins, Colo., 217 pp, Gen. Tech. Report
    RM-43, 1977.

"Biological Effects in the Hydrological Cycle", Proceedings of
    the 3d International Seminar for Hydrology Professors,
    National Science Foundation Advanced Science Seminar,
    July 18-30, 1971, Dept. of Agri. Engineering, Purdue Univ.
    West Lafayette, Ind., 391 pp, 1971.

"Biosphere", The Sept. 1970 issue of Scientific American, vol.
    223, no. 3, 1970.

Commoner, Barry, "The Closing Circle - Nature, Man, and Tech-
    nology, Alfred A. Knopf, New York, 326 pp, 1971.

Dillard, Annie, "Pilgrim at Tinker Creek", Harper's Magazine
    Press, Harper & Row, New York, 271 pp, 1974.

"Ecological Impacts of Snowpack Augmentation in the San Juan
Mountains, Colorado", Harold W. Steinhoff & Jack D. Ives,
editors, prepared for Div. of Atmospheric Water Resources
Mgmt., Bur. of Reclamation, by Colo. State Univ., Univ. of
Colo., & Fort Lewis College, 489 pp, Mar. 9, 1976.

"Ecological Modeling in a Resource Management Framework", ed.
by Clifford S. Russell, Proceedings of a Symposium sponsored by MOAA and Resources for the Future, Johns Hopkins
Univ. Press, Baltimore, RFF Working Paper QE-1, 394 pp,
July, 1975.

Garrison, George A., Ardell J. Bjugstad, Don A. Duncan, Mont E.
Lewis, and Dixie R. Smith, "Vegetation and Environmental
Features of Forest and Range Ecosystems", Forest Service,
USDA, Agri. Handbook No. 475, 68 pp & map, July, 1977.

Grossman, Shelly, "Understanding Ecology", Grosset & Dunlap,
New York, 127 pp, 1970.

Helm, William T., and John C. Peters, "Ecology", pp 195-240 in
Environmental Design for Public Projects, ed. by David W.
Hendricks, Evan C. Vlachos, L. Scott Tucker, Joseph C.
Kellogg, Water Resources Pub., Fort Collins, Colo., 742 pp,
1975.

Hynes, H. B. N., "The Ecology of Running Waters", Univ. of
Toronto Press, 555 pp, 1970.

Kennedy, Charles E., "Wildlife Conflicts in Riparian Management:
Water", pp 52-58 in Importance, Preservation and Manage-
ment of Riparian Habitat: A Symposium, Tucson, Ariz.,
July 9, 1977, Rocky Mt. Forest & Range Exp. Sta., Forest
Service, USDA, Fort Collins, Colo., 217 pp, Gen. Tech.
Report RM-43, 1977.

Kuchler, A. W., "Potential Natural Vegetation of the Conterminous United States", a map $38\frac{1}{4}$ x $60\frac{1}{2}$ in., with Manual to
accompany map of same title, Amer. Geographical Soc. Spec.
publication No. 36, 116 pp, 1964.

Moenke, Helen, "Ecology of Colorado Mountains to Arizona
Deserts", Museum Pictorial No. 20, Denver Museum of Natural History, Denver, Colo., 80 pp, 1971. (This publication
includes 14 pp in color entitled, "Life Zone Displays in
the Walter C. Mead Ecological Hall" by Alfred M. Bailey).

"National Range Handbook", Soil Conservation Service, USDA,
July 13, 1976.

Odum, Eugene P., "The Emergence of Ecology as a New Integrative
Discipline", Science, vol. 195, pp 1289-1293, Mar. 25,1977.

Rapport, David J., and James E. Turner, "Economic Models in Ecology - The Economics of Resource Allocation Provide a Framework for Viewing Ecological Processes", Science, vol. 195, pp 367-373, Jan. 28, 1977.

"Silvics of Forest Trees of the United States", Compiled and revised by H. A. Fowells, Forest Service, USDA, Agri. Handbook No. 271, 762 pp, 1965.

A weed has been defined as a perfectly good plant growing
where we do not want it.  Among living organisms which in the
pursuit of their destiny may interfere with various activities
of the human race, may be listed the higher forms of plants,
animals, birds, and aquatic life, fungae, bacteria, viruses,
actinomyces, bryozoa, nematodes, algae, and hosts of insects.
The eradication, suppression, and control of each type of weed
or pest presents special problems.  The ecological and environmental implications both of epidemics and of elimination are
extremely complex.  (See Topic 38, "Food and Fiber Production")

Techniques of eradication or control may be by mechanical
damage or removal, by burning, or by biocides.  Biocides may be
contact killers, translocatable herbicides, hormones and growth
distorters, or soil sterilants.  Some biocides are specific;
others are general as to their targets.  Carriers may be water
or oil depending on whether the biocide is soluble or in powder
form.  Suitable emulsifiers or wetting agents may be required.

Application of herbicides is usually done by spraying.
Atmosphere inversions are to be shunned when scheduling spraying operations.  Evenings are best.  High temperatures may
cause too rapid evaporation of the carrier.  Aquatic weeds are
controlled by addition of biocides to the water.  Ware (1972)
found that pesticide dusts drifted more than sprays and that
dusts deposited less on the target crop than did sprays if the
sprays were of coarse droplet size.

A definition of potable water is natural water which has
been rendered fit for human consumption by the use of biocides.
Algae cause taste and odor problems and since 1904 the penta-
hydrate form of $CuSO_4$, copper sulfate, has been used to control
algae.  One of the most troublesome forms of life in water
resources management continues to be the algae.  Otto (1970)
reports that studies of environmental parameters of irrigation
canals showed that mat-type blue-green algae grow in a wide
range of water-quality and temperature conditions and do not
require enriched conditions for growth.  He reports that algae-
dical tests of 74 compounds disclosed that only 9 were more
active than copper sulfate and that none provided total control
of blue-green algae mat colonies.

It has been found that once an irrigation project is built
from 40 to 85 percent of the actual expenditures of daily operations of the project are on corrosion protection and aquatic
weed control.  For example, the Madera Canal near Fresno,
California, a concrete-lined canal of about 1,000 cfs capacity,
can lose up to 27 percent of its conveyance when the wetted
perimeter becomes encrusted with about two inches of attached

algae. Unlined canals very rapidly become choked with vegetation which may interfere seriously not only with conveyance but the debris may choke water control and measurement structures sometimes resulting in overtopping of the canal and its ultimate loss.

Bartley's (1977) review of the usage of copper sulfate for aquatic weed control includes construction drawings for a water-powered copper-sulfate dispenser. Allowable concentration of copper in drinking water is one part-per-million (or one milligram per liter) as an upper limit.

Hale (1942) described the use of copper sulfate in the control of 46 microscopic organisms causing taste and odor problems in water. This publication contains 48 photomicrographs of organisms. "Controlling Plant and Animal Pests in Farm Ponds with Copper Sulfate" (undated) includes a table for calculating $CuSO_4$ concentration for farm ponds of various capacities. Color photographs illustrate techniques of treatment not only for control of algae but also for leeches and swimmers' itch.

Otto and Bartley (1965) have prepared an identification guide for aquatic pests in irrigation systems. This guide is illustrated in color with superb botanical drawings by artist David W. Cummingham.

The use of biocides is intimately related to water resource management since applications, not only directly to the water supply but also to field crops, show up sooner or later in some form or other in the surface runoff or groundwater. Bruns and Yoe (1964) report on both greenhouse and field studies of tolerance of certain crops to several aquatic herbicides in irrigation water. Research of this type is a continuing activity.

There is a rapidly-expanding literature on phreatophytes and aquatic weed control. There are professional societies devoted to the subject. The Agricultural Research Service and the Bureau of Reclamation, in cooperation with State Agricultural Experiment Stations and private companies, and the Environmental Protection Agency, are producing an ever-increasing number of reports and instructions on aquatic weed control.

Foresters and rangeland managers deal extensively with biocides. Davis, Ingebo, and Pase (1968) describe the application of picloram (4-amino-3, 5, 6-trichloropicolinic acid), an herbicide potent against a broad spectrum of forbs and woody plants, to control chaparral brush in the Mazatzal Mountains of Central Arizona. It was found that the highest concentration in the streamflow yielded by the 46.5-acre watershed was

0.37 parts per million (ppm). After 16 months and 40 inches of rainfall, picloram was no longer found in the streamflow.

Caro, Edwards, Glass, and Frere (1972) determined the amounts of dieldrin in runoff from treated watersheds near Coshocton, Ohio. Application was 5.6 kg/ha just before corn planting. Dieldrin in runoff was in the range of 0.007 percent in three years to 0.07 percent in one year. When erosion occurred 2.2 percent of the dieldrin was removed in the sediment in the first season after application.

DeVaney's (1968) publication on chemical vegetation control for fish and wildlife management programs includes a description of herbicides and a listing of target vegetation.

Ward (1973) found that big sagebrush control had little effect on elk calving behavior in the Dry Fork drainage basin of the Bighorn National Forest, Wyoming. 96.7 percent of the big sagebrush had to be killed by 2,4-D.

A report by Hodgson, Bruns, Timmons, Lee, Weldon, and Yeo (1962) deals with control of ditchbank weeds which can become very troublesome in canals conveying water only intermittently. Removal of phreatophytes (see Topic 46) with root cutters, bulldozers, etc., can be very expensive and unsatisfactory. Chemical weed killers are now being used where local conditions permit.

The "Herbicide Handbook" (1974) is an authoritative publication of the Weed Science Society of America. Descriptions of herbicides, recommended applications, and toxicities are given.

"Water Operation and Maintenance Bulletin No. 97" (1976) is a 260-page issue dealing in great detail with equipment for the prevention, control, and disposal of weeds on irrigation projects. This issue is illustrated with many photographs and it contains numerous construction drawings.

Although there have been Federal laws dealing with insecticides as long ago as 1910, the Federal Environmental Pesticide Control Act of 1972, PL 92-516, 86 Stat. 1246, revised thoroughly all previous legislation. In 1970 the United States production of pesticides and related products totalled 1,034 billion pounds with a sales value of $870 million. Of the 800 million pounds of pesticides used each year in the United States 40 percent is used by agriculture. Many of the compounds are not only initially toxic but the residue from some of the long-lived biocides may create a continuing hazard as their concentration is built up through the food chain.

There are some 35,000 biocide products including

insecticides, herbicides, plant-growth regulators, rodenticides, bactericides, and fungicides, made up from one or more of the 900 chemical compounds which are currently registered with the U.S. Environmental Protection Agency. The 1972 Act required that about 30 thousand of the biocides must be Federally registered by October, 1974. This deadline was not met. The enormity of the effort required was under-estimated and as of early 1978 no specific deadline has been established. The Congress and the Administration created the 1972 Act but failed to provide the funds and organizational channels to make possible other than a token attempt to tackle this enormous task.

Major provisions of the 1972 Act require classification of a biocide as for "general" or "restricted" use. The EPA may issue a "stop-sale, use and removal" order for pesticides the registration of which has been suspended or cancelled. They may issue permits for experimental use or for research. The EPA is required to monitor the use and presence of pesticides in the environment.

Another provision of the 1972 Act is the requirement that restricted pesticides be applied only by "Certified Applicators". This requirement took effect Oct. 21, 1977. Every state with the exception of Colorado and Nebraska has a procedure for issuing certifications to applicators. In Colorado and Nebraska the certifications are issued by EPA. Any applicator who knowingly violates the 1972 Act in regard to the application of restricted or forbidden pesticides could be subjected to a stiff fine or imprisonment or both.

The recent nation-wide and world-wide concern about the quality of the environment and the impact of the advanced engineering and technology on the health and well-being of individuals has resulted in a situation, the inevitable impact of which could be extremely serious. As new biocides have been developed the organisms which served as the targets have also adjusted to their new environment through evolutionary processes. DDT is no longer effective against flies in the United States. The genetists are under pressure to come forth with a resistant strain about each decade.

Nation-wide public concern about the linkage of the presence in food and the air of biocides to diseases and afflictions such as cancer has resulted in such an extremely stringent Federal requirement on certification as to bring practically to a standstill the development of new biocides. Representatives of chemical companies have said that it now requires 5 to 8 years of time and an investment of from 10 to 15 million dollars for a company to develop a new biocide.

The EPA in 1977 certified only 3 totally-new biocides.

In the coming years when the target organisms have developed
tolerances for the currently certified biocides there will
inevitably be a tremendous increase in crop losses with National and International implications.

Reliance on biological controls should be approached with
caution since most of the few effective biological methods may
be ineffective or very slow-acting in temperate zones.
Blackburn, Sutton, and Taylor (1971) discuss the effectiveness
and limitation of biological control of aquatic weeds by the
following:  insects, snails, the manatee, herbivorous fish,
pathogens, ducks, swans, and through plant competition. Host
specificity is almost a requirement when considering biological controls, to insure against outbreaks.

Oberlander (1977) prepared a review of the Proceedings of
a Symposium, "The Future for Insecticides - Needs and
Prospects". New selective, biodegradable chemicals are needed.
Highly selective biocides have a smaller market than do broad
spectrum biocides. Problems of pollution, resistance by target
insects and toxicity are discussed. An excellent article,
"The Bugs are Coming" (1976), is illustrated with photographs
in color. In the long run, the odds for ultimate survival are
heavily in favor of the insects.

## References

Bartley, T. R., "Investigations of Copper Sulfate for Aquatic
    Weed Control", Water Resources Tech. Publication, Research
    Report No. 27, 24 pp, Bur. of Reclamation, USDI, 1976.

Blackburn, Robert D., David L. Sutton, and Thomas Taylor,
    "Biological Control of Aquatic Weeds", Jour. Irrigation
    and Drainage Division, Proceedings ASCE, pp 421-432,
    Sept. 1971.

Bruns, V. F., and R. R. Yeo, "Tolerance of Certain Crops to
    Several Aquatic Herbicides in Irrigation Water", Agri.
    Research Service, USDA, Tech. Bulletin No. 1299, 22 pp,
    Feb. 1964.

Caro, J. H., W. M. Edwards, B. L. Glass, and M. H. Frere,
    "Dieldrin in Runoff from Treated Watersheds", pp 141-160
    in Watershed Management, Proceedings of the Symposium of
    Aug. 3-6, 1970, Montana State Univ., pub. by ASCE, 1972.

"Controlling Plant and Animal Pests in Farm Ponds with Copper
    Sulfate", 32 pp, Phelps Dodge Refining Corp., 300 Park
    Ave., New York, undated.

Davis, E. A., P. A. Ingebo, and C. P. Pase, "Effect of a Water-
    shed Treatment with Picloram on Water Quality", Forest Ser-
    vice, USDA, Rocky Mt. Forest & Range Exp. Sta., Research
    Note RM -100, 4 pp, 1968.

DeVaney, Thomas E., "Chemical Vegetation Control Manual for
    Fish and Wildlife Management Programs", Bur. of Sport
    Fisheries and Wildlife, USDI, Resource Pub. 48, 42 pp, 1968.

Hale, Frank E., "The Use of Copper Sulfate in Control of Micro-
    scopic Organisms", 44 pp, Phelps Dodge Refining Corp.,
    New York, 1942.

"Herbicide Handbook", 3d edition, 430 pp, Weed Science Soc. of
    America, 425 Illinois Bldg., 113 N. Neil St., Champaign,
    Ill., 1974.

Hodgson, J. M., V. F. Bruns, F. L. Timmons, W. O. Lee,
    L. W. Weldon, and R. R. Yeo, "Control of Certain Ditchbank
    Weeds on Irrigation Systems", Prod. Research Report No. 60
    Agri. Research Service, USDA, Nov. 1962.

Oberlander, Herbert, "Trends in Pest Control", Science,
    vol. 195, no. 4274, pp 169-170, Jan. 14, 1977.

Otto, N. E., T. R. Bartley, with D. W. Cunningham, "Aquatic
    Pests on Irrigation Systems - Identification Guide",
    Bur. of Reclamation, USDI, 72 pp, 1965.

Otto, Naman E., "Algaecidal Evaluation and Environmental Study
    of Mat Producing Blue-Green Algae", Div. of Research
    Report No. REC-OCE-70-25, Bur. of Reclamation, Denver,
    Colo. July, 1970.

"The Bugs are Coming", Time, pp 38-46, July 12, 1976.

Ward, A. Lorin, "Sagebrush Control with Herbicide has Little
    Effect on Elk Calving Behavior", Forest Service, USDA,
    Rocky Mt. Forest and Range Exp. Sta., Research Note
    RM-240, 4 pp, May 1973.

Ware, George W., "Pesticide Drift . . . Dust vs. Spray",
    Progressive Agriculture in Arizona, vol. XXIV, no. 1,
    pp 10-11, College of Agriculture, Univ. of Arizona, Tucson
    Jan. - Feb., 1972.

"Water Operation and Maintenance - Bulletin No. 97", Div. of
    Water Operation and Maintenance, Engineering and Research
    Center, Bur. of Reclamation, USDI, Denver, Colo., 260 pp,
    Sept. 1976.

Irrigation

Since practically all of our food-producing cultivated
crops, berries, and trees require a continuing supply of soil
moisture, food production is dependent on the availability of
soil moisture.  In the humid temperate zones absence of rainfall for a period of even a few weeks may result in considerable reduction of yield or crop failure.  Therefore the
practice of irrigation was developed many hundred years ago to
make it possible to maintain adequate soil moisture during dry
seasons.  The literature on irrigation is extensive.

The objectives of the practice of irrigation are: first,
to provide for an adequate supply of soil moisture for crop
production; second, to control the application of water in such
a way as to prevent erosion; third, to control the water supply
so as not to create water logging and water supply loss through
excessive seepage; and, fourth, to supply just a sufficient
amount of excess water so that salts do not accumulate in the
soil horizons penetrated by the roots of the crop being grown.
(See Topic 80).

Grasses have the ability to survive extended periods when
the soil moisture is deficient for growth by going into a resting phase.  Most cereals are grasses.  In many parts of the
World grain is grown under the dry-land or dry-farming system
of agriculture.  Based on a 104-year record the average precipitation at Denver, Colorado, is 14.58 inches.  In the general
area oats and wheat are grown.  The fields are divided into
strips.  Grain is grown on one strip while the adjacent strip
is left fallow and its bare soil is tilled repeatedly to remove
all growth by cultivation.  This allows a year's precipitation
to soak deeply into the soil.  By alternating cropland and
fallow in successive years grains which require about 20 inches
of water to mature are grown without irrigation.

The water brought to the fields by canals and distribution
systems from surface sources or from groundwater may be applied
to the cropland in a number of ways:  wild flooding, distribution systems of laterals and ditches for surface application or
for subsurface irrigation, drip or trickle irrigation, sprinkler systems, and desert strip farming.  Various surface irrigation methods are depicted in Figure 6-2, page 21.

Subsurface irrigation systems supply water to the soil at
the root depths from perforated pipes buried in the soil or by
periodic raising and dropping of the water table by sub-irriga-
tion.  Fok and Willardson (1971) have prepared a mathematical
analysis of subsurface irrigation system design.

Drip or trickle irrigation systems consist of pipes

releasing water immediately at the plant location without wetting the soil where no plants are growing. Although relatively costly drip irrigation makes very effective use of water. Most of the controlled-environment facilities (see Topic 50) utilize drip irrigation. Olson (1977) stated that the design of a trickle irrigation system requires a delicate balance between four parameters: degree of filtration; type of emission device; water quality; and, management of the system.

Wu (1975) discusses the hydraulic design of drip irrigation main lines and Wu and Gitlin (1973) analyze mathematically the hydraulics and uniformity of drip irrigation.

Drip or trickle irrigation systems are especially suited to arid environments. According to Bengson (1975) drip irrigation was first developed in Israel in the early 1960's. Bengson describes the effective usage of drip irrigation in revegetating steep slopes in an arid region for reclaiming landfills from a mining operation in Arizona. A basic system with filters and fertilizer injectors can cost $300 to $3000 per acre depending on plant density, according to Bengson.

The application of irrigation water through sprinklers is expanding rapidly. This technique makes possible the cultivation of slopes unsuited to surface water conveyance. It permits a uniform application of water to the soil surface over extensive areas in contrast to excessively deep wetting of croplands near ditches characteristic of surface-flow irrigation. Water may be applied through various types of sprinklers among which are: fixed sprinklers; moving sprinkler systems in which the water supply pipes mounted on wheels roll across a rectangular field; and the center-pivot system in which a wheeled pipe swings around the field in the manner of the hands of a clock as is shown in Figure 49-1 on the following page.

The water supplied to a center-pivot sprinkler may be piped in from a surface or groundwater source or from a well drilled at the pivot. The mechanism is costly since the wheels must travel at different speeds depending on distance from the pivot and the sprinklers must be positioned to yield uniform water distribution.

Heermann, Shull, and Mickelson (1974) performed an analysis of center-pivot capacities for Eastern Colorado. System capacities range from 4.5 gpm/acre to 8 gpm/acre with 6.5 gpm/acre being most prevelent. Center-pivot systems are designed for peak evapotranspiration. Chaudhry (1976) has performed a statistical analysis of sprinkler systems.

Figure 49-1  Aerial view of a center pivot sprinkler irrigating
    alfalfa from a well near Bismarck, North Dakota.  In the
    upper left corner can be seen the parallel crop and fallow
    strips of dry farming.  The Missouri River in the back-
    ground flows into Oahe Reservoir.  Bur. of Reclamation
    photo Aug. 26, 1976 by Lyle C. Axthelm.

The Bureau of Reclamation, established in 1902, was the
Federal Agency to which responsibility was assigned for development of irrigation in the Western States.  It may come as a
surprise to many that in the Calendar Year 1975 out of a total
irrigated area in the United States, including Alaska and
Hawaii, of 54,032,574 acres only 9,308,601 acres, or 17.2 percent, were supplied with water from Bureau of Reclamation
projects.

In Calendar Year 1975 total net releases from Bureau of
Reclamation project water supplies were 38,682,106 acre-feet.
Total farm deliveries were 26,015,061 acre-feet; municipal and
industrial water deliveries were 1,567,186 acre-feet; spills
and operational losses were 2,497,564 acre-feet; and miscellaneous deliveries such as stock water, fish and wildlife, construction uses among others, were 404,187 acre-feet.

All deliveries and operational losses total 30,543,998 acre-feet. When this amount of water is subtracted from total releases it is found that transportation losses amounted to 8,138,108 acre-feet or 21 percent of the total releases. (See Topic 57).

For crop year 1975 the gross value of all crops grown on Bureau of Reclamation projects amounted to $4,419,400,000. In contrast the total Federal cost of all in-service Bureau of Reclamation projects from 1902 through 1975 was $6,038,000,000. The wisdom of investment in irrigation projects is evident.

The municipal and industrial deliveries from Bureau of Reclamation projects of 1,567,186 acre-feet in 1975 served a total of 15,911,110 people. Many cities and industries could never have come into existence had water from Reclamation projects not been made available to them in an arid ecosystem. Data on acreages, water volume, and the monetary values are taken from "Federal Reclamation Projects - Water & Land Resource Accomplishments 1975".

Dominy (1968) described the role of irrigation in the West's expanding economy. "Reclamation Project Data" (1961) with a "Supplement" (1966) contain descriptions, photographs, and condensed engineering drawings pertaining to Bureau of Reclamation projects.

A practical reference on irrigation is the farmers bulletin by Lewis (1943). A condensed description of principles and practices of irrigation was prepared by More (1969). Golze (1961) in his book on reclamation in the United States includes a review of the early history of the Bureau of Reclamation.

Interest world-wide in irrigation led to the organization in 1950 of the International Commission on Irrigation and Drainage (ICID). As of 1978 there are about 64 member countries. Congresses are held every third year. The report by Langley, Gray, and Stephens (1972) describes water and land operations and irrigation projects in Bulgaria which the authors observed during tours which are a part of each Congress.

Desert strip farming makes use of a large collector area which harvests water to supply moisture to a smaller farmed area. According to Morin, Parsons, Matlock, and Fangmeier (1973) this technique was used in the Negev Desert prior to the time of Christ to support a population of about 50,000 city-dwelling flood-plain farmers and about 1000 years ago it was also used in Northern Arizona. The authors made use of a computer model to study several collector-area to farmed-area ratios for the growth of grain sorghum at Tucson using rainfall

records for the period 1900-1972. Desert strip farming does
not require massive construction in storage dams or extensive
conveyance systems. Where the geology, topography and soils
are favorable this system could become very valuable.

Even though field and tree crop plants may show no signs
of wilting when they are under moisture stress yields and quality of the crop may be seriously reduced (see Topic 50). It
was found by experience in the eastern humid United States that
irrigation would be very helpful in crop production. Miller
(1968) calculated for the Susquehanna River Basin that by the
year 2020 about 1100 cfs would be removed to supply irrigation
to about 177,000 acres. Demands for irrigation water would be
greatest during dry years when flows are low a condition which
could cause water resource allocation problems.

Figure 49-2  An irrigator is shown using siphon tubes to transfer water to ditches in a young tomato field a few miles
west of Sacramento, Calif., in the U.S. Bureau of
Reclamation's Central Valley Project.
Photo by A. G. D'Allessandro.

The occurrence of brief but severe drought periods at critical stages of growth during growing season in the humid areas are known to have a depressing effect on food production and farm income. Windsor and Chow (1971) formulated a mathematical computer model for the design and analysis of a multi-crop, multi-soil farm irrigation system for humid areas.

Mierau (1977) described the St. Lucie County agricultural area in southern Florida near the Atlantic Coast. Annual rainfall is 51 inches (1300 mm) and potential evapotranspiration for citrus is about 42 inches (1070 mm). However, more than 75 percent of a year's rainfall occurs during the 6-month period May-October. This distribution of the annual precipitation requires drainage and waste of water during the wet months and irrigation during the dry period when the citrus trees are blooming and fruit is set. A major problem, according to Mierau, is inadequate surface storage which prevents carry-over of water from wet periods to dry periods.

As population density increases and the irrigated area also increases in the humid parts of the United States it will inevitably follow that the States will need to abandon the Riparian Doctrine (see Topic 66) and adopt the Doctrine of Prior Appropriation.

## References

Bengson, Stuart A., "Drip Irrigation for Revegetating Steep Slopes in an Arid Environment", Progressive Agriculture in Arizona, vol. XXVII, no. 1, Univ. of Arizona, Tucson, pp 3-5 and 12, Jan.-Feb. 1975.

Chaudhry, Fazal H., "Sprinkler Uniformity Measures and Skewness", Jour. of Irrigation and Drainage Div., Proceedings ASCE, pp 425-433, Dec. 1976.

Dominy, Floyd E., "Role of Irrigation in the West's Expanding Economy", Jour. Irrigation and Drainage Div., Proceedings ASCE, pp 401-418, Dec. 1968.

"Federal Reclamation Projects - Water & Land Resource Accomplishments - 1975", Summary Report 57 pp, Appendix I 284 pp, Appendix II 290 pp, and Appendix III 381 pp, Bureau of Reclamation USDI, 1975.

Fok, Yu-Si, and Lyman S. Willardson, "Subsurface Irrigation System Analysis and Design", Jour. Irrigation and Drainage Div., Proceedings ASCE, pp 449-454, Sept. 1971.

Golze, Alfred R., "Reclamation in the United States", The Caxton Printers, Ltd., Caldwell, Idaho, 486 pp, 1961.

Heerman, Dale F., Hollis H. Shull, and Rome H. Mickelson, "Center Pivot Design Capacities in Eastern Colorado", Jour. Irrigation and Drainage Div., Proceedings ASCE, pp 127-141, June, 1974.

Langley, Maurice N., H. R. Gray, and Larry D. Stephens, "A Brief Review of Water and Land Operations in Bulgaria", ICID Newsletter Supplement No. 5, Special Report, 22 pp, copies available from U.S. Committee on Irrigation, Drainage, and Flood Control, P.O. Box 15326, Denver, Colo.80215

Lewis, M. R., "Practical Irrigation", USDA Farmers' Bulletin No. 1922, 69 pp, Jan. 1943.

Mierau, Ronald, "Water Shortages in Humid Areas", Proceedings Specialty Conference on Water Management for Irrigation and Drainage, of July 20-22, 1977, Reno, Nev., pp 61-73, in vol. 1, 438 pp, ASCE, 1977.

Miller, Howard, "Future Irrigation Demand in the Susquehanna Basin", Jour. Irrigation and Drainage Div., Proceedings ASCE, pp 391-399, Dec. 1968.

More, Rosemare J., "Water and Crops", III(i) in Water, Earth and Man, ed by Richard J. Chorley, Methuen & Co., Ltd., 588 pp, 1969. (Dist. in U.S. by Barnes & Noble, Inc.)

Morin, G. C. A., D. K. Parsons, W. G. Matlock, and D. D. Fangmeier, "Desert Strip Farming - A Way to Make the Desert Green", Progressive Agriculture in Arizona, vol. XXV, no. 4, pp 4-8, July-Aug. 1973.

Olson, Benjamin R.,Jr., "Trickle Irrigation System Design to Fit Management", Proceedings Specialty Conference on Water Management for Irrigation and Drainage, July 20-22, 1977, Reno, Nev. pp 379-381, vol. 1, ASCE, 438 pp, 1977.

"Reclamation Project Data", Bureau of Reclamation, USDI, 890 pp and map, 1961, with Supplement, 1966.

Windsor, James S., and Ven Te Chow, "Model for Farm Irrigation in Humid Areas", Jour. Irrigation and Drainage Division, Proceedings, ASCE, pp 369-385, Sept, 1971.

Wu, I-pai, and Harris M. Gitlin, "Hydraulics and Uniformity for Drip Irrigation", Jour. Irrigation and Drainage Div., Proceedings ASCE, pp 157-168, June, 1973.

Wu, I-pai, "Design of Drip Irrigation Main Lines", Jour. Irrigation and Drainage Div., Proceedings ASCE, pp 265-278, Dec. 1975.

Topic 50     Controlled-Environment Food Production

Photosynthesis

The miracle of photosynthesis has created the Earth's environment. Until recently it was believed that the Earth was the only planet having oxygen and water. Photosynthesis is a process by which carbon dioxide, water, and solar energy are transformed into organic compounds with the release of free oxygen. This process transforms energy into matter. Levine (1969) reported that light of 2 wave lengths is needed to activate 2 photochemical systems. Together they provide the electrons and photons and the energy-rich molecules for photosynthesis in plants. Certain bacteria are photosynthetic but their processes differ from photosynthesis in plants.

The electrons and photons are absorbed to form matter in the fantastically short time of $10^{-12}$ second. The photosynthetic processes which take place in the chloroplasts of green plants are described in detail by Devlin and Barker (1971). Chlorophylls and carotenes are the chemical compounds active in photosynthesis.

In ages past during various carboniferous periods the Earth's atmosphere was very much richer in carbon dioxide than it is now. In those eras the photosynthetic process was extremely active producing organic compounds which ultimately were transformed into what we now recognize as fossil fuels: coal, petroleum, and natural gas. When we burn fossil fuel we are releasing the solar energy which reached the Earth millions of years ago. All life is dependent on photosynthesis and various ecosystems have evolved making use either directly or indirectly of the products of photosynthesis.

In the higher plants the trapping of light energy is followed by the removal of electrons from water and the release of oxygen as described by Tinus (1974). The subsequent process of reduction of $CO_2$ varies with the species. Most plants utilize the Calvin cycle or $C_3$ pathway.

Many xerophytes or succulents keep their stomata closed in the day and open at night which enables them to survive extremely arid climates. Succulents take in $CO_2$ at night and reduce the $CO_2$ through the Hatch-Slack or $C_4$ pathway in which the light energy trapping and the $CO_2$ utilization are separated in time. The $C_4$ pathway is much slower than the $C_3$ pathway and plants following the $C_4$ pathway with few exceptions, among which is the pineapple, are slow-growing. Bassham's (1977) paper includes a detailed discussion of $C_3$ and $C_4$ pathways.

The amount of water found in plant tissues is more than sufficient to satisfy the needs of photosynthesis even when a plant is under moisture stress. Devlin and Barker (1971) report that due to a complexity of factors when relative turgidity of a plant is 40 percent to 50 percent there is practically no photosynthesis. Apple trees showed a 50 percent drop in photosynthesis when the soil was allowed to dry gradually even though the leaves showed no sign of wilting. However sunflower and cotton showed no reduction in photosynthesis even though the leaves were visibly wilted.

Tinus (1974) reported that the photosynthesis of well-watered and well-lighted plants can almost always be increased by increasing the $CO_2$. In the $C_3$ pathway-plants photorespiration is suppressed at concentrations of $CO_2$ above 1,000 ppm. Adding $CO_2$ to greenhouse atmosphere is becoming standard practice.

## Controlled Environment Food Production

Controlled environment food production, usually in greenhouses, makes it possible to produce fresh vegetables and flowers out of season. The yields are usually much greater than those from fields and water requirements are very greatly reduced. The major economic considerations are the costs of the structures and of heating. Solar energy and waste heat from power plants and other industrial processes are the subjects of extensive research. It is estimated that, as of 1977, the size of the greenhouse industry was: in the United States, 20,000 acres (8094 ha); in Western Europe, 40,000 acres (16,000 ha); in Southern Europe, 25,000 acres (10,000 ha); and tens of thousands of hectares in Eastern Europe, the USSR, Asia, and in many developing countries.

The Environmental Research Laboratory of the University of Arizona in the early 1960's initiated research on the development of an integrated power/water/food facility. At the Puerto Penasco facility on the Gulf of California in Mexico a pilot plant operated jointly by the Universidad De Sonora and the University of Arizona produces about 2400 gallons per day of pure water using waste heat from diesel engine-driven generators. Under extremely arid conditions a small amount of water is capable of producing vegetables very efficiently by enclosing the cropped areas under polyethelene covers. These covers are inflated by an internal pressure of .01 to .02 pound per square-inch pressure as described in the bilingual pamphlet, "Power/Water/Food Experiments at Puerto Penasco" (undated).

At the headquarters installations of the Environmental Research Laboratory located at the Tucson International Airport the exhaust gases from the Diesel engines are scrubbed and $CO_2$ is added to the greenhouse atmosphere resulting in significant increases in yields.

At the invitation of Shaikh Zaid Bin Sultan Al-Nahya, ruler of Abu Dhabi, in 1972 the first large-scale power-water-food facility was built on the totally barren Sadiyat Island off the coast of Abu Dhabi in the Persian Gulf. Hodge (1973) describes this artificial oasis. Details concerning the construction, operation, and crop yields of the Abu Dhabi facility are given by Fontes (1973). The installation is aimed to produce about one ton of vegetables per day. The harvest of tomatoes alone was estimated to be sufficient to supply about 29,000 persons at United States levels of consumption.

"Annual Report 1972-1973 Environmental Research Laboratory, University of Arizona - Arid Lands Research Center, Abu Dhabi" includes details of the "food factories" in Abu Dhabi, Puerto Penasco, Tucson shrimp production facility, the commercially-operated Environmental Farms, Inc., south of Tucson, the Fort Yuma Indian Reservation's Quechan Environmental Farms in California, and the Papago Indian Reservation's greenhouse in Sells, Arizona.

An "International Symposium on Controlled Environment Agriculture" was held at Tucson, Arizona, April 7 and 8, 1977 the Proceedings of which have been printed in a 413-page volume consisting of 12 sections with a total of 47 papers. The section topics are: Overview-Industry Background and Situation, Economic Considerations, New Cultivars and Objectives for Plant Breeders, Intercropping of Vegetables, Energy Alternatives, Growing Techniques in Relation to Today's Industry, Vegetable Transplant Production Systems for Open-Field Agriculture, Mineral Nutrient and $CO_2$ Enrichment, Environment Control, Energy Conservation, Greenhouse Designs - Now and Future, and Insect and Disease Control.

Mushrooms are produced in controlled environments. Eggs and chicken production is now industrial engineering utilizing controlled environments. Experiments are underway to grow shrimp. Farm fish protein ponds are very productive. The production of pork and of beef through feeder-lot usage can be considered to be applications of controlled environments.

Bassham (1977, pages 636-637) presents a provocative proposal. He suggests a very large-scale application of $CO_2$ enrichment. He proposes that large areas in the Southwestern United States be covered with huge plastic greenhouses, each one square kilometer (0.386 square mile) in area and 300 m (984 feet) high. With $CO_2$ enrichment photosynthesis would be at the maximum. Alfalfa would be the main crop. Only a very small fraction of the water needed to grow open-field crops would be required in the greenhouses. Protein content of alfalfa can be as high as 24 percent of the dry weight.

In our current era of world-wide increases in population Bassham's proposal is worthy of serious consideration.

## References

"Annual Report 1972-1973 Environmental Research Laboratory, University of Arizona - Arid Lands Research Center, Abu Dhabi", 48 pp, pub. by Univ. of Arizona, Tucson, 1973.

Bassham, James A., "Increasing Crop Production Through More Controlled Photosynthesis", Science, vol. 197, no. 4304, pp 630-638, Aug. 12, 1977.

Devlin, Robert M., and Allen V. Barker, "Photosynthesis", Van Nostrand Reinhold Co., New York, 304 pp, 1971.

Fontes, Miguel R., "Controlled-environment Horticulture in the Arabian Desert at Abu Dhabi", Hort Science, vol. 8, no. 1, pp 13-16, Feb. 1973.

Hodge, Carle O., "Artificial Oases", Hort Science, vol. 8, no. 1, page 2, Feb. 1973.

"International Symposium on Controlled Environment Agriculture" Proceedings of Symposium of Apr. 7-8, 1977, Tucson, Ariz., 413-pp. Available from Environmental Research Lab., Tucson International Airport, Tucson, 85706. 1977.

Levine, R. P., "The Mechanism of Photosynthesis", Scientific American, vol. 221, no. 6, pp 58-70, Dec. 1969.

"Power/Water/Food Experiments at Puerto Penasco", prepared by Universidad de Sonora and the Environmental Research Laboratory of the Univ. of Arizona, Tucson. Pub. in English and in Spanish in one leaflet (undated - about 1974).

Tinus, Richard W., "Impact of the $CO_2$ Requirement on Plant Water Use", Agricultural Meteorology, vol. 14, pp 99-112, pub. by the Elsevier Scientific Pub. Co., Amsterdam, The Netherlands, 1974.

SECTION XI

FORECASTING IN RELATION TO WATER RESOURCES

Topic 51             Hydrologic Forecasting

Land use planners, watershed managers, and others dealing
with environmental management may be called upon to prepare or
to arrange for others to prepare, estimates of forecasts dealing with many of the subjects, singly or in combinations, in
the following list:

Frequency and magnitude of floods.
Incidence and persistence of droughts.
Incidence and persistence of periods of above normal
    precipitation.
Magnitude of flows and their persistence at specific
    locations in particular drainage basins.
Seasonal or annual water yields.
Peak rates of runoff yielded by snowmelt.
Peak rates of runoff from combinations of snowmelt and
    rainfall.
The shape of the hydrograph and volumes to be expected
    from drainage basins for which no hydrologic records
    are available.
Sediment discharge of rivers.
Average annual sediment yield of a drainage basin at a
    specific potential reservoir site.
Evaporation losses from existing and proposed reservoirs
    and from river systems.
Evapotranspiration losses from land areas before and after
    cultural development.
Management of areas occupied by phreatophytes.
Formation and breakup of river and lake ice.
Incidence of floods due to ice jams.
Forecasts of average and of maximum wave heights and char-
    acteristics which might occur on as yet unbuilt
    reservoirs.
Persistence and magnitude of ice pressures on dams and
    hydraulic structures.
Temperatures of flows released from impoundments.
Magnitude of interference with operation of reservoir and
    river systems which might result from biota.
Hydrologic impacts of changes in land use.
Delineation of flood plains for flood insurance purposes.
Water quality characteristics of natural flows and of the
    effects of changes in land use and water utilization
    activities.
Groundwater yield from wells and systems of wells.

Projections of hydrologic and economic life of groundwater
systems.
Changes in quality of urban environments as related to a
shrinking total available water supply.
Hydrologic and water resource analyses and projections of
trends as part of environmental impact statements.

## Runoff Forecasting

Runoff forecasting can be divided into two broad classes,
rate of runoff  or river forecasting, and seasonal water yield
forecasting.  River forecasting makes use of rainfall-runoff
relationships, routing methods, unit hydrographs, recession
curves, and station discharge relationships, among others.  It
may be necessary to prepare forecasts of stage height and to
issue warnings of possible flood damage on very short notice in
some river basins in a matter of hours.

This has led to the development of automatic-transmitting
radio-reporting flood warning systems.  Remotely located, unattended, automatically-reporting river gaging stations have
been developed.  These may be interrogated either by telephone
or by radio communication networks.  Since each river basin
tends to possess individual characteristics and since the
natural forces of geomorphology with accelerations caused by
human endeavor may result in the changes of the river characteristics, rate of runoff forecasting becomes an absorbing and
never-ending activity.

A specialized forecasting endeavor is forecasting the
behavior of water under the effects of tides, flood flows, and
at estuaries.  Another specialized forecasting problem may be
that of forecasting meteorologically the incidence of winds
which could cause waves disruptive to either construction,
operation, or recreation at reservoirs.

## The Philosophy of Forecasting

The "Handbook of Forecasting Techniques" (1975) is a 314-
page analysis of the philosophy of approach to water resources
forecasting.  Thirty-one methods which are discussed are classified into 3 groups: Techniques Using Time Series and Projections with 3 classes; Techniques Based on Models and Simulations with 5 classes; and, Qualitative and Holister Techniques
with 4 classes.

## Reference

"Handbook of Forecasting Techniques", Center for the Study of
Social Policy, Stanford Research Institute, Menlo Park,
Calif., for U.S. Army Engineer Institute for Water Resources, Fort Belvoir, Va., 314 pp, IWR Contract Report
75-7, Dec. 1975.

Topic 52        Seasonal Water-Yield Forecasting

Seasonal water-yield forecasting has as its purpose the prediction of a volume of water which could be yielded from a particular watershed as a result of having received a certain amount of rain, snow, or both. Seasonal water yields deal with total volume such as April through September and are not concerned usually with rates of runoff at which the volume may be generated. In most cases water-yield forecasts are made for drainage basins on which large impoundment structures have been built. Rate-of-inflow forecasts may be critical only when the reservoir is approaching its full capacity. At that time rate-of-runoff forecasting may be necessary for efficient operations and protection of downstream portions of the river should an uncontrolled-spill occur.

The interactions of the many factors influencing seasonal water yield are very complex. Seasonal water-yield forecasting makes use of electronic data processing machinery to assist in the solution of complex multiple correlation and other mathematical techniques in computing the desired forecasts. Ford (1959) presented a thoroughly-tested procedure for computing seasonal water-yield forecasts.

The purpose of correlation analyses is to ascertain through mathematical statistical procedures the cause-and-effect relationships in a system. If it is known from physically-performed measurements or from experience that a one and only independent variable controls the system to such an extent that the result is practically independent of all the other variables, a simple correlation may express the system completely. The spring scale provided with the Federal-State Cooperative Snow System surveying equipment for measuring the water equivalent of snow is an example of a single independent variable system, weight versus elongation. It is known that temperature does have an effect on the response of a spring to a gravity load but in most cases this effect is accepted as being negligible.

In Hydrology very few phenomena can be expressed with a simple correlation. Therefore, extensive use is made of multiple correlation analysis. When more than one independent variable is influencing the behavior of the dependent variable, usually identified by the symbol "Y", multiple correlation (often referred to as regression) analysis expresses mathematically the interaction of the independent variables as they jointly affect the value of the dependent variable.

The performance of linear multiple correlation analyses, manually or with a desk calculator, can be extremely tedious

and time consuming. A study which would take two weeks by
desk-top methods can be performed in seconds on modern high-
speed electronic data processing machinery. An excellent general review of both analog and digital computers and of their
applications in various hydrologic studies is the section by
Dawdy and Matalas (1964) which includes a listing of 192
references.

Additional references on regression analyses are:
Freese (1964), Yevjevich (1964), and Chow (1964). It is not
necessary to be a professionally-capable statistician to make
use of correlation analyses. Many programs are available for
various purposes developed for various computers which range
from pocket-size electronic calculators to the most complicated
and largest data processing machinery. Consultation with someone experienced in this subject is recommended.

There is an extensive literature on water-yield forecasting. The professional periodicals include an ever-increasing
number of publications relating to rate of runoff and seasonal
water-yield forecasting. A number of organizations, some of
which are listed in Appendix C, prepare forecasts available
to the general public.

Topic 18 dealt with a simple correlation analysis of a
linear correlation. Unless clearly stated most simple and
multiple regression (or correlation) analyses treat the data as
if it possessed a linear correlation even if a graph shows a
distinct curvilinearity. Draper and Smith (1966), pages 295-
304, deal with the geometry of non-linear least squares.

Since the managers of water resources utilization projects
are held accountable for their decisions, a great many organizations (private, state, federal, or international) make their
own forecasts which may be considerably different from those
released by the agencies making the publicly-available forecasts.

Shafer and Farnes (1975) review the interpretation of
snow survey data for use in environmental planning including
reservoir management.

Adamcyk, Jolly, and Soloman (1976) make use of regression
equations and hydrologic models in their study of flood forecasting of inflow to Grand Lake Reservoir in Newfoundland. The
drainage basin, with an area of 1942 square miles, is about 100
miles long and 20 miles wide. The reservoir, having a surface
area of 186 square miles, provides storage for a 125-MW hydroelectric power plant. Dickison and Daugharty (1975) describe
snow-cover patterns in the Nashwaak experimental watershed project consisting of two drainage basins in New Brunswick,
Canada.

Problem Assignment - Water Yield Forecasting

Part A

You have reported for duty on May 1st as a water resources specialist in an Area Development Planning Office. The data presented in the table below is given you with the request that you prepare immediately a graph and make a forecast of the 1977 April through September water yield for Clear Creek near Golden, Colorado, area 399 square miles; located one mile west of Golden and 12.5 miles downstream from North Clear Creek; corrected for Berthoud Ditch Diversion. There is no time to explain to you how the "combined index" has been computed with the exception of the statement that it is based on a combination of snow survey data, and there is no time to supply the missing data. There is no time to compute simple correlation by the method of least squares with a desk calculator and no data processing machinery is available. The Area Planning Director wants you to give him not only the forecast but also a range of values for an estimated two chances out of three deviation.

Table 52-1   Water-Yield Forecast Data for Clear Creek Near Golden, Colorado, Drainage Area 399 square miles.

| Water Year | Combined Index | Water Yield Apr.-Sept. 1000 A.F. | Water Year | Combined Index | Water Yield Apr.-Sept. 1000 A.F. |
|---|---|---|---|---|---|
| 1958 | 180.5 | 128 | 1968 | 149.9 | 108 |
| 1959 | 183.9 | 116 | 1969 | 115.5 | 181 |
| 1960 | 166.1 | 145 | 1970 | 223.8 | 180 |
| 1961 | 142.5 | 134 | 1971 | 191.0 | 160 |
| 1962 | 167.1 | 127 | 1972 | 154.7 | 98 |
| 1963 | 111.9 | 63 | 1973 | 135.5 | 173 |
| 1964 | 141.4 | 87 | 1974 | 184.5 | 132 |
| 1965 | 219.0 | 201 | 1975 | 176.0 | |
| 1966 | 88.8 | 68 | 1976 | 129.0 | |
| 1967 | 131.5 | 92 | 1977 | | |

1.  Plot the values, draw a straight line by visual estimate, derive the equation of this line, make your forecast and give your estimate of the most likely volume and state the values of the upper and lower limits.

2.  Number, sign, assemble, and hand in all work sheets in support of your report on this assignment.

Part B

Now that the emergency situation has come to rest you have had an opportunity to supply missing data and to learn about the combined index as it was developed by Jack Washichek,

Snow Survey Supervisor, Soil Conservation Service, Denver, Colorado. His index is based on data from three snow courses described in Table 52-2.

Table 52-2  Description of Snow Surveys

| Snow Survey No. | Name | Elevation Feet | Drainage Basin Location |
|---|---|---|---|
| Sk14S | Berthoud Summit | 11,300 | Fraser River Drainage |
| SK09 | Grizzly Peak | 11,250 | Snake River just west of Loveland Pass |
| SK13 | Berthoud Falls | 10,500 | Clear Creek Drainage |

Washichek's combined index is computed from the following equation in which the April 1st and the May 1st values are the sums of the snow-water equivalents of the three snow courses identified in Table 52-2 for the dates shown.

$$\text{Combined Index} = 2\,(\text{April 1st}) + (\text{May 1st}) \qquad (1)$$

It is to be noted that two of the snow courses are physically located outside the Clear Creek drainage basin. These two snow courses are on the Colorado River side of the Continental Divide in the path of the on-coming air masses which deposit the snow in the headwaters of Clear Creek which is in the Platte River drainage basin. Practically all of the run-off comes from those portions of the Clear Creek drainage basin which are located in the Arapahoe National Forest. By combining the snow-water equivalents of three snow courses for two dates in one combined index Washichek used a simple correlation for the computation of this forecast. He also makes extensive use of multiple correlation analyses.

The combined index can be used for making forecasts as of April 1st or May 1st by assuming values of snow-water equivalents if the forecast is prior to May 1st. The average, the median, or various values arrived at by frequency analyses for chosen return periods can be substituted. Therefore it is possible, with the one equation, to prepare a very large number of forecasts for consideration by the hydrologist when he makes the decision on his forecast for a particular water resources utilization purpose.

3. Using the procedure illustrated in Topic 18 compute the equation of the line for the forecast you made under sub-paragraph 1 and give the values of the upper and lower limits for one standard deviation. (See Topic 17).

4. Compare the forecasts performed by the visual and the mathematical approaches.

5. Discuss with your instructor the handling of the 1969 and 1973 plotting positions.

6. Prepare and hand in a summary report including recommendations for improving the accuracy of the seasonal water-yield forecast for this drainage basin.

## References

Adamcyk, R. J., J. P. Jolly, and S. I. Solomon, "Use of Regression Equations and Hydrologic Models for Flood Forecasting - A Case Study", Eastern Snow Conference, Proceedings of the 1976 Annual Meeting, pp 83-97, 1976.

Chow, Ven Te, "Application of Electronic Computers in Hydrology", Sec. 29, Handbook of Applied Hydrology, Ven Te Chow, ed-in-chief, McGraw-Hill Book Co., 1964.

Dawdy, D. R., and N. C. Matalas, Part III, Analysis of Variance Covariance, and Time Series", Sec. 8, Handbook of Applied Hydrology, Ven Te Chow, ed-in-chief, McGraw-Hill Book Co., New York, 1964.

Dickison, Robert B. B., and David A. Daugharty, "Snow Cover Patterns in the Nashwaak Experimental Watershed, New Brunswick", Eastern Snow Conference, Proceedings of the 1975 Annual Meeting, pp 59-79, 1975.

Draper, N. R., and H. Smith, "Applied Regression Analysis", John Wiley and Sons, Inc., 407 pp, 1966.

Ford, Perry M., "Multiple Correlation in Forecasting Seasonal Runoff", Engineering Monograph No. 2, Bureau of Reclamation, USDI, 2nd revision, 41 pp, June, 1959.

Freese, Frank, "Linear Regression Methods for Forest Research", U.S. Forest Service Research Paper FPL 17, Forest Products Laboratory, Forest Service, USDA, Madison, Wis., Dec. 1964

Shafer, B. A., and P. E. Farnes, "Interpreting Snow Survey Data for Use in Environmental Planning", Western Snow Conf. 43d Annual Meeting, Apr. 23-25, 1975, Proceedings, pp 71-78, 1975.

Yevdjevich, V. M., "Part II, Regression and Correlation Analysis", Sec. 8, Handbook of Applied Hydrology, Ven Te Chow, ed-in-chief, McGraw-Hill Book Co., New York, 1964.

Topic 53   Forecasting Rates of Runoff from Snowmelt

    Snowmelt hydrology involves two phenomena: the first deals
with energy needed to supply the latent heat of fusion to convert ice crystals to liquid water; the second relates to the
synthesis of the hydrograph produced by waters released by the
melting of snow.

    Unless snow is lying on rocks or on very shallow soil,
there is practically no overland flow from snowmelt the hydrograph being composed of subsurface or interflow and groundwater
flow.  Garstka, Love, Goodell, and Bertle (1958) developed a
method of accounting for a day's contribution to the snowmelt
hydrograph.  Figure 53-1 is taken from their page 66.  It
illustrates how the snowmelt hydrograph at the beginning of
the active melt season rises day by day.  This explains why the
cfs for a particular day measured at a gaging station may
appear to have practically no relationship to the heat units.

METHOD OF COMPUTATION OF SNOWMELT HYDROGRAPH

Figure 53-1
    Separation of
    snowmelt hydro-
    graph showing
    contribution
    from one day's
    melt.

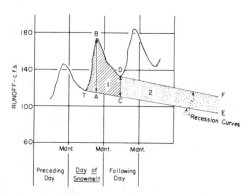

Area I = Volume of a day's snowmelt appearing in the first
       24-hour period. (First day volume)
Area 2 = Volume of a day's snowmelt in recession flow.
Total snowmelt for the day = Area I + Area 2.

    It has been found that both statistical and physical
approaches to determination of heat available for snowmelt are
adequate.  Practically all of the heat which melts snow is
supplied to the exposed upper surface of the snow, very little
coming up from the ground.  Statistical analyses using the
multiple-correlation approach are reported in detail for the
Fraser Experimental Forest, Colorado, by Garstka, Love,
Goodell, and Bertle (1958).

    Light (1941) developed a physical equation for effective
snowmelt.  His complex equation was reduced for the Fraser

312

Experimental Forest by Garstka, Love, Goodell, and Bertle (1958) to

$$D = K U_m \, 0.00184(T_f - 32)10^{-0.0000156h} + 0.00578(e - 6.11)$$

in which    $D$ = effective snowmelt, inches per 6 hours
              $K$ = constant for a particular basin
              $U_m$= average wind velocity, miles per hour at
                  50-ft height
              $T_f$= air temperature, $^\circ$F at 10-ft level
              $e$ = vapor pressure, mb, at 10-ft height
              $h$ = station elevation, feet above mean sea level.

The Light equation presented above gives only theoretical point values of snowmelt. In applying such values to an actual drainage basin, consideration must be given to two modifying factors, namely, the surface roughness and the forest cover ratio. These two factors can be included in a basin constant K which is to modify the theoretical point value. Therefore the basin snowmelt = KD. The basin constant for a drainage basin is the ratio of the observed snowmelt to the theoretical snowmelt computed by the Light equation. The value of K can be obtained through correlation of the two snowmelt values. Theoretically K = 1.0 for a flat basin uniformly covered with snow and without surface obstructions.

The Corps of Engineers, as described in their "Runoff from Snowmelt" (1960), found that the daily springtime snowmelt M in inches may be estimated by the following correlation equations as a function of the mean daily temperature $T_{mean}$, the maximum daily temperature $T_{max}$, and the relative forest cover

   1. For open sites,        $M = 0.06 \, (T_{mean} - 24)$
                               $M = 0.04 \, (T_{max} \; - 27)$

   2. For forest sites,      $M = 0.05 \, (T_{mean} - 32)$
                                 $M = 0.04 \, (T_{max} \; - 42)$

These equations are applicable for $T_{mean}$ in the range of 34 to 66$^\circ$ F and for $T_{max}$ in the range of 44 to 76$^\circ$ F.

Peck (1972) in discussing the snow measurement predicament mentions a citation to a book published in China in 1247 A.D. in which a bamboo snow gage was used at high elevations to provide information on snowfall.

Santeford, Alger, and Meier (1972) found in a two-year snowmelt in the Upper Penninsula of Michigan that, although the ground may have been frozen in early winter, under the protection of snow cover it became unfrozen allowing infiltration which produced a winter-base snow twice that of the summer-base snow.

An investigation dealing with snowmelt as related to various thermodynamic processes is described by Pysklywec, Davar, and Bray (1968) who performed their work in the North Nashwaaksis Stream Basin, New Brunswick, Canada. They used the degree-day method, a U.S. Army Corps of Engineers' generalized snowmelt equation, and regression equations. They concluded that all three methods gave generally comparable results.

Leaf (1970) describes the use of aerial photographs for operational streamflow forecasting in three drainage basins within the Fraser Experimental Forest. He found a linear correlation relating the peak daily discharge in acre feet and the season generated runoff also in acre feet; all three drainage basins plotted on one line. Meier (1969) discusses problems common to snowpacks and glaciers in non-polar glaciology. Garstka reviews developments in snow and ice hydrology in two references (1964) and (1969).

Dincer, Payne, Florkowski, Martinec, and Tongiorgi (1970) in a paper from the International Atomic Energy Agency of Vienna, Austria, describe a very interesting application of measurements of Tritium and Oxygen-18 in snowmelt hydrology. The variations of Deuterium in an annual snowpack are described by Judy, Meiman, and Friedman (1970).

At the Sleepers River Watershed near Danville, Vermont, Bissell and Peck (1973) have demonstrated the feasibility of monitoring snow-water equivalent by using natural soil radioactivity for snow depths less than 40 centimeters. Anderson, Greenan, Whipkey, and Machell (1977) assembled a detailed description of the Danville Watershed with photographs of the NOAA-ARS Cooperative Snow Research Project. This publication includes detailed data for water years 1960-1974.

Degree days above $32^\circ$ F must be used with great care to arrive at point-melt-rates of snow in inches. Point-melt-rate is not the same as a basin index correlation. It has been found that point-melt-rate in inches per-degree day above $32^\circ$ F may vary from 0.015 to 0.20.

It does not matter if a day's contribution of snowmelt is calculated by degree-days, statistical regression analysis, or thermodynamic equations resembling those developed for evapotranspiration as discussed in Topic 40. The snowmelt hydrograph is the result of an assembly of its components as treated in Topic 27.

Figure 53-2 on page 315 taken from page 72 of the report by Garstka, Love, Goodell, and Bertle (1958) shows how solar radiation, wind, air temperature, dew-point temperature, and degree days above $32^\circ$ F interact to produce the snowmelt hydrograph during the period May 13 through July 1, 1948 for

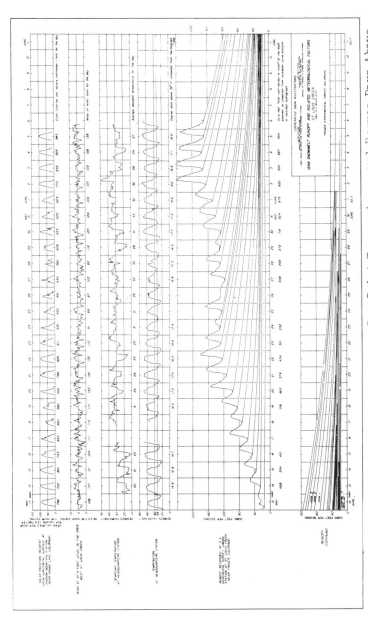

Figure 53-2

Interaction of Solar Radiation, Wind, Air Temperature, Dew-Point Temperature, and Degree Days Above 32° F to Produce the Hydrograph for St. Louis Creek, Fraser Experimental Forest, Colo., May 13 - July 4, 1948; drainage area 32.8 sq. mi. This photographic reduction is included to show how the snow-melt hydrograph is assembled from one day's melt as shown in Figure 53-1.

315

St. Louis Creek, drainage area 32.8 square miles, at the
Fraser Experimental Forest, Colorado. Area 1 of Figure 53-1
accounted for only about 11.2 percent of the snowmelt caused by
a day's heat for the 1948 snowmelt season. The remaining
88.8 percent departed from the drainage basin during the remainder of that summer, as shown in the recession curves.

## References

Anderson, Eric A., Hugh J. Greenan, Ronald Z. Whipkey, and
    Carl T. Machell, "NOAA-ARS Cooperative Snow Research Pro-
    ject - Watershed Hydro-Climatology and Data for Water
    Years 1960-1974", pub. by Office of Hydrology, National
    Weather Service, Md., June, 1977.

Bissell, Vernon C., and Eugene L. Peck, "Monitoring Snow Water
    Equivalent by Using Natural Soil Radioactivity", Water
    Resources Research, vol. 9, no. 4, pp 995-890, Aug. 1973.

Dincer, T., B. R. Payne, T. Florkowski, J. Martinec, and
    E. Tongiorgi, "Snowmelt Runoff from Measurements of
    Tritium and Oxygen-18", Water Resources Research, vol. 6,
    no. 1, pp 110-124, Feb. 1970.

Garstka, W. U., L. D. Love, B. C. Goodell, and F. A. Bertle,
    "Factors Affecting Snowmelt and Streamflow", Bureau of
    Reclamation and U.S. Forest Service, 189 pp, 1958.

Garstka, Walter U., "Snow and Snow Survey", Sec. 10, Handbook
    of Applied Hydrology, Ven Te Chow, ed-in-chief, McGraw-
    Hill Book Co., New York, 1964.

Garstka, Walter U., "Snow and Ice Hydrology", The Progress of
    Hydrology, Proceedings of the First International Seminar
    for Hydrology Professors, July 13-25, 1969. Pub. by
    Dept. of Civil Engineering, Univ. of Illinois at Urbana,
    pp 717-728, 1969.

Judy, Clark, James R. Meiman, and Irving Friedman, "Deuterium
    Variations in an Annual Snowpack", Water Resources
    Research, vol. 6, no. 1, pp 125-129, Feb. 1970.

Leaf, Charles F., "Aerial Photographs for Operational Stream-
    flow Forecasting in the Colorado Rockies", Proceedings
    37th Annual Meeting, Western Snow Conference, Salt Lake
    City, Utah, Apr. 15-17, 1969, pp 17-28. Printed by Colo.
    State Univ., Fort Collins, Feb. 1970.

Light, Phillip, "Analysis of High Rates of Snowmelting", Trans.
    American Geophysical Union, Part I, pp 195-205, 1941.

Meier, Mark F., "Glaciers and Snowpacks: Some Common Problems in Non-Polar Glaciology", The Progress of Hydrology, Proceedings of the First International Seminar for Hydrology Professors, July 13-25, 1969. Pub. by Dept. of Civil Engineering, Univ. of Illinois at Urbana, pp 729-736, 1969.

Peck, Eugene L., "Snow Measurement Predicament", Water Resources Research, vol. 8, no. 1, pp 244-248, Feb. 1972.

Pysklywec, D. W., K. S. Davar, and D. I. Bray, "Snowmelt at an Index Plot", Water Resources Research, vol. 4, no. 5, pp 937-946, Oct. 1968.

"Runoff from Snowmelt", U.S. Army Corps of Engineers, Engineering and Design Manual, EM 1110-2-1406, Jan. 5, 1960. This is a condensation of a part of the following:

>Anonymous "Snow Hydrology - Summary Report of the Snow Investigations", North Pacific Div., Corps of Engineers U.S. Army, Portland, Ore., 437 pp, 30 June 1956.

Santeford, Henry S., Jr., G. R. Alger, and J. G. Meier, "Snowmelt Energy Exchange in the Lake Superior Region", Water Resources Research, vol. 8, no. 2, pp 390-397, Apr. 1972.

There is a similarity in the behavior of water in the soil and in snow.  Both soil and snow on the ground are porous media and the principles of soil physics as they pertain to the flow of a fluid through a porous medium apply.  There is, however, this great difference; a snow pack which at the time of fall may be a "silt loam", through the process of metamorphosis turns into a "gravel".

In the presence of free water whether from snowmelt or rainfall, metamorphosis in the snowpack proceeds at a greatly accelerated rate.  The hydrologic effect of rain on snow is, first, a retention (at times total withholding of the rain) followed by a progressive release as the snowpack ripens and turns into a gravel-like layer.  The snowpack changes the shape of the hydrograph.

Contrary to popular opinion, very little snow is melted by the rainwater.  Wilson (1941) prepared a chart for determining graphically the water melted by rain for various wet-bulb temperatures.  Wilson's chart shows that at a 50° wet-bulb temperature only 1/2 inch of snow water equivalent would be melted by a rainfall of four inches.

A classic work on snow metamorphism is the book by Seligman (1936).  Judy, Meiman, and Friedman (1970) using deuterium as a tracer, have shown that metamorphism and melting greatly reduce the initial variability in the content of deuterium which has been observed to characterize individual snowfalls.  Sommerfeld and LaChapelle (1970) propose a new classification of snow on the ground based on physical processes involved in metamorphism.

Colbeck (Apr. 1976) studied effects of radiation penetration on snowmelt runoff hydrographs.  He found, for practical purposes, that the assumption that all snowmelt takes place at the surface to be sufficient, as shown in his figure 5, page 8. Colbeck (June, 1976) described, with a mathematical analysis, the effect on metamorphism of the flow of water through a dry snow.

Fletcher and Reynolds (1972) describe an analysis aimed at forecasting whether or not a peak rate of runoff from snowmelt would exceed the 10-year peak.  They used Gumbel paper and the plotting positions of the 10-year values were picked off the line.  All values were expressed as a percentage of the 2.33-year value.  They concluded that deep groundwater storage is a very significant factor in this type of analysis.

Zuzel and Cox (1975) have shown that the standard error of daily snowmelt prediction could be decreased by 13 percent by making use of vapor pressure, net radiation, and wind, in statistical predictive equations as compared with the results when using only air temperature.

Bertle (1966) describes and illustrates a method of accounting for the effect of snow compaction on runoff from rain on snow. This method has been verified by analyses of events which took place subsequent to the development of the method. Bertle used two equations from "Runoff from Snowmelt" (1960) for total daily snowmelt in inches, one for open or partly-forested areas with less than 80 percent mean canopy cover, and the other for heavily-forested areas with a mean canopy cover of more than 80 percent.

Garstka (1964) summarizes on page 10-40 other snowmelt equations for forested areas: more than 80 percent cover; 60 to 80 percent cover; 10 to 60 percent cover; and areas with less than 10 percent cover, considered to be open areas. Many equations specify data at certain elevations. For example, wind velocities at the 50-foot level and temperatures of saturated air at the 10-foot level. A discussion of methods of conversion of observations made at other elevations is given in "Runoff from Snowmelt" (1960) and also by Garstka (1964) on page 10-39.

Bertle (1966) derived the following equation for the snow compaction relationship as metamorphism occurs:

$$P_D = 147.4 - 0.474 \ P_W \hspace{3cm} (1)$$

in which

$\hspace{1cm} P_D$ is snowpack depth in percent of initial depth

$\hspace{1cm} P_W$ is initial water content plus added water in percent of initial water content.

Equation (1), which has been found adequate for the extreme condition of a major rain-on-snow event, is based on the following assumptions:

a. The snowpack is homogeneous and free water in the snowpack is distributed evenly throughout the depth of the pack.

b. The compaction curve, Figure 54-1, defines the compaction effect of free water on a fresh snowpack which has a density less than the assumed threshold density. Threshold densities range from 40 to 45 percent. No compaction takes place after threshold density has been reached.

c. Drainage occurs only after the snowpack has reached its threshold density.

319

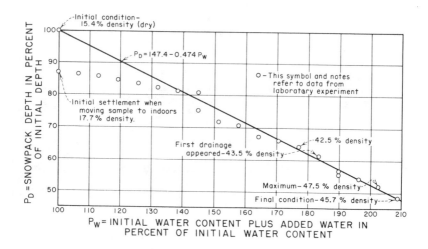

Figure 54-1    Snow Compaction Relationship - Decrease in Snowpack Depth Due to Addition of Water.
Taken from Bertle (1966 page 5).

The degree of agreement between observed and computed
hydrographs of an actual rain-on-snow flood event is shown in
Figure 54-2 on page 321 taken from Bertle (1966, page 32). It
is to be noted that a unit hydrograph in units of three hours
was used in analyses of the hydrograph of the flood of Dec. 21-
24, 1955 in the South Fork of the Yuba River near Cisco,
California, drainage area 51.5 square miles.

The rain-on-snow relationships discussed previously in
this Topic were all based on the assumption, valid for forested
areas, that there was no frost in the soil underlying the snowpack. Dingman (1975 and 1976) has prepared an excellent literature review and synthesis of 172 references dealing with the
hydrologic effects of frozen ground. This report contains,
pages 2 to 7, various definitions of frozen ground.

References

Bertle, Frederick A., "Effect of Snow Compaction on Runoff from
Rain on Snow", Water Resources Tech. Pub., Engineering
Monograph No. 35, Bur. of Reclamation, USDI, Denver, Colo.
45 pp, June, 1966.

Colbeck, Samuel C., "Effects of Radiation Penetration on Snow-
melt Runoff Hydrographs", CRREL Report 76-11, Cold Regions
Research & Engineering Lab., Corps of Engineers, U.S.
Army, Hanover, N.H., 9 pp, Apr. 1976.

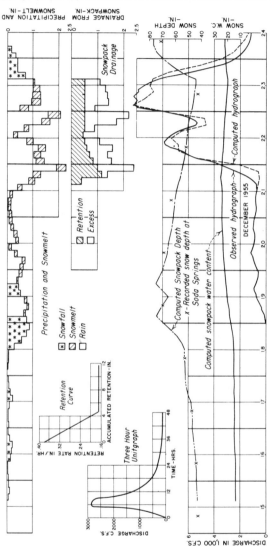

Figure 54-2    Observed and Computed Hydrographs of a Rain-on-
Snow Event, December 1955.    South Yuba River near
Cisco, Calif.    Drainage area 51.5 square miles.
Taken from Bertle (1966 page 32).

Colbeck, Samuel C., "An Analysis of Water Flow in Dry Snow", Water Resources Research, vol. 12, no. 3, pp 523-527, June, 1976.

Dingman, S. Lawrence, "Hydrologic Effects on Frozen Ground - Literature Review and Synthesis", CRREL Special Report 218 Cold Regions Research & Engineering Lab., Corps of Engineers, U.S. Army, Hanover, N.H., 55 pp, Mar., 1975.
(With "Supplement to CRREL Special Report 218", by S. Lawrence Dingman, 3 pp, Feb. 1976.)

Fletcher, J. E., and G. W. Reynolds, "Snowmelt Peak Flows and Antecedent Precipitation", pp 197-199, Proceedings of a Symposium, Watersheds in Transition, Fort Collins, Colo., June 19-22, 1972. Proceedings Series No. 14, Amer. Water Resources Assn., Urbana, Ill., Oct. 1972.

Garstka, Walter U., "Snow and Snow Survey", Sec. 10, Handbook of Applied Hydrology, Ven Te Chow, ed-in-chief, McGraw-Hill Book Co., New York, 1964.

Judy, Clark, James R. Meiman, and Irving Friedman, "Deuterium Variations in an Annual Snowpack", Water Resources Research, vol. 6, no. 1, pp 125-129, Feb. 1970.

"Runoff from Snowmelt", U.S. Army Corps of Engineers, Engineering and Design Manual, EM 1110-2-1406, Jan. 5, 1960. This is a condensation of a part of the following:

  Anonymous "Snow Hydrology - Summary Report of the Snow Investigations", North Pacific Div. Corps of Engineers, U.S. Army, Portland, Ore., 437 pp, 30 June 1956.

Seligman, G., "Snow Structure and Ski Fields: With an Appendix on Alpine Weather by C. K. M. Douglas", MacMillan and Co., Ltd., London, 1936.

Sommerfeld, R. A., and E. LaChapelle, "The Classification of Snow Metamorphism", Jour. of Glaciology, vol. 9, no. 55, pp 3-17, 1970.

Wilson, W. T., "An Outline of the Thermodynamics of Snowmelt", Trans. American Geophysical Union, Part 1, pp 182-195, July, 1941.

Zuzel, John F., and Lloyd M. Cox, "Relative Importance of Meteorological Variables in Snowmelt", vol. 11, no. 1, pp 174-176, Water Resources Research, Feb. 1975.

Topic 55                     Design Floods

It is common experience in water resources management to
learn that there are no streamflow records for a drainage basin
of interest. The carrying capacities of channels, culverts,
spillways, and possible encroachment of flood flows on agricultural, industrial, and urban areas need to be computed as part
of the project planning using the best techniques available
since progress will not wait until decades of data are accumulated.

Topic 31 presented one of the approaches to this problem.
McCuen, Rawls, Fisher, and Powell (1977) have prepared an evaluation of 240 references dealing with flood-flow frequencies
for ungaged watersheds.

A basic relationship for estimating peak rates of flow is
the so-called "rational" formula first expressed in 1851 and
introduced into the American literature in 1889 by Kuichling
as a result of measurements of rainfall and of the flow of
sewers in Rochester, New York, during the period 1877-1888.

The rational formula is given by Ramser (1927) as follows:

$$Q = CIA$$

in which

$Q$ = discharge in cfs
$C$ = a ratio of the theoretical peak (which would
     occur at 100 percent runoff with no storage
     at the time rainfall excess is covering the
     complete drainage basin) to the actual peak.
$I$ = the average intensity of rainfall excess in
     inches-per-hour or for a duration equal to
     or greater than the time of concentration for
     the drainage basin.
$A$ = area in acres.

The $Q$ or peak rate of discharge in most statements of the rational formula is given in cubic feet per second. This is
because, in the English system of units by coincidence, the
flow rate in inches-per-hour-per-acre is arithmetically practically equal, with an error of less than one percent, to the
flow rate in cubic feet per second.

It is a requirement in the rational formula that the
entire area contribute to the flow at the peak rate of discharge. This would mean that the surface runoff from the most
distant part of the drainage basin has had time to reach the
point of outflow. The coefficient $C$ expresses all of the
drainage basin characteristics including physiography, soils,
vegetal cover, shape, etc. The effectiveness of design-flood
estimation when using the rational formula depends on the

choice of the runoff coefficient C.

Kirpich (1940) analyzed Ramser's (1927) data and tabulated times of concentration. Kirpich's analyses were discussed by Langbein (1940). These three engineers were referring to watersheds ranging from 1 to 112 acres in area. However usage of the rational formula has not been restricted to small areas.

Tabulations are given by Chow (1962, page 16) and in "Design and Construction of Sanitary and Storm Sewers" (1969, page 51) of the values of the runoff coefficient C for various types of drainage areas including business, residential, industrial, playgrounds, railroad yards, streets, roofs, and lawns. The value of C may be as low as 0.05 for a lawn on sandy soil at slopes of less than 2 percent, to as high as 0.95 for downtown business areas. Suburban areas usually have a value of 0.25 to 0.40. Cultivated rolling land with a clay loam soil may have a value of 0.50 and moderately steep residential areas consisting of 50 percent impervious surface may have a value of 0.65. The values given would apply to storms of 5- to 10-year frequency. Less frequent storms would require coefficients of higher numerical value.

Chow (1962) discusses 103 formulae for use in estimating the design floods of drainage structures for small basins. Railroad engineers have compiled C's for watersheds ranging in size from 1,000 to 21,000 square miles. Although there are hundreds of estimating formulae Hiemstra and Reich (1967) showed that of 5 of the best methods tested the rational formula appeared to be the most effective.

"The Water Encyclopedia" (1970) contains readily-accessible and useful tables for application of the rational formula to drainage areas of less than 5000 acres. Table 2-26 on page 77 of the Encyclopedia considers relief, soil infiltration, vegetal cover and surface storage in four classes of runoff-producing characteristics giving an array of 16 sub-percentages which can be selected to yield, by addition, a value of C more sensitive to the drainage basin than the single percentage usually available. Table 2-27 on page 78 contains values, in minutes for times of concentration of watersheds of lengths as measured along the main stem from the outlet to the most distant ridge, and differences in elevation between the outlet and the most distant ridge.

Use of the rational formula is world-wide. A reference to a comprehensive study is that prepared by Won (1958). One possible reason for the extensive use of the rational formula could be the similarity of the thermodynamics of high-intensity rainfalls produced by convective storms. Bell (1969) demonstrated a surprising degree of uniformity in depth-duration and depth-frequency relationships for 2-year, 25-year, and 100-year recurrence interval values for one-hour rainfalls as observed in the United States, Australia, South Africa, Hawaii, Alaska, and Puerto Rica.

The study described by Hiemstra and Reich (1967) was published in condensed form by Reich and Heimstra (1967). This condensation was discussed by 10 reviewers in "Discussion of Paper No. 70" (1967). Colby, Dueker, and Lenz (1969) reported on the storm drainage practices of 52 cities, mostly in the mid-west, with frequent references to Manning's "n" and the runoff coefficient C.

Ogrosky and Mockus (1964) describe in detail the approach of the Soil Conservation Service to the hydrology of Agricultural lands. This complicated but effective method has been subjected to continuing development. Wilkes and King (1977) deal with applications of the SCS method in describing procedures for determining peak flows in Colorado including small urban watersheds. The "SCS National Engineering Handbook - Section 4 - HYDROLOGY" (1972) is an excellent book, the acquisition of which is recommended.

Storey, Hobba, and Rosa (1964) summarize the Forest Service's approach to the hydrology of forest lands and range lands. Reich (1972) has performed an extensive study of the influences of the percentage of forest cover on the design floods. This reference deals with drainage basins in both the Eastern and the Western United States. One of the parameters used by Reich is the maximum annual 24-hour precipitation in inches expected to recur once in 2.33 years.

Hewlett, Cunningham, and Troendle (1977) state in describing their R-index method for predicting peak flows from small basins in humid areas, that their method requires no prior assumptions about infiltration capacities of forest lands.

Miller, Frederick, and Tracey (1973) give information for Colorado on precipitation frequency in their Vol. III which is one of eleven volumes in this NOAA Atlas series. An extremely rare rainfall event may not necessarily produce an extremely rare flood event. Gupta, Duckstein, and Peebles (1976) propose a highly mathematical analysis on the joint distribution of the largest flood and its time of occurrence; their analysis deals with runoff records alone.

McCain and Jarrett (1976) have prepared a manual on methods of calculating 10-, 50-, 100-, and 500-year peak discharges and flood depths for natural-flow streams in Colorado. They consider both gaged and un-gaged streams. They state that their methods may not be applicable to heavily-urbanized areas or to reaches affected by backwater.

When a dam is built and a reservoir created special attention must be given to the risks assumed should a major flood
occur in the drainage basin when the reservoir is full (see
Topic 14). A probable maximum flood (PMF) is computed and
routed under the most severe assumed conditions. For the protection of the dam a spillway must be designed to convey the
PMF without endangering the dam as discussed in Topic 56.

Calculation of a PMF is a large and complicated task as
will become evident upon a study of the chapter by Miller,
Clark, and Schamach (1973). A detailed presentation of the
computation of a probable maximum storm or probable maximum
precipitation is given in "Inflow Design Flood Studies" (1977).
This is a complex computation requiring considerable experience
in meteorology and hydrology.

## Problem Assignment - Design Flood

A. 1. Select a drainage basin in a part of the country with
which you are acquainted or in which you have a special
interest. The basin of your choice should have streamflow records. A topographic map with contours is
necessary.

2. Select a rainfall intensity and duration suited to the
application of the rational formula $Q = CIA$ as dis-
discussed in this Topic.

3. Calculate Q. Secure a rating curve or table for your
gaging station and derive the flood depth which would
result from your calculated Q.

4. Prepare a report describing what you did and how you
selected the values you used in this problem.

B. If a recent soil survey map is available those having a
special interest in this subject could compute a design
flood using the SCS method and compare the peak rates
of discharge.

## References

Bell, Frederick C., "Generalized Rainfall-Duration-Frequency
Relationships", Jour. Hydraulics Div., Proceedings ASCE,
pp 311-327, Jan. 1969.

Chow, Ven Te, "Hydrologic Determination of Waterway Areas for
the Design of Drainage Structures in Small Drainage
Basins", Univ. of Illinois Engineering Exp. Station Bulletin No. 462, 104 pp, 1962.

Colby, V. Ardis, Kenneth J. Dueker, and Arno T. Lenz, "Storm
Drainage Practices of Thirty-Two Cities", Jour. Hydraulics
Div., ASCE, pp 383-408, Jan. 1969.

"Design and Construction of Sanitary and Storm Sewers", ASCE
Manuals and Reports on Engineering Practice, No. 37, and
Water Pollution Control Federation Manual of Practice
No. 9. This is a single 332-page publication of the Amer-
ican Society of Civil Engineers, New York, 1969.

"Discussion of Paper No. 70", Purpose and Performance of Peak
Predictions, by Brian M. Reich and Lourens A. V. Hiemstra,
International Hydrology Symposium, Fort Collins, Colo.,
Sept. 6-8, 1967, pub. in vol. 2 of the Proceedings,
pp 360-390, Sept. 1967.

Gupta, V. K., L. Duckstein, and R. W. Peebles, "On the Joint
Distribution of the Largest Flood and Its Time of Occurrence", Water Resources Research, vol. 12, no. 3, pp 295-
304, Apr. 1976.

Hewlett, J. D., G. B. Cunningham, and C. A. Troendle,
"Predicting Stormflow and Peakflow from Small Basins in
Humid Areas by the R-Index Method", Water Resources Bull.,
vol. 13, no. 2, pp 231-253, Apr. 1977.

Hiemstra, L. A. V., and B. M. Reich, "Engineering Judgment and
Small Area Flood Peaks", Hydrology Paper No. 19, Colo.
State Univ., Fort Collins, Apr. 1967.

"Inflow Design Flood Studies", Appendix L, pp 763-837, from
Design of Arch Dams, A Water Resources Tech. Publication,
Bur. of Reclamation, USDI, Denver, Colo., 882 pp, 1977.

Kirpich, Z. P., "Time of Concentration of Small Agricultural
Watersheds", Civil Engineering, vol. 10, no. 6, p 362,
June, 1940.

Kuichling, Emil, "The Relation Between the Rainfall and the
Discharge of Sewers in Populous Districts", Trans. ASCE,
vol. 20, pp 1-56, 1889.

Langbein, W. B., "Time of Concentration of Small Watersheds",
Civil Engineering, vol. 10, no. 8, p 533, Aug. 1940. This
is a discussion of the paper listed above with the same
title by Z. P. Kirpich.

McCain, Jerald F., and Robert D. Jarrett, "Manual for Estimating Flood Characteristics of Natural-Flow Streams in
Colorado", Tech. Manual No. 1, Colo. Water Conservation
Board, Colo. Dept. of Natural Resources, Denver, 68 pp,
1976.

McCuen, Richard H., Walter J. Rawls, Gary T. Fisher, and Robert L. Powell, "Flood Flow Frequency for Ungaged Watersheds: A Literature Evaluation", Report No. ARS-NE-86, 136 pp, Agri. Research Service, USDA, Nov. 1977.

Miller, D. L., R. A. Clark, and S. Schamach, "Flood Studies, Chap. III, pp 37-95 in Design of Small Dams, Bureau of Reclamation, Denver, Colo., 2nd edition, 816 pp, 1973.

Miller, J. F., R. H. Frederick, and R. J. Tracey, "Precipitation - Frequency Atlas of the Western United States", Vol. III, Colorado, NOAA Atlas 2, Natl. Weather Service, NOAA, U.S. Dept. of Commerce, $15\frac{1}{2}$ in. x 21-3/4 in., 67 pp, 1973. This is one of a set of 11 volumes.

Ogrosky, Harold O., and Victor Mockus, "Hydrology of Agricultural Lands", Sec. 21 in Handbook of Applied Hydrology, Ven Te Chow, ed-in-chief, McGraw Hill Book Co., 1964.

Ramser, C. E., "Runoff From Small Agricultural Areas", Jour. of Agric. Research, vol. 34, pp 797-823, 1927.

Reich, Brian M., and Lourens A. V. Hiemstra, "Purpose and Performance of Peak Predictions", Paper No. 70, International Hydrology Symposium, Sept. 6-8, 1967, Fort Collins, Colo., Proceedings Vol. 1, pp 565-572, June, 1967.

Reich, Brian M., "The Influence of Percentage Forest on Design Floods", pp 335-340 in Proceedings of the Sympsoum, Watersheds in Transition, Fort Collins, Colo., June 19-22, 1972 Proceedings Series No. 14, Amer. Water Resources Assn., Oct. 1972.

"SCS National Engineering Handbook - Section 4 - HYDROLOGY", Soil Conservation Service, USDA, as revised Aug., 1972. for sale by Supt. of Documents, GPO, Washington, D.C.

Storey, Herbert C., Robert L. Hobba, and J. Marvin Rosa, "Hydrology of Forest Lands and Rangelands", Sec. 22 in Handbook of Applied Hydrology, Ven Te Chow, ed-in-chief, McGraw Hill Book Co., New York, 1964.

"The Water Encyclopedia", ed. by David K. Todd, Water Information Center, Inc., Port Washington, N.Y., 554 pp, 1970.

Wilkes, S. Glade, and Erke C. King, "Procedures for Determining PEAK FLOWS IN COLORADO, Includes and Supplements - Tech. Release No. 55, Urban Hydrology for Small Watersheds", Soil Conservation Service, USDA, Mar. 1977.

Won, Tae Sang, "A Study on Maximum Flood Discharge Formula", Univ. Seoul, Korea, Scientia Naturalis, vol. 6, Mar. 1958.

SECTION XII

DAMS AND IMPOUNDMENTS

Topic 56        Dams and Impoundments

The construction of barriers across stream channels for
the purpose of impounding water goes back about 5,000 years
according to Biswas (1970, pp 5-14). Dams may be built for a
variety of purposes other than for water supply among which are
recreation, food production, and erosion control. Many city
parks and recreational areas contain ponds, lakes, and lagoons
as part of their esthetic improvement.

"Ponds for Water Supply and Recreation" (1971) includes
detailed instructions for the construction of dams less than
25-feet high for water supply, fish production, and recreation.
Heede (1970) gives details on the design and construction of
rock check dams for controlling erosion in gullies. Arthur
(1973 pp 97-105) discusses a classification of dams for water
supply.

Dams in water resources management may be built for one or
more of the following usages: storage, diversion,and detention.
Materials may be masonry, rock-fill, timber, earth-fill, and
concrete, or various combinations thereof.

Concrete dams may be of the buttress, arch, or gravity
section design. A buttress dam leans on supports; an arch dam
resists displacement by transferring the load to the abutments;
a gravity-section dam is designed with such a cross-section and
weight that any one foot length of the dam has stability because of its weight. As mentioned in Topic 23, page 122, a dam
needs to support a reservoir of a length of only one foot.
Hoover Dam is a gravity section dam built in the form of an
arch.

The hydraulic design of a dam could be either the overflow type, as is Grand Coulee, or non-overflow type in which
inflows exceeding the storage capacity of the reservoir are
conveyed downstream by spillway structures.

Selection of type of dam depends upon:  location, topography, geology, accessibility of material, spillway size and
type, project environmental aspects, limitations of outlet
works, diversion during construction, labor, equipment, and
time estimated for construction.

Thomas (1976) in his book on the engineering of large dams
stated that there are over 10,000 large dams and that about

1,000 are under construction in the World. "Register of Dams
in the United States" (1958) was compiled and edited by Mermel.
"World Register of Dams" (1973) was supplemented by a first updating as of December 31, 1974 and published in 1976, both
published by the International Commission on Large Dams.

The "Handbook of Dam Engineering" (1977) is a compilation
edited by Golze. The Bureau of Reclamation has published a
number of books on dams. "Design of Small Dams" (1973) deals
with dams less than 50 feet high above streambed. "Design of
Gravity Dams" (1974) is a manual for concrete gravity dams.
Figures 56-3 and 56-4 on page 333 show Flaming Gorge Dam, a
single-curvature, thin-arch dam on the Green River in Utah.

The "Earth Manual", 2nd edition (1974) deals primarily
with the use of earth as an engineering material. The distribution of the first formal edition of 1960 attained a total of
28,000 copies world-wide. The "Design of Arch Dams" (1977) is
an 882-page book consisting of 15 chapters and 13 appendices
with ecological and environmental considerations.

The occurrence of an extreme flood (see Topics 14 and 55)
must be considered in the design of a dam. An earthfill dam,
if overtopped would erode very rapidly. A concrete dam's
foundations and abutments may not withstand an extreme flood.
Powerhouses and other structures just below the dam must be
protected against high water or inundation. Therefore an integral part of a dam is the spillway and in many cases the cost
of the spillway may be a considerable part of the total cost of
the dam.

Spillways may be of various types or of combinations of
them. Many designs have been used among which are: free fall,
ogee overflow, side channel, open channel trough or chute,
tunnel, drop inlet shaft or morning glory, baffled apron, cul-
vert and siphon.

Because of the importance of the spillway and in consideration of the costs, it is common practice to perform hydraulic
model studies of spillways for major dams. Burgi and Fujimoto
(1973) report on such studies for the Crystal Dam on the
Gunnison River near Montrose, Colorado. Figure 56-1 shows a
section through the double-curvature thin arch dam and the flip
bucket spillway. The dam is only 10 feet wide at the top. The
discharge capacity of the spillway is 42,350 cfs (1,171 m$^3$/sec)
at a head of 16 feet (4.88 meters). Figure 56.2 shows the
model at a scale ratio of 1-to-36 with a test underway.

According to Thomas (1976) the percentages distribution of
accidents to dams are: for earthfill dams, 25 to 30 percent inadequate spillways, 10 percent inadequate cutoffs, 12 percent
poor construction; for concrete dams, 30 percent inadequate

spillways, 30 percent inadequate cutoffs, 12 percent poor construction; and the remainder for all classes of dams: frost, hostile action, earthquakes, decay, abandonment, etc.

Figure 56-1  Cross Section Through the Spillway of the Crystal Dam, a double-curvature, thin-arch dam on the Gunnison River near Montrose, Colo.  Construction was completed in the fall of 1976 and the reservoir filled in the spring of 1977.  From Burgi, and Fujimoto, 1973.

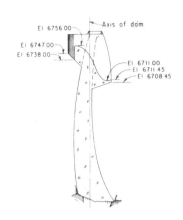

Figure 56-2  Sei Fujimoto and Philip Burgi are conducting tests on a hydraulic model built at the scale of 1-to-36 in the laboratory of the Division of General Research, Bureau of Reclamation, Denver Federal Center, Denver, Colo.  The hydraulic model is of the Crystal Dam spillway river outlet works and stilling basin.

"Lessons from Dam Incidents USA" (1975) reports on 120 incidents, some minor, some serious. It is based on data from 2,000 questionnaires sent to owners, operators, engineers, government agencies and contractors.

Water seepage occurs at practically all newly-constructed dams, the only question being where and how much. Seepings, if anticipated are plugged by curtain grouting as described in pages 211-215 of "Design of Arch Dams" (1977). Grouting consists of injecting water-cement slurries into holes not less than 1½ inches in diameter at pressures up to 100 pounds per square inch.

"Reevaluating Spillway Adequacy of Existing Dams" (1973) is a report by a Task Committee of the American Society of Civil Engineers. It contains a procedural check list and an example problem for the fictional Grapefruit Dam on the Grapefruit River in the valley of which is located the non-existent town of Podunk, population 2500.

"$16.4 Million Sought for Dam Checks" is the title of an article in the Denver Post for Monday, Jan. 23, 1978, page 10. The U.S. Army Corps of Engineers, which was assigned by the Congress the responsibility for safety inspections of non-federally-owned dams, estimated in 1975 that it would cost $367,500,000 to inspect the Nation's 49,500 dams. As of Jan., 1978 only 200 dams have been inspected, according to the article.

Stamm (1971) in his analysis of the achievement of goals subsequent to construction of water-resources projects, stated that not only the visible physical features are needed but especially a technically-competent operation and maintenance staff as well.

Topic 41, Limnology, deals with the physical and biological aspects of lakes and impoundments. "Man-Made Lakes" (1973) is a compilation of pages organized in four categories: Case Studies of Major Man-Made Lakes, Physical Systems, Biological Systems, and Man-Made Lakes in Relation to Man.

Of all the structures built by man only the Egyptian Pyramids offer promise of ultimate survival because they are built of minerals with slopes assembled at less than the angle of repose. The "1976 Annual Report of the Miami Conservancy District" bears on its cover the following statement which is especially pertinent to dam design, construction, and maintenance:

"It should be noted that nature desires always to return an area to its original state, therefore, constant vigilance and extreme care must be maintained, else the tremendous investment is eventually lost."

Figure 56-3  Flaming Gorge Dam on the Green River in Utah.
Night view of construction looking upstream from the left
abutment of this single-curvature, thin-arch dam.
Photo June 28, 1961 by Friend B. Slote.

Figure 56-4  Flaming Gorge Dam on the Green River in Utah.
View of the dam and reservoir looking upstream.  Visitors'
area and switch yard are to the left.  The Flaming Gorge
is just above the top center of the photograph.  Construction was completed Oct. 22, 1963.

333

## References

Arthur, H. G., "Selection of Type of Dam", Chap. IV, pp 97-
105 in Design of Small Dams, A Water Resources Tech. Pub.,
Bureau of Reclamation, USDI, Denver, Colo. 816 pp, 2nd
edition, 1973.

Biswas, Asit K., "History of Hydrology", American Elsevier
Publishing Co., New York, 1970.

Burgi, P. H., and S. Fujimoto, "Hydraulic Model Studies of
Crystal Dam Spillway and Outlet Works, Colorado River
Storage Project", Div. of General Research Report No. REC-
ERC-73-22, Bur. of Reclamation, USDI, Denver, Colo.,
24 pp, Dec. 1973.

"Design of Arch Dams", A Water Resources Tech. Publication,
Bur. of Reclamation, USDI, Denver, Colo., 882 pp, 1977.

"Design of Gravity Dams", A Water Resources Tech. Publication,
Bur. of Reclamation, USDI, Denver, Colo., 553 pp, 1976.

"Design of Small Dams", A Water Resources Tech. Publication,
Bur. of Reclamation, USDI, Denver, Colo., 816 pp, 2nd
edition, 1973.

"Earth Manual - A Guide to the Use of Soils as Foundations and
as Construction Materials for Hydraulic Structures", A
Water Resources Tech. Pub., Bur. of Reclamation, USDI,
Denver, Colo., 810 pp, 2nd edition, 1974.

"Handbook of Dam Engineering", ed. by Alfred R. Golze,
Van Nostrand Reinhold Co., New York, 793 pp, 1977.

Heede, Burchard H., "Design, Construction and Cost of Rock
Check Dams", Rocky Mountain Forest & Range Exp. Station,
Forest Service, USDA, Research Paper RM-20, Fort Collins,
Colo., 24 pp, reprinted June, 1970.

"Lessons from Dam Incidents USA", by the Committee on Failures
and Accidents to Large Dams of the United States Committee on Large Dams, pub. by American Society of Civil
Engineers, New York, 387 pp, 1975.

"Man-Made Lakes - Their Problems and Environmental Effects",
ed. by William C. Ackermann, Gilbert F. White, and
E. B. Worthington, Proceedings of an International Sym-
posium held in Knoxville, Tenn., May 3-7, 1971,
Geophysical Monograph 17, pub. by American Geophysical
Union, Washington, D.C., 847 pp, 1973.

"1976 Annual Report of the Miami Conservancy District, Dayton, Ohio, to: Common Pleas Court of Montgomery County, Ohio", published by Miami Conservancy Dist., 29 pp, 1976.

"Ponds for Water Supply and Recreation", Soil Conservation Service, USDA, Agriculture Handbook No. 387, 55 pp, Jan. 1971.

"Reevaluating Spillway Adequacy of Existing Dams", by Task Committee on Reevaluation of Adequacy of Spillways of Existing Dams of the Committee on Hydrometeorology, Jour. Hydraulics Div., Proceedings ASCE, pp 337-372, Feb. 1973.

"Register of Dams in the United States", compiled and edited by T. W. Mermel, McGraw-Hill Book Co., New York, 429 pp, 1958.

"$16.4 Million Sought for Dam Checks", page 10 of the Denver Post, Denver, Colo., Monday, Jan. 23, 1978.

Stamm, Gilbert G., "Achievement of Goals Subsequent to Construction of Water Resources Projects", published in: Report of the United States Delegation to the Ninth Regional Conference on Water Resources Development of the United Nations Economic Commission for Asia and the Far East, Bangkok, Thailand, 28 Sept. to 5 Oct. 1970. Submitted to the Secretary of State Jan. 1971.

Thomas, Henry H., "The Engineering of Large Dams", Part I, John Wiley and Sons, London, New York, Sydney, Toronto, (Printed in Great Britain) 376 pp, 1976.

"World Register of Dams", pub. by International Commission On Large Dams, 22 et 30 Avenue de Wagram - 75008 Paris, 998 pp, 1973.

"World Register of Dams - First Updating, Dec. 31, 1974", published by International Commission on Large Dams, 22 et 30 Avenue de Wagram - 75008 Paris, France, 299 pp, 1976.

# SECTION XIII

## CONVEYANCE OF WATER

### Topic 57    Conveyance Techniques and Structures

A canal is an artifical open channel built to convey water
to a destination for various purposes among which may be irrigation, power, municipal and industrial usage, or navigation.
Pipeline systems are built for the same purposes. Flow in canals must be controlled so that velocities are so slow that
erosion of the canal sides and bottom does not take place.
This is usually done in canals built in soil by constructing
almost flat slopes; thus the canal may appear to be following
a contour.

There are many techniques and structures for conveying
water on steeper slopes as described by Aisenbrey, Hayes,
Warren, Winsett, and Young (1974). Stilling basins, drops,
chutes, and energy dissipators have been developed. The design
of a canal is a highly technical subject requiring experience
in this field of civil engineering.

As reported in Topic 49, pages 296-297, transmission
losses as a whole amounted to 21 percent of the total releases
of 38,682,106 acre feet in Calendar Year 1975 from Bureau of
Reclamation projects alone. Transmission losses include operational losses, evaporation from the water surface, evapotranspiration, and seepage.

By far the greatest loss from canals is by seepage. Depending on the soils and topography of the area seepage may
either recharge the groundwater or it may cause water-logging
and create swampy areas. Provision for drainage systems (see
Topic 80) is now commonly considered as part of the planning
of an irrigation project.

Seepage losses in canals constructed in soils may average
about 40 percent and in some cases may be very much greater.
Methods of estimation of seepage losses are discussed by
Worstell (1976). On his page 145 he presents a chart for estimating flow loss. He reviews 765 seepage tests made in the
Western United States. Losses averaged in the range of from
0.1 cubic foot per square foot per day to 2 cubic feet per
square foot per day.

Palacios and Day (1977) used a statistical analysis of
water releases and deliveries at an irrigation project in
Mexico as part of their new approach for estimating conveyance
losses and their economic evaluation.

336

Canals may be unlined or lined. Canal linings are classified into 4 broad categories: exposed, buried membrane, earth, and miscellaneous. A detailed description is given in "Linings for Irrigation Canals" (1963).

Exposed linings may be of various types of asphalt, of Portland cement, of soil-cement, or of blocks of various materials. Buried membrane linings may be of hot-applied asphalt, of prefabricated asphalt, of either natural or synthetic rubber, of plastic, or of bentonite. Geier and Morrison (1968) report on buried asphalt membrane linings.

Frobel and Cluff (1976) describe their work on a plastic-reinforced seepage barrier. Use of asphalt increases the resistance to puncture of plain polyethylene film by a factor of about three. Their barrier can be used on slopes.

Hickey (1969) reported on investigations of the use of plastic films for canal linings. Some plants, such as Johnson Grass (Sorghum halepense (L.) also known as Egyptian millet) have been found to perforate both exposed and buried linings. A prior application of a soil sterilant (see Topic 48) has been found to be effective.

Unless the canal right-of-way is fenced both domestic and wild animals puncture exposed linings. Buried membranes and linings are usually protected with a layer of soil or gravel sometimes more than a foot thick.

Depending on the chemical characteristics of the canal flows and on the physical characteristics of the soil, bentonite, a naturally occurring clay, has served as a canal sealant as reported in "Evaluation of Colorado Clays for Sealing Purposes" (1964 reprinted 1977).

Techniques and materials developed for sealing canals have been applied to the sealing of reservoirs and lagoons not only for storing potable water but also in many industrial applications where highly saline or toxic liquids must be managed without polluting surface and groundwater supplies. Some of these installations cover areas greater than 100 acres.

As reported in "Carriage Facilities - Canals" (1977) the U.S. Bureau of Reclamation as of September 30, 1977 had constructed 314 canals totalling 5,988.3 miles (9,637 kilometers), rehabilitated 47 canals totalling 806.1 miles (1,297 kilometers), and had under construction 15 canals totalling 215.2 miles (346 kilometers). The grand totals are: 376 canals, 7,009.6 miles (11,280 kilometers). Since as reported in Topic 49, page 296, the U.S. Bureau of Reclamation supplied water to only 17.2 percent of the irrigated acres in Calendar Year 1975, the magnitude of the Nation's irrigation canals is indicated.

Figure 57-1   Courtland Canal (capacity 751 cfs, bottom width
26 ft; depth of water 8.5 ft.) Bostwick Div., Pick-Sloan
Program, Neb., at the base of a landmark called "Guide-
rock". USBR photo by Lyle Axthelm, June 4, 1963.

Among the largest canals in the USBR system is the All-
American Canal in California. This canal, 80 miles (129 kilometers) long, has a bottom width of 160 feet (49 meters); a
water depth of 20.6 feet (6 meters) and a capacity of 15,155
cfs (429 cubic meters per second).

A canal is a synthetic stream and it may behave either as
a "gaining" or, in most cases, as a "losing" stream as discussed in Topic 44, page 262, and as shown in Figure 44-1,
page 263. When the depth of water is increasing the canal becomes a "losing" stream. When the depth of water is decreasing
the canal becomes a "gaining" stream.

Should the drop in water level occur very rapidly hydrostatic pressures of such magnitude may develop as to displace
even heavy concrete canal linings. To protect against build-
up of drawdown pressures flap-valve weeps are used.

This problem has been encountered in rivers such as the
Mississippi as discussed by Desai (1972). He proposes a highly
mathematical quadrilateral finite element analysis of behavior
of earth banks under drawdown.

Natural lakes and man-made reservoirs behave in a similar
manner. The volume of water in the soil and rock forming the
perimeter of the body of water is called "bank storage". It
may be a sizable portion of the effective storage capacity of
the impoundment. Bank storage is estimated to be 15 percent
for Lake Mead and it could be as high as 100 percent for some
of the Missouri River Basin reservoirs. Only experience in the
actual operation of a reservoir can establish the volumes of
bank storage.

Most canal and reservoir operating criteria include instructions on allowable rates of draw-down. Related problems
in conveyance-system operation are sediment, corrosion, frost
action, and biological aspects as discussed in Topic 48.

References

Aisenbrey, A. J., Jr., R. B. Hayes, H. J. Warren, D. L. Winsett,
and R. B. Young, "Design of Small Canal Structures", a
Water Resources Tech. Publication, Bur. of Reclamation,
USDI, Denver, Colo., 435 pp, 1974.

"Carriage Facilities - Canals", Bur. of Reclamation, USDI,
Denver, Colo., 17 pp, Sept. 30, 1977.

Desai, Chandrakant S., "Seepage Analysis of Earth Banks Under
Drawdown", Jour. Soil Mechanics and Foundations Div.,
Proceedings ASCE, pp 1143-1162, Nov. 1972.

"Evaluation of Colorado Clays for Sealing Purposes", Tech.
Bulletin 83, Civil Engineering Section, Colo. State Univ.
Exp. Station, Fort Collins, 1964, 36 pp, rep. June, 1977.

Frobel, Ronald K., and C. Brent Cluff, "Plastic-Reinforced
Asphalt Seepage Barrier", Jour. Irrigation and Drainage
Div., Proceedings ASCE, pp 369-380, Sept. 1976.

Geier, Fred H., and William R. Morrison, "Buried Asphalt Membrane Canal Lining", Water Resources Tech. Publication,
Research Report No. 12, Bur. of Reclamation, USDI, 50 pp,
1968.

Hickey, M. E., "Investigations of Plastic Films for Canal
Linings", Water Resources Tech. Publication, Research
Report No. 19, Bur. of Reclamation, USDI, 35 pp, 1969.

"Lining for Irrigation Canals", Bur. of Reclamation, USDI,
1st edition, 149 pp, 1963.

Palacios, Enrique V., and John C. Day, "A New Approach for Estimating Irrigation Conveyance Losses and Their Economic
Evaluation", Water Resources Bulletin, vol. 13, no. 4,
pp 709-719, Aug. 1977.

Worstell, Robert V., "Estimating Seepage Losses from Canal
Systems", Jour. Irrigation and Drainage Div., Proceedings
ASCE, pp 137-147, Mar. 1976.

A great many methods have been developed for routing
waves and flows through channels and reservoirs.  New methods
are being developed as needed for specific applications.  All
are based on the law of continuity.  The basic concept is that
the volume of water discharged from any reach during any time
interval must equal the volume of inflow to the same reach during that time interval plus or minus any change in stored water
during that time interval.  This is stated in the equations
quoted as follows from Carter and Godfrey (1960):

"

$$\overline{0} = \overline{I} - \frac{\Delta S}{\Delta t} \tag{1}$$

where    $\overline{0}$  =  mean outflow during routing period $\Delta t$
         $\overline{I}$  =  mean inflow during routing period  $\Delta t$
        $\Delta S$  =  net change in storage during routing period $\Delta t$

Equation (1) is general.  A modification frequently used
is:
$$\frac{\Delta t(0_1 + 0_2)}{2} = \frac{\Delta t(I_1 + I_2)}{2} - (S_2 - S_1) \tag{2}$$

where    0, I, S, and $\Delta t$ are as before, and the subscripts
         identify the beginning and ending of routing period
         $\Delta t$.  The assumption that mean discharge is equal
         to the simple arithmetic average of the flows at the
         end points of the interval can be justified if the
         period is equal to, or less than, the time of travel
         through the reach and no abrupt changes in flow
         occur during the routing period."

A reservoir or lake can be considered to be an extremely
wide and deep portion of a river channel.  Therefore routing of
floods through reservoirs and reservoir operations become
special cases in the application of the law of continuity and,
in some cases, of the energy equation (see Topic 23).  This is
shown in Figure 58-1 taken from Carter and Godfrey (1960,
page 83) on the following page.

The prediction of transient flow in a river having a major
tributary is a common problem in streamflow forecasting.  Fread
(1973) reviews the differential equations pertaining to unsteady flow, describes his procedure, and compares the results
for an idealized problem dealing with the Ohio-Mississippi
junction.

Rutter and Engstrom (1964) have prepared a comprehensive
review of reservoir regulation including reservoir routing.

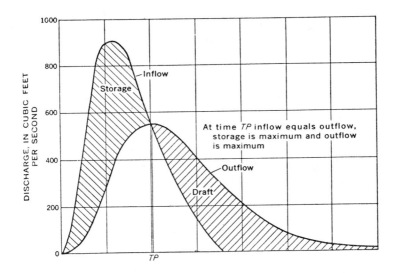

Figure 58-1  Reservoir Inflow and Outflow Relationship

Wycoff and Singh (1976) describe a method for estimating the volume of flood storage required for either a single reservoir or a series of reservoirs without using numeric floodrouting techniques.

Colorni and Fronza (1976) analyze in a highly-mathematical manner with stochastic input, the problem of reliability programming in reservoir management. In dealing with reservoir systems contracted-for deliveries may carry penalties if not met. Their method of analysis is aimed at calculating the optimum reservoir operations which would result from a compromise between profit and risk.

The operational hydrologic and geomorphologic complexity of systems of streams and reservoirs is so intricate that, except for some basic considerations treated by Rutter and Engstrom (1964), very few general approaches are adequate for actual practice. All operating agencies have developed procedures, rule curves, alignment charts, and computer programs specifically applicable to their systems.

References

Carter, R. W., R. G. Godfrey, "Storage and Flood Routing: Manual of Hydrology: Part 3, Flood-Flow Techniques", USGS Water Supply Paper 1543-B, U.S. Govt. Printing Office Washington, D.C. 1960.

Colorni, A., and G. Fronza, "Reservoir Management via
Reliability Programing", Water Resources Research, vol. 12
no. 1, pp 85-88, Feb. 1976.

Fread, D. L., "Technique for Implicit Dynamic Routing in Rivers
with Tributaries", Water Resources Research, vol. 9, no. 4
pp 918-926, Aug. 1973.

Rutter, Edward J., and Le Roy Engstrom, "Hydrology of Flow Control, Part III. Reservoir Regulation", Sec. 25-III, pp
25-60 through 25-97, Handbook of Applied Hydrology,
Ven Te Chow, ed-in-chief, McGraw-Hill Book Co., 1964.

Wycoff, Ronald, and Udai P. Singh, "Preliminary Hydrologic
Design of Small Flood Detention Reservoirs", Water
Resources Bull., vol. 12, no. 2, pp 337-349, Apr. 1976.

There is a certain similarity between reservoir operations and the routing of flow through natural channels. In either case inflow or outflow produces a wedge-shaped volume of water as shown in Figure 59-1 based on Lawler's (1964) Figure 25-II-6. The basic problem of routing is to account in time for volumes and rates of change of the wedge. On rising stages or inflow the direction of flow is left to right. On falling stages or outflow the direction of flow is right to left as shown in the sketch. A sudden increase or decrease in hydraulic head may cause dynamic responses in depth of water (waves) or wedge-dimension changes considerably removed in time and place from the actual amounts of water involved.

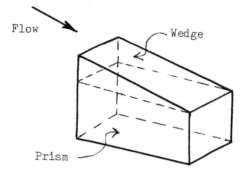

Figure 59-1  Prism and Wedge Storages of Flow, shown on rising stage. On receding stage wedge would point upstream.

Methods of streamflow routing can be classified as follows: (a) hydraulic computation such as the Puls and Muskingum; (b) the statistical which may use graphic, simple statistical computation, coaxial graphic analyses, multiple correlation, or other statistical techniques; (c) the trial and error method; (d) graphic analyses using alignment charts, special slide rules, etc; (e) electric-analogy board assemblies and, (f) electronic automatic data processing machinery either analog or digital or a combination of both.

Himmelblau and Yates (1968) classify flow routing approaches into (a) lumped parameter methods with 4 sub-classes and, (b) distributed parameter methods with 3 sub-classes. They present a third approach based on population balance models which they consider to be balances on unobservable but conceptually countable entities.

Among the factors which tend to complicate routing may be listed: groundwater and bank storage, wind, tributary inflows or diversions, freezing, tides, and effects of operations in other portions of the river system. The individual characteristics of the reservoir and river system are often dominant in indicating the method to be used for the precision necessary for a particular operational objective.

"Unsteady Flow in Open Channels" (1975) is a 3-volume, 1400-page work edited by Mahmood, Yevjevich, and Miller. This deals with unsteady flow in rigid and mobile bed, natural and man-made, open channels. Chow's (1959) book on open-channel hydraulics is a standard reference work.

Mockus (1967) with revisions by Styner (1972) illustrate their chapter on flood routing with numerous examples applying many of the various methods they discuss. This reference is of practical value to those concerned with a specific flow-routing problem.

Thaemert (1971) developed a computer program for calculating steep channel water surface profiles. A steep channel is a waterway whose energy slope is steeper than the critical slope for the rates of flow under consideration.

Garstka (1968), using a computer program developed from the work of Anderson and Anderson (1964), reconstructed the profiles of the flood of June 17, 1965 in Fountain Creek at Pueblo, Colorado, as they might have been if certain channel constrictions caused by flood-plain filling had not been present.

Shearman (1976) of the U.S. Geological Survey describes a computer application for step-backwater and floodway analyses. "Computer Program 723-X6-L202A" (1973) is a program developed by the Corps of Engineers for calculating water surface profiles. All streamflow-routing computer programs require very detailed information on the physical characteristics of the stream channels.

An outstanding attainment in water-resource management is the "Program Description & User Manual for SSARR Model" (1975). This program has been under development and refinement since 1956. The SSARR Model has been of great value in the planning, design, and operation of the complex international Columbia River system. This Model has been refined to include operational river forecasting and river management activities involving flood control, hydropower, navigation, and irrigation, among other usages. This SSARR Model has served as a pattern for the development of other models in use not only in the United States but in many other parts of the World.

References

Anderson, D. G., and W. L. Anderson, "Computation of Water-Surface Profiles in Open Channels", Book 1, Chap. 1, Surface Water Techniques, U.S. Geological Survey, 1964. (This report describes the hydraulic and mathematical reasoning on which their IBM 650/65 program M0059 of Dec. 21, 1967 is based.)

Chow, Ven Te, "Open-Channel Hydraulics", McGraw-Hill Book Co.,
New York, 680 pp, 1959.

"Computer Program 723-X6-L202A, HEC-2 - Water Surface Profiles
Users Manual", Hydrologic Engineering Center, Corps of
Engineers, U.S. Army, Davis, Calif., 137 pp, Oct. 1973.

Garstka, Walter U., "Water Surface Profiles - Flood of June 17,
1965, Fountain Creek At Pueblo, Colorado". 21 pp and 2
charts, unpublished manuscript dated May 28, 1968.

Himmelblau, D. M., and R. V. Yates, "A New Method of Flow
Routing", Water Resources Research, vol. 4, no. 6,
pp 1193-1199, Dec. 1968.

Lawler, E. A., "Flood Routing", Sec. 25-II, Handbook of Applied
Hydrology, Ven Te Chow, ed-in-chief, McGraw-Hill Book Co.,
New York, 1964.

Mockus, Victor, 1967, with revisions by Wendell Styner, 1972,
Chap. 17, "Flood Routing", in SCS National Engineering
Handbook, Sec. 4, HYDROLOGY, Soil Conservation Service,
USDA, pp 17-1 thru 17-93, Aug. 1972.

"Program Description & User Manual for SSARR Model - Streamflow
Synthesis & Reservoir Regulation - Program 724-K5-G0010",
U.S. Army Engineer Division, North Pacific - Portland,
Ore., Sept. 1972, 188 pp and appendix, Revised June, 1975.

Shearman, James, "Computer Program E431 - User's Manual - Computer Applications for Step-Backwater and Floodway
Analyses", Geological Survey, USDI, Open File Report
76-499, 103 pp, 1976.

Thaemert, Ronald L., "Steep Channel Water Surface Profiles",
Thesis No. CET 71-72 RLT6, Civil Engineering Dept.,
Colo. State Univ., Fort Collins, 93 pp, July, 1971.

"Unsteady Flow in Open Channels", a three-volume book based on
lectures of the Institute on Unsteady Flow in Open
Channels, held at Colo. State Univ., Fort Collins, June
17-28, 1974, as well as the bibliographical abstracts
assembled and prepared for this book. Vol. I, 498 pp,
and Vol. II, 450 pp, both edited by K. Mahmood and
V. Yevjevich; Vol. III (Annotated Bibliography), 452 pp,
ed. by W. A. Miller, Jr., and V. Yevjevich, pub. by Water
Resources Publications, Fort Collins, Colo., 1975.

SECTION XIV

DRAINAGE BASIN LAND USE

Topic 60  Management of a Drainage Basin's Water Resource

There are very few examples of integrated land and water resource management of a drainage basin as a whole.  Three examples from the United States are given.

## Wisconsin Valley Improvement Company

The Wisconsin River drainage basin is the ancestor of practically all of the drainage-basin water-resource management developments including the Tennessee Valley Authority.  The Wisconsin River rises a few miles north of the Michigan border and flows throughout practically its entire length within the State of Wisconsin.  Out of a total drainage area of 12,280 square miles, the controlled drainage area is 1,911 square miles.

Virgin forests of pine in the upper reaches of the drainage basin were being logged towards the close of the last century.  The early loggers were granted authority to build small dams for impounding water for sudden release in the spring to transport logs to the sawmills.  Freshly-cut pine logs will float.  All winter the loggers would place the logs in rollways along the stream bottom as shown in Figure 60-1.

Figure 60-1  Log accumulation awaiting transport by flood flow to be released from a "splash" dam.  South Fork of the Williams River, Pocahontas County, West Virginia.  Photograph, date unknown, from the archives of the Yale University School of Forestry and Environmental Studies, New Haven, Connecticut.

The dams constructed by the loggers were built of logs, stone, and soil. Since they had provisions for sudden release of practically the total impoundment, they were called "splash" dams. The residents in the lower reaches of the Wisconsin River became increasingly concerned about the recurrent sudden floods bulked with heavy logs and about the loss of water in the spring.

The first logs to reach the sawmills brought the highest prices. The practice of sneaking in at night and breaching or dynamiting a competitor's splash dam, thereby preventing floating of his logs, was irresistible. At any time of the day or night the down-river residents were pounded with the floods. This was more than they could tolerate and, together with the desire to save the snowmelt water, led to the creation of the Wisconsin Valley Improvement Company, an entity unique in water resources management.

This quasi-governmental organization was created after years of heated argument and analysis by the legislature to manage the water resources of the River, as recorded in Chapter 335 of the Laws of 1907, State of Wisconsin.

By Statute the State of Wisconsin assigned to the Company management responsibilities which are discussed in detail in "One Less River to Boss" (1948). The Company was given several rights among which are included the following: all necessary franchises and all necessary flowage and riparian rights (see Topic 66); the right to charge and collect reasonable and uniform tolls for navigation; the right to make such other tolls a first lien, subject only to taxes, on the water power, dam, franchise, and flowage rights of the person or company benefited (the tolls were fixed in proportion to the benefits conferred); the right of eminent domain as to land, riparian, or water rights required for improvements necessary to accomplish purposes of the Act.

This was an unprecedented grant of authority and the Company has been able to make a success of integrated basin water resource management. According to Sheerar (1978) there have been no defaults. The most recent amendment to the 1907 Act is Chapter 54 of the Laws of 1969 of the State of Wisconsin.

The WVIC owns or operates 21 reservoirs and dams, none of which have hydropower, with a total storage capacity of 400,367 acre feet. There are 26 hydroelectric dams owned and operated by 10 independent corporations. The WVIC acts as the coordinating agency on river flows. The installed capacity of the hydroelectric plants is 149,654 KW and there is in addition 20,759 HP of mechanical power, all of which receive the benefit of the releases of stored water from the WVIC reservoirs. There are no Federally-owned dams in the Wisconsin River drainage basin which is described in a pamphlet, "The Wisconsin River - Namesake of a State" (undated).

## Tennessee Valley Authority

An outstanding example of the management of a drainage basin's water resource, recognized world-wide, is the Tennessee Valley Authority created during the Great Depression for the purpose of developing not only the water resources but also all other resources, land, agriculture, forestry, minerals, and power, for the benefit of the people of the Valley region and of the Nation. A broad description of the TVA is the one written by Lilienthal (1944). There is an extensive literature in many languages on the TVA.

The first Chairman of the Board of the three directors of the TVA was Arthur E. Morgan. According to Cortes-Comerer (1977) Morgan's mother was a hard-driving former high school teacher and his father was a lackadaisical surveyor. Morgan's parents did not think that he would amount to much and they suggested that he become a florist's apprentice. At age 25 Morgan showed no promise of the man he was to become. Morgan died in November, 1975 at age 97 after he had made some of the most significant contributions of this century to water-resources technology, education, and social cognizance.

Since technological advances, population shifts, and national objectives are never static there is a never-ending need of reassessing and reappraising the management programs. An example of one of the steps in this process is "Development of a Comprehensive TVA Water Resource Management Program, Project Status, July, 1974" (Oct. 1974). The TVA found that severely-limiting constraints were being placed on the total water system operation resulting from diversified and conflicting interests relating to quantity and quality of water and to environmental concern.

Evans (1977) in his appraisal of the TVA, reviews its accomplishments. The TVA operates the Nation's largest power-generating system which in 1976 produced over 101 billion kwh. Flood control operations have prevented property damage of 1.38 billion dollars. Navigation traffic in 1975 amounted to 3.92 billion ton-miles, and the waterfront investments by private industry totaled 2.85 billion dollars.

Agricultural sales increased from 113 million dollars in 1933 to 1.4 billion in 1975. More than a million acres have been reforested since 1933 and the Valley provides raw material for a wood-products industry of 1.4 billion dollars. Recreation is available at 110 public parks. Lakeshore developments include 310 commercial areas and 111 camps and clubs. Visits to the lakes exceed 65 million person-days per year.

# Central Valley Project - California State Water Project

The Central Valley of California, located west of the
Sierra Nevada Mountain range, consists of two major drainage
basins, the Sacramento River flowing south, and the San Joaquin
River flowing north. They flow through the Delta into San
Francisco Bay and then to the Pacific Ocean as is shown on
Erwin Raisz' map K in Shimer's (1972) book on land forms. The
fertility of the soil, when irrigated, and the favorable cli-
mate have resulted in some of the World's most productive crop-
land. The Central Valley lies wholly within the State of
California.

The organization of a unified Central Valley Project was
envisioned as early as the 1880's. Water for irrigation and
flood control were the major problems. The citizens of California in the 1920's seemed to favor inviting the Federal
Government's construction and operation of the Central Valley
Project. However, by 1933 the attitude had changed and the
Legislature adopted the "Central Valley Project Act" (Cal.
Stats. 1933 p. 2643). This Act, which was referred to the
electors upon a referendum petition and approved by popular
vote, authorized construction of the CVP by the State.

The State of California, in the midst of the Great
Depression, was unable to secure in 1935 satisfactory terms
for the sale of an issue of $170,000,000 in revenue bonds
authorized by the 1933 Act. The State invited the Federal
Government to assist under the Reclamation Act of 1902, as
described by Montgomery and Clawson (1946).

Both the riparian and the prior appropriation doctrines
(see Topic 66) are active in California. One of the important
provisions of the 1902 Reclamation Act was the one concerning
acreage limitation. A discussion by Sax (1967, p. 121) is
quoted: "In order to prevent monopolization, a number of safe-
guards were enacted. The law provided that water could not be
sold for use on more than 160 acres in any individual private
ownership, that the user had to be a resident or occupant upon
the land, and that water rights were to be appurtenant to the
land." It was later decided that a man and wife could receive
water for up to 320 acres.

The State of California, having never established that it
considered groundwater to be under the riparian doctrine, soon
found the 160-acre limitation most distressing. There is a
voluminous literature on this subject among which is the book
by the then U.S. Senator Sheridan Downey (1947).

Action begun in 1951 culminated in "Bulletin No. 2" (Mar.
1952) and the "Preliminary Report" (May 19, 1953) which were
aimed at the State of California's acquisition of the Central

Valley Project.

The Bureau of Reclamation's Central Valley Project, through 1976, served a total of 456,600 people with a total of 75 billion gallons of municipal, industrial, and non-agricultural water and provided for 5.7 million visitor days at recreational facilities. The CVP for the period 1950-75 accumulated 339.8 million dollars of flood-control benefits. The installed hydroelectric capacity of six power plants of the CVP totals 1,253,000 KW. The cumulative value of the crops produced from 1943 through 1976 by lands irrigated by CVP water is $12,933,592,486, see "1976 Summary Report" (1977).

Meanwhile the CVP continued to grow under the Bureau of Reclamation's and the Corps of Engineers' programs. Plans for State acquisition were dropped and the State proceeded in 1960 with the development of a State-wide water project for integrated future development of all of California's water resources as is discussed by Warne (1966). The Plan is designed to include or supplement rather than to supercede or interfere with all existing local, private, or Federal water resource developments.

The enabling legislation for the California State Water Project, which was approved by the general electorate, is unusual in that it gave the Department of Water Resources a greatly expanded authority beyond their original planning responsibility. The expanded assignments added the roles of designer, constructor, operator, and marketer. It included the conjunctive operation of surface and groundwater resources. It also incorporated associated aspects such as flood control, power generation, irrigation, reuse, fish and wildlife protection, recreation, repulsion of saline water, and other usages such as water quality control and pollution abatement.

The Bureau of Reclamation's CVP and the Corps of Engineers' flood-control reservoirs, together with State and privately-owned facilities, have been integrated operationally through the California State-Wide Federal Interagency Group. As of December 31, 1976 over 2.3 billion dollars have been spent of State money in the development of this plan which now extends from Northern California across the Delta with the California Aqueduct reaching across the Tehachapi Mountains into Southern California. The magnitude of the California State Water Project will become evident in the perusal of the report, "The California State Water Project - 1976 Activities and Future Management Plans" (1977).

The problems relating to the 160-acre limitation, which consists of only 25 words in the Reclamation Act of 1902, have not as yet been resolved. According to Ross (1978) as of April, 1978 a number of lawsuits are pending and might result

in the application of the 160-acre limitation nationwide to all
water released from any reservoir partly financed by Federal
funds. This would include Corps of Engineers, Soil Conservation Service, and various Authorities. Action is being organized aimed at a thorough revision of the 1902 Act.

## References

"Bulletin No. 2 - Feasibility of State Ownership and Operation
    of the Central Valley Project of California", Water Pro-
    ject Authority of the State of California, March, 1952.

Cortes-Comerer, Nhora, "The Extraordinary Genius of Arthur E.
    Morgan", Civil Engineering, vol. 47, no. 10, pp 114-117,
    Oct. 1977.

"Development of a Comprehensive TVA Water Resource Management
    Program - Project Status July 1974", by Water Resource
    Management Methods Staff, Tennessee Valley Authority,
    Knoxville, 83 pp, Oct. 1974.

Downey, Sheridan, "They Would Rule the Valley", 256 pp, 1947.
    (This book was printed privately in San Francisco and
    copyrighted in 1947 by Sheridan Downey, United States
    Senator from California.)

Evans, Paul L., "The Magnificent Obsession of TVA", Civil Eng-
    ineering, vol. 47, no. 10, pp 107-113, Oct. 1977.

Lilienthal, David E., "TVA-Democracy on the March", (originally
    published by Harper Bros. in 1944), Pocket Books Inc.,
    New York, paperback 240 pp, Feb. 1945.

Montgomery, Mary, and Marion Clawson, "History of Legislation
    and Policy Formation of the Central Valley Project",
    Bureau of Agricultural Economics, USDA, 276 pp, Berkeley,
    Calif., March, 1946.

"1976 Summary Report - 75th Anniversary Year", transmitted to
    the Secretary of the Interior by R. Keith Higginson,
    Commissioner of Reclamation, 79 pp, Sept. 20, 1977. (This
    report includes, pp 41-52, an article by Michael C. Robinson
    Public Works Historical Soc., "Water at Work: Reclamation
    1902-1977".)

"One Less River to Boss - The Story of the Wisconsin River",
    reprint from Electrical World, 16 pp, Aug. 14, 1948.

"Preliminary Report to the California Legislature by the Water Project Authority of the State of California Relative to the Acquisition of the Central Valley Project by the State of California", pursuant to Senate Concurrent Resolution No. 24 Resolution Chap. 71, Statutes of 1953, May 19, 1953.

Ross, Jack F., "160-Acre Limitation Controversy", a paper presented at the 20th Annual Convention of the Colo. Water Congress, Denver, Colo., Feb. 23, 1978.

Sax, Joseph L., "Federal Reclamation Law", Vol. 2 of Waters and Water Rights - A Treatise on the Law of Waters and Allied Problems, Robert Emmet Clark, ed-in-chief, The Allen Smith Co., Indianapolis, Ind., 1967.

Sheerar, Lewis L., Manager of Operations, Wisconsin Valley Improvement Co., Wausau, Wisconsin. Private Communication March 8, 1978.

Shimer, John A., "Field Guide to Landforms in the United States", The Macmillan Co., New York, 272 pp, 1972.

"The California State Water Project - 1976 Activities and Future Management Plans", Bull. No. 132-77, 207 pp, Dept. of Water Resources, Sacramento, Calif., Nov. 1977.

"The Wisconsin River - Namesake of a State", pamphlet pub. by Wisconsin Valley Improvement Co., Wausau; Undated.

Warne, William E., "Water Plans of the State of California", Dept. of Water Resources, The Resources Agency, State of Calif., a 34-page pamphlet of the lecture delivered by Warne at the Univ. of Calif. at Irvine, March 1, 1966.

Topic 61     Multiple-Purpose Land Use Management

Land use, always a matter of concern, has become the subject of overwhelming importance as the population of the world
increases. In the United States, as reported by McDonald
(1941), the early conservationists demonstrated remarkable
foresight in their comments on land use. The current programs
deal with the resolution of conflicts concerning the allocation
of the definitely-limited lands to various usages. Clawson
(1973) has written an informative historical overview of land
use planning in the United States.

Clawson emphasizes that much of the land use planning was
done by engineers, sanitary experts, and bankers, among others,
rather than by professional land use planners. It is necessary, he states, to judge all land use planning in the light
of the technological, economic, and social contexts of the
times.

Davis (1976) has prepared an excellent review of the general problems of land use which he illustrates with a number
of examples. Absolute ownership of land does not exist,
according to Davis. He states that the superior authority of
appropriate units of government reserves certain rights or
powers: (1) the right to tax; (2) the right to condemn (to take
title to land for superior public use); and, (3) the police
power (the right of government to protect and promote public
health, safety, morals, and general welfare, and to protect the
rights of adjoining land owners, among other powers). A reading
of his Chapter 13, "Land Use in Review", is recommended.

Other limitations on absolute ownership are easements for
various purposes such as overhead or underground power lines,
cables, and pipelines as needed by public utilities. Flood-
flow encroachment easements are widely used where flooding may
be relatively infrequent thereby allowing other usage of the
land.

The competition between urbanization and agriculture has
become especially intense in many parts of the country. This
is complicated by great expansions of suburban communities in
which the residents expect to have all of the services of highly developed urban centers while enjoying open spaces, rural,
and forest environments. Numerous examples of this are given
in "Land Use: Tough Choices in Today's World" (1977). The
foreword to this volume, written by J. Vernon Martin, states
that in 1852 the population of this country was about 23
million and that there were about 83 acres for each citizen.
As of 1977 there were only about 8 acres per person over half
of which are desert, mountains, or lakes.

353

Residential and especially industrial demands for land near urban centers have caused such extensive increases in land appraisals for tax purposes that many farmers have been forced to sell. This trend has led Congress to study the problem as reported in the article "Congress Focuses on Saving Farmland" (1977). Various approaches such as "development rights", and "transferable development rights" (TDR), which would pay the farmer to keep him on the farm, are being considered.

As discussed in Topic 3 and in "Perspectives on Prime Lands" (1975), the United States has been losing prime agricultural lands at the rate of 2 million acres per year. There are world-wide implications in this trend because, as mentioned in Topic 38, the United States and Canada supply 80 percent of the World's trade in food and feed grain, income from which is important in trade balance.

A considerable portion of the land in the United States is in the public domain made up of National Forests, land under the administration of the Bureau of Land Management, the National Parks, Wilderness Areas, and Military Reservations. The laws pertaining to the management of public lands were the subject of intensive study conducted under the Chairmanship of Wayne N. Aspinall and reported in the 342-page document, "One Third of the Nation's Land" (1970).

Freilich (1977) traces the legal history of zoning, which he considers to be a legislative act supported by police power. His paper contains numerous citations to court decisions. Reading of this paper is recommended.

"Land Use Controls in New York State" (1975) is a handbook on legal rights of citizens primarily in the State of New York. Enabling legislation for local governments, State laws and programs, and Federal laws and programs are discussed. Also New York City's watershed lands and the City's consumer protection laws and programs are mentioned. There is a note starting on page 358 explaining how to interpret legal citations.

Stock ponds or stock-watering reservoirs are necessary for the production of cattle in the open range. It has been found that an animal will not graze beyond a radius of about three-fourths of a mile from water the quality of the forage notwithstanding. Since many of the beef cattle are bred on the open range the construction of stock ponds is an integral part of wildland range management. Langbein, Hains, and Culler (1951) describe the hydrology of stock ponds in Arizona.

In many instances land use development may not be compatable. An example of incompatability is described by Culler and Peterson (1953) in "Effect of Stock Reservoirs on Runoff in the

354

Cheyenne River Basin Above Angostura Dam". The 9100-square-mile drainage basin contained 932 reservoirs with an aggregate storage of 52,360 acre feet and with an aggregate drainage area of 4440 square miles. The construction of the stock ponds reduced the inflow to Angostura Dam to such an extent as to seriously restrict the effectiveness of this reservoir in power generation and irrigation water storage purposes. A more detailed report on these stock ponds was prepared by Culler (1961).

Losses chargeable to stock ponds range from 19,000 acre-feet in a dry year to about 80,000 acre-feet in a wet year in a drainage basin from which discharges range from 50,000 to 180,000 acre-feet.

Seepage losses exceeded evaporation losses by a factor of 3 and in some cases by as much as a factor of 6. Maximum seepage occurred when the stock ponds were full. Maximum losses to Angostura Reservoir were greatest during years of low runoff which are the times when both the stock needed water and reservoir storage was needed. In drought years only 51 percent of the basins would yield runoff to the reservoir and the loss to the stock ponds would amount to about 49 percent. Not all of the seepage could be considered a total loss since some of it would be expected to recharge the groundwater. It was observed that downstream from the stock ponds for a distance of from a few hundred feet to a half mile, vegetal growth was excellent and in some cases the soil was swampy.

The pamphlet by Lynch and Broome (undated) deals with the complex problems of integrating elevation, topography, ecosystems, natural hazards (wildfire, avalanche, flood, climatic, soil, and geologic) with land ownership, the economy, and citizen participation in mountain land use planning.

All of the problems dealing with land use include that of water. In fact in most instances the availability and the seasonal distribution of the water supply is the critical ingredient in making decisions on land use. The world-nature of this is described by Pereira (1973). As discussed in Topics 1 and 3 human endeavors were centered in oases and along stream channels where water was available. However, as presented by Garstka (1972), the current era of massive carry-over storage has made it possible to develop centers of civilization in arid regions ecologically unsuited for that type of land use.

Many of the urban centers acquired water under the doctrine of prior appropriation (see Topic 66) from streamflow yielded by the wildlands. As the unappropriated supply became utilized urban centers have increased their water supply by purchasing prior water rights chiefly from farmers and ranchers.

Such purchases have a major impact on land use. In Nebraska the water right can be acquired only by purchase of the land. On the other hand, in Colorado, a land owner can sell his water right to a higher priority of usage such as domestic without selling his land as part of that transaction. Later on he can sell the land but without the water right. Laws pertaining to transfer of water rights vary with each state and anyone considering the purchase of land or contemplating land use developments should consult a lawyer versed in water law.

Another limitation on absolute ownership is the reservation of mineral rights as is widespread in the Western States.

"National Land-Use Policy and Legislation" (1975) is a position paper prepared by the Task Force on Land-Use Policy Planning of the American Society of Civil Engineers. It proposes 12 objectives which recognize the significance of private ownership and public need together with the necessity of a viable economy.

## References

Clawson, Marion, "Historical Overview of Land-Use Planning in the United States", Chap. 2, pp 23-54 in Environment: A New Focus for Land-Use Planning. Report NSF/RA/E-74-001, Research Applied to National Needs, Natl. Science Foundation, Washington, D.C., 328 pp, Oct. 1973.

"Congress Focuses on Saving Farmland - Million Acres Lost Yearly", The Denver Post, page 1, Section E, Dec. 4, 1977.

Culler, R. C., and H. V. Peterson, "Effect of Stock Reservoirs on Runoff in the Cheyenne River Basin above Angostura Dam", Circular 223, Geological Survey USDI, 33 pp and map, 1953.

Culler, R. C., "Hydrology of Stock-Water Reservoirs in Upper Cheyenne River Basin", USGS Water Supply Paper 1531-A, pp 1-136 (1961).

Davis, Kennth P., "Land Use", McGraw-Hill Book Co., New York, 324 pp, 1976.

Freilich, Robert H., "Courts: The Ultimate Arbiters in Land Use Disputes", pp 22-33 in Land Use: Tough Choices in Today's World. Special publication No. 22, Soil Conservation Society of America, Ankeny, Iowa, 454 pp, 1977.

Garstka, Walter U., "Water Resources in the West", pp 8-14 in Watersheds in Transition, Proceedings of a Symposium held at Fort Collins, Colo. June 19-22, 1972. Edited by S. C. Csallany, T. G. McLaughlin, and W. Striffler. Proceedings Series No. 14, American Water Resources Assn., Urbana, Ill., 405 pp, Sept. 1972.

"Land Use Controls in New York State", Elaine Moss, Ed., The Dial Press/ James Wade, New York, 368 pp, 1975.

"Land Use: Tough Choices in Today's World", Proceedings of a Symposium, Mar. 21-24, 1977, Omaha, Neb., 454 pp, Soil Conservation Soc. of America, Ankeny, Iowa, 1977.

Langbein, W. B., C. H. Hains, and R. C. Culler, "Hydrology of Stock-Water Reservoirs in Arizona", U.S. Geological Survey Cir. 110, 18 pp, Mar. 1951.

Lynch, Dennis L., and Standish R. Broome, "Mountain Land Planning", pub. jointly by Colo. State Forest Service and the College of Forestry and Natural Resources, Colo. State Univ., Fort Collins, 38 pp, undated.

McDonald, Angus, "Early American Soil Conservationists", U.S. Dept. of Agriculture, Misc. Pub. 449, 63 pp, Oct. 1941.

"National Land-Use Policy and Legislation", prepared by Task Force on Land-Use Policy Planning, a position paper presented at the ASCE Natl. Convention, Denver, Colo., Nov. 3-7, 1975. Meeting preprint 2584, 17 pp, 1975.

"One Third of the Nation's Land", A Report to the President and to the Congress by the Public Land Law Review Commission. Prepared under the Chairmanship of Wayne N. Aspinall. 342 pages, U.S. Government Printing Office, June, 1970.

Pereira, H. C., "land Use and Water Resources - In Temperate and Tropical Climates", Cambridge University Press, London, 246 pp, 1973.

"Perspectives on Prime Lands", Background papers for Seminar on the Retention of Prime Lands, July 16-17, 1975, sponsored by the USDA Committee on Land use, 257 pp paperback, pub. by U.S. Dept. of Agriculture, 1975.

Topic 62            Forests and Wildlands

The wildlands are those portions of the land surface of
the Earth which are not urbanized or industrialized and which,
if not bare or covered with snow and ice, are occupied by forests, ranges, or alpine or tundra vegetation.  Practically all
of the fresh water on the surface of the Earth comes from the
wildlands.  This topic is presented in three sections, Forest
Hydrology, Grasslands Management, and Fire in the Environment.

Forest Hydrology

When a forest is reestablished on a denuded area there
begin a series of changes in the hydrologic behavior of the
drainage basins.  As the forest condition becomes dominant the
following changes have been observed:

a. There is a very great decrease in erosion and sediment
   yield.

b. There is an increase in evapotranspirational water loss.

c. There may be a complete absorption of small rains so that
   they produce no runoff.

d. There may be a considerable modification of the shape of
   the hydrograph of rainstorms for which rainfall excess
   forms a small fraction of the total storm.

e. There may be very considerable changes in the water-yield
   effectiveness of snow accumulations.

f. There usually is no discernable effect on the magnitude of
   the peak rates of discharge during major floods.  However,
   during major floods there is very little increase in sediment yield as compared to bare areas or non-forested areas.

g. Total water yield is reduced.

h. Responses to changes in land use take place slowly.

The generalizations stated are of the usual trends.  Sometimes the results of research for specific areas may not
support the general trends.  Removal of the forest, either partial or complete, tends to return, in part, the hydrology of
the area to conditions approaching bare ground, with the important exception that as long as forest soil and litter layer
conditions prevail, erosion remains at the low levels similar
to the forest condition.

It has been established that an unbroken stand of grass is
practically as effective as a forest in its influence on water
yield and on the hydrograph.  Grass has the advantage over the
forest in that the evapotranspirational losses from grass are

usually less than from a forest. It may be difficult if not impossible without tillage practices or the use of biocides to perpetuate grass in a region in which the forest is the climax vegetation, as has been experienced in the Northeastern States.

The first thoroughly organized drainage land-use experiment to determine the effects of forest management on water yield was the "Swiss Emmenthal" experiment, as reported by Engler (1919). The National Research Institute of Switzerland conducted this research during the period 1903-1917. One of a pair of watersheds was mostly forest, the other was mostly grassland. Major differences in the water yield were not observed and the results indicated that a watershed in grassland might be equal to or perhaps better in some respects than a forested watershed insofar as erosion control and water yield were concerned.

The first forest and streamflow experiment in the United States, conducted by the Forest Service and the Weather Bureau, was organized in 1909 just west of Wagon Wheel Gap in the headwaters of the Rio Grande in Colorado. Bates and Henry (1922 and 1928) describe this experiment. Circumstances which led to the organization of the experiment are reviewed by Schiff (1962) in his Chapter 4. Two watersheds, each about 200 acres in area, were calibrated. In 1919 Watershed B, 84 percent of which was an aspen and coniferous forest, was clear-cut and the slash burned. There was an increase in water yield chiefly during the snowmelt season but herbaceous vegetation and aspen protected the soil against severe erosion. The exact findings of the Wagon Wheel Gap experiment remain a subject of controversy.

Garstka (1972) has recommended that the Wagon Wheel Gap experiment be repeated in order to evaluate with physical measurement silvicultural and ecological changes since 1909. This should be done starting in 1979.

The second forest-streamflow experiment in the United States was the White Mountains project conducted for the Forest Service by the U.S. Geological Survey in 1911-12 as described by Langbein (1978). Ten well-instrumented watersheds were selected ranging in area from 0.303 to 20.900 square miles. They were located in the headwaters of the Pemigewassett and the Ammonoosuc Rivers near North Woodstock, New Hampshire. Observations were made from June, 1911 to October 1912.

Analyses were made of individual storms or storm periods rather than for totals of runoff for months or years. The objective was to learn the effects of forests on streamflow. Langbein quotes a report prepared in October, 1913 by M. I. Walters of the U.S. Geological Survey as follows: "Undoubtedly slope has the greater effect, and next in importance would come the condition of the soil cover. The forest effect is last and is of the least importance." Langbein's article, when published, will make fascinating reading.

There is an extensive and rapidly increasing literature on forest watershed management research and practices in all parts of the world. A comprehensive volume, world-wide in scope, is the 813-page "International Symposium on Forest Hydrology" (1967). Pereira's book on land use and water resources (1973) includes numerous references to forest and wildland management in various parts of the World.

A comprehensive summary of the results of 39 studies dealing with the effects of altering forest cover on water yield was prepared by Hibbert (1967). There are a number of publications describing for various regions the general approach to forest management aimed at increasing water yield among which are: Beattie (1967), Lull (1966), Martinelli (1964), and Croft and Bailey (1964).

Although it is becoming widely recognized that the reforestation of an area will reduce the total water yield, effectiveness of the forest in controlling erosion and reducing sediment, for many purposes, more than compensates for the loss of water yield. Examples of an extensive literature dealing with the control of soil erosion and the handling of potentially erosive water in the channels are the two reports by Heede (1968).

The Division of Watershed Management of the U.S. Forest Service, working through the Regional Offices and the National Forest Supervisors, has organized a system of representative watersheds ranging from 50,000 to 150,000 acres. The purpose of this program is to bridge the gap between the research findings and the operational management of drainage basins for increasing water yield. The areas included in this program are commonly referred to as "Barometer Watersheds". Dortignac (1967) deals with forest water yield management opportunities. "Davidson River Barometer Watershed" (1972) is described in a pamphlet issued by the Pisgah National Forest, North Carolina.

Swank and Douglass (1974) found that streamflow was reduced about 20 centimeters (20 percent) fifteen years after two experimental watersheds in the Southern Appalachians at the Coweeta Experimental Forest were converted from a mature deciduous hardwood cover to White Pine. Largest monthly reductions in runoff occurred in the White Pine watershed during the hardwood watersheds' dormant and early-growing seasons.

Douglass (1972) in his annotated bibliography lists 209 publications on watershed management by the Southeastern Forest

Experiment Station for the period 1928-1970.

The American Society of Civil Engineers sponsored a Symposium on "Interdisciplinary Aspects of Watershed Management" which was held at Bozeman, Montana, in August, 1970.

Ffolliott and Thorud (1974) have prepared an informative review of vegetation management for increasing water yield as the techniques pertain to various vegetal zones in Arizona. They conclude that the potential for water yield increase by vegetation management could amount to between 600,000 and 1,200,000 acre-feet per year under average conditions for Arizona as a whole. In some basins the vegetation and climate are such as to offer no promise of water-yield increase by vegetation management.

Hewlett and Helvey (1970) in their analysis of the effects of forest clear-felling on the storm hydrograph conclude that soil-water deficits resulting from evapotranspiration are important in explaining the increases in volume of runoff yielded from deep soil drainage basins in the Southern Appalachians.

A report on 17 experimental watersheds in the Badger Wash Basin 25 miles west of Grand Junction, Colorado, is given by Branson and Owen (1970). Highly significant correlation coefficients were found for percent bare soil and runoff but the relationship between bare soil and sediment yields was found not to be statistically significant. Correlation coefficients for spring vegetation measurements and runoff were found to be higher than those for autumn measurements.

Alexander and Watkins (1977) describe the work at the Fraser Experimental Forest, Colorado. This report includes summaries of findings at this research station which was established in 1937. About three-fourths of this forest lies above the 10,000-foot elevation. This report gives data on runoff increases, in some cases of 25 percent, from areas in the high altitude coniferous forests. Study of this report is recommended.

Leaf and Brink (1973) have designed a mathematical simulation model to determine probable hydrologic changes resulting from watershed management in the Colorado subalpine zone. Their report describes Program WBMODEL with 5 related programs, 2 functions, and with a total of 22 subroutines prepared for the CDC 6400 computer.

Meiman and Grant (1974) describe research on management techniques in alpine forest and clearing aspects for reducing snowwater evaporation losses to increase the water yield. They concluded that evaporation losses from the snow season's precipitation amounted to 60 percent in an alpine setting and

45 percent in both a forest and forest opening, whereas 75 percent of the snow water caught in glacial cirques appeared as runoff during the melt season.

"Research Watersheds" were the subject of a Symposium in Ontario, Canada, at the University of Guelph in 1964. Farrar (1964) lists 15 small research watersheds in Canada. Periods of record range from one to 16 years and sizes range from 20 to 6000 acres.

Ling, Pan, and Lin (1969) list 21 reservoirs in Taiwan and describe the extremely high rates of erosion, with many landslides, produced by intense and heavy typhoons and thunderstorms in the steep mountainous terrain. River and reservoir siltation is extremely rapid. Their Figure 4 shows the abandoned powerhouse of the Tungmen Station now completely buried under the riverbed of the Mukua Chi. Watershed-management programs for several river basins are described.

Australia has few native softwoods. A large portion of import expenditures are for timber products. Extensive plantations of Pinus radiata (Monterey Pine, a native of California) were established. Bell and Gatenby (1969) describe research conducted on 11 catchments ranging in size from 10.4 to 240 acres at the Lidsdale State Forest near Lithgow, west of Sidney, Australia. They found that mature pine and eucalyptus had similar soil-moisture depletion cycles and that largest water yields occurred from a catchment of immature pine. Observations were conducted from December, 1963, to April, 1966.

Dils (1965), in his report on watershed management in New Zealand, includes numerous photographs illustrating the extremely complicated problems in that country including the impacts of exotic wildlife among which are, thar, chamois, deer, opposum, feral pigs, and goats. Control of rabbits is a major problem.

In the United States concern with the quality of the environment has focused attention on drainage-basin land use. The Symposium, "Watersheds in Transition", sponsored by the American Water Resources Association and Colorado State University, was held at Fort Collins June 19-22, 1972 as a United States contribution to the International Hydrological Decade. The 405-page Proceedings was published in October, 1972.

Pfankuch (1975) has prepared an outline for stream-reach inventory and channel-stability evaluation for application to mountain streams in forested areas.

In his text on wildland watershed management Satterlund (1972) includes discussions of hydrologic fundamentals with numerous tables and charts.

Anderson, Hoover, and Reinhart (1976) in their review,
"Forests and Water: Effects of Forest Management on Floods,
Sedimentation and Water Supply", give an outstanding report
which contains 6 figures and 15 tables presenting in condensed
form an extensive wealth of knowledge on pertinent subjects,
including a list of 610 references. A study of this publication is recommended.

Research in forest hydrology was initiated by the TVA in
1934 and since then 6 major watershed studies have been organized, as reported by Ellertsen (1968). He describes the Pine
Tree Branch Watershed on his page 27. Figure 62-1 is a photograph of the stream-gaging station taken in 1941. Figure 62-2
is a photograph of the same station taken in October, 1972.
The following photographs are quoted from the sign erected at
that location:

"TENNESEE VALLEY AUTHORITY

PINE TREE BRANCH EXPERIMENTAL AREA

"This is Pine Tree Branch, a stream draining 88 acres of
sandy soil, highly vulnerable to erosion. TVA acquired
the area to test and demonstrate the benefits of reforestation and other land reclamation practices. When the
project started the watershed was typical of tens of thousands of acres of eroding land in North Mississippi, West
Tennessee, and West Kentucky.

"This structure - called a weir - was built to measure water
and sediment from the watershed above it. Measurement from
1941 to 1945 reflected conditions before the land was
treated. During the winter of 1945-46 simple wire and
brush checks were installed to help control erosion. Planting of 90,000 seedlings mostly Loblolly pine, was completed
in March 1946.

"Up the trail to the right you can see how this young forest
is protecting the soil. Surface water runoff has been reduced about 65 percent as more water soaks into the ground.
Before treatment, 94 percent of the surface runoff of a
given storm occurred the first hour; 25 years later, for
similar storms, first-hour runoff was only 18 percent.
Before treatment, soil washed off this watershed at the
rate of 24.2 tons per acre per year. By 1965 the rate was
only 0.5 ton, a reduction of 98 percent.

"The planted trees were thinned in August 1966. Five hundred cords of pulpwood were cut and 1200 cords were left
standing. By 1990 the 88 acres will have produced an estimated 2-1/2 million board feet of saw timber and 2400 cords
of pulpwood. Its value at current prices will be about
$60,000. An average gross return of $18 per acre per year
for the 45 year growing period."

Figure 62-1  Pine Tree Branch Experimental Area as it appeared
in 1941.  Photo:  Tennessee Valley Authority

Figure 62-2  Pine Tree Branch Experimental Area, October, 1972.
The gaging station is visible on the right.  Detailed
descriptions of these two photographs are given on the
preceding page.  Photo: Tennessee Valley Authority

## Grasslands Management

A major division of the non-forested wildlands consists of
the grasslands. The grasslands are ecological entities examples of which are the prairie lands and grasslands of the
United States and Canada; the steppes of Central Asia; and the
pampas of South America. Tundras and alpine areas are characteristic of sub-arctic climates. Arid shrublands are to be
found in many parts of the World. When domesticated animals
are grazed in wildlands the areas are often referred to as
rangelands. Pereira (1973) in his Chapter 7 has written an
informative review of the effects of grazing animals on
watersheds.

Many forests such as the pinon-juniper and the ponderosa-
pine may have such a low crown density as to support growth of
grass and such forests may be considered to be rangelands.

The principles of soil science (Topic 34) and of ecology
(Topic 47) apply to the grasslands and rangelands. Water is a
critical element in the natural ecology and in the range management of grassland. An example of the importance of water is
given in Topic 61. It was observed long ago that the grazing
animal is very selective in the forage which it browses.
Given a choice, the plants higher in the ecological succession,
that is those demanding higher nutrients in the soil and a more
favorable water supply, are preferred by the grazing animal as
observed by Sampson (1919). The following is quoted from his
page 5:
"Species high in development are grazed with greater relish
than those lower in the succession. Thus, the plants well
up in the development of the type may disappear gradually
or suddenly, according to the degree of disturbance
caused by the adverse factor until the plant stages lower
in the development predominate."

Godden (1926) found that in every case (with the exception
of sodium) plants which were grazed had a higher mineral element content than plants which were not eaten. Usually plants
higher in the ecological succession have a higher ash content
than plants lower in the succession.

Forage utilization, daily intake, and nutrient value of
desert range are the subject of a paper by Cook (1973) who
recommends supplements high in protein, especially in the
winter, for cattle grazing in desert shrublands.

Thilenius (1975) presents the status of our knowledge of
alpine range management including areas at high elevations
above timberline which are usually grazed by sheep. The alpine
wildlands are fascinating in that the plant species have
adapted, with very efficient photosynthesis, to short growing

seasons and intense cold. Some alpine plants carry on photo-synthesis at temperatures of minus 6° C and lichens may photo-synthesize at minus 24° C.

The rangelands and pastures are of great importance in food production since their availability makes it possible to produce meat utilizing land unsuited for growing crops, accord-ing to Hodgson (1976). Various techniques have been applied and are under study for range improvement practices. A com-prehensive review of both beneficial and detrimental effects of such practices on runoff and erosion is given in the paper by Gifford (1975).

Figure 62-3 from Currie (1975) on the following page il-lustrates the effect of moderate and heavy grazing on soil loss and runoff. The leaflet "Grass Waterways in Soil Conservation" (1966) gives practical instructions for the use of 33 grasses and legumes for use in 6 regional areas of the United States to control runoff from terraces, diversions, and contour rows.

Van Haveren and Striffler (1976) conducted research on snowmelt recharge on a shortgrass prairie. They found that topography and vegetation characteristics exert strong controls on snow redistribution on the prairie. Slope exposure and wind were important. Snowmelt recharge efficiency on lee slopes trapped as soil water 46 percent of winter precipitation as compared to only 30 percent in windward slopes.

Three references dealing with rangeland management are: "Range Hydrology" by Branson, Gifford, and Owen (1972); "The Nation's Range Resource (1972); and the Soil Conservation Service's "National Range Handbook" (1976). Cook (1978) states on his page 22, "Production of one pound of weaning weight from rangeland calves requires only about 30 percent as much fossil fuel as a pound of meat from weaner calves produced from har-vested feeds (Cook et al. 1976)". He includes data on acreages, numbers of livestock, and energy requirements. A reading of Cook's article is recommended.

The history of the management of rangelands in the United States in the early days was one of exploitation. Voigt (1976) has written a very detailed review and history of the Nation's management of its rangeland. In his Chapter 25 he summarizes the problems facing our rangelands. Grazing was permitted too early in the year; livestock concentrations were too great; and the livestock was permitted to graze too long. This frontier-type exploitation in the days of the "cattle barons" resulted in such degradation as to cause serious erosion with its correlated filling of stream bottoms and reservoirs and with greatly increased loss of water by surface runoff.

There are about 200,000,000 acres of Federal rangelands.

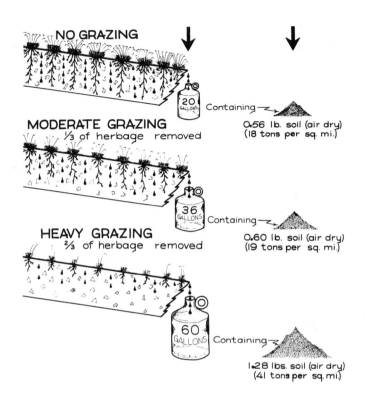

Figure 62-3 Grazing results as reported by Currie (1975 p 9).

For many years the Forest Service and the grazing public were practically at war. Early in the Century stockmen were allowed access to forest and rangelands to graze their cattle at what began as a nominal charge per month. The early permits were for one year; then the time was increased to 5 years and since the 1920's a grazing permit is more or less standard for a 10-year period.

Permittees soon found that their grazing permits increased the value of their stock and of their land as compared with the land of neighbors without grazing permits. The stockmen soon looked on the grazing permit as a property right which was permitted to be transferred with the sale of the property.

Charges were made for grazing by the animal unit month (AUM) which increased from about 5 cents for the AUM in 1936-1946 to about one dollar in 1974-1976. Five sheep were considered to be equivalent to one cattle AUM. As of early 1978 the stockmen considered $1.85 per AUM a fair price whereas the Forest Service and the Bureau of Land Management set the figure at $2.20 per AUM.

The stockmen who have a grazing permit must construct access roads to the grazing land; they must furnish salt; drill wells or build stock ponds; and maintain fences. All improvements which they make to the rangeland become the property of the Federal Government. As of the present time the charges for grazing on Federal land, taking into account other costs to the stockmen, are finally after 70 years approaching some semblance of an equitable balance. Robertson (1978), in his paper on the use of the grazing fee as an incentive for range management, analyzes various approaches to this problem which involves about 25,000 permittees.

Attention now is being centered on research needs for improving the over-grazed and depleted rangelands to a condition of sustained yield for the protection of the watersheds and for dependable production of grazing animals.

Klemmedson, Pieper, Dwyer, Mueggler, and Trlica (1978) list research needs in five categories. Increased demands internationally for grains have called attention to the importance of rangelands for meat production. Rangeland-management research needs to be accelerated since rangelands produce not only forage but also wildlife, water, minerals, and often, wood fiber.

Restoration of devastated rangelands, even with supplemental seeding and fertilization, may take many decades provided that the number of livestock and periods of grazing are controlled in recognition of the flowering requirements of the plants as the rangeland advances in the ecological succession.

Fire in the Environment

Evidence of the use of fire by the aborigines has been observed in many parts of the World according to Aschmann (1977) on his page 132. There is evidence that deliberate burning of vegetation, which may have had its initial start by accident, has been characteristic of human societies for thousands of years. Aschmann mentions references pertaining to the use of fire on the Island of Madeira; in the Mediterranean basin including Libya, Morocco, Sicily, and Spain; and in Chile, California, South Africa, and Australia. The ancient use of fire in "shifting" agriculture is described in Topic 38.

The recent practice of fire prevention and suppression has resulted in many parts of the World in a build-up of fuel to such levels that, when a fire does occur for whatever reason, the resulting intense conflagration has a devastating effect. Dodge's (1972) article on the growing problem of forest fuel accumulation includes 37 references.

Komarek (1965) has written an interesting analysis of the

interactions of fire on the ecology of grassland and on the migration routes of early man. The importance of climate in wildland fires is discussed by Schroeder and Buck (1970). Countryman (1976) has prepared a well-illustrated and very informative pamphlet on radiation and wildland fires in which he includes suggestions for survival if one should be caught in the path of a wildland fire.

The Peshtigo fire of October 8 and 9, 1871 in the lumber-industry town of Peshtigo, Wisconsin, took the lives of 1500 people. An estimated 2 billion pine trees and 1,250,000 acres of forest were destroyed. This cataclysm is described in "Wild Fire - A Study of Modern Fire Fighting" (1972).

There is an extensive literature on wild fires as they pertain to both forests and grasslands. Examples of this are: the report by Albini (1976) on estimating wildland fire behavior; the article by Sneevwjagt and Frandsen (1977) published in Canada which reports on the behavior of experimental grass fires in Canada; and King and Furman's (1976) article describing fire-danger rating networks.

A forest or grassland wildfire changes the ecology and the environment so radically that there was in the past a widespread public feeling against the deliberate usage of controlled fire as a wildland-management technique. Attitudes are changing but not without resistance. Schiff's (1962) book "Fire and Water - Scientific Heresy in the Forest Service" is an interesting history of professional and public attitudes. "Forest and Flame in the Bible" (1955) is a compilation of 40 citations which had been approved for inclusion by leaders of the Protestant, Catholic, and Jewish Faiths.

One of the undesirable effects of wildfire is the immediate, and at times enormous, impact on the hydrology. Satterlund (1972) in his pages 245-248 summarizes reports from the San Dimas Experimental Forest in Southern California. Following denudation by the wildfires of 1938 and of 1953 peak rates of discharge were from 13.0 to 67.7 times as great as were the peak flows before the fire at the same experimental watersheds and for comparable storms.

Another undesirable effect is the very great increase in erosion. There is an extensive literature concerning the effects of wildfire on peak flows, erosion, and on streamflow temperatures and water quality.

Komarek, Komarek, and Carlysle (1973) include 136 illustrations, many of them photomicrographs taken with a scanning electron microscope, in their publication on smoke particulates and charcoal residues from forest and grassland fires. These particulates and charcoal act as environmental cleansing agents.

Wildfire particulates and charcoal are different from industrially-produced substances. In many instances the authors have been able to identify the genera of the plant material.

Brotak and Reifsnyder (1976) found in their study of meteorological conditions that extreme wildfires in the Eastern United States occurred near frontal areas, especially following the passage of a dry cold front.

The Proceedings of the Symposium "Fire in the Environment" (1972) present an excellent treatment of the subject including sections on ecology, public attitudes, alternatives to conflagration, and fire control technology among others.

## References

Albini, Frank A., "Estimating Wildfire Behavior and Effects", USDA Forest Service General Tech. Report INT-30, Intermountain Forest and Range Exp. Station, Ogden, Utah, 92 pp, 1976.

Alexander, Robert R., and Ross K. Watkins, "The Fraser Experimental Forest, Colorado", USDA Forest Service General Tech. Report RM-40, Rocky Mt. Forest and Range Exp. Sta.-Fort Collins, Colo., 32 pp, Sept. 1977.

Anderson, Henry W., Marvin D. Hoover, and Kenneth G. Reinhart, "Forests and Water: Effects of Forest Management on Floods, Sedimentation, and Water Supply", USDA Forest Service General Tech. Report PSW-18/1976, 115 pp, 1976.

Aschmann, Homer, "Aboriginal Use of Fire", pp 132-141 in Proceedings of the Symposium on the Environmental Consequences of Fire and Fuel Management in Mediterranean Ecosystems, Aug. 1-5, 1977, Palo Alto, Calif. USDA Forest Service General Tech. Report WO-3, 498 pp, Nov. 1977.

Bates, C. G., and A. J. Henry, "Stream-flow Experiment at Wagon Wheel Gap, Colo.; Preliminary Report on Termination of First Stage of Experiment", Monthly Weather Review, Supplement No. 17, 55 pp, 1922.

Bates, C. G., and A. J. Henry, "Forest and Streamflow Experiment at Wagon Wheel Gap, Colo.; Final Report on Completion of Second Phase of the Experiment", Monthly Weather Review, Supplement No. 30, 79 pp, 1928.

Beattie, Byron, "Harvesting the National Forest Water Crop", a paper presented at the 36th Annual Convention, Natl. Reclamation Assn., Honolulu, Hawaii, week of Nov. 2, 1967.

Bell, F. C., and M. T. Gatenby, "Effects of Exotic Softwood
Afforestation on Water Yield", Bull. No. 15, Water
Research Foundation of Australia, 93 pp, Mar. 1969.

Branson, Farrel A., Gerald F. Gifford, J. Robert Owen, "Rangeland Hydrology", Range Science Series No. 1, Society for
Range Mgmt., Denver, Colo., 84 pp, Oct. 1972.

Branson, F. A., and J. B. Owen, "Plant Cover, Runoff, and Sediment Yield Relationships on Mancos Shale in Western
Colorado", Water Resources Research, vol. 6, no. 3,
pp 783-790, June, 1970.

Brotak, Edward A., and William E. Reifsnyder, "Synoptic Study
of the Meteorological Conditions Associated with Extreme
Wildland Fire Behavior", pp 66-69 in Proceedings of the
Fourth Natl. Conference on Fire and Forest Meteorology,
St. Louis, Mo., Nov. 16-18, 1976, USDA Forest Service
General Tech. Report RM-32, Rocky Mt. Forest and Range
Exp. Station, Fort Collins, Colo., 1976.

Cook, C. Wayne, "Forage Utilization, Daily Intake, and Nutrient
Value of Desert Range", pp 47-50 in Arid Shrublands, Proceedings of the Third Workshop of the United States/Aus-
tralia Rangelands Panel, Tucson, Ariz. 1973. Pub. by
Society for Range Mgmt. Denver, Colo.

Cook, C. Wayne, "Rangelands and Meat Production", pp 21-23 in
Rangeman's Journal, vol. 5, no. 1, Feb. 1978.

Countryman, Clive M., "Radiation and Wildland Fire", Heat -
its Role in Wildland Fire - Part 5, Pacific Southwest
Forest and Range Exp. Station, Forest Service, USDA,
Berkeley, Calif., 12 pp, 1976.

Croft, A. R., and R. W. Bailey, "Mountain Water", pub. by
Intermountain Regional Office, USFS, Ogden, Utah, May,1964.

Currie, Pat O., "Grazing Management of Ponderosa Pine-Bunch-
grass Ranges of the Central Rocky Mountains: The Status of
Our Knowledge", USDA Forest Service Research Paper RM-159,
Rocky Mt. Forest and Range Exp. Station, Fort Collins,
Colo., 24 pp, Dec. 1975.

"Davidson River Barometer Watershed", Pisgah Ranger District,
Pisgah Natl. Forest, Southern Region Forest Service, USDA,
Folder, 1972.

Dils, R.E., "Watershed Management in New Zealand - Status and
Research Needs", Special Pub. No. 4, Tussock Grasslands &
Mountain Lands Institute, 28 pp, 1965.

Dodge, Marvin, "Forest Fuel Accumulation - A Growing Problem", Science, vol. 177, pp 139-142, 14 July 1972.

Dortignac, Ed. J., "Forest Water Yield Management Opportunities" pp 579-592 in International Symposium on Forest Hydrology, ed. by Sopper and Lull, Pergamon Press, New York, 1967.

Douglass, James E., "Annotated Bibliography of Publications on Watershed Management by the Southeastern Forest Experiment Station, 1928-1970", USDA Forest Service, Southeastern Forest Exp. Station, Asheville, North Carolina USDA Forest Service Research Paper SE-93, March, 1972.

Ellertsen, Birger W., "Forest Hydrologic Research Conducted by the Tennessee Valley Authority", Water Resources Bulletin, vol. 4, no. 2, pp 25-33, June, 1968.

Engler, A., "untersuchungen uder den einfluss des waldes aus den stand der gawasser (Researches on influence of the forest on the disposition of terrestrial and atmospheric waters). Mitteilungen Der Schweizerischen Centralanstalt Fur Vas Forstliche Versuchswesen. vol. XII, 1919, 626 pp, (Partially translated in Forest Service, Division of Sylvics, Translation 100.)

Farrar, J. L., "Research Watersheds in Canada", pp 11-13 in Research Watersheds, Proceedings of Hydrology Symposium No. 4, held at the Univ. of Guelph, May 27-28, 1964. Pub. by Dept. of Northern Affairs and Natl. Resources, Natl. Resource Council of Canada, 1965.

Ffolliott, Peter F., and David B. Thorud, "Vegetation Management for Increased Water Yield in Arizona", Tech. Bulletin 215, Agri. Exp. Station, Univ. of Arizona, Tucson, 38 pp, Sept. 1974. (This reference is an abstract of a 2-3/8-in. report by the same authors under the title, "Water Yield Improvement by Vegetation Management - Focus on Arizona", prepared by the Univ. of Arizona, Tucson, for the USFS Rocky Mt. Forest and Range Exp. Station, Fort Collins, Colo., 1975.

"Fire in the Environment", Symposium Proceedings of the meeting May 1-5, 1972, Denver, Colo., Pub. by USDA Forest Service in Cooperation with the Fire Services of Canada, Mexico, and the United States - Members of the Fire Management Study Group, North American Forestry Commission, FAO, 151 pp, Dec. 1972.

"Forest and Flame in the Bible", USDA Forest Service, Pub. PA-93, 15 pp, reprinted Nov. 1955.

Garstka, Walter U., "Forest and Streamflow Experiment at Wagon Wheel Gap, Colorado, 1909-1926", Page 147 in Symposium Proceedings of the meeting May 1-5, 1972, Denver, Colo. Pub. by Forest Service, USDA, in cooperation with the Fire Services of Canada, Mexico, and the United States, 151 pp, Dec. 1972.

Gifford, Gerald F., "Beneficial and Detrimental Effects of Range Improvement Practices on Runoff and Erosion", pp 216-248 in Watershed Management, Proceedings of a Symposium conducted by the Irrigation & Drainage Div. of the ASCE, Logan, Utah, Aug. 11-13, 1975, 781 pp, 1975.

Godden, W., "Report on the Chemical Analyses of Samples of Pasture from Various Areas in the British Isles", Jour. Agric. Science, vol. 16, pp 78-88, 1926.

"Grass Waterways in Soil Conservation", by M. Donald Atkins and James J. Coyle, USDA Leaflet No. 477, 8 pp, Oct. 1966.

Heede, Burchard H., "Engineering Techniques and Principles Applied to Soil Erosion Control", USFS Rocky Mtn. Forest and Range Exp. Sta., Research Paper RM-102, 1968.

Heede, Burchard H., "Conversion of Gullies to Vegetation-lined Waterways on Mountain Slopes", USFS Rocky Mtn. Forest and Range Exp. Sta., Research Paper RM-40, 1968.

Hewlett, J. D., and J. D. Helvey, "Effects of Forest Clear-Cutting on the Storm Hydrograph", Water Resources Research vol. 6, no. 3, pp 768-782, June, 1970.

Hibbert, Alden R., "Forest Treatment Effects on Water Yield", pp 527-543 in International Symposium on Forest Hydrology, ed. by Wm. E. Sopper and Howard W. Lull, Pergamon Press, New York, 813 pp, 1967.

Hodgson, Harlow J., "Forage Crops", Scientific American, vol. 234, no. 2, pp 63-75, Feb. 1976.

"Interdisciplinary Aspects of Watershed Management", Proceedings of a Symposium held Aug. 3-6, 1970, Montana State University, Bozeman, 411 pp, pub. by ASCE, 1972.

"International Symposium on Forest Hydrology", Proceedings of an NSF Advanced Science Seminar held at Penn. State Univ. Aug. 29-Sept. 10, 1965. Ed. by Wm. E. Sopper and Howard W. Lull, Pergamon Press, New York, 813 pp, 1967.

King, Rudy M., and R. William Furman, "Fire Danger Rating Network Density", USDA Forest Service Research Paper RM-177, Rocky Mt. For. & Range Exp. Sta. Ft. Collins, Oct. 1976.

373

Klemmedson, J. O., Rex D. Pieper, Don D. Dwyer, Walter F. Mueggler, and M. J. Trlica, "Research Needs on Western Rangelands", pp 4-8 in Journal of Range Management, vol. 31, no. 1, Jan. 1978.

Komerek, E. V., Sr., "Fire Ecology - Grasslands and Man", pp 169-220 in Proceedings Fourth Annual Tall Timbers Fire Ecology Conf., pub. by Tall Timbers Research Station, Tallahassee, Florida, 1965.

Komarek, E. V., Betty B. Komarek, and Thelma C. Carlysle, "The Ecology of Smoke Particulates and Charcoal Residues from Forest and Grassland Fires: A Preliminary Atlas", Misc. Pub. No. 3, 75 pp, Tall Timbers Research Station, Tallahassee, Florida, 1973.

Langbein, Walter B., Personal communication of January, 1978 concerning the USGS Experimental Watersheds in the White Mts., New Hampshire, 1911-12. Publication in preparation.

Leaf, Charles F., and Glen E. Brink, "Hydrologic Simulation Model of Colorado Subalpine Forest", USFS Rocky Mtn. Forest and Range Exp. Sta., Research Paper RM-107, May, 1973.

Ling, Kuo-chang, Chi-fen Pan, Yuan-lin Lin, "Sediment Problems and Watershed Management in Taiwan", for the International Hydrological Decade, 51 pp, pub. by Taiwan Power Co., Taipei, Taiwan, Republic of China, Nov. 1969.

Lull, Howard W., "An Annotated Bibliography of Watershed Management Research by the Northeastern Forest Experiment Station, 1931-65", Northeast Forest Service Research Paper NE-48, 1966.

Martenelli, M., Jr., "Watershed Management in the Rocky Mountain Alpine and Subalpine Zones", USFS Rocky Mt. Forest and Range Exp. Sta. Research Note RM26, Dec. 1964.

Meiman, James R., Lewis O. Grant, "Snow-air Interactions and Management of Mountain Watershed Snowpack", Environmental Resources Center Completion Report Series No. 57, 36 pp, Colo. State Univ., Fort Collins, June, 1974.

"National Range Handbook", Soil Conservation Service, USDA, Washington, D.C., Report NRH-1, July 13, 1976.

Pereira, H. C., "Land Use and Water Resources", Cambridge Univ. Press, London, 246 pp, 1973.

Pfankuch, Dale J., "Stream Reach Inventory and Channel Stability Evaluation", A Watershed Mgmt. Procedure, Forest Service Northern Region, USDA, 26 pp, March, 1975.

"Research Watersheds", Proceedings of Hydrology Symposium No. 4 held at Ontario Agricultural College, Univ. of Guelph on May 27-28, 1964, 321 pp, pub. by Dept. of Northern Affairs and Natl. Resources, Natl. Resource Council of Canada, 1965.

Robertson, Joseph H., "The Grazing Fee as an Incentive for Range Management", Rangeman's Journal, vol. 5, no. 1, pp 19-21, Feb. 1978.

Sampson, Arthur W., "Plant Succession in Relation to Range Management", USDA Prof. Paper Bulletin 791, Aug. 27, 1919.

Satterlund, Donald R., "Wildland Watershed Management", The Ronald Press Co., New York, 370 pp, 1972.

Schiff, Ashley L., "Fire and Water - Scientific Heresy in the Forest Service", Harvard Univ.Press, 225 pp, 1962.

Schroeder, Mark J., and Charles C. Buck, "Fire Weather", USDA Forest Service Agriculture Handbook 360, May 1970.

Sneevwjagt, Richard J., and William H. Frandsen, "Behavior of Experimental Grass Fires vs. Predictions Based on Rothermel's Fire Model", Canadian Jour. of Forest Research vol. 7, no. 2, pp 357-367, 1977.

Swank, Wayne T., and James E. Douglass, "Streamflow Greatly Reduced by Converting Deciduous Hardwood Stands to Pine", Science, vol. 185, no. 4154, pp 857-859, Sept. 1974.

"The Nation's Range Resources - A Forest-Range Environmental Study", USDA Forest Service Report No. 19, 147 pp, Dec. 1972.

Thilenius, John F., "Alpine Range Management in the Western United States - Principles, Practices, and Problems: The Status of Our Knowledge", USDA Forest Service Research Paper RM-157, Rocky Mt. Forest and Range Exp. Sta., Fort Collins, Colo., Nov. 1975.

Van Haveren, B. P., and W. D. Striffler, "Snowmelt Recharge on a Shortgrass Prairie Site", Proceedings Western Snow Conference, Apr. 20-22, 1976, Calgary, Alberta, pp 56-62, 1976.

Voigt, William, Jr., "Public Grazing Lands - Use and Misuse by Industry and Government", Rutgers Univ. Press, New Brunswick, N.J., 359 pp, 1976.

"Watersheds in Transition", ed. by S. D. Csallany,
T. G. McLaughlin, and W. D. Striffler, a Symposium held
at Fort Collins, Colo., June 19-22, 1972, Proceedings
Series No. 14, Amer. Water Resources Assn., 405 pp,
Oct. 1972.

"Wildfire - A Story of Modern Firefighting", USDA Forest
Service Publication PA 993, 28 pp, Oct. 1972.

Topic 63          Double Mass Analysis

If the ratio between two quantities is constant the cumu-
lation of values of one quantity when plotted against the cumu-
lation of values of the other quantity will plot as a straight
line. The cumulative sum is called a mass and the plotting of
two masses produces the double-mass curve.

Merriam (1931) applied the double-mass analysis technique
in a study of the consistancy of rainfall records and of runoff
records in the Susquehanna River Basin.

The slope of the curve is the ratio or the constant of
proportionality. The double-mass curve is a straight line unless, for some physical reason, there is a change in the proportionality. A break in the slope of the double-mass curve
discloses the time in which the change of proportionality
occurred. The investigator must ascertain why the change
occurred.

An inherent problem in the analysis of the results disclosed from a double-mass curve is that of ascertaining which
of the two variables changed since this is not self-evident
from the graph. The double-mass curve is an extremely valuable
technique in the analysis of drainage basin behavior since it
portrays a picture of trends. Figure 63-1 shows a double-mass
analysis graph.

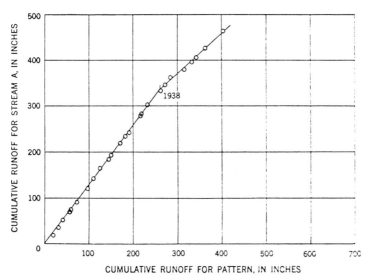

Figure 63-1  Double-Mass Curve of Streamflow Data taken from
    Searcy and Hardison (1960, page 41).

377

A common usage of a double-mass curve for checking the consistency of precipitation data is given by Linsley, Kohler, and Paulhus (1975). Anderson (1965) discusses in greater detail the use of the double-mass curve in the evaluation of watershed behavior.

A comprehensive treatment of the double-mass curve in hydrology was prepared by Searcy and Hardison (1960). This reference considers not only the basic double-mass curve approach but also deals with the residual mass curve and presents a statistical test for significance which can be applied in further analysis of the double-mass curve. Waananen (1969) makes use of the double-mass curve in his analysis of the effects of urbanization on water yield.

Singh (1968) describes an application of a computer to double-mass analysis but Hawkins (1969) takes issue with Singh as to the justification for this use. A computerized method of applying double-mass analyses to a hydrologic series with multiple inconsistencies is proposed by Chang and Lee (1974).

The application of the double-mass analysis method is valid if the physical processes reflected in the system satisfy the following requirements: (a) The control variable must remain unaltered and unchanged throughout the period of observation and measurement; (b) The control variable must be highly correlated to the event being treated; (c) The magnitude of the change should be proportional to the size of the event.

It is a requirement of the double-mass analysis relationship that the intercept in the equation $y = mx + b$ be either zero or not significantly different from zero. If there is a significant value to the intercept spurious breaks may occur in a double-mass curve according to Searcy and Hardison (1960).

If a double-mass plotting indicates a definite break in the slope, the record for one set of conditions may be adjusted to yield computed values of what the record would have been under the conditions prior to the occurrence of the change. Searcy and Hardison (1960, p. 38) present an equation which in their example deals with precipitation for adjustment of records. If a satisfactory explanation cannot be found for the elbow in a double-mass curve it will be necessary to make statistical analyses.

The double-mass technique can be used for estimating missing data. It is not suited for adjusting individual storms. Annual discharge in general is not affected by small differences in the precipitation distribution. Any major change in water use, transbasin diversion, or evapotranspiration in a basin will show up in a double-mass analysis. Schulz (1976) pages 47-53 describes and illustrates double-mass analysis.

Problem Assignment - Double-mass Analysis

Love (1955) describes the hydrologic effect of an insect depredation the results of which lend themselves to double-mass analysis. Engelmann spruce and Lodgepole pine were killed by the Engelmann spruce beetle on the White River Plateau in Western Colorado in a considerable portion of the 762-square-mile drainage basin of the White River above Meeker. Comparisons of streamflow of the White River with streamflow of the Elk River, drainage area 206 square miles, above Clark, Colorado, indicated that there was a considerable increase in the streamflow of the White River after the spruce were killed by the beetle.

Total annual flows of the two drainage basins, expressed in inches,are given in Table 63-1.

Table 63-1  Total Annual Flows of the White and Elk Rivers

| Water Year Oct. 1 - Sept. 30. | Total Annual Flow | | | |
|---|---|---|---|---|
| | White River | | Elk River | |
| | inches | cumulative inches | inches | cumulative inches |
| 1934 | 6.03 | | | |
| 1935 | 8.99 | | | |
| 1936 | 10.30 | | | |
| 1937 | 8.11 | | 23.79 | |
| 1938 | 12.19 | | 26.21 | |
| 1939 | 9.16 | | 18.48 | |
| 1940 | 8.86 | | 18.39 | |
| 1941 | 11.06 | | 17.82 | |
| 1942 | 11.72 | | 20.38 | |
| 1943 | 9.28 | | 21.09 | |
| 1944 | 9.79 | | 19.79 | |
| 1945 | 11.34 | | 26.34 | |
| 1946 | 8.94 | | 19.69 | |
| 1947 | 13.62 | | 23.76 | |
| 1948 | 11.30 | | 19.43 | |
| 1949 | 12.86 | | 26.54 | |
| 1950 | 10.56 | | 22.60 | |
| 1951 | 10.83 | | 21.21 | |

1.  Tabulate summations of the flows.
2.  Plot a double-mass curve for the two rivers with the Elk River on the X-axis. Killing was considered complete in 1947.

379

3. Determine the slopes of the trend lines as indicated by the points for the years before and the years after the beetle kill.
4. Compute the percentage increase in streamflow of the White River subsequent to the beetle kill.
5. Prepare a report describing your work, analyzing the hydrologic processes which could have produced the results observed, and estimating how long the differences in streamflow might prevail.

References

Anderson, H. W., "Detecting Hydrologic Changes in Watershed Conditions by Double-Mass Analysis", Trans. Amer. Geophyical Union, vol. 36, pp 119-125, 1965.

Chang, Mingteh, and Richard Lee, "Objective Double-Mass Analysis", Water Resources Research, vol. 10, no. 6, pp 1123-1126, Dec. 1974.

Hawkins, Richard H., discussion of "Double-Mass Analysis on the Computer by R. Singh, ASCE Proc. 5729, Jan. 1968." Jour. Hydraulics Div., Proc. ASCE, pp 477-479, Jan. 1969.

Linsley, R. K., M. A. Kohler, J. L. H. Paulhus, "Hydrology for Engineers", McGraw-Hill Book Co., New York, 2d edition, pp 81-82 and 133-135, 1975.

Love, L. D., "The Effect on Stream Flow of the Killing of Spruce and Pine by the Engelmann Spruce Beetle", Trans. Amer. Geo. Union, vol. 36, no. 1, pp 113-118, 1955.

Merriam, C. F., "Comparative Analysis of Runoff and Rainfall of Three Drainage Areas", pp 4-8 in Forecasting Water Supply, Natl. Electric Light Assn., Pub. No. 115, Mar. 1931.

Schulz, E. F., "Problems in Applied Hydrology", Water Resources Pub., Fort Collins, Colo., 501 pp, Rev. 1976.

Searcy, James K., and C. H. Hardison, "Double-Mass Curves", pp 31-59 in USGS Water Supply Paper 1541-B, 1960.

Singh, Rameshwar, "Double-Mass Analysis on the Computer", Jour. Hydraulics Div. Proc. ASCE, pp 139-142, Jan. 1968.

Waananen, Arvi O., "Urban Effects on Water Yield", pp 169-182 in Effects of Watershed Changes on Streamflow, ed. by W. L. Moore and C. W. Morgan, Univ. of Texas Press, Austin, 1969.

Topic 64    Remote Sensing in Water Resources and Land Use

Possibly one of the earliest applications of remote sensing was the usage of tethered balloons in the United States
during the Civil War to observe troop movements and positions.

The invention in 1903 by Alfred Maul, a German engineer,
of a rocket-borne camera is described in "The Camera" (1970).
In 1912 Maul fired his rocket near Dresden and secured a photograph of the area from a height of about 2,600 feet, shown on
page 161 of the reference. The camera floated down to earth
by parachute. Decades passed before cameras again flew by
rockets.

Dirgibles and heavier-than-air flying machines, with their
superior camera platforms, led to extensive developments in
photographic recordings and interpretations. Photogrammetry
is a highly developed science based on advanced photographic
techniques and the application of advanced mathematics which
require complex and delicate machinery. Practically all contour maps are now made by photogrammetric techniques.

The development of outer-space satellites led to very
great advancements in remote sensing. Not only the visible
portions of the electromagnetic spectrum are used but observations are now made with microwave, radar, infrared, and ultraviolet portions of the spectrum. The applications of remote
sensing are limited only by the ingenuity and imagination of
those active in this field. Many of the images, either photographic or televised, have been found to be most useful when
the observations are made by other than visible light.

The U.S. Geological Survey has prepared a pamphlet
entitled "Availability of Earth Resources Data" (1976). This
pamphlet refers to the National Aeronautic and Space Administration's Earth Resources Aircraft Program, the Earth Resources
Technology Satellite (ERTS), the LANDSAT, and the EROS facilities. Individual agencies have made extensive aerial surveys.
Among these are the U.S. Agricultural Stabilization and Conservation Service, the U.S. Forest Service, the U.S. Geological
Survey, the U.S. Soil Conservation Service, the National Ocean
Survey, and the Tennessee Valley Authority. Agencies which
have made extensive use of early photography restricted in type
and coverage are the Bureau of Land Management, the Bureau of
Reclamation, the Bureau of Indian Affairs, and the National
Park Service, all of the U.S. Department of the interior. The
Corps of Engineers, U.S. Army, also has made extensive use of
early photography for water resource management applications.
The USGS pamphlet lists the addresses and phone numbers of
locations at which access is available to a tremendous volume

381

of information on aerial photography and on remote sensing.

Another extensive system of remote sensing consists of the weather satellites which are in continuous orbit and which transmit their observations by television. Weather satellites used were the NIMBUS series, the TIROS, the ITOS, the ATS series, the SMS, the ERTS, the EREP, and others as described by Molloy and Salomonson (1973).

The Scientific American for September, 1976 contains on page 30 a LANDSAT image of the Imperial Valley in Southern California. The All-American Canal and the Salton Sea are clearly visible in this special computer-enhanced satellite image of a false-color rendition in which healthy vegetation appears in red. The cover of this issue of the Scientific American shows an enlarged portion of this same view. The cover was taken by LANDSAT 2 in May, 1975 from an altitude of 570 miles.

Remote sensing has been of great value in water resource research and management. Thermal modification of flows in rivers, lakes, and estuaries has been identified. Differences in salinity and in suspended sediment have been pinpointed. Turbidity as it influences the sub-surface environment of estuaries has been recognized. The advancement and departure of major floods have been observed in the Mississippi River and in other rivers. Assisted by multi-color dye tracers complex littoral currents have been identified. Changes in watershed conversions from forested to agricultural and urban land have been recorded; water pollution in lakes and rivers has been traced and pinpointed. The above enumerated subjects and many others are treated in papers, some of which are illustrated by color photographs, in "Remote Sensing and Water Resource Management" (1973).

There is an ever-growing literature on remote sensing and in the following paragraphs a few references are given. Suspended solids and turbidity were studied with color infrared photographs for stereoscopic viewing for the Clark's Fork of the Yellowstone River by Ruff, Keys, and Skinner (1974).

Kiefer and Scherz (1971) discuss sensors for aerial photographs of water resource studies. Their article is illustrated with photographs of lakes and rivers. Aerial interpretations of flood-plain soils is the subject of a paper by Kiefer (1969) in which he presents photographs depicting the work.

Depth to the water table by remote sensing is the subject of a paper by Abdel-Hady and Karbs (1971). Infrared radiometry and infrared thermal imaging airborne techniques can record temperature differences of less than 0.01° C at close range.

Scherz (1971) includes photographs of flow patterns and mixing at a number of places in Wisconsin in his discussion of monitoring water pollution by remote sensing.

Figure 64-1  The photograph shows the location of 3 submerged
           outfalls of an overloaded domestic sewage plant on the Fox
           Ri. r near Appleton, Wisconsin.  Changes in reflectance
           indicated by the white areas are associated with the
           amount of solid present.  Men on the shore or in boats
           could not see the effluent spread nor discern how it
           mixed with the river water.  From Scherz (1971, page 216).

The application of color and color-infrared aerial photographs to identify shrub species are described by Driscoll and Coleman (1974).  Using photographs at scales of 1:800 - 1:1,500 they found that 7 of 11 species of shrubs were identified correctly more than 80 percent of the time on color infrared; 2 were identified 100 percent of the time.  Six were identified more than 80 percent of the time on color photographs.  The technique is best applied to relatively open stands where the crowns do not overlap.  Larger scale photos are needed for low-growing species in dense stands.

Schmugge, Meneely, Rango, and Neff (1977) found that early season observations of soil moisture variations could be made by satellite microwave techniques using 1.55 cm wave length. They describe research conducted in Illinois, Indiana, and Texas-Oklahoma.  This technique could be of value for scheduling irrigation when the root zone is still near the soil surface.

Rango (1977) describes snow cover observations by aircraft and by LANDSAT and various NOAA satellites using both visible and infrared bands and microwaves.  On page 79 he illustrates how natural radiation emission from a snow-covered ground can be interpreted to yield data on the snow-covered area, the snow volume, and the snowpack condition. According to Rango ultimately it should be possible to acquire information on small watersheds in such detail as to be usable in operational wildlife and range management, forest management, and water resource management.

The Salt River Project in Arizona supplies water to 1,200,000 residents. Seventy-six percent of the total municipal, industrial, and agricultural water comes from reservoirs and the remaining 24 percent comes from 255 deep-well pumps.

Kirdar, Schumann, and Warskow (1977) describe the applications of aerial and satellite snow-mapping techniques for the Salt River and the Verde River in Arizona in the drainage basins of which are located the 6 dams of the Salt River Project impounding reservoirs with a total water storage capacity of 2,072,000 acre-feet (256,000 hectare-meters).

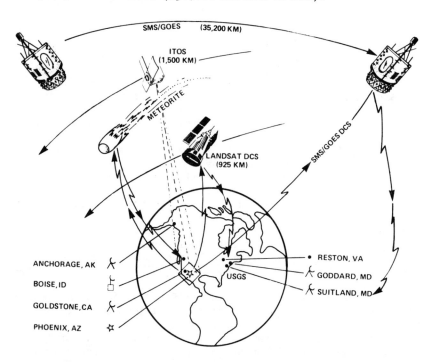

Figure 64-2 The sketch shows the observing satellites and the data-transmitting relay stations operated by the Salt River Project in Arizona to provide information for multipurpose reservoir system management.
From Kirdar, Schumann, and Warskow (1977, page 100).

## References

Abdel-Hady, Mohamed, and Harlan H. Karbs, "Depth to Ground-
    Water Table by Remote Sensing", Jour. Irrigation & Drain-
    age Div., Proceedings ASCE, pp 355-367, Sept. 1971.

"Availability of Earth Resources Data", Geological Survey,
    USDI, 47 pp, U.S. Government Printing Office, 1976.

Driscoll, Richard S., and Mervin D. Coleman, "Color for Shrubs"
    Photogrammetric Engineering, vol. XL no. 4, pp 451-459,
    Apr. 1974. With 6-page supplement pub. by Rocky Mt.
    Forest and Range Exp. Station, Forest Service, USDA, Fort
    Collins, Colo. 1974.

Kiefer, Ralph W., "Airphoto Interpretation of Flood Plain
    Soils", Jour. Surveying and Mapping Div., Proceedings
    ASCE, pp 49-70, Oct. 1969.

Kiefer, Ralph W., and James P. Scherz, "Aerial Photography for
    Water Resources Studies", Jour. Surveying and Mapping Div.
    Proceedings ASCE, pp 321-333, Nov. 1971.

Kirdar, Edib, Herbert H. Schumann, and William L. Warskow,
    "The Application of Aerial and Satellite Snow-Mapping
    Techniques for Multi-Purpose Reservoir System Operations
    in Arizona", pp 95-101 in Proceedings 45th Annual Meeting
    Western Snow Conference, Albuquerque, N.M. Apr. 1977.

Molloy, Martin W., and Vincent V. Salomonson, "Remote Sensing
    and Water Resources U.S. Space Program", pp 6-38 in Remote
    Sensing and Water Resources Management, ed. by
    Keith P. B. Thomson, Robert K. Lane, and Sandor C. Csallany
    Proceedings Pub. No. 17, Amer. Water Resources Assn.,
    437 pp, 1973.

Rango, Albert, "Remote Sensing: Snow Monitoring Tool for Today
    and Tomorrow", pp 75-81 in Proceedings 45th Annual Meeting
    Western Snow Conference, Albuquerque, N.M., Apr. 1977.

"Remote Sensing and Water Resources Management", ed. by
    Keith P. B. Thomson, Robert K. Lane, and Sandor C. Csallany
    Proceedings Pub. No. 17, Amer. Water Resources Assn.,
    437 pp, 1973. (This book contains 46 papers on a wide
    variety of the application of remote sensing.)

Ruff, James F., John W. Keys III, and Morris M. Skinner,
    "Clarks Fork Yellowstone River Remote Sensing Study",
    Jour. Hydraulics Div., Proceedings ASCE, pp 719-729,
    June, 1974.

Scherz, James P., "Monitoring Water Pollution by Remote Sensing", Jour. Surveying and Mapping Div., Proceedings ASCE, pp 307-320, Nov. 1971.

Schmugge, T. J., J. M. Meneely, A. Rango, and R. Neff, "Satellite Microwave Observations of Soil Moisture Variations", Water Resources Bulletin, vol. 13, no. 2, pp 265-281, Apr. 1977.

"Scientific American", vol. 235, no. 3, cover and page 30, Sept. 1976.

"The Camera", one of the volumes of the Life Library of Photography, Time-Life Books, New York, pp 160-161, 1970.

Topic 65     Watershed Management for Water Quality

The beneficial influence of a forest on the quality of water yielded by a drainage basin has been recognized for a very long time. An obvious effect of the removal of a forest, either by harvesting practices or by fire, is the increase in erosion. A number of studies are underway dealing with the effects of denudation on the quality of water. The article by Likens, Bormann, and Johnson (1969) is an example of the results of one of these experiments in which the authors report a great increase in the nitrate concentration in the water yielded by a small, experimentally-denuded watershed. Before the denudation nitrate concentration was 0.9 milligrams per litre, whereas, 2 years afterward, the concentration became 53 milligrams per litre. This is a continuing experiment.

It has been found that a fully developed forest-soil or grassland-soil ecological complex must be present if the purification of waste water is to be accomplished under heavy applications to small areas. This is not the same as the age-old use of effluents as an irrigation supply for farm crops. A very complex ecological system makes up the forest soil condition. The ability of the forest soil to disintegrate organic matter without polluting the water yield was recognized by C. W. Thornthwaite in 1950. As described by Mather (1953) the Seabrook Farms Company, in South Central New Jersey, disposed of the effluent from a large vegetable packing plant by spraying it into a forest.

The surface soil in this area is sandy with the surface layers averaging 79 percent sand, 11 percent silt, and 10 percent clay. During an 8-month period 400 to 600 inches of water were applied by a complex sprinkler system to the 180 acres of a mixed oak forest. As would be expected, there were radical changes in the composition of the forest and in the ground cover.

Subsequent to the work described by Mather, research has been carried out elsewhere in which not only wash water from canning plants but sewage effluent from treatment plants has been disposed of by its application to forest and farmland. Significant reductions in the concentrations of nitrogen and phosphorous were observed. Kardos, Sopper, and Myers (1965) describe the renovation of sewage effluent through application to farm and forest lands. Sagmuller and Sopper (1967) report on the increase in growth of white spruce when irrigated by municipal sewage effluent.

Sopper and Kardos (1972) report on eight years of research dealing with the application of waste water treatment effluents

to a forest ecosystem. The additional nutrients available to
the forest resulted in a very marked increase in growth. Other
benefits are recharge of the groundwater and improved water
quality of the streams. The team at Pennsylvania State University working on the problem is made up of agricultural and
civil engineers, agronomists, foresters, geologists, microbiol-
ogists, biochemists, and zoologists.

The U.S. Army Corps of Engineers has proposed a wastewater treatment plan to take care of the Chicago metropolitan
area according to the article, "Waste Water Study Made" (1972).
The project would consist of giant subterranean cisterns, mammoth tunnels to transport sludge, satellite communities, and
new wildlife and recreation areas. The system would finally
dispose of much of the waste products by applying them to thousands of acres of Indiana and Illinois farmland. It is expected that the population in the Chicago area will increase from
7.2 million to about 11 million by the year 2020.

There are a number of research and action programs,
planned and underway, for the use of sewage treatment plant
effluents on the barren surfaces of soil and parent material
resulting from strip-mining operations. Lejcher (1972) found
that anaerobic digested sewage applied to Southern Illinois
strip-mining areas improved the soil pH and allowed establishment of vegetative cover, in his progress report on this
recently-organized activity.

The disposition of animal waste from the meat-producing
industries has become a major problem. Frink (1970) estimates
that in Connecticut alone poultry farms contain 4 million lay-
ing hens which produce annually an estimated 280,000 tons of
poultry waste. Frink recommends intensive research on the use
of farm and wildlands for disposal of solid waste from meat-
producing industries. He specifically mentions young forest
plantations.

The meat production industry is divided into three broad
functions. Firest, animal breeding; second, feedlot or fatten-
ing process; third, meat packing and distribution. As discussed in Topics 60 and 62 much of the beef cattle is bred on
open ranges or in pastures; hogs are bred on farms and sheep
in pastures and in alpine rangelands.

Hogs are fattened on farms and ranches; sheep depend on
grasslands; and beef cattle are commonly fattened in feedlots.
These are corrals purposely kept small in size so that the
cattle have restricted movement.

The cattle feedlot industry is extensive and highly mech-
anized being in effect industrial engineering. For example,
the Monfort Packing Company of Greeley, Colorado, operates

numerous feedlots in Northeastern Colorado the largest of
which has a capacity of 80,000 head of cattle at one time.
Such a high concentration on a very small area of intensively-
fed animals produces body wastes in tremendous amounts. The
resultant pollution of the local groundwater and especially of
the surface water supply had to be controlled.

This was done by the Environmental Protection Agency in
cooperation with the States involved. The regulations are published in two issues of the Federal Register. The first is
"Feedlots Point Source Category - Effluent Guidelines and Standards" (1974); the second, "State Program Elements Necessary
for Participation in the National Pollutant Discharge Elimination System - Concentrated Animal Feeding Operations" (1976).

Under these rules and regulations no discharge of pollutants from feedlots is permitted. This includes runoff, waste
water such as drinking trough flushing, washing of cattle, and
dust control. The only exception is for runoff which might result from a 25-year, 24-hour storm (see Topics 15 and 19).

Coal mines, underground and strip, have long been recognized as having adverse effects on water quality. Highly acid
mine effluent, polluted with sulphur, has been observed in
Pennsylvania with adverse effects on fish and wildlife. There
is an extensive and increasing literature on the treatment of
toxic mine and mineral industry effluents. May and Striffler
(1967) have prepared an informative summary of the watershed
aspects of stabilization and restoration of strip mine areas.

Aldon, Springfield, and Sowards (1976) describe the demonstration test of two irrigation systems for plant establishment
on coal mine spoils on the Navajo Indian Reservation in New
Mexico. The U.S. Forest Service established the Surface Environment and Mining Program (SEAM) in 1973. This program is
aimed to help land managers with the complex problem of mineral
industry management as it relates to land use and watershed
management. SEAM includes over 130 field studies on hydrology,
re-vegetation, plant adaptability, spoils placement, wildlife,
and remote sensing as is described in the article by Colling
(1977).

The logging of forests to produce lumber, depending on the
techniques used and the intensity of the cut, may have immediate and tremendous impacts on water quality. Patric and
Aubertin (1977) found that diameter-limit cutting of forests on
a watershed in Northeastern West Virginia was not harmful to
forest streams. This study of the effects of logging on water
encompassed a period from 1901 to 1972 as observed at the
Fernow Experimental Forest. Another report dealing with water
quality and quantity is the article by Kochenderfer and
Aubertin (undated). They analyzed 22 years of forest hydrology

at the Fernow Experimental Forest and concluded that it is currently not practical to manage forest land for both increased water yield and marketable timber products but that forest land can be managed for a variety of other uses without impairing water quality if these uses are regulated intelligently.

Swift and Messer (1971) measured stream temperature during 6 forest cutting treatments on small 23 to 70-acre watersheds in the Southern Appalachians. Maximum stream temperatures in the summer increased from a normal $66^\circ$ F to $73^\circ$ F. This increase in temperature exceeded optimum levels for trout habitat. However, where stream bank vegetation was uncut or had regrown the maximums remained unchanged. This research indicates that where water temperature is important, cutting should be carefully controlled near stream bottoms.

"Forest Harvest, Residue Treatment, Reforestation and Protection of Water Quality" (1976) is a compilation of reports presented in 5 chapters on the protection of water quality in the Pacific Northwest. It includes background information, a review of cutting and regeneration practices, logging methods, and various types of erosion together with a treatment of thermal effects.

It has been observed in many parts of the United States that the great increase in soil erosion, sediment transport, and turbidity at a logging operation does not come from the area cut but chiefly, if not exclusively, from the logging roads. "Logging Roads and Protection of Water Quality" (1975) is a study of this problem. This report includes detailed descriptions of the effects of logging and presents design criteria including route reconnaissance, economic evaluation, roadway design, slope stabilization, drainage design, construction specifications, and maintenance problems including road maintenance chemicals.

"Symposium on the Use of Small Watersheds in Determining Effects of Forest Land Use on Water Quality", is the Proceedings of a Symposium held at the University of Kentucky in 1973, edited by Edwin H. White, consisting of 11 papers dealing with this subject. Sopper (1971) summarizes on his pages 38-48 the effect of forested watershed management on discoloration of water, turbidity, erosion, water temperature, nutrient and biocide outflow, and algal growth in streams.

"Managing Water Quality ... A Job of the Miami Conservancy District" (undated) is a well-illustrated brochure describing the work which the District, originally organized for flood-control, is now doing on water quality.

"Drinking Water Quality Enhancement Through Source

Protection", edited by Robert B. Pojasek, is a 34-section book which includes case histories of the effectiveness of source protection in increasing water quality at minimal expense. He proposes that source protection to eliminate or reduce expensive water renovation and cut the cost of waste-water treatment plants be considered.

## References

Aldon, Earl F., H. W. Springfield, and Wayne E. Sowards, "Demonstration Test of Two Irrigation Systems for Plant Establishment on Coal Mine Spoils", pp 201-214 in Fourth Symposium on Surf. Min. and Reclam. NCA/BCR Coal Conf. and Expo. III, Louisville, Ky., Nat. Coal Assn., Wash., D.C., 276 pp, Oct. 1976.

Colling, Gene, "SEAM - Technology Takes on Surface Mining Problems", in Forestry Research, What's New In the West, USDA Forest Service, Fort Collins, Colo., 17 pp, Apr. 1977.

"Drinking Water Quality Enhancement Through Source Protection", Robert B. Pojasek, ed., Ann Arbor Science Publishers, Inc. Ann Arbor, Mich., 614 pp, Sept. 1977.

"Feedlots Point Source Category - Effluent Guidelines and Standards - EPA", Federal Register Part II, vol. 39, no. 32, pp 5704-5710, Thurs. Feb. 14, 1974.

"Forest Harvest, Residue Treatment, Reforestation & Protection of Water Quality", U.S. Environmental Protection Agency, Reg. X, Seattle, Wash., 273 pp, Pub. No. EPA 910/9-76-020, Apr. 1976.

Frink, Charles R., "Plant Nutrients and Animal Waste Disposal", Circ. No. 237 of the Connecticut Agri. Exp. Station, New Haven, May, 1970.

Kardos, L. T., W. E. Sopper, and E. A. Myers, "Sewage Effluent Renovated Through Application to Farm and Forest Land", Science for the Farmer, vol. XII, no. 4, p 4, Summer 1965.

Kochenderfer, James N., and Gerald M. Aubertin, "Effects of Management Practices on Water Quality and Quantity: Fernow Experimental Forest, W. Virginia", pp 14-24 in Municipal Watershed Management Symposium Proceedings, USDA Forest Service Gen. Tech. Rep. NE-13, undated.

Lejcher, T. R., "Strip Mine Reclamation Utilizing Treated Municipal Wastes", pp 371-376 in Watersheds in Transition, ed. by Csallany, McLaughlin & Striffler, Proc. Series No. 14, of the Ft. Collins, Colo. meeting of June 19-22, 1972, Amer. Water Resources Assn., Oct. 1972.

Likens, G. E., F. H. Bormann, and N. M. Johnson, "Nitrification: Importance to Nutrient Losses from a Cutover Forested Ecosystem", Science, vol. 163, no. 3872, pp 1205-1206, Mar. 14, 1969.

"Logging Roads and Protection of Water Quality", Water Div. Region X, U.S. Environmental Protection Agency, Seattle, Wash., Report No. EPA 910/9-75-007, 312 pp, Mar. 1975.

"Managing Water Quality ... A Job of the Miami Conservancy District", a 12-page illustrated pamphlet pub. by The Miami Conservancy District, Dayton, Ohio, orig. undated, up-date 1975.

Mather, John R., "The Disposal of Industrial Effluent by Woods Irrigation", Proceedings of the 8th Industrial Waste Conf. May 4-6, 1953, Purdue Univ. Eng. Ext. Dept., Ext. Series Bull. No. 83, pp 439-454, 1953. (This material appears in the Trans. of the Amer. Geophysical Union vol 34, no. 2).

May, Robert F., and W. David Striffler, "Watershed Aspects of Stabilization and Restoration of Strip-Mined Areas", pp 663-671 in International Symposium on Forest Hydrology, ed. by Wm. E. Sopper and Howard W. Lull, Pergamon Press, 813 pp, 1967.

Patric, J. H., and G. M. Aubertin, "Long-Term Effects of Repeated Logging on an Appalachian Stream", Jour. of Forestry, vol. 75, no. 8, pp 492-494, Aug. 1977.

Sagmuller, C. J., and W. E. Sopper, "Effect of Municipal Sewage Effluent Irrigation on Height Growth of White Spruce", Jour. of Forestry 65:822-823, Nov. 1967.

Sopper, Wm. E., "Watershed Management", Natl. Water Commission Report NWC 71-008, 149 pp, Sept. 1971

Sopper, Wm. E., and L. T. Kardos, "Effects of Municipal Wastewater Disposal on the Forest Ecosystem", Jour. of Forestry pp 540-545, Sept. 1972.

"State Program Elements Necessary for Participation in the National Pollutant Discharge Elimination System - Concentrated Animal Feeding Operations, EPA", Federal Register, Part III, vol. 41, no. 54, pp 11458-11461, Mar. 18,1976.

Swift, Lloyd W., Jr., and James B. Messer, "Forest Cuttings Raise Temperatures of Small Streams in the Southern Appalachians", Jour. of Soil and Water Conservation, vol. 26, no. 3, pp 111-116, May-June, 1971.

"Symposium on the Use of Small Watersheds in Determining
   Effects of Forest Land Use on Water Quality", Proceedings
   of a meeting held at the Univ. of Kentucky, May 22-23,
   1973, ed. by Edwin H. White, pub. by the Univ. of
   Kentucky, Lexington, 106 pp, 1973.

"Waste Water Study Made", The Denver Post, p 86, Sunday,
   Nov. 5, 1972.

SECTION XV

WATER RIGHTS AND WATER LAW

Topic 66        Water Rights and Water Law

The hydrologist, water resources developer or manager, if
he is to be professionally effective, must recognize water law
and rights. Law serves to regulate the relations between men
and groups of men. Without regard to form of government law
tends to express the will of the majority of the people at any
particular time and place. This is especially true of water
law as it applies to water rights, contracts, exchanges, interstate compacts, and international treaties.

Water Rights

Under the riparian rights doctrine equal rights to use
water are possessed by the owners of the land touching the
water course. A fundamental right of a riparian owner, in its
strictest interpretation, is to have the stream flow as it did
in nature unimpaired in quality and undiminished in quantity.
This doctrine developed in the old world where there was a uniform precipitation and abundant water throughout the year.

"One Third of the Nation's Land" (1970), a report by the
Public Land Review Commission under the Chairmanship of
Wayne N. Aspinall, reviews water resources in Chapter 8, pages
141-155. The riparian system is discussed on page 142 in which
3 major features are brought out. The first is that water may
be used only by a riparian land owner on riparian land and
within the natural drainage basin of the stream; second, that
water is neither acquired by use nor lost by non-use; and,
third, that should shortages develop all users would share
proportionately the water available. Strictly applied, this
doctrine becomes unworkable.

Although the history of water rights goes back for over
five thousand years, the doctrine of Prior Appropriation was
developed in the Western United States. Under this doctrine
ownership of land does not include ownership or control of
water simply because the water flows through or is a boundary
of the land. The one who first put the water to beneficial use
acquired a first right to that water. Those who came later
acquired water rights of lower orders of priority.

Trelease (1964) has written a condensed summary on water
law. Sax (1967) summarized the Federal Reclamation law. A
comprehensive review of the general subject is the article by
Thomas (1969) "Water Laws and Concepts". "Legal Aspects of

Drainage in New England" is the subject of a bibliography
(1971).

The legal implications of water not naturally available to
a drainage basin but resulting from atmospheric water resources
practices are discussed by Davis (1969). A day-long Symposium
sponsored jointly by the American Bar Foundation and the American Association for the Advancement of Science together with
several professional societies, on the law in relation to
Weather Modification,was held in Denver, Colorado, as part of
the February 1977 Annual Meeting of the AAAS. Strain (1977) reported on that Symposium.

The complexity of dealing with water resources is illustrated by the decision of Superior Judge Kenneth Eymann as
described in the article, "Judge Decides Steam is Mineral",
(1976). He decided that steam used for electric power generation in a geo-thermal area in California known as the Geysers
in Sonoma County, is a mineral rather than a water resource.

Water Law

With reference to groundwater there are four doctrines:
(a) the English Common-Law Doctrine or Absolute-Ownership Rule;
(b) the American Rule or Reasonable-Use Doctrine; (c) the
California Doctrine or Correlative-Rights Rule; (d) the Doctrine of Prior Appropriation or Prior-Rights Rule. An outstanding presentation with comparisons of the workings of the
four doctrines is contained in the Bulletin by Farmer (1960).

The laws pertaining to groundwater are in a developmental
stage in most states. Radosevich, Nobe, Allardice, and
Kirkwood (1976) describe the evolution and administration of
Colorado water law; included is a review of groundwater law in
their Chapter 8. Rice (1975) has prepared an informative pamphlet including a glossary of terms as used in water engineering in Colorado.

A special case pertaining to some of the areas in the
Southwestern United States, which received grants prior to the
Treaty of Guadalupe Hidalgo of 1846, is the so-called "Pueblo
Right", as described by Clark (1964). This Right, strictly
interpreted, assigns a paramount right to all water needed by a
community for its continued growth. The water referred to
would be all water naturally in the drainage basin in which the
Pueblo is located, to include surface water, including contributing tributaries, groundwater, and impounded flood flows.
The Pueblo Right is perpetual and cannot be lost by failure to
continue its exercise.

The City of Los Angles, California, Las Vegas and Albuquerque, New Mexico, and areas in Arizona and Texas where

pueblo rights were brought into being before the Republic of Texas joined the United States, continue their growth under the Pueblo Water Right concept.

At the direction of the National Water Commission "A Summary Digest of State Water Laws" was prepared in an 826-page volume in which Chapter 14 summarizes the water laws of Indiana. The Indiana Flood Control and Water Resources Commission can arbitrate between the users of surface waters. The Groundwater Conservation Act of 1951 provided that the Department of Conservation may restrict the use of groundwater if it finds that the withdrawal is exceeding or threatening to exceed natural replenishments. The Stream Pollution Control Board determines what qualities and properties of water indicate a polluted condition for streams or other waters of the State. This Board deals with the Federal Government on water pollution matters.

As conflicts and disputes develop over the use of waters from a common source and as the geologic entity of groundwater systems becomes recognized, and furthermore as interactions develop between surface and groundwater, especially with reference to pollution abatement and water-quality control, the Indiana Water Law will inevitably tend toward a modification of the absolute ownership concept of 1860 and take on more of the principles of the doctrine of prior appropriation.

Federal and State Water Law

The concept of Federal vs State and private water rights has been a source of litigation preceding the existence of the United States. Stone (1967) in his Chapter 3 traces the historical development of navigation as a public use.

The navigability concept originally applied to tide waters but it was extended, as reviewed by Stone (1967), to include rivers and lakes. It was then reasoned that, since the rivers were navigable by virtue of water supplied to the navigable portions by inflowing streams such tributaries were considered themselves navigable and therefore under the jurisdiction of the United States.

The concept of navigability which implies that the river bottom itself is no longer private property controlled by the owner or by the State has been subject to challenges. Judge Clause J. Hume, as reported by Meyers (1977), levied a fine of $50.00 each on three individuals whom he considered guilty of trespass when they floated on a raft in the Colorado River through private property near Parshall, Colorado. The fact that the floaters did not cross private land to reach the stream was not considered pertinent. The decision is being appealed.

The concepts of jurisdiction over the water resource in the original 13 Colonies did not carry over into the States created subsequently from land acquisitions and purchases by the United States. The ownership of water in other than in the 13 original States has not yet been resolved. An important United States Supreme Court decision is referred to in the following quotation from "One Third of the Nation's Land" (1970) page 142: "However, in 1955, the Supreme Court in the Pelton Dam decision [4] indicated that the withdrawal or reservation of Federal lands for specified purposes also reserved rights to use water on such lands, even though the legislative or executive action made no mention of water or its use. Under this doctrine such reserved water rights would carry a priority as of the date of the reservation or withdrawal of the lands. [4] Federal Power Commission v. Oregon, 349 U. S. 435 (1955)."

The significance of the Pelton Dam decision in relation to private and state water rights has never been clarified. Another complication is the ownership of water by the Indians. Does their ownership of the land and the natural resources as either set forth or omitted in treaties with the Indian Tribes include the water rights?

A course book in law and public policy dealing specifically with water resource management was prepared as a 984-page volume by Meyers and Tarlock (1971) in which they discuss and analyze specific litigations.

In order to have climatological and hydrologic data admissible in litigations it is necessary that their impartiality and technical validity be established. "Weather Records in Private Litigation" (1974) is a pamphlet prepared by NOAA concerning availability and certification of official weather records. Similarly streamflow and groundwater data to be acceptable in litigation must be certified by the U.S. Geological Survey.

Extremely rapid scientific advances in engineering technology, nuclear physics, space exploration, genetics, and moral and religious codes, together with complexities introduced by management of the environment, require a profundity of technical knowledge by the legal profession not previously recognized as pointed out by Morris (1963).

A definitive work in 3 volumes is "Water Rights Laws in the Nineteen Western States", begun by Wells A. Hutchins (1971) and completed by Harold H. Ellis and J. Peter DeBraal. Land use is intimately related to water rights and water law as discussed in Topic 61.

# References

"A Summary-Digest of State Water Laws", Richard L. Dewsnup, Dallin W. Jensen, editors, Robert W. Swenson, Associate Editor, The National Water Commission, transmitted to the President May 16, 1973.

Clark, Robert Emmet, "New Mexico Water Resources Law", Div. of Government Research, Univ. of New Mexico, Albuquerque, 1964.

Davis, Ray J., Principal Investigator, Univ. of Arizona, "The Legal Implications of Atmospheric Water Resources Development and Management", prepared for the Bur. of Reclamation, Oct. 1968. Pub. by Bur. of Reclamation, Denver Federal Center, Denver, Colo. Jan. 1969.

Farmer, Edward J., "Colorado's Ground-Water Problems . . . . Water and the Law", Bulletin No. 505-S, Colo. State Univ. Exp. Station, Fort Collins, Colo. Jan. 1960.

Hutchins, Wells A., completed by Harold H. Ellis and J. Peter DeBraal, "Water Rights Laws in the Nineteen Western States", in 3 volumes:
    Vol. I, Chapters 1-9, 650 pp, 1971,
    Vol. II, Chapters 10-20, 756 pp, 1974.
    Vol. III, Chapters 21-23, 793 pp, 1977.
All 3 volumes are identified as Misc. Publication No. 1206. Natural Resources Economics Div., Economic Research Service, USDA, Washington, D.C.

"Judge Decides Steam is Mineral - California Energy Issue", The Denver Post Page 14E, June 6, 1976.

"Legal Aspects of Drainage in New England", A Bibliography, Report WRSIC 71-212, Water Resources Scientific Information Center, UDSI, Washington, D.C., 125 pp, Oct. 1971.

Meyers, Charles J., and A. Dan Tarlock, "Water Resource Management" (A course-book in Law and Public Policy) The Foundation Press, Inc., Mineola, N. Y., 984 pp, 1971.

Meyers, Charlie, "Colorado River Floaters Fined - Private Property Trespass", The Denver Post, page 36, Apr. 27, 1977.

Morris, Edward A., "Lawyers and Scientists", Calif. State Bar Journal, July-Aug. 1963.

"One Third of the Nation's Land", A Report to the President and to the Congress by the Public Land Law Review Commission, prepared under the Chairmanship of Wayne N. Aspinall. 342 pages, U.S. Government Printing Office, June, 1970.

Radosevich, G. E., K. C. Nobe, D. Allardice, and C. Kirkwood, "Evolution and Administration of Colorado Water Law: 1876-1976", Water Resources Publications, Fort Collins, Colo., 280 pp, 1976.

Rice, Leonard, "Water Engineering in Colorado", Leonard Rice Consulting Water Engineers, Inc.; 31 pages, Denver, Colo. Jan. 1975.

Sax, Joseph L., "Federal Reclamation Law", Vol. 2 of Waters and Water Rights - A Treatise on the Law of Waters and Allied Problems, Robert Emmet Clark, ed-in-chief, The Allen Smith Co., Indianapolis, Ind., 1967.

Stone, Albert W., "Section 37. Use of Inland Waters for Navigation and Recreation", in Vol. 1 of Waters and Water Rights - A Treatise on the Law of Waters and Allied Problems, Robert Emmet Clark, ed-in-chief, The Allen Smith Co., Indianapolis, Ind., 598 pp, 1967.

Strain, Peggy, "Weather Modifying in Quandary of Law", The Denver Post, page 30, Feb. 23, 1977.

Thomas, Harold E., "Water Laws and Concepts", EOS, Trans. Amer. Geophysical Union, vol. 50 no. 2, pp 40-50, Feb. 1969.

Trelease, Frank J., "Water Law", Section 27, Handbook of Applied Hydrology, Ven Te Chow, ed-in-chief, McGraw-Hill Book Co., New York, 1964.

"Weather Records in Private Litigation", Environmental Information Summaries C-1, NOAA, Natl. Climatic Center, Asheville N.C., 4 pp, Sept. 1974.

# SECTION XVI

## PROJECT PLANNING

Topic 67    Project Planning Principles and Standards

The hydrology of a drainage basin is fundamentally important in water resource project planning but it may or may not
be the critical consideration. Constraints on water resource
development may be classified as: technical, among which are,
geology, hydrology, engineering design and construction; economic and budgetary; and legal. Technical considerations have
rarely prevented development of a project.

Economic considerations involve the computation of the
benefit-cost ratios. In other words, is the project worth the
investment? Benefits are classified as direct, indirect, and
intangible. In computing alternative costs for multiple-
purpose projects which might include water supply, irrigation,
hydropower, navigation, flood control, pollution control, recreation, and possibly others, the Separable Costs - Remaining
Benefits approach is used. The tentative designs are made and
total costs computed as if the project were to be built only
for one of the multiple purposes. This is done for each of the
multiple purposes.

Senate Document No. 97 (1962) established guidelines used
for many years in the United States. Dixon's (1964) Section
26-I in the Handbook of Applied Hydrology is a condense treatment of project planning as it was performed up to the early
1970's.

"Pamphlet No. 1120-2-1" (1967) describes 18 major steps in
the conception, authorization, and construction of Corps of
Engineers' projects for water resources development as pursued
prior to the early 1970's. Schad and Boswell (1968) have
written a very informative review of Congressional handling of
Water Resources legislation before the environmental crusade.

Analysis of the alternative costs indicates whether or not
it would be better to build the project for a single purpose
or to combine several purposes. For example, a municipal water
supply reservoir may require just as extensive a foundation
preparation and a spillway as would a much larger flood-control
dam at the same site. For economic justification and arrival
at a benefit-cost ratio, a judicious balance is attained between separate and multiple-purpose costs and the benefits.
For each estimated benefit, the added cost to a multiple-
purpose project must be less than the cost of an alternative
single-purpose feature.

Economic and political considerations often exert major influences on decisions on water resource development as reviewed by Smith (1966) in his fascinating book on the politics of conservation. White (1969) analyzes six major strategies which have been employed to approach decisions on water management. There is not sufficient water available in most river basins to satisfy the complete requirements of any of the multiple purposes for which water resources are developed. An example of an extensive literature dealing with the recreational aspects of water is the review by Gomez and Crane (1968) of competition for recreation water in California.

"River Management" (1967) is a 258-page volume containing a total of 17 papers dealing mostly with river management in England under four general subjects: (1) Problems of Measurement in Relation to River Management; (2) River Management in Relation to River Flow; (3) Control of River Quality; (4) The Present State of Knowledge and Problems Awaiting Solution.

Maass, Hufschmidt, Dorfman, Thomas, Marglin, and Fair (1962) prepared an outstanding work on the design of water resource systems. This book was among the first to describe and illustrate simulation of a river basin system including analyses of mathematical models of river systems with digital electronic data processing machinery.

Kuiper's (1965) Chapter 11 is a condensed treatment of economic analysis of water resource planning, including a section on the mathematics of finance, pages 406-411.

Whereas decades ago benefit-cost ratios were the main criteria in evaluating the soundness of a project, the public awareness of the environment introduced a need for consideration of intangibles for which no monetary values could be assigned.

Major (1977) distinguishes between multiobjective and multipurpose water resource planning in the following quotation from his pages 1 and 2: "The terms multiobjective, referring to the multiple economic, social, environmental, and other objectives of water development, and multipurpose, referring to the multiple functions, navigation, flood control, etc., of water projects, are not synonymous. Purposes can vary and still be aimed at the same objective, and one purpose can fulfill more than one objective. For example, projects for the purpose of navigation as well as those for the purpose of water supply can be designed for the objective of increasing the income of a region, while a navigation project can contribute both to the objective of regional income and to the objective of increasing national economic growth. His monograph describes four cases of multiobjective planning. The North Atlantic Regional Water Resources Study (NAR) which included the States of Virginia, part of West Virginia, Delaware, Maryland, New Jersey, Pennsylvania, New York, and the six New England States, was performed with the Corps of Engineers as the executive agency.

The Rio Colorado, Argentina, study was carried out by the Massachusetts Institute of Technology under a contract with the Sub-secretariat of State for Water Resources of Argentina. The Rio Colorado rises from snowmelt in the Andes and flows east through arid lands to the Atlantic Ocean.

The Big Walnut Creek, Indiana, study is an interesting case of a multiobjective trade-off between flood-control, recreation, water-quality control, and Indianapolis water-supply interests on the one hand, and ecological and wildlife interests on the other. In this case the intangibles added 3 million dollars to the cost of the project to make it acceptable to all interests.

The United Nations' Industrial Development Organization performed a study for an irrigation scheme for a hypothetical less-developed country assigned the name of Managua. Objectives were to increase the national and regional incomes and especially to increase the income of small farmers tilling 10 hectares or less.

Land use and water resource planning are based on population projections. In the late 1950's and early 1960's it was accepted that, according to forecasts, the population of California would reach 55,000,000 by the year 2020. According to Creighton (1976) current projections of population by 2020 are for a population ranging from 26,500,000 to 43,000,000. Land use and public work programs, which have a long lead time, need to be revised. Creighton's report is a demonstration study of alternative-futures planning of the total water needs for Lake, Napa, Yolo, and Solano Counties in California.

Many of the continuing reevaluations of the Nation's approach to the water resource originated in a comprehensive report, "Water Policy for the Future"(1973).

Principles and standards made effective October 5, 1973 are described in "Water and Related Land Resources - Establishment of Principles and Standards for Planning" (1973) and are still in effect as of early 1978. This reference from the Federal Register consists of 167 pages of the detailed discussion plus a 13-page final environmental statement.

"Water Resource Policy Study - Issue and Option Papers" (July 15, 1977) is a reference from the Federal Register in which the number of project planning issues are presented for discussion. Among the issues are goals and objectives; cost sharing; policy considerations and alternatives; and water conservation.

"Water Resource Policy Study" (July 25, 1977) is an assembly of statements pertaining to the broad subject. Included are comments from the EPA and a section on Federal reserved water rights.

Since the water resource pervades all human endeavors it is logical that the policy formulation remain dynamic.

## References

Creighton, James L., "Alternative Futures Planning", a report prepared by Synergy Consultation Services, Saratoga, Ca., for the Div. of Planning Coordination, Bur. of Reclamation USDI, Denver, Colo., Aug. 1976.

Dixon, J. W., "Water Resources, Part I, Planning and Development", Sec. 26-I, Handbook of Applied Hydrology, Ven T. Chow, ed-in-chief, McGraw Hill Book Co., N.Y. 1964.

Gomez, Amalio, and Dale A. Crane, "Competition for Recreation Water in California", Jour. Irrigation and Drainage Div., Proceedings ASCE, pp 295-307, Sept. 1968.

Kuiper, Edward, "Water Resources Development - Planning, Engineering and Economics", Butterworths, London, 483 pp, 1965.

Maas, Arthur, Maynard M. Hufschmidt, Robert Dorfman, Harold A. Thomas, Jr., Stephen A. Marglin, Gordon Maskew Fair, "Design of Water-Resource Systems - New Techniques for Relating Economic Objectives, Engineering Analysis, and Governmental Planning", Harvard Univ. Press, Cambridge, Mass. 620 pp, 1962.

Major, David C., "Multi Objective Water Resource Planning", Water Resources Monograph 4, Amer. Geophysical Union, Washington, D.C., 81 pp, 1977.

"Pamphlet No. 1120-2-1 - Survey Investigations and Reports - Major Steps in the Conception, Authorization and Construction of Corps of Engineers' Projects for Water Resources Development", Office of the Chief of Engineers, Dept. of the Army, Washington, D.C., 5 pp, 1 May 1967.

"River Management - Proceedings of a Symposium Organized by the Dept. of Civil Engineering, Univ. of Newcastle upon Tyne, 20 and 21 September 1966", ed. by Peter C. G. Isaac, Prof. of Civil & Public Health Engineering, Univ. of Newcastle upon Tyne, pub. by Univ. of Alabama Press, Univ. Ala., USA, 258 pp, 1967.

Schad, Theodore M., and Elizabeth Boswell, "Congressional Handling of Water Resources", Water Resources Research, vol. 4
no. 5, pp 849-863, Oct. 1968.

"Senate Document No. 97 - Policies, Standards, and Procedures
in the Formulation, Evaluation, and Review of Plans for
Use and Development of Water and Related Land Resources",
87th Congress, 2d Session, 1962.

Smith, Frank E., "The Politics of Conservation", Pantheon Books
New York, 338 pp, 1966.

"Water and Related Land Resources - Establishment of Principles
and Standards for Planning", Water Resources Council,
Federal Register, vol. 38, no. 174, Mon. Sept. 10, 1973.
(This document consists of 167 numbered pages plus a 13-
page Final Environmental Statement, Eff. Oct. 3, 1973.)

"Water Policies for the Future", Final Report to the President
and to the Congress of the United States by the National
Water Commission, U.S. Govt. Printing Office, 579 pp,
June, 1973.

"Water Resource Policy Study - Issue and Option Papers", Water
Resources Council, Federal Register, vol. 42, no. 136,
Part VI, pp 36788-36795, Fri. July 15, 1977.

"Water Resource Policy Study", Water Resources Council, vol. 42
no. 142, Part IV, Mon. July 25, 1977.

White, Gilbert F., "Strategies of American Water Management",
The Univ. of Michigan Press, Ann Arbor, 155 pp, 1969.

Topic 68      Hydrologic and Hydraulic Models

The scarcity of complete climatological and hydrologic installations for drainage basins of various sizes has led to the use of models for various research and practical purposes. Models make it possible to manipulate variables, to impose extreme conditions, and to manipulate time scales. For many purposes they may be much less expensive than an exhaustive and often not indicative analyses of fragmentary data of natural events.

In general models may be classified in two broad systems: (a) the lumped model in which all of the drainage characteristics are modeled to some extent; and, (b) a distributed model in which only certain factors or phenomena are modeled. The various types of models are:

(1) The iconic or "look-alike" model. Reduced scale models such as miniatures of drainage basins are iconic. In order to attain a behavior in the model approximating that in the prototype it is often necessary to distort the scale ratio of an iconic model in accordance with the principle of fluid dynamics.

(2) The analog model is one in which a set of properties of one physical system is represented by the behavior of the properties of another physical system. The electrical analog tray, salt flow models, and resistance-capacitance boards are examples of analog models. This is not the same as the analog analyses of transients by digital computers.

(3) The symbolic model in which the properties and relationships are expressed by symbols. The unit hydrograph is a symbolic model. Mathematical expressions of hydrologic properties or systems are symbolic models. (See Topic 89, Mathematical Modeling)

The behavior of flowing water continues to elude rigorous mathematical analysis. Even a slight change in a dimension or rate of flow may result in a radical change in behavior. Hydraulic models are constructed to save effort, time, and money, and to develop the most effective design.

An iconic model is shown in Figure 56-2, page 331 of Topic 56, at a scale ratio of 1-to-36. This shows hydraulic model tests being conducted at the Bureau of Reclamation's Engineering and Research Center, Denver, Colorado, on the spillway and river outlet works for the Crystal Dam on the Gunnison River in Colorado. Listings of available laboratory reports can be secured by writing to: Bureau of Reclamation, Engr. & Research Center, Attn: Code 922, P.O. Box 25007, Bldg. 67, Denver Fed. Center, Denver, Colo. 80225.

"Summary of Capabilities - 1978" is an illustrated 95-page publication describing the unusual facilities and the extensive world-wide activities of the U.S. Army Engineer Waterways Experiment Station, Vicksburg, Mississippi. Figures 68-1 (which follows) and 68-2 (shown on the following page) depict some of the activities of this Station.

Figure 68-1  Working demonstration model depicts flood control, river channel stabilization, navigation, hydro-electric power production, harbor protection, conservation, recreation, and watershed management among other water-resource management activities.  The model is open to the public year-around at the U.S. Army Engineer  Waterways Experiment Station, Vicksburg, Mississippi.
U.S. Army Corps of Engineers photograph.

A unique facility built by the Station is described in "The Mississippi Basin Model" (undated).  This 600-acre model represents the Mississippi River System from Sioux City, Iowa, to the Gulf of Mexico.  Model-to-prototype ratios are 1-to-2000 for horizontal dimensions and 1-to-100 for vertical dimensions. Time is compressed so that 5.4 minutes on the model equal one day on the prototype.  Information on the list of the extensive publications available from the Center may be obtained by writing to:  Chief, Public Affairs Office,
                 Waterways Experiment Station, Corps of Engineers
                 Dept. of the Army, P. O. Box 631
                 Vicksburg, Mississippi  39180

Figure 68-2  Hydraulic model of Imperial Beach, California,
about 10 miles south of San Diego at the scale of 1-75.
Tests are being conducted on several groins and off-shore
breakwater layouts to study the direction of sediment
transport. Waves of different heights and periodicities
can be generated at this facility located at the U.S. Army
Engineer Waterways Experiment Station, Vicksburg, Miss.
U.S. Army Corps of Engineers photograph.

"David Taylor Model Basin - A Brief History" (1971)
attributes to Benjamin Franklin the creation of the first
"model basin", a narrow wooden trough filled with water.
Franklin had observed in a Dutch  canal that the shallower the
water the slower the barge traveled. He verified this in his
model by timing the travel of a board pulled by a string attached to a weight.  Figure 68-3 shows a ship model under test.

The extensive facilities of shallow, deep, low-speed and
high-speed basins and tanks are described in the folder "Hydrodynamic Basins" (undated).

Another specialized facility is the Coastal Engineering
Research Center located at Fort Belvoir, Virginia,  as described by Saville, Weggel, and Fusch (1974). The "Publications
List - October 1977" is a 29-page compilation of references to
reports on a wide variety of subjects dealing with coastal
engineering and beach erosion.

Many private research institutes and Universities possess
excellent hydraulic model laboratories.  An outstanding facility, both indoor and outdoor, for hydraulic modeling is at the

407

Foothills Engineering Research Center, Colorado State University, Fort Collins.

Figure 68-3  A remote-controlled, self-propelled ship model is undergoing maneuvering tests in the J-shape basin at the David W. Taylor Naval Ship Research and Development Center near Bethesda and Annapolis, Maryland. This Center is described in the folder, "David Taylor Naval Ship R & D Center" (undated).
Official U.S. Navy photograph.

The use of models in hydrology can have great advantages. However, there is the limitation that most models do not provide for a free interaction of various factors involved in nature. Therefore the interpretation of the results of model studies must be performed with extreme caution. The model prototype comparison and verification of the behavior in nature of the systems being modeled provide the only valid test. Sample plots as used in forest and agronomic research and lysimeters are models of watershed response (See Topic 37).

Glover, Frink, and Phillips (1967) describe an electric analog which has made it possible to study interchanges between surface and groundwater flows in the Snake River Plain of Idaho. This analog consists of a 4 x 8-foot quarter-inch-thick peg board on which the resistance and capacitance components can be arranged for various runs with observations being made by voltmeters and an oscillograph. Numerous sources of power introduce current to represent flows of various rivers and water systems.

One of the early approaches to the systemization of small watershed data was the work performed by Laurenson, Schulz, and Yevjevich (1963). A more detailed description of this endeavor together with illustrations of the data provided and a listing of 195 small watersheds is in "Research Data Assembly for Small Watershed Floods - Part II" (1967).

An endeavor to bridge the abyss of unknown width between the results of computer modeling and physical reality on a very small scale is the indoor physical watershed model described by Ven Te Chow (1967).

At the Engineering Research Center of Colorado State University there is a unique outdoor model, the "Experimental Rainfall-Runoff Facility". This facility makes it possible to program precipitation events of many different types with artificially-created storms. Since the model is outdoors it also yields data on behavior under natural conditions. A comprehensive report on this has been prepared by Dickinson, Holland, and Smith (1967).

The Agricultural Research Service of the U.S. Department of Agriculture has been assembling in great detail hydrologic data on experimental watersheds. An example of this is "Hydrologic Data for Experimental Agricultural Watersheds in the United States-1963" (1970).

Smith and Woolhiser (1971) report on an investigation in which equations of infiltration and overland flow were combined into a mathematical model of a simple watershed the behavior of which was compared with data from a hydrologic laboratory soil flume at the CSU Engineering Research Center and from a small experimental watershed located near Hastings, Nebraska.

Riley and Hawkins (1976) describe their work on hydrologic modeling of rangeland watersheds. In contrast to many more intricate mathematical models, which are treated in Topic 89, Riley and Hawkins deal only with the summer rainstorms excluding snowmelt. This choice reduces greatly the complexity and size of the mathematical model since many watershed simulation models expend a major part of their effort in dealing with snowmelt. The authors compare their model with the physical behavior of the West Branch of Chicken Creek, a 217-acre (87.8 hectares) small watershed in the Wasatch Mountains west of Farmington, Utah, about 20 miles northeast of Salt Lake City. The authors conclude that hydrologic modeling remains to a large degree the sophisticated application of sound judgement.

Damelin and Shamir (1978) use a hydraulic simulator as a basic element in a mathematical model to determine optimum pumping policies of a system containing two stations in a series connected by canals and reservoirs. The prototype for this study consists of Lake Kinneret (the Sea of Galilee), the Jordan Canal, the Zalmon Reservoir, the Netufa Canal, and the Eshkol Reservoir. Part of the water-conveyance system is a 108-inch dimater pipeline. All of these features are in Israel.

References

Chow, Ven Te, "Laboratory Study of Watershed Hydrology", Proceedings, IHS Symposium Sept. 6-8, 1967, Fort Collins, Colo., vol. 1, pp 194-202, June, 1967.

Damelin, Elliott, and Uri Shamir, "A Simple Hydraulic Simulator", Water Resources Bulletin, vol. 14, no. 1, pp 12-23, Feb. 1978.

"David Taylor Model Basin - A Brief History", pamphlet pub. by the Naval Historical Foundation, Washington Navy Yard, Washington, D.C., Series 11 - No. 15, Spring, 1971.

"David Taylor Naval Ship R & D Center", an 8-page folder pub. by the Center, Bethesda, Md., undated.

Dickinson, W. T., M. E. Holland, and G. L. Smith, "An Experimental Rainfall-Runoff Facility", Hydrology Paper 25, Colo. State Univ., Fort Collins, Sept. 1967.

Glover, Robert E., John W. Frink, H. Boyd Phillips, "Snake Plain Analog Studies", Jour. Irrigation & Drainage Div., Proceedings ASCE, pp 97-110, Dec. 1967.

"Hydrodynamic Basins", a 6-page folder pub. by The Naval Ship Research and Development Center, Bethesda, Md., GPO 886-932, undated.

"Hydrologic Data for Experimental Agricultural Watersheds in the United States - 1963", Misc. Pub. No. 1164, Agri. Research Service, USDA, in coop. with State Agri. Exp. Stations, July, 1970.

Laurenson, E. M., E. F. Schulz, and V. M. Yevjevich, "Research Data Assembly for Small Watershed Floods", Report No. CER63EML-EFS-VMY37, Engineering Research Center, Colo. State Univ., Fort Collins, Sept. 1963.

"Research Data Assembly for Small Watershed Floods - Part II", Report No. CER67-68-13, Colo. State Univ. Exp. Station, Fort Collins, General Series 856, Sept. 1967.

"Publications List-Oct. 1977", Coastal Eng. Research Ctr. and Beach Erosion Bd., U.S. Army Corps of Engrs. (CERC) Kingman Bldg., Fort Belvoir, Va., 1977.

Riley, J. Paul, and Richard H. Hawkins, "Hydrologic Modeling of Rangeland Watersheds", pp 123-138 in Watershed Management on Range and Forest Lands, Proceedings of the 5th Workshop of the United States/Australia Rangelands Panel Boise, Idaho, June 15-22, 1975, ed. by Harold F. Heady, Donna H. Falkenborg, and J. Paul Riley, pub. by Utah Water Research Lab., Utah State Univ., Logan, 222 pp, Mar. 1976.

Saville, Thorndike, Jr., J. Richard Weggel, and Kenneth Fusch, "The Coastal Engineering Research Center", Military Engineer, no. 434, pp 368-371, Nov.-Dec. 1974.

Smith, Roger E., and David A. Woolhiser, "Mathematical Simulation of Infiltrating Watersheds", Hydrology Paper No. 47, Colo. State Univ., Fort Collins, Jan. 1971.

"Summary of Capabilities - 1978", U.S. Army Engineer Waterways Exp. Station, Vicksburg, Miss., 95 pp, 1978.

"The Mississippi Basin Model", U.S. Army Engineer Waterways Exp. Station, Vicksburg, Miss., 13 pp & 1 plate, undated.

Topic 69   Multiple-Purpose Reservoir and River Systems

Very few reservoirs are designed and operated for a single purpose. The objectives to be obtained from a reservoir system may include domestic and municipal water supply, irrigation, power, flood control, navigation, recreation, water quality control, and mosquito abatement among others. Often conflicts develop between the different objectives. For example water supply and irrigation interests would like to retain as much water as possible in the reservoir. Flood control requires empty space in a reservoir. Hydropower is best attained with a steady supply of minimum fluctuations in a high reservoir level.

In multiple operation of reservoirs and river systems no one interest can be satisfied completely and all objectives must be balanced and integrated to attain the best possible overall management. Hirsch, Cohon, and ReVelle (1977) have prepared a mathematical analysis of three methods aimed at attaining gainful joint operation of multiple reservoir systems.

The operation of multiple-purpose reservoir and river systems requires the integration of fluvial geomorphology, erosion and sedimentation, fluid mechanics, hydrology, and meteorology. The application of this knowledge requires data gathering and communication networks, computer technology, agricultural and industrial management, and hydroelectric power system interactions with other sources of electric energy. Rutter and Engstrom (1964) provide a general background for this subject.

Multiple purpose reservoir and river system operations are a proving ground for the knowledge usually compartmented into separate subjects. There are constraints placed on the freedom of decision not only by meteorological and hydrological considerations but also by water rights doctrines, State and Federal laws and International treaties.

There is a tremendous difference between theoretical considerations of separate components of a system and the actual operation in a responsible and efficient manner of the water resources of a reservoir and river system. The literature on the subject is expanding rapidly and only a few of the references available are listed. Each reservoir and river system is an individual and the techniques successfully worked out for one may not be applicable directly to another system.

An excellent discussion of the methods used in the construction of Rule Curves is given by Kuiper (1965). Rule Curves provide guidance for the day-to-day operation of a reservoir. They can be expanded to provide complete instructions

for reservoir regulation. Kuiper discusses reservoirs in parallel and in series and also combinations of the two in his
pages 297-309.

Operation studies for single reservoirs and especially for
reservoir systems are tedious and time-consuming if done with
desk-top calculators. Therefore much of the recent work is being done with electronic data processing machinery. Rockwood
(1966) and (1970) gives brief descriptions of this approach as
applied to the Columbia River Basin. This International stream
is being operated in accordance with the "SSARR Model" (1975).

The Columbia River system includes 56 hydroelectric projects 31 of which are Federal and 25 non-Federal as described
in "Multi-Purpose Dams of the Pacific Northwest" (undated)
(see Topic 91). The whole multi-purpose system is managed by
an interagency group which prepares an annual report the most
recent of which is the "Columbia Water Management Report for
Water Year 1977" (1978). This comprehensive report consists of
147 pages with numerous tables and 56 charts.

The International Boundary Commission of the State Department deals with integrated operation of streams in which Canada
and Mexico have a direct interest. The Columbia River system
is managed under a Treaty signed January 17, 1961 between the
United States and Canada. This is described in the illustrated
pamphlet "Columbia River Treaty" (1975).

An envisioned computer configuration for water resource
management is shown in Figure 69-1 as revised by the Tennessee
Valley Authority in March, 1978. This figure, shown on the
following page, is taken from "Development of a Comprehensive
TVA Water Resource Management Program - Project Status July
1974".

Many rivers in Texas begin and end entirely within that
State. Under enabling legislation a number of river basin
authorities have been created among which are the Brazos River
Authority and the Colorado River of Texas Authority.

The Missouri River drainage basin's water resources are
being developed under two divisions of a broad interagency
approach. The "Annual Operating Plan, Western Division" (1978)
is the 26th annual report for the Pick-Sloan Missouri Basin
Program of the U.S. Bureau of Reclamation. The U.S. Army Corps
of Engineers also issues an "Annual Operating Plan" (1977) for
the Missouri River main stem reservoirs. Both of these reports
include a text and numerous tables, maps, and charts.

Anderson's (1967) computer application to the Lower Mekong
River parallels that of the SSARR (1975).

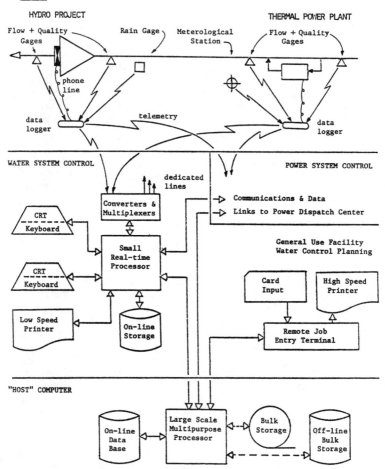

Figure 69-1  Envisioned computer configuration for water
       resource management as revised by the TVA March, 1978.
       See page 67 of "Development of a Comprehensive TVA Water
       Resource Management Program" (1974).

## References

Anderson, James A., "Computer Application to System Analysis,
    Lower Mekong River, Computer Program No. 24-K3-G001",
    U.S. Army Engineer Div., North Pacific, Portland, Ore.,
    Aug. 1967.

"Annual Operating Plan, 1977-78, Missouri River Main Stem Res-
    ervoirs, and Summary of Actual 1976-77 Operations",

prepared for Interagency Coordination - U.S. Army Engineer Div., Missouri River, Reservoir Control Center, Aug., 1977.

"Annual Operating Plan - Western Division, Pick-Sloan Missouri Basin Program, 1977-1978", Bureau of Reclamation, USDI, Denver, Colo., Apr. 1978.

"Columbia River Treaty - Joint United States - Canadian Development of River Resources", Bonneville Power Admin. USDI, 31 pp, Portland, Ore., Apr. 1975.

"Columbia River Water Management Report for Water Year 1977", Columbia River Water Mgmt. Group, U.S. Army Corps of Engineers and Bonneville Power Admin., Portland, Ore., Jan. 1978.

"Development of a Comprehensive TVA Water Resource Management Program - Project Status July 1974", by Water Resource Mgmt. Methods Staff, TVA, Knoxville, 83 pp, Oct. 1974.

Hirsch, Robert M., Jared L. Cohon, and Charles S. ReVelle, "Gains from Joint Operation of Multiple Reservoir Systems" Water Resources Research, vol. 13, no. 2, pp 239, 245, Apr. 1977.

Kuiper, Edward, "Water Resources, Development, Planning, Engineering, and Economics", Butterworths, London, 482 pp, 1965.

"Multi-Purpose Dams of the Pacific Northwest", Bonneville Power Admin. USDI, Portland, Ore., 60 pp, undated.

Rockwood, David M., "Water Management of the Columbia River", Annual Report, Chief of Engrs. US Army, vol. 2 for 1966, pp xv - xviii.

Rockwood, David M., "River Control by Computer", Military Engineer, No. 405, Jan-Feb, 1970.

Rutter, Ed. J., and LeRoy Engstrom, "Part III, Reservoir Regulation", Hydrology of Flow Control, Sec. 25-III in Handbook of Applied Hydrology, Ven Te Chow, ed-in-chief, McGraw-Hill Book Co., New York, 1964.

"SSARR Model - Streamflow Synthesis & Reservoir Regulation, Program Description & User Manual for Program 724-K5-G0010" U.S. Army Engineer Div., North Pacific, Portland, Ore., 188 pp, plus 13 page appendix, Sept. 1972. rev. June 1975.

Topic 70    <u>Navigation and Inland Waterways</u>

The construction of canals and river channel improvements for navigation have been practiced for many centuries. Beckinsale (1969) reports that treaties concerning navigation on the River Po date back to 1177 A.D. and on the Rhine River to 1255 A.D. Beckinsale's section on "The Human Use of Open Channels" describes navigation world-wide. One of the simplest usages of an inland waterway is to transport logs. See Figure 60-1, page 346 of Topic 60.

In the United States the history of canals is in effect the history of the Nation. There were extensive systems of canals in Pennsylvania which are described by Shank (1975). An entrancing feature of the canal between Hollidaysburg and Johnstown was the construction of the Allegheny Portage Railroad, authorized in March, 1831, which moved sectional barges mounted on flat cars on rails across the summit of the Allegheny Mountains. The Portage Railroad tunnel, 900 feet long, was the first railroad tunnel built in America. The motive power was horses as shown by Shank (1975, page 29).

The Erie Canal, which was a major influence in the development of the West, connected the Atlantic Ocean with the Great Lakes. Langbein (1976) has made a thorough study of the hydrologic and environmental aspects of the Erie Canal. Langbein's (1977) article, also on the Erie Canal, presents some interesting facets of the construction, fluid mechanics, hydrology, barge design, and financial problems which faced the intrepid supporters of the Erie Canal.

Extensive settlements took place and many cities were founded along the old canals. Just about at the peak of the construction of the canals the steam-engine railroad became practical and many of the canals drifted into oblivion and were abandoned.

The New York State Department of Transportation has issued a map, "Barge Canal System & Connecting Waterways" (1975). A folder primarily aimed at recreational usage has been issued by the same organization entitled "Cruising the Canals - New York State" (1975).

One of the problems is that of recreational usage by small pleasure craft of very large locks built for commercial traffic. Recreational usage of the inland waterways and especially of the Gulf-Intercoastal waterway and the Great Lakes region is growing and there are many instances of congestion where recreational craft wait to pass through locks.

There is extensive literature on the joint United States-Canada St. Lawrence Seaway which allows ocean-going vessels to go as far west as Duluth, Minnesota, and Chicago, Illinois. Condensed information on the engineering achievement is given in the folder "The St. Lawrence Seaway" (undated) in which it is stated that a ton of grain can be hauled by freighter from Chicago to Liverpool at less cost than a railroad can haul it from Chicago to an Atlantic coast port, or a tractor-trailer can haul it from Chicago to Detroit.

An ingenious water-conserving technique is used in the "World's Highest Lift Locks" (1976) shown in Figure 70-1.

Figure 70-1  Hydraulically-operated counter-balanced lift
    locks in operation on the canal connecting the Trent and
    Severn Rivers near Peterborough, Ontario, Canada.  Hahn
    (1978) describes the locks, construction of which began in
    1896 and which was completed in 1904.  The locks have been
    in continuous operation since.  The lift is 65-feet high;
    the lock chambers are 140-feet long and 33-feet wide.  The
    hydraulic, mechanical, and electrical parts were renovated
    in 1964 at which time automatic electrical controls were
    installed to replace the original manual controls.

Photograph taken by Thomas F. Hahn in the summer of 1976.

The model shown in Figure 68-1, page 406, includes a standard navigation lock.

417

The management of inland waterways involves the application of fluvial geomorphology. Kuiper (1965) reviews the basic concepts in his Chapter 9, "Navigation". (See Topics 32 and 33.)

The inland-waterway program in the United States began in 1824 when a small appropriation was made to the U.S. Corps of Engineers for the removal of snags and sand bars which were interfering with navigation on the Mississippi and Ohio Rivers. An informative review of our inland-waterway program is given in Chapter 5, Sec. B, of "Water Policy of the Future" (1973). As of that year the United States had 25,000 miles of commercial navigable waterways, 15,000 miles of which have a depth of 9 feet or more and 9,000 miles have a depth of 12 feet or more.

Commercial traffic in 1970 on the inland-waterway system, exclusive of the Great Lakes, totalled 204 billion-ton miles which is more than 4 times the traffic carried by the waterways system in 1950. About one-third of the tonnage moved in 1970 was petroleum and petroleum products. Coal accounted for about one-fifth of the tonnage, and grain, grain products, and soy beans accounted for one-twentieth of the tonnage. About 10 percent of the Nation's inter-city traffic has moved on the inland waterway system. Of the total inter-city traffic 44 percent moves by rail, 20 percent by trucks, and 20 percent by oil pipeline.

The Tennessee Valley Authority has developed a very efficient inland waterway system which is part of the Mississippi River System. Stockton, California, has a port which accepts ocean-going vessels. The lower Colorado River, Arizona - California, at one time served as an inland waterway.

Additional references concerning the extensiveness and importance of inland waterways are to be found in: "Big Load Afloat: U.S. Inland Water Transportation Resources" (1965); and "Waterborne Commerce of the United States" (1975). The "Second International Waterborne Transportation Conference" (1978) is the subject of a Proceedings of the October, 1977 conference held in New York, published in a 746-page volume by the American Society of Civil Engineers in 1978.

With the current National need for the conservation of energy thought should be given to the reactivation of the surprisingly extensive system of old canals and to the improvement of existing inland and coastal waterways for non-motorized recreation and for industrial usages.

References

"Barge Canal System & Connecting Waterways", map by New York State Dept. of Transportation, Albany, 1975.

Beckinsale, Robert P., "The Human Use of Open Channels", Sec.
III(i), pp 331-343 in Water, Earth and Man, ed. by Richard
J. Chorley, Methuen & Co. Ltd, London, 588 pp, 1969.

"Big Load Afloat: U.S. Inland Water Transportation Resources"
American Waterways Operators, Arlington, Va., 1965.

"Cruising the Canals", a folder, Waterways Maintenance Subdivision, New York State Dept. of Transportation, Albany.

Hahn, Thomas F., President, American Canal Society, Shepherdstown, W. Virginia, personal communication, Feb. 10, 1978.

Kuiper, Edward, "Water Resources Development - Planning, Engineering and Economics", Butterworths, London, 483 pp, 1965.

Langbein, W. B., "Hydrology and Environmental Aspects of Erie
Canal (1817-99)", USGS Water Supply Paper 2038, 92 pp, 1976.

Langbein, Walter B., "Our Grand Erie Canal: 'A Splendid Project
A Little Short of Madness'", Civil Engineering, vol. 47,
no. 12, pp 75-81, Oct. 1977.

"Second International Waterborne Transportation Conference",
Proceedings, Oct. 1977 Urban Trans. Div. Conf. New York,
pub. by ASCE, 746 pp, 1978.

Shank, William H., "The Amazing Pennsylvania Canals", pub. by
American Canal & Transportation Center, York, Pa., 80 pp,
3d edition, 4th printing, Jan. 1975.

"The St. Lawrence Seaway", a folder pub. jointly by, Great
Lakes Pilotage Admin., U.S. Dept. of Commerce, Washington,
D.C., and Nautical & Pilotage Div. Dept. of Transport,
Ottawa, Canada, undated.

"Waterborne Commerce of the United States", calendar year 1975,
5 vols., Waterborne Commerce Statistics Center, P.O. Box
61280, New Orleans, La.

"Water Policies for the Future", Final Report to the President
and to the Congress of the United States by the National
Water Commission, U.S. Govt. Printing Office, Washington,
D.C., 579 pp, June, 1973.

"World's Highest Lift Locks", p 7 in American Canals, Bulletin
of the American Canal Society, no. 19, Box 842,
Shepherdstown, W.Va., 8 pp, Nov. 1976.

FLOODS

Topic 71                    Flood Flows

Under extreme conditions of maximum probability flood
potential, when a rainfall excess situation has been established, the effect of forests may be inconsequential on the
extreme flood. Hurricane Camille of late August, 1969 resulted
in extremely high peak rates of discharge along the Appalachian
Mountains. In the Blue Ridge Mountains rainfall from 5 to
about 30 inches in a day was reported. Extensive landslides
occurred carrying with them the forest cover. There is physiographic evidence that this was not the first of such storms in
this region. A complete report is given by Camp and Miller
(1970).

Sopper and Lull (1970) have prepared a bulletin which includes examples of the type of information which is needed for
all forested watersheds to provide a basis for sound decisions
on forest hydrology as it affects land use and improvement and
intelligent management of the environment.

The assumptions that there is safety from floods because
the drainage basin may be forested has been shown to be unten-
able. The most damaging types of floods insofar as the downstream channels are concerned are those which are yielded by
forested drainage basins since the discharge is clear and extremely erosive, as explained by Garstka (1972).

"Fire-Flood Sequences....on the San Dimas Experimental
Forest" (1954) reviews behavior of experimental watersheds in
the chaparral area of Southern California. Table 71-1 compares
the behavior of two watersheds following the fire of 1953.

Table 71-1  Peak Flows from Watersheds I and II, San Dimas
Experimental Forest, California, produced by storms
following the 1953 fire in the evergreen chaparral cover.

|  | Dry soil conditions | Wet soil conditions |
|---|---|---|
| Watershed I 32 percent burned | 67.7 times normal | 15.6 times normal |
| Watershed II 3 percent burned | 3.7 times normal | 1.2 times normal |

The normal rate of erosion for Watershed I was established at
2,000 cubic yards per square mile per year. Immediately after

the 1953 fire the erosion rate on this watershed was 28 times
the erosion rate from unburned watersheds in the area.

Kraebel (1934) describes the runoff and erosion which were
produced by the La Crescenta flood of January 1, 1934.  Wildfires of late November 1933 denuded large areas in Los Angeles
County on the San Gabriel Mountain front.  The fires were
followed by a series of storms.  In a 38-hour period the average catch of 7 raingages in the Verdugo Watershed was 12.56 inches.  Runoff from unburned watersheds averaged about 51 cfs
per square mile as compared to 500 to 1900 cfs per square mile
from burned-over canyons.  Figure 71-1 was taken in the Verdugo
Watershed.

Figure 71-1  Scoured channel of Pickens Creek in the burned-over
Verdugo watershed as it was left by the Jan. 1, 1934 flood.
The upper tape marks the high-water level; the middle tape
outlines the probable pre-storm channel; and the bottom
tape outlines the scoured channel.

Photograph by Walter U. Garstka, spring, 1934.

The June 20-24, 1972 floods of the Susquehanna River at Harrisburg, Pennsylvania, reached a peak discharge on June 24 which was the highest in 185 years. The mean discharge of the Susquehanna River on June 24, 1972 was 918,000 cfs. The momentary maximum occurred at 2 a.m. at about 1,000,000 cfs. The previous highest peak was 654,000 cfs on June 2, 1889, as reported in "Water Resources Review for June, 1972".

A very comprehensive report has been prepared by Thorud and Ffolliott (1973) on the Labor Day, 1970 storm and floods in Arizona. An official raingage recorded 11.4 inches of precipitation between 10 p.m. of September 4, and 10 p.m. of September 5 at Workman Creek, located in the Sierra Ancha Mountains of Central Arizona. This was almost twice the previously recorded maximum 24-hour rainfall of 6 inches. Twenty-three lives were lost and the total property damage was estimated at $8,500,000. Most of the floods originated in forested watersheds. Debris jams in the channels added significantly to the damage. Storage in reservoirs was increased by about 160,000 acre feet as a result of the flood flow.

A debris flood is not the same as a high-water flood. Depending chiefly on the characteristic of the soil and the velocities, flowing water may suspend sizable amounts of mineral material (see Topics 32 and 33). Water has a density of one; rock has an average density of about 2.54. Any suspension is denser than water and as the proportion of minerals increases so does the density. Such a debris-bulked flow or "mud-flow" is capable of transporting large rocks. Its behavior is different from that of clear water flow, as described by Croft (1967). Much of the destructiveness of floods is caused by debris flows and not by simple inundations.

The Rapid City, South Dakota, flood of June, 1972 resulted from the rain of 12 inches or more which fell June 9 on the east slopes of the Black Hills and fed the three streams flowing through the City. According to the U.S. Department of Commerce the rainfall was about 4 times as great as can be expected once in 100 years and flood-flow peaks ranged up to 62 times as high as the 50-year flood estimated by the U.S. Geological Survey. Orr (1973) reported that the land, much of it forested, could not retain the amount of water which the rains produced. The damage, greatly compounded by encroachment on the natural channels of the streams, amounted to 200 lives lost and 100 million dollars in property damage. White (1975) in his Chapter V, pages 57-75, has given a thorough review of the history of floods at Rapid City. He analyzes alternatives for future consideration.

West Virginia's Buffalo Creek flood of February 26, 1972 is reported by Davies, Bailey and Kelley (1972). In a 3-hour period this flood killed at least 118 people, destroyed 500

homes, left 4,000 homeless and did over $50,000,000 property
damage. Rains were not excessive. The flow which would have
been less than a 10-year flood jumped, as a result of failure
of dams built of coal-mine waste, to a discharge 40 times
greater than the 50-year flood.

In September, 1969 rain fell intermittently for 38 days
produced by a storm stalled against the Atlas Mountains in
Tunisia as reported in "Tunisian Flood a Major Disaster" (1970).
Frank E. Clarke, who was in Tunisia at the time of this flood,
reports in this news release that, in an area having an average
annual precipitation of three inches, 15 inches fell on the
first day alone. These floods, which are described in detail
in "Tunisie - Les inondations de septembre-octobre 1969 en
Tunisie" (1970) killed 600 people, left 300,000 homeless, and
swept away 70,000 homes. More than a million cattle, camels,
and sheep were lost, 10,000 olive trees uprooted, and thousands
of desert wells destroyed. Ancient Roman bridges which had
withstood the tests of centuries were destroyed when rivers
flowed as much as 35 feet above usual levels during this truly
rare hydrologic event.

Kruszewski (1963) emphasizes the importance of river regulation structures to reduce flood damage resulting from summer
floods in several rivers in Poland.

Channel degradation and aggredation take place in a stream
bed with each flood. Lane and Borland (1954) include cross-
sections of the Colorado River at Yuma, Arizona, for three
years, 1912, 1916, and 1929, as shown in Figure 71-2 on the
following page. Channel scour may endanger structures along
riverbanks.

A flash flood occurred on the night of July 31-August 1,
1976 in the Big Thompson River canyon east of Estes Park, Colorado. A superbly illustrated publication on this flood is "The
Big Thompson Disaster" (1976). Additional references are given
in Topic 13, pages 72 and 74. More than 12 inches of rain fell
on a small area; 139 people lost their lives, 316 homes, 56 mobile homes, and 52 businesses were destroyed and hundreds of
other buildings were damaged by inundation or debris flows.
Discharge at the mouth of the canyon was 31,200 cfs.

Shank (1974) has written a history of two centuries of
floods in Pennsylvania. His Chapter V is on the great Johnstown flood of May 31, 1889 in which about 3000 people lost
their lives. This was a debris flow partly bulked by the failure of an upstream fishing club dam. Eye witnesses described
the flood as a "wall of water, yellow-brown in color, and about
30 to 40 feet high" according to Shank, page 31.

On July 20, 1977 Johnstown was flooded again. Discharges

were estimated to be as great as or even greater than those of
the flood of 1889. A floodway through the center of town was
over-topped by a depth of 10 feet. Detailed reports on this
flood are being prepared by the U.S. Geological Survey.

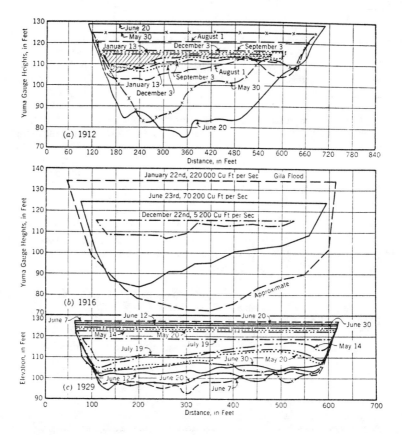

Figure 71-2  Changes of a Colorado River Cross Section at Yuma,
    Arizona. See Lane and Borland (1954) page 1076.

The great flood of 1913 in the Miami River, Ohio, is
covered in Topic 72.

The U.S. Geological Survey publishes Water Supply Papers
reporting on floods. An example of this type of report is
"Summary of Floods in the United States During 1965" prepared
by Rostvedt and others (1970). Separate reports are published
on outstanding flood events an example of this is the paper by
Mathai (1969) in which is included the flood of June 16-17,
1965 at Denver, Colorado, in the South Platte River basin.

# References

Camp, J. D., and E. M. Miller, "Flood of August 1969 in Virginia", Open-file Report, USGS Water Resources Div., Richmond, Va., 120 pp and map, 1970.

Croft, A. Russell, "Rainstorm Debris Floods", Agri. Exp. Sta., College of Agri., Univ. of Arizona, Tucson, 36 pp, May, 1967.

Davies, W. E., J. F. Bailey, and D. B. Kelley, "West Virginia's Buffalo Creek Flood: A Study of the Hydrology and Engineering Geology", USGS Circ. 667, 1972.

"Fire-Flood Sequences...on the San Dimas Experimental Forest", Tech. Paper No. 6, Forest Service, USDA, Calif. Forest & Range Exp. Sta., Berkeley, 29 pp, March, 1954.

Garstka, Walter U., "Water Resources in the West", pp 8-14 in Watersheds in Transition, Proceedings of a Symposium held at Fort Collins, Colo. June 19-22, 1972. Ed. by S. C. Csallany, T.G. McLaughlin, and Wm. Striffler, Amer. Water Resources Assn. Series No. 14, 405 pp, Sept. 1972.

Kraebel, Charles J., "The La Crescenta Flood", American Forests, June, 1934.

Kruszewski, Todeusz, "Flood Damages to Hydraulic Structures and Land Melioration Works", orig. pub. in Gospodarka Wodna, no. 11, pp 419-422, 1963. Trans. No. TT 67-56045 by Karol Jurasz, available from U.S. Dept. of Commerce, Clearinghouse for Federal Scientific & Tech. Information, Springfield, Va., Trans. pub. 1968.

Lane, E. W., and W. M. Borland, "River-Bed Scour During Floods" Trans. ASCE, vol. 119, pp 1069-1089, 1954.

Matthai, H. F., "Floods of June 1965 in South Platte River Basin, Colorado", USGS Water Supply Paper 1850-B, 64 pp with maps, 1969.

Orr, Howard K., "The Black Hills (South Dakota) Flood of June, 1972: Impacts and Implications", USFS Rocky Mtn. Forest and Range Exp. Sta., General Tech Report Rm-2, Mar. 1973.

Rostvedt, J. O., and others, "Summary of Floods in the United States During 1965", USGS Water Supply Paper 1850-E, 1970.

Shank, William H., "Great Floods of Pennsylvania - A Two-Century History", pub. by Amer. Canal and Transportation Center, York, Pa., 2nd ed. 4th printing, 91 pp, Nov. 1974.

Sopper, Wm. E., and Howard W. Lull, "Streamflow Characteristics of the North-eastern United States", Bull. No. 766, Penna. State Univ., College of Agriculture. Agri. Exp. Sta., Univ. Park, Pa., June, 1970.

"The Big Thompson Disaster", (A collection of editorial and pictorial material concerning Colorado's tragic flash flood of July 31, 1976) pub. by the Lithographic Press, P.O. Box 455, Loveland, Colo., 2nd printing, 1977.

Thorud, David B., and Peter F. Ffolliott, "A Comprehensive Analysis of a Major Storm and Associated Flooding in Arizona" Agricultural Exp. Sta., Univ. of Arizona, Tucson, Tech. Bulletin 202, 30 pp, May, 1973.

"Tunisian Flood a Major Disaster", Geological Survey, USDI, Earth Science Feature News Release, Tues. Jan. 27, 1970.

"Tunisie - Les inondations de septembre-octobre 1969 en Tunisie", UNESCO, report N° de Serie: 1957/BMS.RD/SCE, Paris, juin 1970.

"Water Resources Review for June, 1972 - Streamflow and Groundwater Conditions", USGS and Canada, Dept. of the Environment, Inland Waters Branch, pub. monthly by the USGS, Washington, D.C.

White, Gilbert F., with the collaboration of Waltraud A. R. Brinkmann, Harold C. Cochrane, and Neil J. Ericksen, "Flood Hazard in the United States: A Research Assessment" Program on Technology, Environment and Man, Monograph #NSF-RA-E-75-006, Institute of Behavioral Science, Univ. of Colorado, 141 pp, 1975.

Topic 72                    Flood Control

The term "flood control" has several meanings.  We really
do not control as yet the incidence of floods.  We attempt to
reduce or mitigate the inconvenience or destruction resulting
from the occurrence of flows of various magnitudes taking place
in river channels which we have preempted for our use.  Under
natural conditions any high or even extreme rate of discharge
is a force of nature, an expression of dynamic ecology, often
of benefit to the drainage basin's total environment.

White (1975) lists the following six approaches for coping
with flooding: (1) control and protection works; (2) flood
proofing; (3) forecasting and warning systems; (4) land-use
management; (5) flood insurance; and, (6) relief and rehabilitation.  There is another and widely practiced approach: do
nothing.

Control and protection works hydrologically have two general approaches: the first is the construction of dams to impound flood flows; and the second is to increase the conveyance
of water in channels so that gage heights remain below damaging
elevations.  One of the great historic floods in the United
States occurred in the Miami River Valley, Ohio, in 1913.  On
Sunday, March 23d rain, which amounted to a total of more than
9 to 11 inches by March 27, began to fall.  Detailed descriptions of the flood, the damage, and the steps which were taken
subsequent to the flood are described in detail by Morgan
(1951) see Topic 60.  One of Arthur E. Morgan's great attainments was the organization and construction of the Conservancy
District which is described in the pamphlet, "The Story of the
Miami Conservancy District" (1945).  This has served as a prototype for numerous other districts.

Since experience has shown that effective flood control
could be incompatible with other multiple purposes the people
in the river basin decided that they would make flood control
preeminent.  Therefore the dams in the river basin were built
with ungated outlets hydraulically designed to automatically
release stored water at rates not exceeding downstream safe
channel capacities.  Figure 72-1 is a picture of a plaque
which dedicates the dams to flood control only.

Dams and impoundments are treated in Topic 56.  As channel
encroachments continue and as valley bottom population grows,
there is an increasing concern about the safety of the dams.
Peck (1976) has written an informative question-answer review
of dams in his article "Let's Get It Straight About Those Dams".

Another approach to protection works is the channel

427

improvement. This may consist of the construction of levees, of concrete chutes, or the utilization of bypass channels. An outstanding example of the latter technique is the Yolo Bypass between Sacramento and Davis, California. This Bypass, a natural feature of the drainage pattern, is dedicated to the passage of high rates of discharge. Although the Bypass is farmed there are no habitations; the highway between Sacramento and Davis is a causeway. Where the topography permits a bypass is one of the most effective ways of disposing of flood flows. The cover of "Water Conditions and Flood Events in California - Water Year 1975-76" (1977) shows a photograph of the Tisdale Weir and Bypass which is one of five structures controlling the flow of the Sacramento River into the Sutter and Yolo Bypass system.

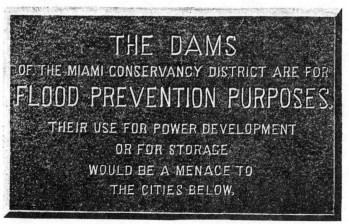

THE DAMS

OF THE MIAMI CONSERVANCY DISTRICT ARE FOR

FLOOD PREVENTION PURPOSES.

THEIR USE FOR POWER DEVELOPMENT

OR FOR STORAGE

WOULD BE A MENACE TO

THE CITIES BELOW,

Figure 72-1   Inscription on granite block placed at each of the five dams of the Miami Conservancy District by order of the Board of Directors and on recommendation of the engineers of the project. See Morgan 1951, page 473.

Flood proofing is a technique for protecting structures, usually business or industrial, against influx of water. An excellently illustrated pamphlet showing detailed architectural and engineering drawings has been prepared by Sheaffer (1967).

Forecasting and warning systems require extensive and highly detailed instrumentation and a flood-proof communication system. Telephone lines are highly vulnerable to flood damage and radio, microwave, and satellite communication components are necessary. "New England Leads the Way" (1972) describes what is referred to as the World's largest flood control and hurricane protection system. The National Oceanic and Atmospheric Administration has published pamphlets pertinent to warning systems. These are: "Tornado" (1973); "Spotter's

Guide" (1973); and, "Floods, Flash Floods, and Warnings" (1973).

Land-use management involves the control of developments in areas subject of flooding. Goddard (1971) states that ecologically-acceptable flood management nowadays is of a degree of interest which at least equals other considerations. His article presents case histories among which are Bear Creek in Alabama and Mississippi, the coastal marsh near Houston, Texas, and Upper Mill Creek near Cincinnati, Ohio. An interesting example discussed by Goddard is the flood control problem at Prairie du Chien, Wisconsin. It is proposed that 205 buildings be removed from the flood plain and relocated on higher ground.

Flood insurance could develop into a technique for the management of land use for flood control. Topics 86, 87, and 88, Urban Hydrology, discuss these approaches in greater deail. It has been very difficult to apply land-use measures for flood control. Historically the river channels were the avenues of travel and commerce even before the days of recorded history. Canal construction followed river channels and then railroads followed river channels and canals. Cities were built in the flood plains as a natural sequence. Whereas a traffic jam on a highway can back up vehicles for miles, water being free in three dimensions simply increases its depth as it departs from the drainage basin. The channel belongs to the river.

The TVA has constructed an extensive and very effective flood control system. Goddard and Gray (1966) describe programs for managing flood losses. Figure 72-2, shown on the following page, is a chart of flood damage prevention measures.

Relief and rehabilitation measures are temporary survival adjustments for those who for various reasons have found it necessary to live in a high-risk flood zone.

A basic reference on flood control is the Bulletin prepared by White (1964), "Choice of Adjustment to Floods". The Handbook of Applied Hydrology, edited by Ven Te Chow, contains in Section 25, "Hydrology of Flow Control", 5 parts all of which pertain to flood control (1964).

Although flood control dams and levee systems have been extremely effective in flood control their very high cost and the preemption of land has led to the consideration of other approaches. Increasing attention is being directed to non-structural flood control. An example of this is the paper by Wright and Wright (1975).

Ball, Bialas, and Loucks (1978) discuss structural flood control plans. Bialas and Loucks (1978) state that in recent years annual flood damage has increased in spite of vast

429

·investments in flood protection works. They suggest a mathematical optimization technique for the planning of non-structural flood plain control management.

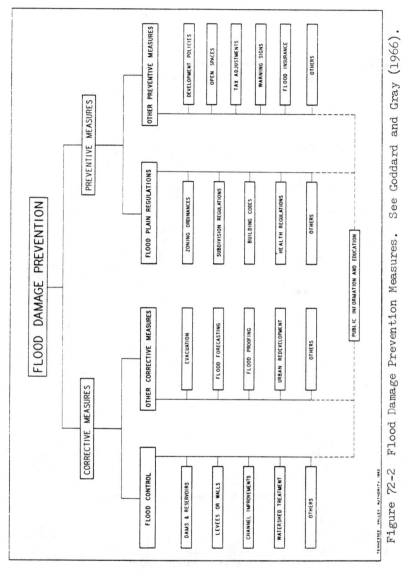

Figure 72-2 Flood Damage Prevention Measures. See Goddard and Gray (1966).

References

Ball, Michael O., Wayne F. Bialas, and Daniel P. Loucks, "Structural Flood Control Planning", Water Resources Research, vol. 14, no.1, pp 62-66, Feb. 1978.

Bialas, Wayne F., and Daniel P. Loucks, "Nonstructural Floodplain Planning", Water Resources Research, vol. 14, no. 1,
pp 67-74, Feb. 1978.

"Floods, Flash Floods and Warnings", National Weather Service,
NOAA, U.S.Dept. of Commerce, pamphlet NOAA/PA 71009, 1973.

Goddard, James E.,and Aelred J. Gray, "Emerging Program for
Managing Flood Losses", Paper presented at the Aug. 14,
1966 Annual Conference of the American Institute of Planners, Portland, Ore., 1966.

Goddard, James E., "Flood-Plain Management - Must be Ecologically and Economically Sound", Civil Engineering, vol. 41,
no. 9, pp 81-85, Sept. 1971.

"Hydrology of Flow Control", Sec. 25, in Handbook of Applied
Hydrology, ed. by Ven Te Chow, McGraw-Hill Book Co., 1964.

Morgan, Arthur E., "The Miami Conservancy District", McGraw-
Hill Book Co., New York, 504 pp, 1951.

"New England Leads the Way - The story of the world's largest
flood control and hurricane protection system ...",
New England Div., U.S. Army Corps of Engineers and Applied
Systems Unit, Motorola, Inc., 15 pp, pub. by Motorola, Inc.
Washington, D.C., 1972.

Peck, Ralph B., "Let's Get it Straight About Those Dams",
Military Engineer, vol. 70, no. 453, pp 20-23, Jan. Feb.
1978.

Sheaffer, John R., and others, "Introduction to Flood Proofing-
An Outline of Principles and Methods", Center for Urban
Studies,The Univ. of Chicago, 61 pp, Apr. 1967.

"Spotter's Guide for Identifying and Reporting Severe Local
Storms", NOAA, U.S. Dept. of Commerce, NOAA/PA70011,
pamphlet 16 pp, 1973.

"The Story of the Miami Conservancy District", pub. by the
District, Dayton, Ohio, pamphlet 48 pp, 1945.

"Tornado", NOAA, U.S. Dept. of Commerce, Natl. Weather Service
pamphlet, 0-524-059, 16 pp, 1973.

"Water Conditions and Flood Events in California - Water Year
1975-76", Bulletin No. 202-76, Dept. of Water Resources,
State of California, 76 pp, July, 1977.

White, Gilbert F., (with and appendix by John Eric Edinger), "Choice of Adjustment to Floods", Research Paper No. 93, Dept. of Geography, Univ. of Chicago, 150 pp, 1964.

White, Gilbert F., with the collaboration of Waltraud A. R. Brinkmann, Harold C. Cochrane, and Neil J. Ericksen, "Flood Hazard in the United States: A Research Assessment" Institute of Behavioral Science, Univ. of Colorado, Boulder, Monograph NSF-RA-E-75-006, 141 pp, 1975.

Wright, Kenneth R., and Ruth M. Wright, "Non-Structural Urban Flood Control", ASCE Natl. Convention, Nov. 3-7, 1975, Denver, Colo., meeting preprint 2526, 22 pp, 1975.

SECTION XVIII

QUALITY OF WATER AND OF AIR

Topic 73              Water Quality

A classification of the quality of water depends on the
purpose for which it is to be used. Seawater, which is very
corrosive and non-potable, may serve very well as a coolent in
thermal power plants or in industry. Water for irrigation must
have a total dissolved solid content not exceeding plant tolerances. In medicinal or photographic industries very precise
limitations may be set on various bacteriological and chemical
constituents.

Chapter 9, "The Pollution of Surface Waters", in the book
by Moran, Morgan, and Wiersma (1973), is an informative treatment of the subject. Their Chapter includes many excellent
drawings and photographs. A condensed technical discussion of
water quality is the Section written by Powell (1964).

One of the most important criteria for water quality insofar as living organisms are concerned, is the dissolved oxygen content (DO). This is a function of temperature. The
colder the water temperature the higher is its capability of
holding oxygen in solution.

Swenson and Baldwin (1965) have prepared a highly informative Primer on water quality. Figure 73-1, on page 434, shows
how the quality of water may change as it moves through the
water cycle. A comprehensive book, "Water Quality in a
Stressed Environment" (1972), has been edited by Pettyjohn.
The reading of this is recommended.

The acidity or alkalinity of water has a critical bearing
on the use to which it may be put. The convenient term "pH" is
used to express acidity or alkalinity. Numerically pH is the
negative logarithm, to the base 10, of the hydrogen ion concentration in an aqueous solution. At pH 7.0 there is an exact
balance between the hydrogen ion $H^+$ and the hydroxyl ion $OH^-$
and the solution is neutral. As the number of $H^+$ ions increases the pH becomes numerically less than 7.0 and the solution
becomes acid. Since the non-linear expression is logarithmic a
pH of 6.0 has ten times as many $H^+$ ions as pH 7.0 and a pH of
5.0 has 100 times as many $H^+$ ions as at pH 7.0. Figure 73-2,
on page 435, from Feth (1973) indicates the ranges of pH which
are acceptable for certain usages. Feth's paper includes a
glossary of water quality terms.

433

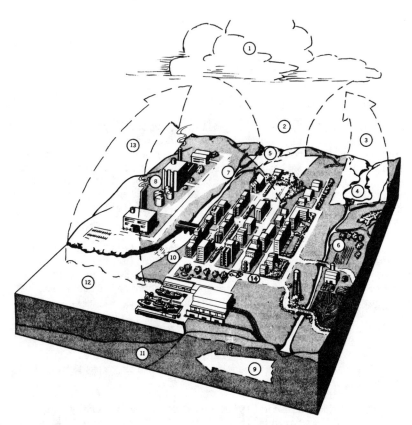

Figure 73-1  How Water and Air Quality Change.  (Based on
    Swenson and Baldwin 1965, page 5)

1. Water vapor mixes with gas and dust in clouds
2. Vapor condenses around small particles to form rain or snow
3. Evaporation increases minerals in surface waters
4. Changes in water quality of lakes
5. Quality of surface water is modified by contact with soil and air
6. Irrigation increases concentration of salts in water
7. Surface-water quality modified by chemical reaction among salts, sediments and biological materials
8. Cities and factories add chemical and organic pollutants to water and air
9. Groundwater modified chemically and physically by minerals and gases dissolved from the rocks
10. Salt water from ocean mixes with fresh water
11. Mixing along salt-fresh water interface
12. Water quality in ocean altered by physical, chemical, and biological processes
13. Dust and spray are picked up by air movement over land and water surfaces
14. Vehicular and other hydrocarbon combustion contributing to smog

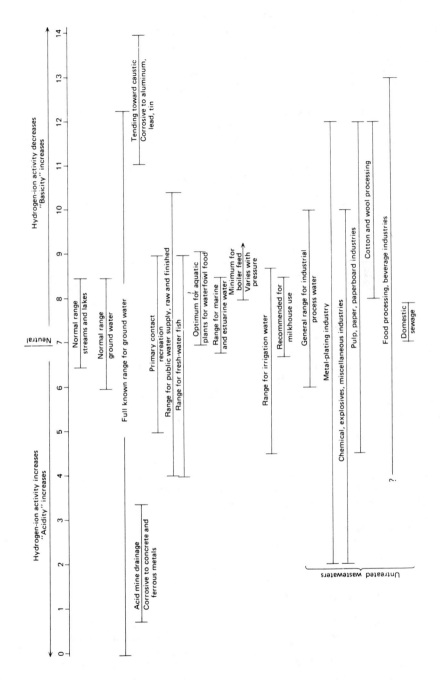

Figure 73-2  Acidity and Alkalinity (pH ranges) in Relation to
    Water Use.  (See Feth 1973, page I-20)

"Subsurface Water Pollution" is the subject of a selective annotated bibliography published in 3 volumes by Ballentine, Reznek, and Hall (1972). They classify subsurface water contamination as belonging to one of 3 categories: (1) introduction of pollutants through injection wells; (2) percolation from surface sources; and (3), intrusion of salt water.

A comprehensive assembly presented in an integrated form on pollution control has been published under the title, "Modern Pollution Control Technology", in two volumes totalling 2,080 pages (1978).

Two sources of information on water quality, in which there are great increases in the literature, are the American Water Works Association, 6666 West Quincy Avenue, Denver, Colorado, and the Environmental Protection Agencies' national, regional, and local offices.

Decades ago it was common to use the statement "Dilution is the solution to pollution" in connection with industrial, urban, and other forms of stream pollution. With the national interest in restoring the quality of water in the streams, dilution is no longer acceptable. One of the best publications describing stream life and the pollution environment is the article by Bartsch and Ingram (1959). The responses of a flowing stream to the sudden addition of various pollutants are charted in elapsed time in days and stream distances in miles. Their article, the reading of which is recommended, is illustrated with 8 figures 4 of which are reproduced in this Topic. These figures appear on pages 437, 438, 439, and 440.

An outstanding example of the restoration of a river is described by Turnpenny and Williams (1977). The Ebbw Fawr River in the extreme end of the South Wales coal fields had practically no life for over a century. Steel works in the valley, which were in operation since about 1850, produced iron, sheet steel, and plate, with the waste water flowing freely into the Ebbw Fawr River. High levels of toxic metals such as chromium, zinc, copper, nickle, lead, and manganese existed in the river in such high concentrations as to be toxic to almost all life, especially to fish. An extensive system of water quality control which went into effect in 1973 was found to be so effective that by 1977 several species of fish had returned for the first time in over a century.

Green (1978) describes the restoration of the Thames River at London, England. More than a century and a half ago the establishment of a gas works and the wide-spread use of Sir William Crapper's invention of the water closet changed the character of the pollution entering the Thames River. Before the use of the water closet most of London's human waste lay in streets or festered in about 200,000 cesspools until it was

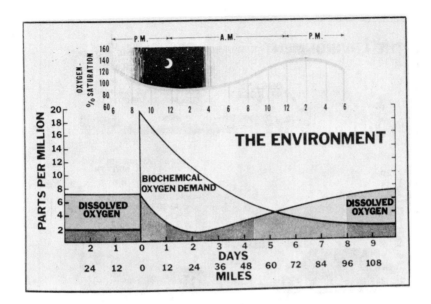

Figure 73-3 Dissolved oxygen content fluctuates according to
    available light, a result of photosynthesis. This chart
    shows the impact of a pollution load introduced at the
    point zero days and zero miles.
    (See Bartsch and Ingram, 1959, page 105)

carted off to fertilize gardens in the surrounding countryside.
The gas works effluents contained cyanides, phenols, and
ammonia. The Thames was truly lifeless.

In the summer of 1976 dissolved oxygen levels in the
Thames were the highest observed in any summer since 1882 when
records began. The restoration of the Thames, as is evidenced
by the return of fish including salmon which has practically no
tolerance to pollution, and wildlife, is evidence of the success of the restoration. In a 17-year period this required an
expenditure of 200 million dollars of taxpayers' money in
addition to heavy expenditures by industries in their endeavor
to conform with the stringent pollution-control standards.

The examples of the Ebbw Fawr and the Thames prove that
rivers can be restored. They also point out that successful
restoration may require constant supervision, massive expenditures of public and private funds, and the passage of decades
before success can be attained.

McKee and Wolf (1963) have prepared an informative review
of the literature on many pollutants and their effects.

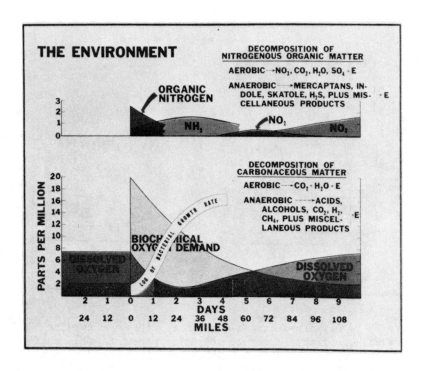

Figure 73-4  When a heavy load of nitrogen and carbon compounds
in sewage is introduced into a stream, bacterial growth
is accelerated and dissolved oxygen is utilized.  As the
proliferating bacteria consume the introduced compounds
the biological oxygen demand (BOD) declines.
(See Bartsch and Ingram, 1959, page 106)

The standards for the quality of water for human consumption are the subject of extensive research and appraisal,
especially as they pertain to metals, biocides, synthetic organic industrial chemicals, and radioactive substances.

Public Law 92-500 of 1972 (See Topic 81) assigned to the
Environmental Protection Agency the responsibility for regulat-
ing pollution from practically all sources including sewage
and industrial wastes, biocides, fertilizers, and water contam-
inants.  Public Law 93-523, signed in 1974, authorized the EPA
to set up nationally drinking water standards.  It provided
that drinking water regulation was to be supervised and
enforced by states.

Many of the provisions of the previous legislation were
redefined, modified, extended, and reauthorized in the Clean

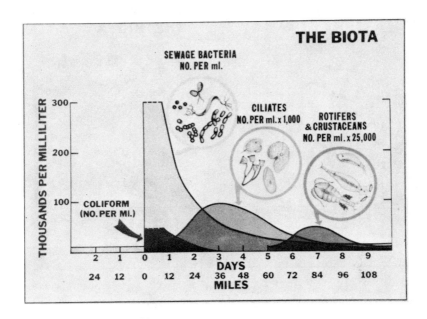

Figure 73-5  The bacteria, whose numbers expand greatly as
    shown in Figure 73-4, finally become food for the ciliates
    which in turn serve as food for the rotifers and crusta-
    ceans.  (See Bartsch and Ingram, 1959, page 108)

Water Act of 1977.  Committee Print, Serial No. 95-12, 95th
Congress, 1st Session, is "The Clean Water Act Showing Changes
Made by the 1977 Amendments".  This 125-page Committee Print is
very valuable in that omissions from existing laws are enclosed in heavy black brackets; new material is printed in
"italic"; existing laws in which no change was made is shown
in Roman type.  The "Federal Water Pollution Control Act"
(commonly referred to as the Clean Water Act) was signed by
President Carter on December 27, 1977 and became PL-95-217.

Problem Assignment - Reuse of Streamflow

1.  Select a river basin in which are to be found a number of
    cities or industrial establishments.

2.  Tabulate the times and volumes of unadjusted diversions
    made at intakes reported in U.S. Geological Survey Water
    Supply papers or in-state publications.

3.  If groundwater pumping is practiced it may be necessary to
    take into account the volumes pumped.

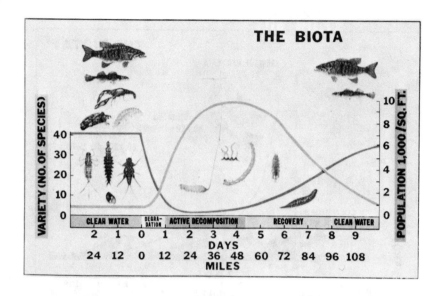

Figure 73-6  The ecological complexes involved in the process
by which a flowing stream purges itself of a sudden pollution load are fascinating in their intricacy and in the
numbers of organisms participating in these processes.
For example, the sludge worm, Tubifec, can prosper in
water having as little as one-half of one part per million
of dissolved oxygen.  Sludge worms are very valuable in
destroying organic sewage pollution.  Needle-thick in size
and only 1-1/2 inches long, from 7,000 to 14,000 sludge
worms may be found per square foot of bottom surface in
sludges.  (See Bartsch and Ingram, 1959, page 109)

Problem assignment - continued

4.  Set up an accounting sheet and compare the sums of the
    diversions with the measured flow at the lowermost stream
    gaging station.  Usually the sum of the diversions exceeds
    many times the actual flow measured at the lowermost gaging
    station.

5.  Interpret the results in terms of reuse.

References

Ballentine, R. K., S. R. Reznek, and C. W. Hall, "Subsurface
    Pollution Problems in the United States", Tech. Studies
    Report: TS-00-72-02, Office of Water Programs, EPA,
    Washington, D.C., 24 pp, May, 1972.  This publication is
    supplemented by a selective annotated bibliography in 3
    parts:  Part I, Subsurface Waste Injection; Part II,

Saline Water Intrusion; and Part III, Percolation from Surface Sources.

Bartsch, Alfred F., and William M. Ingram, "Stream Life and the Pollution Environment", Public Works, vol. 90, no. 7, pp 104-110, July, 1959.

Feth, J. H., "Water Facts and Figures for Planners and Managers", U.S. Geological Survey Circ. 601-I, 30 pp, 1973.

Green, Timothy, "Father Thames has cleaned up his act, at long last", Smithsonian, vol. 9, no. 2, pp 102-108, May, 1978.

McKee, J. E., and H. W. Wolf, "Water Quality Criteria", Pub. 3-A, State Water Quality Control Board, Sacramento, Calif. 1963.

"Modern Pollution Control Technology", Research and Education Assn. New York, 2 vols., 2080 pp, 1978.

Moran, Joseph M., Michael D. Morgan, and James H. Wiersma, "An Introduction to Environmental Sciences", Little, Brown, and Co., Boston, 389 pp, 1973.

Powell, Sheppard T., "Quality of Water", Section 19 in Handbook of Applied Hydrology, ed by Ven Te Chow, McGraw Hill Book Co., New York, 1964.

Swenson, H. A., and H. L. Baldwin, "A Primer on Water Quality", Geological Survey, USDI, 27 pp, 1965.

"The Clean Water Act Showing Changes Made by the 1977 Amendments", Committee Print Serial 95-12, 95th Congress, 1st Session, Government Printing Office, 125 pp, Dec. 1977.

Turnpenny, Andrew, and Ron Williams, "Ebbw Fawr - a River Restored", New Scientist, vol. 73, no. 1039, pp 388-390, Feb. 17, 1977.

"Water Quality in a Stressed Environment - Readings in Environmental Hydrology", ed. by Wayne A. Pettyjohn, Burgess Pub. Co., Minneapolis, Minn., 309 pp, 1972.

The atmosphere is a mixture of gases primarily nitrogen and oxygen. However the presence of small amounts of other gases and isotopes of the principle gases exerts a tremendous impact on the quality of the air as it pertains to life. Volcanos, fumaroles, geysers, wildfires, and various compounds released by growing vegetation and by decomposition products of plants and animals all have exerted an influence on air quality. The interaction between ultraviolet radiation and ozone and the presence of carbon dioxide and of water vapor in the air influence the makeup of radiation reaching the surface of the Earth especially from the Sun. There is reason to believe that during the carboniferous era the carbon dioxide content of the atmosphere was considerably greater than it is at present.

Man has exerted an effect on air quality dating back to the bronze age. Air is considered of good quality if concentrations of particulates and of gases or of natural and synthetic organics are so low as not to endanger health. The concentrations which may occur at any particular location depend on the industrial complex, the size of the area involved, the type of irritants or pollutants, and the density of population. Air flow patterns which depend on the topography and the occurrence of meteorological conditions work together in establishing an inversion layer which affects air quality.

Smoke resulting from the incomplete combustion of wood, coal, and oil, is extremely complicated chemically. It consists of a great array of organic compounds, particulate matter, and of gases, among which carbon dioxide, carbon monoxide, various oxides of nitrogen and of sulphur, and hydrocarbons may be found. When diffusion of smoke is suppressed by low wind velocities especially when combined with an inversion layer, in the presence of water and under the influence of ultraviolet radiation, several hundred compounds not found in the smoke as first emitted, are synthesized in the atmosphere. The resulting product is smog. Under meteorological conditions operating as the "inshore-offshore" wind in the daily heating and cooling of land and/or water surfaces, each day's production of smog is added to that of the preceding day resulting in a buildup of concentrations which may attain toxic levels.

Schaefer (1970) related auto exhaust, pollution, and weather patterns. His discussion centers on particles of the size ranging from 0.05 micron to one micron, the majority of which are smaller than 0.5 micron. Particles in these ranges are invisible even under a microscope. Table 74-1 from his page 31 lists the pollution ranges of particle concentrations

per cubic centimeter. Schaefer reports that concentrations
exceeding 500,000 particles per cc have occurred in restricted
places and the air along roads frequented by automobiles commonly exceeds 150,000 particles per cc.

Table 74-1  Pollution Ranges (Indicated by Condensation Nuclei)

| Typical Source | Concentration of Particulates (per cc) | Degree of Pollution |
|---|---|---|
| Oceanic and polar air | Less than 1,000 | Clean |
| Country air | 1,000-5,000 | Light |
| Suburban air | 5,000-50,000 | Medium |
| Urban and industrial air | More than 50,000 | Heavy |

(See Schaefer, 1970 page 31)

As particles grow to sizes of 0.1 to 0.4 micron in diameter, their light scattering produces a bluish haze. Schaefer
believes that the engineering efforts to clean up visible
emissions from automobile exhausts and chimneys by reducing
particle size to the invisible range are self-defeating. A
single 50-micron (0.002-inch) particle can produce 10 million
smaller-size particles which have a residence time in the atmosphere of weeks or months whereas the 50-micron particles
would settle in less than 15 minutes if emitted from a 100-
meter (300-foot) high chimney. A study of Schaefer's paper is
recommended.

An interpretation by Schaefer of the influence of air
pollution on inadvertent weather modification is given in his
paper (1975) in which he discusses ice crystals from polluted
air, misty rain and dust-like snow, potential ice nuclei from
auto exhausts, and other sources of ice nuclei. His thinking
about air pollution research is given in his pages 195-196.

Numerous instances can be found in the literature of dead-
ly accumulations of smog. As a result of a combination of
micrometeorology and physiography Los Angeles, California,
Salt Lake City, Utah, and Denver, Colorado, have smog problems.
Crutzen (1977) outlines the chemical steps in the creation of a
photo-chemical smog. The inefficiency of the internal combustion engine coupled with the chemistry of the fuels which it
burns have been found to produce most of the smog-forming combustion products.

As a result of stringent pollution requirements there have
been very significant reductions in the 5 major pollutants, as
reported in "Trends in the Quality of the National Air" (1977),
a report by the Environmental Protection Agency. During the
period 1970-75 particulates have been reduced by 33 percent,
sulphur oxides by 4 percent, nitrogen oxides by 7 percent,

443

hydrocarbons from all sources by 9 percent, and carbon monoxide by 15 percent. The percentages apply to all emissions.

Mudd (1977) discusses the physiological effects of air pollutants, chiefly ozone. Fosberg and Fox (1976) describe the use of wind-field models combined with dispersion models to allow planners to incorporate air quality into land-use planning.

Heavy industrial concentrations, especially of thermal power plants burning vast quantities of coal, have been known to greatly increase the sulphur dioxide content of the air in their vicinity.

Air quality degradation by the Arizona Public Service Company's Four Corners power plant near Shiprock, New Mexico, was described by Wolff (1972). The low-grade coal burned at this plant is almost one-quarter ash. In addition to the usual problems of sulphur and nitrogen, the Four Corners plant suffered from heavy particulate emissions. In a modern thermal power plant the coal, pulverized into a dust approaching talcum powder in size, is burned in a blow-torch-like flame. There is no ash pit and the incombustible components exit through the smoke stack as "fly-ash".

The Kingston Steam Plant of the Tennessee Valley Authority when operating at its full capacity of 1,700,000 kilowatts, consumes 16,193 tons of coal per day. Assuming an ash content as low as five percent, there could be thrown out of the smoke stacks 1,620,000 pounds of fly-ash per day. Because of particulates and of sulphur emissions this steam plant is adding new electrostatic precipitators and two 1,000-foot-tall smoke stacks. These additions are estimated to cost $64,000,000. The stacks are of such height as to extend above the inversion layer which has been observed in the valley. Figure 74-1 on the following page is a photograph of the Kingston Plant taken October 4, 1977. According to the folder, "Kingston Steam Plant" (undated), at full capacity, the condensers require 967,000 gallons per minute of cooling water.

Pollutants in the atmosphere have changed the precipitation, as is described in "Acid Showers Bring Discolored May Flowers" (1977). Fox (1977) presents numerous figures and maps describing the quality of precipitation in the Eastern United States. Acid precipitation has an influence not only on the vegetation but also on the soil.

Chapter 7 "The Contaminated Atmosphere" in the book by Moran, Morgan, and Wiersma (1973) is an informative review of the subject.

Figure 74-1  Kingston Steam Plant of the Tennessee Valley
    Authority. This coal-burning plant consumes 16,193 tons
    of coal per day when operating at full capacity of
    1,700,000 kw. The 1,000-foot-tall smoke stacks were
    built to penetrate an inversion layer.
    Photograph by TVA, Oct. 4, 1977.

An extensive research project involving 60 scientists and
several hundred graduate students has been organized to examine
the ecological, geochemical, hydrologic, and meteorologic
functions of 8 small watersheds in the Hubbard Brook Valley in
New Hampshire, as reported in "Yale and Cornell Study Pollution's Effect on Forest" (1977). The principal investigator
for this project is Dr. F. Herbert Bormann of the Yale University School of Forestry and Environmental Studies. Highly acid
rain with a pH ranging from 2.5 to 5.6 (see Topic 73) has been
recorded. It was also found that the forest removes lead from
the atmosphere. The chief source of atmospheric lead has been
tetraethyl lead used to control rates of combustion in gasoline
engines. Recent developments in the petroleum industry technology has yielded lead-free gasolines now in increasing use.

An unexpected pollutant is the production of colorless and
odorless methane from sanitary land fills as described by Stone
(1978). A slow migration of methane from a sanitary land fill
caused an explosion in a National Guard Armory at Winston-
Salem, North Carolina, in 1969. Three guardsmen were killed

and 25 injured. The closest section of the building was 30 feet (7 meters) from the land fill.

A sanitary land fill can be considered as a man-made bog and the biological decomposition of the organic materials produces methane, which has been known for centuries under the name of "marsh gas". The experiences described by Stone indicate that extreme caution must be exercised when constructing buildings on a sanitary land fill. Stone on his page 53 describes five methane control systems.

Two gases naturally present in the atmosphere are under intensive study. One is ozone which is found chiefly in the upper elevations of the atmosphere. Ozone filters out the ultraviolet radiation and a reduction in the concentration of ozone in the higher elevations could presumably increase the concentration of ultraviolet radiation at the surface of the Earth with possible extensive impact on all life. Ultraviolet is known to induce skin cancer. The physics and chemistry of the maintenance of an effective ozone layer are extremely complicated.

The atmospheric concentration of carbon dioxide is also a matter of intensive concern and study. Stuiver (1978) states that in the middle of the 19th century air had a $CO_2$ content of approximately 268 parts per million and a total increase in atmospheric $CO_2$ of 18 percent since 1850. About 46 percent of the increased release of $CO_2$ has been stored in oceans leaving an air-borne fraction of 53 percent. Although the concentrations of $CO_2$ may seem to be very small, having been observed as about 330 parts per million in 1976, the effect which the $CO_2$ may have on the Earth may be extremely far-reaching. $CO_2$ operates to create the "greenhouse" effect since it is transparent to short-wave infrared but is opaque to long-wave heat.

Woodwell (1978) ascribes the steady increase in the $CO_2$ content of the air to a combination of greatly accelerated combustion of fossil fuels and the reduction of the forests and wildlands which has been experienced world-wide in the last few decades. Woodwell considers the forest vegetation as of very great importance. Agricultural land is much less efficient in removing $CO_2$ from the atmosphere by photosynthesis than is natural vegetation. In his closing paragraph Woodwell states that no national or international policy can continue to function in disregard of the possibility of world-wide climatic changes. Carbon dioxide can no longer, in his opinion, be considered an innocuous gas since it is rapidly moving toward becoming a major force affecting the future of the present World order.

In many parts of the World where there have been great concentrations of industry and of population density, the limiting factor for human endeavors may not be the land or the water supply but the quality of the air.

References

"Acid Showers Bring Discolored May Flowers", Civil Engineering
vol. 47, no. 10, p 30, Oct. 1977.

Crutzen, Paul, "Chemistry of Photochemical Smog", a paper presented at the AAAS Annual Meeting, Denver, Colo. Feb. 24,
1977. (Paul Crutzen is on the staff of the Natl. Center
for Atmospheric Research, Boulder, Colo.)

Fosberg, Michael A., and Douglas G. Fox, "An Air Quality Index
to Aid in Determing Mountain Land Use", pp 167-170 in
Proceedings of the 4th National Conference on Fire and
Forest Meteorology, St. Louis, Mo., Nov. 16-18, 1976.
USDA For. Service Gen. Tech. Rep. RM-32, 239 pp.

Fox, Douglas, "Precipitation Quality and Its Effects on Stream
Water Quality and the Forest in General", a 36-page paper
presented at and included in the Proceedings of the
"208" Symposium - non-point sources of pollution from
forested land held at the Southern Ill. Univ. at Carbon-
dale, Oct. 19-20, 1977.

"Kingston Steam Plant", a folder No. F73I10R, TVA, Knoxville,
Tenn. 4 pages, undated.

Moran, Joseph M., Michael D. Morgan, James H. Wiersma, "An
Introduction to Environmental Sciences", Little, Brown and
Co., Boston, 389 pp, 1973.

Mudd, J. B., "Biological Effects of Air Pollutants", a paper
presented at the AAAS Annual Meeting, Denver, Colo. Feb.
24, 1977. (J. B. Mudd is on the staff of the Univ. of
Calif. at Riverside.)

Schaefer, Vincent J., "Auto Exhaust, Pollution and Weather
Patterns", Bull. of the Atomic Scientists, pp 31-33,
Oct. 1970.

Schaefer, Vincent J., "The Inadvertent Modification of the
Atmosphere by Air Pollution", pp 177-196 in The Changing
Global Environment, S. Fred Singer, ed., D. Reidel Pub.
Co., Dordrecht, Holland, 1975.

Stone, Ralph, "Preventing Underground Movement of Methane from
Sanitary Landfills", Civil Engineering, vol. 48, no. 1,
pp 51-53, Jan. 1978.

Stuiver, Minze, "Atmospheric Carbon Dioxide and Carbon Reser-
voir Changes - Reduction in Terrestrial Carbon Reservoirs
Since 1850 has Resulted in Atmospheric Carbon Dioxide
Increases", Science, vol. 199, pp 253-258, Jan. 20, 1978.

"Trends in the Quality of the Nation's Air", pamphlet, 18 pp,
    Environmental Protection Agency, Office of Public Affairs
    (A-107), Washington, D.C., March, 1977.

Wolff, Anthony, "Showdown at Four Corners", Saturday Review,
    pp 29-31, June 3, 1972.

Woodwell, George M., "The Carbon Dioxide Question", Scientific
    American, vol. 238, no. 1, pp 34-43, Jan. 1978.

"Yale and Cornell Study Pollution's Effect on Forest", Yale
    Alumni Magazine and Journal, p 23, Jan. 1977.

The effort to make available adequate quantities of potable water is in effect part of the history of civilization. (See Topics 1, 2, and 3). Many centuries ago it was discovered that water could be secured from wells and the digging of wells is an ancient practice. As mentioned in Topic 44 the ancient Persians learned how to dig tunnels into mountain aquifers. The Roman water systems, some parts of which are still in use, conveyed water by gravity. The systems included canals, tunnels, inverted siphons, and aqueducts. According to Smith (1978) aqueducts made up only about 5 percent of the systems.

The first piped water supply in the United States was built in Boston in 1652 along what is now known as Conduit Street. In 1746 Schaeffer piped water from a spring to the community now known as Schaeffertown, Pennsylvania. This, according to "The Story of Water Supply" (1976) was the first water supply in the United States built to serve an entire town. During the period 1652-1800 there is record of only 9 water works in what is now the United States. Now more than 45,000 water works supply billions of gallons daily to the people of the United States and Canada. The "Story of Water Supply" (1977), a pamphlet illustrated with numerous cartoon-like drawings, is an informative publication.

A superb volume of historical interest is the "Comprehensive Treatise of the Water Supply of Cities and Towns" written by William Humber and published in 1879. This volume includes 50 double plates of articles of a quality suitable for framing and over 250 illustrations, originally executed as wood cuts.

Municipal water supply may come from streams, from lakes, and/or from groundwater. With the technological attainment of water demineralization (see Topic 42) saline water and ocean water can be considered to be sources of potable water supply. An informative publication on water quality as it pertains to domestic use is the Bulletin by Swenson and Baldwin (1965).

Many cities have outgrown their original local water supply sources and have found it necessary to go long distances for water which is derived from other drainage basins. Among these are New York, which makes almost no use of the Hudson River for its supply; San Francisco, which imports water from the high Sierras; and, Los Angles, which gets water from the Colorado River 400 miles away.

Denver receives a greater part of its supply from a transbasin diversion of the headwaters of the Colorado River. The publication, "Features of the Denver Water System", (1976) contains numerous photographs of this system. An example of a report dealing with the complicated problems facing a city seeking to increase its dependable source of water is the progress report dated June, 1977 entitled, "Water Supply for a Growing Kansas City Metropolitan Region - Problems & Possible Solutions".

Chicago and a few other large cities secure their water from nearby lakes. Although many communities are located along streams, the cost of dams and the possibly questionable quality of surface water have led many cities to depend mostly on groundwater. Albuquerque, New Mexico, pumps all of its water from the valley fill of the Rio Grande; Tucson, Arizona, is dependent entirely on groundwater some of which may be up to 25,000 years old; Miami, Florida, Honolulu, Hawaii, and a great many cities in the mid-west depend on groundwater. Highly efficient systems of groundwater withdrawal have been developed making use of well points driven horizontally from a deep shaft. This arrangement in plan view would resemble the spokes of a wheel. Millions of gallons a day can be pumped from a suitable aquifer by this system.

Differences in water quality were recognized in India about 2000 B.C. Foul water was improved by boiling and exposure to sunlight. Siphons were used in ancient Egypt about 1450 B.C. to draw clear water from jars after the sediment of the Nile had settled. Cyrus the Great is reported to have transported boiled water in silver flagons in carts drawn by mules about 600 B.C. Hippocrates, the father of medicine, about 400 B.C. is said to have asserted that rain water should be boiled and strained. About 1885 laboratory examination of London water first disclosed that bacteria could be removed by filters. In 1872 the first successful filters were installed in Poughkeepsie, New York. Clorine was first applied to destroy disease-producing bacteria in water in 1912. The information in this paragraph is from "The Story of Water Supply" (1976).

A modern water treatment plant is a very complicated physical and chemical process especially since industrial technology has introduced into the raw water many heavy metals, synthetic organic industrial chemicals, and biocides. Figure 75-1 on the following page from Swenson and Baldwin (1965) depicts one of the larger water treatment plants.

As discussed in Topic 3, water may be either consumptively or non-consumptively used. For the United States as a whole it is commonly considered that an acre foot of water will supply four persons for a year. Urban water requirements vary with the geologic area but they average 150 gallons (568 litres) per day. Residential use averages 60 gallons; industrial use about 50 gallons; commercial, about 20 gallons; public, about 10

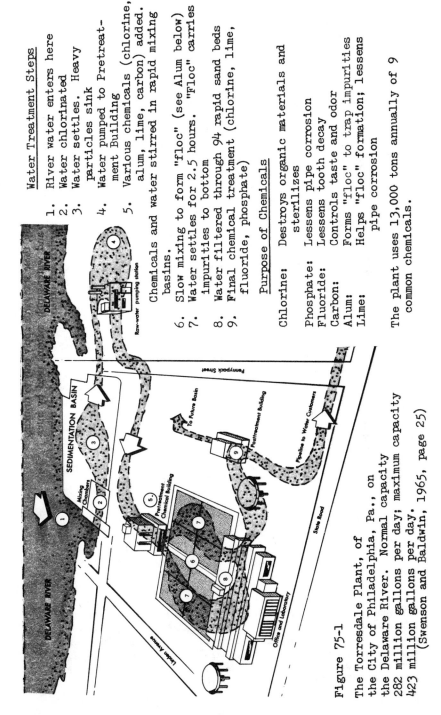

## Water Treatment Steps

1. River water enters here
2. Water chlorinated
3. Water settles. Heavy particles sink
4. Water pumped to Pretreatment Building
5. Various chemicals (chlorine, alum, lime, carbon) added. Chemicals and water stirred in rapid mixing basins.
6. Slow mixing to form "floc" (see Alum below)
7. Water settles for 2.5 hours. "Floc" carries impurities to bottom
8. Water filtered through 94 rapid sand beds
9. Final chemical treatment (chlorine, lime, fluoride, phosphate)

## Purpose of Chemicals

Chlorine:  Destroys organic materials and sterilizes
Phosphate: Lessens pipe corrosion
Fluoride:  Lessens tooth decay
Carbon:    Controls taste and odor
Alum:      Forms "floc" to trap impurities
Lime:      Helps "floc" formation; lessens pipe corrosion

The plant uses 13,000 tons annually of 9 common chemicals.

Figure 75-1

The Torresdale Plant, of the City of Philadelphia, Pa., on the Delaware River. Normal capacity 282 million gallons per day; maximum capacity 423 million gallons per day. (Swenson and Baldwin, 1965, page 25)

451

gallons; and losses about 10 gallons. Except for the very
small amount of water lost from the body by evapotranspiration,
the largest consumptive use is for the watering of lawns. In
many cities about 85 to 90 percent of the water flowing
through the taps reappears as return flow to the waste water
works.

A great many industrial uses are non-consumptive. Much
industrial usage is for cooling purposes which results in thermal modification. Production of steel may require as much as
110,000 gallons of water per net ton of rolled steel. Five
hundred  gallons are needed to produce a gallon of gasoline.
Over 90,000 gallons are required to produce a ton of paper
board. Some industrial usages pollute the water in various
ways. As recognition of the limitations on water supply develops a rapidly-growing field for research and industrial
development and engineering deals with the reuse of water.

The "Manual of Individual Water Supply Systems" (1973)
lists in its Table 1, page 15, the requirements in gallons per
day for various types of establishments and usage. Table 2,
page 17, lists the rates of flow for certain household plumbing and farm fixtures in gallons per minute at various
pressures of pounds per square inch.

"The Water Encyclopedia" (1970) gives on page 243 the use
of water in an average home in Akron, Ohio: washing, one percent; drinking and food preparation, 5 percent; bathing, 37
percent; lawn watering, 3 percent; toilet flushing, 41 percent;
dishwashing, 6 percent; household cleaning, 3 percent; and
clothes washing, 4 percent. On pages 244-245 figures are
given on water requirements for public buildings, schools,
camps, farm animals, and poultry. Water requirements for residential use differ greatly depending on the life style and the
climate of the area. A general figure used for drinking and
preparation of food in a residence is 4 percent.

"Water Conservation in California" (1976) gives the following totals for residential use in California in 1972: ext-
erior, 44 percent; interior, 56 percent. Of the 56 percent
interior use the utilization was: toilet flushing, 42 percent;
bath, 32 percent; kitchen, 8 percent; laundry 14 percent; and
cooking, 4 percent.

Not much is being done in most areas about lawn-watering
efficiency. In arid regions one of the greatest demands on
municipal water may be for the irrigation of vegetation not
native to the area. Applications of new technology to save
residential water are aimed primarily at internal usage. Several techniques have been developed or are under consideration.
Dual-flushing toilets using a low volume for liquid human
waste and a higher volume for solids can reduce toilet water

requirements up to 75 percent. The modern English toilet can operate on 2 gallons of water for flushing solids and one gallon for flushing liquids. However such toilets cannot be used in the United States because under the Uniform Plumbing Code a slope of 1/4-inch per foot is prescribed for drain lines. The English toilet uses a steeper slope. Automatic washing machines and automatic dishwashers are high in their water requirements, especially of hot water. Vallentine (1967) states on page 206 that domestic sewage is 99.9 percent water.

According to "Water Conservation in California" (1976) about 25 percent of California's 21 million residents are children in kindergarten, primary, and secondary schools. A concerted effort has been organized in California and in Colorado to include water conservation education in the school systems. An example of this approach is "The Official Captain Hydro Water Conservation Workbook" originally prepared by Johnson and Akutagawa (1975) for the East Bay Municipal Water District, Oakland, California. This pamphlet, in addition to cartoons, contains carefully-planned problem assignments which incorporate a tremendous amount of information on the water resource.

A visit to a municipal water treatment plant is recommended. Only then can one appreciate the complexity, the precision, and the efficiency of the whole process on which our health and survival depend.

References

"Features of the Denver Water System", Produced by the Office of Public Affairs, Denver Water Dept., Denver, Colo., 71 pp, Dec. 1976.

Humber, William, "A Comprehensive Treatise on the Water Supply of Cities and Towns with Numerous Specifications of Existing Waterworks", manuscript completed Jan., 1876, pub. by Geo. H. Frost, Chicago, 298 pp, and 50 double plates, 1879.

Johnson, Bob, and Ben Akutagawa, "The Official Captain Hydro Water Conservation Workbook", East Bay Municipal Utility District, Oakland, Calif., 32 pp, 1975. (Reprint distributed by the Denver Water Dept. 1978).

"Manual of Individual Water Supply Systems", Water Supply Div., Environmental Protection Agency. Report No. EPA-430-9-73-003, 155 pp, 1973.

Smith, Norman, "Roman Hydraulic Technology", Scientific American, vol. 238, no. 5, pp 154-161, May, 1978.

Swenson, H. A., and H. L. Baldwin, "A Primer on Water Quality",
Geological Survey, USDI, 27 pp, 1965.

"The Story of Water Supply, by 'Willing Water' - A Trip Behind
Your Water Faucet", pamphlet pub. by Amer. Water Works
Assn., Denver, 15 pp, 1976.

"The Story of Water Supply, Featuring, 'Willing Water'", pamphlet pub. by Amer. Water Works Assn., Denver, Cat. No.
70001, 15 pp, 1977.

"The Water Encyclopedia", ed by David Keith Todd, Water Information Center, Port Washington, N.Y., 559 pp, 1970.

Vallentine, H. R., "Water in the Service of Man", Penguin
Books, Baltimore, Md., 224 pp, 1967.

"Water Conservation in California", Bull. No. 198, Dept. of
Water Resources, State of Calif., Sacramento, 95 pp, May,
1976. (Reprinted March, 1977)

"Water Supply for a Growing Kansas City Metropolitan Region -
Problems & Possible Solutions", prepared by Kansas City
Urban Study, U.S. Army Corps of Engineers, Kansas City,
Mo., Progress Report, 1977.

The number of people in the United States who have their own supply of domestic water was estimated to be about 41 million in 1970. In 1956 about 50 million Americans were served by local and suburban wells at which time that was 30 percent of the total population, according to Ackerman and Lof (1959) page 405. In recent years there has been a great increase in the number of small water-supply systems as part of the effort to restore the quality of streamflow.

The hydrologic implications of small water-supply systems for communities of perhaps a few dozen people may be far-reaching. With the development of turbine pumps there was a great increase in the non-urban water supply. Domiciles with groundwater wells and septic tanks were in effect an excellent example of the reuse of water. As population density increased water-well pollution was observed which led to small water treatment systems and to a great increase in the number of small waste-water treatment installations. This development was coupled with the creation of sanitary districts. The net result is that water is no longer recycled through the septic tanks but is now conveyed away from the area. Groundwater levels have been lowered. The long-range result could be restriction of water use or importation of water, or both.

"Water Policies for the Future" (1973) page 7, Section B, deals with improving groundwater management. An excellent publication is "Manual of Individual Water Supply Systems" (1973). This Manual deals with selection of a water source, pumping, distribution and storage, and water treatment if required.

Flack (1976) has compiled a bulletin on the design of water and waste-water systems for rapid growth areas. This publication deals in detail with the design, construction, and operation of systems in the rigorous winter-time conditions prevailing in the Colorado Rockies.

Although a few individual water systems make use of streams or lakes, an overwhelming number depends on groundwater. The State of Colorado considers the groundwater and the surface water as being one source insofar as water rights are concerned. It is possible in Colorado to sell a water right but to retain title to the land. In the State of Nebraska water rights cannot be sold separately from the land. A problem in Colorado (and in other states either already having a similar water-right interpretation or contemplating its adoption) is that of a complicated procedure relating to "augmentation" of water supply which must be followed for any new communities in an area in which there are no available water rights. There is a provision for an individual to be allowed a very small amount of water for use in his domicile for his own personal use as a resident.

White, Bradley, and White (1972), in their book on domestic water use in East Africa, report that 9 out of 10 households drew water from outside the house. Expenditures for the betterment of the water supply did not result in improvement either in water use or in health. They raise the question (page 12) as to what is a socially desirable investment in water supply.

During the drought in Northern California in early 1977 water rationing had been in effect for several months. Drinking water was being sold in vending machines in supermarkets for 20 cents a gallon in the purchaser's own container, according to the photograph captioned, "Getting Water Wherever They Can" (1977).

The "Manual of Individual Water Supply Systems" (1973) includes in its Appendix C emergency disinfection methods for sterilizing water to make it safe for drinking. A common method is boiling vigorously for at least one full minute. Another method makes use of chlorine found in common household bleaches to be used as recommended in Table 76-1.

Table 76-1 Emergency Disinfection Using Household Bleach

| Available Chlorine[1] | Drops per quart of clear water [2] |
|---|---|
| 1 percent | 10 |
| 4-6 percent | 2 |
| 7-10 percent | 1 |

[1] If strength is unknown, add 10 drops per quart to purify
[2] Double amount for turbid or colored water.

(From Manual of Individual Water Supply Systems, 1973, p 140)

The treated water should be mixed and allowed to stand for 30 minutes. If it does not have a slight odor of chlorine the dosage should be repeated and the water allowed to stand another 15 minutes.

Problem Assignment - Cost of Drinking Water

Calculate the cost of an acre-foot of drinking water purchased at a vending machine at 20 cents a gallon.

## References

Ackerman, Edward A., and George O. G. Lof, with the assistance of Conrad Seipp, "Technology in American Water Development", pub. for Resources for the Future, Inc. by The John Hopkins Press, Baltimore, 710 pp, 1959.

Flack, J. Ernest, "Design of Water and Wastewater Systems for Rapid Growth Areas", Environmental Resources Center, Colo. State Univ., Fort Collins, 149 pp, 1976.

"Getting Water Wherever They Can", Photograph with caption, The Denver Post, page 13 AA, Wed., Apr. 20, 1977.

"Manual of Individual Water Supply Systems", Water Supply Div., Environmental Protection Agency, Report No. EPA-430-9-73-003, Washington, D.C., 155 pp, 1973.

"Water Policies for the Future", Final Report to the President and to the Congress of the United States by the National Water Commission, 579 pp, June, 1973.

White, Gilbert F., David J. Bradley, and Ann U. White, "Drawers of Water - Domestic Water Use in East Africa", Univ. of Chicago Press, Chicago and London, 306 pp, 1972.

Topic 77          Wastewater Treatment

Two broad categories of wastewater are surface runoff and
sewage.  In an urban industrial area surface runoff is made up
of flows from rainfall excess, from impervious areas such as
roofs, streets and airport pavements, and from bare soil or
vegetated areas.  Surface runoff may come also from street
washing and fire fighting.  "The Design and Construction of
Storm Sewers" (1969) deals in engineering detail with these
subjects.  Surface runoff may contain heavy metals such as
chromium, cadmium, zinc, lead, copper, iron, and also organic
materials consisting of rubber dust, fallout from smoke, oils,
hydrocarbons,and synthetics which drip from motor vehicles.

Storm runoff is not potable and the sudden and often extremely large volumes if permitted to enter sewage treatment
plants would have very disruptive effects on their operation.
Therefore it is a modern practice to separate the storm runoff
from sewage flows.  Where completely separate drainage facilities do not exist a bypass is often constructed to separate
the storm flows from the sewage flows.  Figure 77-1, shown on
the following page, taken from "A Primer on Wastewater Treatment" (1976),shows this type of arrangement.

Sewage is made up of waste water from domiciles, hotels,
and industry.  Sewage treatment plants have been designed to
deal with 8 general categories of pollutants: (1) oxygen-
demanding waste made up of human waste and waste from the food
industry, paper product mills, tanning plants, among others;
(2) disease causing agents, which includes microbes which
could cause disease either by drinking or by contacting; (3)
plant nutrients such as carbon, nitrogen, and phosphorous
compounds which may over-stimulate the growth of algae and
other water plants causing disagreeable taste and odors; (4)
synthetic organic chemicals such as detergents and industrial
chemicals some of which are highly toxic at low concentrations;
(5) inorganic chemicals and mineral substances which include
acids and alkalis, and solid matter from metal working and
from agricultural irrigation practices; (6) sediments such as
soils, sands, minerals; (7) radioactive substances; (8) heat,
which is an ecological modifier.

The design, construction, and operation of a wastewater
treatment plant is a highly technical activity involving engineering, hydraulics, biology, chemistry, and physics.  "Wastewater Treatment Plant Design" (1977) is a highly technical
engineering practice manual dealing in detail with plant design.

There are 3 broad classifications of treatment.  One
method of disposal, which was in common use and which is still

458

in use in some parts of the country, is that of pouring the
sewage directly into a flowing stream. Primary treatment consists of screening out floating debris and then allowing the
sewage to stand in a sedimentation pond. In the past about
one-third of the municipalities in the United States treated
their sewage only in the primary stage. Sometimes the effluent
was chlorinated to kill pathogenic microbes and to reduce
odors. Primary treatment is no longer acceptable since it did
very little to restore the water quality.

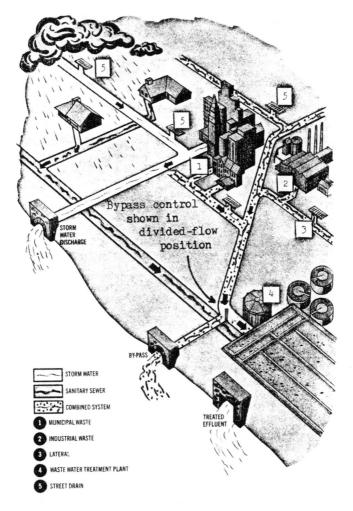

Figure 77-1    Wastewater Collection System showing separate
    storm water and sanitary sewers and a combined system
    with bypass control.  From A Primer on Wastewater Treat-
    ment, 1976.

Secondary treatment can remove up to 90 percent of the organic matter in sewage. This process makes use of bacteria to consume the organic matter in a food chain. Secondary treatment resembles in many ways the natural river purification processes described in Topic 73. Baker (1978) describes the Lawton advanced wastewater treatment plant built for the City of Lawton, Oklahoma.

One of the products of a secondary treatment plant is a sludge consisting of components which are not digested in the process. A major problem facing municipalities is that of disposing of the sludge which may contain significant amounts of heavy metals. Extensive work is underway in using the sludge as a fertilizer on farmland. Incorporation of sludge in the non-fertile soils exposed to the surface when strip mines are being reclaimed is being studied.

Bouwer, Bauer, and Dryden (1978) report on the renovation of sewage effluent by land treatment. They list 3 basic types of land treatment systems: (1) irrigation-type where water enters the surface soil slowly; (2) infiltration-percolation type for high rates of groundwater recharge, and (3) surface-flooding type, an overland flow system. Advantages of land treatment are: wastewater is kept separated from surface run-off; nutrients in the wastewater are used for plant production; and renovated water is produced suitable for reuse with the least environmental and health hazards. Sopper (1971) reviews the renovation of municipal wastewater through forest irrigation. See Topic 65, page 387.

For many purposes secondary treatment is not acceptable and the current trends are toward further treatment. Tertiary treatment, which includes denitrification, removal of polymers, reduction of metal content through electrodialysis, among other approaches, has been shown to produce treated water superior to that found naturally in some areas. In the Santee River Reclamation Project near San Diego, California, the sewage is kept in lagoons for 30 days and then the effluent, after chlorination, is pumped to land immediately above the surface of lakes and allowed to trickle through the sandy soil into the lakes. The resultant water is of such good quality that residents of the area can swim, boat, and fish in the water as described in "A Primer of Wastewater Treatment" (1976) page 6.

At one time it was a common practice to chlorinate wastewater treatment plant effluent. Since it was found that compounds of chlorine and certain amines were toxic to fish, discretion is now being exercised on post-treatment chlorination.

Ozone has been used in Europe for more than 70 years, according to Miller and Rice (1978), not merely as a substitute for chlorine for drinking water disinfection, but also because of ozone's effectiveness in viral inactivation and as a powerful oxidant. Humic material after ozonization is more biodegradable than is humic material after chlorination. Although costs of ozonization are somewhat higher than costs of chlorination, recent doubts about the effects of chlorinated water on human health indicate that ozonization will increase greatly in the near future.

The history of many areas shows that at first a low-density population depends on septic tanks. As a small community develops a small independent wastewater treatment plant is built. With increasing population density the small plants are inactivated and a metropolitan treatment plant is built. The first inhabitants are required to pay for three systems in succession as their area is transformed into a megalopolis. Advanced land use planning could save costly wasted effort and disturbance of the environment. A visit to a large wastewater treatment plant can be illuminating on this activity which is gaining in importance as the technology supporting civilization increases in complexity.

References

"A Primer on Wastewater Treatment", Environmental Protection Agency, Washington, D.C., 27 pp, July, 1976.

Baker, John M., "Lawton Advanced Wastewater Treatment Plant", Military Engineer, no. 454, pp 78-81, Mar.-Apr., 1978.

Bouwer, Herman, W. J. Bauer, Franklin D. Dryden, "Land Treatment of Wastewater in Today's Society", Civil Engineering, vol. 48, no. 1, pp 78-81, Jan. 1978.

"Design and Construction of Sanitary and Storm Sewers", ASCE Manual of Engr. Practice No. 37 and Manual WPCF No. 9, pub. by ASCE, 332 pp and index, 1969.

Miller, G. Wade and Rip G. Rice, "European Water Treatment Practices-Their Experience With Ozone", Civil Engineering, vol. 28, no. 1, pp 76-77, Jan. 1978.

Sopper, William E., "Renovation of Municipal Wastewater Through Forest Irrigation", pp 275-291, in Biological Effects in the Hydrological Cycle, Proceedings of the 3d International Seminar for Hydro. Prof., Purdue, Univ. July 18-30, 1971, pub. by Purdue Univ., Indiana, 391 pp, 1971.

"Wastewater Treatment Plant Design", ASCE Manual of Engr. Practice No. 36 and WPCF Manual No. 8, pub. by ASCE, 560 pp, 1st pub. July, 1930, rev. edition as of June, 1977.

As of 1972 about 49 million persons in the United States
were served by about 15 million individual sewage disposal
systems. Roughly one-fourth of the new homes under construction were designed to use individual wastewater disposal systems. Human wastes are called sewage, often referred to as
black water. Other wastewater from individual homes is made up
of dishwashing, bathing, household cleaning and laundry water.
This type of wastewater is commonly referred to as gray water.
In cold regions or areas of critical deficiency in water supply
the gray water may be stored and used to flush toilets.

Human excreta are a major factor in public health since
many diseases such as dysentery, infectious hepatitis, typhoid,
and paratyphoid, together with various types of diarrhea, are
transmitted from one person to another through fecal contamination of food and/or water. This contamination is largely due
to the improper disposal of human waste. Direct dumping of
human waste into streamflow is no longer permitted. Cesspools
which are simple storage tanks with provision for loss of water
by percolation are seldom allowed. Depending on the soil characteristics a seepage tank may be acceptable for gray water
disposal.

Disposal of sewage essentially is a controlled oxidation,
the end products being carbon dioxide and water in an ideally
efficient system. The oxidation may take place aerobically,
that is in the presence of oxygen, or anaerobically in the absence of oxygen. Most individual wastewater disposal systems
make use of an anaerobic septic tank one design for which is
shown in Figure 78-1 on the following page. A septic tank must
be water-tight and air-tight and the destruction of sewage is
performed by bacteria which feed on the inflow. Certain relationships must be maintained between the capacity of the tank,
the rates of sewage inflow, and the size of the leaching field.

The percolation characteristics of the soil are extremely
important, since for each gallon of water flowing into the
tank a gallon must flow out and be disposed of in the leaching
field. A septic tank-leaching field combination, when properly
designed and installed, is a very effective and trouble-free
system which requires no energy input. Periodic emptying of
sediment and greasy scum, sometimes years apart, performed by
specialists is the only maintenance needed.

Flack (1976) has compiled an informative publication on
the design of water and wastewater systems in which he includes
163 references. Acquisition of this publication is
recommended.

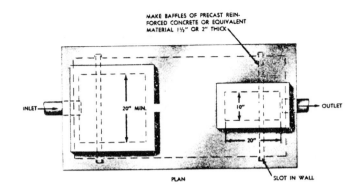

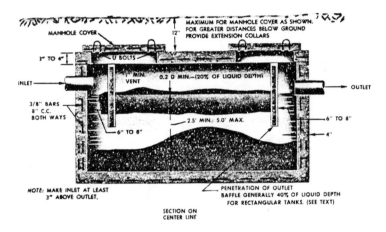

Figure 78-1  Septic Tank, an anaerobic system.  A rectangular
design is shown but septic tanks may be of various shapes
and capacities.
From Manual of Septic Tank Practice (1972) page 33.

There are numerous developments pertaining to individual
disposal systems.  This subject is of such importance that
many states have legal requirements concerning the choice and
suitability of individual disposal systems.  For example, in
Colorado, before an individual system can be constructed, percolation tests are made and inspections by county sanitarians
are conducted to make certain that the system will not endanger
public health, as described in "Guidelines for Establishing
Rules and Regulations Applying to Individual Sewage Disposal
Systems" (1974).

Newer developments in individual disposal systems make use
of the aerobic process.  These systems are very efficient.
Many of them require 110-volt AC electric power since they

463

include stirring devices or air injection systems. They are considered to be much more efficient than the standard septic tank but they require a dependable source of power.

Other newer developments make use of the composting principle. Several of these systems, which were developed in the Scandinavian Countries, reduce the waste to sterile compost which can be used in gardening. One of the systems has an electric heating pad to maintain a temperature favorable to the growth of the composting microbes. Another new system makes use of gas, usually propane, to incinerate the waste. These systems also require electric energy at various voltages depending on the design.

Another technique widely used and suitable for use in small communities is the sewage lagoon. This is a pond usually 3 to 5 feet deep designed in such a way that the inflow will have time to spread throughout rather than to take a short-cut to the outflow. A sewage lagoon is an oxidation system in which the waste products are broken down in an oxygen-rich water with the oxygen being supplied by the growth of algae as described in "A Primer on Wastewater Treatment" (1976), page 6. The engineering and biological design of a sewage lagoon is critical. Lagoons are highly efficient and in most instances relatively odorless and trouble free. Problems may be encountered in cold regions.

An increasing problem of waste disposal is that connected with outdoor recreation including boating, camping, and recreational vehicles. Holding tanks are now provided at dock facilities and at private and public campgrounds.

Evans (1977), page 14, describes problems with gravity sewers in mountainous areas. Steep slopes result in extremely high velocity flow with reduced velocities in flatter segments. He discusses long-way around layouts and pressure and vacuum systems.

Ward (1977) reports on research dealing with evaporation-transpiration beds to be used instead of leaching fields to dispose of the effluent from a septic tank. Leaching fields do not work in shallow soils at high elevations where the rock is near the surface and where frost depths may approach 10 to 11 feet. Ward's report has an excellent compilation of evaporation, evapotranspiration, and solar energy information including 33 selected references.

Not all of the various aerobic and composting systems are approved in all states. Taking into account the importance of the problem, the rapidly developing technology and the increasingly stringent regulations for wastewater disposal systems, it is recommended that anyone interested should consult with local public health authorities before proceeding with a selection of a wastewater disposal system.

References

"A Primer on Wastewater Treatment", Office of Public Affairs (A-107), Environmental Protection Agency, Washington, D.C., 27 pp, July, 1976.

Evans, Norman A., "Water Research: Solving Colorado's Water Problems", Colo. Water Resources Research Institute of The Environmental Resources Center, Colo. State Univ., Fort Collins, 36 pp, Nov. 1977.

Flack, J. Ernest, "Design of Water and Wastewater Systems - for Rapid Growth Areas", Environmental Resources Center, Colo. State Univ., Fort Collins, 149 pp, 1976.

"Guidelines for Establishing Rules and Regulations Applying to Individual Sewage Disposal Systems", Colo. Dept. of Health, Denver, 18 pp, as amended Feb. 30, 1974.

"Manual of Septic-Tank Practice", Public Health Service, Bureau of Community Environmental Mgmt., U.S. Dept. of Health, Education, and Welfare, Rockville, Md., DHEW Pub. No. (HSM) 72-10020 (formerly PHS Pub. No. 526) 92 pp, rev. 1967. (reprinted 1972).

Ward, John C., "Evaporation of Wastewater from Mountain Cabins", Environmental Resources Center, Colo. State Univ., Fort Collins, Completion Report Series No. 77, 123 pp, Mar., 1977.

SECTION XIX

ENVIRONMENTAL ASPECTS OF WATER-RESOURCE UTILIZATION

Topic 79          Environmental Quality

Many people think that the environmental crusade of the
current decade is something new.  However, observers and
philosophers have expressed concern about the environment for
centuries.  George Perkins Marsh, who served as Ambassador to
Italy from the United States, 1861 to 1882, was fascinated by
man's impact on nature.  His long period of service in the
Mediterranean permitted him to travel extensively and his
mastery of 20 languages gave him direct access to the cultures
and beliefs of people of many lands.  His book, "Man and
Nature", first published in 1864 and reprinted in 1965, is a
classic.  Smith (1966) in his book, "The Politics of Conservation", traced the history of the battles of major conservation
movements in the United States.

A distinction should be made between the natural ecology
and the environment.  The dynamic balance of nature is
expressed in ecosystems.  When man mastered fire and learned to
fabricate metals he embarked on a series of modifications of
the natural ecology for which there is no end.  Development of
intellectual capabilities to learn by experience and to pass
along through the process of education to succeeding generations
the sum of accumulated experience and knowledge, advanced man
far beyond his biological relatives the great apes.

Man's manipulation of the natural ecology has produced
what is called the environment which may be not at all similar
to the natural ecosystems of the regions occupied by man.  As
technology becomes more complex and the interdependence of man
on the resources becomes increasingly intricate, especially
with concentrations of population numbering into the millions,
there has developed a nostalgic yearning for simplification and
a return to nature.  It was inevitable that some action would
be taken in this direction and in 1969 PL 90-190 (83 Stat.
852), the "National Environmental Policy Act of 1969" was
passed and signed into law January 1, 1970.  This law established in the Executive Office of the President the Commission
on Environmental Quality.  "Quest for Quality" (1965) a U.S.
Department of the Interior Conservation Yearbook is a superbly
illustrated presentation.

The following paragraphs are quoted from "In Productive
Harmony" (1976):

"NEPA established in the Executive Office of the President a
Council on Environmental Quality (CEQ), charged with

responsibility to study the condition of the Nation's enviro-
ment, to develop new environmental programs and policies, to
coordinate the wide array of Federal environmental efforts, to
see that all Federal activities take environmental considerations into account and to assist the President in assessing
environmental problems and in determining ways to solve them.

"To ensure that environmental amenities and values are given
systematic consideration equal to economic and technical considerations in the Federal decision-making process, NEPA requires each Federal agency to prepare a statement of environmental impact in advance of each major action, recommendation
or report on legislation that may significantly affect the
quality of the human environment. Such actions may include new
highway construction, harbor dredging or filling, nuclear power
plant construction, large-scale aerial pesticide spraying,
river channeling, new jet runways, munitions disposal, bridge
construction and more."

Subsequent to the NEPA Act a series of other laws were
passed which pertain to the environment all of which are concerned with the water resource in some way. A list of pertinent Federal laws follows:

PL 92-500, Oct. 18, 1972 (86 Stat. 816) Federal Water
Pollution Control Act Amendments of 1972. See Topic 81.

PL 92-516, 1972 (86 Stat. 1246) Federal Environmental
Pesticide Control Act of 1972.

PL 93-205, Dec. 28, 1973 (87 Stat. 884) Endangered Species
Act of 1973.

PL 93-523, Dec. 16, 1974 (88 Stat. 1660 et Seq.) Safe
Drinking Water Act.

PL 94-469, Oct. 11, 1976 (90 Stat. 2003) Toxic Substances
Control Act.

PL 94-580, Oct. 21, 1976 (90 Stat. 2795) Resource Conservation and Recovery Act of 1976.

PL 95-217, Dec. 27, 1977 (91 Stat. 1566) Clean Water Act
of 1977. See Topic 81.

"Federal Environmental Law" (1974) is a legal reference
work edited by Dolgin and Guilbert. Goldfarb (1978) reviews the
judicial mechanisms as a result of which NEPA has attained such
a tremendous impact. The CEQ was required to prepare annual
reports an example of which is their first entitled, "Environmental Quality" (1970).

Zealous concern for the saving, improvement, and perpetuation of the quality of the environment has resulted in legislation prescribing acceptable standards for water and air. It
is difficult to name any aspect of human endeavor which has not

467

been touched upon by the environmental quality legislation and regulations.

References

"Environmental Quality - The First Annual Report of the Council on Environmental Quality", (together with the President's Message to Congress) U.S. Govt. Printing Off., 326 pp, Transmitted to the Congress, Aug. 1970.

"Federal Environmental Law", edited by Erica L. Dolgin and Thomas G. P. Guilbert, Environmental Law Institute, West Pub. Co., 1600 pp, 1974.

Goldfarb, William, "Litigation and Legislation - NEPA AT SEVEN" Water Resources Bulletin, vol. 14, no. 1, pp 212-214, Feb. 1978.

"In Productive Harmony - A Brief Explanation of Environmental Impact Statements", a folder, 12 pp, U.S. Environmental Protection Agency, Washington, D.C., rev. June, 1976.

Marsh, George Perkins, "Man and Nature - or Physical Geography as Modified by Human Action", orig. pub. in 1864, reprinted by the Harvard Univ. Press as edited by David Lowenthal, 472 pp, 1965.

"Quest for Quality", U.S. Dept. of the Interior Conservation Yearbook, 95 pp, 1965.

Smith, Frank E., "The Politics of Conservation", Pantheon Books, Division of Random House, New York, 338 pp, 1966.

Topic 80     The Environmental Impact Statement

PL 90-190, The National Environmental Policy Act of 1969, (see Topic 79) requires the preparation of an Environmental Impact Statement (EIS) in advance of each major action on legislation that may seriously affect the quality of the human environment. A condensed explanation of the purpose, actions, preparation, review, and explanation of the rules, has been prepared by the Environmental Protection Agency and is presented in the folder, "In Productive Harmony" (1976). The EPA has issued also a "Manual for Preparation of Environmental Impact Statements for Wastewater Treatment Works, Facilities Plans, and 208 Areawide Waste Treatment Management Plans" (1974). Another EPA Manual is "Environmental Impact Assessment Guidelines for Selected New Source Industries" (1975). "Preparation of Environmental Impact Statements - New Source NPDES Permits" appears in the Federal Register for January 11, 1977.

An Executive Order relating to the responsibilities of the Council on Environmental Quality appears in "Environmental Protection - Environmental Impact Statements" in the Federal Register for May 25, 1977. This reference also includes Executive Orders on exotic organisms, floodplain management, off-road vehicles on public lands, and protection of wetlands.

The volume of literature pertaining to Environmental Impact Statements as they affect various activities is tremendous. Black (1975) states that the EIS should not be looked upon as an encyclopedia of local ecology but should accurately represent what impact a proposed action and its alternatives may have on the subject environment.

Whitlatch (1976) proposes mathematical procedures for the preparation of an EIS. Bradley (1976) has prepared an environmental impact analysis of the Central Arizona Project as teaching material for courses in public works and environmental administration.

More than 25 states have laws paralleling in various ways PL 90-190. Polayes (1977) has prepared a detailed analysis of state environmental policy acts for Minnesota, Massachusetts, and North Carolina. Brown (1974) in his paper on environmental issues, effects and solutions, discusses the controversies involved in the preparation of an EIS. Brown is quoted from his page 511: "Our issue today, of more immediate concern, involves one of the many interfaces between the manmade environment and the natural environment. The issue concerns protecting and enhancing the natural environment and at the same time maintaining and improving the quality of life we now enjoy. Most of the controversy has pitted ecologists, environmentalists, biologists, and concerned citizens against administrators, engineers, economists, landowners, and other concerned citizens. The issue involves alteration of our nation's watercourses and streams. Strong opposition has been voiced about the environmental impacts of federally-assisted water development projects and particularly channel work for drainage or flood protection."

McNabb (1976) warns environmentalists that benefit-cost ratios are a fact of economic life and that if the EIS had existed 200 years ago the industrial revolution would probably never have happened. He states that it is no secret that the EIS and other planning procedures have been used as legal weapons to bury projects to which environmentalists are opposed. McNabb wrote that agreements are not permanently won by persons who want to stop actions; they are won by those who propose better alternatives. Server (1977) prepared a list of projects which have been either delayed or cancelled because of the EIS procedures.

Strabala (1977) reports that between 1974 and 1983 the United States will spend about $200 billion for environmental improvement. Although it is estimated that in the last 6 years about 17,600 jobs were lost because of environmental restrictions Strabala quotes Senator Gary Hart as saying that environmental programs created one million jobs in 1975 alone.

Speth (1978), who is a member of the Council on Environmental Quality (CEQ), refers to two incidents in which well-intentioned projects have created havoc with a nation's food supply and with public health. A biocide used by farmers in Indonesia to control rice pests also killed the fish in the paddies, resulting in the destruction of a vital source of protein. Following the introduction by the United States of a piped potable water supply there was a spread of dysentery and trachoma in the Ryukyu Islands. Writing in support of a proposed form of international EIS Speth states that the developing nations, to which most of the United States non-military assistance goes, have a right to know when a project may introduce health, safety, or environmental problems.

There is increasing concern about the over-use of the EIS. Schindler (1976) reports that enormous sums have been spent on EIS's with little or no scientific return and that continuing preparation for release of voluminous but relatively inconclusive EIS's can have several effects. Among these are an increase in prices for natural resources, a decline in public credibility for environmental science and scientists, a reduction in the overall quality of scientific personal, and the degradation of natural resources. Fairfax (1978) believes that the National Environmental Policy Act and the Environmental Impact Statement have wasted the environmentalists' resources on processing paper, which could lead to a disaster in the environmental movement.

A major portion of the EIS's prepared to date touch upon the water resource in some manner or other. If the EIS is to attain its objective of being a tool for progress in enhancing and maintaining the quality of the human environment, the following suggestions are offered: a limit should be placed on the size and bulk of the Statements; the opponents of a proposed action should be required, by an amendment to PL 90-190, to prepare an EIS analyzing the impact not only on the natural ecology but especially on the human environment if the action proposed is not approved; and, they should be required to submit alternatives.

## Problem Assignment - Environmental Impact Statement

Environmental Impact Statements are public documents and are available for analysis and review. Comments by the public are welcome. Find out what projects, in an area in which you are interested, are currently going through the EIS review process. Learn where an EIS is available for public inspection and secure a copy from, or inspect it at, the issuing office. Analyze the EIS and submit comments to the appropriate issuing or reviewing office. Prepare a report evaluating the appropriateness of the proposal and of the opponents' positions, if any.

## References

Black, Peter E., "Environmental Impact Statements in Planning Water and Related Land Resources", Water Resources Bulletin, vol. 11, no. 5, pp 881-886, Oct. 1975.

Bradley, Michael D., "Environmental Impact Analysis: The Central Arizona Project as an Example", College of Business and Public Admin., Univ. of Arizona, Tucson, Report PW-76-9, 54 pp, July, 1976.

Brown, Lynn A., "Environmental Issues, Effects, and Solutions", pp 511-528 in Agricultural and Urban Considerations in Irrigation and Drainage, selected papers from the Irrigation and Drainage Div., and Colo. Section, ASCE Conf., Fort Collins, Colo., Apr. 22-24, 1973, pub. by ASCE, 1974.

"Environmental Impact Assessment Guidelines for Selected New Source Industries", U.S. Environmental Protection Agency, Washington, D.C., Oct. 1975.

"Environmental Protection - Environmental Impact Statements", Federal Register, Part VI, pp 26967-26968, vol. 42, no. 101, Wed., May 25, 1977.

Fairfax, Sally K., "A Disaster in the Environmental Movement", Science, vol. 199, pp 743-748, Feb. 17, 1978.

"In Productive Harmony - A Brief Explanation of Environmental Impact Statements", a folder, U.S. Environmental Protection Agency, Washington, D.C., 12 pp, rev. June, 1976.

"Manual for Preparation of Environmental Impact Statements for Wastewater Treatment Works, Facilities Plans, and 208 Areawide Waste Treatment Management Plans", Office of Federal Activities, EPA, Washington, D.C., 35 pp, July, 1974.

McNabb, Scott, "Environmentalist's Views on No. 3", The Denver Post, p 21, Fri. Oct. 22, 1976.

Polayes, Joanne R., "State Environmental Policy Acts and the Public", Working Paper No. 6, Yale Univ. School of Forestry and Environmental Studies, New Haven, 55 pp, June, 1977.

"Preparation of Environmental Impact Statements - New Source NPDES Permits", EPA, Federal Register, vol. 42, no. 7, Part V, pp 2450-2459, Tues., Jan. 11, 1977.

Schindler, D. W., "The Impact Statement Boondoggle", Science, vol. 192, no. 4239, p 509, May 7, 1976.

Server, Kenneth R., "Economic Impact of Environmental Impact Statements", The Denver Post, p 8, Sat., Mar. 12, 1977.

Speth, Gus, "Environmental Impact of Foreign Aid Projects", The Denver Post, p 25, Fri., Feb. 24, 1978.

Strabala, Bill, "Environment Goals Aid Economy: Hart", The Denver Post, p 26, Sun., June 12, 1977.

Whitlatch, Elbert E., Jr., "Systematic Approaches to Environmental Impact Assessment: An Evaluation", Water Resources Bulletin, vol. 12, no. 1, pp 123-127, Feb., 1976.

Topic 81    PL 92-500 and the Clean Water Act of 1977

In the 55th Congress, Third Session, an Act was passed on March 3, 1899 entitled, "An Act making appropriations for the construction, repair, and preservation of certain public works on rivers and harbors and for other purposes" which contained a series of sections dealing with the deposition of refuse in navigable waters. The beginning section on this subject is Section 13, entitled, "Depositing refuse in navigable waters forbidden", as published on page 1152 of the Statutes of the United States printed in 1899. The pertinent sections of that appropriations Act are commonly referred to as "The 1899 Refuse Act". The provisions forbidding the deposition of refuse appear to have been forgotten for many decades. Pettyjohn (1972) analyzes section by section the enforcement of the 1899 Refuse Act through citizen action. Subsequent to the "Oil Pollution Act of 1924" a series of very important Federal Acts were passed which are identified in "Federal Water Pollution Control Act ..." (1971).

On the closing day of the 92nd Congress, October 18, 1972, both the Senate and the House over-rode a Presidential veto to pass the "Federal Water Pollution Control Act Amendments of 1972", PL 92-500, Oct. 18, 1972 (86 Stat. 816). The impact of the passage of this Act has been extremely far-reaching. The law set two general goals for the United States: (1) to achieve wherever possible by July 1, 1983, water clean enough for swimming and other recreational uses, and clean enough for the protection and propagation of fish, shellfish, and wildlife; (2) and, by 1985 to have no discharges of pollutants into the Nation's waters.

The law for the first time extends the Federal pollution control program to all United States waters. Previously only interstate waters were covered by Federal legislation. Also, for the first time, the law authorizes the Federal government to seek an immediate court injunction against polluters when water pollution presents "an imminent and substantial endangerment" to public health, or when it endangers someone's livelihood.

PL 92-500 included provisions for extensive grants for the construction of wastewater facilities and for states to carry on water pollution control programs. A new system of permits was established to replace the 1899 Refuse Acts programs. The law clarified relationships between the Federal water pollution control program and the National Environmental Policy Act of 1969 (NEPA).

Penalities for violating the provisions of PL 92-500 range

473

from a minimum of $2,500 to a maximum of $25,000 per day, and up to one year in prison for the first offense, and up to $50,000 a day and two years in prison for subsequent violations.

PL 92-500 has had an influence either directly or indirectly on agriculture, forestry, the mineral industry, and practically every manufacturing activity.

On December 27, 1977 President Carter signed into law the Federal Water Pollution Control Act as amended in 1977. This Act, PL 95-217 of December 27, 1977 (91 Stat. 1566, 33 USC 1251), states in Sec. 518 that the Act may be referred to as "The Clean Water Act" of 1977. This Act revises in practically all major respects PL 92-500.

According to Goldfarb (1978) three types of pollutants other than heat are now recognized. These are toxic pollutants, conventional pollutants, and non-conventional pollutants. Terms such as Best Available Technology (BAT), Best Conventional Pollutant Control Technology (BCT), are used in connection with the National Pollutant Discharge Elimination System (NPDES) as administered by the EPA. BCT will probably fall between BAT and BPT, Best Practical Control Technology Currently Available.

In the 125-page Committee Print, 95th Congress, 1st Session, "The Clean Water Act Showing Changes Made by the 1977 Amendments" (1977), the existing law in which no change was proposed is printed in roman, proposed omissions are enclosed in black brackets, and new material is printed in italics. This is an informative reference on this long and complicated Act.

As the Nation demands more and more electric energy the disposal of excess heat from both thermal and nuclear power plants has created a new problem, that of thermal modification. An excellent discussion of some of the ecological impacts of this subject is given by Clark (1969). Much remains to be done on pollution control since, to date, the techniques in use on larger volumes of water seldom succeed in restoring the water to its quality before use.

Exhaustive historical research has shown that in many parts of the country the water in streams under natural conditions prior to heavy encroachment by agricultural, industrial, and urban activities would at times fail to meet the drinking water standards.

References

Clark, John R., "Thermal Pollution and Aquatic Life", Scientific American, vol. 220, no. 3, pp 19-27, Mar. 1969.

"Federal Water Pollution Act as amended by the Federal Water
    Pollution Control Act Amendments of 1961 (public Law 87-
    88), the Water Quality Act of 1965 (Public Law 89-234),
    the Clean Water Restoration Act of 1966 (Public Law 89-
    753), and the Water Quality Improvement Act of 1970,
    (Public Law 91-224). Appendices:
        Reorganization Plan No. 2 of 1966
        Executive Order 11507 - Prevention, Control, and
            Abatement of Air and Water Pollution at Federal
            Facilities.
    U.S. Environmental Protection Agency, Washington, D. C.
    Sept. 1971.


Goldfarb, William, "Litigation and Legislation - The 1977
    Amendments", pp 491-493, Water Resources Bulletin, vol. 14,
    no. 2, Apr. 1978.

Pettyjohn, Wayne A., "Enforcement of 1899 Refuse Act Through
    Citizen Action", pp 277-285 in Water Quality in a Stressed
    Environment, Readings in Environmental Hydrology, Ed. by
    Wayne A. Pettyjohn, Burgess Pub. Co., Minneapolis, Minn.,
    309 pp, 1972.

"The Clean Water Act Showing Changes Made by the 1977 Amend-
    ments", 95th Congress, 1st Session, Committee Print,
    Serial No. 95-12, Printed for the use of the Senate
    Committee on Environment and Public Works, U.S. Government
    Printing Office, 125 pp, 1977.
    (PL 95-217 was signed into Law Dec. 27, 1977 - 91 Stat.
    1566, 33 USC 1251.)

The Federal Water Pollution Control Act of 1972 (PL 92-500) under its Section 208 called for specific planning of area-wide waste treatment management programs. It recognized non-point sources of pollution which are intermittent, diffuse, and were not contained in pipes or clearly-defined channels. Expenditures for point sources of pollution such as outflows from wastewater treatment plants, industries, etc., could be ineffective if without an area-wide waste management program.

The Clean Water Act of 1977 (PL 95-217) includes numerous deletions and extensive changes (see Topic 81). The states are held responsible for regional 208 plans which are subject to approval by the Governor. The Environmental Protection Agency through its regional offices is to make the ultimate decisions on the acceptability of the plans. Although the Federal share of the costs was to be 100 percent for grants made before June 30, 1975, very few applications met that deadline, so most of the 208 costs are supported 75 percent by Federal funds.

Major steps in performing a Section 208 study aimed at the solution of a documented water quality program are:
a. Acquisition of field data,
b. Assessment of the problems both present and future,
c. Identification of control alternatives,
d. Selection of the best alternative which might or, might not be the one of lowest cost, but which must be politically acceptable.

There are 3 other Sections of the Clean Water Act which are related to Section 208. Section 201 has as its purpose the assistance in the development and implementation of waste treatment management plans and practices. Grants authorized under Section 201 may be used to construct wastewater treatment works serving residences and small business establishments. Innovative approaches are welcome. Section 303 relates to the establishment of water quality standards.

Section 404 deals with permits for the discharge of dredged or fill material at specified disposal sites in navigable waters. As given in PL 92-500 Section 404 was interpreted to be so all-inclusive as to cover a farmer digging a ditch or a logger placing a temporary fill in a channel as part of an access road to timber. The Clean Water Act of 1977 includes extensive revisions of Section 404.

The Clean Water Act of 1977 in its revised Section 208 authorizes a state to take over the issuance of permits for dredged or fill material under Section 404. As it now stands all permits for dredged and fill material are issued by the U.S. Army Corps of Engineers with the advice and approval of the Administrator of the EPA.

The EPA has prepared a "Manual for Preparation of Environmental Impact Statements for Wastewater Treatment Works, Facilities Plans, and 208 Areawide Waste Treatment Management Plans". Under Section 208 it is permissible to plan separate storm sewer systems to carry flows from areas which are recognized as urban land. However, such programs cannot be funded under Section 201. Other sources of funds may be available.

Dobrowolski and Grillo (1977) report on their experience in dealing with area-wide wastewater planning in northeastern New Jersey. The Bergen County Sewer Authority serves 115 square miles providing sewage service for 507,000 people in 43 municipalities. They conclude that planning should be carried out concurrently on Sections 303, 208, and 201 since there are interrelationships which must be considered if the best possible plan meeting the requirements of the 3 sections is to be developed. Their 303 recommends immediate action on a tertiary treatment plant that could cost over $100 million. This level of treatment will be necessary since the effluent flows into a tidal estuary.

Goldrosen (1977) discusses the role of 208 planning in protecting drinking water sources particularly in the Old Colony area of Massachusetts. This 208 planning area covered 172 square miles with a population in 1975 of about 200,000 people in 13 communities. Sources of water consist about equally of surface and groundwater and these sources are interrelated hydrologically because of the local geology.

Blackman, Wills, and Celnicker (1977) summarize the problems arising when municipal-industrial waste treatment NPDES permit approaches are attempted to control irrigation return flows. Bulkley and Gross (1977) draw on the experience of the Thames Water Authority in England and other organizations in Wales. They compare the British water authorities with those of Chicago, Detroit, and Cleveland. They conclude that the British experience should be valuable in the 208 area-wide water quality management approaches.

Galbraith (1976) has prepared a report on the Teton County 208 planning dealing with water quality investigations in the Bridger-Teton National Forest in northwest Wyoming.

The EPA's position on water quality management 208 programs as they relate to agriculture is presented in a format of 16 questions and answers appearing in "Yellowstone - Tongue A.P.O., A Water Quality Management Project" (1977). The area covered in this report consists of Carter, Custer, Fallon,

Powder River, Rosebud, and Treasure Counties in Montana. These counties, together with Big Horn County, are the location of some of the most available, low-ash-content coal. Strip mines and power plants are either being constructed or are in the planning stages in these areas.

The Section 208 approach to water quality control is new and unprecedented in a number of respects: it places responsibility on local groups to carry out the water quality management planning under state supervision; it incorporates concepts of land use previously not included; it is related to other Sections of the Clean Water Act dealing with financing, construction, and activation of area-wide wastewater treatment approaches. The impact on the quality of the Nation's water as a result of the 208 activities will inevitably be far-reaching.

Billions of dollars are authorized and many millions have been appropriated and expended in pursuit of the inescapably necessary goals and policies which are expressed in Section 101 (a) of PL 95-217.

It would not be wise to proceed with the construction of wastewater treatment plants on a vast scale to meet the July 1, 1983 deadline. The plants as designed in the past are approaching obsolescence since in view of rapidly evolving technology, especially on tertiary treatment and revision of standards on acceptable water quality, new concepts need to be considered.

Legal interpretations, usually decisions by the Courts, and the promulgation of administrative procedures, always follow new legislation. Before any program is initiated under Section 208 it would be advisable for one to become thoroughly informed on the latest information.

## References

Blackman, William C., Jr., Carroll G. Wills, and Arnold C. Celnicker, "PL 92-500 v. Pollution by Irrigation Return Flow", Jour. Irrigation and Drainage Div., Proceedings ASCE, vol. 103, no. IR2, pp 207-220, June, 1977.

Bulkley, Jonathan W., and Thomas A. Gross, "Innovative Management Concept for 208 Planning", Jour. of Water Resources Planning and Mgmt. Div., Proceedings, ASCE, vol. 103, no WR2, pp 227-240, Nov. 1977.

Dobrowolski, Frank, and Leonard Grillo, "Experience With the 303-208-201 Study Relationships", Water Resources Bull., vol. 13, no. 3, pp 455-460, June, 1977.

Galbraith, Alan F., "Water Quality Investigations on the Bridger-Teton National Forest", A Report to the Teton County 208 Planning Agency, Wyoming, 31 pp, Dec. 17, 1976.

Goldrosen, John, "The Role of Section 208 Planning in Protecting Drinking Water Sources", Chap. 4, pp 39-61 in Drinking Water Quality Enhancement Through Source Protection, ed by Robert B. Pojasek, Ann Arbor Science Pub. Inc. Ann Arbor, Mich., 614 pp, 1977.

"Manual for Preparation of Environmental Impact Statements for Wastewater Treatment Works, Facilities Plans, and 208 Areawide Waste Treatment Management Plans", Office of Federal Activities, U.S. Environmental Protection Agency, Washington, D.C., 35 pp, July, 1974.

"Yellowstone-Tongue A.P.O. - A Water Quality Management Project - Agricultural Report", a 12-inch by 15-inch publication, 16 pages, pub. cooperatively by the ASCS, The Conservation Districts, and the Yellowstone-Tongue A.P.O., Broadus, Montana, June, 1977.

The draining of low-lying water-logged land is an ancient practice. McGill, Bennett, Moody, and Vittetoe (1974) report that in 1773 George Washington and others surveyed the Dismal Swamp area of Virginia and North Carolina for land reclamation and water transportation. About 30 years later some of the facilities were constructed. Extensive land-drainage programs were pursued in New England and the Atlantic coastal states. In the central states there were some very large drainage projects. The locale of a novel by Gene Stratton-Porter (1909) was a swampland in Northern Indiana called the Limberlost. This has since been drained and is now farmland.

An outstanding example of the effectiveness of drainage is in The Netherlands where large areas called polders have been reclaimed from the sea and are now in agricultural production. This activity was developed more than a thousand years ago.

Many drainage practices were put into effect in the organic soils of the Lake states. This modification of the environment had far-reaching effects completely changing the ecology of the area and influencing the migration of wild fowl.

According to Brown (1974) nearly 200,000 miles of the Nation's 3.5 million miles of waterways have been modified in the past 150 years. About 130 million acres of wetlands have been drained. Much of the early work in stream channels was not properly planned, engineered, or financed. This experience led to Federal assistance in drainage projects.

A drainage system, which may consist of open channels, pumping, or **subsurface** drain tile installations, changes the elevation of the water table thereby affecting the ecology, the erosion, and sedimentation patterns, the fish and wildlife, the hydrology, and the esthetics of the area. Because of the visible impact of drainage practices the legal aspects have been accorded much attention. An example is "Legal Aspects of Drainage in New England", a bibliography (1971) which includes references with abstracts to 87 litigations.

Poland (1974), in his paper on groundwater overdraft, describes many instances of subsidence. Subsidence resulting from water level decline has occurred in California, Nevada, Arizona, Texas and Louisiana. In the San Joaquin Valley of California subsidence of up to 29 feet (9 m) has been measured, with 5,200 square miles (13,500 $km^2$) being affected to some extent. Poland states that the principle causes of subsidence are changes in elevation and gradient of natural drainage patterns and water transport structures in the subsurface; destruction

of water wells from compressive rupture of casing; and, tidal
encroachment and saline water intrusions in low-lying coastal
areas.

In Florida suburban developments accompanied by land
drainage and private boat docks resulted in saline water intrusions. (See Topic 45) The pumping of water from mines can
result in pollution of surface streamflow often with highly
acid and toxic water. This is also true of oil fields.

Duvel, Volkmar, Specht, and Johnson (1976) describe the
environmental impact of stream channelization in Pennsylvania.
They studied six watersheds. Channelized streams provided a
poor fish habitat, especially for trout, as a result of uniform cross-sections, very shallow water, very few pools, and
absence of overhanging vegetation.

The actual practice of drainage other than groundwater
pumping is based on an application of soil physics, hydraulics,
and civil engineering. Mathematical analyses of drainage
systems can become exceedingly complex. Bouwer and
van Schilfgaarde (1963) proposed a simplified method of predicting fall of water table on drained land. The dynamic
interactions between soil, the precipitation, and the outflow
of a drainage system are so intricate that in a great many instances field experiences are necessary before detailed engineering information can be made available.

Toksoz and Kirkham (1971) have prepared a highly mathematical analysis of steady drainage of layered soils in which
the upper layer may have a hydraulic conductivity 5 to 10 times
that of the lower layer. In their first paper they deal with
two-layered and three-layered soils. Their second paper includes nomographs for easy calculation, applying their
equations, of buried drain tile spacing in two-layered soils.

Special problems arise when it is desired to use pipe-
underdrains to convey high-level groundwater into an open
concrete-lined channel. Mevorach and Zanker (1978) analyse the
operation of flap-valves needed to prevent sediment from entering the pipe drains.

There is an extensive literature relating to drainage
practices in the publications of the various professional soci-
ties of soil scientists, agronomists, agricultural engineers,
civil engineers, industrial engineers, petroleum geologists,
and in the publications of the International Commission on
Irrigation, Drainage, and Flood Control, and of its U.S.
Committee. "Drainage Manual" (1978) has practical information.

Because of salt concentrations in the surface of soils in
arid land it has been found necessary in many parts of the

World to apply water much beyond that needed for plant production to maintain a salt balance, a practice which requires construction of drainage systems. Therefore, irrigation projects
are often designed and built concurrently with drainage projects. Excessive irrigation water applications have created
swamplands in portions of the projects thereby taking out of
cultivation a considerable fraction of the land for which the
irrigation projects were organized. Trickle and drip irrigation methods are being expanded very rapidly to supply just
sufficient irrigation water to satisfy evapotranspiration
demands where the quality of the water available is acceptable
to the crop plants.

Tabor (1974) discusses the relationship of drainage at
the Wellton-Mohawk Project in the Gila River Valley in Southwestern Arizona and the Mexico salt problem. Tabor reviews the
history of irrigation, salinity, and international relations
between the United States and Mexico. The Treaty of 1944
promised Mexico 1,500,000 AF of Colorado River water per year.
See Topic 42 for a discussion of saline water demineralization
in the Yuma area.

It is recommended that anyone facing a land drainage problem consult with the State Agricultural Extension Service,
possibly through a County Agent. If the project is potentially
a large one the State Engineer, The State Department of
Resources or of Conservation, and possibly the EPA and the U.S.
Army Corps of Engineers could become involved.

References

Bouwer, Herman, and Jan van Schilfgaarde, "Simplified Method of
    Predicting Fall of Water Table in Drained Land", Trans.
    American Society of Agricultural Engineers, vol. 6, no. 4,
    pp 288-296, 1963.

Brown, Lynn A., "Environmental Issues, Effects, and Solutions",
    pp 511-528 in Agricultural and Urban Considerations in
    Irrigation and Drainage, Proceedings of a Conf. held at
    Fort Collins, Colo., Apr. 22-24, 1973, pub. by ASCE,
    1974, 800 pp, 1974. (Brown's Ref. 6 pertains to the 3-vol.
    "Report on Channel Modification" prepared by Arthur D.
    Little, Inc., for the Council on Environmental Quality,
    U.S. Govt. Printing Off., Washington, D.C. March, 1973.)

"Drainage Manual - A Guide to Integrating Plant, Soil, and
    Water Relationships for Drainage of Irrigated Lands", A
    Water Resources Tech. Publication, Bur. of Reclamation,
    USDI, Washington, D.C., 1st edition, 286 pp, 1978.

Duvel, William A., Jr., Robert C. Volkmar, Winona L. Specht, and Fred W. Johnson, "Environmental Impact of Stream Channelization", Water Resources Bulletin, vol. 12, no. 4, pp 799-812, Aug. 1976.

"Legal Aspects of Drainage in New England - A Bibliography", Water Resources Scientific Information Center, Office of Water Resources Research, USDI, Washington, D.C., 125 pp, Oct. 1971.

McGill, H. N., Allyn C. Bennett, Wendell B. Moody, and Gene C. Vittetoe, "Effects of Surface Drainage on Stream Flow", pp 501-510 in Agri. and Urban Considerations in Irri. and Drainage, Proceedings of a Conf. held at Fort Collins, Colo., Apr. 22-24, 1973, pub. by ASCE 1974, 800 pp, 1974.

Mevorach, J., and K. Zanker, "Hydrodynamic Performance of Pipe Underdrains", Jour. of Irrig. and Drainage Div., Proceedings ASCE, vol. 104, no. IR1, pp 127-142, Mar., L978.

Poland, J. F., "Subsidence in United States Due to Ground-Water Overdraft--A Review", pp 11-38 in Agri. and Urban Considerations in Irri. and Drainage, Proceedings of a Conf. held at Fort Collins, Colo., Apr. 22-24, 1973, pub. by ASCE, 800 pp, 1974.

Stratton-Porter, Gene, "The Girl of the Limberlost", pub. 1909 by Doubleday, Page & Co., 1972 printing by Grosset & Dunlap, New York.

Tabor, C. C., "Wellton-Mohawk Drainage and the Mexican Salt Problem", pp 285-309 in Agri. and Urban Considerations in Irri. and Drainage, Proceedings of a Conf. held at Fort Collins, Colo., Apr. 22-24, 1973, pub. by ASCE, 1974.

Toksoz, Sadik, and Don Kirkham, "Steady Drainage of Layered Soils: I, Theory", Jour. Irrig. and Drainage Div., Proc. ASCE, vol. 97, no. IR1, pp 1-16, Mar. 1971.

Toksoz, Sadik, and Don Kirkham, "Steady Drainage of Layered Soils: II, Nomographs", Jour. Irri. and Drainage Div., Proc. ASCE, vol. 97, IR1, pp 19-37, Mar. 1971.

In many parts of the World drainage basins which are forested in the higher altitudes may be arid and semi-arid at
lower elevations. A considerable part of the area of many
National Forests in the Southwestern United States consists of
arid and semi-arid lands.

Regions are classified as either arid or semi-arid because
of deficiency of precipitation as a result of the interaction
of the circulation of the atmosphere, the position of the
oceans, and the land forms of the continents. Thornthwaite
(1931) presents a more detailed classification. In the arid
regions precipitation is not only relatively scarce but rainfall may come purely at random. When precipitation does come
it may be torrential causing high rates of runoff. Arid and
semi-arid drainage basins tend to lie at lower elevations
where the precipitation-yielding mechanism is of the convective
type. This tends to produce extremely high intensities of
rainfall over relatively small areas. A general discussion of
the subject is given by Christian and Parsons (1964).

The nonharmonic cycles of wet years and dry years are especially important in arid and semi-arid regions. A succession
of years of such deficiency in precipitation as to affect plant
and animal life and to reduce the water supply for human
endeavors is considered to be a drought. Hudson and Hazen
(1964) review the subject of droughts and low streamflow.

Due to the nature of the rainfall, flows in arid and semi-
arid regions may often pick up such a tremendous suspended
sediment load as to change the characteristics of the flow.
Instead of flow of water in open channels subjected to the laws
of hydraulics, the "bulked" or "mud flow" becomes a heavy
media moving like a viscous mass. Many of the high water marks
to be found as a result of floods in arid and semi-arid
regions may have been created by this viscous flow rather than
by open channel flow of water transporting sediment. An
informative bulletin illustrated with many photographs of debris
floods has been written by Croft (1967).

A major problem facing water resource developers is the
scarcity of data applicable to undeveloped areas for which no
meteorological records are available. Bell (1969) showed that
rainfall-duration-frequency relationships for short-duration
convective storms showed a surprising consistency for such
diverse places as the continental United States, Alaska,
Hawaii, Puerto Rico, South Africa, and Australia.

The "Walnut Gulch Experimental Watershed" is located in

the arid Southwest near Tombstone, Arizona. In this instru-
mented drainage basin of 58 square miles the stream channels
are dry 99 percent of the time. The Agricultural Research Service, USDA, established an extensive instrumentation in this
area in 1953. Many reports and publications are in the literature emanating from the Walnut Gulch Experimental Watershed.

Another arid-zone experimental area is the Santa Rita Experimental Range south of Tucson, Arizona. Martin and Cable
(1974) describe the responses of managed semi-desert grass-
shrub ranges to precipitation, grazing, and soil texture. They
also write about mesquite control.

Various techniques have been developed for modifying the
micro-climate of cropland in arid and semi-arid regions. One
of these is the planting of shelter belts. Van Deusen (1976)
writes about the need for renovation of shelterbelts in the
Great Plains. Between 1935 and 1942 more than 200 million
seedling trees and shrubs were planted in 18,000 miles of
shelterbelts and windbreaks. About 30,000 farmers were
assisted in these plantings by the U.S. Forest Service. The
shelterbelts were beneficial in almost every instance.

Van Deusen (1978) describes the disruptive impact on
shelterbelts by the center-pivot sprinkler irrigation system.
In the states of the Great Plains from one to 16 million acres
of land are damaged annually by wind erosion with a 40-year
average of 5 million acres. The shelterbelts in the past were
planted along section lines and property lines but it may be
necessary to change the pattern of planting to conform with
center-pivot irrigation development.

Gindel (1966) investigated in Israel the increase in soil
moisture as a result of the conveyance of water from dew and
mist following intake of woody zerophytes by leaves and plant
tissues. He found increases of soil moisture of 30 to 50 percent in the dry months, June to October, in permeable soils
beneath Tamarix aphylla and T. pseudopalassi and 12.5
to 30.8 percent in rendzina soil beneath Aleppo pine.

In the section on absorption of atmospheric moisture by
woody xerophytes in his volume on "The Ecodynamics of Forest-
Water Relationships in Arid Climates" Gindel (1970) stresses
the importance of dew and mist in maintaining the survival of
plants in arid zones. He reports that dry crops such as maize,
wheat, barley, and sesame, flourish in the western valley of
Israel where there is heavy dew but they do not do as well in
the eastern section of the valley where there is less dew.
Gindel, on his pages 76 and 77, quotes several passages from
the Bible indicating that the importance of dew was recognized
thousands of years ago.

The drought in the Sahel zone in the Sub-Sahara area of West Africa was mentioned in Topic 22, page 117. Glantz (1976) found that the introduction of the inappropriate technology of deep wells was a major contributor to the severe impact of the drought of about 1967 to about 1974. At least 100,000 people and about 40 percent of the 25 million cattle were lost. Water from deep wells changed the life style of the people. Nomads settled on marginal lands to raise crops. The number of cattle increased while the utilization of the open range was forsaken. The deep wells were not a part of the delicate ecosystem developed over the centuries. As the drought developed and wells dried up, devastation set in. Englebert's (1974) article on the Sahel region depicts the severe effects of the drought including desertification.

A very valuable reference on the arid and semi-arid regions is "Deserts of the World" (1968) edited by McGinnies, Goldman, and Paylore. The early pages of this book include maps of the areas of the world's continents showing the locations of extremely arid, arid, and semi-arid areas. This volume, based on work performed at the University of Arizona's Office of Arid Lands Studies with the assistance of a major contract from the U.S. Army Research Office, is a United States contribution to the International Hydrological Decade.

"Earth's Creeping Deserts" (1977) is an article which summarizes the spread of desertification. In half a century 251,000 square miles (650,000 sq. km) along the Sahara's southern fringe, have changed from farming and grazing to desert.

Cluff (1972) proposes a method of augmenting streamflow at stock ponds by water harvesting techniques using impervious plastic-lined gravel-filled catchments.

Villagers, about a quarter of a million people, near the town of Nsukka in Eastern Nigeria must walk at least 5 miles to the nearest spring since there is no piped drinking water. Most of the annual rainfall of 66.2 inches falls between April and October on soils of lateritic origin. Households collect runoff in pits and store the water in 50-litre earthenware pots. An average household of 20 people may have 50 pots in which the water attains natural purfication and clarification in a 5-month storage period.

Egbuniwe (1978) reports that wood ashes from the burning of tropical woods such as iroko, obeche, upke, and akpu, when added to the recently-filled storage jars, clarified the iron-bearing water and reduced coliform bacteria to acceptable levels in 3 days. This was accomplished without resorting to advanced technology, investments in equipment, and in chemicals.

The desert is a fragile ecosystem. Hastings and Turner (1972) have prepared a fascinating book in which are included 97 pairs of photographs. Elapsed time between two views in the same pair may be as long as 75 years. Their book deals only with the arid and semi-arid regions of the Sonoran Desert, the desert grasslands of the San Pedro and the Santa Cruz Valleys in Arizona, and the oak woodlands of the same valleys. In a great many instances it is difficult to discern much change in the vegetation in the elapsed time.

A 40-year photographic record of plant recovery on an abused watershed has been prepared by Gary and Currie (1977). Their report is illustrated with 14 pairs of photographs, taken in 1937 and again in 1977, of the semi-arid Ponderosa pine, Douglas fir, quaking aspen, shrubs and grasses, comprising the forest in the Front Range of the Rocky Mountains in the Trail Creek drainage basin about 30 miles (48 km) northwest of Colorado Springs, Colorado. The average elevation of the area is about 7,500 feet (2288 m).

They concluded that tree planting, done in the 1930's by the Civilian Conservation Corps, was more effective than natural reseeding; that ground cover has reduced erosion losses; and that reestablishment of more palatable grasses has been very slow. Considerably more than 40 years will be needed to rebuild the ecosystem of this area.

"Desertification - Environmental Degradation in and Around Arid Lands" (1977), edited by Glantz, is an assembly of 12 papers, world-wide in scope, on an increasingly pressing environmental management problem.

References

Bell, Frederick C., "Generalized Rainfall-Duration-Frequency Relationships", Jour. Hydraulics Div., Proceedings ASCE, pp 311-327, Jan. 1969.

Christian, Francis G., and Walter J. Parsons, Jr., "Semiarid Regions", Chap. 9, pp 286-300 in Hydrology by C. O. Wisler and E. F. Brater, John Wiley and Sons, New York, 2nd edition, 3d printing, Mar. 1965.

Cluff, C. Brent, "Multipurpose Water Harvesting Systems - A Possible Method of Augmenting Streamflow Through Reduction of Inefficient Earth Stock Tanks in Stream Channels on Semiarid Watersheds", pp 251-256, in Watersheds in Transition, a Symposium held at Fort Collins, Colo. June 19-22, 1972, ed. by S. C. Csallany, T. G. McLaughlin, and W. Striffler, Proceedings Series No. 14, Amer. Water Resources Assn., 405 pp, Sept. 1972.

Croft, A. Russell, "Rainstorm Debris Floods", Agri. Exp. Station, Univ. of Arizona, Tucson, 36 pp, May, 1967.

"Desertification - Environmental Degradation in and Around Arid Lands", ed. by Michael H. Glantz, Westview Press, Boulder, Colo., 346 pp, July, 1977.

"Deserts of the World - An Appraisal of Research into their Physical and Biological Environments", edited by William G. McGinnies, Bram J. Goldman, and Patricia Paylore, A United States Contribution to the International Hydrological Decade, The Univ. of Arizona Press, Tucson, 788 pp, 1968.

"Earth's Creeping Deserts - A Tide of Ecological Refugees from Land Turning to Sand", pp 58-59, Time, Sept. 12, 1977.

Egbuniwe, Nnamdi, "Rural Water Supplies from Laterite Runoff", Water Resources Bulletin, vol. 14, no. 2, pp 466-469, Apr. 1978.

Englebert, Victor, "Drought Threatens the Tuareg World", National Geographic, vol. 145, no. 4, pp 544-571, April, 1974.

Gary, Howard L., and Pat O. Currie, "The Front Range Pine Type - A 40-Year Photographic Record of Plant Recovery on an Abused Watershed", General Tech. Report RM-46, Rocky Mt. Forest and Range Exp. Station, Forest Service, USDA, Fort Collins, Colo., 17 pp, Nov. 1977.

Gindel, I., "Attraction of Atmospheric Moisture by Woody Xerophytes in Arid Climates", Commonwealth Forestry Review, vol. 45 (4), no. 126, pp 297-321, Dec. 1966.

Gindel, I., "The Ecodynamics of Forest-Water Relationships in Arid Climates", Science Series No. 1, College of Forestry and Natural Resources, Colo. State Univ., Fort Collins, 206 pp, 1970. (This was written while Dr. Gindel was visiting professor at CSU.)

Glantz, Michael H., "Water and Inappropriate Technology: Deep Wells in the Sahel", pp 527-540 in Water Needs for the Future: Legal, Political, Economic, and Technological Issues in National and International Perspectives, Proceedings of a Conf., of Oct. 8-9, 1976 held at the Univ. of Denver, College of Law, pub. as vol. 6, special issue by the Denver Journal of International Law and Policy, Univ. of Denver, 1976. (Copyright 1977)

Hastings, James Rodney, and Raymond M. Turner, "The Changing Mile - An Ecological Study of Vegetation Change With Time in the Lower Mile of an Arid and Semiarid Region", The Univ. of Arizona Press, Tucson, 317 pp, 1965, 3d printing 1972.

Hudson, H. E., Jr., and Richard Hazen, "Droughts and Low Streamflow", Sec. 18 in Handbook of Applied Hydrology, ed by Ven Te Chow, McGraw-Hill Book Co., New York, 1964.

Martin, S. Clark, and Dwight R. Cable, "Managing Semidesert Grass-Shrub Ranges - Vegetation Responses to Precipitation, Grazing, Soil Texture, and Mesquite Control", Forest Service, USDA Tech. Bulletin 1480, 45 pp, Apr. 1974.

Thornthwaite, C. Warren, "The Climates of North America, According to a New Classification", The Geographical Review, vol. XXI, no. 4, pp 633-655, Oct. 1931.

Van Deusen, James L., "Shelterbelt Renovation in the Great Plains", pp 181-186 in Shelterbelts on the Great Plains, Proc. Symposium, held by Great Plains Agri. Council, Denver, Colo., Apr. 1976, Pub. 78, 218 pp, 1976.

Van Deusen, James L., "Shelterbelts on the Great Plains: What's Happening", Jour. of Forestry, vol. 76, no. 3, pp 160-161, Mar., 1978.

"Walnut Gulch Experimental Watershed", Agri. Research Service, USDA, in Cooperation with U.S. Soil Conservation Service, Univ. of Arizona, and Local Ranchers, 28 pp, undated. (The Watershed is near Tombstone, Ariz., headquarters are at the Southwest Watershed Research Ctr. ARS, USDA, Tucson, Ariz.)

Topic 85    Arctic and Sub-Arctic Water Resources

The arctic and sub-arctic regions are characterized by a
short growing season and by the presence of water in the form
of ice throughout much of the year. The annual precipitation
is low in amount, usually less than 15 inches, and often similar to arid and semi-arid regions of the temperate zones.
Much of the arctic region's exposed soil surface is permafrost
or permanently frozen ground. During the short and intense
summers some of the permafrost may thaw out at the surface.
Chow (1964, Section 10, page 48) has prepared a map of permafrost for the Northern Hemisphere.

A general discussion of permafrost is given by Stearns
(1966) in which he shows in his Figure 53 the tree line for the
North Pole region. A review of the characteristics of cold
regions, especially of the northern hemisphere, is to be found
in the monograph by Gerdel (1969). McKay (1976) includes in
his chapter on hydrological mapping, Fig. 1.31, a map of permafrost by physiographic regions of Canada.

"The World We Live In" (1955) presents in its chapter
entitled "The Arctic Barrens", pages 197-218, a superbly illustrated description of the frozen desert ringing the polar sea.

Since frozen soil is physically and physiologically dry,
the removal of liquid water through the formation of ice in a
soil in the process of freezing sets up a capillary tension
which tends to bring additional water to the freezing layer.
As this water freezes it produces ice lenses underground or ice
"flowers" which project up from the surface. Upon melting, the
sudden release of water beyond field capacity of the soil results in fluidity causing failure of foundations, pavements,
pipelines, and other structures. Arctic and sub-arctic construction requires maintenance of frozen foundations. A
classic work on cold region engineering is "Permafrost or Permanently Frozen Ground and Related Engineering Problems" by
Muller (1943 and 1947).

Tundra and permafrost are found above timberline in the
Rocky Mountains. Industrial, research, and recreational facilities in these areas must be constructed and operated in a
manner similar to that which has been developed for the arctic
and sub-arctic regions. Conveyance of water, even in pipes,
and the disposal of waste and sewage become special problems
which are reviewed by Monney, Hill, Oien, Rowland, and Vail
(1968). To protect utility systems, utilidors have been found
to be very effective, according to Alter (1969). A utilidor is
a passageway which may be built out of concrete or wood, or be
in effect a tunnel, in which electrical conduits, steamlines,

490

water supply and sewer lines, are installed in complete protection from outside weather.

Navigation is restricted by freezing of lakes and rivers. The Great Lakes of the United States and Canada are usually closed to traffic most winters. Ice breakers are specially designed ships used to open up passageways through ice covers. Induced melting of ice cover at the confluence of the Chena and Tanana Rivers in Alaska is described by Cook and Wade (1968). About 35 tons of fly ash and coal dust were applied in 10 hours from converted aircraft. The treatment was effective as was indicated by the observation that the dusted river channel opened 9 days before the remainder of the river.

Water in storage as ice is not restricted to continental glaciers such as in Greenland and in the Antarctic. It has been estimated that over 40 million acre-feet of frozen fresh water is in storage in glaciers in the State of Washington alone. This volume of water is about equal to the amounts stored in all the reservoirs, lakes, and rivers in that State. The Geological Survey has prepared a folder, "Glaciers - A Water Resource" (1976) based on information supplied by Mark Meier and Austin Post. This publication is a very concise monograph with illustrations on the importance of glaciers in hydrology. Meier's (1964) Section on ice and glaciers is an excellent treatment of the subjects.

Colonization and utilization of the water resources and especially the mineral resources of the arctic and sub-arctic regions is inevitable. As these endeavors expand, a knowledge of cold-region engineering is fundamental to natural resource utilization with a minimum of permanent damage to the exceedingly fragile arctic and sub-arctic environment.

Becker (1972) reviews the obstacles of muskeg and permafrost which had to be overcome in the construction of the 364-mile Anchorage-Fairbanks Highway. Becker describes the rolling surcharge technique. A photograph on page 766 of this reference shows styrofoam insulation being laid as a base for a pavement. A major problem in arctic and sub-arctic highway maintenance is that of disposing quickly of flowing water to prevent the water from inducing thawing in the roadway base.

An informative publication presenting a wealth of data in readily usable form is the "Design Manual - Cold Regions Engineering" (1967). Engineers have made use of the favorable characteristics of frozen soil and of frozen aquifers by installing refrigeration systems to create artificial freezing as reviewed by Sanger (1968). The "Proceedings of the Conference on Soil-Water Problems in Cold Regions" (1975) is an assembly of 13 papers dealing with this subject. Dingman (1975 and 1976) reviews 172 references in his synthesis of literature on the hydrologic effects of frozen ground.

Martinec, Moser, de Quervain, Rauert, and Stichler (1977) describe the use of parallel sampling using deuterium, tritium, and oxygen-18 ratios to determine snow accumulation, snowmelt water, and evaporation from snow in a lysimeter. Proportions of concentrations of the three elements changed in the percolating water as compared to those in the snowpack. Tritium was found to be least indicative in the conduct of this assessment. A broad discussion of snow and winter hydrology was written by Garstka (1964).

Beschta (1975) used linear, quadratic, and cubic equations in his regional analyses as part of the development of a method for estimating snowfall amounts as measured at the time of fall (not snowpack accumulations) based on temperature and precipitation measurements only. He used data from Alaska, Arizona, Minnesota, Montana, New England, and Oregon. No general equation was evident but the relationships for a given region were found to be significant.

Construction of dams on permafrost is exceedingly dangerous since any impoundment which prevents downward penetration of the frost ultimately results in the collapse of the dam and of its appurtenant structures. Batenchuk, Biyanov, Toropov, and Myznikov (1968) report on the construction of an earth dam for the Vilyui Hydroelectric Plant in the far north on a tributary of the Lena River in Siberia, where minimum temperatures of -63° C (-81° F) have been observed. The dam site is on bedrock. Their report, with numerous charts, tables, and photographs, describes the technological processes, the equipment used, and the quality control methods applied. They used electrical resistance heating of earth material stockpiles to prevent freezing.

One of the early investigations of ice pressure against dams is described by Monfore and Taylor (1948). The coefficient of expansion of ice is nearly five times that of steel. Michel (1970) has prepared a comprehensive discussion, including mathematical treatment, of ice pressure on engineering structures.

A very condensed and informative discussion of the great Trans-Alaska Pipeline controversy is given by Friggens (1972). The Alaskan oil is viscous and a temperature of 135° F must be maintained to permit flow. The oil is heated in transit by friction generated by pumping pressures of up to 1,180 pounds per square inch. The pipeline is heavily insulated.

Brew (1974) prepared an example of an environmental impact analysis for the Trans-Alaska Pipeline. He listed a total of 41 principle unavoidable effects. The pros and cons of the pipeline controversy were presented by Patton (1973). Sloan Zenone, and Mayo (1976) showed the location of icing along the Trans-Alaska Pipeline route on a series of maps and photographs.

Hodgson and Raymer (1976) have prepared an excellently-illustrated description of the 800-mile-long Trans-Alaska Pipeline. Their pages 694-696 show the anatomy of the pipeline. An ingenous non-mechanical refrigeration system using liquid and vaporized ammonia maintains the footings of the pipeline supports below freezing. The pipeline, 48-inches in diameter, required 78,000 vertical supports in the 425 miles subjected to permafrost risk.

Practically all of the fears of environmental disaster have been shown to be unfounded to date and the American Society of Civil Engineers bestowed its Outstanding Civil Engineering Award on the Trans-Alaska Pipeline in April, 1978, describing it as one of the most extraordinary projects in engineering innovation and attention to ecological impact, possibly of all time, as reported in "Trans-Alaska Pipeline OCEA Choice", 1978.

There is an extremely sensitive response of water near the freezing point to the formation of ice under turbulent flow conditions. Water does not freeze instantly throughout. At a few thousandths of a degree below the freezing point some of the water substance, which exists in many configurations in nature, solidifies. In still water the first microscopic crystals link, form platelets, and then rapidly form an unbroken ice layer. Water has its greatest density at $39.2^{\circ}$ F or $4^{\circ}$ C and as it cools below $4^{\circ}$ C it expands and ice cover forms on the surface. See Logan (1974) figures 1 and 3.

However, under turbulent flow conditions the ice crystals that form do not cluster but remain suspended individually throughout the flow. A turbulent stream has the same temperature throughout. It takes 80 calories per gram to melt ice and conversely when water freezes it releases 80 degrees calories per gram. This acts as an equalizer to replenish heat which is lost from the turbulent flow. The crystals suspended in a turbulent flow are called frazil and, as the amount of ice increases, a frazil slush forms which is different from solid ice. Carstens (1970) on his page 8 presents a diagram showing the typical history of supercooling. Water at a temperature of about $-0.07^{\circ}$ C freezes in about 3 minutes. A frazil-bulked flow no longer requires 80 calories of heat to be lost since most of the flow may already be ice and the loss of a few hundredths or even thousandths of a degree will result in the flow freezing.

Foulds and Wigle (1977) describe stages in the formation of frazil ice. Their article is illustrated with photographs.

They state that the rate of ice build-up on an underwater object can be phenomenal. Intakes to power plants and to waterworks are often blocked when frazil crystals adhere to the trash rack and build up an arch action which in a very short time cuts off the flow. Schaefer (1950) on his page 889 includes a photograph of a powerplant intake trash rack encrusted with a frazil ice build-up. Frazil ice has been known to plug intakes to powerplants and water works and in a very short time cause shutdowns of multi-million dollar installations. See Hayes (1974) pages 23-39.

To provide ice-free diversions it is necessary to have a reservoir of sufficient depth so that higher density frazil-free water can be withdrawn. Water treatment plants cannot operate with frazil-bulked flows.

When frazil ice builds up on the stream bottom it becomes anchor ice. A number of papers on frazil and anchor ice are to be found in "The Role of Snow and Ice in Hydrology" (1973). A classic work on streamflow under winter conditions is the book by Barnes (1928). See Burgi and Johnson (1971) page 2.

The U.S. Army Cold Regions Research and Engineering Laboratory of Hanover, New Hampshire (CRREL) has compiled the "USA CRREL Technical Publications" (1972) and (1976) in which hundreds of references are abstracted, with author and subject indices included. In 1961 CRREL resulted from the combination of the Snow, Ice, and Permafrost Research Establishment (SIPRE) of 1949 and the Arctic Construction and Frost Effects Laboratory of 1953. Without the research knowledge and experience of CRREL and its predecessors the Trans-Alaska Pipeline would have been impossible.

"Snow and Ice Hydrology in the United States - Current Status and Future Directions" (1976) is a 61-page final report of the Work Group on Snow and Ice Hydrology of the National Research Council. The Work Group made 4 recommendations which are summarized as follows:

(1) Lead agencies should be identified and especially charged with responsibility of coordinating and disseminating data;

(2) A national data system should be activated for providing necessary information on snow and ice to operating agencies and to researchers;

(3) Research funding agencies including the National Science Foundation need to increase their allocation of funds for snow and ice hydrology;

(4) Resources of the research-funding and research-conducting agencies should be directed to the synthesis of research results especially on in-depth studies of primary chemical and physical processes affecting snow and ice.

494

There are many organizations conducting research on the arctic and sub-arctic. One of these is the University of Alaska's Institute of Arctic Environmental Engineering. The Arctic Institute of America has extensive publications and bibliographies. Many Universities have organizations or institutes which conduct research on the arctic regions on various aspects such as ecology, wildlife resources, meteorology, geology, and mineral resources. Exploration and research in the Antarctic is being conducted under international treaties.

References

Alter, Amos J., "Water Supply in Cold Regions", Cold Regions Science and Engineering Monograph No. III-C5a, U.S. Army Cold Regions Research and Eng. Lab., Hanover, New Hampshire, Jan. 1969.

Barnes, Howard Turner, "Ice Engineering", Renouf, Montreal, Canada, 364 pp, 1928.

Batenchuk, E. N., G. F. Biyanov, L. N. Toropov, and Yu. N. Myznikov, "Winter Construction From Cohesive Earth in the Far North - (Dam-Core Construction for the Vilyui Hydroelectric Plant)", original in Russian, Energiya, Moskva, 1968. Trans. by the Israel Program for Scientific Translations, Jerusalem, 1969. Pub. for the U.S. Dept. of the Interior and the Natl. Science Foundation, Washington, D.C. Trans. No. TT 69-55098.

Becker, John C., "Alaska Builds Highway Over Muskeg and Permafrost", Civil Engineering, vol. 42, no. 7, pp 75-77, July, 1972.

Beschta, Robert L., "A Method for Estimating Snowfall Amounts", Water Resources Bulletin, vol. 11, no. 6, pp 1209-1219, Dec. 1975.

Brew, David A., "Environmental Impact Analysis: The Example of the Proposed Trans-Alaska Pipeline", U.S. Geological Survey Circ. 695, 16 pp, 1974.

Burgi, P. H., and P. L. Johnson, "Ice Formation - A Review of the Literature and Bureau of Reclamation Experience", Div. of General Research, Report REC-ERC-71-8, Engr. & Research Ctr., U.S. Bur. of Reclamation, Denver, Colo. 27 pp, Sept. 1971.

Carstens, Torkild, "Heat Exchange and Frazil Formation", Paper No. 2.11, 17 pages in I.A.H.R. Symposium: Ice and its Action on Hydraulic Structures, held at Reykjavik, Iceland, 7-10 September 1970.

Chow, Ven Te, "Permafrost Line In Arctic Region", Fig. 10-20 in Section 10, Snow and Snow Survey, by Walter U. Garstka, Handbook of Applied Hydrology, ed by Ven Te Chow, McGraw Hill Book Co., New York, 1964.

Cook, R. G., and M. D. Wade, Jr., "Successful Ice Dusting at Fairbanks, Alaska, 1966", Jour. Hydraulics Div., Proceedings ASCE, pp 31-41 in vol. 94, no. HY1, Jan. 1968.

"Design Manual - Cold Regions Engineering", NAVFAC DM-9, prepared by Naval Facilities Engineering Command, Dept. of the Navy, Washington, D.C., U.S. Govt. Printing Office, Washington, D.C., Dec. 1967.

Dingman, S. Lawrence, "Hydrologic Effects on Frozen Ground - Literature Review and Synthesis", CRREL Special Report 218, Cold Regions Research & Engineering Lab., Corps of Engineers, U.S. Army, Hanover, N.H., 55 pp, Mar., 1975. (With "Supplement to CRREL Special Report 218", by S. Lawrence Dingman, 3 pp, Feb. 1976.)

Foulds, D. M., and T. E. Wigle, "Frazil - The Invisible Strangler", Jour. Amer. Water Works Assn., vol. 69, no. 4, pp 196-199, Apr. 1977.

Friggens, Paul, "The Great Alaska Pipeline Controversy", Reader's Digest, pp 125-129, Nov. 1972.

Garstka, Walter U., "Snow and Snow Survey", Section 10 in Handbook of Applied Hydrology, ed. by Ven Te Chow, McGraw Hill Book Co., New York, 1964.

Gerdel, Robert W., "Characteristics of the Cold Regions", Monograph 1-A, Cold Regions Research and Eng. Lab., Corps of Engineers, U.S. Army, Hanover, N.H., Aug. 1969.

"Glaciers - A Water Resource", Geological Survey, USDI, Folder INF-73-8, 24 pp, 1976.

Hayes, R. B., "Design and Operation of Shallow River Diversions in Cold Regions", Div. of General Research, Report REC-ERC-74-19, Engr. & Research Ctr., U.S. Bur. of Reclamation, Denver, Colo., 39 pp, Sept. 1974.

Hodgson, Bryan, and Steve Raymer, "The Pipeline: Alaska's Troubled Colossus", National Geographic, vol. 150, no. 5, pp 684-717, Nov. 1976.

Logan, T. H., "Prevention of Frazil Ice Clogging of Water Intakes by Application of Heat", Div. of Design, Report REC-ERC-74-15, Engr. & Research Ctr., U.S. Bur. of Reclamation, Denver, Colo. 20 pp, Sept. 1974.

Martinec, J., H. Moser, M. R. de Quervain, W. Rauert, and
W. Stichler, "Assessment of Processes in the Snowpack by
Parallel Deuterium, Tritium, and Oxygen-18 Sampling",
Proceedings of the Grenoble Symposium, Aug.-Sept. 1975,
IAHS Pub. No. 118, pp 220-231, 1977.

McKay, Gordon A., "Hydrological Mapping", Chap. 1, pp 1-36 in
Facets of Hydrology ed. by John C. Rodda, John Wiley and
Sons, printed in Great Britain, 1976.

Meier, Mark F., "Ice and Glaciers", Sec. 16 in Handbook of
Applied Hydrology, ed. by Ven Te Chow, McGraw Hill Book
Co., New York, 1964.

Michel, Bernard, "Ice Pressure on Engineering Structures",
Monograph III-B1b, U.S. Army Corps of Engineers, Cold
Regions Research and Engineering Lab., Hanover, N.H.,
June, 1970.

Monfore, G. E., and Frank W. Taylor, "The Problem of an Expanding Ice Sheet", Branch of Design and Construction, Bur.
of Reclamation, USDI, Denver, Colo., 16 pp, Mar. 18, 1948.

Monney, Neil T., Millard M. Hill, A. Oien, S. J. Rowland, and
F. L. Vail, "Arctic Construction Problems and Techniques",
Jour. Construction Div., Proceedings ASCE, vol. 94,
no. CO1, pp 89-93, Jan. 1968. (The five authors were all
members of the U.S. Navy's Naval Facilities Engrg.
Command, Seattle, Wash.)

Muller, Siemon William, "Permafrost or Permanently Frozen
Ground and Related Engineering Problems", J. W. Edwards
Pub., Ann Arbor, Mich., 1947. (This publication is
essentially a reprint of Report No. 62 under the same
title prepared by the U.S. Geological Survey for the
Intelligence Branch, Office, U.S. Army Chief of Engineers,
March, 1943.)

Patton, E. L., "The Trans-Alaska Pipeline Story", Transportation Engineering Jour., Proceedings ASCE, vol. 99, no.
TE-1, pp 139, 144, Feb. 1973.

"Proceedings - Conference on Soil-Water Problems in Cold
Regions", Meeting of the Special Task Force, Div. of
Hydrology, Amer. Geophysical Union, held at Calgary,
Alberta, Canada, May 6-7, 1975, pub. by Dept. of Water
Science and Engineering, Univ. of Calif. at Davis, 211 pp,
1975.

Sanger, Frederick J., "Ground Freezing in Construction", Jour.
Soil Mechanics and Foundations Div., Proceedings ASCE,
vol. 94, no. SM1, pp 131-158, Jan. 1968.

Schaefer, Vincent J., "The Formation of Frazil and Anchor Ice in Cold Water", Trans. Amer. Geophysical Union, vol. 31, no. 6, pp 885-893, Dec. 1950.

Sloan, Charles E., Chester Zenone, and Lawrence R. Mayo, "Icings Along the Trans-Alaska Pipeline Route", USGS Prof. Paper 979, 31 pp, 1976.

"Snow and Ice Hydrology in the United States - Current Status and Future Directions", Final report of the Work Group on Snow and Ice Hydrology of the U.S. Natl. Comm. for the International Hydrological Decade, Natl. Research Council, Natl. Academy of Sciences, Washington, D.C., 61 pp, 1976.

Stearns, S. Russell, "Permafrost (Perennially Frozen Ground)", Part 1, Sec. A2, Cold Regions Research & Engr. Lab., U.S. Army Materiel Command, Hanover, N.H., Aug. 1966.

"The Role of Snow and Ice in Hydrology", Proceedings in two volumes of the Banff Symposia of Sept. 1972, pub. by UNESCO-WMO-IAHS and UNESCO-OMM-AISH, printed in Canada, 1973.

"The World We Live In", by the Editorial Staff of Life and Lincoln Barnett, a 11-inch by 14-inch, 304-page book, pub. by Time Inc., New York, 1955. Distribution by Simon and Schuster, Inc.

"Trans Alaska Pipeline OCEA Choice - Board of Direction Acts at Pittsburgh Meeting", ASCE News, vol. 3, no. 5, p 1, May, 1978. Also see Civil Engr., pp 59-71, June, 1978.

"USA CRREL Technical Publications", Special Report 175, U.S. Army Corps of Engineers, Cold Regions Research and Engr. Lab., Hanover, N.H., 375 pp, June, 1972.
    (The above report is supplemented by a publication of the same title.)

SECTION XX

URBAN HYDROLOGY

Topic 86     Urban and Industrial Area Hydrology

The hydrology of urban and industrial areas includes an
adequate supply of water of good quality, provision for disposing of surface runoff and flood flows, and provision for a
wastewater conveyance and disposal system. Inherent in the
planning, construction, and operation of the hydrologic features is the land use plan which may be of great importance in
affecting the decisions on these 3 major hydrologic requirements of cities and industries.

There are numerous instances where land use planning envisioned a single family suburban-type development for which
the water supply and wastewater systems were designed. However
very often, as a result of rezoning subsequent to the construction of the hydrologic facilities, high-rise apartments have
been built. Consequently requirements for water-related services far exceeded the design capacities originally planned.

Hauser (1970) stated that the World's population did not
reach one billion until 1850. The second billion came in the
following 80 years and the third in only 30 years. Hauser
believes that if the present birth and mortality trends continue the global population could be 7.5 billion by the year
2000. Cities of a million or more developed about 170 years
ago. If one uses the United Nation's definition of an urban
area as one having a population of 20,000 people or more,
slightly more than 2 percent of the World population was in
urban areas in the year 1800. Hauser projects that by the year
2000 the World's urban population may be between 40 and 50
percent. Such an increase in urbanization will inevitably
create competition for water resources, especially for food and
fiber production, in many parts of the World.

The transformation of a flood plain of the Salt River
Valley in Phoenix, Arizona, into an urban and industrial area
is described by Womack (1975). Farmland supplied by water in
open canals and laterals over a period of 60 years became practically completely urbanized. It was found necessary because
of rising land values and because of the cost of fencing to
protect against drownings and to reduce maintenance due to
debris, to place the water conveyance systems underground.

The population of Phoenix grew tremendously without requiring an increase in the water supply. The average popula-
lation density of 20 people per acre required on the average

5 acre feet per year which by a fortunate coincidence about equalled the irrigation supply. When the irrigated farmland was exhausted and urbanization encroached on the desert, water-supply problems arose.

Romm (1977) has analyzed the relationship between water supply, land use, and urban growth. He concludes (page 284):

"Available water supply does not determine the combination of water requirements or land uses, supported by that supply. Rather, it is economics, historical trends, and, at the very center, community goals and associated policies that define and direct the social, economic, and environmental lifestyle of an area. A valley with the existing sources of supply of Santa Clara County has enough water to adequately support any number of land-use and population variations. Water supply only becomes 'not enough' when it cannot support a set of community goals that are made taking future water supply for granted and that will require a greater supply than is available.

"Land-use projections represent a more reliable basis than population projections for the determination of future supplemental water requirements and the design of water distribution systems."

Feth (1973) has tabulated the hydrologic effects of changes of land use and water use associated with urbanization. This is reproduced in Table 86-1 on page 501.

In the humid part of the United States it was common practice, going back more than 100 years in some instances, for municipal water supply companies to own the land of the drainage basin which served as a source of the water for their impoundments. The New Haven Water Company lands in Connecticut are an example. As population density increases there has been a steady pressure for conversion of the forested water supply drainage basins to urbanization. Great pressure is exerted by developers, especially when land is being assessed as city lots rather than as forested land. "Report of the Connecticut Council on Water Company Lands" (1977) is a detailed presentation of environmental, legal, hydrologic, and social implications of such changes in land use. Obviously if all of a water company's lands are urbanized contaminated surface runoff may be unacceptable for domestic use.

Wilber and Hunter (1977) studied the transport of lead, zinc, copper, nickel, and chromium in stream runoff and in sediment in the Saddle River drainage basin in Northern New Jersey. Sources of heavy metals are domestic waste waters, industrial activities such as plating, oil and coal refining, paint and biocide manufacture, with small amounts contributed by precipitation. Lead, zinc, and copper were the major

Table 86-1   Hydrologic effects during a selected sequence of changes in land and water use associated with urbanization.

| Changes in land or water use | Possible hydrologic effect |
|---|---|
| Transition from preurban to early-urban stage: Removal of trees or vegetation, Construction of scattered city-type houses and limited water and sewage facilities. | Decrease in transpiration and increase in storm flow. Increased sedimentation of streams. |
| Drilling of wells ----------------------------- | Some lowering of water table. |
| Construction of septic tanks and sanitary drains __ | Some increase in soil moisture and perhaps a rise in water table. Perhaps some waterlogging of land and contamination of nearby wells or streams from overloaded sanitary drain system. |
| Transition from early-urban to middle-urban stage: Bulldozing of land for mass housing; some topsoil removal; farm ponds filled in. | Accelerated land erosion and stream sedimentation and aggradation. Increased flood flows. Elimination of smallest streams. |
| Mass construction of houses; paving of streets; building of culverts. | Decreased infiltration, resulting in increased flood flows and lowered ground-water levels. Occasional flooding at channel constrictions (culverts) on remaining small streams. Occasional over-topping or undermining of banks of artificial channels on small streams. |
| Discontinued use and abandonment of some shallow wells. | Rise in water table. |
| Diversion of nearby streams for public water supply. | Decrease in runoff between points of diversion and disposal. |
| Untreated or inadequately treated sewage discharged into streams or disposal wells. | Pollution of streams or wells. Death of fish and other aquatic life. Inferior quality of water available for supply and recreation at downstream populated areas. |
| Transition from middle- to late-urban stage: Urbanization of area completed by addition of more houses and streets, and of public, commercial, and industrial buildings. | Reduced infiltration and lowered water table. Streets and gutters act as storm drains creating higher flood peaks and lower base flow of local streams. |
| Larger quantities of untreated waste discharged into local streams. | Increased pollution of streams and concurrent increased loss of aquatic life. Additional degradation of water available to downstream users. |
| Abandonment of remaining shallow wells because of pollution. | Rise in water table. |
| Increase in population requires establishment of new water-supply and distribution systems, construction of distant reservoirs diverting water from upstream sources within or outside basin. | Increase in local streamflow if supply is from outside basin. |
| Channels of streams restricted at least in part to artificial channels and tunnels. | Increased flood damage (higher stage for a given flow). Changes in channel geometry and sediment load. Aggradation. |
| Construction of sanitary drainage system and treatment plant for sewage. | Removal of additional water from area, further reducing infiltration recharge of aquifer. |
| Improvement of storm drainage system -------- | |
| Drilling of deeper, large-capacity industrial wells_ | Lowered water-pressure surface of artesian aquifer; perhaps some local overdrafts and land subsidence. Overdraft of aquifer may result in salt-water encroachment in coastal areas and in pollution or contamination by inferior or brackish waters. |
| Increased use of water for air conditioning ------ | Overloading of sewers and other drainage facilities. Possibly some recharge to water table, owing to leakage of disposal lines. |
| Drilling of recharge wells --------------------- | Raising of water-pressure surface. |
| Wastewater reclamation and utilization --------- | Recharge to ground-water aquifers. More efficient use of water resources. |

From page I 14 of "Water Facts and Figures for Planners and Managers", by J. H. Feth, USGS Circular 601-I, U.S. Government Printing Office, 30 pp, 1973.

contributors of heavy metals in storm water. These 3 metals accounted for 90 to 95 percent of the total metals observed of which lead and zinc accounted for 89 percent. Mercury and cadmium, even at human subtoxic levels, may render fish and shellfish unmarketable. Peak contributions of heavy metals in storm runoff occurred in the first 30 minutes.

Cherkauer and Ostenso (1976) report on the effect of salt on small artificial lakes in Milwaukee, Wisconsin. In 1966-67 the total consumption of salts, chiefly sodium chloride with some calcium chloride, which were applied to driving surfaces to keep them free of snow and ice, exceeded 6.5 million tons in the United States. The authors found a pronounced saline stratification in these artificial lakes. Sodium chloride (common salt) requires the input of heat to dissolve in water; calcium chloride releases heat when dissolved. The more northern the climate, the greater is the proportion of calcium chloride required.

The folder, "Water in the Urban Environment: Real Estate Lakes" (1976), is an informative publication dealing with the planning, location, and management of small bodies of water. Real estate lakes, which add greatly to the quality of an area and to the value of property, may be natural. Usually they are the result of topographic adjustments and modifications of surface runoff drainage patterns. Large excavations such as those resulting from the mining of gravel deposits, rather than despoiling the environment, have turned out to be urban improvements if handled with intelligence.

Barker (1976) found that planting strips, which are components of street rights of way, constitute an important public land resource in urban areas. They make up a total of about 2,000,000 km (1,240,000 miles) or 60,000 ha (148,000 acres) in the United States. Aprroximately one hundred million trees could be planted on this land on about a 12 metre (40-foot) spacing. The esthetic impact of trees and their beneficial influence on the microclimate are widely recognized. Broadleaf deciduous species are especially beneficial since they provide shade in the summer, reducing air conditioning power requirements, and permit the sunlight to come through in the winter. Obviously planting-strip vegetation other than in a humid region will require irrigation.

Cook and Haverbeke (1977) present a detailed discussion illustrated with numerous charts and recommendations for controlling suburban noise with plant material and solid barriers. Their bulletin includes analyses on specific properties for which photographs and sound data in decibels are included. A difference of one decibel is the smallest change in loudness which can be detected ordinarily by the human ear. A quiet library has about 25 decibels; a noisy street corner about

80 decibels; 130 decibels are at the threshold of pain. The decibel scale is not linear.

Lull and Sopper (1969) discuss the influence of both total and partial urbanization of forested watersheds in the northeast with special reference to interception, infiltration, overland flow, soil moisture storage, evapotranspiration, total runoff, peak flows, and water quality. They conclude that urbanization may increase peak flows by 1.2 to 5 times the rate of discharge as compared to the previous conditions. During development and construction, and even after construction, sediment yields are increased from 5 to 10 times those from protected forested watersheds. Annual potential evapotranspiration was reduced in the range of 19 percent to 59 percent of that under previous forested conditions and the annual volume of runoff was increased in the range of 15 percent to 41 percent as a result of urbanization. Davis (1970) emphasizes the growing importance of urban forestry.

Patric and Gould (1976) use double-mass analysis in their study of the effects of shifting land on riverflow in Massachusetts. About 80 percent of Massachusetts had been cleared for farming at one time or another. About 100 years ago much of the land began to revert to forest so that now about 65 percent of the State is forested. The authors believe that decreasing streamflow contributed to the decline of water power as the prime energy source for the industries in Massachusetts.

Patric and Gould refer in their reference 3 to a 1949 publication by C. E. Knox and R. M. Soule describing the oldest streamflow record in the United States. Beginning in 1948 flows at the Merrimac River at Lowell, Massachusetts, were reported, but only for that part of each work day when the mills were operating.

The Hydrologic Engineering Center of the U.S. Army Corps of Engineers at Davis, California, assembled the 15 papers of their "Proceedings of a Seminar on Urban Hydrology" (1970). These papers by professional hydrologists are of direct interest to anyone dealing with land use and urban hydrology.

An example of an excellent presentation of management alternatives for consideration by the citizens is the "Water Supply for a Growing Kansas City Metropolitan Region - Problems and Possible Solutions", Progress Report (1977). It presents 4 alternatives, extending to the year 2025, each of which is described concisely with a map, tables of dates of completion of components, costs, and with discussions of economic, social, and environmental impacts.

Flack, Weakley, and Hill (1977), in their Handbook on

achieving urban water conservation, review residential water conservation including water-saving devices, recycling, metering, water-use restrictions, conveyance problems, building code modifications, horticultural changes, pricing, and public education. Specific case histories are included. A study of this reference is recommended. The National Water Commission in its report, "Water Policies for the Future" (1973) pages 305-306, made 5 recommendations relating to urban use.

Continuing sources of information on urban and industrial area hydrology are the programs, conferences, and publications of several divisions of the American Society of Civil Engineers among which are the Urban Planning and Development Division, Urban Transportation Division, Highway Division, Environmental Engineering Division, Pipeline Division, Irrigation and Drainage Division, and the Water Resources Planning and Management Division.

References

Barker, Philip A., "Planting Strips in Street Rights-of-Way: A Key Public Land Resource", pp 263-274 in, Trees and Forests for Human Settlements, ed. by John W. Andresen, Centre for Urban Forestry Studies, Univ. of Toronto Press, Toronto, Ontario, 417 pp, 1976.

Cherkauer, Douglas S., and Nile A. Ostenso, "The Effect of Salt on Small, Artificial Lakes", Water Resources Bulletin, vol. 12, no. 6, pp 1259-1266, Dec. 1976.

Cook, David I., and David F. Van Haverbeke, "Suburban Noise Control with Plant Materials and Solid Barriers", Research Bulletin EM 100, report of a study conducted jointly by the Univ. of Nebraska, Lincoln, and the Rocky Mt. Forest and Range Exp. Station, U.S. Forest Service, Fort Collins, Colo., 74 pp, Mar. 1977.

Davis, Kenneth P., "Land: The Common Denominator in Forest Resource Management - Emphasis on Urban Relationships", Jour. of Forestry, vol. 68, no. 8, pp 628-631, Oct. 1970.

Feth, J. H., "Water Facts and Figures for Planners and Managers", USGS Cir. 601-I, U.S. Government Printing Off., Washington, D.C., 30 pp, 1973.

Flack, J. Ernest, Wade P. Weakley, with Duane W. Hill, Colo. Water Resources Research Institute Completion Report No. 80, Colo. State Univ., Fort Collins, 207 pp, Sept. 1977.

Hauser, Philip M., "What to Do as Population Explodes, Implodes, Displodes", Smithsonian, vol. 1, no. 9, pp 21-25, Dec. 1970.

Lull, Howard W., and Wm. E. Sopper, "Hydrologic Effects from Urbanization of Forested Watersheds in the Northeast", U.S. Forest Service Research Paper NE-146, N.E. For. Exp. Station, Upper Darby, Pa., 1969.

Patric, James H., and Ernest M. Gould, "Shifting Land Use and the Effects on River Flow in Massachusetts", Jour. Amer. Water Works Assn., vol. 68, no. 1, Jan. 1976.

"Proceedings of a Seminar on Urban Hydrology", 1-3 Sept. 1970, The Hydrologic Engr. Ctr., U.S. Army Corps of Engineers, Davis, Calif., 1970.

"Report of the Connecticut Council on Water Company Lands", prepared by the Council, Hartford, Conn., 121 pp, Feb. 1977.

Romm, Jerri Kay, "Water Supply, Land Use, and Urban Growth", Jour. Water Resources Planning and Mgmt. Div., vol. 103, No. WR2, pp 271-284, Nov. 1977.

"Water in the Urban Environment: Real-Estate Lakes", a folder, prepared by the U.S. Geological Survey, 19 pp, U.S. Govt. Printing Office, Washington, D.C., 1976.

"Water Policies for the Future", Final Report to the President and to the Congress of the United States by the National Water Commission, 579 pp, Washington, D.C., June, 1973.

"Water Supply for a Growing Kansas City Metropolitan Region - Problems & Possible Solutions", prepared by Kansas City Urban Study, U.S. Army Corps of Engineers, Kansas City, Mo., Progress Report, 1977.

Wilber, William G., and Joseph V. Hunter, "Aquatic Transport of Heavy Metals in the Urban Environment", Water Resources Bulletin, vol. 13, no. 4, pp 721-734, Aug. 1977.

Womak, Donald E., "From Farm to City", ASCE Natl. Convention of Nov. 3-7, 1975, Denver, Colo., Meeting Preprint 2590, 12 pp, 1975.

505

Topic 87          Flood Plain Delineation

The delineation of a flood plain is an administrative
decision based on statistical analyses of the frequency and recurrence intervals of meteorological events, of accumulated
streamflow data, and of the application of fluid mechanics,
combined with streamflow routing techniques. The following
Topics provide a background to this problem: 14, 15, 19, 20,
21, 53, 54, 55, 56, 57, 58, 59, 71, 72, and 86.

The problem is not one of routing streamflow in natural
channels. It is complicated by channel encroachments, by
streambed modifications such as channelization to increase the
velocity, thereby reducing the heights of flow, and by the
storm sewer systems and the points at which surface storm run-
offs enter the main channels. Ardis, Dueker, and Lenz (1969)
report on storm drainage practices of 32 cities in Wisconsin
with a 1960 population of 6,000 or more. Figure 87-1, shown
below, from their page 405, shows the relationship between average annual installed feet of storm drainpipe, average 1966 population density, and the average annual expenditures for storm
drainage. It must be kept in mind that the reported expenditures are in terms of March, 1967 dollars.

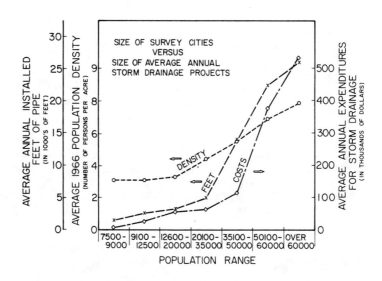

Figure 87-1  Size of Survey Cities vs. Size of Average Annual
   Storm Drainage Projects Expenditures.
   From Ardis, Dueker, and Lenz (1969) page 405.

506

The choice of size and complexity of storm drain systems is an administrative decision. It is based on a balance between the value of the property, flood recurrence interval, and the money available. One of the imponderables is the value to be placed on human life. It would be a simple technological solution to build a storm-sewer system for a thousand-year flood but the costs would be so enormous as to exceed the value of the property being protected. In that event financial support could not be secured.

Grigg, Botham, Rice, Shoemaker, and Tucker (1975) analyze urban drainage and flood control projects from the economic, legal, and financial aspects. This is a comprehensive report dealing with the District made up of all of the County of Denver and of parts of five adjacent counties: Adams, Arapahoe, Boulder, Douglas, and Jefferson. It encompasses about 1200 square miles. This Urban Drainage and Flood Control District is supported by a tax levy not to exceed 0.5 of a mill. This District has prepared a report: "Feasibility Evaluation - Methodology for Evaluation of Feasibility: Multi-Jurisdictional Urban and Flood Control Projects" (1977). A study of these two references is recommended.

Wilkes and King (1977) have prepared a procedure for determining peak flows in Colorado. This report includes and supplements the Soil Conservation Service Technical Release No. 55, entitled "Urban Hydrology for Small Watersheds" of January, 1975. The report by Wilkes and King is a highly technical presentation applying the Soil Conservation Service's soil series hydrologic classification to Colorado conditions.

McCain and Jarrett (1976) have written a manual for estimating flood characteristics of natural flow streams in Colorado (see their pages viii & ix). This is also a highly technical report prepared as part of the State of Colorado's approach to flood insurance, which is described in Topic 88. According to information from the Federal Insurance Administration, manuals paralleling the one written by McCain and Jarrett are being prepared separately for each of many states.

Weiss (1975) gives 8 equations which he presents in detail, with supporting statistical and hydrologic-meteorologic analyses, in his paper on flood formulas for urbanized and non-urbanized areas in Connecticut. He used flow records from a total of 105 stream gaging stations in this densely-populated State for the derivation of his equations. A concise review of various hydrologic methods and techniques underlying the hydrology of urban areas is given by Jens and McPherson (1964).

Maynard (1969) describes the use of building codes and local subdivision control in flood plain management in Iowa. He concludes that the goals of flood plain regulation, which are to protect the floodways and to provide flood control, can be attained by zoning and subdivision regulation, housing codes including building and plumbing, and the acquisition of easements where possible.

White and Haas (1975) list 15 natural hazards affecting habitations: hurricanes, floods, tornadoes, lightning, hail, windstorms, frost, urban snow, earthquakes, tsunami, landslides, snow avalanches, coastal erosion, drought, and volcanoes. To this list should be added the hazard of wildfire. Many communities in forested mountain areas, especially in suburban developments in the chaparral region of Southern California, are located in areas of wildfire hazards.

White and Haas discuss many of the hazards and they describe the research methodology they use in their studies. A considerable portion of their book discusses the distinctive opportunities which are open for managing communities and for alleviating or reducing the potentials for extensive damage. A reading of this book is recommended. They also mention the striking changes which have taken place in the housing industry in the United States since 1960. Mobile homes shipments have been increasing steadily in proportion to single-housing construction. In 1971 30 percent of all single-family unit starts were mobile homes and 20 percent of the total family housing was in mobile homes. It was estimated that mobile homes accounted for 94 percent of all single-family sales under $15,000 in 1971.

White and Haas state that the 1970 census indicated that, out of a sample of 2 million mobile homes, slightly more than half were outside of standard metro areas and that about the same number were in rural non-farm locations. Mobile homes are more vulnerable to wind storms, hurricanes, and tornadoes than are structures on solid foundations. Many mobile home parks in the past were located in flood plains.

The U.S. Water Resources Council has published a pamphlet "Floodplain Management Guidelines For Implementing E.O. 11988" (1978).

Section 2.5, Hydrologic Analyses, and Section 2.6, Hydraulic Analyses, are statements of requirements which are included in the Federal Insurance Adminstration's "Guidelines and Specifications for Study Contractors" (1977).

Kresan (1974) prepared a report describing, with maps, photographs, and text, a self-guided tour of flood hazards in the urban area of Tucson, Arizona. This is an excellent approach to public education so that the inhabitants of a flood area can become acquainted, firsthand, with their immediate environment.

Powell, James, and Jones (1975) present an approximate method for quick flood plain mapping. They illustrate their method with examples. Their paper includes maps of the vicinity of Greensboro, Georgia; Berlin, Wisconsin; Danville, Pennsylvania; and Point of Rocks, Maryland.

## References

Ardis, Colby V., Kenneth J. Dueker, and Arno T. Lenz, "Storm Drainage Practices of Thirty-Two Cities", Jour. Hydraulics Div., Proceedings ASCE, vol. 95, no. HY1, pp 383-408, Jan. 1969.

"Feasibility Evaluation - Methodology for Evaluation of Feasibility: Multi-Jurisdictional Urban Drainage and Flood Control Projects", prepared by the Urban Drainage and Flood Control Dist., Denver, Colo., Feb. 1977.

"Floodplain Management Guidelines for Implementing E.O. 11988", U.S. Water Resources Council, Washington, D.C., 52 pp, Feb. 10, 1978. (This is a reprint from the Federal Register, vol. 43, no. 29, pp 6030-6055, Fri. Feb. 10, 1978.)

Grigg, Neil S., Leslie H. Botham, Leonard Rice, W. J. Shoemaker, and L. Scott Tucker, "Urban Drainage and Flood Control Projects Economic, Legal and Financial Aspects", Completion Report Series No. 65, Environmental Resources Center, Colo. State Univ., Fort Collins, 220 pp, July, 1975.

"Guidelines and Specifications for Study Contractors - Flood Insurance Study", U.S. Dept. of Housing & Urban Development, Federal Insurance Admin., Washington, D.C. Oct. 1977.

Jens, Stifel W., and M. B. McPherson, "Hydrology of Urban Areas", Section 20, Handbook of Applied Hydrology, ed. by Ven Te Chow, McGraw-Hill Book Co., New York, 1964.

Kresan, Peter L., "Flood Hazards in the Tucson Area - A Discussion and Self-Guided Tour of Flood Hazards in the Tucson Basin, Arizona", Dept. of Geosciences, College of Earth Sciences, Univ. of Arizona, Tucson, 11 pp, Oct. 1974.

Maynard, Jim L., "Building Codes and Local Zoning and Subdivision Control for Flood Plain Management", Chap. 16, pp 183-193 in Flood Plain Management - Iowa's Experience, ed. by Merwin D. Dougal, Iowa State Univ. Press, Ames, 270 pp, 1969.

McCain, Jerald F., and Robert D. Jarrett, "Manual for Estimating Flood Characteristics of Natural-Flow Streams in Colorado", Tech. Manual No. 1, Colo. Water Conservation Board, Colo. Dept. of Natural Resources, Denver, Colo., prepared in cooperation with the U.S. Geological Survey, 68 pp, 1976.

Powell, Roy F., L. Douglas James, and D. Earl Jones, Jr., "Approximate Method for Quick Flood Plain Mapping", Meetin Preprint 2559, ASCE Natl. Convention, Denver, Colo., Nov. 3-7, 1975. 30 pp, 1975.

Weiss, L. A., "Floodflow Formulas for Urbanized and Non-urbanized Areas of Connecticut", pp 658-675 in Watershed Management, Proceedings of a Symposium held at Utah State Univ., Logan, Aug. 11-13, 1975. Pub. by ASCE, 781 pp, 1975.

White, Gilbert F., and J. Eugene Haas, "Assessment of Research on Natural Hazards", The MIT Press, Cambridge, Mass., and London, England, 487 pp, 1975. (Second printing 1977.)

Wilkes, S. Glade, and Erke C. King, "Procedures for Determining Peak Flows in Colorado", Incorporates and Supplements Technical Release No. 55 Urban Hydrology for Small Watersheds which was pub. by the Soil Conservation Service, USDA, Jan. 1975. This reference is pub. by the SCS, March, 1977.

Topic 88  Flood Plain Management and Flood Insurance

Whipple (1968) reported that, although many fine flood
control projects have been built, the National total flood damage has increased rather than decreased, due primarily to economic encroachments in the protected areas. Some way must be
found to control project-induced developments since very few
flood-control structure systems guarantee absolute protection.
The flood plain, geologically, belongs to the river.

The concept of Federal flood insurance programs is not
new. During the period 1936-1973 the Federal Government spent
an estimated 9 billion dollars on flood protection work. In
1956 Congress passed the Federal Flood Insurance Act but failed
to appropriate funds. The history of Federal flood insurance
is given on page 43 of the "National Flood Insurance Program"
(1974).

The Housing and Community Development Act of 1977 (PL 95-
128) became law on October 12, 1977. Several significant
changes in the flood insurance program resulted from some of
the provisions of this law. Changes apply to both the Regular
and the Emergancy programs. The most important change is the
extension of the closing date for entry into contracts for
flood insurance from September 30, 1977 to September 30, 1978.

Major conclusions of several studies on public attitudes
was that many people in high-flood risk areas are seriously
uninformed about the risk of flood damage and that they were
overly optimistic in their belief that their property would not
be flooded. Many thought that public help would bail them out
when the inevitable flood disaster struck.

The flood insurance program is administered by the Federal
Insurance Administration of the Department of Housing and Urban
Development. Region VIII, headquartered in Denver, has prepared
a very informative assembly entitled, "Questions and Answers on
the Flood Insurance Program", (1978). The acquisition of this
publication consisting of 59 questions and answers  is
recommended. The following are quoted from this reference:

"19. Q. What types of losses are covered?
     A. All direct losses by 'flood' are covered. 'Flood' is
        defined in the policy as a general and temporary con-
        dition of partial or complete inundation of normally
        dry land areas, from overflow of inland or tidal
        waters, or from the unusual and rapid accumulation or
        runoff of surface waters from any source, or from
        mud 'flows'. Also covered are losses resulting from
        land collapse caused by water activity exceeding est-
        ablished levels. The flood policy will not cover

511

damage caused by a loss in progress.

"20. Q. What is a 'loss in progress'?

A. A 'loss in progress' is a situation where flood damage to a structure or its contents had started prior to inception of the policy.

"22. Q. Are losses from water seepage, sewer back-up or hydrostatic pressure covered?

A. Only when directly caused by a general condition of flooding.

"47. Q. What is meant by 'flood plain management'?

A. 'Flood plain management' means the operation of an overall community program of corrective and preventive measures for reducing flood damage, including (but not limited to) emergency preparedness plans and any measures aimed at the future use of the flood plain. Flood plain management includes specific local codes and ordinances which provide standards for the location and design of new development within flood-prone areas. These measures may be adopted in any manner that is legally enforceable for a particular community. Typically they take the form of zoning, subdivision or building requirements or a special purpose flood plain ordinance."

For purposes of flood insurance it was necessary to establish a flood plain. This was done after extensive study. It was agreed that a 100-year flood would serve as a reasonable compromise between financial commitments on buildings and the recurrence interval of the flooding. (See Topic 19)

Informative articles on the flood insurance program have been published by the League of Women Voters (1975), "Environmental Update on Water - Flood Plain Management and the National Flood Insurance Program"; and by the Sierra Club, "Water Over the Bridge - Dollars and Sense on the Floodplain" (1975).

The essential feature of the Federal Flood Insurance Program is that individual owners, small businesses, condominia, and certain local government facilities, can purchase Federally subsidized insurance at low cost. Insurance is available through local insurance agents. The cost of the insurance is relatively low, amounting to $25.00 a year for $10,000 insurance for home owners. A typical cost for $35,000 structural home insurance and $10,000 for contents is $123 a year. There is, however, a very important requirement; subsidized insurance can be purchased only in areas which are in a designated flood hazard area which has been adopted by the local governmental agencies and for which there have been prepared detailed maps on which is delineated the 100-year flood.

There is a specific ban against the sale of Federally-subsidized flood insurance in hazard areas as long as the communities have failed to comply with zoning and delineation. Furthermore reasonable construction practices and building code requirements need to be in force. If these requirements were not in force the investment of taxpayers' money would be wasted.

The magnitude of the National flood insurance program is indicated by the following information, as of June 15, 1977, secured from the Federal Insurance Administration:

| | |
|---|---|
| Eligible Communities | 15,569 |
| No. of Policies in Force | 1,046,217 |
| Amount of Coverage | $30,762,125,000 |
| No. of Claims Paid | 66,513 (est.) |
| Amount Paid in Claims | $ 206,136,122 (est.) |

It has been estimated by the Federal Insurance Administration that by the Year 2000 the flood insurance program will have saved the taxpayers and the flood victims about $1,700,000,000 a year.

The flood insurance program has been slow in spreading to areas of high flood risk. Novoa and Halff (1977) describe the management of flooding in Peaks Branch, a stream in East Dallas, Texas, in which 5,000 buildings would be partially inundated by a 100-year flood. Their article deals with the analyses of alternative flooding remedies ranging from no action to complete redevelopment. They discuss both structural and non-structural alternatives with the cost ranging from $5,600,000 to $16,300,000.

Nationally there has been a very slow spread of the Federally-subsidized insurance program even though the figures in the table on the amount of insurance and the number of communities involved appear impressive. For example the flood of June, 1972 at Rapid City, South Dakota, in which 236 people lost their lives, required flood disaster assistance of about one hundred million dollars. Only 29 flood insurance policies had been sold in the area that was decimated by this flood. Tropical storm Agnes, which cost the Nation 3.1 billion dollars, produced among other devastating floods, the one at Wilkes-Barre, Pennsylvania. Only 2 flood insurance policies had been sold in this area.

The Big Thompson Canyon Flood occurred between Loveland and Estes Park, Colorado, on the night of July 31-August 1, 1976. (See Topics 13 and 71). In this extreme event 139 people lost their lives and 316 homes, 56 mobile homes, and

52 businesses were destroyed. Hundreds of others were damaged. Subsequent to this flood the 100-year floodway was delineated and any building which suffered more than 50 percent damage may not be repaired and reoccupied. According to Schmidt (1978) several land-purchase programs to remove areas from future habitation are under way. The lands and properties of 38 owners who suffered more than 50 percent damage are to be purchased by Federal funds and incorporated into the Roosevelt National Forest.

Although under the 1968 Act the Federal share of insurance was 90 percent, the flood disaster Act of 1973 reduced this to 55 percent. The "Floodplain Management Guidelines for Implementing Executive Order 11988" have been published in the Federal Register, Part VI, vol. 43, no. 29, pages 6030-6055, of Friday, February 10, 1978. This section of the Federal Register is available as a reprint entitled, "Floodplain Management Guidelines for Implementing E.O. 11988", published by the Water Resources Council. The Federal Insurance Administration has prepared "Flood Insurance Study - Guidelines and Specifications for Study Contractors" (Oct. 1977).

Shows (1977) describes the workings of the National Flood Insurance program in the coastal zone using the experiences of Hurricane Eloise. He concludes that there could be an undesirable indirect effect that underpricing flood risk could have on location decisions on the coastal flood plan. Currently the Federal Insurance Administration is reviewing 50,000 claims in order to make adjustments in rates.

Although it was envisioned in 1968 that land use and watershed management could make some contributions to flood control, Foster (1976) found that watershed management to reduce flood peaks has not been very attractive. The watershed land owner must pay the cost of his land-use improvements. Although these may be cost-shared through some Federal programs the beneficiaries living in the flood plain pay nothing. A basic reference on the subject of floodplain management is the report by White (1964) on choices of adjustments to floods, including several non-structural approaches.

The Federal Register, Part IV for Friday, February 17, 1978, pages 7140-7148, "Mandatory Flood Insurance Purchase Requirements", was issued by the Department of Housing and Urban Development. Banks are required to supply evidence of flood insurance purchase as a condition of financing under FHA and VA. The states of Maine, Georgia, Oregon, and Florida are exempt from the requirements of Federal Flood Insurance for State-owned structures and for contents because they have established State plans for hazard insurance. This issue of the Federal Register includes complex details of changes in the amounts of available insurance coverage and other details.

A list of Housing and Urban Development Regional offices and
the regional flood insurance staff addresses and phone numbers
are given in this issue of the Federal Register. It would be
wise for anyone considering Federal flood insurance to contact
the Federal Insurance Administration for the most recent
information and procedures.

## Problem Assignment - Urban Land Use and Flood Control

A decision must be made concerning a 150-year-old city
which is facing problems critical to its survival. The State
Department of Natural Resources, the EPA, the U.S. Army Corps
of Engineers, FHA, VA, FIA, and several other agencies of the
Department of Housing and Urban Development are involved,
among others. The water supply system is on the verge of
breakdown; the water treatment plant has been operating beyond
its safe normal capacity; industrial and urban developments
have been served by water mains added to the old existing
mains. In order to deliver water at the extreme extensions
water pressure has been stepped up to a point where rupture of
the old pipes is occurring with frequent interruptions to service and with mounting maintenance costs. The wastewater
treatment plant is obsolete and cannot meet tertiary treatment
effluent standards now required. Many of the buildings cannot
meet modern structural, electrical, and fire-safety standards.
Urbanization has increased flood peaks so that the constricted
channel cannot carry runoff from even medium-size storms.

You have been hired as a water resources environmental
consultant to analyze the possible contribution to the rehabilitation of the city if an upstream multi-purpose reservoir
were to be built. The decision to be made is one of either
removal of all structures from the 100-year floodway or building a dam which would assure a dependable water supply for
domestic, industrial, and municipal use and to provide flood
control.

Your particular assignment is: how much flood control capacity in acre feet would be needed in the proposed reservoir
to meet safe channel capacity requirements. Other specialists,
bankers, and investors will consider the results of your
computation in assembling proposals and alternatives for
analysis.

The safe capacity of the stream flowing through this city
is 500 cfs. The geologic explorations show that there is no
limit on the height of the proposed dam. Outlet works are
being designed to permit constant discharge under conditions of
changing depth of water in the proposed reservoir. All reservoir releases are to be controlled.

Exhaustive statistical analyses and hydrometeorological studies have provided the background for the decision to use the hydrograph shown as the design flood, as given in Figure 88-1.

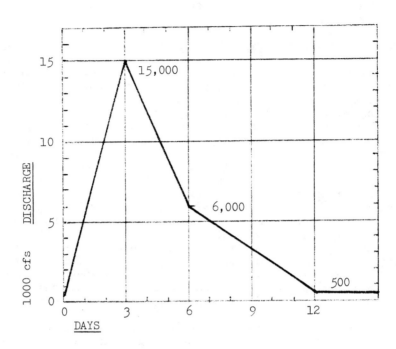

Figure 88-1  Flood Design Hydrograph

Perform your computation and prepare a report to be submitted to the organization which retained your services as a consultant.  Append to the report all work sheets.

References

"Environmental Update on Water - Flood Plain Management and the National Flood Insurance Program", The League of Women Voters Education Fund, Washington, D.C., Pub. No. 534, 4 pp, Jan. 1975.

"Floodplain Management Guidelines for Implementing Executive Order 11988", The Federal Register, Part VI, vol. 43, no. 29, pp 6030-6055, Fri., Feb. 10, 1978. (This has been published by the Water Resources Council, Washington, D.C. as a 52-page separate under the same name and date.)

Foster, John H., "Flood Management: Who Benefits and Who Pays", Water Resources Bull., vol. 12, no. 5, pp 1029-39, Oct. 1976.

"Mandatory Flood Insurance Purchase Requirements", Dept. of Housing and Urban Development, Fed. Insurance Admin., Federal Register, Part IV, vol. 43, no. 34, pp 7140-7148, Fri. Feb. 17, 1978.

"National Flood Insurance Program", Dept. of Housing and Urban Development, Washington, D.C., Government Printing Office, 48 pp, Jan. 1974. (This publication gives the history of Federal Flood Insurance and discusses Pl 93-234, Pl 91-152 and PL 90-448.)

Novoa, Jose I., and Albert H. Halff, "Management of Flooding in a Fully-Developed, Low-Cost Housing Neighborhood", Water Resources Bulletin, vol. 13, no. 6, pp 1237-1252, Dec. 1977.

"Questions and Answers on the National Flood Insurance Program" An assembly of 59 entries prepared by the Regional Office, Reg. VIII, Federal Ins. Admin., Dept. of Housing and Urban Development, Denver, Colo., Mar. 8, 1978.

Schmidt, Ann, "Thompson Land-Buy Scheduled", The Denver Post, page 2, Sat. June 3, 1978.

Shows, E. W., "National Flood Insurance and the Coastal Zone: A Case Study of Hurricane Eloise", Water Resources Bull., vol. 13, no. 5, pp 973-982, Oct. 1977.

"Water Over the Bridge - Dollars and Sense on the Floodplain", Sierra Club Bulletin, pp 17-18, Nov./Dec. 1975.

Whipple, Wm. Jr., "Optimum Investment in Structural Flood Control", Jour. Hydraulics Div., Proceedings ASCE, pp 1507-1515, Nov. 1968.

White, Gilbert F., "Choice of Adjustment to Floods", Dept. of Geography Research Paper No. 93, Univ. of Chicago, 1964.

## MATHEMATICAL MODELING

Topic 89                Mathematical Modeling

Hydrologic and hydraulic models are discussed in Topic 68. In water-resource management there are a great many systems which cannot be modeled iconically or by analogs. For example, readjustments of land use, translocation of population and of industries in regional and urban planning, cannot be manipulated for experimental purposes. Studies of this type can be done only with mathematical modeling. Although mathematical model studies were performed in the past with desk-top mechanical calculators, the complexities of the system and the vast input of data required prevented wide-spread use until automatic electronic data processing machinery was developed.

An informative introductory series of articles is given in a special section of Time magazine entitled, "The Computer Society" (1978). Fantastic progress has been made with computers. They are now used routinely in a great many fields of endeavor at great savings of time, money, and in many cases with significant increases in accuracy. For example, surveying instruments are now practically all electronic. Many of the electronic levels and theodolites are linked to computers so that all of the computations, including angles, areas, and elevations are done in the field.

An entrancing new development is that of computer films which produce a moving display, sometimes in color, of complex systems. These resemble in general animated film cartoons but the images, instead of having been drawn by hand, are of cathode ray tube displays showing the output of very complex computers. Computer films are described by Robinson (1978).

An outstanding example of the application of computers to routine reservoir and power operations is the SSARR Model (1975) as described in Topic 69. The speed with which computers operate, practically at the speed of light, has made it possible in reservoir and river operations to compute dozens of alternatives while a storm is underway so that a plan of operation can be chosen and adjusted before or during the time the hydrologic event is taking place.

There are a number of constraints facing anyone using computers. With few exceptions the computers are digital mechanisms; that is, they process data submitted to them as numbers. A few computers are of the analog type in which transients such as hydraulic and electronic systems, which are constantly varying, can be analyzed. Another constraint is that the computers, being digital, need to be provided with mathematically rigorous expressions of equations which are to be used in the analyses of the data. The investigator is bounded by these two constraints. Taking into account data and mathematical equation constraints, it is not surprising that many of the results of mathematical modeling have turned out to be unrealistic when compared with physical systems which they endeavored to represent. It may be that some of the best science fiction is being written by computers. The realism of the analyses depends on the completeness and the indicativeness of the data and the results depend on the equations which have been selected by the investigator and which he fed into the computer in the programming.

Andrews, Radziul, Gilman, Graeser, Daniels, Kelley, Cobb, and Rosenkranz (1977) discuss computer application in water and wastewater management. Among their numerous summaries and recommendations they conclude: (a) a computer dedicated to forecasting needs and power savings is cost effective; (b) for computer application it is necessary to establish a realistic level of expectation with a reliable system of instrumentation and basic control; a computer cannot make a water or wastewater treatment operate any better than its design permits; (c) it is necessary that the sensors for flow, pressure, liquid level, and time, be those which have been proven in performance since any deviation in the quality of the input data defeats the value of the computer system. One of their recommendations was that the door into the computer room be built large enough to permit entry of the computer and that, insofar as overall performance is concerned, what is outside the computer is more important than what is inside.

Fox (1976) has written an assessment of problems of modeling atmospheric effects. Extensive use is being made by city planners, and especially by meteorologists, of atmospheric models of air pollution and its removal by dry deposition and precipitation scavenging. On his page 184 Fox states that one of the more fundamental difficulties in large-scale meteorological modeling is to know what equation to solve. Atmospheric models are becoming increasingly important as National consideration is being focused on the use of coal as a principal source of energy. The burning of coal introduces some exceedingly complex problems in environmental management.

The National Center for Atmospheric Research (NCAR) at Boulder, Colorado, and the U.S. Bureau of Reclamation's Office of Atmospheric Resources Management make extensive use of atmospheric mathematical modeling.

Basic references on simulation with a digital computer of the hydrology of the watershed are the reports by Linsley and

Crawford (1960) and Crawford and Linsley (1966). Chapter 10, Computer Simulation of Streamflow, presented by Linsley, Kohler, and Paulhus (1975), is a condensed description of this simulation program which has been known as the Stanford Watershed Model. This Model makes use of 15 parameters for computing the rainfall-runoff relationships. These parameters include, among others, interception, storage, average infiltration rate, interflow, Manning's "n" for overland flow, evapotranspiration, and groundwater recessions. The snowmelt routine of the Stanford Watershed Model makes use of 10 parameters among which are lapse rate, compensation for deficiency of raingage catchments of snow, percent of forest cover, water equivalent of snowpack, and theoretical evaporation equations. Numerous applications have been made of the Stanford Watershed Model Concept.

An important reference work making use of simulation techniques of river basin systems using digital computers is the book, "Design of Water-Resource Systems", by Maas, Hufschmidt, Dorfman, Thomas, Marglin, and Fair (1962). In this volume Reedy reviews the conventional methods of analyses which had been developed by the Bureau of Reclamation, the Corps of Engineers, the Soil Conservation Service, and the Tennessee Valley Authority. Bower, Hufschmidt, and Reedy (1962) discuss the role of operating procedures by simulation analyses as they may influence the design of water resource systems. The transition from hypothetical computations to the actual operations of reservoir, river, and hydropower systems requires judgement, flexibility, and experience since the actual operation must deal with hydrologic, meteorologic, social, and economic requirements as they interact in the real world.

"Systems Approach to Water Management" (1976) is an assembly of 11 papers edited by Asit K. Biswas. This book provides information on various hydrologic, water quality, ecologic, estuarine, and economic models as they may be applied in water resource planning and management especially in relation to multiple objective developments.

Slack (1972) states that a stochastic model is usually selected for its theoretical ability to serve as an apparent analogy with real-world processes by preserving certain statistics. His paper is a philosophical discussion of the part which bias, illusion, and denial, play in introducing data uncertainties in an assumed model.

Riley and Hawkins (1976) have prepared a simplified mathematical simulation model for hydrologic modeling of rangeland watersheds. They call attention to the fact that their model includes no snowmelt routine. This is a major simplification since in many hydrologic models the snowmelt handling occupies a major portion of such models. Their model uses linear reservoirs and transfer functions thereby avoiding abrupt threshold infiltration by assuming linear disposition of time and soil moisture infiltration rates across the watershed. Their article includes a discussion of its application to an existing watershed in Utah. A study of their 11 questions on page 137 concerning the mathematical modeling process as a whole, and of their summary, is recommended.

Hwang, Williams, Shojalashkari, and Fan (1973) describe a mathematical model for a river basin which receives thermal as well as organic wastes. The effects of thermal changes on BOD and DO are analyzed in the highly non-linear model. They illustrate the mathematical methods by applying the procedure to the Chattoochee River Basin below Atlanta, Georgia.

Nicolson, Pyatt, and Moreau (1970) describe the use of an optimization model which is based on a complete knowledge of meteorologic and hydrologic data for the period of interest. They present a methodology for selecting among water quality alternatives with special reference to the effects on the quality of downstream waters which have been released from reservoirs. They describe a test case involving the Clark Hill Reservoir on the Savannah River in Georgia.

An application of mathematical modeling by computer to farm forestry planning is described by Coutu and Ellertsen (1960). In order to obtain maximum profits a farmer must integrate his woodland activities with other farm operations to make the best overall use of available land, labor, and capital. The authors used a linear programming model.

In order to save time and investment in expensive physical models, aeronautical, structural, mechanical, civil, chemical, and hydraulic engineers, among others, have been making extensive use of mathematical models. Dale (1977) has compiled and indexed an extensive listing of publications of the U.S. Army Engineer Waterways Experiment Station. In the listing are numerous references to mathematical modeling on a great variety of subjects. The pamphlet "Data Processing in the Bureau of Reclamation" (1977) describes the extensive, west-wide integrated computer system of the Bureau which is centered in its Engineering and Research Center. This computer system can store on discs more than 3.9 billion characters at any one time. It can transfer data between the main memory and extended core storage at the rate of 2.5 million words per second, each word consisting of 10 characters, and it can perform one million multiplications in one second.

A fascinating application of mathematical modeling is the Colorado River Simulation Model known by its acronym, "CORSIM". This is an activity dealing with all of the White River and the Colorado River basins in Western Colorado exclusive of the

Gunnison River. Fleming (1975) describes the purpose, organization, and functions of this privately-financed study of the water resources and water rights of the subject area. Virgin flow data are now being updated so that information will be available for the water years, 1941 through 1977. Participants in this activity are two municipalities, two major water districts, a public utility, and 12 private companies chiefly major energy interests.

The magnitude of CORSIM is indicated by the following: the study area is approximately 14,000 square miles; the range of elevations is from 4365 feet to 14,421 feet above sea level; there are 1075 virgin flow features; 342 reservoirs; and 2695 water rights. The computer time for processing a 30-year run involving 118 sub-routines is less than 10 minutes. Analyses of this type would be completely out of the question had it not been for the availability of computers.

There is an increasing volume of literature on mathematical modeling and on the verification of mathematical models with their physical prototypes. Anyone considering a mathematical model study in whatever field of endeavor should take the time to make a thorough review of the literature on verification of mathematical models. Practically every month, professional society symposia, University-sponsored Institutes, Seminars, and work groups and task force meetings are being held. Attendance at one or more of such meetings is recommended.

## References

Andrews, John F., Joseph Radziul, Harold D. Gilman, Henry J. Graeser, James E. Daniels, Harold A. Kelley, William A. Cobb, and William Rosenkranz, "Computer Application in Water and Wastewater Management: A Panel Discussion", Jour. AWWA, vol. 69, no. 5, pp 246-255, May, 1977.

Bower, Blair T., Maynard M. Hufschmidt, and William W. Reedy, "Operating Procedures: Their Role in the Design of Water-Resource Systems by Simulation Analyses", Chap. 11 in Design of Water-Resources Systems by Arthur Maas and others, Harvard Univ. Press, Cambridge, Mass., 620 pp, 1962.

Coutu, Arthur J., and Birger W. Ellertsen, "Farm Forestry Planning through Linear Programming", Report No. 236-60, TVA Division of Forestry Relations, Norris, Tenn. 31 pp, Dec. 1960.

Crawford, N. H., and R. K. Linsley, "Digital Simulation in Hydrology: Stanford Watershed Model IV, Stanford Univ., Dept. Civ. Eng. Tech. Report 39, 1966.

Dale, Virginia, "List of Publications of the U.S. Army Engineer Waterways Experiment Station", Special Projects Branch, Tech. Information Center, Vicksburg, Miss., July, 1977.

"Data Processing in the Bureau of Reclamation", A folder, 12 pp, GPO No. O-228-805, Washington, D.C., 1977.

Fleming, David E., "The CORSIM Project", a paper presented at the Annual Meeting of the Amer. Soc. of Civil Engineers, Denver, Colo., Nov. 3-7, 1975; the manager of the CORSIM Project for the Participants is the David E. Fleming Co., of Denver, Colo., in a joint venture with Parsons, Brinkerhoff, Quade and Douglas, New York, Nov. 4, 1975.

Fox, Douglas G., "Modeling Atmospheric Effects - An Assessment of the Problems", pp 173-198 in Water, Air, and Soil Pollution 6, D. Reidel Pub. Co., Dordrecht-Holland, 1976.

Hwang, C. L., J. L. Williams, R. Shojalashkari, and L. T. Fan, "Regional Water Quality Management by the Generalized Reduced Gradient Method", Water Resources Bull., vol. 9, no. 6, pp 1159-1181, Dec. 1973.

Linsley, R. K., and N. H. Crawford, "Computation of a Synthetic Streamflow Record on a Digital Computer", Int. Assoc. Sci. Hydrol. Pub. 51, pp 526-538, 1960.

Linsley, Ray K., Jr., Max A. Kohler, and Joseph L. H. Paulhus, "Hydrology for Engineers", Chap. 10, Computer Simulation of Streamflow, pp 319-337, 2d edition, McGraw Hill Book Co., New York, 482 pp, 1975.

Maas, Arthur, Maynard M. Hufschmidt, Robert Dorfman, Harold A. Thomas, Jr., Stephen A. Marglin, and Gordon Maskew Fair; with the following other authors: Blair T. Bower, William W. Reedy, Deward F. Manzer, Michael P. Barnett, Myron B. Fiering, and Peter Watermeyer, "Design of Water-Resource Systems - New Techniques for Relating Economic Objectives, Engineering Analysis, and Governmental Planning", Harvard Univ. Press, Cambridge, Mass., 620 pp, 1962.

Nicolson, Gilbert S., Edwin E. Pyatt, and David H. Moreau, "A Methodology for Selecting Among Water Quality Alternatives", Water Resources Bull., Jour. Amer. Water Resources Assn., vol. 6, no. 1, pp 23-33, Jan.-Feb. 1970.

Reedy, William W., "Conventional Methods of Analysis", Chap. 8 in Design of Water-Resource Systems by Arthur Maas and others, Harvard Univ. Press, Cambridge, Mass, 1962.

Riley, J. Paul, and Richard H. Hawkins, "Hydrologic Modeling of Rangeland Watersheds", pp 123-138 in Watershed Management on Range and Forest Lands, Proceedings of the Fifth Workshop of the United States/Australia Rangelands Panel, Boise, Idaho, June 15-22, 1975, ed. by Harold F. Heady, Donna H. Falkenborg, and J. Paul Riley, pub. by Utah Water Research Lab., Utah State Univ., Logan, 222 pp, Mar. 1976.

Robinson, Arthur L., "Computer Films: Adding an Extra Dimension to Research", Science, vol. 200, no. 4343, pp 749-752, May 19, 1978.

Slack, J. R., "Bias, Illusion, and Denial as Data Uncertainties" pp 122-132 in Vol. 1, Proceedings of the International Symposium on Uncertainties in Hydrologic and Water Resource Systems, held at the Univ. of Ariz. Tucson, Dec. 11-14, 1972; pub. by the Natl. Science Foundation and the Univ. of Ariz., 1972.
       (The Proceedings are in three volumes, totalling
       1661 pages.)

"SSARR Model - Streamflow Synthesis & Reservoir Regulation, Program Description & User Manual for Program 724-K5-G0010", U.S. Army Engineer Div., North Pacific, Portland, Ore., 188 pp, plus 13 page appendix, Sept. 1972, rev. June, 1975.

"Systems Approach to Water Management", ed. by Asit K. Biswas, McGraw-Hill Book Co., New York, 429 pp, 1976.

"The Computer Society", A special section, pp 44-59 in Time, vol. 111, no. 8, Feb. 20, 1978.

SECTION XXII

ENERGY

Topic 90   Alternative Sources of Energy and the Water Resource

Fundamentally all energy is a component of the astro-
physical system of the Universe.  The fossil fuels, coal, oil,
and gas, are in effect solar radiation converted to matter
through photosynthesis (Topic 50) in ages past (Topic 28).
Until recently energy released for human use resulted from a
change in valence which accompanies chemical reactions; for
example, from the burning of wood or from muscle power.  Within our lifetimes nuclear fission has become another manner of
utilization of astrophysics.  All of the alternative sources
of energy involve the water resource in some way, either as a
participant in the reaction, as a coolant, or as a mechanism
of kinetic energy.  In energy reactions water may be absorbed,
released, thermally modified, or polluted.  The alternative
sources of energy are listed in Table 90-1 which is based on
page 11 of "The Role of the Bonneville Power Administration in
the Pacific Northwest Power Supply System" (1977), page 527.

Hubbert (1969) in his chapter on energy resources gives
an excellent review of this broad subject, a reading of which
is recommended.  Hubbert states that half of the World's cumulative production of petroleum occurred during the 12-year
period following 1956.  In the United States one-half of the
cumulative coal production occurred in the 38-year period
starting in 1930.  Most of the World's consumption of energy
from fossil fuels, during its entire history, occurred during
the 25-year period, 1923-1968.

Bartlett (1976) has written a series of 5 articles on the
exponential function which is the mathematical expression underlying the analysis of growth.  An example of an exponential
function is equation (1) in Topic 27.  The theme of Bartlett's
presentation is that the greatest shortcoming of the human
race is man's inability to grasp the significance of the exponential function.  The relationship between a percentage rate
of growth and doubling time has been reduced by Bartlett to:

$$\text{Doubling time} = \frac{70}{\text{percent growth per unit time}}$$

If a growth rate of 3 percent a year is assumed the
doubling time becomes 23.1 years; at 6 percent it becomes 11.5
years; and at 10 percent, 6.93 years.  A thought-provoking
application of this concept of growth rate and doubling times
is given by Bartlett (1976) in his article, "The Forgotten
Fundamentals of the Energy Crisis" (1976).

An excellent general review of the subject of energy is the September, 1971 "Scientific American". This issue contains 11 articles, four of which deal respectively with the flow of energy in the biosphere, in a hunting society, in an agricultural society, and in an industrial society. Especially thought-provoking is the article by Dyson (1971) on "Energy in the Universe", pages 51-59. Dyson, who deals with the flow of energy in the astronomical sense, believes that a delicate balance which exists among gravitation, nuclear reactions, and radiation, keeps the energy of the Universe from flowing too fast. Dyson's general attitude is one of optimism for the future of our human race in the Universe.

When dealing with energy it is necessary to use quantitative units. Fowler and Kryger (1977) have prepared a glossary of terms. A British Thermal Unit (BTU) is the amount of energy needed to raise one pound of water one degree Fahrenheit. Klein (1974) discusses at length the complexity of detailed definitions of the BTU.

A small calorie is the amount of heat needed to raise one gram of water one degree Celsius. The Calorie is the amount of heat needed to raise one kilogram of water $1^{\circ}$ C; the Calorie, or kilocalorie is equivalent to 1000 small calories.

The basic metric unit of energy is the joule which is the energy produced by a force of one newton operating through a distance of one meter. One BTU equals 1055 joules and one Calorie equals 4.185 joules. A watt, the metric unit of electric power, equals the work of one joule per second and a kilowatt is 1000 watts. One kilowatt-hour equals 3,413 BTU's. One megawatt equals 1000 kilowatts or one million watts.

A quad is one quadrillion ($10^{15}$) BTU's. Large amounts of energy are expressed in quads in the United States. A quad is equal to the amount of energy in 172,000,000 barrels of oil. Each barrel contains 42 gallons of crude oil which weigh about 306 pounds.

The terms used in expressing energy in electric power, transportation, heat, and radiation, are so complicated and the expressions may require so many digits, that it has been very difficult to compare or add data. In "Living in a Glass House 1 - Home Energy Budgeting" (1977) the Bonneville Power Administration proposes the new approximate unit: the "Enerjoule". This is equal to 100,000,000 or $10^8$ joules. For approximate, but not exact, usage one Enerjoule is equivalent to the energy in one gallon of gasoline or oil, one therm of natural gas, 10 pounds of coal, 30 killowatt-hours of electric power, or roughly about 100,000 BTU's (actually 94,880).

Table 90-1    Sources of Energy and Their Impacts

| Energy Source | Impact on Water and Air Quality and on Environment |
|---|---|
| Muscle power, human and animal | Minor |
| Coal | Major, depending on environment at mines and where burned. |
| Biomass | Variable depending on environment at source & where used. |
| Municipal waste | Variable, on air, water quality, and visual effects. |
| Wind | Major, on visual environment. |
| Hydro | Land disturbance & visual effects with possible impact on fish. |
| Petroleum products burned in engines, combustion turbines, & in furnaces at thermal powerplants | Major, on air quality, possible impact on water quality including thermal modification. |
| Geothermal | Major, on water & air quality & possibly on esthetic, solid waste, & flora and fauna. |
| Nuclear fission | Possibly major, on water & air quality with implications of radioactivity, thermal & visual pollution on the environment and/or human health. |
| Nuclear fusion | Same as above |
| Solar | Land disturbance and esthetic impacts on environment. |
| Fuel cells | Minor |
| Hydrogen | Land disturbance and visual pollution. |
| Primary and secondary cells | Minor |
| Magnetohydrodynamic | Land disturbance, air & water pollution & possible impact on human health. |
| Tidal power | Land disturbance, flora, fauna, and visual impacts. |
| Ocean thermal energy conversion | Land and water surface disturbance and visual effects. |
| Energy storage | Variable |

Muscle power, especially human, remains of prime importance in
all technological activities since mechanisms and manufacturing processes are controlled by intellects directing muscular
movements. Krendel (1967) found that man's production of
power for useful work is the equivalent to about one-tenth
horsepower or 75 watts. Beasts of burden and draft animals
are important in all parts of the World.

Coal first became a source of energy in the 12th or 13th Century when it was discovered that black rocks found on the
northeast coast of England would burn. This discovery was
followed by mining of coal for domestic heat, for use in mineral industry, and ultimately for heat for the steam engine.

Singer (1977) compares the economics of land values for
agriculture and for coal with costs of restoration. He states,
for example, that prime wheat land in North Dakota sells for
up to $300 an acre. Mined lignite may reach a value of
$300,000 an acre. The costs of restoration of this land may
run from a few hundred to several thousand dollars an acre.
Singer reports that in New Mexico from $4,000 to $5,000 an
acre is being spent by mining companies to speed up reseeding,
and to restore land which after restoration may be worth only
about $55 an acre.

He raises some fundamental questions: what would be the
best social use of funds earmarked for restoration; should
they be spent (a) for restoration of strip-mined land? (b) for
restoration of eroded farmland? or (c) restoration of city
slums? Singer brings up another thought-provoking comparison:
if the total United States coal production of 6 hundred million
tons per year were to be concentrated in the deep beds of
Wyoming's Powder River Basin, the amount of land disturbed
would be between 10 to 20 square miles per year. A reading of
Singer's guest editorial is recommended.

Young and Blair (1975) in their pages 242-243 show a
three-dimensional drawing of a deep coal mine. Their very informative article deals with life in a coal-mine town. The
reading of this is recommended. Glover (1976) reviews the
surface mine reclamation loss of West Virginia where coal has
been mined for more than 100 years. A condensed statement of
West Virginia's new approach is that if you can't reclaim it
don't mine it.

Williams (1975) concludes that there is probably sufficient water in the western states to support practically any
rate of coal development. However, it may be necessary to
construct storage reservoirs and possibly to modify agricultural developments because of possible reduction of surface
water and groundwater supplies in the future.

Smoke-stack effluents from the burning of coal, unless subjected to extensive treatment, could be a major air and water pollutant. In addition to fly ash (see Topic 74, page 445) the effluents may contain radioactive substances and a great array of metals, many of which are toxic. Walker (1978) analyzes the smoke plumes from power plant smoke stacks as they are affected by air temperature and lapse rate gradients. The famous London fogs which were created under inversions are described. In December, 1952, about 2,000 tons of sulphur dioxide were thrown into the air of London each day. An inversion trapped the sulphur dioxide and the smoke for 4 days; the sky became yellow, then brown, and finally black. About 4,000 people died as a direct result of pollution and it is estimated that another 8,000 died from respiratory problems brought about by this air pollution.

The actual usable energy produced from a ton of coal in the ground is surprisingly small. To begin with, according to "Energy and the Environment" (1975), 42 percent of the coal never leaves a deep mine and 20 percent is lost in strip mining. For a ton of coal in the ground 1140 pounds are removed from a deep mine and 1600 pounds from a strip mine. Another 8 percent is lost in processing and one percent in transporting coal from the mine to the power plant so that 1040 pounds are delivered from the deep mine and 1450 pounds from a strip mine. Transportation of coal by truck or rail requires consumption of energy not only to move the coal but also to transport the incombustible ash and water. Additional energy is required to pulverize and dry the coal and to remove air pollutants and particulates from the flue gases.

When coal is burned 62 percent of the energy is lost. Therefore the extracted energy equivalent at the power plant is 400 to 550 pounds of coal. About 10 percent of the electrical energy generated is lost in the transmission system. If the electricity is used for light, 90 percent of the power consumed is lost as heat. The result is that only 50 pounds of the energy from the original ton of coal in the ground is put to use. Petroleum fuels also are subjected to inefficiency losses all along the line. Increasing the efficiency of the energy system as a whole would make a great contribution to the Nation's energy resource.

Power plants cause thermal modification of the water used as a coolant in the condensers. Gurfinkel and Walser (1972) have presented an analysis of the design of hyperbolic air cooling towers as they may be affected by winds, earthquakes, temperature changes, and base restraints. Hyperbolic towers, which may be about 400 feet high and 300 feet wide, are a clearly visible component of a power plant.

Dunrud and Osterwald (1978) have prepared a very thorough

analysis, illustrated with photographs in color, of the effects of coal-mine subsidence in the western Powder River Basin in Wyoming, with supplemental information from North Dakota, Montana, Colorado, and New Mexico. They conclude that when modern surface mining procedures are employed, rather than underground room-and-pillar mining, surface mining may be the best way to produce coal in an area where the overburden is about 60 m (200 feet) thick. This is especially applicable to some of the western strip mine areas where high-quality, low-sulphur, and low-ash coal may be found in seams up to about 17 m (50 feet) thick. Environmentally it is much easier to restore a strip mine area than to get involved with abandoned underground mines with the dangers of subsidence and coal mine fires.

Judy and Gartner (1977) conducted a Section 208, areawide waste treatment management project in a number of counties in southeastern Montana where surface-mineable coal, oil fields, and uranium deposits are found. They concluded that construction and population growth on a short-term basis will have a greater impact on water quality than strip mining.

Instead of surface transportation of coal from the mine to power plants by rail or truck, coal slurry pipelines have been proposed. A very comprehensive report on this is "A Technology Assessment of Coal Slurry Pipelines" (1978). A suspension of powdered coal is conveyed in a slurry consisting of about 50 percent water. There is sufficient water at present for this system. However, the following paragraph is quoted from page 99 of this reference:

"The uncertainty arises when future coal slurry pipeline water use is contrasted with future alternative water uses. Future alternative energy uses include present municipal and agricultural uses plus projected increased municipal, agricultural, industrial, and energy-related uses."

An alternative water source is to recycle water recovered from the coal slurry pipeline. The disadvantages are the added cost of a return-flow pipeline and the cost of separating water from the coal. About two-thirds of the water could be recycled. In view of the uncertainty of future developments and the inevitable conflicts with the legality of water rights, transbasin diversions, and priorities, a major research effort should be concentrated on recycling of the water as part of the coal slurry pipeline development. The mining, processing, transportation, and combustion of coal to yield energy are all tied in with the water resource.

Biomass combustion, the burning of the products of photosynthesis, has been from ages past a source of heat energy. A
subject of fundamental world-wide concern is that of the
atmospheric balance which is discussed in detail in Topic 74.
Bormann (1976) warns against mismanagement of forest and land
surfaces in the pursuit of energy. He concludes that conservation of natural ecosystems is an inseparable linkage to the
conservation of fossil energy.

Burgess (1978) has computed that a thermal power station
running at 60 percent operating efficiency would consume
600,000 tons of wood per year to produce one megawatt of electric energy per year. Environmental quality considerations
raise serious constraints on total forest fuel production for
energy. There are also complex ecological and silviculture
problems.

Burwell (1978) concludes that using biomass combustion as
an indirect source of solar energy through the photosynthesis
process does not offer promise of becoming a major source of
energy. Harvested wood residues and cull trees from silviculture could be important in certain areas if economically
feasible. Likens, Bormann, Pierce, and Reiners (1978) found
that a deforested ecosystem in northern hardwoods may require
60 to 80 years to recover.

Municipal waste Haughey (1978) states that within the next
few months the city of Mountain View, California, plans to
bring on the line methane gas recovery from a sanitary land
fill at a demonstration plant which is to recover, purify, and
inject the methane into Pacific Gas and Electric Company's
distribution system.

Cox, Willson, and Hoffman (1974) report that in 1971 the
amount of moisture and ash-free solid organic waste (SOW) generated in the United States was about 799,000,000 metric tons
(879,000,000 U.S. short tons) equivalent to a daily per capita
production of 10.67 kg (23.5 lbs.). In the same year, 1971,
only 509,000,000 metric tons (560,000,000 tons) of coal were
produced. Their article describes research on the conversion
of organic waste to fuel gases, chiefly, methane, carbon
dioxide, hydrogen, and carbon monoxide. Their product has a
heat value about equal to that of natural gas.

"Fuels from Biomass" (1977) includes a photograph of a
Department of Energy's experimental facility at Albany, Oregon,
which converts a ton of wood chips, sugar beet tops, and corn
stalks into about two 42-gallon barrels of heavy fuel oil.

Incinerators are widely used by cities to burn solid
wastes. In some instances the heat is scavenged. Many sewage
treatment plants use methane generated in their digesters.

Wind is indirectly an application of solar energy transformed into mechanical energy through atmospheric circulation (see Topic 7). Sailing vessels were, and are, powered by wind. In the 19th and 20th Centuries extensive use was made of windmills in Holland as sources of energy for activities connected with the reclamation of polders. Until the turn of this Century thousands of windmills were found in the United States. Figure 90-1, taken from Wilson (1896), shows a ground-tumbler type of windmill built of scrap lumber in the Great Plains in the 1890's. This figure appears on page 533.

Wilson's reference entitled, "Pumping Water for Irrigation", is U.S. Geological Survey Water Supply Paper No. 1. This report is illustrated with drawings of ancient water diversion mechanisms such as the paecottah and the latha from India, the Egyption shadoof, the tilting trough, the bullock-powered water bag or mot, draft-animal-powered geared water wheels, and the double zig-zag balance of Asia Minor. Wilson's paper is illustrated with drawings of some fascinating water pumps and mechanical elevators some of which are shown as having been powered by various types of windmills and water wheels.

Torrey (1976) has written a book describing the history of windmills. He classifies windmills into 5 families: horizontal, post, smock, American, and aerodynamic, with some designs which include concepts from more than one of the "families". Persian (Arab) windmills are mentioned as being used for grinding grain as early as the 10th Century. The first windmills recorded in America are thought to have been built by the French on the banks of the St. Lawrence River about 1629.

The largest windmill built to date, known as the Smith-Putnam Mill, was located on Grandpa's Knob in the Green Mountains west of Rutland, Vermont. The turbine was located on a 110-foot-tall tower. The windmill, built by the Central Vermont Public Service Corporation, operated intermittently for 1100 hours during a three and one-half year period providing power for the public utility. This mill is described by Torrey (1976) in Chapter 12. At 30 mph the mill would deliver up to 1250 kw. Each of the two blades weighed 8 tons. The mill withstood gales up to 115 mph and finally broke up, due primarily to a bearing failure.

An informative article entitled "Can We Harness the Wind?" has been written by Hamilton and Kristof (1975). A map, indicating the parts of the United States where average wind speeds are of sufficient velocity to give serious consideration to the use of wind power, is included on page 819. Wind power increases as the cube of the velocity.

Figure 90-1  Ground-Tumbler Type of Windmill Built of Scrap
    Lumber in the Great Plains in the 1890's. (See Wilson
    1896.)

Fowler and Fowler (undated) in their discussion of wind
power, state that in 1850 windmills in America supplied the
equivalent of 1.4 billion horsepower-hours-of-work for pumping
water and turning sawmills. The energy was about the equivalent of that supplied in 11.83 million tons of coal. In the
1930's the electrification of extensive non-urban areas under
the sponsorship of the Rural Electrification Administration
(REA) provided a convenient and low-maintenance alternative
source of energy so that by 1950 small-scale windmills became
a thing of the past. The current emphasis on energy conservation has resulted in new interest in large-scale and possibly
extensive wind-powered installations.

"Energy from the Winds" (1978) is a pamphlet which describes some of the advanced aerodynamic concepts of wind-power
research. Consideration is being given to rotors up to 300
feet in diameter.

Hydro power, both mechanical and electrical, with related
power system management problems, is discussed in Topic 91.

Petroleum is a complex liquid generally considered as having
been derived from plant and animal debris which was buried
under sediment during the geologic past. It is now found only
in basins filled with sedimentary rock. The search for petroleum engages the professional services of a great many geologists. Extensive knowledge of the World's sedimentary rock

533

notwithstanding, the drilling of oil and gas wells continues to be a gamble.

The petroleum group of fossil fuels, all of which in effect are concentrated sunshine of ages past, consists of oil varying in viscosity from natural gas liquid, known as "casing-head" gasolines, to heavy oils such as are found in Alaska, which flow only at higher temperatures. The natural gases consist of methane, ethane, propane, butane, and pentane. Propane and butane are available as LPG (Liquified Petroleum Gases) commonly known as "bottled gas".

Tar sands are sands which contain crude oil of such high viscosity that it cannot be pumped from the ground. A large-scale commercial operation extracting oil from tar sands is in successful production in northeastern Alberta, Canada. There are a few natural deposits of asphalt among which are the La Brea tar pits of Southern California, and the pits which yielded the Bitumen of Judea, used centuries ago to waterproof canals. A truly solid hydrocarbon, gilsonite, is found in limited quantities. Gilsonite was used for automotive storage battery cases before hard rubber and plastics came into common usage.

Another form of petroleum is that found in fine-grain sedimentary rocks called collectively "oil shale". The first reference to oil from shale goes back to the 14th Century when dark, sulphurous oil named "icthyol" was released from shale containing fish fossils in Austria and Switzerland. In the mid-19th Century there were many small oil shale processing plants producing candle wax, kerosene, lubricants, and combustible gases. This industry was abandoned when Edwin Drake drilled his oil well near Titusville, Pennsylvania, on August 27, 1859.

The yield of oil from oil shale varies from about 10 gallons per ton to as much as 140 gallons per ton. To be of commercial interest oil shale should yield from 25 to 65 gallons per ton in the United States. Foreign deposits containing 10 to 25 gallons per ton have been mined on a large scale.

"What Everyone Should Know About Oil Shale" (1977) is a non-technical pamphlet with cartoon-like illustrations which contains a wealth of information on oil shale. Another pamphlet illustrated with photographs and maps is "Oil Shale, A Potential Source of Energy" (1974).

Extensive research has been conducted by the Bureau of Mines, USDI, in Colorado and Wyoming. The Anvil Points Experiment Station in Garfield County, Colorado, has been extracting oil from shale using a high-temperature retort.

534

Several environmental problems have been encountered in the extraction of oil from shale. One stems from the fact that the spent shale is more bulky than when mined. Spoil banks may occupy large areas since return of the spent shale to the mines is not considered economically feasible. Of serious concern to water quality is the fact that the spent shale may contain large amounts of salts which would seriously degrade surface water and possibly groundwater supplies which would interfere and prevent other usages. It may be necessary to construct large evaporative lagoons to dispose of the salt water. Experiments have been conducted on the use of nuclear devices to distill the oil from shale in place underground. Detailed reports are not available although some of the initial gases yielded were said to be radioactive. Another possibility under study is controlled burning of the shale underground in a manner similar to a coal mine fire.

A related activity is the production of new fuels from coal. It has been demonstrated on a large scale that synthetic oils and combustible gases can be manufactured from coal through three basic processes as described by Fowler (undated). These are: hydrogenation which is the addition of pure hydrogen; pyrolysis, heating in the absence of oxygen; and catalytic conversion using carbon monoxide and hydrogen to yield liquid fuels.

Another and very important use of petroleum from whatever source is as the raw material from which possibly thousands of compounds and substances are synthesized. These may range from synthetic rubber, plastics, and protective coatings, to synthetic fibers, food additives, and medicines. The Royal Embassy of Saudi Arabia in a full page newspaper statement on "Sun Day", Wednesday, May 3, 1978, stated that the first objective of Saudi Arabia is to stretch out the oil, of which they possess 25 percent of the Earth's oil resources, to benefit not only their own people but also the World's economy. They expressed the belief that oil must be conserved for petrochemicals and other long-range usages.

Coal-oil mix offers considerable promise according to Peracchio (1978). Such a mix can be burned in existing power plants with practically no modifications. As part of the production of synthetic fuels at coal conversion plants it should be possible to manufacture a suitable oil which would then serve to transport pulverized coal directly to market. This would be an oil-coal slurry which would not result in transbasin diversion of water and would not require a looped pipeline for the return of the fluid.

Geothermal heat has been used by man for many centuries. The Romans used water from natural hot springs in their baths. Geysers are surface evidence of geothermal heat. There are

3 broad forms of geothermal reservoirs: hydrothermal or hot
water reservoirs; the geocompressed zones in which gas, heat,
and water are retained under great pressure; and the hot rock
reservoirs. Weaver (1977) on pages 568-569 presents 3-dimen-
sional sketches in color of the various forms of geothermal
reservoirs together with a map of the World showing the locations of existing and potential geothermal developments. Geothermal resources could produce 140,000 megawatts over a life
expectancy of 30 years which would be the equivalent to the
output of 140 nuclear plants.

The first application of geothermal energy for power generation was accomplished at Larderello, Italy, in 1905. The
dry steam geothermal field is at present most easily managed.
The only large-scale application of this in the United States
is at the Pacific Gas and Electric Company's steam-driven
turbine installation at the Geysers, about 90 miles northeast
of San Francisco, California. This plant was built in 1960
and is producing sufficient electrical energy to supply about
one-half of the electrical needs of the City of San Francisco.
By the 1990's Pacific Gas and Electric Company plans to develop
the Geysers to a level of 2,000 megawatts or almost the capacity of two Hoover Dam power plants.

Fowler and Fowler (undated), in their appraisal of world-
wide potentialities for geothermal energy, state that two-
thirds of Turkey is believed to have geothermal potential and
they refer to a UN survey which suggested that the geothermal
potential of Ethiopa, if developed, could satisfy the present
electrical needs of all Africa.

Both Larderello and the Geysers are the dry-steam type.
Other geothermal areas may involve considerable environmental
problems. Gases such as hydrogen sulphide and others may be
expelled in large quantities. Much of the water which is at
high temperatures and pressures may carry in solution vast
quantities of inorganic material. When brought to the surface,
as is happening in the Yellowstone National Park, reduction of
pressure and temperature results in extensive deposits of some
of the minerals. Geothermal wells may range in depth from 200
to 900 feet and drilling costs may amount up to $150,000 per
well.

"Natural Steam for Power" (1975) discusses the interaction
of groundwater and geothermal heat. The temperature in a deep
well or mine increases about one degree Fahrenheit for each
100-foot depth on the average. This rate of increase is much
greater in geothermal areas. The potential for geothermal
energy world-wide is tremendous. However, it will take very
large investments in research and exploration to develop this
resource. Although geothermal energy cannot satisfy all of
the World's needs it can be extremely important in many areas.

Kazmann (1978) proposes underground storage of otherwise wasted heat by superheating water to be injected into saline aquifers for later withdrawal for space heating. This provocative concept, in effect an artificial geothermal energy source, could cut National fuel needs about 10 percent according to Kazmann.

Nuclear Fission is a subject on which there is a vast volume of literature. A classic reference is the book by Smyth (1945), "Atomic Energy for Military Purposes". An informative reference is the book by Hogerton (1963) on atomic energy. Fowler (undated) has prepared a very informative Factsheet 12 on conventional reactors. Acquisition of this and others in the series of 19 Factsheets is recommended to anyone having more than a passing interest in energy. A condensed pamphlet on the general subject is "Nuclear Energy" (1976).

Moran, Morgan, and Wiersma (1973) have written an excellent, illustrated discussion of the structure of matter, including nuclear changes in the fission of Uranium 235 in their Chapter 3, pages 49-68. A reading of this Chapter is recommended as a quick review of nuclear physics. Einstein's mass-energy equation of 1905 is given in Topic 4 on page 16. "Nuclear Energy Resources - A Geologic Perspective" (1975) is an informative pamphlet describing the geology of the occurrence of uranium and thorium.

The current electric-power-producing nuclear plants all operate on the fission of radioactive uranium. The proper description would be that these are thermal power plants similar to the coal or oil-burning power plants except that the heat comes from the fission of radioactive material. There is as yet no practical direct conversion of nuclear energy to electricity. Overall efficiency of the system in the conversion of nuclear heat to electricity is about 33 percent.

The heat comes from the fission reaction of elements encased in fuel rods which resemble a very long pencil. When only a very small percentage of the potential heat has been released the rods must be removed. This brings about a fundamental problem in the fission nuclear energy business. The fuel elements must be reprocessed. At present there is no commercially-operating nuclear fuel reprocessing plant. The quantities of radio active waste material from military and civilian applications of nuclear materials have been increasing steadily.

The present conventional reactors yield heat energy from the fission of Uranium 235, an isotope which makes up only 0.7 percent of common uranium ore most of which is Uranium 238. In the conventional reactor Plutonium 239 is created.

According to Fowler (undated), Factsheet 12, the nuclear fuel cycle for a 1000-megawatt light-water conventional reactor is: out of 126 thousand tons of uranium ore 239 tons of uranium oxide $(U_3 O_8)$ are created. This weight is converted to 300 tons of uranium hexafluoride $(U F_6)$ gas. When treated in a gaseous diffusion plant the yield is 42.3 tons of enriched uranium which in turn yields 28.3 tons of fuel. After removal from the reactor the fuel rods are placed in storage. If the rods are reprocessed the 28.3 tons of uranium fuel yields 27.2 tons of recovered uranium, 50 pounds of plutonium, and 1,760 pounds of waste which must go into storage.

According to Carter (1977) there were 200 underground tanks of up to 1.3 million gallons capacity, holding a total of 75 million gallons of military nuclear waste in solution at Hanford, Savannah River, and Idaho Falls installations.

Schmidt (1978) reports that there are 70 million gallons of toxic corrosive liquid waste from the nuclear weapons program alone as well as 50 million cubic feet of radioactive tools, clothing, and worn-out machinery. In addition there are 5,000 tons of spent fuel from nuclear reactors and 140 million tons of radioactive tailings from uranium mining.

According to Parmenter (1978) 69 existing nuclear power plants are supplying 12 percent of the Nation's power. Another 133 plants are either under consideration or under construction.

At present the spent fuel elements are being stockpiled. The volume of high-level and low-level waste from reprocessing, of fuel is greater than that of the material not reprocessed. Some of the waste products are so radioactive as to remain dangerous for more than 24,000 years which is the half-life of Plutonium 239.

Reprocessing is an extremely complicated, intricate, and expensive procedure since it must be done by remote control in laboratories and factories completely isolated from our environment. If a gasoline engine needs to have its carbon removed it is done simply by removing the cylinder head and doing the work. In the nuclear fission world the engine would be removed, broken up, and the pieces dissolved in corrosive chemicals. The metals in solution would then be separated, precipitated, and extracted, and the metals machined and manufactured into components. The engine would then be assembled, the carbon having been eliminated.

In the past 30 years no solution acceptable to the general public has been discovered for the storage and disposal of nuclear waste. Costs of moving and storage will run into billions. Before disposal waste must be sealed in non-corrosive canisters and where possible converted chemically to ceramic substances. "National Security - Safeguarding of Nuclear Materials" (1976) is a folder describing the systems used. "Nuclear Energy - Shipping of Nuclear Wastes" (1978) describes in an illustrated pamphlet the extreme precautions taken in shipping and storage of low-level wastes, high-level wastes, transuranium wastes, and other wastes.

One method of disposal of radioactive wastes under serious consideration is to bury them thousands of feet underground in dry salt beds which are geologically extremely stable and which have no groundwater. Strata of rock salt possess a unique characteristic. When bent or twisted they flow like pitch rather than fracturing like glass. That is why petroleum geologists usually search for salt domes under which natural gas and petroleum may be trapped.

Another possibility is described in "Nuclear Waste Disposal" (1978). Scientists from the National Oceanic and Atmospheric Administration and Yale University propose that nuclear waste be deposited in cracks in the Atlantic Ocean floor where they would be buried under sediment as part of the Earth's creation of future sedimentary rocks. Such disposal could leave the waste undisturbed for as long as 250,000 years.

Nuclear waste is accumulating world-wide in such vast quantities that decisions must be reached without further delay on methods of storage and disposal before an accident occurs. This decision requires international understanding and concurrence. A mechanism exists for this in the form of the International Atomic Energy Agency (IAEA) which was organized in 1957 within the framework of the United Nations.

According to Fowler (1977) in his Factsheet 13 on the breeder reactors, the neutrons released from fission create fissionable nuclei out of material that would not otherwise serve as a nuclear fuel, such as the non-fissionable uranium ore and thorium. The breeder reactor is unique in that it operates in such a manner as to produce more fuel than it consumes. By reprocessing the spent fuels from conventional reactors and using them in breeder reactors about 60 to 70 times as much energy can be yielded from uranium as can be produced in conventional reactors. Plutonium is the fissionable element in the nuclear fission bomb. One pound of Plutonium 239 can theoretically provide the same amount of energy as would be released by the burning of 3 million pounds of coal.

Although there is no active fuel reprocessing plant in the United States, it is known that France is about to have a plant in commercial operation. Silcock (1978) reports that the British Government has approved construction of a mammoth reprocessing plant at Windscale in Northern England. West Germany and Japan are interested in reprocessing plants, and it is reasonable to expect that other nations possessing large numbers of conventional reactors will want to operate reprocessing plants. This is especially true of the nations which have had to rely on imported petroleum as their chief source of energy. To them, the breeder reactor is looked upon as an absolute necessity.

In international diplomacy, as analysed by Yergin (1978), the distinction between nuclear energy and nuclear bomb proliferation is becoming exceedingly complex since both involve the United States' position against Plutonium 239 recycling. Uranium ore is now available in international commerce and since the technology of the breeder reactor has been physically demonstrated, the activation of the breeder reactor by nations other than ours is just a matter of time.

"Environment and Safety - Plutonium in the Environment" (1976) describes plutonium and its beneficial and harmful usages in the human environment. Most of the World's plutonium has fallen on water. A study of Lake Michigan disclosed that about 97 percent of the plutonium which fell on the Lake is in the bottom sediment.

There is wide-spread, world-wide concern about the possibility of illegal diversion of plutonium to non-power generation usages. In the hands of unfriendly or irresponsible groups or individuals diverted plutonium could endanger all of the human race.

Drozd, Hohenberg, and Morgan (1974) found evidence of a spontaneous nuclear fission chain reaction which occurred near the Oklo mine site, in the Republic of Gabon, Central Africa. Xenon isotopic studies confirmed the occurrence of this natural nuclear fission event more than one billion years ago. The active time of this natural reactor was between 14,000 and 70,000 years. The authors state that their analyses do not imply that the chain reaction operated continuously over that period of time. Some geologists estimate that the plutonium from the Okla reactor was trapped naturally for the hundreds of thousands of years it took for it to lose all of its radioactivity.

Taking into account such factors as national patriotism, necessity of energy for human and economic survival, the rising cost of depleting reserves of the World's oil, and the wide-spread knowledge of fuel reprocessing and breeder reactor technology, it is totally unrealistic to continue to think that our Nation can control internationally the production of plutonium. Complete control of plutonium is no longer a topic of conversation; it is an absolute necessity calling for international effort.

Nuclear fusion is the mass-energy reaction which powers our
Sun. It is also the reaction which takes place in the hydrogen
bomb. Fowler in his Factsheet 14 has presented a very informative description of the nuclear physics, the technology, and
the environmental effects and safety of nuclear fusion. He
lists 5 references.

The reaction is one which involves deuterium and tritium.
The relatively rare light metal, lithium, is necessary to produce tritium. Deuterium when combined with oxygen yields
"heavy water" which is found in nature with one molecule of
heavy water to 6,500 molecules of ordinary water; or one pound
of deuterium is found in 60,000 pounds of water. Considering
the waters of the Earth, it is estimated that there are 10
trillion tons of deuterium present, a practically infinite
resource.

The total energy released from a ton of deuterium would
be equivalent to that released in the combustion of 60 million
tons of coal. There are, however, a number of extremely great
obstacles. The fusion reaction takes place at temperatures of
50 to 100 million degrees Celsius. In the hydrogen bomb such
temperatures are attained for an infinitesimal fraction of
time by conducting the fusion reaction within a conventional
nuclear fission bomb.

Several approaches are under study to attain this tremendous heat. First, it is necessary to produce "plasma" which is
a deuterium-tritium mixture stripped of electrons so that the
plasma consists of charged electrons and nuclei. The plasma
may be heated by (1) induced electric current; (2) by injection
into the plasma of energetic nuclear particles; and, (3) by
compressing the plasma in magnetic pinched devices. Another
tremendous problem is that of sustaining under control the
fusion reaction.

Ashworth (1977) has written a somewhat optimistic users'
perspective on the fusion reaction. At present, although extensive research is being conducted, estimates of nuclear
fusion as a sustaining source of energy place the time of
attainment at least 50 years in the future.

Solar energy is commonly thought of as referring to the use of
incoming solar radiation for conversion to energy. Photosynthesis converts solar radiation to matter. There are 2 general
catagories of usage of direct solar energy. One is the solar
energy conversion to heat; the other is solar-photovoltaic conversion to electric energy. Solar-thermal conversion is classified by Fowler in his Factsheet 5 into 3 broad systems: central reservoir, distributed, and total energy.

The central reservoir facility either focuses or reflects

incoming solar energy so that it is concentrated at boilers or heat-exchangers from which the heat is conveyed to points of utilization. These systems may require heavy investments in equipment and controls so that reflectors may move with the sun to maintain concentrated beams. Efficiency may approach 90 percent but this system requires clear skies or direct sunlight. The central system solar furnace in the Pyrenees can on a clear day produce temperatures as high as 6000 degrees F. One advantage of the central system is that it allows electric energy generation with conventional steam turbine-generator technology.

The distributed collector system receives either direct or diffused solar radiation on cloudy days and the heat is transferred to a substance such as water, oil, molten metal, or air, depending on the complexity of the design and the purpose for which the heat is needed. Flat-plate collectors of this type are becoming widely used for space heating and domestic water heating. One problem in both of these systems is that they require a heat storage. Large water tanks or crushed rock are commonly used.

Fowler's 3d classification, the total energy system, is one that would provide heat, refrigeration, and electricity. This is currently a subject of considerable research.

Shaffer (1977) suggests that solar ponds could serve as low-cost energy storage facilities. His article includes suggestions for the design of such ponds. He states that the solar radiation reaching the surface of the Earth is about 13,000 times the World's current annual energy requirement.

The U.S. Department of Housing and Urban Development has established, in cooperation with the U.S. Department of Energy, the National Solar Heating and Cooling Information Center, Rockville, Maryland. Two of the information pamphlets prepared by this Center are: "Solar Energy and Your Home" (1978) and "Passive Design Ideas for the Energy Conscious Consumer" (undated). An "active" solar heating design uses solar energy collectors, fans, pumps, heat exchanges and storage, whereas a "passive" design needs little hardware, uses no energy in itself, and may be low in cost.

The pronouncement "Sun Day" (1978) by the Royal Embassy of Saudi Arabia, contains information that the pioneering solar energy facility for both heating and cooling of the Terraset Public Elementary School in Reston, Virginia, was funded by Saudi Arabia only after funds from other sources were not available. This solar energy facility is a global "first", according to the pronouncement.

An example of photovoltaic conversion is the photoelectric cell. In the silicon cell, widely used in photo-

graphic light meters, the radiant energy is converted directly
to electric current the voltage of which is indicated by the
deflection of a needle. Recent photographic applications make
use of a conducting cell, such as cadmium sulfide, the resistance of which changes depending on the incident radiation.
Both types of photoelectric cells have applications in solar
energy. According to Fowler (Factsheet 4) a 1000-watt direct
solar cell generator is in operation by the MITRE Corporation
near Washington, D.C. It consists of 20 panels each of which
contains about 700 individual cells. The installation cost
$30,000. In contrast conventional power plants can be built
and placed in operation for less than $1,000 per kilowatt.
Extensive research is underway on photovoltaic energy. There
are many applications in science and industry and in satellite
engineering where photovoltaic cells are now in service.

"Solar Electricity from Photovoltaic Conversion" (1978)
discusses the solar cells, solar modules, economics, and future
prospects of this subject. Johnston (1977) includes diagrams
and photographs of photovoltaic conversion. He concludes that
there is a possibility that in the future solar cells might
produce 30 percent of our total electric needs or about 10 percent of the Nation's energy needs.

"State Solar Legislation" (1978) gives citations to laws
pertaining to solar energy including incentives, solar access
standards for solar systems, and building code provisions.
"New Book Tackles Solar Law Worries" (1978) describes the problems which are to be treated in a forthcoming book by
Sandy F. Kraemer. The problem is that of protecting solar
energy users from shadow. An excellent illustrated review of
the solar energy has been written by Wilhelm and Kristof (1976).
"Solar Energy - A Bibliography"(1977) is a compilation of
thousands of references.

The Solar Energy Research Institute (SERI) was created by
PL 93-473, the Solar Energy Research, Development, and Demonstration Act of 1974, signed Oct. 26, 1974. It is located at
Golden, Colorado, and is operated by the Midwest Research Institute, of Kansas City, Missouri, under a contract issued by the
U.S. Department of Energy. SERI was dedicated by the President
on "Sun Day", May 3, 1978.

Fuel cells  A fuel cell electric power generating system demonstrated its capabilities in the moon landings of 1971 to 1973
and it has been used to provide electric power to 50 apartments, houses, commercial establishments, and small industrial
buildings, according to "Fuel Cells: A New Kind of Power Plant"
(1978). This folder includes charts showing the operation of a
fuel cell. The chemical energy that bonds atoms of hydrogen
and oxygen is converted directly to electric energy. Efficiencies in excess of 75 percent have been attained. A hydrogen-

rich fuel which might be coal, oil, hydrocarbon gas, or hydrogen, is fed down the anode (negative electrode) and air, the source of oxygen, is fed down the cathode (plus electrode). The hydrogen and oxygen combine to form water which departs from the cell as steam and the excess electrons flow from the cell as an electric current. It is estimated by the Department of Energy that by 1985 about 20,000 megawatts of fuel-cell electric power could be produced at a saving of more than 100 million barrels of oil. Environmentally, fuel cells have the advantages of being non-polluting, quiet, and portable if necessary.

Hydrogen is an unusual fuel. Although the energy content per cubic foot is less than one-third that of natural gas, its energy content per pound is almost 3 times that of gasoline making it the highest in energy content of any fuel known.

Hydrogen is very common in nature but in its uncombined, elemental state it is extremely rare. Water, for example, is $H_2O$. Considerable energy must be expended to produce gaseous hydrogen. Hydrogen as a fuel must be considered a technique of energy storage as is mentioned in "Hydrogen Fuel" (1978). Several million pounds of hydrogen are produced annually in the United States for use in the chemical industries, in petroleum refining, and in the manufacture of ammonia and methyl alcohol. For such purposes hydrogen is produced by reacting natural gas and light oil with steam at high temperatures. Food processing, for example hydrogenation of cooking fat, uses hydrogen in much purer form produced by electrolysis.

Research is being conducted to use hydrogen as a fuel either in internal combustion engines or in fuel cells to provide peaking electric power in areas where pumped storage hydropower is not feasible. Extensive research is underway to improve the effectiveness of the electrolysis cell. Another possibility is to use the electric current produced from central solar heat systems to separate hydrogen from water thereby storing the solar energy. It has been suggested that the experimental gas-cooled nuclear reactors, which have reached temperatures of 1100 degrees C (1922° F), be used to break down water by heat alone.

Hydrogen liquifies at -267° C (-420° F). Storage in liquified form requires expensive refrigeration facilities and the loss of the equivalent of perhaps 25-30 percent of the stored hydrogen's energy value. However, hydrogen can be stored as a compound with certain metals with which it forms hydrides. Metals and alloys which form such hydrides are magnesium-nickle, magnesium-copper, and iron-titanium. Hydrogen has been used as a fuel in rocket propulsion and it has been used successfully in the engines of aircraft, naval vessels, and motor vehicles.

Hammond, Metz, and Maugh (1973) in their Chapter 18 on hydrogen, state that widespread production of hydrogen by electrolysis would produce vast quantities of oxygen as a by-product. They suggest use of some of this oxygen for the processing of municipal sewage.

It is anticipated that the burning of hydrogen can very greatly increase the efficiency of the World's energy resources.

Primary and secondary cells are commonly referred to as batteries. A primary cell is one which generates electric current from chemical reactions. The dry cell, used in flash lights, in portable radios, hearing aids, and a great variety of other applications, is expended as it produces the electric current. This chemical reaction is not reversible and primary cells cannot be recharged effectively.

Secondary cells are storage batteries. The ordinary lead-sulphuric acid storage batteries are very widely used in automobiles and other vehicles. The efficiency of most batteries is very low and extensive research is underway on a large number of combinations of chemical compounds which could store electric energy in the form of chemical changes. Some systems, such as lithium-sulfur and sodium-sulfur, operate at temperatures from $300^{\circ}$ to $450^{\circ}$ C (about $570^{\circ}$ to $840^{\circ}$ F). It is envisioned that new materials in storage batteries might make it possible to store as much as 5 to 8 times the electricity per pound as is stored in the lead-acid batteries.

According to the folder "Energy Conservation - Large Scale Storage of Electricity in Batteries" (1977) a 2.5-megawatt battery facility is being built in the system served by the Public Service Electric and Gas Company in Somerset County, New Jersey, about 20 miles southwest of Newark. This facility, known as BEST (Battery Energy Storage Test) is to use the zinc-chloride battery storage design, among others. The direct current released from this facility is to be inverted to AC and used for peaking purposes.

Magnetohydrodynamics (MHD) is a process which holds promise of providing clean and efficient electric-current generation directly from combustion of petroleum or powdered coal. When the hot ionized gases in a flame pass between the poles of a magnet electrons are removed thereby producing an electric current. Weaver and Kristof (1972) describe the MHD process on pages 673 -675 of this reference. They report that it has been calculated that efficiences may reach as high as 60 percent or one and one-half times that of the conventional fossil fuel-burning, steam-powered plant. After part of the energy from the ionized gases has been converted to electricity, the hot gases could then be used to heat a conventional steam turbine-generator assembly system.

Tidal power   The harnessing of tidal power provides a source of
energy which does not depend on radiation.  Gravity forces exerted by the Moon and the Sun on the waters of the oceans produce a periodic rise and fall.  Two high tides and two low
tides occur about every 24 hours.  Where the fluctuations of
levels impinge on coast lines and estuaries, dams are built to
direct the waters through hydroelectric turbine generators.
At least a 5-foot difference in depth between water in the reservoir created by the dam and the ocean-side of the dam is
necessary; however, the greater the difference the more efficient would be the tidal power.

According to the Department of Energy's fact sheet, "Tidal
Power", (1978) the largest tidal power plant currently in operation is the 240,000-kilowatt (240 mw) Rance Station located
near St. Malo, France.  The average output for the period 1960-
1967 was 65,000 mw hours which would provide enough power for
more than 16,000 average homes in the United States.  China
may have more than 100 small tidal power plants.  The USSR has
a 400-kilowatt  experimental tidal plant near Murmansk.  South
Korea, Canada, France, England, the USSR, and the United States
are all studying tidal energy seriously.

Two areas of exceptionally high tides are the Passamaquoddy Bay region along the United States-Canada border in
Maine, and the Cook Inlet region in Alaska.  The Passamaquoddy
tidal project has been under consideration for almost 50 years.
There are numerous advantages and disadvantages to tidal power.
The effects of air and water pollution would be minimal.  Some
types of recreation would be enhanced but there would be
changes in the ecology in fish and wildlife, and scenic
environments of the area..

In the past there were serious problems with synchronization and with storage of electrical  energy during non-generat-
ing periods.  Now, however, with AC-DC-AC power systems (see
Topic 91) it could be possible, in conjunction with other
thermal and hydro systems, to use very effectively the output
of a tidal power plant.

Another energy storage system which could be very advanta-
geously applied to tidal power plants is that of using the
power to electrolize water for the production of hydrogen.  For
this system, the Cook Inlet or other locations anywhere in the
World which may be far removed from centers of industry could
still convert astrophysical energy of the tides to hydrogen
fuel.

A comprehensive reference on tidal power is the book by
Bernshtein (1961).  A translation of this from the Russian was

published in 1965. Shaw and Thorpe(1971) suggest the integration of pumped storage (see Topic 91) with tidal power to allow for steady base-load operation of a thermal power plant. They present a detailed description of a combined operation planned for the Severn Estuary near Bristol, England, and Cardiff, Wales.

Ocean thermal energy conversion would make use of temperature differences which occur in the ocean when the surface waters are heated by the Sun. According to the pamphlet "Ocean Thermal Energy Conversion" (1977) more than 70 percent of the solar energy reaching the Earth falls on the oceans and other bodies of water. Beginning in 1926 Georges Claude, a Frenchman, already famous for developing industrial applications of acetylene, helium, and neon, and for his work in liquifying gases, succeeded in producing 22 kw of electric power at a facility which was built on the Cuban coast. His experimental facility conveyed cold water from a depth through large pipes. He used a boiler-condenser system which operated on steam at temperature differences of only $24^{\circ}$ F.

It has been estimated that 180 trillion kilowatt-hours of power could be generated annually from the Gulf Stream flowing along the East Coast of the United States. This amount of energy would be about 75 times the projected energy consumption of all the United States by 1980. A conversion plant could operate 24 hours a day and not be dependent on intermittent sunshine since the oceans are a tremendous reserve of solar energy.

A favorable advantage of this system could be an increase in the production of commercial fish, an important source of protein. It is known that the Humboldt Current, which has a natural upwelling of nutrient-rich cold water off the coast of Peru, produces fish supplying about 20 percent of all commercial fish in the World.

Structural problems of stability in heavy seas and of corrosion of equipment could be very important. The long-range effect of removing heat from the ocean could have global repercussions if it affected the circulation patterns of the ocean currents. The Department of Energy is planning construction of a 25 mw demonstration plant in the early 1980's according to the pamphlet "Ocean Thermal Energy Conversion" (1977). Fowler and Fowler (Factsheet 6) have written an informative review of potentialities and problems.

Othmer and Roels (1973) proposed a combined approach to produce power, demineralize water, and to culture algae, shell fish, crustaceans, and seaweed in mariculture ponds in their entrancing article dealing with ocean thermal energy consumption.

Energy storage  At present there is no simple way to store
large amounts of electrical energy.  The broad categories of
energy storage requirements are (a) to provide a mobile source
of electric energy for transportation; (b) methods of transporting and storing heat energy; and, (c) methods of storage
of both electric and heat energy to meet peak demands.  See
Topic 91 for discussions of hydropower, pumped storage, and
systems management.  Fowler (Factsheet 16) presents an excellent review of the economics of developing systems of energy
storage to meet peak demands.  It is not economical to build a
power system having the capacity for peak demands which may
prevail for only a small part of the energy-consuming cycle.

Energy storage may be accomplished in various ways.  The
mechanical storage can be done by fly-wheels which can attain
efficiencies of about 70 percent.  The folder, "Fly Wheels:
Storing Energy as Motion" (1977) is a very informative review
of the subject.  Fly wheels can be used for regenerative brak-
ing in conjunction with electrical propulsion.  When applied
to a subway system, power requirements were cut 20 to 30
percent.

The booklet, "Energy Conservation - Energy Storage" (1976)
contains illustrations of a high-temperature lithium-sulfur
storage battery and of a gyrobus which has been used in Switzerland and in the Belgian Congo.  This bus drew electric power
from an overhead pole to spin a flywheel which in turn drove
an electric generator powering the road wheels.  The power
poles were about one-half mile apart and the bus stopped at
each pole.  The bus was 35-feet long; weighed 24,000 pounds;
its capacity was 35 people seated and 35 standing.

Pumped storage discussed in Topic 91 is widely used and
only about one-third of the energy is lost in a cycle.  Economically it is very favorable since the pumping is done with
power for which there might be no market, whereas the generation is timed for peak demand times.  Compressing air is
another way of storing the heat.  Efficiency is very low unless
the heat generated when compressing the air is stored to pre-
heat the air when energy is needed.

Thermal storage offers a great potential.  More than one-
half of the Nation's energy consumption is for heating.  Water,
rocks, bricks, and heat pumps have been used.  Storage of heat
at high temperatures offers a number of problems and there is
not much experience with this subject.  Chemical storage has
potentials since it provides for high-energy density when
released and can be managed in a stable system.

Magnetic storage is the subject of much research.  This
technique would require the use of superconductors operating
at temperatures approaching absolute zero.  At extremely low

temperatures many substances have practically no electrical resistance and large amounts of electric energy might be stored with little or no loss.

Metz (1978) believes that the energy storage aspects of the use of solar power have been exaggerated. He gives (page 1473) the following costs for storage of energy: thermal storage of hot water in tanks, $4.00 per kilowatt-hour; lead-acid storage batteries, $50.00 per kwh; hydroelectric pumped storage, $10.00 per kwh; hot water storage in underground aquifers possibly as low as 5 cents per kwh; compressed air, flywheels, and superconducting systems $25.00 to $75.00 per kwh. For comparison, energy from the combustion of coal or oil is available at a cost of about one cent per kilowatt-hour.

Energy - General  Since about one-fifth of the Nation's total energy consumption is for space heating and water heating, a great deal of attention is being focused on building design and construction features which would reduce energy requirements. Karheck, Powell, and Beardsworth (1977) analyzed the prospects for district heating in the United States. Such systems have been used in Europe for a long time. Denmark serves 32 percent of its population with district heating using refuse incinerators, electric plants, and oil-burning boilers for heat. The Soviet Union is said to supply 70 percent of its urban heat and 54 percent of entire space and water heat requirements by district heating. Whereas in the United States high-pressure steam is used in most district heat systems, the European practice is to use hot water for heat transport. The authors conclude that 50 to 55 percent of the population of the United states could be served economically by district heating.

Bahadori (1978) has written a fascinating article illustrated with photographs and drawings of passive cooling systems developed in Iranian architecture. He describes four approaches: the wind tower; the air vent; the cistern; and the ice-maker. Wind towers may be up to 34 meters (112 feet) high. Air vents in curved roofs, the design for which dates back to about 3000 B.C.,vent the hot air. Air flowing through tunnels, past fountains, over subterranean streams or cisterns, picks up moisture and its temperature drops as the relative humidity increases. Ice-makers, which are passive cooling systems, are illustrated on page 154 in Bahadori's article. Cisterns and ice-makers appeared in Iran about 900 A.D. The Iranian passive cooling systems require no energy other than the Sun and wind. A study of this reference is recommended.

In contrast to the Iranian developments and the excellent architecture developed centuries ago by the American Indian, an example of which are the pueblos of New Mexico and Arizona suited to the desert environment, our current practice is to build flat-roof, one-story ranch houses for which the costs of

air-conditioning using electrical energy can be as high as
$200 per month for a one-family residence.

A fossil fuel plant is about 50 percent efficient and a
conventional nuclear power plant is about 33 percent efficient,
as measured in terms of electrical energy produced. The
difference is lost as heat much of it in the cooling water.
"Symposium: Beneficial Uses for Thermal Discharges" (1973) is
an assembly of 8 papers which deal with utilizing waste heat in
integrated systems for water pollution control; for soil warming using subsurface water pipe systems; for the use of radiative cooling basins instead of condenser towers; for ecological
management of thermal discharges; for heating food production
complexes such as greenhouses; and for aquaculture including
fish production.

The discussion of alternative sources of energy in this
Topic brings out the importance of water which is involved in
practically all of the alternatives. The need for energy
arises in many instances from activities which deal with the
water resources as they apply to human endeavors.

## References

"A Technology Assessment of Coal Slurry Pipelines", Office of
    Technology Assessment, Congress of the United States,
    155 pp, Mar. 1978.

Ashworth, Clinton P., "A User's Perspective on Fusion - Part
    II", a paper presented at the Annual Meeting of the AAAS,
    in the Symposium on Energy, Denver, Colo., Feb. 25, 1977,
    33 pp, 1977.

Bahadori, Mehdi N., "Passive Cooling Systems in Iranian Arch-
    itecture", Scientific American, vol. 238, no. 2, pp 144-
    154, Feb., 1978.

Bartlett, Albert A., "The Forgotten Fundamentals of the Energy
    Crisis", a paper given at the Third Annual Conference on
    Energy, Univ. of Missouri at Rolla, Oct. 12-14, 1976.

Bartlett, Albert A., "The Exponential Function", The Physics
    Teacher, vol. 14, no. 7, Oct. 1976. (Dr. Bartlett is with
    the Dept. of Physics and Astrophysics, Univ. of Colo. at
    Boulder. This reference is pub. in 5 parts.)

Bernshtein, L. B., "Tidal Energy for Electric Power Plants",
    1961. Trans. from the Russion by A. Baruch of the Israel
    Program for Scientific Translations. Available from U.S.
    Dept. of Commerce, Clearinghouse for Federal Scientific &
    Tech. Information, Springfield, Va. Trans. No. TT 64-
    11028, 378 pp and map. 1965.

Bormann, F. H., "An Inseparable Linkage: Conservation of
Natural Ecosystems and the Conservation of Fossil Energy",
BioScience vol. 26, no. 12, pp 754-760, Dec. 1976.

Burgess, Robert L., "Potential of Forest Fuels for Producing
Electrical Energy", Jour. of Forestry, vol. 76, no. 3,
pp 154-157, Mar. 1978.

Burwell, C. C., "Solar Biomass Energy: An Overview of U.S.
Potential", Science, vol. 199, no. 4333, pp 1041-1048,
Mar. 10, 1978.

Carter, Luther J., "Radioactive Wastes: Some Urgent Unfinished
Business", Science, vol. 195, pp 661-666 and 704,
Feb. 18, 1977.

Cox, John L., Warrack G. Willson, and Edward J. Hoffman,
"Conversion of Organic Waste to Fuel Gas", Jour. Environmental Engineering Div., Proceedings ASCE, vol. 100,
no. EE3, pp 717-732, June, 1974.

Drozd, R. J., C. M. Hohenberg, and C. J. Morgan, "Heavy Rare
Gases from Rabbit Lake (Canada) and the Oklo Mine (Gabon)
Natural Spontaneous Chain Reactions in Old Uranium
Deposits", Earth and Planetary Science Letters, vol. 23,
pp 28-33, 1974.

Dunrud, C. Richard, and Frank W. Osterwald, "Effects of Coal
Mine Subsidence in the Western Powder River Basin,
Wyoming", Geological Survey, USDI, Open-File Report 78-
473, 71 pp, Denver, Colo., 1978.

Dyson, Freeman J., "Energy in the Universe", Scientific
American, vol. 224, no. 3, pp 50-59, Sept. 1971.

"Energy Conservation - Energy Storage", a folder, 10 pp, Energy
Research and Dev. Admin., Office of Public Affairs,
Washington, D.C., June, 1976.

"Energy Conservation - Large-Scale Storage of Electricity in
Batteries", a folder, 14 pp, Energy Research & Dev. Admin.
Office of Public Affairs, Washington, D.C., Mar. 1977.

"Energy and the Environment", Citizens Workshop Handbook,
Energy Research and Dev. Admin., Washington, D.C., 32 pp,
1975.

"Energy from the Winds", a folder, U.S. Dept. of Energy, Office
of Public Affairs, Washington, D.C., 10 pp, Feb. 1978.

"Environment & Safety - Plutonium in the Environment", Energy
    Research and Dev. Admin., Office of Public Affairs,
    Washington, D.C., a folder, Sept. 1976.

Fowler, John M., and Kathryn Mervine Fowler, "Factsheet 3,
    Wind Power", 4 pp, undated. (Complete reference for this
    and the following Factsheets given with Fowler and Kryger
    below.)

Fowler, John M., "Factsheet 4, Electricity from the Sun I -
    Solar Photovoltaic Energy", 4 pp, undated.

Fowler, John M., "Factsheet 5, Electricity from the Sun II -
    Solar Thermal Energy Conversion", 4 pp, undated.

Fowler, John M., and Kathryn Mervine Fowler, "Factsheet 6,
    Solar Sea Power - Ocean Thermal Energy Conversion", 4 pp,
    undated.

Fowler, John M., and Kathryn Mervine Fowler, "Factsheet 8,
    Geothermal Energy", 4 pp, undated.

Fowler, John M., "Factsheet 12, Conventional Reactors", 6 pp,
    undated.

Fowler, John M., "Factsheet 13, Breeder Reactors", 6 pp, 1977.

Fowler, John M., "Factsheet 14, Nuclear Fusion", 6 pp, undated.

Fowler, John M., "Factsheet 15, New Fuels from Coal", 4 pp,
    undated.

Fowler, John M., "Factsheet 16, Energy Storage Technology",
    6 pp, 1977.

Fowler, John M., and King C. Kryger, "Factsheet 18, Alternative
    Energy Sources - A Glossary of Terms", 8 pp, undated.
    A series of 19 Factsheets was  produced by the National
    Science Teachers Association under contract with the U.S.
    Energy Research and Dev. Admin.  The Factsheets may be ob-
    tained from: ERDA-Technical Information Center, P.O. Box
    62, Oak Ridge, TN 37830.

"Flywheels: Storing Energy as Motion", U.S. Dept. of Energy,
    Office of Public Affairs, Washington, D.C., a folder,
    Nov. 1977.

"Fuel Cells: A New Kind of Power Plant", U.S. Dept. of Energy,
    Office of Public Affairs, Washington, D.C., a folder,
    Feb., 1978.

"Fuels from Biomass", U.S. Dept. of Energy, Office of Public Affairs, Washington, D.C., a folder, Nov. 1977.

Glover, Frank W., Jr., "Surface Mine Reclamation in the Mountain State", Soil Conservation, pp 4-7, Aug. 1976.

Gurfinkel, German, and Adolf Walser, "Analysis and Design of Hyperbolic Cooling Towers", Jour. Power Div., Proceedings ASCE, vol. 98, no. PO 1, pp 133-152, June, 1972.

Hamilton, Roger, and Emory Kristof, "Can We Harness the Wind?", National Geographic, vol. 148, no. 6, pp 812-829, Dec. 1975.

Hammond, Allen L., William D. Metz, and Thomas H. Maugh II, "Energy and the Future", Amer. Assn. for the Advancement of Science, Washington, D.C., paperback, 184 pp, 1973.

Haughey, Richard D., "Methane Gas", a letter to the editor, Civil Engineering, vol. 48, no. 5, pp 36-38, May, 1978.

Hogerton, John F., "Atomic Energy Deskbook", Reinhold Publ. Corp, New York, 673 pp, 1963.

Hubbert, M. King, "Energy Resources", Chapt. 8, pp 156-242 in Resources and Man - A study and recommendations by the Committee on Resources and Man, Natl. Academy of Sciences-Natl. Research Council, pub. by W. H. Freeman and Co., San Francisco, 259 pp, 1969.

"Hydrogen Fuel", U.S. Dept. of Energy, Office of Public Affairs Washington, D.C., a folder, Jan. 1978.

Johnston, W. D., Jr., "The Prospects for Photovoltaic Conversion", American Scientist, vol. 65, no. 6, pp 729-736, Nov.-Dec., 1977.

Judy, Clark H., and Ambrey Gartner, "Areawide Water Quality Management in an Energy Development Area", Water Resources Bulletin, vol. 13, no. 4, pp 835-841, Aug. 1977.

Karkheck, J., J. Powell, and E. Beardsworth, "Prospects for District Heating in the United States - District heating can effect a significant reduction in fossil fuel consumption", Science, vol. 195, pp 948-955, Mar. 11, 1977.

Kazmann, Raphael G., "Underground Hot Water Storage Could Cut National Fuel Needs 10%", Civil Engineering, vol. 48, no. 5, pp 57-60, May, 1978.

Klein, H. Arthur, "The World of Measurements", Simon and Schuster, New York, 736 pp, 1974.

Krendel, E. S., "Man- and Animal-Generated Power", pp 9-209 & 9-210 in Standard Handbook for Mechanical Engineers, 7th ed., T. Baumeister ed-in-chief, McGraw-Hill, New York, 1967.

Likens, G. E., F. H. Bormann, R. S. Pierce, and W. A. Reiners, "Recovery of a Deforested Ecosystem", Science, vol. 199, no. 4328, pp 492-496, Feb. 3, 1978.

"Living in a Glass House 1 - Home Energy Budgeting", Bonneville Power Admin., U.S. Dept. of Energy, Portland, Ore., 12 pp, Nov. 1977.

Metz, William D., "Energy Storage and Solar Power: An Exaggerated Problem", Science, vol. 200, no. 4349, pp 1471-1473, June 30, 1978.

Moran, Joseph M., Michael D. Morgan, and James H. Wiersma, "An Introduction to Environmental Sciences", Little, Brown and Co., Boston, 389 pp, 1973.

"National Security - Safeguarding of Nuclear Materials", Energy Research and Development Admin., Office of Public Affairs, Washington, D.C., a folder, Sept. 1976.

"Natural Steam for Power", Geological Survey, USDI, a folder, 1975.

"New Book Tackles Solar Law Worries", Rocky Mountain News, p 18 Sat. Apr. 29, 1978

"Nuclear Energy - Nuclear Energy", Energy Research and Dev. Admin., Office of Public Affairs, Washington, D. C., a folder, Sept. 1976.

"Nuclear Energy Resources - A Geologic Perspective", Geological Survey, USDI, a pamphlet, 15 pp, 1975.

"Nuclear Energy - Shipping of Nuclear Wastes", Energy Research and Dev. Admin., Office of Public Affairs, a folder, Washington, D.C., Aug. 1977.

"Nuclear Waste Disposal", p 41 in Offshore Technology, The Military Engineer, vol 70, no. 453, Jan.-Feb., 1978.

"Ocean Thermal Energy Conversion", U.S. Dept. of Energy, Office of Public Affairs, Washington, D.C., a folder, Nov. 1977.

"Oil Shale: A Potential Source of Energy", Geological Survey, USDI, a folder, 15 pp, 1977.

Othmer, Donald F., and Oswald A. Roels, "Power, Fresh Water, and Food from Cold, Deep Sea Water", Science, vol. 182, no. 4108, pp 121-125, Oct. 12, 1973.

Parmenter, Cindy, "Nuclear-Power Plants Waste - A Where-to-Put-it Dilemma", Denver Post, p 1, Sun. June 4, 1978.

Parmenter, Cindy, "Public Disillusioned About Finding Any N-Disposal Solution", Denver Post, p 29, Sun. June 4, 1978.

"Passive Design Ideas for the Energy Conscious Consumer", A National Solar Heating and Cooling Information Center Publication, Franklin Institute Research Laboratories in cooperation with U.S. Dept. of Housing and Urban Dev., and U.S. Dept. of Energy, Rockville, Md., 32 pp, undated.

Peracchio, Adrian, "Coal-Oil Mix May Serve as Plug in Energy Drain", Denver Post, p 9-E, Sun. June 11, 1978.

Schmidt, Ann, "Solve Disposal of Waste or Lose N-Energy: Hart", Denver Post, p 37, Sun., Mar. 19, 1978.

"Scientific American", Special Issue on Energy and Power, vol. 224, no. 3, Sept. 1971.

Shaffer, Lloyd H., "Solar Ponds: Low Cost Solar Energy Management Systems", Energy, vol. 11, no. 3, pp 18-20, Summer, 1977.

Shaw, Thomas L., and Geoffrey R. Thorpe, "Integration of Pumped-Storage with Tidal Power", Jour. Power Div., Proceedings, ASCE, vol. 97, no. PO 1, pp 159-180, Jan., 1971.

Silcock, Bryan, "British Challenge U.S. Nuclear Policy", The Denver Post, p 19, Sun. May 7, 1978.

Singer, S. Fred, "Soil and Coal: A Cost-Benefit Inquiry", Science, vol. 198, no. 4314, guest editorial, Oct. 21, 1977.

Smyth, Henry D., "Atomic Energy for Military Purposes", Princeton Univ. Press, Princeton, N.J., 264 pp, 1945. (This is the Official Report on the Development of the Atomic Bomb under the Auspices of the United States Government, 1940-45).

"Solar Electricity from Photovoltaic Conversion", a folder, U.S. Dept. of Energy, Office of Public Affairs, Washington D.C., 9 pp, Mar. 1978.

"Solar Energy - A Bibliography", U.S. Energy Research & Development Admin., Office of Public Affairs, Tech. Information Center, Washington, D.C., Report No. TID-3351-R1P2, Mar. 1976.

"Solar Energy and Your Home", A National Solar Heating and Cooling Information Center Publication, Franklin Institute Research Laboratories in coop. with U.S. Dept. of Housing and Urban Dev., and U.S. Dept. of Energy, Rockville, Md., a folder, 20 pp, Apr. 1978.

"State Solar Legislation", A National Solar Heating and Cooling Information Center Publication, Franklin Institute Research Lab. in cooperation with U.S. Dept. of Housing and Urban Dev., and U.S. Dept. of Energy, Rockville, Md., 6 pp, Jan., 1978.

"Sun Day - A Special Day- A Special Relationship", from the Royal Embassy of Saudi Arabia, Washington, D.C., The Denver Post, p 11, Wed. May 3, 1978.

"Symposium: Beneficial Uses for Thermal Discharges", 8 papers appearing on pp 178-228 of the Jour. of Environmental Quality, vol. 2, no. 2, Apr.-June, 1973.

"The Role of the Bonneville Power Administration in the Pacific Northwest Power Supply System including its Participation in the Hydro-Thermal Power Program", Summary Report, 54 pp, of A Program Environmental Statement and Planning Report, Bonneville Power Admin., Portland, Ore., Aug.1977.

"Tidal Power", Dept. of Energy Fact Sheet, Office of Public Affairs: Information, Washington, D.C., 4 pp, May, 1978.

Torrey, Volta, "Wind-Catchers - American Windmills of Yesterday and Tomorrow", The Stephen Greene Press, Brattleboro, Vermont, 226 pp, Nov. 1976, 2nd printing, Mar. 1977.

Walker, Jearl, "The Amateur Scientist - What plumes of smoke tell about the structure of the atmosphere", Scientific American, vol. 238, no. 5, pp 162-171, May, 1978.

Weaver, Kenneth F., and Emory Kristof, "The Search for Tomorrow's Power", National Geographic, vol. 142, no. 5, pp 650-681, Nov. 1972.

Weaver, Kenneth F., "The Power of Letting Off Steam - Geothermal Energy", National Geographic, vol. 152, no. 4, pp 566-579, Oct. 1977.

"What Everyone Should Know About Oil Shale", A Scriptographic
Booklet, 15 pp, pub. by Channing L. Bete Co., Inc.,
Greenfield, Mass., 1977.

Wilhelm, John L, and Emory Kristof, "Solar Energy, the Ultimate
Powerhouse", National Geographic, vol. 149, no. 3, pp 380-
397, Mar. 1976.

Williams, Theodore T., "Water Conflicts in Western Coal Development", ASCE Natl. Convention Nov. 3-7, 1975, Denver,
Colo., Meeting Preprint 2588, 26 pp, 1975.

Wilson, Herbert M., "Pumping Water for Irrigation", Water
Supply and Irrigation Paper No. 1, Geological Survey,
USDI, Govt. Printing Office, 57 pp, 1896.

Yergin, Daniel, "Nuclear Power Slips in Europe", The Denver
Post, p 19, Sun., May 7, 1978.

Young, Gordon, and James P. Blair, "Will Coal Be Tomorrow's
'Black Gold'?", National Geographic, vol. 148, no. 2,
pp 234-259, Aug., 1975.

When water falls the kinetic energy which it acquired by having been lifted to a higher elevation, is converted to mechanical energy and to heat, although the amount of heat generated is very small. Hydropower is, in effect, a form of solar energy since the water attained the high elevation through the evaporation, atmospheric-transport, and precipitation processes. In pumped storage it is lifted mechanically. The mechanical energy has been extracted from falling water for centuries. Water wheels have powered all types of machinery, factories, sawmills, and flour mills. The hydraulic ram is an ingenious application of the energy of flowing water.

Albertson, Barton, and Simons, in their Chapter 12, refer to a centrifugal pump invented by Demour in 1730. This consisted of a rotating pipe in the form of a "T". If the lower end of the vertical member of the pipe was submerged in liquid and the unit spun on this vertical axis, water was lifted and thrown out of the horizontal arms of the T. There is a vast sum of knowledge on turbines and pumps which are discussed in this reference.

The development of the electric generator late in the 19th Century provided an important use for hydraulic turbines. Goncharov's (1972) book contains a discussion of the fundamentals of the theory of hydraulic turbines and their design as they relate to electric power generation. Gubin (1970) wrote about draft tubes of hydroelectric stations. Once water has expended its energy in spinning a turbine it should depart with a minimum of back pressure. Otherwise effective power-producing head is lost.

The first alternating current hydropower for commercial purposes was generated near Telluride, Colorado, early in 1891 to provide power for a mine. This power plant was built by L. L. Nunn, a dynamic lawyer-promoter, who at that time was the manager for eastern interests of the Gold King Mine. His brother, P. N. Nunn was familiar with the work of George Westinghouse whose faith in alternating current at a time when direct current was the prevailing practice, placed Westinghouse in the class of crackpot theorists. P. N. Nunn later became chief engineer for the Ontario Power Company at Niagara Falls. A more detailed history of the Ames Power Plant appears on pages 298 through 302 of the 75th Anniversary Issue of Electrical World, dated August, 1962. Figures 91-1 and 91-2 are taken from an out-of-print pamphlet supplied through the courtesy of Harry Wright (1978) who has personal knowledge of the Ames Power Plant which was the World's first. It preceded by two months the Lauffen-Frankfort experiment in Germany.

Figure 91-1   Sketch of the Ames Power Plant built in late 1890
which was the first high-voltage, AC, commercial power
application.   It was located on Howard's Fork of the San
Miguel River in San Miguel County, Colo.   (Wright 1978)

Figure 91-2   The Westinghouse 100-hp generator produced a
3000-volt, 133-cycle, single-phase, alternating current
when driven by a belt connected to a 6-ft.-diameter Pelton
water wheel operating under a head of 320 feet fed by a
4000-foot-long cast iron pipe from a small reservoir at
the Ames Power Plant.   The motor was identical with the
generator.   (Wright 1978)

Table 2 on page 2 of "Energy in Focus - Basic Data" (1977) gives the historical energy consumption patterns for selected years from 1860 through 1976. Fuel wood supplied 83.5 percent of a total energy consumption of 3.5 quads in 1860. This shrank to 3.3 percent of 34.0 quads in 1950. Coal supplied 16.4 percent of 3.1 quads in 1860. This increased to 72.8 percent of 21.3 quads in 1920 and shrank to 18.6 percent of 74.2 quads in 1976. Petroleum and natural gas supplied 0.1 percent of 3.1 quads in 1860, and in 1950 they supplied 55.9 percent of a total of 34.0 quads, and 74.5 percent of 74.2 quads in 1976. Hydropower supplied 2.6 percent of 9.6 quads in 1900. This increased to 4.1 percent of a total of 34.0 quads in 1950 and to a percentage of 4.2 of 74.2 quads in 1976. Nuclear power supplied 0.3 percent of a total of 67.1 quads in 1970 and this has increased to 2.7 percent of 74.2 quads in 1976.

Although the discharge of the Nation's hydro-electric energy capacity has decreased from 30 percent in the 1930's to 20 percent in the 1960's and to less than 15 percent in 1978, the actual contribution to the Nation's power from hydroelectric development has increased from 7800 megawatts in 1930 to 31,900 megawatts in 1960 and to 69,000 megawatts in 1978, according to "Water Power-Use of a Renewable Resource" (1978). The trends of these two sets of figures is the result of a vast increase in the total energy available because of tremendous growth in the use of oil for power.

In addition to the environmental advantages of hydropower generation, non-consumptive, non-polluting, quiet, and infinitely renewable at no cost, there are other very important advantages. All electric currents generated by rotating magnetic fields are in the form of a sine wave. This wave in the United States has a frequency of 60 hertz (60 cycles per second). Since the sine-wave voltage goes through zero twice in each cycle, it is necessary that the output of all generators in a linked power system alternate practically exactly at 60 hertz. The leeway of normal operating range is extremely small and the frequency must be maintained between 60.01 and 59.99 cycles per second.

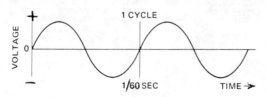

Figure 91-3  The form of the sine wave which the voltage of a single-phase 60-cycles per second alternating current exhibits as it passes from zero to positive maximum, through zero to negative maximum and back to zero in one cycle. (From "A.C.-D.C. - How it Works" 1972)

The common electric clock is a synchronous motor which runs exactly in step with generating systems' frequency control. According to "Better Control of Electric Power Systems" (undated) during the severe winter of 1976-1977 frequency control problems produced a Nation-wide time error of one-half minute. When any one of the generators in a power system loses its speed due to overload or voltage drop, its output is out of phase with the sine-wave pattern of the rest of the system resulting in surges of voltage and amperage of such magnitude that safeguard equipment, such as circuit breakers, opens the circuit to protect generator windings against melting.

The loss of a generator places the load on the remaining generators in the system and unless power can be supplied almost instantaneously from a spinning reserve or storage, one generator after another is removed from the line by its protective equipment and the entire system collapses like a row of falling dominoes. This may result in blackouts such as the one which occurred in the Northeast in 1965 affecting about 30 million people. Since it is not possible as yet to store electric energy efficiently in large quantities, an electrical generating system, which may be made up of hydropower, nuclear, and thermal power-plants, must have an operating reserve or instant backup generating facilities.

On the night of July 13, 1977 the New York City area suffered another blackout. A comprehensive description of this is given in the Time Magazine (1977) article "Blackout '77 - Once More With Looting". The Consolidated Edison Company had almost no reserve and on this hot and humid night it was importing about one-third of the electricity it was supplying. An unusual occurrence of intense electrical storms, which lasted almost an hour, progressively knocked off the line practically the entire system. Since there was almost no hydropower reserve, adjacent power systems could not supply power to the New York area without themselves blacking out. About 25 hours elapsed before the whole system was back on the line. It is possible to bring up to speed and place on the line hydropower generators from a standing start to full capacity in about one minute. A spinning reserve, that is a hydropower generator turning at synchronous speed, but without output, can be fully loaded in much less than a minute.

A thermal system operates in an entirely different manner. The removal of a steam turbine-driven generator from the line is followed in a progressive sequence by automatically-controlled steps with cutoff of steam pressure to the turbine (the boiler pressure up to 1100 pounds per square inch must be reduced at a controlled rate to prevent explosive drops) and the furnace fires must be banked slowly enough so that destructive thermal stresses do not occur in the boilers and steam systems. After a certain time the thermal plant finally comes to rest.

Approximately the same procedure, although somewhat more complicated, must be followed in a nuclear power plant. It may
take several days to bring a system of thermal power plants
back on the line. The steps in reactivating a thermal plant,
especially a nuclear plant, must be followed in reverse order
to that of the shutdown. Finally when the steam turbines have
come up to full speed and the output is synchronized, the
thermal plant has power on the line.

Wherever possible power networks make use of hydropower.
If it is not available on a continuing basis pumped storage
facilities are built. The power demand of an area varies with
the time of day; peaking during the day and evening and dropping at night. A pumped-storage power plant uses the excess
output of a thermal system at night by consuming the power to
pump water to a higher elevation. The machinery at a pumped-
storage project is designed so that the generator can work as
a motor while the turbine can serve as a pump. During the
day, at the periods of peak demand, the facility serves as a
turbine-generator supplying synchronized power to the system.

The largest privately-owned pumped-storage project in
operation is the Consumer Power Company's Ludington Project
near Lake Michigan with a generating capacity of 1,009
megawatts. The highest head pumped-storage project currently
operating is the Cabin Creek Project of the Public Service
Company near Georgetown, Colorado. This plant pumps up to
455,000,000 gallons of water in one 24-hour period. The two
generating units add 324,000 kilowatts of capacity to the
state-wide system.

Consideration is being given to the construction of pumped
storage projects below ground in areas where the topography
does not permit elevating water. Caves and mines in conjunction with a surface reservoir would be used.

In many parts of the United States where pumped-storage
facilities are not available, gas turbines are being used to
provide power for peaking. Although gas turbines are only 20
percent efficient in yielding energy from the combustion of
natural gas, they have served very effectively. The pamphlet
"Gas Turbines for Efficient Power Generation" (1978) includes
diagrams and drawings of gas turbines. The hot exhaust gases
can be used as a source of heat for other applications.

Another approach to the problem of synchronization is the
use of extra-high voltage direct-current (EHV-DC) transmission.
All electric currents generated by a rotating armature are
alternating currents. In automotive work the alternators are
generators producing AC at higher voltages which is then converted to 12 volts DC. Recent invention of high voltage mercury arc valves in Sweden has made it possible to handle

562

energy at 125,000 volts and 1800 amperes. The folder, "A.C.-D.C. - How it Works" (1972) includes diagrams of valve circuits and of assemblies.

An extremely high voltage direct-current transmission line costs about one-third less than an AC line of the same capacity but this is not the greatest advantage. AC current converted to DC can be carried long distances much more efficiently than the same amount of power can be carried as AC. However, there is still another and very great advantage. At the receiving end the mercury facility can then invert the DC to AC in perfect synchronization with the AC network. In this way it is no longer necessary to attempt to maintain synchronization over thousands of miles of lines and of hundreds of generators.

Clifford and Schmidt (1974) describe the research on the digital representation of a DC transmission system and its controls. Mahoney (1971) describes the direct current, 750,000 volt line, 853 miles long, which connects the South-western power system centered in Los Angeles, to the Pacific-Northwest Bonneville Power system.

The advent of low-cost oil and thermal power plants resulted in a major change in the Nation's electric power. Lilienthal (1977) has written a provocative article illustrated with excellent photographs in color, of the lost megawatts as water flows over the Nation's myriad spillways. At one time there were hundreds of small factories and power plants which generated their own power, first mechanically from falling water, and later from hydropower installations. As oil became available hundreds of these power plants were abandoned. Lilienthal's recommendation is that the lost megawatts in these small power plants be recovered. There are now available synchronous and induction generators which could make it possible for small power plants to be part of an extensive power network.

According to Skuderna (1978) the Department of Energy and the Bureau of Reclamation are currently conducting a joint project aimed at the standardization of hydraulic and electric components aimed at the development of a family of standardized package-deal assemblies which could be installed as needed. The large installations are all individually designed and built. The development of such more or less mass-produced systems should make it economically feasible to reactivate and expand the small hydropower systems.

Park and Helliwell (1978) describe the discovery that very low-frequency (VLF), one to 8 kilohertz, radio waves radiated by electrical power transmission lines, leak into the magnetosphere out to distances of many Earth radii. There they interact with the corpuscular radiation trapped in the Earth's magnetic field. The wave power may grow by a factor of 1000 or

563

more due to the wave-particle interactions. Their energy is dissipated by collisions with ambient gas producing ionization, heat, optical emissions, and x-rays. Observations which were made at Eights, Antarctica, showed that the wave activity tended to occur during daytime when power consumption was high in Eastern Canada. Research is being conducted to learn what, if any, effects this man-made wave activity may have on the energetic electrons trapped in the Earth's radiation belts.

Hammond (1978) reports that the World's largest hydro-electric plant is under construction by Brazil and Paraguay on the Parana River. This plant, known as the Itaipu facility, is to have a capacity of 12.6 gigawatts and it will produce 70 billion kilowatt-hours per year or about 3 times the production of Grand Coulee. Transmission will be by extra-high voltage DC. Paraguay's power systems are at 50 hertz, whereas Brazil uses 60 hertz. The AC-DC-AC systems will make it possible for both countries to develop the hydropower site previously too remote from centers of power demands.

The World's second largest hydroelectric power project, according to "Oil Cash Funds Hydro Switch", (1978) is part of the multi-purpose development of the Caroni River in Venezuela. The Venezuelans were a driving force behind the Organization of Petroleum Exporting Countries (OPEC). This organization invoked the sudden and unprecedented oil price rise of 1973-74 which jolted the World's economy. Venezuela appreciates the fact that its oil will not last forever and it is investing oil money into hydropower, irrigation, and flood control. The development envisions an investment by 1980 of 52,000 million dollars. By 1985 the Guri power plant will have a generating capacity of 10.0 gigawatts placing it second only to Itaipu's 12.6 gigawatts.

References

"A.C.-D.C. - How it Works", a folder, 6 pp, Bonneville Power Admin., Portland, Ore., 1972.

Albertson, Maurice L., James R. Barton, Daryl B. Simons, "Fluid Mechanics for Engineers", Prentice-Hall, Inc., Englewood Cliffs, N.J., 551 pp, 1960.

"Better Control of Electric Power Systems", Energy Research and Development Admin., Office of Assistant Administrator of Conservation, pamphlet, 10 pp, Washington, D.C. (Undated)

"Blackout '77 - Once More With Looting", Time, pp 12-26, July 25, 1977.

Clifford, James F., and Albert H. Schmidt, Jr., "Digital Representation of a DC Transmission System and Its Controls", pp 503-510 in Stability of Large Electric Power Systems, ed. by Richard T. Byerly and Edward W. Kimbark, The Institute of Electrical and Electronics Engineers, N.Y., 1974.

"Energy in Focus - Basic Data", Folder, 13 pp, Fed. Energy Admin., Washington, D.C., May, 1977.

"Gas Turbines for Efficient Power Generation", a folder, U.S. Dept. of Energy, Office of Public Affairs, Washington, D.C., Feb., 1978.

Goncharov, A. N., "Hydropower Stations - Generating Equipment and its Installation", 1972. Trans. from the Russion by the Israel Program for Scientific Trans.; Th. Pelz, Translator; TT 74-50023, available from U.S. Dept. of Commerce Natl. Tech. Info. Service, Springfield, Va. 367 pp, 1975.

Gubin, M. F., "Draft Tubes of Hydro-Electric Stations", 1970. Trans. from the Russion by Jagan Mohan, New Delhi, India. Pub. by Amerind Pub. Co., Pvt. Ltd, New Delhi. Trans. No. TT 72-52000, 246 pp, 1973.

Hammond, Allen L., "Itaipu: Direct-Current Transmission", Science, vol. 200, no. 4343, p 754, May 19, 1978.

Lilienthal, David E., "Lost Megawatts Flow Over Nation's Myriad Spillways", Smithsonian, vol. 8, no. 6, pp 82-89, Sept. 1977. (This article was reprinted as a whole in The Military Engineer, no. 454, pp 82-85, Mar-Apr. 1978. A panel insert on page 82 by the editor of the Military Engineer refers to a Corps of Engineers' 90-day study of small hydropower generation.)

Mahoney, William M., "EHV-DC System Ties Los Angeles to Northwest", Jour. Power Div., Proceedings ASCE, vol. 97, no. PO1, pp 181-201, Jan. 1971.

"Oil Cash Funds Hydro Switch", in World Water, vol. 1, no. 1, pub. in London, England, pp 49-51, May, 1978.

Park, C. G., and R. A. Helliwell, "Magnetospheric Effects of Power Line Radiation", Science, vol. 200, no. 4343, pp 727-730, May 19, 1978.

Skuderna, John E., Bur. of Reclamation Engineering and Research Center, Denver, Colo., Interview of June 15, 1978.

"Water Power - Use of a Renewable Resource", pamphlet, 12 pp, U.S. Dept. of Energy, Fed. Energy Regulatory Commission, Washington, D.C., Apr. 1978.

Wright, Harry, Montrose, Colo.; information and illustrations concerning the Ames Power Plant were supplied through the courtesy of Mr. Wright who also made available the out-of-print report, "The First 50 Years - A Romance of Electricity on the Western Slope". This was published about 1963 by the Western Colorado Power Company. June 3, 1978.

SECTION  XXIII

RECREATION

Topic 92                    Recreation

Although few users of outdoor recreation facilities are
cognizant of it there is an extensive, highly professional activity connected with the planning, organization, and administration of outdoor recreational facilities.  Dearinger (1968),
in his research report, "Esthetic and Recreational Potential of
Small Naturalistic Streams Near Urban Areas", has prepared a
thorough analysis of this subject.

There are many forms of outdoor recreation.  Broad general
classes include parks and picnic areas, the National forests
and the undeveloped wildlands which could include wild and
scenic rivers and the wilderness.  Wherever it may be, outdoor
recreation involves the water resource in 4 major ways: (1) an
adequate supply of safe drinking water; (2) waste water facilities and disposal; (3) provision for swimming, fishing, and
boating; and, (4) adequate precipitation or irrigation to maintain the recreational facilities without ecological and scenic
degradation.

Possibly the greatest need for outdoor recreational facilities affecting the greatest number of people is for provision
of open-space recreation in metropolitan areas as discussed by
Winslow (1977).  One of the greatest problems in urban recreational open space is that of securing funds for natural and
scenic areas.  The highly organized facilities such as golf
courses, tennis courts, and swimming pools in many areas are
privately financed.

"Outdoors USA", the Yearbook of Agriculture for 1967, is an
excellent general reference.  Allen's (1974) book, "Our Wildlife Legacy", deals with wildlife, its management and with
biopolitics.

Douglass (1975) in his Chapter 15, "Water-Oriented Recreational Development", refers to a study in which it was found
that almost one-half of the Nation's population preferred
water-based activities to any other type of outdoor recreation.
National forest and wildland users, it was found, prefer water-
based recreation in a natural setting.  The construction of
swimming pools is not recommended away from urban or suburban
areas.

Recreational resource development involves ecology, land-
use planning, and consideration of alternatives for urban,

suburban, industrial, and surface transportation corridor developments as they interact with each other and especially as they involve measurements of scenic beauty.

Stankey (1977) has written a thought-provoking article on social aspects of outdoor recreation planning. He deals with the concepts of recreational preference of substitutability, carrying capacity, dependent satisfactions, externalities (many of the external benefits of outdoor recreation and of costs have no direct economic measure), and cost effectiveness. A reading of this paper is recommended for those interested in recreational planning.

Elsner (1977) reviews the state-of-the art methods for research planning and for determining the benefits of outdoor recreation. York, Gahan, and Dysart (1976) describe their work on modeling water-related recreational benefits drawing on their experience in the Great Santee Swamp in central South Carolina. Gilbert (1971) reviewed the public relations and media publicity aspects of natural resource management and development. He includes in his book a number of case studies among which are the Yellowstone elk controversy of 1967, the Wyoming fencing controversy, 1967, and the defeat of the proposed Amendment No. 3 of 1960 in Colorado.

Recreational and scenic areas continue to function as water-yielding drainage basins. The pamphlet "Water in the Great Smoky Mountains National Park" (1972) is a description of this Park including considerations of hydrology, drainage basin geomorphology, erosion, and floods. The average precipitation is 890 billion gallons of water per year and, of this rainfall, 390 billion gallons are evaporated and 5 billion gallons are available for streamflow, replenishing lakes and the groundwater system.

"Statistical Abstract 1977" is the annual report prepared by the National Park Service, USDI. Acreage administered in 294 areas amounted to 31,323,618.41 acres. Total number of visitors in Calendar Year 1977 was 262,603,433 persons of which 17,560,237 stayed overnight.

One of the problems facing outdoor recreation development specialists is that of overuse. Areas of special appeal may attract visitors in such vast numbers that their presence tends to destroy the quality of the area. Garrett (1978) has written a superbly illustrated article entitled "Grand Canyon - Are We Loving it to Death?"

Many National parks have found it necessary to rotate areas assigned for campground use. The intense traffic concentration tends to destroy the forest litter, expose roots, and visibly degrade the area. When campgrounds show signs of deterioration they are closed and the public directed to other locations. Hinds (1976) described, with photographs, the aspen mortality in Rocky Mountain campgrounds.

Years ago many picnic and campground areas were located along streambanks. The current practice of the U.S. Forest Service is to provide no facilities within 100 feet of flowing streams or shorelines.

Solid waste at outdoor recreation facilities has become a major problem as reported by Spooner (1971). Because of reductions in appropriations coupled with increased usage, the USFS has found it necessary to ask recreational facility users to carry out all of their debris. Another problem is that of providing wood for camp fires. This includes the related problem of cleanup of the area and the intelligent handling of camp fire sites.

Sanitation problems are increasing as the number of people engaged in outdoor recreation rises. Douglass (1975) treats water supply in his Chapter 13 and sanitation in Chapter 14.

Surgenor (1977) describes the water supply and sanitation problems in the back country.

The White Mountain National Forest is within a day's drive of 62 million people in eastern Canada and the United States. Over two million visitor days are generated annually. The Appalachian Mountain Club built the first hiker refuge on the shoulder of Mount Madison in 1888. At present the Club manages 8 mountain huts, 18 lean-to shelters, and over 300 miles of hiking and ski trails. Water supply and waste disposal systems are a continuing management problem.

Although special studies have been conducted on wastewater disposal by filter beds and spray irrigation, the majority of the sites are serviced by helicopter. Expensive helicopter flyouts remove entirely the waste and potential for drinking water contamination. Extensive studies have been made of drinking water quality. Fecal contamination comes from human, wildlife, and occasionally from domestic pets. Human contamination is rare but failure of a sewage disposal system could be catastrophic.

Recent water-quality legislation no longer permits discharge of sewage from commercial or recreational vehicles into inland waterways or lakes. Portable toilet facilities are now available small enough to be carried in a row boat. Shore-line facilities have dumping stations similar to those provided for travel trailers and motorized recreational vehicles at trailer campgrounds.

Winter sports areas, especially ski resorts, have many problems resulting from the intensity of usage during only part of the year. Oversnow vehicles and cross-country ski touring have resulted in administrative problems and work loads unknown in the past. "Snowshoe Country" by Jaques and Jaques (1944) is illustrated with outstanding drawings of winter in the Superior National Forest of Minnesota, and the Quetico Provincial Park, Canada.

Four-wheel drive and all-terrain vehicles, first developed for utilitarian and military purposes, have become adjuncts to outdoor recreation.

Wildfowl hunting in wetlands, both coastal and inland, is another use of the outdoors for recreation. The waters in wetlands are apt to be polluted by waste products from the complex ecosystem of wildlife.

Construction of large dams and the creation of man-made lakes have serious impacts on both commercial and sport fishing. In the "Design of Arch Dams" (1977), page 368, is to be found a brief discussion of fishways. Anadromous fish, such as the salmon, which ascend rivers from the sea so that they can breed in fresh water, must be provided access past dams to headwaters. This is done by flumes, fish locks, and tankers. Fish ladders, although very expensive, have been found to be very effective. These are synthetic rapids built past the dam at a slope of 10 horizontal to 1 vertical consisting of a series of pools of such height that the fish can ascend by leaping from pool to pool.

Another problem at hydroelectric power plants results from the sudden decompression of fish as water is released from the penstocks. Nitrogen goes into solution in the blood stream of the fish at the high pressures common at many powerplants. Sudden decompression causes bubbles to form in the blood stream often with fatal results. Research is being conducted on several approaches to this problem.

Helm and Peters (1975) describe in detail highway construction as it affects the quality of fishing facilities of a natural stream. They show on pages 236-237 photographs of the Clark Fork River and of a scale model of I-90 in western Montana. The quality of the fishing was preserved since stream meander lengths were reconstructed.

Public Law 90-542:82 Stat 906 of August 2, 1968 is the Wild and Scenic Rivers Act which declares it a National policy to preserve certain rivers in their natural free-flowing condition and to retain their scenic, recreational, geologic, fish and wildlife, historic, cultural, and other values.

It is not necessary to preserve the entire river throughout
its length.  For example, the Rio Grande is a scenic and wild
river for that portion which flows through the gorge near
Taos, New Mexico.

Chapter XV, "Ecological and Environmental Considerations"
in Design of Arch Dams (1977) deals with fish and wildlife,
recreation, and design considerations as part of the planning
and construction of large engineering dams.  The construction
of Flaming Gorge Dam on the Green River in Utah-Wyoming
created the 3.8-million acre-foot Flaming Gorge Reservoir as
part of the Colorado River Storage Project.  (See Topic 56,
page 333)  After closure of the Dam it was found that the
oxygen-deficient water released from the deep reservoir was so
cold that it resulted in a great reduction of fish production,
especially trout, in the river below the dam for a distance of
about 60 miles.  Before closure in 1967 anglers spent 124,400
hours on the River taking 71,200 fish weighing a total of
71,912 pounds.  In 1976 anglers spent 25,175 hours with a harvest of 12,100 fish weighing only 8.022 pounds.  The above
figures are given by Scher (1978) in his article "How They
Tricked Mother Nature at Flaming Gorge".  Figure 92-1 shows
the improved discharge control structures.

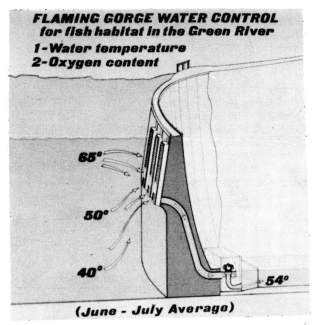

**FLAMING GORGE WATER CONTROL**
**for fish habitat in the Green River**
**1-Water temperature**
**2-Oxygen content**

65°

50°

40°

54°

**(June - July Average)**

Figure 90-1  Schematic drawing of the operation of the Flaming
Gorge fish habitat water quality control.  Drawing pro-
vided by the Upper Colorado Regional Office, Bureau of
Reclamation, USDI, Salt Lake City, Utah.

The Bureau of Reclamation designed the reservoir-discharge facility which would control the dissolved-oxygen content and the temperature of the water discharging into the Green River below Flaming Gorge Dam. This facility was installed at a cost of over 4.5 million dollars. Scher's article includes photographs of this facility taken at the time of installation. Each of the three steel withdrawal control structures is 220 feet long and weighs 600 tons. The structures can be raised or lowered by 95,000-pound lifting capacity hoists. The temperature of water released during the months of fish growth will be 10 to 20 degrees F warmer than it was before these structures were installed.

## References

Allen, Durward L., "Our Wildlife Legacy", Funk and Wagnalls, New York, 422 pp, paperback edition, 1974.

Dearinger, John A., "Esthetic and Recreational Potential of Small Naturalistic Streams Near Urban Areas", Univ. of Kentucky, Water Resources Institute, Lexington, Research Report No. 13, 260 pp, 1968.

"Design of Arch Dams", A Water Resources Tech. Pub., Bur. of Reclamation, USDI, Denver, Colo., 882 pp, 1977.

Douglass, Robert W., "Forest Recreation", Pergamon Press Inc., New York, 2nd edition, 336 pp, 1975.

Elsner, Gary H., compiler, "State-of-the-Art Methods for research, planning, and determining the benefits of outdoor recreation", USDA Forest Service General Tech. Report PSW-20/1977, Pac. Southwest Forest and Range Exp. Sta., Berkeley, Calif., 62 pp, 1977.

Garrett, W. E., "Grand Canyon - Are We Loving it to Death?", National Geographic, vol. 154, no. 1, pp 16-51 with map insert, July 1978.

Gilbert, Douglas L., "Natural Resources and Public Relations", The Wildlife Society, Washington, D.C., 320 pp, 1971.

Helm, William T., and John C. Peters, "Ecology", Chap. 5 in Environmental Design for Public Projects, ed. by D. W. Hendricks, E. C. Vlachos, L. S. Tucker, and J. C. Kellogg, Water Resources Publications, Fort Collins, Colo., 742 pp, 1975.

Hinds, T. E., "Aspen Mortality in Rocky Mountain Campgrounds", Rocky Mt. Forest and Range Exp. Sta., Forest Service, USDA, Fort Collins, Colo., Research Paper RM-164, 20 pp, Mar. 1976.

Jaques, Florence Page, illustrations by Francis Lee Jaques, "Snowshoe Country", The Univ. of Minnesota Press, Minneapolis, 110 pp, 1944, 2nd printing 1945.

"Outdoors USA", U.S. Dept. of Agriculture Yearbook, 90th Cong. 1st Sess., House Document No. 29, 408 pp, 1967.

Scher, Zeke, "How They Tricked Mother Nature at Flaming Gorge", Empire Magazine, The Denver Post, Denver, Colo., pp 10-13, Mar. 26, 1978.

Spooner, Charles S., "Solid Waste Management in Recreational Forest Areas", Solid Waste Mgmt. Office, U.S. Environmental Protection Agency, Washington, D.C., 96 pp, 1971.

Stankey, George H., "Some Social Concepts for Outdoor Recreation Planning", Part IV - A Sociologist Among the Economists, Proceedings of a Natl. Symposium on Outdoor advances in application of economics, pp 154-161, Forest Service, USDA, Gen. Tech. Rep. WO-2, 1977.

"Statistical Abstract, 1977", National Park Service, USDI, prepared by Branch of Science, Denver Service Ctr., NPS, Denver, Colo., 27 pp, 1977.

Surgenor, Sara H., "Problems in Protecting Backcountry Water Supplies", Chap. 29, pp 527-544 in Drinking Water Quality Enhancement Through Source Protection, ed. by Robert B. Pojasek, Ann Arbor Science Publishers, Inc., Ann Arbor, Mich., 614 pp, 1977.

"Water in Great Smoky Mountains National Park", pamphlet, 15 pp, Geological Survey, USDI, Washington, D.C., 1972.

Winslow, Darrell G., "Providing Recreation and Open Space in a Metropolitan Area", pp 325-328 in Land Use: Tough Choices in Today's World, Proceedings of a Natl.Symposium, Mar. 21-24, 1977, Omaha, Neb., pub. by Soil Conservation Soc. of America, Ankeny, Iowa, 454 pp, Spc. Pub. No. 22, 1977.

York, David W., Lawrence W. Gahan, and Benjamin C. Dysart, "Modeling Water-Related Recreation Benefits", pp 409-413 in Jour. of the Water Resources Planning and Management Div., Proceedings ASCE, vol. 102, no. WR2, Nov. 1976.

Topic 93 The Wilderness

The Wilderness Act, PL 88-577 of September 3, 1964, created a new classification of public land. The legislative history of this Act is given in the "United States Code - Congressional and Administrative News" (1964). The movement which
culminated in the passage of the Wilderness Act has many roots
among which were the writings of Henry David Thoreau. His
book, "Walden; or Life in the Woods", published in 1854, in-
stituted thinking about the value of the wilderness far beyond
the boundaries of the United States.

Aldo Leopold, a forester, is credited with expressing recent concepts of the wilderness. He was one of the founders
of the Wilderness Society. His section on the Wilderness,
pages 264-270 in "A Sand County Almanac" (1949) is a concise
statement of the values of the wilderness, and the book is a
classic on conservation.

"National Forest Wildernesses and Primitive Areas" (1973)
includes a tabulation and a map. Buckman and Quintus (1972)
have prepared a report listing a total of 291 natural areas
according to a classification made by the Society of American
Foresters. Angier (1972) includes a number of valuable suggestions of a practical nature in his Chapter, "Water, Water
Everywhere". "Man, Leisure, and Wildlands - A Complex Interaction" (1975) is a 286-page assembly of 39 papers dealing with
various aspects of the subject.

Douglass (1975) tabulates 8 Federal Acts pertaining to
recreation. Among these is the Wilderness Act of 1964. His
Chapter 4, "Public Pleasure and Legislative Response" (pages
49-68) includes an analysis of the Wilderness Act. To many
people the wilderness is an area offering an opportunity for
escape and temporary release from the regimentation and pressures of everyday life. In spite of extensive publicity concerning the value and the utilization of the wilderness, a very
small percentage of the users of the outdoor recreational facilities make use of the wilderness and primitive areas.

Table 93-1, shown on the following page, lists the number
of visitor days making use of various recreational facilities
in the U.S. Forest Service Region 2, The Rocky Mountain Region.
This Region includes all of Colorado and parts of Wyoming,
South Dakota, Nebraska, and Kansas. The information provided
by Mittmann (1978) is taken from the Forest Service Recreation
Information Management (RIM) data assembly which is stored in
a computer. Similar information is publicly available for all
Forest Service Regions. Only 3.5 percent of the visitor-days
account for wilderness-primitive area usage. This figure does

not separate between visits in a legally-designated wilderness area and a primitive area.

Table 93-1  Number of Visitor Days - 1977.  U.S. Forest Service
Region 2 - Headquarters, Denver, Colorado.

| Recreational Facility | Visitor Days |
|---|---|
| Established camps and picnic grounds | 4,844,300 |
| Visitor information service sites | 204,200 |
| Other public use sites | 103,000 |
| Developed sites (by permit) | 1,635,000 |
| Winter sports sites | 2,208,500 |
| Dispersed use* (exclusive of wilderness and primitive areas) | 14,767,700 |
| Wilderness and primitive areas | 856,500 |
| Total | 24,619,200 |

*Dispersed use includes camping, fishing, ski touring, hiking, hunting, snowmobiling etc.

A great many people, when entering a wilderness area, expected to be completely alone.  Travel by individuals or small parties in most wilderness areas is relatively rare. Most wilderness travel is by pack train.  Certain famous wilderness areas have had such concentrated use that restrictions had to be enforced, according to the article "Camping Restrictions Set for Bridger Wilderness" (1978).  Pack trains entering the Bridger Wilderness will be restricted in 7 areas. The pack trains entering these areas will be limited to a maximum of 10 persons and 15 horses each.  Further restrictions are  that only gas stoves or fully enclosed fires will be permitted and camping will be not less than 200 yards removed from major lakes, streams, and trails.

Restrictions had to be imposed on other wilderness areas including the Boundary Water's Canoe Area in Minnesota, the San Jacinto and San Gorgonio in California, and on the Mt. Whitney Trail in the John Muir Wilderness in California. Stankey and Baden (1977) discuss 5 basic rationing systems which could regulate social and ecological impacts on a wilderness.  The 5 systems are: reservation, fees, queuing (first come, first served), lottery, and merit.  It is obvious that serious administrative problems are inherent in the application of any of these rationing systems and acceptance by the public would be necessary.  One example of rationing was the National Park Service's restrictions on the use of the Colorado River for boat trips in the Grand Canyon National Park. Most of the openings were allotted to commercial operators and as a result many private parties were denied access to the River.

Attendance at National parks has increased to such an extent, as discussed in Topic 92, that, according to Steif (1978) people have overflowed into National forests. It is obvious that there must be a management system developed for the wilderness. Lucas (1973) concludes that the wilderness cannot survive if managed on the draw-a-line and leave-it-alone philosophy. The reading of his article is recommended.

Stankey, Lucas, and Lime (1976) describe the crowding in parks and wilderness areas. Schoenfeld (1976) in his article "Who's Minding the Wilderness Store?" analyzes the management philosophies of the Forest Service, the National Park Service, and the Fish and Wildlife Service, together with several divergent state policies.

Public Law 88-578, the Land and Water Conservation Fund Act of 1965, (as amended by PL 90-401 and PL 91-485) provides funds to state and local governments and to Federal agencies for the acquisition and development of outdoor recreation on a planned, Nation-wide scale. Sixty percent of the LWCF is to go to state governments on a 50-50 matching basis. Federal agencies may get 40 percent of the money for land acquisition with the provision that 85 percent of the land which might be added to National forests must be east of the 100th Meridian. At first there was no direct appropriation for funding activities under this Act. The income was derived from the sale of surplus land, existing tax on motorboat fuels, and income from the sale of Golden Eagle passports. Later the off-shore mineral receipts were automatically deposited in the fund. The funding has been more than adequate, according to Douglass, (1975) and the surplus income of about 70 million dollars was developed between 1965 and 1971 but subsequent appropriations eliminated any surplus. The authorized funding amounts to $900,000,000 for Fiscal Year 1978, according to Tiedt (1978).

PL 88-578 has had a tremendous impact on the development of recreational facilities. It is now administered by the Heritage Conservation and Recreation Service, USDI. This organization combines the functions of the former Bureau of Outdoor Recreation and the archeological and historic functions previously in the National Park Service.

PL 90-543, the National Trails Act of 1969, authorized the creation of a trails system. Two major existing trails, the Appalachian and the Pacific Crest were included. A total of 31 recreational and scenic trails on public and private land were included in the National Trails System as of 1973. The Colorado Mountain Trails Foundation is coordinating the

576

National Trails System activities for the Colorado Trail which is being designed for the hiker, horseback rider, and ski tourer. It will travel near but not necessarily along the Continental Divide. Reifsnyder (undated) has written a planning guide for the construction of high mountain huts along the Colorado Trail. "Mountain Trails: Some Guide Lines on Environmental Inventory and a Selected Bibliography" (undated) has been prepared by the Colorado Mountain Trails Foundation.

It is not necessary to be in a climax virgin forest, grassland, or desert to reap the benefits of wilderness experience. In fact, in the East it is difficult to find a true wilderness condition of any size since much of the forest is now in the 5th or 6th cutting. Reifsnyder (1973) in his Totebook on the Austrian Alps says that after centuries of use the Austrian trails and forest are in much better ecological and scenic condition than those that exist in most of our country. Campfires are not allowed, no wood is cut, tenting is almost unknown, and nearly everyone sleeps overnight in a hut over 500 of which have been constructed in Austria. There is very little evidence of the presence of man on the Austrian trails. What is carried in is carried out and the only item left is human spoor which is properly disposed of with no surface evidence.

The insistent pressures by the proponents of the Wilderness movement may be ill-advised. It is true that the more widely publicized wilderness areas are suffering from lack of administration and over use. However, the creation of more and larger areas is not the solution. Very few people are physically capable or intellectually interested in traveling alone in the wilderness. Parks, campgrounds, and trail systems would satisfy the desires of most people without increasing the pressure on the few famous wilderness areas. Foster (1976) in his paper on recreation needs from 1980 to the 21st Century, recommends a shift of program emphasis away from quantity in areas and facilities. It is necessary that emphasis be placed on the quality of a facility for a particular recreational purpose. This shift will be difficult since it will require tremendous readjustments in traditional thinking and administrative approaches.

An example of quantity approach is described by Monberg (1978). Her summaries of various contemplated Congressional actions lead to the conclusion that if the wilderness proponents were completely successful 10 to 15 percent of all forested land in the United States could end up designated as Wilderness. It is doubtful if the public would accept this.

The U.S. Forest Service is going through the process of completing its Nation-wide study of roadless areas. Their report "RARE II - Draft Environmental Statement - Roadless Area

Review and Evaluation" (1978) was released in June, 1978 by John R. McGuire, Chief, U.S. Forest Service. A total of 2686 roadless and undeveloped areas are considered in 154 National forests and 19 National grasslands. Two maps are included with this report. One shows the location of the National Wilderness Preservation System and wilderness proposals; the other shows the ecosystems of the United States with an explanatory text printed on the back. A total of 21 state and/or regional supplements have been prepared in extension of the RARE II report presenting in much greater detail the environmental impact analyses.

Ten options are outlined in the RARE II reports. The total area under consideration is about 62 million acres. The options vary from no change to total withdrawal of vast areas and their incorporation into the National Wilderness Preservation System.

Thompson (1978) in his letter to the editor, presents the problems facing a private lumber company with reference to massive lockups of forests in the wilderness system. Margolf (1978) expresses the attitude of the mineral industries toward massive lockup of the Nation's lands into the wilderness. He emphasizes that the importance of accessibility for exploration and development for mineral resources should be considered. He states that minerals are where they are and no regulation, law, rule, or investigation can change the location of a mineral deposit.

The passage of the Wilderness Act of 1964 had a tremendous impact on hydrologic data-gathering activities. van de Erve (1968) described prophetically the devastating effect of the Wilderness Act on hydrologic research and hydrologic data acquisition. Garstka (1972) states that subsequent to the passage of the Wilderness Act many existing hydrologic stations, some with many decades of record, were being terminated. It is known that a major flood from a forested area can be extremely destructive since the flood waters are clear and very aggressive in the downstream reaches. Without instrumentation these flood cannot be forecasted. There are many examples of this type of flood; a recent one was the Big Thompson flood in Colorado in 1976.

A specific instance of the continuing impact of the Wilderness Act on hydrologic data is to be found on page 117 of "Columbia River Water Management: Report for Water Year 1977" (1978). In 1976 the Forest Service and the Soil Conservation Service signed a memorandum of understanding regarding temporary installation of automated data sites in wilderness areas. Installations may be permitted at existing snow courses temporarily for a period not to exceed about 10 years so that data for correlation with installations outside the wilderness areas may be established while both sites are operated concurrently. Installations are to be removed from the area when adequate correlations are established. Only miniaturized and unobstrusive types of equipment, to be camouflaged to blend with the terrain can be installed!

Should 10 percent of the forested land be locked up in wilderness areas the devastating impact on hydrologic research and operational management of the Nation's water resources could be extremely profound as it would affect all activities. Wildernesses remain water-yielding drainage basins and the legal classification of their land use does not remove them from performance as part of water-resource management systems.

## References

Angier, Bradford, "Survival With Style", National Wildlife Federation, Washington, D.C., 320 pp, 1972.

Buckman, Robert E., and Richard L. Quintus, "Natural Areas of the Society of American Foresters", 38 pages with 3-page supplement, pub. by Soc. of Amer. Foresters, Washington, D.C., 1972.

"Camping Restrictions Set for Bridger Wilderness", The Denver Post, page 15, Fri. June 2, 1978.

"Columbia River Water Management Report for Water Year 1977", prepared by Columbia River Water Mgmt. Group, Portland, Ore., 132 pp and 58 charts, Jan. 1978.

Douglass, Robert W., "Forest Recreation", Pergamon Press Inc., New York, 2nd edition, 336 pp, 1975.

Foster, Charles H. W., "Recreation Program Needs: 1980 to the 21st Century", Working Paper No. 3, Yale Univ. School of Forestry and Environmental Studies, New Haven, Conn., 11 pp, June 12, 1976.

Garstka, Walter U., "Water Resources in the West", pp 8-14 in Watersheds in Transition, Proceedings of a Symposium held at Fort Collins, Colo., June 19-22, 1972. Ed. by S. C. Csallany, T. G. McLaughlin, and W. Striffler. Proceedings Series No. 14, 405 pp, Amer. Water Resources Assn., 1972.

Leopold, Aldo, "A Sand County Almanac", A Sierra Club/Ballantine Book, 1st ed. 1949 by Oxford Univ. Press, paperback edition, Sept. 1970.

Lucas, Robert C., "Wilderness: a Management Framework", Jour. Soil and Water Conservation, pp 150-154 in vol. 28, no. 4, July-Aug., 1973.

"Man, Leisure, and Wildlands: A Complex Interaction", Proceedings of a research symposium, held at Vail, Colo., Sept.
14-19, 1975. Eisenhower Consortium Bulletin 1, 286 pp,
pub. by Rocky Mt. Forest & Range Exp. Sta., Fort Collins,
Colo., 1975.

Margolf, Charles W., "Getting from 'Here' to 'There'", an
address given May 8, 1978 to the Colo. Chapter of ASCE
Denver, Colo., 31 pp. (Mr. Margolf is Director of Western
Coal Operations, Mining Div. of W. R. Grace & Co.) 1978.

Mittmann, Hubertus J., Conference of June 15, 1978.
(Mr. Mittman is regional landscape architect, US Forest
Service, Reg. 2, Denver, Colo.)

Monberg, Helene C., "One of Ten Acres in U.S. Likely to be Designated as Wilderness", The Denver Post, p 11, Mar.20,1978

"Mountain Trails: Some Guide Lines on Environmental Inventory
and a Selected Bibliography", pub. by Colo. Mountain
Trails Foundation, Littleton, Colo., 25 pp, undated.

"National Forest Wildernesses and Primitive Areas", a folder,
Forest Service, USDA, No. FS-25, Washington, D.C., Apr.
1965, rev. Jan. 1973.

Reifsnyder, William E., "High Mountain Huts: A Planning Guide",
pub. by Colo. Mountain Trails Foundation in cooperation
with Forest Service, USDA, 44 pp, distributed by Colo.
Mt. Trails Foundation, Littleton, Colo., undated.

Reifsnyder, William E., "Hut Hopping in the Austrian Alps",
A Sierra Club Totebook, 207 pp, The Sierra Club, San
Francisco, Calif., 1973.

"Roadless Area Review and Evaluation - RARE II - Draft Environ-
mental Statement 78-04", Responsible Official,
John R. McGuire, Chief, Forest Service, USDA, Washington,
D.C., 112 pp, and 2 maps, June, 1978.

Schoenfeld, Clay, "Who's Minding the Wilderness Store? -
Diverse Wilderness Management Can be Desirable or
Dangerous", Jour. Soil and Water Conservation, pp 242-247,
Nov.-Dec. 1976.

Stankey, George H., and John Baden, "Rationing Wilderness Use:
Methods, Problems, and Guidelines", Forest Service, USDA,
Research Paper INT-192, Intermountain Forest and Range
Exp. Sta., Ogden, Utah, 20 pp, July, 1977.

Stankey, George, H., Robert C. Lucas, and David W. Lime, "Crowding in Parks and Wilderness", a reprint from Design and Environment, 4 pp, Fall, 1976.

Steif, William, "The U.S. and You - Parks Overflow to National Forests", The Rocky Mountain News, Denver, Colo., Page 35-C, May 26, 1978.

Tiedt, Glenn F., of Heritage Conservation and Recreation Service, USDI, Denver, Colo. Personal communication of July 12, 1978.

Thompson, Michael C., "Letter to the Editor", Park County Republican and Fairplay Flume, Fairplay, Colo., p 4, Thurs., May 11, 1978. (Mr. Thompson is the forester for the Edward Hines Lumber Company of Chicago, Ill. This company operates 9 plants for processing sawlogs in Colorado, Wyoming, South Dakota, and eastern Oregon.)

"United States Code - Congressional and Administrative News", 88th Congress - 2nd Session, vol. 2, Legislative History: Wilderness Act, pp 3615-3633, 1964.

van de Erve, J., "The Effect of the Wilderness Law on the Collection of Hydrologic Data", Proceedings, 36th Annual Meeting, Western Snow Conference, held Apr. 16-18, 1968 Lake Tahoe, Nev., pp 19-26. Pub. by Colo. State Univ., Fort Collins, Colo., Apr. 1969.

SECTION XXIV

SOCIAL SCIENCES

Topic 94     Social Sciences in Water Resources

The prevailing attitude of modern organized society toward
the water resource is one of somnolent security in the belief
that water, for whatever demand may be placed on it, will always be available. This may be punctuated by periods of panic
when a drought occurs. These attitudes are depicted in
Figure 94-1 taken from Foehner (1977).

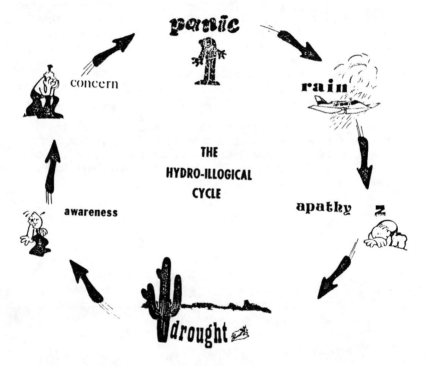

Figure 94-1  The Hydro-Illogical Cycle (from Foehner, p 7,1977)

Kaynor (1972) discusses the planning for the Springfield-
Chicopee-Holyoke Standard Metropolitan Statistical Area in
which 21 cities and towns lie astride the Connecticut River and
its local tributaries. As a result of 118 interviews of
approximately one and one-quarter hours average duration an
appraisal was attained of four initial hypotheses: (1) fragmen-
tation; (2) apathy; (3) conflict; and, (4) distorted perception. The appraisals tended to support all of the hypotheses

except the one on conflict. Expected antagonisms did not come
to the surface.

During the period 1961-1967 the northeastern United States
suffered the worst drought in its recorded history. Hogarty
(1971) describes this drought which affected about 22,000,000
people in the Delaware River basin alone. New York City gets
about one-third of its water requirements from the Delaware
River. Hogarty describes patterns of local actions and the
response of state and Federal governments.

As the urban centers expand into "suburban sprawls" there
has developed a desire in many urban centers to control the
population growth. Some of the proponents of limiting population growth have attempted to do so through the control of the
water resource. In many parts of the old world where serfdom
existed as a social system, the people were part of the real
estate and their freedom of travel was restricted. One of the
fundamental concepts of liberty in our United States is that
there is freedom of movement. There is a custom of human relationship in the Arab world reaching back into antiquity,
according to Abdun-Nur (1978); any traveler, even an enemy,
arriving at an oasis must be provided with food and water.

Restrictions on the expansion of water-supply systems have
been proposed as a means of controlling growth. Such an
approach is unenforceable. As people come into an area they
must be provided with water and if the water supply system has
been developed to its limit, the newcomer can only be taken
care of by a reduction of the supply available to those who
came first. In an arid region the water obviously surplus to
immediate human personal needs is the water used for irrigation
of lawns and ornamentals not ecologically native to the area.

White (1962), in his analysis of the changing role of
water in arid lands, calls attention to the desire of people
settling in arid zones to attempt to recreate the ecosystem of
the area from which they came. White calls attention to the
situation where people, who have settled in the deserts of
Arizona, attempt to maintain lawns, trees, and shrubs to which
they were accustomed, for example, in Connecticut. The impact
on the water resource of such a nostalgic practice is far-
reaching since the creation of the synthetic environment
requires a great deal more water for irrigation than is necessary to meet the personal needs of the residents.

The need to provide a relaxing and pleasing environment
as it pertains to homes, gardens, communities, and cities, is
universal. Nuzum (1975) has written an excellent chapter (his
pages 307-335) on visual harmony. How this need is to be satisfied when population increases while water supply remains
constant, will turn out to a major sociological challenge.

583

The history of water resource development is treated in Topics 1, 2, and 3. The current era of massive carry-over storage (Garstka 1972) is unprecedented in history since it has made it possible for concentrations of population in the desert areas which are ecologically totally unsuited for supporting urban and industrial centers.

De Jong (1977), in his paper on residential preference attributes and population redistribution migration behavior, analyses 47 preference characteristics. An unexpected finding, the reverse of the trend of the last 70 years, is a preference for a non-urban environment.

The concept of man against nature, according to Glacken (1970), is outmoded. Most races and cultures have acknowledged that they are part of the natural ecosystem and that their survival depends on integrating their demands with the ecosystem. According to Abdun-Nur (1978) there is a statement in the Koran that: "Out of water are created all living things". Glacken compares Eastern and Western philosophies concerning man's relationship to the environment. A reading of Glacken's paper is recommended. Burch (1971) has written a thought-provoking sociological essay entitled, "Day Dreams and Nightmares", in which he traces the sociological institutional and organizational attitudes of our Nation toward the environment.

Four milestones in man's sociological interaction with the environment are: (1) the mastery of fire and with its assistance the refining of metals to make tools; (2) the usage of fossil fuels, first coal and then oil, to provide energy freeing man of muscle power; (3) the realization that there is a definite limit to the supply of fossil fuels; and (4) the realization that on the Earth there remains no true wilderness, no virgin territory, and no frontier; what is left is only undeveloped territory.

The industrial revolution was powered by energy from coal. With the development of technology for releasing the flexible and practically unbounded energy from the burning of petroleum, man took off like a rocket on a delirious outburst of technological progress which has not yet ended. This progress, coupled with petroleum-based food production (see Topic 38) has supported a great increase in the World's population so that man is no longer a part of the natural ecosystem.

Stahr (1971) refers to the recent sudden concern with the environment as a reaction to what he calls, "ecosystem overload". Whenever the natural processes cannot recycle waste substances dumped on them, ecosystem overload develops.

A sociological reaction to the realization that there is no frontier and no wilderness is the desire to preserve, in their current state, areas as yet unexploited by an industrial society. This is evidenced by the movement to establish wild and scenic rivers and wildernesses. The yearning for a return to a life in closer contact with the natural ecosystem has resulted in the extensive world-wide activation of primitive areas and national parks (see Topics 92 and 93).

One evidence of the sudden concern with the depredations of the natural ecosystem is the passage of the Endangered Species Act. The life processes of all species require water and therefore practically all analyses of endangered species to date involve the water resource.

A classical example of the impact on water resources is the case involving the Tennessee Valley Authority's Tellico Dam, a practically completed structure costing about $100,000,000, and the Snail Darter, a fish about 3 inches long said to exist only in that part of the river to be inundated by waters impounded by Tellico Dam. The Supreme Court of the United States in its decision of June 15, 1978, Number 76-1701, acting on the Writ of Certiorari to the United States Court of Appeals for the Sixth District in the matter of Tennessee Valley Authority vs. Hiram G. Hill, Jr., et al, ruled that the TVA could not complete Tellico Dam and could not impound water. This ruling was based strictly on the Endangered Species Act PL 93-205 of Dec. 28, 1973, as a law of the land and not on the impact on human endeavors of the perpetuation of a species whose evolutionary future is in serious doubt. Such considerations, the U.S. Supreme Court stated, must be resolved by the Congress.

Adler (1973) in his book "Ecological Fantasies" discusses the myths and the facts relating to pollution and improvement of the environment including water resources. He reports that, although the United States has only 6 percent of the World's population it uses about 40 percent of the World's non-renewable natural resources. About one-half of the World's industrial pollution is contributed by the United States. The reader is urged to study Adler's book.

Driver and Knopf (1977) have analyzed the interrelationships of personality, outdoor recreation, and expected consequences. Their analyses suggest that personality variables do have an influence on the extent to which a chosen activity is pursued. However, peer group pressures, educational levels, past experiences, skill levels, facility availability, time on hand, and income levels might influence choice just as much as, or possibly more so, than do personality traits.

Many people are afraid of the wilderness; others accept an outdoor recreational experience as an occasion for release of repressions. As the number of people making use of recreational facilities increase there has followed an inevitable increase in antisocial behavior in the parks. According to the article "Crime Assumes 'Grand' Proportions Along Canyon" (1977), in 1963 there were 94 criminal cases handled in state and Federal courts in the Grand Canyon National Park. In 1976 over 1,000 cases were reported. The National Park Service employees now must know not only the natural history of their areas but also criminal law, mob psychology, and traffic management. Such knowledge is becoming increasingly necessary as millions of people visit the natural recreational areas each year.

Brown (1978) refers to two mega-cultures, the Rich and the Poor. Of the total World's population, two-thirds are in the Poor mega-culture. If the Poor were to suddenly disappear the World's total resource consumption would be reduced by only 10 percent. Management of natural resources requires providing the general public and governmental bodies with sufficient information so that intelligent decisions can be reached concerning natural resources. Stephens (1973) describes the problems and techniques of the transfer internationally of knowledge of irrigation and drainage.

A problem which is increasing in complexity is that of applying to practice the products of research for the social good. There are instances where a lack of communication between scientists and practioners resulted in investments in effort and money on activities or programs without due regard to knowledge and experience available. Cohan and Simmons (1973) discuss the transfer of the products of engineering research to practice. Two-way communication and feedback are stressed.

Burch, Cheek, and Taylor (1972) have edited an informative assembly of 16 papers entitled: "Social Behavior, Natural Resources, and the Environment". Fitzsimmons and Salama (1973) analyzed the relationship between social-psychological systems and water resource development. This is a 428-page thorough analysis of the subject. Another volume dealing with the social sciences in the management of water resources is "Man and Water" (1974) edited by L. Douglas James. This book is made up of 9 papers.

Fitzsimmons, Stuart, and Wolff (1977) have prepared a Social Assessment Manual. They present techniques for evaluating the beneficial and adverse social effects of alternative plans for planning water resource projects. Their analytical procedure includes 13 catagories under "Life, Protection and Safety", 20 catagories under "Health", 18 under "Family and Individuals", 3 major catagories under "Attitudes, Beliefs and Values", and 3 major catagories under "Environmental Considerations", to begin with. The total number of catagories in their analyses amount to 359.

A guiding principle in the democratic form of government is that decisions be reached so that actions produce the greatest good for the longest time for the greatest number of people at least cost. This principle underlies a government's right of eminent domain, often applied to highway and public building construction. Burdge and Ludtke (1972) analyze the social impacts on displaced rural families when they are moved from their land designated for a flood control reservoir.

Emotional disorders and deterioration of health, especially among older people, have been observed in association with forced migrations. However, favorable attitudes towards reservoir projects tend to reduce apprehension over moving and contribute towards willingness to accept loss of a social structure.

The sudden realization of the fact that the natural ecology was fast disappearing and that the Earth was beginning to stagger under ecosystem overload has been called the Environmental Crisis which brought into being a group of dedicated and zealous individuals and organizations referred to broadly as "preservationists". One of the most articulate of these is David A. Brower. McPhee (1971) has written a fascinating account entitled "Encounters with the Archdruid" in which he describes field trips and meetings between Brower and Charles Park, a mineral engineer, Charles Fraser, a resort developer (who is said to have defined a druid as a religious figure who sacrifices people and worships trees), and Floyd Dominy when he was Commissioner of the U.S. Bureau of Reclamation.

The World-encompassing problem of the storage and disposal of nuclear wastes was mentioned in Topic 90. La Porte (1978), a political scientist, presents 5 speculations about future sociopolitical attitudes and impacts towards the management of radioactive nuclear waste. The root of the problem is the extremely long-term toxicity of the wastes. Included in La Porte's list of 27 references is a tabulation of present and estimated future amounts of high-level, transuranic, and low-level wastes. This problem will last for thousands of years.

An informative illustrated article by Farney (1974) deals with the disposal of radioactive wastes. Various approaches have been proposed. One idea was to use outer space. This has been rejected, not only because of tremendous costs but also because of the danger of possible accidental demolition of the rocket vehicle at time of firing and a remote chance of a boomerang orbit. Transmutation, polar and sea-bed disposals have been considered. The best possibilities are geologic disposal or surface storage in massive warehouses. Whatever the decision, there must be absolutely no possibility, however remote, of contaminating the World's water resources.

References

Abdun-Nur, Edward, Personal communication of Apr. 15, 1978.
(Mr. Abdun-Nur is an American civil engineer of Arab
extraction and a resident of Denver, Colo.)

Adler, Cy A., "Ecological Fantasies - Death from Falling Water-
melons", Green Eagle Press, New York, Sept. 1973. The 3d
printing of this book, May, 1975, 350 pp, is being distributed by Water Resources Publications, Fort Collins,
Colo.

Brown, Harrison, "The Human Future Revisted: The World Predicament and Possible Solutions", W. W. Norton & Co., Inc.,
New York, 287 pp, 1978.

Burch, William R., Jr., "Daydreams and Nightmares - A sociological essay on the American environment", Harper and Row,
New York, paperback, 175 pp, 1971.

Burdge, Rabel J., Richard L. Ludtke, "Social Separation Among
Displaced Rural Families: The Case of Flood Control
Reservoirs", Paper No. 5, pp 85-108 in Social Behavior,
Natural Resources, and the Environment. Edited by
William R. Burch, Jr., Neil H. Cheek, Jr., and Lee Taylor,
Harper and Row, Pub., New York, 374 pp, 1972.

Cohan, Howard J., and W. P. Simmons, "How Engineering Research
is Reduced to Practice in the Bureau of Reclamation",
pp 148-154 in Transfer of Water Resources Knowledge,
Proceedings of the First International Conference on Transfer of Water Resources Knowledge, Sept. 1972, Fort
Collins, Colo., ed. by Evan Vlachos. Water Resources Pub.
Fort Collins, 562 pp, June, 1973.

"Crime Assumes 'Grand' Proportions Along Canyon", The Denver
Post, p 22, Mon. Nov. 7, 1977.

DeJong, Gordon F., and Population Issues Research Office,
Pennsylvania State University, University Park, "Residen-
tial Preference Attributes and Population Redistribution
Migration Behavior", a paper presented at the Annual
Meeting of the Amer. Assn. for the Advancement of Science,
Denver, Colo., Feb. 24, 1977.

Driver, B. L., and Richard C. Knopf, "Personality, Outdoor
Recreation, and Expected Consequences", Environment and
Behavior, vol. 9, no. 2, pp 169-193, June, 1977.

Farney, Dennis, "Ominous Problem: What to do with Radioactive
Waste", Smithsonian, vol. 5, no. 1, pp 20-27, Apr. 1974.

Fitzsimmons, Stephen J., and Ovadia A. Salama, "Man and Water -
A Social Report", prepared by Abt Associates Inc., Cambridge, Mass., for Div. of Planning Coordination, Bureau
of Reclamation, USDI, 428 pp, Nov. 1973.

Fitzsimmons, Stephen J., Lorrie I. Stuart, and Peter C. Wolff,
"Social Assessment Manual", An Abt Associates Study, prepared for Div. of Planning Coordination, Bureau of Reclamation, USDI, pub. by Westview Press, Boulder, Colo.
289 pp, 1977.

Foehner, Olin H., "Weather Modification - A Major Resource
Tool", Proceedings 45th Annual Meeting, Western Snow Conf.
Apr. 18-21, 1977, Albuquerque, N.M., pp 1-7, 1977.

Garstka, Walter U., "Water Resources in the West", pp 8-14
from Watersheds in Transition, Proceedings of a Symposium
held at Fort Collins, Colo., June 19-22, 1972. Edited by
S. C. Csallany, T. G. McLaughlin and W. Striffler, Proceedings Series No. 14, American Water Resources Assn.,
Urbana, Ill., 405 pp, Sept. 1972.

Glacken, Clarence J., "Man Against Nature: An Outmoded Concept"
pp 127-142 in The Environmental Crisis - Man's Struggle
to Live With Himself, ed. by Harold W. Helfrich, Jr.;
this volume contains 14 papers, pub. by Yale Univ. Press,
New Haven, 187 pp, 1970.

Hogarty, Richard H., "The Metropolis Runs Dry", Jour. Irrigation and Drainage Div., Proceedings ASCE, vol. 97, no.
IR 4, pp 559-570, Dec. 1971.

Kaynor, E. R., "Citizen Input in River Basin Management: Range,
Intensity, and Effectiveness", pp 50-54 in Watersheds in
Transition, Proceedings of a Symposium held at Fort
Collins, Colo. June 19-22, 1972. Ed. by S. D. Csallany,
T. G. McLaughlin, W. D. Striffler, Pro. Series No. 14,
Amer. Water Resources Assn., Urbana, Ill., Sept. 1972.

La Porte, Todd R., "Nuclear Waste: Increasing Scale and Sociopolitical Impacts", Science, vol. 201, no. 4350, pp 22-28,
July 7, 1978.

"Man and Water - The Social Sciences in Management of Water
Resources", ed. by L. Douglas James, an assembly of 9
papers, The University Press of Kentucky, Lexington,
258 pp, 1974.

McPhee John, "Encounters With the Archdruid", (Narratives about
a conservationist and three of his natural enemies),
Farrar, Straus, and Giroux, New York, 245 pp, 1971.

Nuzum, Dwayne C., "Visual Harmony", pp 307-335 in Environmental Design for Public Projects, ed. by David W. Hendricks, Evan C. Vlachos, L. Scott Tucker, and Joseph C. Kellogg, Water Resources Publications, Fort Collins, Colo. 742 pp, 1973.

"Social Behavior, Natural Resources, and the Environment", ed. by William R. Burch, Jr., Neil H. Cheek, Jr., and Lee Taylor; this is an assembly of 16 papers in 6 sections dealing with the title subject. Harper and Row, New York, 374 pp, 1972.

Stahr, Elvis J., "Antipollution Policies, Their Nature and Their Impact on Corporate Profits"; this is one of 4 papers in Economics of Pollution. The other 3 papers are by Kenneth E. Boulding, Solomon Fabricant, and Martin R. Gainsbrugh, New York Univ. Press, 158 pp, 1971.

Stephens, Larry D., "The Role of the International Commission on Irrigation and Drainage in the Transfer of Water Resources Knowledge", pp 132-142 in the Proceedings of the First International Conference on Transfer of Water Resources Knowledge, Sept. 1972, Fort Collins, Colo. Ed. by Evan Vlachos. Water Resources Publications, Fort Collins, 562 pp, June, 1973.

White, Gilbert F., "The Changing Role of Water in Arid Lands", Riecker Memorial Lecture No. 6, Univ. of Arizona Bulletin Series, vol. XXXII, no. 2, pp 1-15, 1962.

WATER RESOURCES IN THE FUTURE

Topic 95         Water Resources in the Future

Ackermann, Allee, Amorocho, Haimes, Hall, Meserve, Patrick, and Smith (1978) all of whom are recognized authorities in hydrology and water resources, summarize a more extensive report in their review of scientific and technological considerations in water resources policies. This includes issue differences, findings, policy recommendations, and research directions in 10 catagories. Among the many points given in their summary and concluding comments the most indicative is that no new technologies exist which offer promise of substantially increasing water supply in the near future. A study of this paper is recommended.

There are a number of known potentialities for increasing the water supply substantially in some parts of the country. These are: weather modification, reuse of water, saline water demineralization, and reservoir evaporation loss reduction.

Transport of icebergs has been an intriguing possibility. Schulz (1974) in his informative review of icebergs in the arctic region, lists 11 references. Icebergs could be anchored off-shore in Southern California primarily to provide a source of fresh water. Saudi Arabia's Prince Mohammed Al Faisal financed in part the First International Conference on Iceberg Utilization which was held at Iowa State University in October 1977, according to an article in the Denver Post: "Saudi Prince Backs Project" (1977).

In the recent California drought of 1977, according to Smith (1977) California farmers overcame the drought in the Central Valley by drilling about 10,000 wells. There have been great increases in the number of wells supplying water to center-pivot irrigation systems throughout the Great Plains.

Tucson, Arizona, is completely dependent on groundwater which is withdrawn from deep wells as a mining operation. There is nothing inherently wrong in mining water providing that the land-use planners admit that they are mining and that there is no future for the development short of importation of water by transbasin diversion. Should transbasin diversions fall short of current and anticipated demand several adjustments might follow: one would be the departure of population and industry until a balance is attained between supply and demand; another would be an adjustment of life-style by conversion of grass and exotic broad leaves to desert vegetation.

Ambroggi (1977) proposes the use of underground reservoirs to control the water cycle. He reports that at any one time about two-thirds of the fresh water on Earth is groundwater. The application of this concept would be unworkable in the United States under present water laws.

The time has come for the Congress to appoint a task force made up of the American Bar Foundation, Federal and State research and action agencies, environmental interests, and members of both local, state, and National legislative bodies to present specific recommendations for establishing a Management Authority which would return areas of over-extended groundwater usage to the "safe-yield" basis.

Wade (1976) has written an article about Edward Goldsmith, a British writer, who has prepared blueprints for a de-industrialized society. Although some of Goldsmith's remedies may be impractical and utopian he is amassing a following which has demonstrated political power in some parts of the World.

A world-wide problem related to the water resource is that of energy. Hitch (1977) in his guest editorial, "Unfreezing the Future", states that, in the past transitions from old to new sources of energy were pleasant. Now, however, it is necessary to acknowledge that we will have to pay for energy in higher costs with undesirable side effects such as pollution and some risk of danger. The only alternative would be to minimize the combination of the three.

It has been estimated that the World's known supply of commercially usable petroleum and of uranium ore as used in the conventional fission reactor is about the same. Both will peak at about 1990 to 2010 A.D. As discussed in Topic 90 the breeder reactor would produce 60 to 70 times as much energy from uranium as does the conventional fission reactor. In order to move toward a more favorable balance of trade in international commerce it is necessary that we spend less of our income on importing oil. In which case the only immediate source of energy is the breeder reactor. It could be less damaging to the environment than would be the almost total conversion to the burning of coal. It is necessary that the United States resume actively the development of the breeder reactor.

The water-coal slurry discussed in Topic 90 has many undesirable consequences on the water resource. It is suggested that conversion of coal to oil be greatly accelerated and the oil produced, not necessarily of lubrication grade, be used to transport fuel as a coal-oil slurry which can be burned in conventional power-plant furnaces. The overall impact of this on the water resource would have to be determined since conversion of coal would require water. However, there would not be the

loss by consumptive use as in a transbasin diversion with all
of its environmental and legal complications.

The heat efficiency of thermal power plants and many
industries is very low. Waste heat to an unknown extent could
be used to generate electricity for electrolizing water to
produce hydrogen and oxygen. While emissions from the internal
combustion engine have been reduced at great cost, the overall
improvement on air quality in urban centers is very low because
of the increase in the number of vehicles. Hydrogen-burning
vehicles in urban centers may be needed to replace those burning gasoline especially where local conditions produce smog.
The recommendation was made in Topic 90, page 546, to generate
hydrogen and oxygen with hydroelectric power at remotely-
located tidal power plants. Some of the processes of conversion of coal to oil require hydrogen.

As the demand for domestic and industrial water increases
with population migrations to the arid regions, one of the few
sources of water for such developments would be to take water
away from irrigation. When this takes place a new National
policy would have to be formulated which would transfer food
production to the East and the South with extensive impact on
life style and land-use patterns.

Saunders (1976) stated that transmountain diversions will
have to be built in the future if we are to make use of our
water resources. One technique of attaining a transbasin
diversion is that of the undersea aqueduct. Armstrong (1972),
in his description of such an aqueduct, includes drawings of an
artist's conception of an off-shore pipeline if built in the
Pacific Ocean from off the mouth of the Columbia River to
Southern California.

In late 1964 the Ralph M. Parsons Company, a private
international engineering and construction firm headquartered
in Los Angeles, California, published a brochure, "NAWAPA -
North American Water and Power Alliance". This bold concept,
estimated to cost $100 billion, would tie together the waters
of most of Canada and of the United States and of northern
Mexico in 10 major water and hydropower systems.

NAWAPA could irrigate 56 million acres, carry from 110
million to 250 million acre feet of water per year, and generate from 60 to 180 million kilowatts of power. This 3-nation
project, which elicited world-wide attention, is described in
"Newsweek" magazine for February, 22, 1965.

Although NAWAPA appears to have engineering feasibility
and economic justification, violent opposition was voiced by
the environmentalists. There are also complex international
water law problems. It is likely that NAWAPA as a whole will

never be built but many of its subsystems possess merit, and inevitably will be built in the future.

The environmentalists, conservationists, and preservationists, with the support of recent legislation, have had a profound influence in delaying or stopping completely many worthwhile power and water resources projects. While these delays are in force time is running out on many projects of increasingly insistent importance. It now takes about 12 years to go through the maze of Environmental Impact Statements, hearings, reviews, etc., to get clearance for construction of a powerplant. A reading of Schaumburg's (1974) article entitled, "Enviropolitics is a Pollutant Too", is recommended.

This situation has led to the evolution of a new professional activity; that of environmental mediators as described by Lake (1977). One reason for this new profession, according to Lake, is that the usual adversary proceedings of environmental confrontations do not lend themselves to realistic judicial decisions since the courts are seldom equipped to do their own technical fact finding, and to balance trade-offs between claims in conflict.

Lear (1977) describes the success of the new mediators in resolving a conflict of over 20-years' standing on a highway in the vicinity of Seattle, Washington. Lear also writes about the successful mediation of a 14-year-old dispute centering on the Snohomish River.

Brown (1978) has written a provocative book which is a sequel to one he published 25 years ago under the title, "The Challenge of Man's Future", The Viking Press, New York (1954). Brown's Chapter VIII, Global Changes, in his 1978 book, is an informative essay on the changes, some caused by man, in the three components of our environment: land, water, and air. Brown's prediction of 1954 has turned out to be surprisingly accurate. His Chapter X, The Future, and Chapter XI, What We Can Do, in his new book, should be considered as required reading.

---

In conclusion, the water resource, a gift to mankind from Nature operating through the hydrologic cycle, is to be appreciated and not exploited. Not only our welfare, but our future survival depends on the intelligent management of the water resource and I am sure we are capable of meeting this responsibility.

# References

Ackermann, William C., David J. Allee, Jaime Amorocho, Yacov Y. Haimes, Warren A. Hall, Richard A. Meserve, Ruth Patrick, and Philip M. Smith, "Scientific and Technological Considerations in Water Resources Policy", Eos, vol. 59, no. 6, pp 516-527, June, 1978.

Ambroggi, Robert P., "Underground Reservoirs to Control the Water Cycle", Scientific American, vol. 236, no. 5, pp 21-27, May, 1977.

Armstrong, Ellis L., "The Undersea Aqueduct - A New Concept in Transportation", Transportation Engineering Journal, Proceedings ASCE, vol. 98, no. TE 2, pp 303-310, May, 1972.

Brown, Harrison, "The Human Future Revisited: The World Predicament and Possible Solutions", W. W. Norton & Co. Inc., New York, 287 pp, 1978.

Hitch, Charles J., "Unfreezing the Future", guest editorial in Science, vol. 195, no. 4281, p 825, Mar. 4, 1977.

Lake, Laura M., "Environmental Mediators Pioneer New Profession", a paper presented at the Annual Meeting, Amer. Assn. for the Advancement of Science, Denver, Colo., Feb. 25, 1977. (Dr. Lake is on the staff of the Univ. of Calif. at Los Angeles.)

Lear, John, "The New Mediators", RF Illustrated, (a publication of the Rockefeller Foundation, New York), vol. 3, no. 4, p 5, Sept. 1977.

"NAWAPA - North American Water and Power Alliance", a brochure the Ralph M. Parsons Company, Los Angeles, 27 pp, 1964.

"Saudi Prince Backs Project - Icebergs Studied as Source of Water", The Denver Post, p 6, Mon. Oct. 3, 1977.

Saunders, Glenn G., "Water for the Future: Concluding Remarks", pp 567-570 in Denver Journal of International Law and Policy, vol. 6, special issue, 587 pp, pub. in 1977. This issue is the Proceedings of the Conference held at the Univ. of Denver College of Law, Oct. 8-9, 1976, entitled, Water Needs for the Future: Legal, Political, Economic, and Technological Issues in National and International Perspectives.

Schaumburg, Frank D., " ' Enviropolitics' is a Pollutant Too", The National Observer, p 24, week ending May 4, 1974.

Schulz, E. F., "Harvesting Glacier Ice", pp 73-85 in Proceedings 42nd Annual Meeting Western Snow Conference, Apr. 16-20, 1974 held at Anchorage, Alaska, 105 pp, printed by Colo. State Univ., Fort Collins, 1974.

Smith, Roger, "California Farmers Overcome Drought with 10,000 Wells", The Denver Post, p 2BB, Wed. Aug. 17, 1977.

Wade, Nicholas, "Edward Goldsmith: Blueprint for a De-industrialized Society", Science, vol. 191, pp 270-272, Jan. 23, 1976.

CONVERSION FACTORS

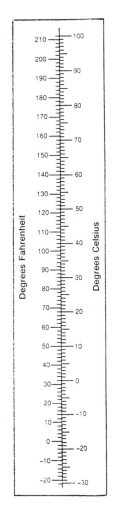

| One acre-foot (AF or af) | = | 325,851 U.S. gallons |
| | | 271,000 Imperial gallons |
| | | 43,560 cubic feet |

| One cubic-foot persecond (cfs or cusec) | = | 86,400 | Cubic ft. per day |
| | | 1.9835 | AF per day |
| | | 0.646 | Million gallons per day |
| | | 0.9917 | Inch per hr per acre |
| | | 3,600 | Cubic ft. per hr |
| | | 448.8 | U.S. gallons per minute |

One cubic foot = 7.48 U.S. gallons

One Imperial gallon = 7.48 U.S. gallons

One inch of runoff per sq. mi. = 53.3 AF
One square mile = 640 acres

One mile per hr. = 1.466 ft. per second
60 mi. per hr. = 88 ft. per second

One horsepower (hp) = 0.746 kilowatts (KW)

One inch of rain yields about 27,200 gallons per acre or about 100 tons per acre.

Page I 17 of "Water Facts and Figures for Planners and Managers", by J. H. Feth, USGS Circular 601-1 (1973) contains a nomograph for converting gallons per minute, million gallons per day, cubic feet per second, acre-feet per day, and acre-feet per year.

Water attains its maximum density at a temperature of 39.3° F at which it weighs 62.424 pounds per cubic foot. The weight of water at 32° F (just before it solidifies) is 62.416 lbs/cu.ft. At the boiling point the weight is 59.483 lbs/cu. ft. At 50° F the weight is 62.408 lbs/cu.ft. It is customary in the English system to assume the weight of water to be 62.4 lbs/cu.ft.

# SELECTED ENGLISH TO METRIC SYSTEM CONVERSION FACTORS

| English Unit | Multiply by | To get metric equivalent |
|---|---|---|
| **Length** | | |
| inches (in) | 25.4 | millimetres (mm) |
| | 2.54 | centimetres (cm) |
| | .0254 | metres (m) |
| feet (ft) | .3048 | metres (m) |
| miles (mi) | 1.6093 | kilometres (km) |
| **Area** | | |
| square inches (in$^2$) | $6.4516 \times 10^{-4}$ | square metres (m$^2$) |
| square feet (ft$^2$) | .092903 | square metres (m$^2$) |
| acres | 4046.9 | square metres (m$^2$) |
| | .40469 | hectares (ha) |
| | .40469 | sq. hectometres (hm$^2$) |
| | .0040469 | sq. kilometres (km$^2$) |
| square miles (mi$^2$) | 2.589 | sq. kilometres (km$^2$) |
| **Volume** | | |
| gallons (gal) | 3.7854 | litres (l) |
| | .0037854 | cubic metres (m$^3$) |
| million gallons (10$^6$ gal) | 3785.4 | cubic metres (m$^3$) |
| cubic feet (ft$^3$) | .028317 | cubic metres (m$^3$) |
| cubic yards (yd$^3$) | .76455 | cubic metres (m$^3$) |
| acre-feet (ac-ft) | 1233.49 | cubic metres (m$^3$) |
| | .0012335 | cubic hectometres (hm$^3$) |
| **Volume/Time (Flow)** | | |
| cubic feet per second (ft$^3$/s) | 28.317 | litres per second (l/s) |
| | .028317 | cubic metres per second (m$^3$/s) |
| gallons per minute (gal/min) | .06309 | litres per second (l/s) |
| | $6.309 \times 10^{-5}$ | cubic metres per second (m$^3$/s) |
| million gallons per day (mgd) | .043813 | cubic metres per second (m$^3$/s) |
| **Mass** | | |
| pounds (lb) | .45359 | kilograms (kg) |
| tons (short, 2,000 lb) | .90718 | tonne (t) |
| | 907.18 | kilograms (kg) |

APPENDIX B

GLOSSARY

Ability-to-pay principle - The pricing of goods or services on
the basis of family income or some other measure of financial
capability rather than on the basis of benefits received.
(See benefits-received principle.)

Acre-foot - The quantity of water required to cover 1 acre to a
depth of 1 foot; equal to 43,560 cubic feet or 325,851
gallons.

Alternative futures - A range of different future economic,
social, and demographic patterns of development, each depending on a different set of assumptions with respect to public
policies, life-styles, patterns of consumption, etc., and any
one of which could materialize. Contrasts with a single projection of future population, production, water requirements,
etc.

Appropriation (funds) - At the Federal level, the process
whereby Congress enacts a statute permitting expenditure of
funds, sometimes repeatedly over a period of several years,
for construction of authorized projects or implementation of
authorized programs.

Appropriation doctrine - The system of water law adopted by
(and dominant in) most Western States. The basic tenets of
the appropriation doctrine are (1) that a water right can be
acquired only by diverting the water from a watercourse and
applying it to a beneficial use and (2) in accordance with
the date of acquisition, an earlier acquired water right
shall have priority over other later acquired water rights.
The first in time of beneficial use is the first in right,
and the right is maintained only by use. Water in excess of
that needed to satisfy existing rights is viewed as unappropriated water, available for appropriation by diversion and
application to a beneficial use. (See riparian doctrine.)

Aquifer - A saturated underground body of rock or similar material capable of storing water and transmitting it to wells
or springs.

Area of origin - In the case of interbasin water transfers,
the area exporting water.

Assimilative capacity - The ability of bodies of water to purify themselves after absorbing waste discharges or to dilute
such wastes and thus render them innocuous.

Authorization - At the Federal level, the process whereby
Congress enacts a statute approving construction of a project
or implementation of a program, frequently specifying a maximum amount to be appropriated for the purpose (but not
appropriating the required funds).

Benefit-cost analysis - Comparison of the expected benefits of
a water project with the anticipated costs of that project.
Ordinarily, unless the computed benefits exceed the computed
costs, the project is not considered feasible.

Benefits-received principle - The pricing of goods or services
on the basis of benefits received by users; those who use a
service pay for the service. (See ability-to-pay principle.)

Best known technology - for water pollution control is a short-
hand term to describe those techniques and methods known by
the National Water Commission to be under consideration in
the spring of 1972 when the Commission's estimates of cost of
various pollution control measures were prepared. Does not
necessarily bear any relationship to the term "best available
technology" as used in the Federal Water Pollution Control Act
Amendments of 1972.

Best management practices (BMP) - A term used to describe agricultural and forestry land use management techniques as they
pertain to the Clean Water Act of 1977. (Popovich, 1978)

Biochemical oxygen demand - The requirement for oxygen when
organic matter decomposes in bodies of water; oxygen-demand-
ing wastes lower dissolved oxygen levels in water which in
turn adversely affect aquatic life. Also called "BOD".

Biota - The flora and fauna of a region.

Conjunctive management - The situation where management of two
or more water resources, such as a ground aquifer and a surface water body, is integrated.

Consumptive use - Water withdrawn from a supply which, because
of absorption, transpiration, evaporation, or incorporation
in a manufactured product, is not returned directly to a surface or groundwater supply; hence, water which is lost for
immediate further use. Also called "consumption".

Cost allocation - The apportionment of the costs of a multi-
purpose water project among the various purposes served.

Cost effectiveness - Comparison of alternative ways to achieve
a given objective in order to identify the least-cost way.

Cost-sharing - The assignment of the responsibility for paying
the costs of a water project among two or more entities as,
for example, among the Federal Government, a State government,
and individual users.

Depletion - The withdrawal of water from surface or groundwater
reservoirs at a rate greater than the rate of replenishment.

Desalting - The technical process of converting sea water or
brackish water to fresh water or otherwise more usable condition by removing dissolved solids. Also called "desalini-
zation" and "desalination".

Discharge - The rate of flow of a spring, stream, canal, sewer, or conduit.

Discount rate - The interest rate used in evaluation of water (and other) projects for the purpose of calculating the present value of future benefits and future costs, or otherwise converting benefits and costs to a common time basis.

Diversion - See "withdrawal".

Divide - A ridge which separates two river basins or drainage basins.

Drainage basin - The land area from which water drains into a river, as for example, the Columbia River Basin is all the land area which drains into the Columbia River. Also called "catchment area", "watershed", or "river basin".

Ecology - The study of the interrelationships of living organisms to one another and to their surroundings.

Ecosystem - Recognizable, relatively homogeneous units, including contained organisms, their environment, and all of the interactions among them.

Effective economic demand - In an economic sense, demand for a product (goods or service) is reflected by the quantities consumers will purchase at alternative price levels. With respect to a water project or program, effective economic demand is the willingness and ability of those who benefit to pay the full costs of the output of the project or program.

Effluent - The outflow of used water from a sewer, holding tank, industrial process, agricultural activity, etc; sometimes treated, other times not.

Eminent domain - The right of a government to acquire private property for public use, even from an unwilling owner, upon payment of compensation to the owner; occasionally conferred upon private entities vested with a public interest such as utilities.

Estuary - The lower course of a river which flows to the sea and which is influenced by the tides; or an arm of the sea itself that extends inland to meet a river flowing to the sea; the reaches of a river into which sea water intrudes and mixes with fresh water from land drainage.

Eutrophication - Overfertilization of a water body due to increases in mineral and organic nutrients, producing an abundance of plant life which uses up oxygen, sometimes creating an environment hostile to higher forms of marine animal life.

Evaluation - Examination of a proposed water project to determine feasibility.

Evaporation - Conversion of liquid water into water vapor;
hence, the dissipation of water from water surfaces and the
ground into the atmosphere.

Evapotranspiration - Water dissipated to the atmosphere by
evaporation from water surfaces and moist soil and by plant
transpiration.

External diseconomy - A harmful effect on one or more persons
or firms which stems from the activity of other persons or
firms; the activity yields private benefits or advantages to
the individuals or firms engaged in it but results in social
costs, disadvantages, or economic penalties to others; for
example, where expansion of wood pulp production benefits a
pulp mill but results in discharge of additional effluents
into a stream harmful to recreationists and other users of
the downstream water resource. Also called "externality".

Flood plain - The land area bordering a river which is subject
to flooding.

Floodway - The riverbed and immediately adjacent lands needed
to convey high velocity flood discharges.

Floodway fringe - Lands immediately adjacent to floodways which
are still subject to flooding but which are not needed for
high velocity flood discharge and are flooded less frequently
and for shorter durations than floodways.

Groundwater - Water that occurs beneath the land surface and
completely fills all pore spaces of the rock material in
which it occurs.

Groundwater mining - The condition when withdrawals are made
from an aquifer at rates in excess of net recharge; sooner
or later the underground supply will be exhausted or the
water table will drop below economic pump lifts.

Headgate - A device to control water flow, placed at the
entrance to a pipeline, canal, or irrigation ditch; the point
at which water is diverted from a river into an irrigation
ditch.

Headwaters - The place where a river originates.

Humid region - An area of the country with ample rainfall, generally considered to be in excess of 20 inches annually.

Hydrologic cycle - The circulation of water from the sea,
through the atmosphere, to the land; and thence (with many
delays) back to the sea by overland and subterranean routes,
or directly back into the atmosphere by evaporation and
transpiration.

Instream use - Use of water which does not require withdrawal
or diversion from its natural watercourse. For example, the
use of water for navigation, waste disposal, recreation, and
support of fish and wildlife.

Interbasin transfer - The physical transfer of water from one watershed to another.  On a large scale the transfer of large quantities of water from one major river basin to another.

Interstate compact - In the case of water resources, agreements between two or more States for dealing with water resources problems involving more than one State and beyond the legal authority of one State alone to solve.  Such agreements require the consent of Congress.  The Federal Government may participate in some compacts in which case the agreement is called a Federal-interstate compact.

Inverse condemnation - The act of taking property by governmental action prior to filing eminent domain proceedings.  In such cases the property owner must file suit to recover compensation.

Joint costs - The costs of those parts of a water project which cannot be isolated as to a single purpose.  For example the cost of a dam structure itself which simultaneously serves two or more purposes such as power production, flood control, and navigation.  (See separable costs.)

Lacustrine - Pertaining to lakes generally as distinguished from other bodies of water such as rivers, oceans, groundwater aquifers, and estuaries.

Leaching - Removal of salts and alkali from soils by water which percolates through the soil.

Littoral rights - The water rights of landowners adjacent to lakes, equivalent to the riparian rights of landowners bordering a stream.  (See riparian doctrine.)

Marginal cost pricing - Charging a price for goods  or service equal to the incremental cost of the last unit produced.  Marginal cost pricing generally has the attribute of leading to the most efficient use of scarce resources.  When marginal cost pricing does not prevail, efficiency can be improved by moving resources away from industries where prices are below marginal costs and into industries where prices are above marginal costs.

Mouth of a river - The point where a river empties into another river or into the sea.

Multiple use - In the case of water resources, development of a particular water resource to serve two or more purposes simultaneously.

No discharge policy - The policy which prohibits discharge of any harmful substance into a water body.  Strictly applied, the policy would forbid discharges which are within the capacity of a water body to assimilate and render harmless.

Nonpoint-source - The diffuse discharge of waste into a water
body which cannot be located as to specific souce, as with
sediment, certain agricultural chemicals, and acid mine
drainage.

Nonreimbursable cost - A cost of a water project which will not
be repaid out of project revenues but which will be borne instead by the construction or operating entity and funded by
the government.

Once-through process - The withdrawal of water from a water
body for use in cooling or processing and subsequent return
of that water, usually at a higher temperature or other
altered condition, into the same body of water from which it
came. Contrasts with water recycling processes.

Pathogenic bacteria - Bacteria capable of causing disease.

Peak pricing - The technique of pricing goods or services higher at times of peak demand and lower at times of reduced
demand to discourage consumption "on peak" and encourage consumption "off peak", thus to make more efficient use of plant
capacities.

Phreatophytes - (literally, "well plants") plants that send
their roots down to the water table, or to the capillary
fringe immediately above the water table; some of which consume relatively large quantities of water.

Point-source - A specific site from which wastewater is discharged into a water body and which can be located as to
source, as with effluent, treated or otherwise, from a municipal sewage system outflow from an industrial plant, or
runoff from an animal feedlot.

Precipitation - Any form of rain or snow falling to the earth's
surface.

Recycling process - In the case of water, the withdrawal of
water for use in cooling or processing and the subsequent re-
conditioning and reuse of that same water over and over,
usually with relatively small additions of "makeup" water required to compensate for losses through evaporation or
otherwise.

Regulation (stream) - The artificial manipulation of the flow
of a stream, as by the storage of water and its later release.

Reimbursable costs - Those costs of a water project which are
expected to be recovered, in whole or in part, usually from
direct beneficiaries, and repaid to the funding entity.

Reservoir -- A pond, lake, aquifer, or basin, either natural or
artificial, in which water is stored, regulated, or
controlled.

Residual - Material or energy flow, the value of which is less than the cost of using it.

Return flow - The portion of withdrawn water that is not consumed by evapotranspiration and that returns instead to its source or to another body of water.

Riparian doctrine - The system of water law historically recognized by the Eastern States. The riparian doctrine protects landowners adjacent to lakes and streams from withdrawals or uses which unreasonably diminish water quantity or quality. Under the riparian doctrine, individuals have a right to make reasonable use of the stream waters flowing by lands they own so long as that use does not substantially diminish either the quantity or the quality of the water passing to landowners downstream. Where diversions or uses have been unreasonable, they either have been enjoined or riparian owners adversely affected have been compensated for interference with their rights. (See appropriation doctrine.)

River basin - see "drainage basin".

Runoff - the part of precipitation that appears in surface streams.

Sediment - Soil or mineral material transported by water and deposited in streams or other bodies of water.

Separable costs - The costs of a water project which can be isolated and exclusively allocated to a single purpose. For example, the costs of turbine generators at a hydroelectric plant. (See joint costs.)

Site-specific - Phenomena which occur under certain conditions at a particular site but which would not necessarily occur at another site.

Sovereign immunity - The doctrine under which the Federal Government cannot be sued without its consent.

Standard metropolitan statistical area (SMSA) - An integrated economic and social unit with a large population nucleus. There are over 245 SMSA's in the United States. Each contains at least one central city with 50,000 inhabitants or more, or two adjoining cities constituting, for economic and social purposes, a single community with a combined population of a least 50,000, the smaller of which must have a population of at least 15,000. Each SMSA includes the county in which the central city is located, and adjacent counties that are metropolitan in character and economically and socially integrated with the county of the central city.

Storage - The impoundment in surface reservoirs or accumulation in underground reservoirs of water for later use or release.

Streamflow - The discharge in a surface stream course.

Sustained yield - In the case of groundwater aquifers, the quantity of water which can be withdrawn annually without, over a period of years, depleting the available supply.

Transpiration - The process in which plant tissues give off water vapor to the atmosphere.

User charge - A charge made upon direct beneficiaries (users) of a water project, designed to recover part or all of the cost of the project.

Watershed - A geographic area which drains into a particular water body. (See drainage basin.)

Water table - The upper level of an underground water body.

Withdrawal - The diversion and removal of water from a natural watercourse. Also called "diversion".

## References

With the exception of "Best management practices" (Popovich, 1978) all definitions in this appendix are from Water Policies for the Future (1973). Additional definitions of terms are given by Langbein and Iseri (1960) and in the Glossary of Meteorology (1959). "Thesaurus" lists 6,585 terms.

"Glossary of Meteorology", ed. by Ralph E. Huschke, pub. by American Meteorological Society, Boston, Mass., 638 pp, 1959.

Langbein, W. B., and Kathleen T. Iseri, "General Introduction and Hydrologic Definitions", (Manual of Hydrology Part 1, General Surface-Water Techniques), USGS Water Supply Paper 1541-A, 29 pp, 1960.

Popovich, Luke, "If at First You Don't Succeed", Jour. of Forestry, vol. 76, no. 3, pp 168-171, March, 1978.

"Thesaurus of Water Resources Terms", Bureau of Reclamation, USDI, Government Printing Office, 339 pp, 1971.

"Water Policies for the Future", Final report to the President and to the Congress of the United States by the National Water Commission, U.S. Government Printing Office, Washington, D.C., 579 pp, 1973.

APPENDIX C

SOURCES OF HYDROLOGIC DATA

Information on climatology is given in Topic 9; on snow measurements in Topic 16; and on surface water measurements in Topic 24.

Precipitation amounts and maximum and minimum temperatures have been recorded by cooperative observers since weather records were first kept, originating in the U.S. Army. For many years the Weather Bureau assembled and published these observations in Climatological Bulletins, usually prepared separately for each state. A year's record was reported in 13 issues, one for each month and an annual summary.

In the past when these bulletins were distributed at no charge, many libraries acquired them. However, as a result of differences in appropriations, which once authorized free distribution, and reorganizations of the Weather Bureau, few libraries possess complete assemblies of the bulletins. It is suggested that anyone interested in rainfall and weather records contact a National Weather Service office to learn where any particular series of data may be obtained. State agricultural experiment stations and state agricultural colleges usually have a complete file of weather records.

All accumulated records are being reduced for computer storage and are available at the

> National Climatic Center
> Environmental Data Service, NOAA
> Dept. of Commerce
> Asheville, North Carolina  28801

Additional references to compilations of climatological data are given on pages 44 and 45 of Topic 9.

The National Oceanic and Atmospheric Administration (NOAA) operates 5 additional facilities in its Environmental Data Service.  These are:

> National Geophysical and Solar-Terrestrial Data Center,
>     Boulder, Colorado
> National Oceanographic Data Center
> Environmental Science Information Center
> Center for Experiment Design and Data Analysis
>     (the above 3 in Washington, D.C.)
> Center for Climatic and Environmental Assessment, Columbia,
>     Missouri

Snow depth as measured at the time of fall is reported in the climatological data summaries of the National Weather Service.

607

Several snow survey systems report upon snow depth and snow-water equivalent. Most of the organizations performing snow surveys in addition to publishing bulletins usually calculate seasonal water yield forecasts (see Topic 52). In the Western United States, exclusive of California, the Soil Conservation Service, USDA, is in charge of snow survey and forecasts. Reports may be obtained by writing to the Snow Survey Supervisor at the following addresses:

| | |
|---|---|
| Alaska | Room 129, 2221 East Northern Lights Blvd., Anchorage, Alaska 99504 |
| Arizona | Room 3008, Federal Bldg., Phoenix, Ariz. 85025 |
| Colorado | P.O. Box 17107, Denver, Colorado  80217 |
| New Mexico | same as above |
| Idaho | Room 345, 304 N. 8th St., Boise, Idaho  83702 |
| Montana | P.O. Box 98, Bozeman, Montana  59715 |
| Nevada | P.O. Box 4850, Reno, Nevada  89505 |
| Oregon | 1220 S.W. Third Ave., Portland, Oregon  97204 |
| Utah | 4012 Federal Bldg., 125 So. State St., Salt Lake City, Utah  84138 |
| Washington | 360 U.S. Court House, Spokane, Washington 99201 |
| Wyoming | P.O. Box 2440, Casper, Wyoming  82602 |

The snow survey system in the northeastern United States is operated under the sponsorship of the Eastern Snow Conference. Data is compiled by the U.S. Geological Survey at Albany, New York, Augusta, Maine, and Boston, Massachusetts. Snow survey bulletins and a winter snow summary are published by the National Weather Service, NOAA, U.S. Dept. of Commerce, Silver Spring, Maryland.

The State of California operates its own snow survey system. Bulletins are issued by the Water Supply Forecast and Snow Surveys Unit, California Dept. of Water Resources, P.O. Box 388, Sacramento, California  95802.

In Canada snow survey and forecast bulletins are published by a number of organizations. For British Columbia, by the Ministry of the Environment, Water Investigations Branch, Parliament Bldgs., Victoria, B.C. V8V 1X5; for Yukon Territory, by the Dept. of Indian and Northern Affairs, Northern Operation Branch, 200 Range Rd., Whitehorse, Yukon Territory Y1A 3V1; and for Alberta, Saskatchewan, and N.W.T., by the Water Survey of Canada, Inland Waters Branch, 110-12 Avenue S.W., Calgary, Alberta T3C 1A6.

The Meteorological Branch, Dept. of Transport, of Canada, publishes from its Toronto, Ontario, office snow cover data

for all of Canada at the end of each winter. Included in this report are records on snow survey for New Foundland, Prince Edwards Island, Nova Scotia, New Brunswick, Quebec, and Ontario. In addition to the regular snow survey the Division of Research of the Ontario Dept. of Land and Forests makes weekly observations on snow depth and crust conditions as part of its research on snow cover characteristics as they relate to wildlife population.

In addition to snow survey observations at established snow courses under special conditions of frozen soil, snow cover, and flood threat during years when such conditions prevail, the U.S. Army Corps of Engineers, in cooperation with numerous other agencies, perform snow surveys in the Northeast, the Mid-west, and in the Plains States, for the purpose of securing data for rate-of-runoff forecasting of complex floods. The Tennessee Valley Authority operated in the late 1940's a snow survey system on both the east and west slopes of the highway over Newfound Gap in the Great Smoky National Park.

The official agency for measuring streamflow in the United States is the Water Resources Division of the U.S. Geological Survey. For the period about 1912 to about 1960 the Geological Survey published in its series of Water Supply Papers, data on surface runoff, lakes, rivers, groundwater, and water quality. The divisions and subdivisions of the United States used in the Water Supply Papers are shown in Figure C-1 on the following page. Tabulations are available from the Geological Survey which list the numbers of the Water Supply Papaers for each of the Part and Volume numbers pertaining to the subdivisions shown on the map in Figure C-1.

During the period 1960-1965 publications of annual water resources reports by the Geological Survey in its Water Supply series ceased. Since that time individual states or combinations of states publish separate volumes in cooperation with the Geological Survey and others.

Some of the larger libraries in their Government Documents Division have a complete series of Water Supply Papaers. Many state agricultural colleges also have a complete series. The new annual water supply papers published for each state are released either by the field center offices of the Water Resources of the Geological Survey or by state agencies. Issuing offices are usually located at the state capitols.

Rapid advances are being made in the precision of observations, techniques of reduction of raw data, and conversion to computer storage. The U.S. Geological Survey established its National Water Data Storage and Retrieval System (WATSTORE) in November, 1971. This system, operated at the National Water Data Exchange, U.S. Geological Survey, 421 National Center,

Reston, Virginia, 22092, was designed to modernize water data processing procedures and techniques.

Another computerized system, also operated by the Geological Survey at Reston, Virginia, is the National Water Data Exchange" (NAWDEX) which serves as a central clearing house and a management center for many different types of data. Access to both of these systems is available from numerous field offices of the Geological Survey.

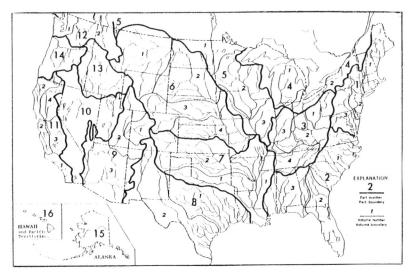

Figure C-1  Areas covered by the volumes on surface-water supply as published by the U.S. Geological Survey in its Water Supply Paper series. The large digits and the heavy lines pertain to Part numbers and Part boundaries. The small digits and the dotted lines pertain to Volume numbers and their boundaries. (From USGS Circular 666)

In addition to the data being collected by agencies such as the National Weather Service and the Geological Survey, there is a tremendous volume of water-resource-related information being compiled by irrigation districts, power companies, research institutes, universities, and individuals. Other Federal agencies such as the Agricultural Research Service and the Forest Service, both of the U.S. Dept. of Agriculture, have extensive accumulations of data pertaining to their research activities.

The Environmental Protection Agency maintains the Storage and Retrieval System (STORET) in its Office of Water and Hazardous Materials in Washington, D.C. This system contains about 40 million observations pertaining to a great number of parameters describing physical, chemical, biological, and radio-

logical characteristics as they apply to water quality.  Access
to STORET is available at EPA Regional Offices.

Water quality data is available at, and in many instances
is published by, State Health Departments.  Air quality data is
being assembled by the Environmental Protection Agency on a
National basis.  The repository for this data is:  The Office
of Air Quality Planning and Standards, Monitoring  and Data
Analyses Division, EPA, Research Triangle Park, North Carolina,
27711.  Satellite observations (see Topic 64) are available
from:  Satellite Data Services Branch, NOAA, World Center Bldg.
Room 606, Washington, D.C.  20233.

Many states have extensive series of publications on a
variety of subjects many of which touch upon the water
resource.  A very useful bibliography with a supplement is
"Water Publications of State Agencies", edited by Gerald J.
Geifer, David K. Todd, with the assistance of Mary Louise Quinn
Water Information Center, Port Washington, New York, 319 pp,
1972.  This publication is followed by "First Supplement, 1971-
1974" to Water Publications of State Agencies, edited by
Gerald J. Giefer, David K. Todd, and with the assitance of
Beverly Fish, Water Information Center, Huntington, New York,
189 pp, 1976.

The acquisition and preparation for analysis of data often
has turned out to be a task requiring two-thirds of the effort
expended on the activity.  Care should be taken, depending on
the purpose for which the analysis is being performed, to make
certain as to the character of the data available or secured.
Many organizations have raw data immediately available.  In
some cases preliminary data releases have been issued and these
may be followed, sometimes years later, by the final official
data.  The acceptability of water resources data in litigation
is discussed in Topic 66, page 397.

The magnitude of the problem of water-resource-related
data collection and reduction can be appreciated when it is
realized that about 30 Federal agencies, hundreds of State,
county, and city agencies, and an unknown number of other organizations collect water data in the United States.

In response to the Office of Management and Budget Circu-
lars A-62 (1963) and A-67 (1964) the first of a proposed 10-
chapter handbook was released on Sept. 2, 1977.  This release
included the introduction to the "National Handbook of Recommended Methods for Water-Data Acquisition", and Chapter 5,
"Chemical and Physical Quality of Water and Sediment", dated
January, 1977, 193 pages.  This was followed by revision sheets
dated January, 1978.  This series is released by: Chief, Office
of Water Data Coordination, U.S. Geological Survey, MS-417,
National Center, Reston, Virginia  22092.

# AUTHOR AND NAME INDEX

Burdge, R. J., 587, 588
Burges, S. J., 109
Burgess, R. L., 531, 551
Burgi, P. H., 330, 331, 334, 494, 495
Burke, M., 86, 89
Burnett, R. W., 39, 40
Burson, Z. G., 86, 89
Burt, W. V., 236, 238
Burwell, C. C., 531, 551
Buswell, A. M., 17, 18
Butler, S. S., 25, 93, 95
Butz, E., 10, 11
Buzyna, G., 117, 120
Byerly, R. T., 565
Byers, H. R., 40, 61

Cable, D. R., 485, 489
Cabrera, G., 264, 269
Camp, J. D., 420, 425
Campbell, C. J., 280, 281
Campbell, R. E., 222, 229
Carlson, E. J., 272, 273, 276
Carlysle, T. C., 369, 374
Caro, J. H. 290, 292
Carson, M. A., 194, 196
Carstens, T., 493, 495
Carter, G. F., 113, 119
Carter, L. J., 538, 551
Carter, R. W., 340, 341
Celnicker, A. C., 477, 478
Cervione, M. B., Jr., 131, 132
Chadwick, D. G., 86, 90, 269
Chandler, R. F., Jr., 178, 184
Chang, F. J., 163, 166
Chang, M., 71, 74, 378, 380
Changnon, S. A., Jr., 59, 61, 62, 64, 80, 82
Chapman, R. D., 118, 119
Chase, E. B., 265, 271
Chaudry, F. H., 295, 299
Cheek, N. H., Jr., 586, 590
Cheng, R. T., 273, 276
Cherkauer, D. S., 502, 504
Chorley, R. J., 2, 3, 4, 25, 145, 147, 196, 201, 300, 419
Chow, V. T., 5, 7, 19, 25, 34, 68, 82, 90, 101, 104, 106, 107, 108, 109, 111, 119, 121, 125, 127, 132, 152, 153, 154, 156, 157, 160, 196, 220, 230, 232, 240, 271, 299, 300, 308, 311, 322, 324, 326, 328, 342,

344, 345, 399, 403, 409, 410, 415, 429, 431, 441, 489, 490, 496, 509
Christian, F. G., 484, 487
Church, J. E. 85, 90
Clark, F. E., 423
Clark, J. R., 474
Clark, R. A., 42, 44, 326, 328
Clark, R. E., 395, 398, 399
Clark, R. H., 185, 189, 214, 219
Claude, G., 243, 547
Clifford, J. F., 563, 565
Clawson, M., 349, 351, 353, 356
Cloud, P., 242, 243, 253
Cluff, C. B., 217, 218, 219, 337, 339, 486, 487
Cobb, W. A., 519, 522
Cochrane, H. C., 426, 432
Cohan, H. J., 586, 588
Cohon, J. L., 412, 415
Colbeck, S. C., 318, 320, 322
Colby, B. R., 171, 174
Colby, V. A., 325, 326
Coleman, E. A., 198, 201
Coleman, M. D., 383, 385
Colling, G., 389, 391
Colorni, A., 341, 342
Commoner, B., 284, 285
Connor, S. V., 6
Constant, C., 201, 203
Conway, H. M., Jr., 41, 44
Cook, C. W., 365, 366, 371
Cook, D. I., 502, 504
Cook, R. G., 491, 496
Corbett, D. M., 129, 131
Corbett, E. S., 66, 68
Corey, M. W., 244, 255
Cortes-Comerer, N., 348, 351
Countryman, C. M., 369, 371
Coutu, A. J., 521, 522
Cox, D. C., 265, 270
Cox, J. L., 531, 551
Cox, L., 200, 201, 319, 322
Coyle, J. J., 373
Craig, R. F., 181, 183
Crane, D. A., 401 403
Crawford, N. H., 520, 522
Creighton, J. L., 402, 403
Criddle, W. D., 228, 229

Guy, H. P., 163, 164, 165, 166, 167, 169

Haas, J. E., 508, 510
Hagan, R. M., 183
Hahn, T. F., 417, 419
Haimes, Y. Y., 267, 270, 591, 595
Hains, C. H., 354, 357
Haise, H. R., 183, 225, 229, 230
Hale, F. E., 289, 293
Halff, A. H., 513, 517
Hall, C. W., 275, 276, 436, 440
Hall, F. R., 140, 144
Hall, W. A., 591, 595
Hallam, A., 241, 253
Halley, E., 213
Hamilton, E. L., 198, 201
Hamilton, R., 532, 553
Hammad, H. Y., 165, 167
Hammond, A. L., 206, 211, 545, 553, 564, 565
Harbaugh, T. E., 27
Harbeck, G. E., Jr., 216, 219, 231
Hardison, C. H., 120, 377, 378, 380
Hare, P. E., 113, 119
Harleman, D. R. F., 217, 220
Harmon, R. W., 213, 219
Harrington, A. W., 129, 132
Harrison, W., 273, 276
Harrold, L. L., 136, 137, 188, 189, 197, 199, 202
Hart, G. E., 228, 230
Hart, H. E., 224, 228, 231
Hastings, J. R., 487, 489
Haughey, R. D., 531, 553
Haugseth, L., 251, 253
Haupt, H. F., 228, 229
Haurwitz, E., 40
Haury, E. W., 2, 4
Hauser, P. A., 499, 504
Haushild, W. L., 163, 167
Hawkins, R. H., 378, 380, 409, 411
Hayes, R. B., 336, 339, 494, 496
Hazen, R., 111, 120, 484, 489
Heady, H. F., 62, 64, 411, 524

Hebert, D. J., 234, 235, 236, 239
Heckler, W., 129, 131
Hedman, E. R., 159, 160
Heede, B. H., 129, 130, 132, 162, 167, 329, 334, 360, 373
Heerman, D. F., 295, 300
Heindl, L. A., 26
Helfrich, H. W. Jr., 589
Helliwell, R. A., 563, 565
Helm, W. T., 284, 286, 570, 572
Helvey, J. D., 361, 373
Henderson, P. B., 131, 132
Hendricks, D. W., 286, 572, 590
Hendricks, S. B., 209, 211
Henry, A. J., 6, 359, 370
Hershfield, D. M., 80, 83
Hess, W. N., 61, 62
Hewlett, J. D., 26, 140, 141, 144, 145, 147, 191, 196, 325, 327, 361, 373
Hibbert, A. R., 200, 203, 360, 373
Hibbs, C., xii
Hickey, M. E., 337, 339
Hidore, J. J., 117, 120
Hiemstra, L. A. V., 324, 325, 327, 328
Higginson, R. K., 351
Hill, D. W., 503, 504
Hill, G. A., 207, 211
Hill, I., 204
Hill, M. M., 490, 497
Hill, R. H., 41, 45
Himmelblau, D. M., 343, 345
Hinds, T. E., 569, 572
Hirsch, R. M., 412, 415
Hirshburg, R. I., 235, 239
Hitch, C. J., 592, 595
Hitschfeld, W. F., 61, 64
Hjorth, P., 127, 128
Hobba, R. L., 325, 328
Hobbs, P. V., 17, 19, 56, 57, 61, 62, 64
Hodge, C. O., 303, 304
Hodgson, B., 493, 496
Hodgson, H. J., 366, 373
Hodgson, J. M., 290, 293
Hoffman, E. J., 531, 551
Hogarty, R. H., 583, 589
Hogerton, J. F., 537, 553
Hohenberg, C. M., 540, 551

625

629